FROM YALTA TO BERLIN

FROM YALTA TO BERLIN

THE COLD WAR STRUGGLE OVER GERMANY

W. R. SMYSER

St. Martin's Press
New York

ISBN 0-312-06605-8

Library of Congress Cataloging-in-Publication Data
Smyser, W. R., 1931–
    From Yalta to Berlin : the Cold War struggle over Germany / W.R. Smyser.
        p.   cm.
    Includes bibliographical references and index.
    ISBN 0-312-06605-8
    1. Germany—Politics and government—1945–   2. Cold War.
3. Germany—Foreign relations—Soviet Union.   4. Soviet Union—
Foreign relations—Germany.   5. United States—Foreign
relations—1945–1989.   6. German reunification question (1949–1990)
I. Title.
DD257.4.S59   1999   98–55304
943.087—dc21   CIP

Book design by Letra Libre Inc.

First edition: August 1999
10   9   8   7   6   5   4   3   2   1

CONTENTS

Six pages of illustrations appear between pages 136 and 137.

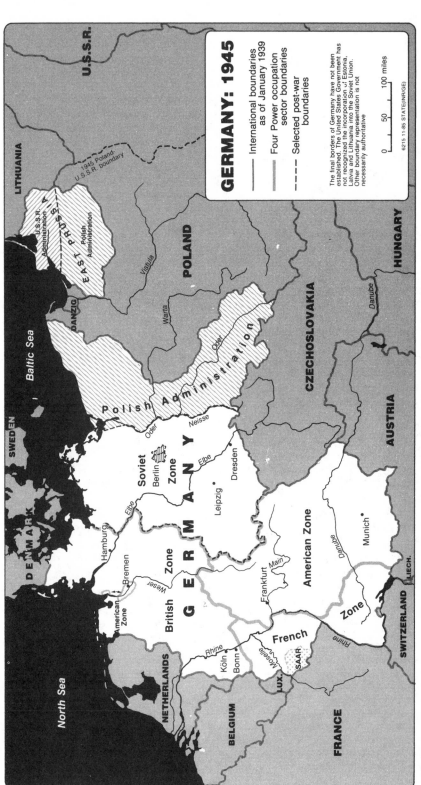

Germany divided into Occupation Zones, 1945. Reproduced from *Documents on Germany 1944–1985*, Department of State publication 9446.

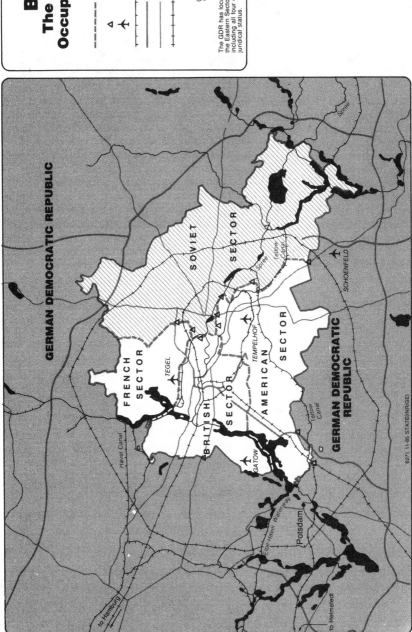

BERLIN:
The Four Power Occupation Sectors

Sector limit
Check point
Airport
Canal
Major highway (Autobahn)
Road
Railroad

0   5 miles

The GDR has located the seat of its government in the Eastern Sector of Berlin. However, Greater Berlin, including all four occupied sections, retains Four Power juridical status.

GERMAN DEMOCRATIC REPUBLIC

FRENCH SECTOR

SOVIET SECTOR

BRITISH SECTOR

AMERICAN SECTOR

GERMAN DEMOCRATIC REPUBLIC

TEGEL

Spree

Teltow Canal

SCHOENFELD

TEMPELHOF

GATOW

Teltow Canal

Havel Canal

Spree

Potsdam

Elbe-Havel Waterway

to Hamburg

to Helmstedt

6271 11-85 STATE(INR/GE)

Berlin divided into Occupation Sectors, 1945. Reproduced from *Documents on Germany 1944–1985*, Department of State publication 9446.

Street Map of Central Berlin

United Germany, 1994

FOREWORD

GERMANY HAS BEEN A SIGNIFICANT FACTOR IN MY LIFE, both personally and professionally. Alongside Russia, or perhaps I should say the former Soviet Union, no country other than my own has proved of such consuming interest over the years. As a matter of principle, therefore, I can only welcome any new dispassionate study of Germany like Dr. Smyser's.

My family is of German origins on both sides. I learned to speak German before English, thanks to a nanny at home in Chicago. I have vivid memories of the fateful summer of 1914, when I was seven, as my father whisked us across Europe from our holiday in the Tyrol in the wake of the assassination in Sarajevo. We were in Munich when England declared war on Germany. We wore little American flags in our lapels so as to avoid harassment as despicable Britons. I recall following the war closely, selling war bonds once the U.S. had entered it and, as a sixth grader, taking the part of Walter Rathenau, the German foreign minister, in a school debate on the Paris Peace Conference.

Germany was also to provide, albeit indirectly, my entree into the worlds of finance and government. In 1929, not long out of Harvard, I was commissioned by Bacon, Whipple, a Chicago brokerage firm, to go to Germany to report on whether German securities might be a better investement than American securities at their then high prices. I went armed with several letters of introduction, including one I made use of even before my departure for Europe. It was to Clarence Dillon, the illustrious New York investment banker. He offered me a job as his personal assistant at Dillon, Read on my return. The acquaintances I made at that firm in the 1930s, particularly with Jim Forrestal, then a partner, were later to prove instrumental in my move to Washington.

That seven month tour of Europe, with its focus on my report on German securities—which I did not recommend buying—was memorable in many ways. An especially happy period was spent at the Pension Nauman on Nickolsburger Platz in Berlin in the company of, among others, Alexander Calder, the sculptor. Berlin was also the base camp for my first, if inadvertent, excursion into the Soviet Union when hiking with my great Harvard friend, Freddy Winthrop. Completely lost, we accidentally crossed the Finnish border and walked on in heavy rain until we came across a fisherman who told us that we were in Russia and should get out fast.

It was a few years later, in 1937, that I got my first sight of Adolf Hitler, and at rather close range, too. I had been told by a correspondent for a Chicago newspaper that I ought to check out what he called this "madman," so I drove down to Munich with my wife—we were on a motoring vacation—and booked into the Eden Hotel. My second floor room had a little balcony overlooking the square and the next day Hitler gave a speech from the first floor, immediately beneath my feet. I had never heard anything like it before. It was quite an experience for me. I used to think people gave quiet and judicious speeches; he ranted and raved with true passion and hatred. Just as disturbing on that vacation were our first observations of the Hitler Youth Corps, whose look of arrogance and disdain sent a shiver of apprehension down my spine.

I recall being with my parents at their ranch in Colorado when Germany invaded Poland, forcing Britain and France to declare war. Like many Americans at the time and influenced by my own German-American ancestry, I thought the U.S. should remain neutral in the conflict, as we did initially. But it soon became apparent that the more Germany conquered, the more endangered became our own security. When, in the summer of 1940, the invitation to serve in Washington came from Jim Forrestal, who was serving as one of FDR's six special administrative assistants, I did not hesitate to go. Several assignments intervened, but as the war in Europe ended I found myself in Germany again. I managed to locate some of our German relatives and even tried to visit the Pension Nauman in Berlin, but it was in ruins. One of the more memorable episodes was interrogating Albert Speer, mastermind of Germany's war production effort, which we did in Holstein, in territory not yet occupied by the Allies. He attributed Germany's defeat to the incompetence, softness and stupidity of the group around Hitler. I think he hoped I could get him off being accused as a war criminal but I let him know that was above my pay grade.

From that point on, my association with Germany was to remain principally in the fields of policy, the facts of which are mostly in the public domain, from the Marshall Plan, the Berlin Airlift and the creation of NATO all the way to our strategic arms negotiations with the Soviet Union. I still consider the Berlin crisis of 1948 to be the most parlous moment for America, far closer, in my view, to drawing us into conflict with the Soviet Union than the later Cuban missile crisis. Not the least reason for this was that I knew the U.S. was ill-prepared militarily for war, whereas I thought the Soviet Union had combat-ready divisions in abundance. But we took the necessary risks and our policies worked.

Over the years, I came to know all the post-war German Chancellors. I admired Konrad Adenauer, a courageous man who never let himself or anybody else down. I became a close friend of Helmut Schmidt, a man of considerable intelligence, and found Helmut Kohl to be very much my kind of fellow, with a fine sense of humor. I did not always agree with them. I was, for example, initially dubious about Schmidt's proposal in 1977 that the U.S. deploy intermediate-range weapons in Europe to offset the deployment of Soviet SS-20 missiles. I was unpersuaded by the military arguments, believing that the Pershing Two was not the right missile for the purpose, and was concerned that deployment might prove politically divisive, especially in West Germany. But once NATO adopted the "twin track" policy in 1979, I thought we had no other choice but to stick with it, because we could not abruptly back away from our commitments.

Equally, although I had no problem with Kohl's view that Germany would be better off in an economically successful and integrated Europe, I always placed greater emphasis on the importance of German-American relations than I did on intra-European cooperation. The two were not incompatible to my mind but as long as the Cold War lasted it was logical for America to cultivate the closest of ties with Germany and for Germany to contribute substantially to the Western alliance. And so it did, thanks initially to Adenauer's leadership and our own persuasive arguments, much to the frustration of Moscow.

Dr. Smyser, particularly with his access to much secret and now declassified Soviet information, throws welcome light onto many of these issues. If only we knew then what we know now, we might have slept easier at night.

—Paul H. Nitze

PREFACE

AS DUSK FELL ON AUGUST 3, 1914, WITH DECLARATIONS OF WAR flying all around Europe, the British foreign secretary, Sir Edward Grey, looked out the tall windows of his Whitehall office and said: "The lamps are going out tonight all over Europe. We shall not see them lit again in our lifetime."

Sir Edward's prophecy came true. The lamps did not come on again until 1990, when the last of the European empires surrendered its leaden grip on the eastern half of the continent.

Germany did more than any other state to keep the lamps dark. It twice launched wars that engulfed Europe and the world. Then, defeated and divided, it became the principal prize in a new and different war.

No nation's fury, no nation's fate, had a greater impact on the twentieth century. German philosophers spawned the most venomous ideologies. Their disciples launched the most murderous wars. German scientists conceived the most noxious weapons. German armies, in victory and defeat, shifted entire nations and redrew their maps. Germany seared its ideas, its triumphs, and its brutalities into the conscious and subconscious memories of three generations.

From 1945 to 1990 the struggle over Germany helped shape the world. It formed the central vortex of the Cold War, sucking in every state in Europe and many beyond. It had no fixed boundaries, becoming the center of a titanic global conflict between opposite concepts of government and society.

No matter where the Cold War antagonists might clash at any moment, they always had the struggle over Germany in mind. They evaluated virtually every crisis in terms of its effect on the central European balance. And they evaluated every German crisis in terms of its effect on Europe and beyond.

The struggle over Germany ended only when all participants received what they had needed from the beginning, although none received it in the form in which they had first thought they wanted it. The German people themselves—and especially the Berliners—played important and ultimately decisive roles.

In writing this book, I have tried to give all elements of the struggle over Germany their due. I set forth the factors that shaped the struggle and determined the outcome. I focus on the core of the conflict but also cite relevant factors on a wide periphery. I record what happened and why, sometimes offering comment as well as narrative.

I concentrate at length on the most decisive moments, when the future balanced on a knife's edge or when new leaders set new directions. I also describe, if in less detail, what happened in between, because the struggle over Germany never paused for breath. For good reason, I look at the people as well as the leaders.

An author owes his readers a word about his own role in the events he describes. In my case, it was a very active role. I have been closely involved in German matters for much of my life. I lived in Adolf Hitler's Germany for two years before Pearl Harbor. I served with U.S. forces in Germany for two years during the 1950s, with General Lucius Clay and for four more years in Berlin during the early 1960s, and then for four years as political counselor at the U.S. Embassy in Bonn during the late 1970s. I have continued to visit Germany frequently and to write about it.

I was involved in much of what I describe here, sometimes as player and sometimes as close observer. I am both witness and historian, sometimes going by my research, sometimes by my recollections, often by both.

An author must also make clear what he wants to contribute. Thousands of books and articles touch on matters covered in this book, but none has reviewed the entire story of German division from beginning to end and tried to understand its meaning. I want to do that. I want to present new, not old, data and analyses. I do not want to enter into all debates, especially the old ones. I try to draw fresh conclusions about how the Cold War shaped what we now see and what we can expect.

New information about Germany, especially about German unification, now appears almost every day from old files or new memoirs. Scholars can now examine many former East German documents although the foreign office of united Germany keeps East German foreign ministry files confidential. Several major American institutes, such as the Cold War International History Project or the National Security Archive, are publishing and analyzing Soviet and East German documents. American scholars concentrate on those documents most pertinent to U.S. concerns. German scholars are concentrating on those about Germany. Soviet and East German diplomats and intelligence officers have told their stories, some more truthfully than others.

Russia has opened many files, although not the presidential archives which might tell us what top Soviet leaders thought or at least what they wrote and said. We have seen more than we had long expected to see even if some areas still remain closed. More files, including those of the Stalin era, may yet open.

I have not tried to duplicate other research but have used it where I regard it as reliable. Because this book concentrates on the United States, the Soviet Union, Germany, France, and England, I have used sources from all those countries. American scholars can no longer ignore European, especially German, material on the Cold War. German-language versions of memoirs often contain more information than English translations. I have used both where necessary and have tried particularly to bring recent German-language research to English-language readers.

An author must proceed when the record is complete enough to tell what he or she thinks is a full story. That is what I have tried to do, pulling currently available information into an analysis that will, I believe, stand the test of time. Later documentation may challenge some of my conclusions, but I do not expect it to reverse them entirely.

The research and writing of this book were supported by a generous grant from the United States Institute of Peace. I also received a grant from the German Marshall Fund to study the diplomacy of détente and to conduct interviews in Germany.

Several persons in particular helped with my research: the staff of the Ralph J. Bunche Library of the U.S. State Department, especially William Sullivan; Hannelore Köhler of the German Information Service in New York; and Christian Ostermann of the Cold War International History Project. A number of scholars and practitioners, including J. D. Bindenagel, Karl H. Cerny, John Mapother, Karl-Heinz Schmidt, and Robert Zoellick, reviewed all or parts of the manuscript and offered helpful suggestions and information. I thank those institutions and persons for their help, but they bear no responsibility for my conclusions.

Although the struggle over Germany ended happily for many, it proved fatal to some. This book is written in memory of those who died, whether flying in the Berlin Airlift, trying to climb over the Wall, or in ways that we may never know.

For Cameron

BISMARCK AND THE GERMAN QUESTION

PRINCE OTTO VON BISMARCK, GERMANY'S "IRON CHANCELLOR," IN 1871 united Germany under Prussian domination after successive victories over Denmark, Austria and France. When he and the new German emperor, Wilhelm I, proclaimed the German Reich in the Hall of Mirrors of the Palace of Versailles, Bismarck assumed that he had made Germany strong enough to put an end to invasions of German territory by foreigners coveting a strategic location for themselves or for their garrisons. He thought there would be no more "German question," as the fighting and wrangling over German lands had become known.

Bismarck could be excused for his optimism. He had brought together under one roof the multiplicity of German minidomains whose weakness had for centuries invited attack by France, Russia, Sweden, Austria or other neighbors that wanted either to control some part of Germany or to prevent others from controlling it. Those attacks had killed millions of Germans and had left towns, castles and farms in ruins. Bismarck thought that a strong Germany, united finally, although later than other European states, could protect its interests and its people. But Bismarck made two fateful mistakes, creating a German Empire that contained the seeds of its own destruction.

First, he tied German unity to Prussian autocracy. Having helped to defeat the German liberals, idealists and humanists who had tried to unite Germany on a democratic foundation in 1848 and 1849, Bismarck united Germany under the Hohenzollerns. This condemned the German Empire to one disaster after another, at home and abroad, under the swaggering and myopic Prussian ruling class.

Second, Bismarck annexed Alsace-Lorraine from France, gaining an irreconcilably vengeful enemy. Germany had not won peace or security. Instead, it had to live under the unrelenting threat of a war that Bismarck's ceaseless and often devious maneuvers could only postpone and that Germany would lose. After France and its allies imposed their own vindictive peace at Versailles in 1919, Hitler's wars of revenge and conquest left even more destruction and a monstrous legacy of shame. Bismarck's Reich spawned a new German question: how to cope with the raging Gargantua in the heart of Europe.

The world and Germany itself paid a high price for Bismarck's mistakes. The united Germany he had created became an even greater tinderbox than the divided Germany had been. After World War II, the victors decided not to give it another chance.

Only half a century after Bismarck's death in 1898, Germany again lay divided and under foreign occupation, more thoroughly defeated and devastated than ever. Prussia itself had been legally abolished and most of its territory split between Russia and Poland.

But once again—as before 1871—a divided Germany incited avaricious rivalry. The four powers that had defeated Hitler's Reich argued over the remains. They wanted either to control all of Germany or at least to prevent each other from controlling it. They did not launch a military conflict over Germany as European kings and emperors had in the past. Instead, they fought by all other means in what became known as the Cold War. They preferred to keep Germany divided than to risk losing control over whatever part they held.

Finally, in September 1990, the four powers and the Germans agreed on terms that let Germany unite again. Thus ended not only the division of Germany but the Cold War as a whole.

The Cold War had some unexpected benefits. It served as the essential incubator for a modern German state. It softened wartime emotions on all sides, forestalling yet another vindictive peace. And it gave Germans time to rediscover and to nourish the democratic roots in their own history, to accept their losses, to recognize and to respect the legitimate fears of their neighbors, and to understand and try to compensate for the suffering that Hitler had caused.

Time became both healer and creator. During its four decades, the Cold War drew old enemies into new relationships. It let Germany define its future in a reconciliation that others would accept. Europe and the world created institutions in which Germany could join and contribute.

Recently available evidence gives new insights into the history of the Cold War over Germany. It is now clear that Josef Stalin did not want a divided Germany but did not make the decisions necessary to prevent it. His satrap, Walter Ulbricht, played a more autonomous and more pernicious role than we knew.

Nikita Khrushchev put missiles into Cuba to win West Berlin, not to protect Cuba itself. Ulbricht's successor Erich Honecker may have plotted the removal of West German chancellor Willy Brandt against the wishes of Soviet leader Leonid Brezhnev.

In the West, we can now see that British foreign secretary Ernest Bevin shaped Cold War Germany and Europe more than he had been credited with doing. Later, U. S. president John F. Kennedy suffered from inexperience and slanted advice. He blundered but recovered. New documents show that Kennedy and others could have prevented construction of the Berlin Wall by quick action. In the bitter aftermath, French president Charles de Gaulle almost outmaneuvered Kennedy and did outmaneuver British prime minister Harold Macmillan in Germany and Europe.

At the end, the Republican presidents Ronald Reagan and George Bush finished what the Democrat Harry Truman had started. Mikhail Gorbachev made choices that other Soviet leaders had wanted but failed to make. But he came too late and history punished him, as he had himself foreseen.

The struggle over Germany showed how time can affect politics and policy. Solutions impossible in 1946 or 1958 became possible by 1970 or 1990. The passage of time, the stability of German democracy and policy, and the depth of Soviet exhaustion brought back the unity that many Germans had sought but that others had squandered.

The Soviet Union and the West could end the Cold War only when the Germans could fill the space between them. And although the Germans could not win the struggle over their own country, neither could it be won without their help. It ended as it had to end, not on the battlefield but on the streets, in the churches, atop the Berlin Wall and in the conference room. It ended so that all could win, and did.

The most silent became the most articulate and the most powerless became the most powerful. They gave the lie to Bismarck's assertion that Germany would be forged in "blood and iron." They corrected his mistakes. And the peace they brought ended not only the Cold War but the long conflict that had racked Europe and the world since Bismarck's defeat of the German liberals and his humiliation of France.

Nonetheless, the German question does not go away. It mutates into a new form, no longer about a divided Germany that tempts others or a united Germany that terrifies them. What is that new form? What can the United States, Europe and others now expect from the new united Germany? And how did the Cold War provide both a new German question and perhaps an answer?

ONE

MAKING PEACE WHILE MAKING WAR

ADOLF HITLER AND HIS "THOUSAND-YEAR REICH" MET THEIR DOOM during the winter of 1942–1943, ten years after he had come to power.

Field Marshal Erwin Rommel, beaten at Egypt's El Alamein in October 1942, would never reach the Suez Canal. Field Marshal Friedrich von Paulus surrendered what remained of the German Sixth Army at Stalingrad in February 1943. Five months later, Hitler himself masterminded and lost the greatest armored engagement of all time, the battle of Kursk in Russia. By the summer of 1943, Germany was losing more U-boats than it could build. The Allies had landed successfully in North Africa and Italy. In the Pacific, Japan had lost the crucial naval battle at Midway.

Germany began a wide if slow retreat across Russia, North Africa and Europe. But Hitler fought on, like a third-rate chess player who will not admit defeat until he is checkmated. He and his allies still occupied much of Europe and of the Pacific Ocean. Allied victory would not come quickly.

ROOSEVELT, STALIN AND CHURCHILL

Like Napoleon, Hitler had spawned a mighty coalition of enemies, which Great Britain's prime minister Winston Churchill called the "Grand Alliance."

The leaders of the Grand Alliance, President Franklin Roosevelt of the United States, Marshal Josef Stalin of the Soviet Union and Churchill himself, knew by 1943 that they would win the war. But they also knew that they would win only if they remained united. Several major campaigns, in France, the Philippines, Germany and Japan, had not even begun. If any ally faltered or withdrew, the others could still lose.

The Allied leaders also knew that they would have to agree on the fate of Germany and its allies. But they had virtually nothing in common except their wish to defeat the Axis powers. Each had his own interests and his own views.

Roosevelt came the closest to being an idealist, although he had made a brilliant political career as a pragmatist. Like most Americans, he believed that the world should no longer be divided into spheres of influence. He did not share Secretary of State Cordell Hull's faith that global problems could best be solved through a new and improved League of Nations. But Roosevelt did believe that Americans could solve international problems better than the Europeans had done.

After the Japanese attack on Pearl Harbor on December 7, 1941, had brought the United States into the war, Roosevelt had agreed with U.S. Army Chief of Staff George C. Marshall that postwar political considerations should be subordinated to the needs of victory.[1] Roosevelt attached special importance to gaining and keeping Stalin's confidence until both Germany and Japan were beaten. He thought it would be unwise to make or seek specific commitments about the postwar shape of Europe while the war was going on. But he knew that he would have to begin planning for peace.

Churchill lived in both the idealist and the practical worlds. A master writer and speaker, he relished words that could articulate great ideals. When Hitler's forces threatened England, Churchill's powerful rhetoric helped to mobilize the British people and their friends.

Like Roosevelt, Churchill wanted to keep Stalin fully committed to the war effort. He felt an obligation to Stalin because the Soviet Union carried the burden of the European land war against the Wehrmacht until the Western Allies opened other fronts in Italy and France. Although he knew that Stalin did not share his or Roosevelt's democratic ideals, he wanted to reach arrangements that would keep Stalin in the war.

Stalin, despite his communist ideology, saw the world in the most practical terms of the three leaders. To him, realities mattered more than words. On December 16, 1941, he told British foreign secretary Anthony Eden in Moscow: "Declarations—that is like algebra; treaties or agreements—that is practical arithmetic. We prefer arithmetic to algebra." He dismissed sweeping pledges except for propaganda. He saw little purpose in a new League of Nations after the failure of the last. Stalin did not want a new and untried world order. He wanted precise arrangements that would give the Soviet Union secure borders.[2]

The darkest and most xenophobic of the three leaders, Stalin wanted to outdo the founder of the Soviet Union, Vladimir Lenin, in spreading world revolution and the czars in establishing an empire. But his mistrust of others could work against him. Maxim Litvinov, who had served as Soviet foreign commissar for several years during the 1930s and as ambassador to Washington during the early 1940s, condemned Stalin as narrow-minded and rigid. He complained that Stalin had surrounded himself with the "half-wit" Vyacheslav Molotov, the "careerist" Lavrenti Beria and the "fool" Nikita Khrushchev.[3]

Stalin felt that the West never helped him as much as it should have. He thought that the Allies had not established a European front against Hitler until they had seen that the Soviet Union would dominate Europe if they did not act. He remembered that Lenin had wanted a link with Germany as the key to world revolution. Now Stalin wanted that link. He also wanted recognition as a full global partner.

Whatever their differences, all three Allies agreed that they had to deal harshly with Germany. Having narrowly escaped defeat twice in less than thirty years, all three wanted to make certain that Germany could never threaten them again. Roosevelt toyed actively with permanent dismemberment and perhaps de-industrialization. Stalin and Churchill also wanted to do whatever was necessary to save their nations from more German attacks.[4]

With the prospect of victory before them, Roosevelt and Churchill met in Casablanca, Morocco, in January 1943. Roosevelt seized the occasion to announce that the Allies wanted the "unconditional surrender" of Germany, Italy and Japan. Churchill would have preferred to allow a separate arrangement for Italy, but he fully supported Roosevelt's language and especially unconditional surrender for Germany.[5] It immediately became the main Allied war objective.

Neither Roosevelt nor Churchill had discussed the insistence on unconditional surrender with Stalin before announcing it. Stalin had been invited to Casablanca but had begged off. He supported the demand but let it be known that he would have preferred to be consulted.

By mid-1943 Churchill and Roosevelt wanted to begin more precise discussions with Stalin, especially as they kept hearing rumors (perhaps inspired by the Kremlin itself) of a separate peace between Stalin and Hitler.[6] Eden sent a memorandum to Soviet Foreign Minister Molotov on July 2, proposing that the Allies apply the principles of unconditional surrender to all European Axis states, occupy the defeated states, install control committees to govern occupied territories, and establish a European steering committee that would include large and small victorious powers.

Eden's proposal jolted Stalin into action although he did not formally reply. He decided that the Soviet Union needed to establish its long-term objectives clearly. Realizing the importance of the task, he assigned the responsibility to a committee headed by his close associate Marshal Kliment Voroshilov.

Voroshilov and his committee warned that a peace treaty with Germany might take a long time to reach and that during the interim the Germans might play off the Allies against each other. He argued that Stalin should leave nothing to chance but should make certain that even the initial cease-fire arrangements reflected Soviet security interests and territorial claims. The cease-fire should be designed to serve as an acceptable status for Germany until a peace treaty was signed. The Soviet Union would be safe even if its friends changed their minds after the war was over. Stalin accepted that proposal.

Having recognized that they needed to talk, the three Allied leaders had to decide where. They agreed to meet in Teheran before the end of 1943. That was as far from Soviet territory as Stalin wanted to venture. They also agreed to establish the European Advisory Commission (EAC) as a coordinating and planning body. The EAC was to meet in London on a continuing basis and was to make recommendations on the terms of surrender to be imposed upon each of the European enemy states and on the machinery required to ensure fulfillment of those terms.[7]

The Teheran summit conference served two purposes. The more immediate, but less important one, was to discuss Allied strategy for the remainder of the war. The other, more far-reaching, was to discuss the future shape of Europe. At the meeting, the two purposes came into conflict, for the Allied leaders could not discuss disagreements about the future of Europe while trying to coordinate military plans. In particular, the Western Allies felt that they could not question Stalin's designs too closely while they still needed his help against Germany and perhaps against Japan.

At Teheran, the Allies agreed that Poland's borders should be shifted to the west. Stalin made it clear that the Soviet Union would seize eastern Poland. Churchill then said that Poland might "move westward" to remain viable even if its eastern territories became part of the Soviet Union. He added that "if Poland were to step on some German toes, that could not be helped." Stalin suggested that Polish territory extend as far west as the Oder River.[8]

Using three matches to represent potential borders, Churchill showed Poland moving westward, which apparently pleased Stalin because it showed that Churchill agreed with him. All three Allies concurred that the Oder would mark most of Poland's western border. Stalin also said that the Soviet Union wanted Königsberg in East Prussia as a warm-water port, with neither Roosevelt nor Churchill raising any objection.

The Allies discussed the portion of the Polish-German border south of the Oder but did not decide it clearly. They spoke of the Neisse River serving as that border but did not specify whether they meant the eastern or western Neisse, both of which flowed northward into the Oder but about 200 kilometers (120 miles) apart. They did not use a map during their discussions.[9]

Having decided that Germany would lose its eastern territories to Poland, all three leaders agreed tentatively that the remainder of Germany should be divided into smaller states as it had been before 1871.

Roosevelt proposed splitting Germany into five parts: (1) Prussia to the northeast; (2) Hanover and the lowland part of Germany to the northwest; (3) Saxony and the Leipzig area to the east; (4) Hesse-Darmstadt and Hesse-Kassel to the west; and (5) Bavaria, Baden, and Württemberg to the south. While those five sections would be self-governing, a planned United Nations organization would control such strategically sensitive areas as Kiel, the Kiel canal, and Hamburg as well as the Ruhr and the Saar coal- and steel-producing regions.

Churchill showed some support for Roosevelt's plan but added that he believed that the most important point was to treat Prussia sternly. Other German states could be in some kind of Danubian or other confederation, and things should be made easier for them.

Stalin said that he liked the idea of dividing Germany but wanted to study it further before making concrete proposals. He added that he questioned making new confederations, Danubian or otherwise. He concluded that the Allies would have to recognize that the Germans would want to reunite no matter what division they might impose.

All three agreed that they had only begun to address the future shape of Germany, and they decided to pass the subject to the EAC for further discussion.

By the end of the Teheran Conference, the Big Three leaders of Churchill's Grand Alliance had at least preliminarily decided the general postwar shape of Germany. Germany was to lose Königsberg and all the territory east and northeast of the Oder as well as some territory south of the Oder in Silesia, although the shape and size of the latter area remained unclear. The rest of Germany might be partitioned, but the three Allies had not agreed on the principles to govern that partition. They did not want to argue about details while the war raged. The EAC thus did not follow up with any decision on dismemberment. It did, however, by early 1944, agree on the broad shapes of temporary occupation zones.[10]

Teheran reflected the punitive attitude of the Allies toward the Hitler regime and toward Germany itself. But the Allies thought not only in terms of revenge. They also wanted to prevent another Hitler. The occupation arrangements thus tried to avoid repeating one mistake made at the Versailles peace conference after World War I. This time, the Allies would not let Hitler saddle someone else—especially a democratic government—with the blame for his defeat, as the German military had done with the "stab-in-the-back" charge against the Weimar Republic after 1918. Germany was to be thoroughly defeated, and was to know it, so that the forces of tyranny and militarism would be fully expurgated.

But Roosevelt and Churchill also wanted to avoid the mistake made at Versailles of forcing the German economy to collapse after the war as it had done after World War I. This collapse, which led to staggering inflation followed by ruinous depression, had helped bring Hitler to power.

The "lessons of Versailles," therefore, gave the three Allies and their EAC representatives two mutually contradictory objectives: on the one hand, to punish Germany and especially Hitler and the Nazis for the war; on the other, to avoid putting the Germans into such a desperate situation that they would turn again to political extremism. These contradictory aims were to complicate policy toward the occupation and toward reparations.

YALTA DIVIDES GERMANY

The Teheran summit left many questions open because the Big Three did not want to jeopardize their cooperation against Hitler. As the war progressed, however, they began to realize that they would have to try to agree on those questions.

Allied armies advanced inexorably. German soldiers sometimes put up fierce resistance, especially on the Russian front, but they had no strategic plan and little incentive to keep fighting. Tens of thousands deserted, although they were shot when caught. Members of the German high command increasingly resented Hitler's irrational orders, which often compelled German forces to remain in indefensible positions, losing not only battles but major units. Those who had long opposed Hitler on moral grounds found friends among those who realized that he would lose the war. They plotted to kill Hitler and tried to do so on July 20, 1944. But the attempt failed, the plotters were hanged on meathooks and the war went on.

Soviet forces became the dominant presence in Europe. By the summer of 1944 they entered Poland. But Stalin did not order a direct advance into Germany. Instead, he ordered the Red Army to conquer all of eastern Europe and the Balkans on a wide front. The Red Army stood at the Oder River only at the beginning of 1945. By then the Western Allies had reached Germany's western borders.

The Allies tried to advance on the diplomatic front as their armies were advancing on the military front. But they could not agree on what was to become of the country they were defeating. Their delegates to the European Advisory

Commission differed on many basic issues.[11] The EAC delegates could not agree on how long an Allied control system was to function, although they did agree that it should be temporary.[12] Nor could they decide on a longer-term regime to succeed the occupation. They produced no formal political document of surrender, no common occupation policy declaration, no dismemberment plan and no reparations schedule. They could not even agree on whether the Allies should leave some German authority in place after they entered Germany.[13]

The EAC delegates did, however, concur that each zonal commander would have supreme authority in his zone while broad policy was to be made by unanimous agreement in an Allied Control Council (ACC).[14] This virtually decided the division of Germany because each occupier could do as he wished in his zone and could veto any policy to be applied all across Germany.[15] Both the U.S. and Soviet forces insisted on these rules because they did not want their commanders subject to outside control.

The EAC also produced three largely technical agreements:

(1) draft instructions for German unconditional surrender,
(2) a protocol on the occupation zones and Berlin, and
(3) an agreement on the control machinery for Germany.[16]

The EAC agreed on the outline of the occupation zones by early 1944, but only in September did Roosevelt agree to accept the zone in southern Germany that the others had assigned to the United States. He had wanted the northwest area because he mistrusted the French Resistance leader Charles de Gaulle and did not want U.S. forces to depend on supply routes through France. He had also wanted the Ruhr. But Churchill had argued that British forces had always been north of U.S. forces during the Allied advance, and shifting forces around would be very difficult. Roosevelt finally accepted Churchill's argument, but did not like having the U.S. occupation zone landlocked. He made more careful arrangements for transit traffic through the British zone than he ever made for traffic to Berlin through the Soviet zone.[17]

Allied leaders faced policy disagreements at home as well as abroad. The fiercest took place in Washington and concerned the long-term future of Germany. Secretary of the Treasury Henry J. Morgenthau proposed turning Germany into an agricultural country to make certain that it could never again constitute a threat. Morgenthau also wanted total dismemberment of Germany and deliberate creation of economic chaos. Both Secretary of State Cordell Hull and Secretary of War Henry Stimson opposed the Morgenthau Plan, as it came to be known. They thought that U.S. interests in Europe would be better served by having a prosperous and democratic instead of an impoverished and vengeful Germany. Roosevelt first accepted and then abandoned the Morgenthau Plan, although it was to surface again in U.S. occupation policy.[18]

American attitudes toward Germany began to shift as it became evident that relations with Moscow might deteriorate after the war. The U.S. government began to hear ever more worrisome reports about Soviet intentions. George Kennan, counselor at the U.S. Embassy in Moscow, wrote at the end of 1944 that the United States could not hope for cooperation with the Soviet Union in Europe.[19]

In London as in Washington, foreign policy experts argued that Germany would have to be permitted and perhaps encouraged to reemerge as a viable state because Europe needed a stable Germany for economic survival and to help hold back the Soviet Union strategically. But Churchill himself wanted to punish Germany more than his experts did.

French leaders had their own differences. They had begun to discuss post-war plans for Germany during 1943, but they received very little information about the ideas being discussed in Washington, London or Moscow. Some of the leaders of the French Resistance, including de Gaulle, favored a return to the military controls over Germany tried after World War I. Others, however, including some French socialists, believed that France and Europe should befriend Germany and integrate it into a future West European confederation.[20]

By 1944, as de Gaulle became the leader of the new French government, his views became French policy. He wanted to detach all the land west of the Rhine River from Germany, with most of it to be under French occupation although some parts were to be under the Belgian or Dutch flags. De Gaulle said that France would not annex those parts of Germany but that "the flag of the French army" would fly over them. He wanted the French occupation zone to cover most of Baden-Württemberg, including the city of Stuttgart. He also wanted France to have its own full share of reparations.[21]

De Gaulle saw a parallel with Poland. As Stalin wanted the land east of the Oder for Poland, de Gaulle wanted the land west of the Rhine for France. He wanted the Ruhr to be permanently removed from German sovereignty, to be internationalized, and to have its mineral resources and its steel mills expropriated and turned over to an international authority that would trade freely with all the states of the world including Germany.

While others thought and planned, the Red Army took control of eastern Europe. Churchill flew to Moscow in October 1944 to try to apply his spheres-of-influence concept. He gave Stalin a paper proposing the following division of influence between Moscow and the West:

Romania: 90 percent Moscow/10 percent West
Bulgaria: 75 percent Moscow/25 percent West
Yugoslavia: 50 percent Moscow/50 percent West
Hungary: 50 percent Moscow/50 percent West
Greece: 10 percent Moscow/90 percent West[22]

Stalin glanced at the paper and initialed it instantaneously. Churchill thought the initials signaled agreement. More likely, though, they signaled derision. Stalin already occupied all the listed states except Greece and parts of Yugoslavia. He could dismiss Churchill's percentages as irrelevant, for he himself would decide what would really happen in all of eastern Europe and over most of central Europe.

Stalin showed his power even more clearly when the two men discussed Poland. Stalin insisted that the Polish people had shown their preference for the so-called Lublin government, which the Red Army had brought to Poland, and that it would govern until a more permanent government might be chosen. Churchill could not change Stalin's mind, for the Soviet dictator intended to exercise full influence over Poland.

Stalin and Churchill also discussed the future of Germany, with both considering some form of dismemberment. Stalin reiterated that he wanted the city of Königsberg. But they agreed that no firm decisions could be made without Roosevelt's participation at another summit.

De Gaulle made his own pilgrimage to Moscow two months later. When he told Stalin that France wanted all of Germany west of the Rhine River, Stalin said he would not accept that. De Gaulle also told Stalin that France wanted a treaty with the Soviet Union. Stalin agreed. They signed a treaty of mutual assistance on December 10, 1944.

The separate bilateral talks and the futile EAC sessions showed that the Big Three needed to meet again. No other forum could decide the future of Germany. If there was ever to be a common policy, only Roosevelt, Churchill and Stalin could define it.

Between February 4 and 12, 1945, the Big Three met at the resort town of Yalta in the Crimea. The Western Allies did not want to go there but Stalin would not leave Russia.[23] De Gaulle tried to visit all of the Big Three capitals just before the Yalta Conference to present his views and demand admittance, but Roosevelt and Churchill would not receive him.[24]

The Yalta Conference opened under the somber reality of the Red Army's occupation of eastern Europe. Roosevelt and Churchill recognized that they had little chance to bring Western-style freedom to Poland and its neighbors, but they believed that they still had to try. They also needed to discuss Germany. Roosevelt wanted to get two additional items: Stalin's agreement on a United Nations voting formula and his pledge to join the war against Japan as soon as possible after the Allies had defeated Hitler.

Early during their meetings at Yalta, Roosevelt told Stalin that he did not expect U.S. forces to remain in Germany more than two years after the end of hostilities. Such a swift withdrawal would leave Great Britain and France as the sole major Western powers in Europe. That prospect colored all discussion on Germany at Yalta.

Unlike Teheran, the Yalta meeting did not dwell on military matters. The war had virtually ended. The Western and the Soviet armies would soon meet somewhere in defeated Germany, although no one could predict exactly where or when. The Big Three could thus concentrate on the postwar settlement.

The Big Three discussed Germany several times. For the most part, they approved the documents produced by the European Advisory Commission. All knew that those texts did not resolve the truly difficult issues, but they still preferred to ignore those issues when they could.

The discussion over possible dismemberment of Germany did not go as it had at Teheran. Roosevelt did not repeat his previous proposal. Churchill said that he favored dismemberment "in principle," but he did not repeat his earlier suggestions either. He had already come to believe that the West would need a united Germany to balance Soviet power in Europe. Stalin opposed dismemberment openly.[25] But the Big Three did not want to dismiss the notion completely, so they decided to establish a Dismemberment Committee to study "the procedure for the dismemberment of Germany."

The principals did approve EAC proposals for three occupation zones in Germany as well as for a Berlin divided into three sectors. They decided to accept the borders between those zones and sectors as temporary dividing lines.

The leaders further agreed that France would receive an occupation zone, although Stalin insisted that it should be taken out of the U.S. and British occupation areas. Stalin also agreed to give France a seat on the Allied Control Council. But he did so only toward the end of the conference in response to a personal appeal from Roosevelt. He clearly did not like de Gaulle's plans for Germany.

The Yalta Conference may have agreed on occupation zones, but it did not agree on reparations. Although Stalin urged Roosevelt and Churchill in the strongest terms to grant major reparations to compensate the Soviet Union for its World War II losses, he could not win them over.

Stalin presented a plan under which Germany would pay $20 billion in reparations, with half of that amount to go to the Soviet Union. For two years,

German industry was to be dismantled and shipped as reparations. After that, Germany was to pay reparations in kind for another ten years.

Churchill and Roosevelt recognized that the Soviet Union deserved reparations. But they would not accept a specific target, especially such a high one. Roosevelt feared that the United States and other Western countries would end up paying the bill as they had after World War I because they would be forced to rebuild the German economy after it had been destroyed for reparations. Churchill shared those fears.

Roosevelt and Churchill did not believe that they needed to provide indefinite help to Moscow. After all, the United States and Great Britain had helped the Soviet Union during the war itself. They had sent Moscow over 10 million tons of armaments, costing a total of more than $6 billion, and about a third as much again in non-military aid. The shipments had included food as well as thousands of tanks, artillery pieces and trucks, absolutely essential to Stalin's war effort.[26]

Stalin became angry during the final Yalta discussion on this topic. He reminded the Western leaders that the Soviet Union had suffered more from the war than any other country. At that point, Roosevelt wanted to accept Stalin's demands, but Churchill refused. Finally, at Roosevelt's urging, Churchill reluctantly accepted the $20 billion figure as a "basis for discussion" but not as an agreed figure. The Yalta reparations protocol stated that the British delegation believed that "no figure on reparations should be mentioned."[27]

The Yalta agreement to disagree over reparations left the wartime alliance shaken. It must have frustrated Stalin, whose military position was never more dominant than at the time of the Yalta Conference. But he also must have recognized that he could not do much. The most important reparations would have to come from the Ruhr industrial basin, an area in the projected British zone of occupation and which Western troops would reach first.

While the Allies could perhaps postpone some decisions about Germany, they could not postpone decisions about Poland, the problem that dominated the Yalta Conference. They focused mainly on two issues: Poland's western borders, which directly affected Germany as well as Poland, and Poland's future government, which affected Germany less directly but would change the West's perception of Stalin and thus Western thinking about Germany.

Soviet behavior in eastern Europe appalled Churchill. He realized that Moscow would dominate the area. He could even agree to that, albeit reluctantly, as he had shown in the spheres of influence that he had offered Stalin. But he objected deeply, even emotionally, to the combination of repression and cynicism that marked Stalin's domination. Churchill could not accept having a British ally behave as Soviet forces and Soviet administrators did. He told Stalin at Yalta that an eagle would still "let the small birds sing" even if it were strong enough to stop them. Stalin did not appreciate the point.

The two leaders argued fiercely about the future government of Poland. Stalin still favored the Lublin government. Churchill favored the Polish government in exile in London. He also bitterly resented Stalin's decision to hold back the Red Army while German forces massacred Warsaw's resistance fighters after Stalin himself had urged an uprising against the Nazis. But Churchill could not change the reality that Stalin had conquered Poland and would decide its future.[28]

The dispute about Poland's government helped shape the discussion about its western border. At Teheran, the Big Three had agreed that Poland should be shifted westward without fixing the precise boundaries. But at that point Churchill had still expected Poland to be an independent state. By the time of Yalta, Churchill realized that Poland would be a Soviet satellite. This sharpened the disagreement about its western border. Pushing Poland to the west would merely give Stalin even greater domination over eastern Europe, helping him rather than the Poles.

The plan that Stalin and Molotov presented for Poland's western frontier incorporated the German Baltic port of Stettin into Poland in the north. The border then continued directly south along the Oder and the western Neisse River to the Czech border. Both Roosevelt and Churchill questioned having the border run along the western Neisse, which would effectively remove all of Silesia from Germany. They suggested that the border turn eastward along with the Oder River itself and then turn south again along the eastern Neisse. This would still have left upper Silesia in Polish hands but would have left about 3 million Germans south of the Oder River in Germany instead of including them in Poland.[29]

Churchill questioned whether Poland could absorb that much territory and that many Germans. He warned that the "Polish goose" might choke on so much "German food." Stalin dismissed this problem by observing that most Germans were fleeing ahead of the Soviet army and that there was a lot of empty land for Poles to take.

Churchill and Roosevelt had lost this argument before Yalta. On December 18, 1944, *Pravda* had published an article drawing the border as Stalin and Molotov were to propose at Yalta. Although the article ostensibly was written by a representative of the Polish Lublin government, Stalin obviously had made his decision.[30] Under those circumstances, Churchill and Roosevelt could do nothing, especially because even the London Polish government in exile favored the western Neisse border.

Given the disagreement, the conference communiqué stated only that Poland should receive "substantial" compensation "in the north and west" for the land that it was giving up in the east, with the final border delineation to "await the peace conference."[31] The area was ostensibly to be "under Polish administration." But no one could leave Yalta without recognizing that a new Polish-German border would be part of the price that Germany would pay for Hitler's war.

When the Yalta Conference ended, each of the Big Three had won and lost. Roosevelt had made his gains outside Europe, obtaining Stalin's agreement to his United Nations voting formula and Soviet entry into the war against Japan. Stalin had made his gains in eastern Europe, with Roosevelt and Churchill accepting Poland's shift westward and major if unspecified Soviet reparations from Germany. Churchill had scored his gains in western Europe, getting French membership in the Allied Control Council to help him balance the Soviet Union after the expected departure of the United States from Europe. But he left the meeting deeply embittered, realizing that the cause for which England had entered the war, a free Poland, had been lost.

Churchill and Roosevelt also saw for the first time that Stalin would not yield where he had control. Although the Yalta Conference produced a "Declaration on Liberated Europe," pledging democratic freedoms in countries from which the Nazis had been expelled, Churchill and Roosevelt knew by then that their kind of freedom would not prevail any more under Stalin than it had under Hitler.

Yalta divided Europe between those states that were under the rule of the Red Army and those that were to join the West in one association or another. It did so in fact, but not formally. It also divided Germany, ostensibly into occupation zones but ultimately into separate states.

TRUMAN JOINS AT POTSDAM

After Yalta, the war rolled on. Allied armies fought their way across German territory from east and west and met at Torgau in what was to become the Soviet zone. Before committing suicide in the rancid air of the chancellery bunker on April 30, 1945, Hitler appointed Admiral Karl Dönitz, commander of Germany's northern forces, to succeed him as chancellor and head of state. Facing a hopeless military situation, Dönitz decided that German forces had to capitulate. The instrument of surrender was signed at Reims on May 7. At Soviet insistence, it was signed again at Berlin on the following day.

The surrender instrument did not constitute a surrender by the German government but only by the German armed forces. The first paragraph stated that:

> We, the undersigned, acting by authority of the German High Command, hereby surrender unconditionally to the Supreme Commander, Allied Expeditionary Forces, and simultaneously to the Supreme High Command of the Red Army, all forces on land, at sea, and in the air who are at this date under German control.[32]

The Dönitz government continued to function out of its capital at Flensburg in northern Germany for almost three more weeks until the Western Allies unceremoniously arrested its members. As this was a unilateral step, there was no surrender document by a German chief of state or head of government. The German government did not formally yield its authority and sovereignty. Constitutional lawyers were to write countless volumes on the legal implications of this action, but the immediate effect was to leave a nation without central institutions.[33]

The four Allies took sovereignty over Germany into their own hands on June 5, 1945, issuing a document in which they assumed supreme authority, including the powers of the German government, the German high command, and all state, municipal and local governments. This document, which came to be known as the Berlin Declaration, announced the rules for the occupation of Germany and of Berlin as well as for the Allied control machinery.[34] Thus the German state had been replaced by a new Allied structure.

The Berlin Declaration did not clarify what had happened to Germany's territories east of the Oder-Neisse line. It spoke of Germany's territory "as of 31 December 1937" but did not mention Königsberg, Prussia, Pomerania, or Silesia as areas to be occupied by any of the four powers. It pretended that the territories under four-power occupation represented the German boundaries of 1937, which they did not. The Allies never assumed formal responsibility for the separation of the territories to be administered by Poland. They left that for a peace treaty or for a future German state.

Although Germany had been defeated and occupied, the Allies still faced vexing issues left over from Yalta, such as dismemberment and reparations. They needed to make more decisions and to agree on implementing arrangements. Thus they needed to meet again.

Stalin again insisted that they meet on Soviet territory, in the historic city of Potsdam in the Soviet occupation zone near Berlin. It had not been as badly destroyed as major German cities. The Allies met there for two weeks between July 17 and August 1, 1945. It seemed a fitting place to decide the future of Germany for Frederick the Great of Prussia had built his retreat, Sans Souci, there.

Churchill had pressed hard for another Big Three meeting. He could see the wartime spirit of cooperation fade before his eyes. He saw Soviet armies imposing thinly veiled dictatorships on east and central European states. He saw American forces leaving Europe for Asia or for home. He hoped to be able to influence Stalin and also to take the measure of the new American president, Harry S. Truman, whom he had never gone out of his way to meet during his visits to Washington. He also wanted to raise some questions again, especially regarding the Oder-Neisse line.

Churchill became a forlorn figure at Potsdam, trying to persuade Stalin and Truman with the power of his oratory even as they held the high cards. Before the conference, he had tried to persuade Truman to delay withdrawing U.S. forces from the part of the Soviet occupation zone that they had conquered, at least until he had won some concessions from Stalin. Truman disagreed. As a final humiliation, Churchill and Eden had to leave before the end of the conference and learn that the British people had voted them out of office.

Churchill's successor, Clement Attlee, had worked in the British war cabinet for many years and had been present at Potsdam from the beginning of the conference. He continued Churchill's policies but could have no impact on the conference itself. Eden's successor, Ernest Bevin, quickly showed himself to have a strong personality and firm views but also could change nothing.

Truman, the new man at the table, had not wanted to come. He thought that he had more urgent business in Washington than in Potsdam and he did not like to sit around and talk. Instead, he liked to make decisions and carry them out. He had the atomic bomb very much on his mind, being notified during the conference that the A-bomb test in New Mexico had succeeded beyond expectations. His impatience finally forced through some of the most difficult Potsdam decisions because he thought that further discussion would change nothing.

Truman differed from Roosevelt in many respects. He did not come from an aristocratic family in the American Northeast but from a middle-class family in the American heartland. Instead of acting on intuition and accumulated knowledge, as Roosevelt had, he read his briefs and studied the subjects at hand carefully. He prepared himself for the Potsdam meeting much more thoroughly than Roosevelt had prepared himself for Teheran or Yalta.

Stalin faced the most delicate task at Potsdam. His forces dominated much of Europe but, once the fighting ended, had become a wasting asset. He had to find a way to use temporary military preponderance for permanent political and economic gain. He had established a security zone in eastern Europe but wanted influence across all of Europe. When Averell Harriman, the U.S. ambassador in

Moscow, congratulated him for having come as far west as Potsdam, Stalin replied that Czar Alexander I had reached Paris.

Stalin wanted to strengthen the Soviet Union and to obtain a wider range for Soviet power. He thought that German reparations could modernize the Soviet economy. He hoped to get part of the German navy. Most of all, he wanted a voice in the affairs of Germany as a whole.

Arguments about the German-Polish border dominated much of the Potsdam Conference. Churchill tried tenaciously to limit the area of Germany that was to be turned over to the Poles.[35] He repeated his Yalta argument that the border should be at the eastern, not the western, Neisse.[36] But Soviet, not British, forces sat in Silesia. Although Churchill later asserted that he would not have accepted the western Neisse border if he had remained for the entire conference, there was little that he, Attlee or Truman could do.

Truman, who had not taken part in the Teheran or Yalta discussions, tried another approach. He said that the Big Three were at Potsdam to speak of the Germany of 1937 and that this included the territories east of the Oder River. But Stalin corrected Truman to say that they were speaking of "the Germany after the war," for the Germany of 1937 no longer existed. Truman said that the United States was prepared to recognize the Soviet claim to Königsberg but that the Soviet Union could not unilaterally give the Poles "a zone of their own." He asked "are we going to give Germany away piecemeal?"

Stalin would not agree that the new Polish territories constituted an occupation zone. He saw occupation zones as temporary, and he intended the Polish shift to be permanent. He told Truman that he did not believe that the Poles would leave. With that, Truman realized that Stalin expected the Poles to stay even after the Americans and other occupiers had left.

Stalin had pushed Poland before him. Millions of Poles had fled before the Red Army, many going into former parts of Germany such as East Prussia, Pomerania and Silesia all the way to the western Neisse. Millions of Germans had fled before them and before the Soviets, with many dying in flight. No one wanted or tried to keep count. No Western army would challenge the transfer of land to Poland. All was decided long before the Potsdam Conference, although the formal Potsdam document reaffirmed that "the final delimitation of the western frontier of Poland should await the peace settlement."

The Allies resented the increasingly obvious Soviet determination to convert eastern Europe into a bastion. Churchill and Eden cited the brutal methods used by Stalin to impose communist-dominated regimes on Romania, Bulgaria and later Hungary to charge that the Soviet dictator was violating the Yalta "Declaration on Liberated Europe" as well as the agreement on relative spheres of influence. Churchill worried privately that Stalin would use the Soviet position in Romania and Bulgaria to control Turkey and the Dardanelles, which would allow Moscow to challenge Britain in the Mediterranean. Stalin and Molotov in turn complained about Western policies in Greece and elsewhere.

Stalin, like the Western leaders, did no better at Potsdam than at Yalta. Neither Truman nor his British colleagues would accept any fixed target for Soviet reparations from Germany. Molotov repeatedly claimed that the Big Three had agreed on a figure at Yalta, but he got nowhere with Truman's new secretary of state, James Byrnes, with Eden or with Bevin.

Truman and Churchill objected to the $20 billion total for the same reasons as before but with renewed intensity. Having observed Stalin's actions in eastern Europe, they saw even less reason to repeat the post–World War I experience, when reparations had crushed the fledgling Weimar democracy and had forced the United States and Britain to subsidize them. Truman also knew that the U.S. Congress would never authorize funds which would help support the Red Army's conquests.

The Western Allies had seen that Stalin was already carting away reparations from German and "Polish-administered" areas under Soviet military control but was not counting those items as reparations. Byrnes and Molotov sparred over the amount by which those dismantlings should reduce final Soviet claims, with Molotov asserting that they represented "war booty" rather than reparations. Byrnes demanded a full accounting but did not receive it.

Byrnes and Truman chose to make the best of a bad bargain by tying reparations to Stalin's Polish demands. Truman said that he would not agree to Soviet reparations numbers as long as parts of Germany were being given away to Poland. He argued that the rest of Germany could not be expected to meet claims based on the larger area covered by the 1937 boundaries. He wondered out loud if reparations from the Polish "zone" were being counted against the total claim. Stalin refused even to discuss the subject, not wanting to choose between reparations and the Oder-Neisse line.

When he finally did have to choose, Stalin chose the Oder-Neisse line, as Byrnes had expected. And Byrnes chose to reach an agreement on that basis, despite objections from his British colleagues. He stopped challenging that border, but in exchange demanded that each occupying power draw reparations primarily from its own zone of occupation with no overall target. Stalin and Molotov had to agree. But they still wanted and got an accord that the Soviet Union would receive 15 percent of German industrial equipment that was not needed in the Western zones. In exchange, they promised to ship food, minerals and other commodities from their zone. Stalin negotiated an additional 10 percent of unneeded German industrial equipment from the Western zones without having to pay any compensation.[37]

But the Soviet leader could not compel Truman and the British to accept both his territorial and his reparations claims. Stalin's troops occupied Poland and eastern Germany, but Truman's and Churchill's troops occupied the areas from which Stalin wanted to take his main reparations. Stalin must have asked himself if he should not have marched directly on the Ruhr instead of occupying the Balkans.

Raw power drove the Potsdam negotiations from start to finish. Stalin could give away a quarter of Germany to Poland and his army could take anything within reach, but he could not get anything from the western parts of Germany. Churchill's Grand Alliance had fulfilled its purpose and lost its common interest.

Nonetheless, the Big Three were able to reach six decisions that shaped the future of Europe and the struggle over Germany.[38]

First, they decided to establish a Council of Foreign Ministers (CFM) that was to meet regularly to prepare peace treaties for Germany and its allies. They decided that the council would begin by writing the peace treaties for Italy and the smaller German satellites Bulgaria, Finland, Hungary and Romania. It would only later write a treaty for Germany.

Second, the Big Three agreed to treat Germany as a single economic unit with "equitable distribution" of essential goods throughout all of occupied Germany, and they agreed that German administrative machinery was to manage the economy under appropriate Allied control and direction.

Third, the Big Three abandoned the Morgenthau Plan although they agreed on a set of economic principles that adopted elements from it. Truman himself disliked the Morgenthau Plan and refused to take the treasury secretary to Potsdam although Morgenthau had wanted to go. Morgenthau thereupon resigned. Nonetheless, the Big Three agreed to rid Germany of its cartels, trusts and other monopolistic arrangements. They also agreed that German war potential should be eliminated and that agriculture and "peaceful domestic industries" should be promoted.

Fourth, the Big Three tacitly agreed that there would not be a complete or permanent dismemberment of Germany. They did not record this decision in the protocol of the conference, except insofar as they decided to treat Germany as an economic unit and closed down the commission on dismemberment. By the time of Potsdam, Stalin had decided that he preferred a united to a dismembered Germany. So had Churchill. Truman had no reason to disagree with them.

Fifth, the Big Three also tacitly agreed to the deportation of remaining ethnic Germans from Czechoslovakia, Hungary and Poland. Within the next several years, those states expelled virtually all ethnic Germans. Although the Big

Three stipulated that any deportations should be conducted in an "orderly and humane manner," the Germans were usually expelled unceremoniously without any chance to take anything. Hitler's Wehrmacht had left so many bitter memories in the lands it had occupied that no one wanted to treat Germans gently.

Sixth, the Big Three opened the way for the formation of a German government that would be in a position to accept the terms of a peace treaty. In artfully vague language, they agreed that the Council of Ministers would prepare a peace treaty for Germany "to be accepted by the Government of Germany when a government adequate for the purpose is established."[39] But they reached no agreement about when such a German government would be established, how it was to be established, who might have the authority to establish it, or what kind of government it was to be. The Big Three thus showed that they did not envision the permanent occupation of Germany, but their imprecise language revealed that they differed about its long-term future.

Many basic issues were left undecided. The Big Three did not formally agree on Germany's future external or internal borders. They did not formally divide Germany except into occupation zones, but neither did they establish any single German government authority. On some of the most important issues regarding Germany's future, Potsdam left no clear legacy.

Yet Potsdam may have left a lasting legacy for Germany in Truman's and Stalin's attitudes toward each other. Truman found Stalin difficult and sometimes unpleasant to deal with, although he liked the Soviet leader's decisive style. He was very disappointed that Stalin refused to discuss the internationalization of major waterways, a subject Truman regarded as important and which had interested him for some time. Truman raised the matter during the conference but met with a stone wall from Stalin, who wanted to keep control of the Danube. When Truman personally appealed to Stalin at least to enter the subject in the conference record even if nothing had come of it, Stalin rejected the request in crude terms. Even before the interpreter had finished translating his remarks, Stalin forcefully repeated, in English, "No! I say no!" These remarks, the only English words Stalin spoke during the entire conference, left Truman flushed and angry.

Truman, who had found himself in an unpleasant confrontation with Molotov over Poland even before meeting Stalin, told his daughter Margaret that he had learned at Potsdam that the police state of the communists was no different from that of the Nazis.[40] He quickly recognized that Stalin's wishes in Germany differed from his own. He complained that nothing had really been achieved at Potsdam although he had spent more than two weeks there. He vowed never again to attend a conference like Potsdam and did not do so.[41] Thereafter, he dealt with Stalin in a manner very different from Roosevelt's.

There had been signs that Roosevelt himself had become disheartened about Stalin. He had said shortly before his death: "We can't do business with Stalin. He has broken every one of the promises he made at Yalta."[42] But Roosevelt had not briefed Truman on this, and the new president formed his own opinion.

Stalin in turn disliked Truman. Although Truman had not challenged Soviet policies as persistently as Churchill and often had appeared to mediate between British and Soviet positions at Potsdam, he had several times put his views forward in a blunt way that may have surprised a dictator unaccustomed to open challenges. Truman had also canceled Lend-Lease financial aid to the Soviet Union immediately after the end of the war in Europe, an action that was required under U.S. legislation but was badly explained and did not accord with what Stalin might have expected from a friendly partner. Stalin later told Nikita Khrushchev that Truman was "worthless."[43]

The Potsdam results suffered from several fatal flaws. Mainly, France did not attend. This absence made a mockery of some of the most important conference decisions, for Charles de Gaulle felt neither inclined nor obliged to carry out the accords reached by his allies.

Churchill and Truman had asked Stalin to let de Gaulle join at Potsdam. Churchill, increasingly daunted by the prospect that an exhausted Britain would be left alone to face Soviet power in Europe, had genuinely hoped for French participation despite his own well-honed personal aversion toward de Gaulle. Truman, although he had not inherited Roosevelt's animosity against the general, had resented how slowly the French were withdrawing to their assigned zone of occupation. He had to threaten a cut-off in aid to France in order to get French forces out of Stuttgart, a city de Gaulle wanted although it was in the American-designated occupation zone. Truman supported Churchill in wanting French participation at Potsdam but saw no reason to press the point.[44]

Stalin said that he would let France join at Potsdam only if Poland did, knowing that neither Churchill nor Truman would accept that bargain. Stalin did not object if London and Washington wanted to give some of their occupation area to France, but he did not want to let France participate in decisions about Germany. He had given France a seat on the Allied Control Council for Germany only in response to Roosevelt's personal plea at Yalta, but Potsdam was too important to admit de Gaulle. Stalin may also have disliked de Gaulle's open determination to dismember Germany.

Not surprisingly, de Gaulle rejected most of the results of the Potsdam meeting. In notes handed to the Big Three five days after the meeting, de Gaulle agreed to join the Council of Foreign Ministers while adding pointedly that France would participate in "every important question concerning Europe." He accepted the Oder-Neisse border and the transfer of Königsberg to the Soviet Union but said that other German frontiers should be examined by "all the interested powers" (including France). And de Gaulle reserved the right to present French views on reparations.

De Gaulle did not like the occupation zone that Washington and London had granted him. He believed that the area was too small and too close to the French border to have the strategic and political reach he wanted. Wags called it the "brassiere" because it was split into two barely connected and approximately equal areas. The French leader showed his displeasure by waiting until July of 1945 to accept.

At Potsdam, the Big Three faced their differences for the first time. At Teheran and Yalta, which took place while they still needed each other to fight Hitler, they had been able to make grand statements about the future of Germany and Europe while postponing or delegating issues on which they disagreed. By Potsdam, that was no longer necessary or possible. They no longer deluded themselves or anyone else.

Potsdam became a contentious summit precisely because the Big Three could no longer postpone problems—not because Truman had replaced Roosevelt or Attlee would replace Churchill, but because disagreements could no longer be concealed. Eden complained that the Soviet Union used the meeting "to grab as much as she can get."[45] The Potsdam meetings contained the first really acrimonious debates of any Big Three gathering.

Nonetheless, the Big Three did make an important bargain by indirection, as they had at Yalta. Stalin got what he wanted most, a forward border between Germany and Poland. The Americans and the British got what they wanted most, a viable future Germany. Although Byrnes may have angered the British and the Soviets, he proposed the formula that worked. Truman and Attlee agreed to let Poland take about one-quarter of prewar German territory, but they saved the German economy from the hyperinflation and depression that had followed World War I. By insisting that each state take its reparations largely from its own occupation zone, they freed their own zones and thus most of Germany from Soviet reparations demands.

Truman, Byrnes, Attlee and Bevin yielded German land, land which Hitler's armies had already lost, but they preserved the German economy and the German state. It was not a great bargain. But, as in all bargains, each side paid what it had to pay to get what it wanted most.

At Potsdam, the struggle *against* Germany ended and the struggle *over* Germany began. Although the Big Three no longer spoke of dismemberment or even wanted it, they actually instituted it. Without a common policy, each occupying power did what it wanted to do in its own occupation zone. The zones became the dismemberment areas, with some zonal boundaries becoming the functional equivalent of state boundaries.

Potsdam, the last of the Big Three summits, projected a united German state but left a divided one. It projected Allied cooperation but reflected Allied division. It could not solve the German question, leaving that question for the occupiers and for the occupied.

TWO

THE OCCUPATION BEGINS

THE PEACE THAT SETTLED UPON EUROPE IN JUNE OF 1945 FOUND A devastated continent with tens of millions dead, lamed, destitute or uprooted. Not even the Thirty Years' War or the Napoleonic wars had ravaged the continent so cruelly and so widely. None remained untouched.

The victors now had to write the peace treaties. They had chosen to write those for Germany's allies first, perhaps thinking they would be easy to negotiate. Instead, the treaties proved excruciatingly difficult.

THE WEST MEETS MOLOTOV

The Council of Foreign Ministers first met from September 11 to October 2, 1945, in London. It began with a bitter argument, as Vyacheslav Molotov challenged the right of France and of Nationalist China to participate in the council.[1] The French complained that Stalin appeared to take no notice either of their interests or of the Franco-Soviet treaty. Harry Truman appealed directly to Stalin, but Stalin rejected Truman's appeal. This consigned the council to immediate deadlock, for Ernest Bevin and James Byrnes would not permit any Allies to be excluded.

The East-West split deepened further after the procedural issues had been resolved by a compromise letting France and China join for their immediate areas of interest. The foreign ministers had opposite views about the future of the eastern Mediterranean and of eastern Europe, strategic areas that the British and the Soviets saw as their own respective spheres of interest. When the discussion turned to a peace treaty for Italy, Molotov asked for a Soviet trusteeship over the former Italian possession of Tripolitania (Libya). Bevin rejected the demand outright. Molotov then wanted Yugoslavia to receive the Italian port of Trieste, occupied by British and American forces. Both Bevin and Byrnes rejected that. Molotov's demand to renegotiate the Montreux Convention to give Soviet warships easier access to the Mediterranean received the same treatment, as did his demands for a significant Soviet role in the occupation of Japan and in negotiating a peace treaty for it.

The Western Allies, and especially the British, recognized that Stalin wanted to escape from the confines of Europe to play a role in the Middle East and around the Mediterranean. Bevin would not yield that kind of power to the Soviet Union. He feared for the British lifeline through the Mediterranean and the Suez Canal as well as for the oil fields of the Middle East.

Molotov in turn rejected Western demands for democratic processes and governments in eastern Europe. As Great Britain wanted to continue dominating the Mediterranean, Moscow wanted to dominate eastern Europe. In doing so, however, Molotov denied the political freedoms and human rights that Stalin had ostensibly supported during the war. Although the eastern Europeans had nominally formed coalition governments, the communist and pro-Soviet parties ruled ever more obviously and more completely.

When the foreign ministers did comment on Germany, they made no progress. Molotov reiterated Stalin's call for four-power control over the Ruhr. The Western participants rejected this, and Molotov in turn rejected Western requests for open access to the Soviet occupation zone. The French used the meeting to demand the separation of the Rhineland from Germany, to make the Saarland part of the French economic system, and to have the Ruhr internationalized. No one agreed.

Although the CFM had scheduled no further meetings, Byrnes took it upon himself (much to Bevin's annoyance) to ask Molotov for a meeting of Big Three foreign ministers in Moscow in December. Molotov agreed. No substantive progress came out of that meeting. But Byrnes, Molotov and Bevin did cobble together a plan for further negotiations, which would culminate in a peace conference for Germany's allies in Paris in 1946.

Truman did not like what Byrnes had done. He complained that Byrnes had not protested as much as he should have about Moscow's destruction of democracy in eastern Europe, about Soviet forces that had remained in Iran after the war and about Stalin's refusal to agree to freedom of navigation on international waterways. He told Byrnes that he was "sick of coddling the Soviets."[2] In response, Byrnes took a harder stand in later meetings.

The Paris Conference (April 15 to May 16 and June 15 to July 12, 1946) produced several peace treaties. Those permitted Soviet troops to stay in Bulgaria, Hungary and Romania, acknowledging Moscow's dominant role in the area.

The foreign ministers scheduled only a few days for discussions on Germany (April 29, May 15–16, and July 9–12). They barely had time to restate known positions, let alone to bargain. Therefore, the discussions aggravated rather than resolved East-West differences on Germany.[3]

Byrnes tried to break that deadlock by offering what he regarded as an uncontroversial proposal for an agreement to keep Germany de-militarized for twenty-five years under four-power guarantees even after a peace treaty. Bevin and the French foreign minister, Georges Bidault, supported it. But Molotov rejected it, arguing that Germany had already been de-militarized. When Byrnes tried again, Molotov remained adamant. Byrnes finally concluded that Molotov would reject any proposal that gave the United States any long-term voice on Germany. He decided that Stalin expected and wanted America out of Europe.

Byrnes and Bevin again rejected Molotov's proposal for four-power control over the Ruhr, as they did not want any part of the German economy to have separate status. Bevin also feared that Stalin would use any role in the Ruhr to try to control the economy of the entire British zone and perhaps of all the Western occupation zones. Instead, Byrnes and Bevin proposed uniting the entire German economy in accordance with the Potsdam agreement. Molotov, while arguing in favor of German unity in principle, rejected that proposal. So did Bidault, as France remained the occupation power most opposed to German unification of any kind. Nor would either Bevin or Byrnes agree to Molotov's wishes for reparations. Instead, they complained that their two countries had to pay $520 million a year to feed their zones of Germany because the Soviets would not send food from their zone as they had promised. Byrnes also pointed out that the Soviets had already taken reparations from Silesia and Königsberg. The Yalta stalemate on reparations persisted.

Molotov spoke as if Stalin did not want Germany to have a peace treaty for a long time. On July 10, 1946, near the end of the discussion on Germany, he said that the Soviet Union would not be able to conclude such a treaty until it was fully satisfied that the new German government had carried out all its obligations, including its reparations obligations, for several years. Byrnes emerged from the meeting stunned, recognizing that under those circumstances a peace treaty with Germany could not be reached "for years to come" and that this might force a change in U.S. plans to leave Europe.[4]

The CFM meetings in London and Paris showed Bevin in the same role of major partner that Churchill had held during the wartime summits before

Potsdam. By the time of the Paris council meeting, Bevin had begun to give Great Britain a powerful voice. But Bevin did not like to keep talking. He wanted to reach agreements.

Bevin did not look the traditional role of His Majesty's Foreign Secretary. Born into the working class and proud of it, he looked and acted like the manual laborer he had long been. But his untutored manner masked a shrewd mind with an uncanny ability to grasp the heart of any issue. Having been given wide leeway by Attlee, Bevin could deal on more than even terms with his American, Soviet and French colleagues. He protected Britain's traditional interests as best he could at a time when London no longer had the resources or the respect of old. He also increasingly stiffened the U.S. position while putting Britain squarely against Molotov and on the side of the Americans.

Like many other members of the European trade union movement, Bevin despised the communists. He made no bones of his personal dislike for Molotov, whom he taunted by calling him "Mowlotov" and whom he occasionally irritated by likening Soviet tactics in eastern Europe to Hitler's. Molotov would in turn bait Bevin by discourteous behavior and by trying to drive wedges between the British and American positions. But Bevin's tenacity matched Molotov's. Stalin complained that Bevin was no gentleman.

The London and Moscow meetings had convinced Bevin that Molotov wanted to keep talks going while Soviet forces consolidated their hold on the areas they occupied. He feared that Molotov would agree to a German peace treaty only when it would lead to Soviet control over all of Germany and would permit Moscow to dominate continental Europe. He decided, like Bidault, that Germany had to be divided, but for different reasons and along different lines. He wanted to build up Western occupation zones as independent areas free of Soviet influence. He saw this as the only way to keep American forces in Europe to help Great Britain against the Soviet Union.

Bevin exerted an increasingly strong influence on Byrnes, encouraging him to look for alternatives to a reunited Germany and discouraging him about prospects of a deal with Stalin.[5] The Soviet effort to gain U.S. atomic secrets through a spy ring based in Canada reinforced Bevin's words. So did the disdain that the Soviets showed toward the United Nations, with Molotov not even attending the opening session of the General Assembly in 1946.

By the end of 1946, the Council of Foreign Ministers had finished the treaties with the smaller states and could begin the work on a treaty for Germany. But relations among the foreign ministers had suffered during the contentious process of negotiation. Molotov's prickly manner and stubborn tactics had angered his Western colleagues even more than the substance of his positions.

Byrnes, tired of the tedious and fruitless proceedings, brought Molotov to agreement on the satellite peace treaties only by threatening to abandon the CFM process entirely. He remained long enough to sign the treaties as his last act before leaving office.

STALIN TAKES OVER HIS ZONE

Long before the Council of Foreign Ministers had begun to talk about the future of Germany, the armies and the administrators of the wartime allies were busily deciding that future. They did so by their presence, by their occupation policies, and by their relations to each other as well as to the Germans. They shaped the future of Germany more than the diplomats did. They also limited the choices that the diplomats could make.

The Wehrmacht, having mounted futile urban defense efforts with teenage draftees in Berlin and some other cities, had stumbled into the prisoner-of-war camps as the war ended. The Nazi apparatus had melted away. German society, exhausted and rudderless, had disintegrated. The Allied armies found before them not the suicidal resistance fighters they had expected but only clumps of bent figures scratching through the rubble for any remnants of their families and of their possessions.

The Allies contributed to Germany's disintegration by carrying out their decrees that dissolved the German state, divided the country into separate occupation zones, and conferred absolute authority upon each occupation commander within his zone. With those decrees, they set the course of Germany for decades.

The Big Three had not divided Germany equally. The American and Soviet occupation commanders ruled over the two largest zones of about 107,000 square kilometers (66,340 square miles) and 17 million Germans each, with both zones also containing millions of refugees. The British commander ruled a zone of only 97,000 square kilometers (60,140 square miles) but he had the largest single concentration of industry in the Ruhr valley and the largest population (over 22 million) as well as several million refugees. The French commander ruled over 40,000 square kilometers (24,800 square miles) and 5 million Germans but few refugees.[6]

The shock of the occupation hit the Soviet zone especially hard because Stalin and his German administrators had decided to impose immediate social and economic changes that would revolutionize the zone itself and serve as a model to all Germans. Stalin knew that one day he and the Soviet Union would have to deal with a revived Germany. He wanted to make certain that the new

Germany had a social, economic and political order that would not make war on the Soviet Union. This meant the total destruction of Germany's political and military hierarchies and their social and economic foundations.

Stalin did not see the German question as Churchill or Roosevelt had seen it or as Attlee or Truman might. The Anglo-Saxons could retreat behind the Channel and the Atlantic. But the Russians shared a continent with the Germans. They had a land barrier in the form of Poland, but Stalin had seen how quickly the Germans could overrun that.

Stalin wanted and even needed a united Germany. A divided Germany would leave him with the least desirable part of the country. His occupation zone had few assets. It had a narrow coast on the Baltic without a major seaport (Stettin having been given to Poland), medium-quality soils and sandy marshes in Pomerania and the Mark Brandenburg, and the Saxon industrial area that had once been the pride of Germany but that had been eclipsed by the Ruhr. The Soviet zone could produce food and some industrial goods but not much else. In raw materials, its only interesting assets were uranium ore and cheap but low-quality brown coal.

Stalin did not need to be reminded that the part of Germany that he controlled did not give him real influence over Germany itself. And it certainly gave him no influence at all over Europe as a whole. He needed and wanted to do better. Meeting with Soviet officials and German communist leaders in Moscow on June 4, 1945, he said that he expected to achieve German unity with the united *Kommunistische Partei Deutschlands* (German Communist Party, hereafter KPD) as the driving force. They were to lay out plans to bring all of united Germany into the Soviet sphere of influence.

Stalin knew this would not happen quickly. He thought that a united Germany might begin as a bourgeois state, which it had been before Hitler. But he recalled that the communist and socialist parties had been major forces in German politics during the Weimar Republic. As he would now instruct the communists to work together with the socialists, he thought that a united Germany would be friendly to the Soviet Union and would gravitate toward Marxism over time. He wanted to negotiate for conditions that would produce such a result and that would win him economic aid in the meantime.[7]

Stalin saw a united Germany as a strategic necessity. Even a bourgeois Germany would have close economic links with the Soviet Union and would give Stalin influence deep into western Europe. In a politburo meeting on Germany at the end of May 1945, Stalin said that talk of an "agriculturalized" or splintered Germany was illusory and unrealistic. He wanted a united Germany that would have good relations with Moscow. He sent Anastas Mikoyan, his most trusted politburo economic expert, to review the situation in Germany immediately after the war and to recommend ways to use the German economy to help the Soviet Union.[8]

Pending unification, the Soviet zone was to serve as a base for Soviet influence under the direction of German communist administrators. Having established the National Committee for Free Germany during the summer of 1943, Stalin could move quickly at the end of the war. He dispatched KPD teams into Germany immediately behind the Soviet front lines.[9]

On April 30, 1945, well before the Potsdam meeting, the *Gruppe Ulbricht* entered Berlin. Stalin had selected its leader, Walter Ulbricht, as the Soviet point man for Berlin and Germany. Ulbricht had headed a study group about postwar Germany at the Soviet Foreign Ministry. Other teams of German communists went into other parts of the Soviet zone. There, as planned, they established German local authorities as well as newspapers, radios, and book publishers. The KPD received authorization from the Soviet occupiers to begin to function the next day. The KPD trade union, the *Freier Deutscher Gewerkschaftsbund* (Free German Trade Union, hereafter FDGB) began functioning five days later.

The Soviets and Ulbricht made certain that German personnel directors at all levels were KPD members who had lived and served in the Soviet Union. Because of their generally good information about Germany from the KPD underground, the Soviets and Ulbricht knew whom to trust. They dismissed and blacklisted only the core Nazis and the senior figures instead of reaching into the middle levels as the Western Allies tried to do. But there could be no question about who was to be in charge. When Ulbricht brought his group into Germany, he told them that "all must look democratic, but we must have things firmly in hand."[10]

By July 14, Ulbricht and Soviet occupation commander Marshal Georgi Zhukov had laid the basis for eleven central organizations to deal with basic administration and governance throughout the Soviet zone and to serve as the basis for an all-German administration once Germany was united. Although the Soviets exercised supreme authority only in their zone, they were laying plans for a united German state.[11]

In choosing Walter Ulbricht as his man in Germany, Stalin had selected a person like himself. Ulbricht lacked popular appeal but knew how to achieve control. His high-pitched voice and impenetrable Saxon accent prevented him from becoming a persuasive orator even if he had wanted to be one. But his strength lay in organization. He had helped to organize the KPD in Germany after World War I and had risen to become a KPD member of the German parliament during the latter years of the Weimar Republic.

When Stalin had wanted to reshape the KPD during the mid-1920s from a worker-oriented trade union organization into a tough new cadre party fit to infiltrate and to direct events from behind the scenes, he had relied on Ul-bricht—whose KPD code name was *Zelle* (Cell)—to direct the change-over and to keep control for Moscow.[12]

Ulbricht had fled Germany when Hitler came to power, traveling to France and later participating briefly in the Spanish Civil War. Soviet officials recognized him as a potential leader for German communism. They brought him to Moscow, where he spent World War II. He became a Soviet citizen and served in the bureaucracy of the international communist movement, the Comintern, preparing himself and the KPD for the postwar order. He survived the Stalinist purges by changing positions as necessary and reputedly by denouncing his own rivals within the KPD. He earned a reputation for the ruthless exercise of power. Nobody knew KPD organization and personnel better than Ulbricht. Nobody could be relied on to control it better.

Stalin had said in April of 1945 that each victor of the war would introduce his own political and social system as far forward as his own armies could advance.[13] This is what he and Ulbricht proceeded to do. And the reforms that they carried out went much deeper than any carried out by the Western occupiers, for they sought a much more radical transformation.

As a first step, in September the Soviet military administration announced a massive land reform. All the Allies had agreed during the war that postwar Germany should break up the vast estates that formed the power base of the reactionary Prussian *Junker* military and political elite. Ulbricht and Stalin looked further ahead, envisaging land reform as a step toward creating a new class of small farmers who would help to anchor a new type of German political system based on an alliance between workers and farmers. They began their land reform in September 1945, right after the Potsdam Conference. They paid a high price for their haste because land reform during the fall harvest and planting seasons severely cut yields.[14] But they had to move quickly, for they wanted their reforms to take hold before any possible unification. They subdivided the large estates in the north and even many of the smaller holdings in the south.[15]

The reform gave over half a million German farmers their own land and proved popular initially despite its impact on production. It also showed how closely Stalin had studied German matters and how carefully he wanted to proceed. At a meeting in Moscow, he specifically instructed Ulbricht and his fellow KPD leader Wilhelm Pieck to set the lower limit for land holdings at 100 hectares, not at the smaller 50 hectares that Ulbricht preferred. He wanted to stop the owners of medium-size holdings from opposing the KPD and did not want the Soviet zone to be completely incompatible with the Western zones.

Stalin and Ulbricht next proceeded with the nationalization of industry in the Soviet zone, claiming that it all had belonged to Nazis, militarists and war criminals. The Soviets themselves assumed ownership over about 25 percent of industry in the form of *Sowjetische Aktiengesellschaften* (Soviet stock companies, hereafter SAG). They nationalized much of the remainder. By the middle of 1946, they had ended private ownership of any significant industrial holdings. Within less than a year after the arrival of the Red Army, Stalin and Ulbricht had transformed the economic and social order of the Soviet-occupied area.

Stalin took as much as possible from the Soviet zone. He ordered the dismantling of countless plants, often having them taken directly to the Soviet Union. Of more than 1,000 factories that the Soviets had identified for dismantling, they shipped 250 in 1945 and another 200 during early 1946. Thus, within a year of their arrival, the Soviets had removed more than half of the functioning industrial capacity of the Soviet zone.[16]

Ulbricht failed to see how Germans would react to reform. Under pressure from Stalin, he moved arbitrarily and almost impetuously to complete the program quickly. He did not anticipate that such dramatic changes, imposed on a people desperate for stability after twelve years of dictatorship and war, went further than the people could bear.

Only after completing the land reform and nationalization campaigns did Stalin and Ulbricht grasp the opposition that they had fomented. The workers, who were to be the foundation of the new German system, opposed the dismantlings and most of the reforms because they lost their jobs. They also feared being conscripted to work in uranium mines near Wismut under conditions that killed many and ruined the health of countless others. Roundups of laborers for those operations, along with other work disruptions, drove many East Germans to flee to the Western zones early in the Soviet occupation. By June 30, 1946, barely a year into the occupation, the Soviet authorities already had to begin blocking migration from their zone.

Ulbricht and Stalin also wanted to organize a strong left-wing organization in the Soviet zone as the solid foundation for a party that could operate reliably throughout all of Germany. They knew that Hitler had come to power in large measure because the German Left had not united against him during the 1920s and early 1930s. The German Communist Party had fought the German Socialist Party more than the conservatives, permitting the senile field marshal Paul von Hindenburg to become president of Germany and letting Hitler come to power while they campaigned against each other. They wanted to unite the Left this time.

Immediately after the war, the reconstituted *Sozialdemokratische Partei Deutschlands* (Social Democratic Party of Germany, hereafter SPD) invited the KPD to join in a new united party of the Left. Ulbricht rejected the offer, wanting to have the KPD fully under control before diluting it with outsiders. He also thought the KPD could benefit from Soviet prestige and from its anti-Hitler struggle to become the leading party of the Left, and he wanted to wait for that.[17]

By the spring of 1946, Ulbricht realized that he had miscalculated. Communist parties had done poorly in Austrian and Hungarian elections during the fall of 1945. In Germany's western zones, where the widely respected SPD leader Kurt Schumacher railed against communism, the SPD was gaining more support than the KPD. Schumacher, who had spent the war years in Hitler's concentration camps instead of in Moscow, owed nothing to Stalin. He had a powerful personality and a fiery speaking style dramatized by the crippled form to which beatings and torture in the camps had reduced him. Ulbricht feared that the SPD would become the stronger party. Having organized the KPD enough to feel confident that it could prevail in a joint party, he himself proposed a merger with the SPD. By that time, however, the SPD had drawn back from its original proposal. Even Soviet zone SPD leaders like Otto Grotewohl decided there was little to be gained from joining with Ulbricht, and they rejected his belated approach.

Stalin watched the situation unhappily. The communist failure to gain popular support could cripple his plan to unite Germany under a nationwide party of the Left. In early 1946, he called Ulbricht to Moscow and instructed him to form such a united party in the Soviet zone before May Day. On his orders, the new Soviet occupation commander, Vassily Sokolovsky, pushed the SPD leaders toward a union with the KPD. He exerted powerful pressure upon Grotewohl and others, threatening them with arrest and with denial of space and resources for party work if they failed to comply. Soviet forces did arrest recalcitrant SPD members and sometimes deported them to the Soviet Union without telling their families until well after the event if at all. A number of those arrested met their deaths in prison either in the Soviet occupation zone or in the Soviet Union itself.

Word of those arrests and disappearances spread rapidly. Many SPD figures and others faded into silence or into flight to the Western occupation zones. Many withdrew from political life, practicing the "inner emigration" that they had learned under Hitler.

Schumacher thundered against the merger. He warned that the KPD would use the SPD only for a "blood transfusion," exploiting the SPD's support and reputation while planning to destroy both. But Grotewohl could not resist both Ulbricht and Stalin. He agreed to the merger despite his own reservations.[18]

The Soviet zone KPD-SPD merger created the *Sozialistische Einheitspartei Deutschlands* (German Socialist Unity Party, hereafter SED) during a meeting on April 21–22, 1946. The German commentator Wolfgang Leonhard, who was then a member of the KPD and could see Ulbricht's and Sokolovsky's tactics from the inside, called it a *diktatorische Vereinigung* (dictatorial union). Western SPD figure Egon Bahr commented years later: "The hand of the Social Democrats was first seized and was then chopped off."[19] The photo in which Grotewohl shook Pieck's hand to cement the union showed him looking pained and downcast even as Pieck and Ulbricht glowed triumphantly.

Grotewohl had good reason to look downcast. Ulbricht's KPD members took ever more direct and full control of the SED. They destroyed the SPD organization across the Soviet zone.[20] By the time of the second SED congress, held from September 20 to 24, 1947, the SPD had a much less prominent role than in the first "unity" congress of 1946, while former KPD members participated more fully and confidently. Only two of twenty-two speakers were former SPD members.[21]

The second SED congress showed a much more openly subservient attitude toward the Soviet Union and Soviet ideology than the first congress. Party leaders went out of their way to pledge their loyalty to Moscow. Grotewohl praised the Soviet model at length in a speech that had a chilling effect on his former SPD colleagues. They fully realized by then, if they had not realized it before, that the man who had led them into union with the KPD was ready to accept a turn toward Soviet-style communism, Stalinism and absolutism.[22]

Sokolovsky also gave the SED a greater role within the administration of the Soviet zone by turning over some of the authority held by the Soviets. On June 4, 1947, he ordered the establishment of the *Deutsche Wirtschaftskommission* (German Economic Council, hereafter DWK) under SED control as the civilian administration for the Soviet zone. Ulbricht and Sokolovsky had planned this step for some time.[23]

Ulbricht used the DWK to complete SED control over the civilian administration of the Soviet zone. He instructed the party to staff DWK offices as much as possible except for technical functions. He wanted to use the DWK to replace the Soviet authorities and to begin establishing a separate East German civilian administration.

No matter what tactics Stalin and Ulbricht might try, however, they faced impossible odds in trying to win over the Germans in the Soviet zone because of the way Soviet soldiers had behaved when they had entered Germany. Those soldiers had left an explosive mixture of fear and revulsion among the population of the zone and especially among German women.

As Soviet forces had first entered German territory in East Prussia and Silesia in 1944, they had begun a systematic campaign of terror that drove the Germans before them. Inspired by Zhukov's order that "we will get our terrible revenge for everything," the Soviet army had gone on a rampage.[24] Rape became the most singular and most feared hallmark of the Soviet campaign. Aflame with a passion for conquest and revenge, the Soviet soldiers had often pillaged every home in a village for food, alcohol and loot, then had raped every woman or girl, and finally had left the village in flames.

Although some Soviet commanders had tried to put a stop to the extremes of violence, sometimes shooting soldiers for rape, and although they had fully recognized that they were destroying property that would one day be Soviet or Polish, the Red Army had roared ahead in wrath. It had laid waste the land and won even the hardest battles with furious intensity while its commanders tried to outdo each other in the speed and destructiveness of their advance.

Pillage had served a strategic purpose east of the Oder. It had so terrified the Germans that most had fled before the invaders and had left their property to the Poles. Stalin could rightly say at Yalta that the Germans had already abandoned the lands that the Red Army had turned over to Polish administration.

But that strategic purpose vanished when the Soviet forces entered Germany itself. Stalin wanted good relations with the new Germany. The Soviet command tried to rein in its troops as they prepared to cross the Oder for their final push on Berlin. A *Pravda* article recalled Stalin's order of the day of February 23, 1942: "It would be laughable to identify Hitler's cliques with the German people, with the German state. Historical experience shows that Hitlers come and go; the German people, the German state, remain."[25] Zhukov gave specific instructions that his troops were to exercise restraint and self-discipline in their relations with the German population.

Nonetheless, Soviet soldiers and even officers behaved much as they had before. They raped, burned and looted, letting out their rage on the German population and especially on women of almost any age. Years later, German women would not speak of those experiences except with loathing, if indeed they spoke of them at all. Estimates based on newly released documents and on contemporary records indicate that perhaps as many as two million German women were raped, sometimes repeatedly and in the most humiliating manner, and that all lived in dread of it.

Ulbricht and his team used contrived explanations, blaming the rapes on "Nazi vandals" dressed in Soviet uniforms. Ulbricht did not want to criticize the Red Army in public although angry Germans condemned the communists for not intervening against the Soviet forces. He spoke to Zhukov on July 12, 1945, about the "rumors" of Soviet military attacks on the civilian population, and

Zhukov promised to look into the matter. But other KPD officials openly admitted that the Soviet forces had sullied the communist cause, with one remarking that it would have been better for the KPD if the war had ended before the Soviet troops had entered Germany.

After mid-1947 the Soviet troops were confined to their camps to try to end the problem. In March 1949, as Stalin and Ulbricht were considering the creation of the German Democratic Republic, the Soviets decreed heavier punishment for rape. But by then the damage had been done. The Red Army had committed crimes and blunders in Germany as massive as Hitler's forces had committed in the Soviet Union. The Soviet image never recovered. Many of the women, whose husbands or brothers or sons had been killed under Hitler's orders, might have welcomed the army that had freed them from Nazi tyranny. Instead, they came to fear and despise the Red Army.

A senior SED official, Hermann Matern, noted that the rage of German women had critically damaged the SED in Soviet zone elections. Another wrote that it would have been difficult to find a woman in the entire state of Mecklenburg who would be ready to vote for the SED. Ulbricht's failure to confront Moscow on this subject began to open what was to become a deep gulf between the SED and the East German people.[26]

The Berlin local elections of September 1946 told the story. There, where the Western occupation forces made certain that SPD candidates could run on tickets separate from the SED, the SPD outpolled the SED by 44 to 30 percent, even in the Soviet sector. It received over 50 percent of the votes in every Western sector, with the SED averaging only 15 percent. This defeat, like the earlier defeat for the Austrian and Hungarian communist parties, showed that the communists and the Soviets had forfeited popular support almost immediately after the war. The KPD had fewer followers after 1945 than during the 1920s.[27] Soviet soldiers had occupied all of Berlin from April to June before permitting the Western Allied forces to enter the sectors they had been assigned. During those months they had left an indelible impression totally contrary to Stalin's professed intent.

Even as these problems developed, Stalin and Ulbricht disagreed about major policy issues. Although Stalin inspired fear in most persons, and although he could have revoked Ulbricht's authority with a flick of his finger, he never fully imposed his will on his own proconsul. Either Ulbricht had mastered the art of deception to such a degree that he could fool Stalin, or Stalin decided not to remove the man he had himself appointed. Ulbricht's ability to pursue policies that undermined Stalin's supposed goals remains one of the mysteries of German postwar history.

Stalin and Ulbricht followed virtually opposite strategies. Stalin wanted and expected German unification. For him, the Soviet occupation zone offered a base from which the KPD and SED could exert influence over Germany as a whole and could ultimately bring communism to all of Germany. He wanted to move fast to create a solid communist structure in the Soviet zone, but needed to carry it off without alienating the Western Allies or the Germans outside the zone. He needed a subtle lieutenant who could execute a complex mix of policies, knowing exactly how far and how fast to move at any given moment.[28]

Ulbricht could not—or would not—act with that kind of subtlety. He may not even have cared. Ulbricht saw the Soviet zone as his top, and perhaps his only, priority. He did not attach as much importance as Stalin to advancing communism throughout Germany as a whole. Nor did he worry as much as Stalin might have wished about the reaction that some of his—or Stalin's—policies would generate in the Western occupation zones.

Although Ulbricht had to work under Stalin's direction and on the basis of the Soviet dictator's plan, he had his own views and his own methods. He often carried out Stalin's instructions ruthlessly, pushing through both the land reform and the nationalization of industry faster and in a more draconian manner than Stalin had wished. Vladimir Semyonov, the political adviser to Marshal Sokolovsky, often had to hold Ulbricht in check. Many Soviet officials complained that Ulbricht followed policies that might be appropriate in nations fully under Soviet occupation but inappropriate in one part of Germany when Moscow did not control other parts.[29]

Ulbricht did not manage an all-German policy. He treated the KPD in the Western zones as a subsidiary organ, forcing it to echo his own propaganda line instead of one that might have been more successful locally. Semyonov complained that Ulbricht kept all the best communist officials for the Soviet zone, leaving the KPD in the Western zones starved for first-rate talent.

Ulbricht did not develop good relations with non-communist parties. When Stalin wanted to establish parties that would appeal to German conservative groups in order to widen the Soviet base of support, Ulbricht objected and dragged his feet. He also objected when Soviet officials proposed reestablishing the SPD as a separate party in the Soviet zone because the forced merger had alienated socialist support. Ulbricht made it easy for the Allied occupation authorities to block the SED from their zones. A Soviet official concluded that Ulbricht had harmed communist efforts in the Western zones.[30]

Stalin wanted to work with and through the Allied occupiers, whether he liked them or not. He wanted to merge the zones when the time came. Ulbricht never accepted these notions. He provoked a much more negative reaction than necessary within the Soviet zone itself and within the Western zones. While serving his own purpose by establishing his concept of a socialist society in his part of Germany, he was not serving Stalin's purpose. Stalin wanted the German administration in the Soviet zone to reflect some political diversity, even if in mock form, in order to show Germans elsewhere that the Soviet zone had not become a communist fief. Ulbricht, however, used every opportunity to centralize control overtly under the SED.[31]

The Soviet occupiers recognized that Ulbricht's approach was not fully in line with Stalin's wishes, but they proved no match for Ulbricht. He always listened carefully to Stalin's wishes and promised to carry them out but imposed his own system in what was to become his own state.[32]

Stalin did not always help his own cause. He often protected narrow Soviet interests at the expense of Ulbricht's support in the Soviet zone. He refused to permit East German prisoners of war to return from the Soviet Union although many SED officials believed that such a release would have helped the Soviet image throughout Germany. After U.S. aid began flowing into Western Germany in 1947, he refused to lower Soviet reparations demands although even the most loyal SED leaders warned Soviet officials that the contrast between American aid and Soviet reparations claims damaged the SED.[33]

Stalin may also have misunderstood the logic of events. He spoke of wanting German political unity, but rejected any and all steps toward German economic unity as a first step. He treated the Soviet zone as a separate domain, turning down all Western requests for food from that zone. The Western occupiers had no incentive to cooperate with him. He and Molotov turned down every proposal toward uniting Germany or any part of Germany if it did not completely match their wishes. For example, they rejected several efforts by U.S. occupation commander General Lucius Clay to establish trizonal offices without the French.[34]

Stalin preferred a controlled process with guaranteed results to open political competition. Ulbricht gave him that control, but only in the Soviet zone and in a way that alienated the Germans whom Stalin's and Ulbricht's power could not reach. Stalin may have wanted German unity, but he chose the wrong man and the wrong way to implement it. The Soviet zone went its own way, not by Stalin's design but by default, in the hands of a man who wanted to keep what he had rather than to appeal to what he did not have.[35]

By the end of 1947, Ulbricht had won. The Soviet zone had developed a separate identity on the basis of its own system, impossible to merge with the Western zones without major societal and political upheaval on one side or the other. And the bitter mood between the SED and the people left Stalin no choice but to support Ulbricht with the kind of force that appalled all Germans.

The differences between Moscow and Ulbricht were to reverberate for decades. As late as 1990, Soviet president Mikhail Gorbachev's aide Vadim Zagladin told a French official that the Soviet Union had always wanted German unity but that the East German communist leadership had opposed and prevented it.[36] Ulbricht, however, blamed Germany's division on the West.

BEVIN, BYRNES AND BIDAULT
LINK THE WESTERN ZONES

The Western occupiers faced the same problems as the Soviets, including a ruined land, a broken people and an economy in shambles. Many of their wishes matched Stalin's. They wanted to make certain that no German army would ever again attack its neighbors. They wanted to reform German society and politics, although not as profoundly as Stalin and Ulbricht. They also wanted to find out which Germans had been Nazis and which Germans could be trusted. Like the Soviets, they faced a refugee problem, but one that proved more severe and longer-lasting because many Germans who had first fled to the Soviet zone later fled west.

The Western victors had not prepared as well as the Soviets. They had no organized cadre of Germans ready to begin work, and they had few concrete plans. Most Western leaders, and especially most Americans, lacked Stalin's historic vision of the German people separate from Hitler. They had very little idea about what to expect and even less idea about what to do beyond the immediate task of beginning the occupation.

Each Western occupier brought different sets of attitudes and perspectives. Each largely pursued its own separate policies, especially at first. Each also faced its own particular problems in its zone. The occupation agreement had created ministates that shared little beyond language, recent history, and despair. Each zone became very much an entity of its own during the first year of the occupation.[37]

The Americans, demobilizing quickly and expecting to leave Germany within two years, pursued two contradictory policies. On one hand, they followed a punitive occupation doctrine heavily influenced by the Morgenthau Plan. That doctrine, contained in a Joint Chiefs of Staff paper known as JCS 1067 and approved in April 1945, firmly pursued the "four D's": demilitarization, de-cartelization, de-nazification and democratization. It specifically stressed that Germany should not be treated as a liberated but as a defeated nation. It forbade any fraternization with German civilians and decreed that occupation authorities were not to take any action that would strengthen the German economy. The U.S. attitude hardened even more as the Allies saw the horrors of the Nazi concentration camps and came to know of the murder of millions of Jews as well as Gypsies, homosexuals, invalids and others.

General Lucius Clay, deputy military governor under General Dwight D. Eisenhower and later under General Joseph McNarney, took charge of the American zone. He concentrated on German affairs and on the four-power occupation mechanism while Eisenhower and McNarney concentrated on military matters. Clay thus became well known to the Germans and to the Allies even before he became full military governor in the spring of 1947.

Clay had not pursued a typical military career. He had begun in the engineer corps, not in infantry or armor. Having never held a combat command, he had first resisted his assignment to Germany because he wanted to lead a combat unit in the final assault on Japan. But he possessed assets ideal to his new position, combining a superb analytical and organizational mind, intense determination and a genius for lightning improvisation. He had spent many years in the Pentagon handling logistics, procurement and budgets. Thus he could solve many occupation problems more effectively than any combat commander. He also could call on a wide range of contacts in Washington, whether in the administration itself or in the U.S. Congress.

Most important, Clay had been born in the American South, in those states that had been defeated in the American Civil War and been traumatized by Yankee occupation. He vowed that he would not leave a similar legacy of resentment in Germany. Unlike many in Washington, he wanted to establish foundations for future friendship with Germany. In that sense, he matched Stalin. He did not want a peace of revenge but of conciliation.

Clay wanted to prepare Germany for the early departure of the American occupation force, moving as soon as possible toward a German civilian administration under occupation control. He pursued a more active and more widespread de-nazification program at the middle and lower levels than any other occupier, although he did not make the wholesale upper-level societal changes that Ulbricht made. He searched earnestly for "good" Germans who could help to run the occupation. He found quite a few, mainly men who had been politically active in Weimar Germany and whom Hitler had fired and often jailed. Among them, he found an economist named Ludwig Erhard who during the war had run the risk of writing a memorandum advocating free-market policies for a defeated Germany. He called on Erhard to administer the German economy in the U.S. zone.

Clay decided earlier than the other Western powers and earlier than the U.S. government itself that the Allies should begin encouraging German democratic political life. He began in 1945 to open political contacts to the Germans.

Although he followed the broad guidelines of JCS 1067, he interpreted those guidelines more and more liberally as time went on and as he gained ever more confidence that Germany could function as a democracy. He was determined to give it the chance. Some U.S. civilian officials accused him of "localitis," of having become too sympathetic to the Germans, but he believed that experience vindicated his policies.[38]

Clay kept overall control in U.S. military hands but allowed some limited administrative authority for local government. By October 1945 he had established civilian administrations in the German *Länder* (states) under U.S. occupation and had established a council of the minister-presidents of those states as a zonal coordinating body. Having studied German history and the long-standing differences between German states, Clay thought he could develop a system that would be compatible with German traditions as well as with the American federalist model.

Clay learned of the anger that Soviet soldiers had provoked in the Soviet zone and wanted U.S. forces to behave properly. But the Americans did face a disciplinary problem through much of 1946 and 1947. It came not as a wave of rapes, although some rapes were committed, but in the form of the double temptations of the German black market and of German women. American soldiers could pay low post exchange (PX) prices for nylon stockings, American cigarettes and Parker pens, the main standards of value on the black market. A soldier could sell these items at huge profit and establish a grateful German woman in a room or apartment where he could join her on overnight or weekend passes.

As these habits spread, the U.S. army in Germany grew lax and ill-disciplined. Incidents multiplied and German disgust grew. When he became commander, Clay reversed the trend by instituting a strict new training program and by cracking down hard on black-market transactions. Although the problem did not disappear until after the Germans had introduced a solid currency, Clay's willingness to discipline his own soldiers helped win German respect.[39]

Clay believed that Secretary of State James Byrnes agreed with his policies and with his attitudes. Having known Byrnes—a fellow Southerner—for many years, he also knew that Byrnes had a sophisticated understanding of politics. During the summer of 1946, when Molotov spoke of a united Germany, Clay feared that the Soviets would win the contest for German public opinion. Molotov could make it appear that only Moscow supported German unity. The Germans also knew they would have to deal with Moscow because the Red Army would remain long after the Americans had gone. Clay wanted the Germans to hear that they had an alternative. He therefore persuaded Byrnes, who trusted him fully, to come to Stuttgart to deliver a ringing reply to Molotov.

Byrnes did so, outlining a firm but friendly U.S. attitude that would help create a prosperous and democratic Germany. He said the following, written by Clay:

> "We will not shirk our duty. We are not withdrawing. We are staying here and will furnish our proportionate share of the security forces."[40]

Byrnes became the first American to tell the Germans that the United States would remain engaged in Europe and would support them. In one speech, he reversed both the Morgenthau Plan and the expectations of U.S. withdrawal by 1947. Clay reported that he later found Byrnes signing autographs for Germans from the rear platform of his train at a station stop. He saw this as a sign that German public opinion had sought an American assurance and genuinely welcomed it.[41]

But Byrnes left office in 1947, to be followed by George Marshall. Although Marshall had hoped to negotiate a German settlement with Moscow, his advisers thought it would not be possible to reach a satisfactory agreement. Those advisers included Soviet experts Charles Bohlen and George Kennan, who was later to publish the "containment" theory and who already believed that Germany should remain divided because Stalin would give up the Soviet zone only in exchange for a chance to dominate all of Germany.[42] Marshall increasingly listened to their views, especially as Molotov's speeches and negotiating tactics vindicated them.

In the spring of 1947, as Marshall stopped in Germany on his way to the Moscow meeting of the Council of Foreign Ministers, Clay confronted him and his advisers, saying that the United States should make another determined effort to unite Germany and adding that his own relations with Sokolovsky remained good. Clay thought that Germany could be united and insulated from the increasingly acrimonious East-West debates. He did not want the Soviet zone or Berlin to pass under long-term Soviet control. But Clay did not carry the day with Marshall, who remained skeptical.

Clay carried on an especially sharp debate with John Foster Dulles, then a consultant to Marshall. Dulles wanted to offer Molotov an agreement to separate the Ruhr from the rest of Germany and put it under international control. Clay could contemplate a special economic regime for the Ruhr in a united Germany, but he opposed making the Ruhr a separate entity. He feared that this would foment everlasting German hatred of the West as well as a reactionary German irredentist movement. He protested strongly but unsuccessfully. Dulles did not, however, make the offer because Molotov's diatribes offended him. Clay later wondered if Molotov ever knew what his coarse negotiating style had cost Moscow.[43]

Ernest Bevin faced a different problem. Like Churchill, he believed that Great Britain had become too weak to face the Soviet Union alone. But at first Bevin did not know where to turn. He could not turn to Washington because U.S. forces planned to withdraw. Nor could he turn to France, with de Gaulle wanting to amputate both the Rhineland and the Ruhr from the British zone. Bevin could only hope that time would work in his favor, forcing either Paris or Washington to rethink.

In the meantime, the British moved more slowly than the Americans to install a German government at any level. When they did, they followed not the federal but the English model, establishing centralized administration throughout their zone. Although they permitted some degree of local autonomy, they did not permit as much as Clay had. Like the Soviets, they did not want the German *Länder* in their zone to deal with each other directly.

Bevin also pursued a very different economic policy from Clay. He did not introduce the Erhard style of free-market economics but favored a more centrally planned and directed system. England's new Labour government, committed to socialism, nationalized more German firms than any other Western occupier. London also introduced the principle of codetermination, under which German workers received a voice in the basic policy decisions of their enterprises. That system, later adopted throughout all of Germany, was to remain in place as *Mitbestimmung.*

London found its occupation zone a real burden. Germany had a lower priority than the British Empire or the British pound. The Germans in the British zone were to take care of themselves. But they could not take care of themselves. The British zone had the highest industrial and population density in Germany. It had not fed itself for centuries and could not do so in the chaos of defeat and division. As the Soviets refused to ship food from their zone and from Poland, the Ruhr's traditional food suppliers, the British occupiers faced severe shortages. At a time of food rationing at home, Attlee and Bevin had to send food to Britain's former enemy.

To solve these problems, Bevin proposed the "Bevin Plan," under which the economies of all the occupation zones would be free to send their surplus production to each other. He hoped to get food from other zones and to be able to export iron and steel in return. Clay liked the plan and began to discuss it with the British occupation commander, General Brian Robertson. But Stalin and Ulbricht opposed it.

At the beginning of 1946, the Lord Mayor of Bremen decided it was high time for a German initiative to revive German economic unity. He invited the minister-presidents of all German states to a conference on the subject. Neither the French nor the Soviet occupation commanders permitted German officials from their zone to go, but Clay and Robertson did. The conference encouraged civilians in the British and American zones to cooperate.

At first, Clay did not favor separate cooperation with the British because he still hoped to reach an agreement with Sokolovsky for tri-zonal cooperation. But such hopes soon became pointless. Molotov, while preaching German unity, frustrated four-power cooperation on almost every subject. In May 1946, Clay decided to stop reparations shipments to the French and the Soviet zones. In so doing, he hoped to force both Paris and Moscow to open their borders, but he failed. At that point, the sheer economic logic of joining the British industrial and the American agricultural areas became overwhelming.

British-American talks on the subject went on throughout the summer. By September, London and Washington agreed on the economic merger of their zones. On January 1, 1947, they created Bizonia, a single economic area reaching from the North Sea and Hamburg through the industrial heart of western Germany all the way to Austria and the Alps. Frankfurt became the Bizonia capital.

Many British officials, including Bevin, favored the division of Germany along East-West occupation boundaries. They saw Bizonia as the first step. After Bevin had warned the British cabinet in May of 1946 that "the danger of Russia has become certainly as great as, and possibly even greater than, that of a revived Germany," a divided Germany with an American as well as British presence seemed to offer the only hope.[44]

In 1946, Bevin still wondered if Clay, Truman and Byrnes would support such a policy. By 1947, he realized with delight that Clay had begun to consider this possibility and that Washington was also starting to lean in that direction.[45]

Charles de Gaulle personally directed French occupation policy toward Germany from the end of the war until his resignation in January, 1946. Like Stalin, de Gaulle could not put a wide body of water between himself and Germany. He had to find another solution.[46]

De Gaulle, stiff, aloof, imperious and unbending, was romantic about the nation but logical about power. He had lived his life under the German threat. As a young officer, he had shared the fascination of the German military for armored warfare and for the strategic implications of the tank. He had fought honorably and with some success against the German invaders before the French government had capitulated in 1940. He had then moved to London, created the Free French Resistance movement, and returned after the war as the leader of the new French provisional government. He directed French policy for only eight postwar months before his contempt for the French political game made him resign the presidency. During that brief time he formulated basic principles that were to have a lasting effect on Germany.

De Gaulle did not want France ever again to be threatened by a hostile German army directly on its border. Like Louis XIV, Napoleon or Georges Clemenceau at Versailles after World War I, he wanted the Rhineland separated from Germany and linked to France as well as to Belgium and Holland. He did not wish to annex those territories, but he did not want to permit German forces there. De Gaulle also demanded that the Ruhr be separated politically as well as economically from Germany. It should be placed under the control of those states that used its coal, such as France, Italy, Switzerland, the Netherlands, Belgium and Luxembourg, although they would not annex its territory.

If his World War II allies did not agree to separate the Rhineland and the Ruhr from Germany, de Gaulle wanted to keep Germany divided into the postwar occupation zones. De Gaulle said he would use his veto in the Allied Control Council and in the Council of Foreign Ministers to reject any proposals for German unification. From the summer of 1945, French delegates to the ACC and the CFM steadfastly rejected every effort by any or all of the other three occupying powers to establish any central German administrative bodies, no matter how technical their function might appear. In March of 1946, Paris even vetoed the formation of nationwide German political parties that the other victors—and especially the Soviets—wanted to approve.

De Gaulle also wanted to begin developing European structures to contain Germany. He told his German listeners when he visited the French zone in October 1945 that Germany should have a European mission and that the Rhineland should be fitted into a European entity. He offered a new framework and a new purpose for Germany even as he vetoed every attempt to return to the old.

The Big Three, despite their irritation at France, could not overcome de Gaulle's objections. General Clay, determined to establish German unity and ready to do it without France, even proposed the merger of the American, British and Soviet zones into "Trizonia." But Sokolovsky rejected that.

De Gaulle pursued a relatively friendly occupation policy. The French denazification program did not match the American program in its thoroughness. Once the main Nazis and their followers had been removed and punished, other Germans could proceed to live normal lives. The French zone, essentially self-supporting, recovered its economic bearings faster than any of the other zones. Paris also carried out a very active cultural policy, bringing in French theater, French art and French motion pictures as well as French-language training. De Gaulle made a more conscious and consistent effort than any other occupier to win German public opinion.

De Gaulle had his eye on another prize. The coal-rich Saarland, a small part of the southern Rhineland, had been in dispute between Germany and France since the days of Louis XIV. From the beginning of the occupation, de Gaulle gave the Saarland a separate status from other parts of the French occupation zone. On August 30, 1945, he put the Saarland under a special French commission and separated it from the French occupation zone. In December, de Gaulle seized the Saar coal mines for France. A year later, the French government established a customs border between it and other parts of Germany. By November 1947, France had integrated the Saarland's economy into the French.

De Gaulle may have triumphed, at least in the short run, by keeping Germany divided into four zones. But France could not play a lone hand indefinitely. Before his resignation, de Gaulle himself had begun to worry more about the Soviet than the German threat. Successive French governments drew ever closer toward British and American policies but continued to want a European solution.

As Bizonia developed, the French foreign minister, Georges Bidault, began associating the French zone more closely with the other Western zones. On January 1, 1947, the French permitted open trade with Bizonia. But French public opinion remained violently anti-German, and any accommodation with Germany would bring down a French government. Bidault promised American and British officials that French policy would evolve. Nonetheless, he warned them that it would happen only after France had seen the results of the CFM discussion on Germany.

On July 21, the French ambassador informed Marshall that France would be prepared to join its zone to Bizonia if the CFM did not reach agreement on Germany. After Paris had first helped prevent German unification, it prepared to join Britain and the United States in integrating the Western zones.

All these debates affected the daily lives of the Germans in the Western zones very little. They worried much more about finding food. The Germans in all the Western zones, and especially in the American and British zones, suffered from severe food shortages during the first three years of the occupation. Malnutrition became the most severe problem facing Western administrators. German food stocks had been exhausted during the chaos of the early occupation. A succession of poor harvests and harsh winters deepened and prolonged the crisis. Children faced starvation diets. Workers could not produce because they collapsed in the middle of their work. Any jobs that promised adequate lunches, such as positions with the occupation forces, drew almost overwhelming numbers of applicants.

During much of the war, the German population had received a daily ration of 3,000 calories per person but the Allies could not maintain that level. As of August 1945, food rations were set between 950 and 1,150 calories per day, only half of the 2,000 calories regarded as essential for a working population and below even the 1,550 regarded as a minimum ration. But the Allies could not supply enough to meet even those low targets. In November 1945, Clay visited Washington to arrange urgent food imports into Germany. But with Morgenthau Plan and JCS 1067 thinking still very powerful, Germany had a very low priority and Clay did not get as much as he wanted.

During the winter of 1945–1946, the crisis worsened. Although the Americans had brought 600,000 tons of grain to feed the population in their zone, Clay had to give half to the British and French zones to avoid chaos and food riots throughout the Western occupation zones. Thousands of children died from sickness and malnourishment. Industrial production fell. Clay feared that the population in the U.S. zone would turn in despair toward communism, for the Soviet zone could obtain adequate rations from Germany's traditional grain belts. Clay suspected that the Soviets had deliberately stopped food shipments from their zone to undermine support for the Western Allies.

At Clay's request, former U.S. president Herbert Hoover went to Germany in 1946 to review the food situation. Hoover, who had administered U.S. relief programs for Europe after World War I, agreed with Clay and ordered larger food shipments to the occupation zones. Even those, however, proved inadequate during the bitter winter of 1946–1947, as railroads and canals froze and storage bins collapsed. The German ration sank to starvation levels. Food riots took place throughout the country.

Clay hounded Washington with increasingly alarmist messages about the human tragedy and the political fallout from the food shortages. He finally got Truman's personal attention and the president sent Hoover to Germany again in March 1947. Hoover returned with a grim report and with a set of recommendations that fully supported Clay's views. Because American thinking on Germany and Europe was shifting, Marshall endorsed Hoover's proposals and supported a new and more generous U.S. occupation doctrine, JCS 1779, which replaced JCS 1067 on July 11, 1947. The food crisis eased.

Hoover also arranged for former U.S. Army rations to be provided as noon meals for over 3 million German children, a move that Clay believed helped more than any other to convince Germans that the United States wanted to help. After the bounteous 1948 harvest, which boosted food stocks in Germany and worldwide, and after a currency reform that was to make farm produce worth selling, the Western occupation zones did not face any more food problems.[47]

The Western commanders had started the occupation with separate policies. By the end of 1947, however, they had begun to merge both their policies and their zones. They had not done so primarily for the sake of the Germans. Instead, they needed to cut their own costs and to find a way of governing for what looked increasingly like a long road ahead. They also had begun to realize that the differences that separated them from each other did not matter as much as those that separated them from the Soviets and from Walter Ulbricht.

THREE

STALIN'S INDECISION

THE COUNCIL OF FOREIGN MINISTERS (CFM) FINALLY BEGAN discussing the German question in depth at its fourth session, beginning on March 10, 1947. It met in Moscow for seven particularly dreary weeks after the coldest winter in memory. The ministers had first planned to meet for three months but shortened the session because they were going nowhere.

The ministers had become accustomed to disagree, having reached peace treaties for Germany's allies only after sustained and bitter debate. They had also experienced real conflicts of interest and war scares over Turkey and other Middle Eastern states.[1] The wartime mood of cooperation had evaporated completely.

The situation in Germany remained fluid. Nothing had been locked in stone. But the occupation zones had begun to go their separate ways. The foreign ministers would have to act fast and decisively if they wanted to arrest the momentum toward separation.

COLD DAYS IN MOSCOW

The meetings in Moscow got off to a rocky start when Molotov opened with a broadside against the West. He denounced Bizonia, arguing that it undermined the prospect for the united Germany which Moscow still favored. He reiterated the Soviet demand for $10 billion in reparations and again asked for joint control over the Ruhr. He accused the West of violating the Yalta and Potsdam agreements.

Bevin replied by demanding full freedom of movement throughout Germany as a start toward full German economic unity by July 1, 1947. Presenting Bizonia as a potential first step in the direction of full German unity, he invited others to join. He asked for new and higher limits on German industrial production so as to permit Germany to export more and to pay for the food imports now being subsidized by the Allies. He rejected Molotov's demand for greater reparations, saying that Germany needed to be able to produce if it was not to bankrupt the occupiers.

Bidault agreed more with Molotov than with Bevin. He rejected Bevin's demands for German economic unity, opposed any increase in German production, and demanded more reparations. He said that France needed to get its own production going before facing German competition. He demanded that the Saarland become part of the French economic area. But he disagreed with Molotov over German unification, saying that the Allies had to remove both the Rhineland and the Ruhr from German control before France could support any steps toward uniting the rest of Germany.

Marshall, new to these meetings and thinking that he had come to negotiate, not wrangle, found these arguments a shocking waste of time. He entered the discussion carefully and gradually. Citing desperate conditions in Germany, he warned that the Allies had to bring the country back to its feet unless they wanted to choose between subsidizing the Germans or letting them die. He urged redrawing the Oder-Neisse border to give Germany more food-producing areas while letting Poland keep the southern part of East Prussia as well as Upper Silesia. Molotov denounced this as unacceptable.

The ministers also disagreed sharply about the future German government envisaged in the Potsdam agreement. Bevin and Marshall, worried about Soviet domination from the earlier seat of German government now in the Soviet sector of Berlin, favored a loose federal and democratic system under which most government functions would go to the *Länder*. Bidault advanced an extreme form of federalism, with virtually no powers given to the central government. Molotov alone favored a centralized German government.

The ministers then recessed for a week while their deputies tried the impossible task of elaborating texts that would reflect whatever consensus might exist. During that recess, President Truman announced the U.S. aid program to Greece and Turkey that came to be known as the Truman Doctrine. Bevin feared that this announcement would jeopardize the CFM by its strongly anti-communist tone, but Molotov never mentioned it.

Following Truman's theme, Marshall told the reconvened CFM that the United States would continue to exercise its "responsibilities" in Europe. Thus he officially notified the Soviet government that Washington had reversed Roosevelt's Yalta prediction. He went even further than Byrnes at Stuttgart, suggesting that Washington had decided on a long and perhaps indefinite American presence in Europe. As for Germany itself, Marshall said that the United States opposed dividing the country and wanted to establish a united government on democratic principles.

Marshall returned to Byrnes's Paris proposal for a treaty that would demilitarize Germany for 25 years. Bevin agreed, as he had in Paris. Bidault also agreed in principle. Molotov, however, demanded that the Allies first agree on four-power control over the Ruhr. Marshall did not press his proposal, but Molotov apparently did not recognize what this should have told him about Marshall himself and about evolving American attitudes.

The meetings continued fruitlessly, with no compromise on any topic. No foreign minister said anything new, the deputies could reach no agreement, and the entire process finally ran out of steam. The ministers agreed to adjourn until the fall and then to meet in London.

Marshall, who had not yet learned to go as quickly to the top in the Soviet system as his successors did by the 1970s and 1980s, had not asked to call on Stalin before the CFM meeting. But he decided to have a personal talk with the Soviet leader before he left Moscow to help sort out his impressions. Speaking in his usual spare style, he told Stalin that he was disappointed that the CFM session had failed. He warned that the American people were losing their wartime sympathy for the Soviet Union. Finally, he said the United States did not want to impose any system on any country but could not permit economic chaos.

Stalin replied to Marshall in the same calm manner. He explained Soviet actions and policies at the CFM and in general, giving no sign that Molotov's instructions would change. At the very end of his remarks, however, he said that it would be wise to remain patient. There was room for compromise on all matters, including de-militarization, reparations, economic unity and a political structure for Germany. One should not give way to pessimism but should be ready to advance slowly.

Stalin may have thought that he had persuaded Marshall to wait for the next CFM in London, but he failed to anticipate how the American would react to seven wasted weeks in Moscow and to Stalin's own remarks. The secretary of state left Moscow not only disgusted and discouraged but also convinced that Stalin wanted to delay the talks because he expected the situation in Germany to deteriorate further. Marshall had recognized the desperation in the Western occupation zones and in western Europe as a whole. He felt that he could not afford to wait and hope that another CFM session would produce results.

Stalin and Molotov did not know it, but they had lost control over the negotiating process. After the Moscow meeting, Marshall accepted Bevin's view that the West had to act in Germany and Europe without waiting for Soviet concurrence or for further talks. Bevin reported to Attlee that Stalin had made as bad a mistake as his 1939 pact with Hitler by rejecting all U.S. proposals, including the treaty against German militarization.[2]

Stalin then also lost control of the process in Germany itself. After the Moscow meeting, Soviet officials told some of the German communist leaders that the upcoming London meeting would bring about the political and economic unity of Germany. But the German communists replied that the Soviet zone was not ready for unification. Ulbricht informed Stalin that he would need more than a few months to get ready to compete effectively in a united Germany and that Stalin should delay pushing for German unity if he wanted to be successful over the whole of Germany. The summer adjournment did not give Ulbricht enough time. He warned that unification would be risky except under carefully controlled conditions.[3]

Although he did not know of Ulbricht's warning to Stalin, Marshall had reached a similar conclusion. He also felt that any further delay in Germany would play into communist hands. Germany had gone for two years without a treaty and without any prospect of having one. No German knew what to do, what to eat, where to live, where or how to work, or what the future would hold. Riots and strikes raged throughout the Western zones. Marshall concluded that Stalin did not really want to compromise but wanted only to paralyze the West with vague promises while Germany fell into chaos and under communist control. The American did not know that, although Stalin may have wanted a united Germany, he had to stall because the SED was not yet ready to build the kind of Germany he wanted.

Marshall on April 28 replied to Stalin's comments indirectly in a radio address reporting on the Moscow meeting and adding that there was no time left for further empty talks: "We cannot ignore the factor of time. The patient is sinking while the doctors deliberate." He concluded by urging action "without delay."[4]

On June 5, 1947, Marshall proposed what came to be known as the Marshall Plan, offering U.S. aid for European recovery if the Europeans would formulate a joint proposal. Bevin and Bidault seized the initiative to convene a meeting of European states, including the Soviet Union and the east Europeans. Stalin at first seemed interested, sending Molotov to Paris to attend.

Molotov wanted American aid to be administered separately by each state under its own authority rather than through a common agency. In effect, he wanted to have the Marshall Plan follow the Lend-Lease model of World War II rather than the internationally coordinated administration Marshall envisioned. When he realized that the Marshall Plan might bring an American presence to eastern Europe along with American aid, he left Paris and forced east European delegations to leave with him.[5] Marshall and Bevin, relieved that they did not have to include the Soviet Union, went ahead with plans for west European recovery.

Even Bidault, who had once hoped that the CFM could help to lay a firm foundation for future French security, had decided that he could not work with Molotov. He complained after the Moscow meeting that Molotov and other Soviet leaders were "obstinate, simple-minded, and in bad faith." Molotov repeatedly went out of his way to insult France and Bidault, once even deliberately and ostentatiously slighting Bidault in a toast.[6] This increased Bidault's readiness to work with Bevin and Marshall.

By 1947, de Gaulle's Franco-Soviet treaty of 1944 had become a dead letter. Molotov would not support French proposals to separate the Rhineland or the Ruhr from Germany any more than Bevin or Marshall would. But the British and the Americans at least offered some prospects for cooperation whereas the Soviets offered none. Under the circumstances, France had no choice.[7]

Stalin retaliated. In September 1947, he created a communist coordinating system for Europe by establishing the Cominform, in part succeeding the worldwide Comintern which he had abolished in 1943. The Cominform included the communist parties of France and Italy as well as most east Europeans but did not include the SED. Communist-inspired strikes followed in France and Italy as the battle for Europe began in earnest and in the open.

Ulbricht and Sokolovsky had their own reply to Bizonia and to the closer links between the Western occupation zones. On June 4, 1947, even before Marshall's speech, Sokolovsky had ordered the establishment of the *Deutsche Wirtschaftskommission* as the civilian administration for the Soviet zone and perhaps as the precursor for a potential German civilian government that Ulbricht wanted to have in place before the London CFM session.

On November 25, 1947, the Council of Foreign Ministers reconvened in London. By then, however, it was virtually an anachronism. Marshall, Bevin and Bidault had almost given up on the entire diplomatic process and only came to see if there might be one last chance for a deal. They held little hope.

Bevin wanted to bring the negotiating process to an end quickly, not only because he feared chaos in Germany but because of an economic crisis in Britain itself. He wanted Germany to begin to contribute to its own recovery and to stop costing more than the English people could pay.

Stalin still wanted to try to unite Germany in order to extend his influence over all of Germany, although Ulbricht had warned him that the SED was not

ready. On November 21, the eve of the London CFM session, the Soviet communist party politburo agreed that the Soviet delegation to the meeting was to try to
conclude a peace treaty that would lead to a united Germany. Stalin wanted the
CFM to agree on an all-German government and a formal peace conference.[8]

Molotov faced an immense task. He had to reach agreement on a united Germany which would permit an extension of Moscow's influence throughout the
entire country while protecting Ulbricht's fledgling communist system. And he
had to negotiate complex unification terms without yielding on his demands for
reparations. In addition, he had to appeal to German and European public opinion. Nor could he forget that Stalin, while wanting agreement, might punish any
Soviet foreign minister who hinted too openly at compromise.

Molotov could not carry out this task. It would have required a master
diplomat, which he was not. His statements stressed, as in the past, that only the
Soviet Union favored German unity. But his presentations reflected Ulbricht's
warning that he could not yet compete in a united Germany although he already
had the DWK as a potential all-German administration.

Molotov's tactics varied from day to day. He sometimes spoke in glowing
terms about the prospects for a united Germany and for a democratic system in
which all German political forces could participate. At those times, the Western
ministers worried that Molotov might be winning German public opinion and
that they would be led into traps or into interminable talks. A German central
government, which the Western powers feared because it might put all of Germany under Ulbricht's capital in Berlin, might sound attractive if one did not
look at all the demands and conditions that Molotov attached.

On other days, Molotov firmly reiterated all those demands and conditions.
Trying to prevent a reversal of the agricultural and industrial reforms in the Soviet zone, he insisted that the Western occupiers should agree in advance to conduct the same reforms and to impose the same state control over production in
their zones. He also insisted on a German political process that would give
weight not only to political parties but to "democratic" organizations of the kind
created in the Soviet zone. He thought the Western foreign ministers should
agree to let Ulbricht's institutions expand across all of Germany instead of challenging and perhaps discarding them.

Molotov's determination to make sure of a socialized Germany even if the
KPD could not win power did not appeal to the West. Bevin and his colleagues
suspected that Molotov talked about German unity only to score propaganda
points while really wanting to have the SED take control.

Molotov also continued to insist on $10 billion in reparations, now to be
paid out of current German production instead of by further dismantling of

German industry. He demanded four-power control over the Ruhr. The Soviet Union would thus receive German economic support no matter what might happen in a united Germany.

Molotov continued his vituperation about alleged Western breaches of the Potsdam agreement, particularly disturbing Marshall, who could never accustom himself to such tirades and who felt that the negotiators were fiddling while Europe burned. Molotov also rejected every Western proposal, leading other foreign ministers and reporters in London to call him "Mr. Nyet." He did not promote the spirit of mutual understanding that might have led to agreement.

The Western foreign ministers rejected the political and economic mortgages which Molotov placed on Germany's future. They believed that Molotov wanted reparations out of current production because Moscow had taken all it could out of its own zone and now needed to tap into the Western zones. Marshall knew that the U.S. Congress would never agree to provide aid for Germany if that aid funded reparations for Moscow. He and especially Bevin feared that Molotov's conditions would give Moscow permanent control over the German economy.

Even as the CFM sat in London, western Europe teetered ever closer to the edge of disintegration. American food aid had only just begun to arrive. Clay reported that he had never seen German morale so low. France ran out of cereal grains and coal, and the French economy neared collapse. The communist party in Italy called for strikes and demonstrations. Great Britain faced financial meltdown, with one run after another against the pound.[9] Bevin, Bidault and Marshall began talking to each other much more about meeting their common needs in western Europe than about the CFM.

Molotov realized what was happening and tried to change tactics. But, although he stressed his wish for German unity more clearly than before, he still did not send a clear signal for compromise. If Stalin wanted an agreement that would unite Germany, Molotov muddied the message. He continued to punctuate his proposals with long harangues and lists of conditions. The Western foreign ministers listened with deepening mistrust, concluding that Molotov made positive comments only to win public opinion and not to reach agreement. They wanted to deal with Europe's problems instead of giving Molotov a platform for propaganda and polemics. They agreed among themselves to end the CFM session, with Bevin to move for adjournment when the time seemed ripe.

Molotov still did not temper his rhetoric. On December 15, he poured forth such a vial of calumniation that Marshall had heard as much as he could bear. Not waiting for Bevin to take his cue to end the meeting, Marshall himself proposed that the CFM adjourn without setting a date for another session. Bidault and a delighted Bevin agreed on the spot.

Molotov remained alone in his seat as the Council of Foreign Ministers ended abruptly without having written the peace treaty for Germany that he had been instructed to negotiate. General Clay, who had attended many CFM meetings, wrote that it was the only time he had seen Molotov wince. The Soviet foreign minister had not intended his remarks to end the talks. Now he would have to explain to Stalin how he had failed.[10] And he would never have another chance to negotiate seriously about Germany.

Soviet internal documents described the collapse of the London meeting as a "fiasco."[11] Stalin's hopes for a united Germany lay in ruins. So did his hopes for a voice in the Ruhr, for major reparations and for influence across the center of Europe. For him, more than for the West, the Council of Foreign Ministers had proven to be a disaster. Molotov had gained nothing that the Red Army had not won in battle.

But Stalin understood what was to follow. In January 1948, he told a group of east European communist officials that "the West will take over Western Germany and we will make Eastern Germany our own."[12]

With the collapse of the CFM talks, the Western foreign ministers felt released from bondage. Now they could address the urgent problems in their occupation zones without having to lose time in fruitless negotiations. Bevin again took the lead. Under his chairmanship, the three laid plans for increasing the industrial output of their zones and exchanged further ideas for creating a democratic German government.

Most important, Bevin began making arrangements that would guarantee French security if Paris were to join Bizonia. On March 4, 1947, before the Moscow CFM, Britain and France had signed the treaty of Dunkirk, establishing a military alliance ostensibly directed against the risk of German aggression but with the Soviet threat clearly in mind.

By the end of the year, Bevin used the Dunkirk Treaty to arrange the kind of Anglo-French military cooperation that would give Bidault a defense against the Soviet Union. Bidault thought Marshall had been too conciliatory toward Molotov for too long, and he wanted closer links with Britain. As the French could no longer count on a separate Rhineland as a territorial safety belt, they would join in a general security pact.[13]

Bevin had no illusions that French and British resources alone could protect western Europe against the Soviet Union. Before they had left London, Bidault and Marshall had accepted Bevin's ideas for closer transatlantic as well as west European cooperation.

Thus, four-power diplomacy on postwar Germany had come to an end by 1948. Having negotiated peace treaties for the minor players, the ministers could not succeed in their most important mission. The Soviet Union had been confined to its own zone with Walter Ulbricht and his SED. The Western powers would work together and with their German friends. The united German government envisioned in the Potsdam agreement would have to wait, as the World War II victors put German unity into limbo.

SWEPT UP IN CONFRONTATION RHETORIC

Stalin and the West had many conflicts of interest during the immediate postwar years. They disagreed about eastern Europe, the Mediterranean, Trieste, Turkey, Iran, Japan, the atom, and other subjects. And they increasingly saw Germany in that disputatious setting.

Leaders and intellectuals on both sides began to explain separate East-West arguments as evidence of a systemic conflict. They weighed each problem in the context of that wider and deeper contradiction. Germany added to that context and suffered from it.

Stalin threw the first stone in public, saying at an election rally on February 9, 1946, that the United States and Great Britain were ganging up to deny the Soviet Union its security. He said that cooperation with capitalist countries had been only temporary. He added that the Soviet people would be sufficiently well armed to resist any attack.[14] Although Stalin may have intended these remarks as mere rhetoric, the speech drew wide attention in the West and came to be cited as the opening salvo of the Cold War.

Stalin may have had reason to vent his frustration. The West, and especially the United States, had failed to meet his hopes for aid. He had requested an American loan for $10 billion shortly after the war as a form of continued Lend-Lease. The U.S. State Department lost the request and lost it again when Molotov resubmitted it. Stalin could not have been expected to believe that the U.S. government would lose such a request by accident. When U.S. ambassador Averell Harriman paid his farewell call on January 23, 1946, two weeks before Stalin's speech, Harriman evaded questions about the status of the loan. Stalin concluded that Truman had rejected it.[15]

Stalin also had to recognize that the Western states would not grant him a global role. In all discussions about Japan, the Mediterranean or the Middle

East, Western leaders made clear that only they could have interests and forces all around the world. The Soviet Union could have a regional role, but it was not to be a Great Power in the widest sense.

The West replied to Stalin within weeks in a speech by Winston Churchill. Although Churchill had left office, he still felt more acute anguish about Soviet domination of eastern Europe than any other Western leader. Churchill believed that Stalin had misled him about Moscow's postwar plans during the Big Three meetings and other wartime talks.

Churchill's chance came when Truman invited him to speak at Westminster College in Fulton, Missouri, promising to introduce him personally. In long and rolling phrases, Churchill charged that the Soviet Union had installed police states in every east European country except Czechoslovakia. He also accused Stalin of building a communist regime in Moscow's German occupation zone. He warned that:

> From Stettin in the Baltic to Trieste in the Adriatic, an Iron Curtain has descended across the Continent. Behind that line lie all the capitals of the ancient states of central and eastern Europe—Warsaw, Berlin, Prague, Vienna, Budapest, Bucharest and Sofia.[16]

Truman, despite his admiration for Churchill, distanced himself from Churchill's rhetoric. He had not yet made up his mind about U.S. policy toward Moscow. He said (incorrectly) that he had not seen the speech before delivery, and he tried to balance his position by inviting Stalin also to make a speech in Missouri.[17] Stalin ignored the invitation. He had already denounced Churchill's speech, asserting in a *Pravda* interview that "Churchill and his friends bear a striking resemblance to Hitler and his friends" and warning that war was "inevitable" if the West did not recognize Soviet security interests.[18] Churchill's "friends" threatened with the "inevitable" war obviously included Truman.

But Churchill did not stand alone. Truman received another message from a source closer to home. This one warned him and Byrnes that they should stop trying to reach any kind of agreement with Stalin on Germany or any other subject.

In a cable that came to be known as the Long Telegram, George Kennan, in charge of the U.S. Embassy in Moscow after Harriman's departure, wrote in stark terms about an impending clash between the Soviet and Western systems. He warned in February 1946 that a combination of Russian paranoia and messianic communism would lead the Soviet Union into an irreconcilable conflict with the West. He wrote that the traditional Russian sense of insecurity would force the Soviet Union into a "deadly struggle for total destruction" with the West without any hope of compromise.[19]

Kennan pointed particularly to Soviet military preparations, writing that the Soviet Union was highly sensitive to "the logic of force" and would strive for the "maximum development" of its armies. He told Washington, then eager to demobilize, that the only way to impress Stalin was to have "sufficient force" and the will to use it. He added that Moscow did not seek a "general military conflict" and would withdraw when faced with "strong resistance," but that the Soviets would try to take full advantage of any situations in which they were the stronger.

A month later, Ernest Bevin received a similar message from Frank Roberts, head of the British Embassy in Moscow. Going beyond Kennan's general analysis, Roberts warned that Moscow wanted to win control over Germany. He wrote that: "Anglo-Soviet differences are also coming to a head in Germany itself, where the Russians . . . are now encouraging the communists to advocate a united 'democratic' Germany in full control of the Ruhr."[20] He added that Stalin wanted Soviet control over eastern Germany and communist influence throughout all of Germany.

Truman decided that he needed to learn more. He asked Clark Clifford, whom he had recently appointed as counsel to the president, to analyze Soviet policy. In response, Clifford produced a memorandum that sounded the alarm on Soviet policy toward Europe and that spoke of a global Soviet military and political threat.[21]

Drawing extensively on Kennan's Long Telegram, Clifford warned Truman that the Soviet Union was committed to the ultimate triumph of communism over capitalism and would be an irreconcilable foe although it would not start a war unless it felt sure to win. He drew up a long list of Soviet failures to carry out wartime agreements with the West and warned that Stalin was gearing up to present a direct challenge to the United States.

With respect to Germany, Clifford wrote that Stalin wanted a united Germany only in order to control the whole country from its capital in Berlin. He wrote that Stalin would not accept any agreement on Germany which did not give him a chance to win over the entire country, and he asserted that Stalin wanted to use reparations to make Germany a Soviet dependent.

Clifford recommended that the United States join with other Western states "to build up a world of our own which will pursue its own objectives." He added that the United States "should maintain military forces powerful enough to restrain the Soviet Union and to confine Soviet influence to its present area." He concluded that Soviet leaders would "work out with us a fair and equitable settlement when they realize that we are too strong to be beaten and too determined to be frightened."

Truman reacted with alarm because he did not want Clifford's memorandum to force his hand. Wanting to pay off the huge U.S. deficit from World War II, he did not want to expand the military budget. He told Clifford to destroy all copies of the report.

At least some Soviet officials saw corresponding threats from the West. In September 1946, the Soviet ambassador in Washington, Nikolai Novikov, analyzed U.S. policy in the same alarmist terms in which Kennan and Roberts had analyzed Soviet policy. He wrote that "American monopolistic capital" would try to expand American influence into Europe and Asia because the devastation wrought by the war offered good openings for U.S. economic and political penetration. He wrote that Truman had reversed Roosevelt's friendly policies toward the Soviet Union and that the United States was building up its armed forces to prepare for war.

Novikov, close to Molotov and undoubtedly well informed about the debates between the Soviet and Western foreign ministers, saw Germany as a key arena for U.S. plots against Soviet interests. He pointed out that the American occupation authorities had left the German capitalist structure intact, neither nationalizing German industry nor reforming German agriculture as the Soviets had done in their zone. Novikov wrote that U.S. efforts to negotiate an early end to the occupation of Germany, before Germany had been fully de-militarized and "democratized," revealed U.S. intentions to revive Imperial Germany to use in a war against the Soviet Union.

In Stalin's Russia and Molotov's foreign ministry, no ambassador would have sent such a telegram without being told to send it and what to write. Molotov probably asked for the cable and told Novikov what it should say. His personal copy shows frequent underlining and other signs of approval. He also asked that the cable be kept in his personal files, perhaps to explain (to Stalin?) why he had found it so difficult to reach agreement with the West.[22]

In 1947, the American side of the debate went public. Kennan, who had first sounded the alarm from Moscow, wrote an article entitled "The Sources of Soviet Conduct" in the journal *Foreign Affairs* of July 1947. The article, written under the pseudonym "X" to protect Kennan's identity as a government official, poured cold water on any prospects of accommodation with Stalin and with the Soviet system.[23] As a public document written by a well-placed member of the American east coast Establishment, the article shaped the thinking of all American political and intellectual figures and forced open discussion. Truman could not ignore it or the commentary it provoked. Nor could he resist its conclusions any longer.

Kennan argued against any negotiations with Stalin, as the Soviet leader would regard any agreement with the West as a tactical maneuver. The Soviet system, Kennan wrote, was sensitive only to "contrary force" and to the sheer logic of power. This meant that Truman would find it hard to reach an agreement with Stalin and could not expect Stalin to keep whatever agreement might be negotiated. Kennan recommended that the West pursue a strategy of firm "containment," holding back the thrust of Soviet expansion until the system lost its momentum and collapsed.

Projecting into the future, Kennan wrote that those characteristics of the Soviet system "will be with us . . . until the internal nature of Soviet power is changed." He added, however, that the collapse of the communist power system would change the Soviet Union almost instantly from the strongest to the weakest of states.

Kennan's article set forth the arguments for a redirection of U.S. thinking, for a break in East-West negotiations, and (to Kennan's distaste) for a military buildup. Although it did not offer specific advice on Germany, Kennan's reasoning suggested that there would be little point in trying to reach agreement on Germany until the West had built the kind of power position that Stalin would respect.

Kennan, more influential under Marshall than under Byrnes, had favored the division of Germany well before the Yalta and Potsdam conferences. He thought it would be an illusion to hope that Germany could be administered jointly with Moscow and believed the only hope for the West lay in dividing Germany and building up the western portions to prevent the Soviet Union from reaching the North Sea by dominating a united Germany.[24] After such advice, it was little wonder that Marshall cut off the dialogue with Molotov.

Stalin chose Andrei Zhdanov, the Kremlin's propaganda chief, to reply. Zhdanov, speaking at the first meeting of the Cominform during September 1947, well before the London CFM, portrayed American capitalism as an implacable and irreconcilable foe in words similar to Kennan's portrayal of Soviet communism.[25]

Zhdanov asserted that Washington wanted to achieve global hegemony and that the United States was trying to enslave Europe by creating an Atlantic system. That plan, he predicted, would divide Europe into "two camps." Zhdanov asserted that Marshall wanted to use U.S. aid "to restore the power of imperialism in the new democracies and to compel them to renounce economic and political cooperation with the Soviet Union." Like Novikov, he warned that the United States wanted to restore German capitalism and to use a revived Germany to gain control over eastern Europe.

Zhdanov's argument, coming on the heels of electoral defeats for communist parties in France and Italy, may have shown Stalin's deepening doubts whether such parties could take over in western Europe as he had originally hoped.[26] That may have influenced him to want to make assurance doubly sure before negotiating for a united Germany. It almost certainly convinced Ulbricht, if that was still necessary, that he did not want open competition in Germany as a whole.

Such speeches and articles rendered negotiations on Germany pointless. Once Soviet and Western leaders and analysts mistrusted each other so deeply and denounced each other so openly, little hope remained for compromise on such a sensitive area as central Europe.

The Allied Control Council, the main four-power coordinating mechanism for occupied Germany, reflected the increasingly hostile attitudes of the four powers toward each other. Discussions in the council turned ever more acrimonious. General Clay, who believed longer than other U.S. officials that the four powers could continue to cooperate in Germany, watched the deteriorating state of relations with growing concern.[27]

Clay had experienced the heady days of summer 1945, when the four powers in the ACC had enjoyed warm personal and professional relations and when they could agree on most topics. Stalin had obviously given his ACC representatives more accommodating instructions than he had given to Molotov, or the ACC representatives had interpreted them more positively. During the early months of the ACC, the Soviets and Americans often had agreed more with each other than with the British or the French. They had wanted to restore German unity, which de Gaulle had blocked, and they had favored a slower restoration of the German economy than Robertson did. Clay often found himself trying to mediate British-Soviet disputes.

But signs of trouble had begun to multiply, especially due to Stalin's and Ulbricht's determination to keep the Soviet occupation zone as their exclusive preserve. The Soviets consistently took unilateral measures in their zone, leaving others to wonder why they did not coordinate or at least discuss their ideas before acting. Soviet occupation commander Sokolovsky kept Western offices out of his zone. He would not permit an American consulate to open, although American forces had fought there and the U.S. government needed to get information about casualties.

The occupation powers also had to deal with the growing divergences in German attitudes toward them, with Berlin being the site of the first clash. Western Allies had long wanted to replace the city's Soviet-appointed administration with an elected government. When the Soviets agreed and the SED suffered a defeat, the Soviets would not permit the government and the new governing mayor, Ernst Reuter, to sit in the old Berlin city hall which was in the Soviet sector. The Allied occupation authority in Berlin, the Kommandatura, never recovered from the angry arguments that followed.

Once the Council of Foreign Ministers began discussing Germany formally in early 1947, the ACC found itself increasingly drawn into the debates between Molotov and the Western ministers. After the disputatious Moscow meeting, the ACC could no longer pretend to function as an effective instrument for the occupation of Germany. Each zonal commander did what he wanted without even pretending to consult with others.

The low point came at the last meeting of the ACC before the opening of the London CFM meeting. Sokolovsky read a long list of alleged Western failures to comply with wartime agreements. Clay reported that the meeting represented a total departure from the norm, for in the past Sokolovsky had tried—like his Western colleagues—to maintain a collegial atmosphere even when he and others disagreed. Clay concluded that both the ACC and the CFM were on the verge of breaking up.

WHY GERMANY WAS DIVIDED

The temporary occupation lines that Roosevelt, Stalin and Churchill had drawn at Yalta began to look more permanent by 1947. Goods and persons could not cross some of the lines. Social structures and political organizations developed differently on opposite sides. Germany once again lay divided, as it had been for centuries.

Germany lay divided not because the occupiers feared Germany itself but because they feared each other in combination with Germany. All were afraid that Germany's weight could decide the winner in the new battle looming between them. They decided that they would rather have their own slices than risk letting their prospective opponents have the whole.

Divided and defeated, Germany could threaten nobody. But united and recovered, it could help to threaten any of the occupying states if it joined with one or more of the others. Although the wartime Allies had agreed at Potsdam to form a German government and to sign a peace treaty with it, the CFM could not begin to agree on how to form that new government. It could not even agree on how to manage the occupation. No one dared to let the other have an advantage.

Germany represented a zero-sum game. A united Germany in the hands of either Stalin or the West meant an absolute gain for one and an absolute loss for the other. None of the leaders wished to gamble on that. Even in ruins, Germany still mattered. Faced with this risk, the wartime allies chose the safe way out.

Stalin had the most contradictory ambitions, offensive and defensive at the same time. The documents that Moscow has released over the past several years, as well as some of the memoirs recently published by Soviet officials, show that the Soviet leader did not want a divided Germany and that he was prepared to accept a non-communist regime there for the immediate future if it was friendly. But if he could not have a communist government over all of Germany quickly, he wanted an agreement that would at least assure him about its prospects as well as about reparations and the Ruhr. He also wanted protection for the SED. No Western government could agree to that, especially in the disputatious atmosphere that Molotov generated and after they had all seen how Stalin gained and exercised control over eastern Europe.

Stalin made several fundamental mistakes in his German policy. His decision to place much of Germany "under Polish administration" proved to be the most important. Stalin had little bargaining strength. If East Prussia and Silesia had been under Soviet occupation, he would have had almost half of Germany in his occupation zone. When he gave those areas to Poland, however, Stalin lost his chance to negotiate about Germany. He could offer the Western Allies no incentive to unite Germany. Why should they have given him influence over their valuable parts of Germany in exchange for his denuded rump? Stalin paid a price in Germany itself for his Polish insurance against German aggression.

Stalin may have deliberately chosen security over influence. The decision to push Poland westward, like the decision to occupy the Balkans before attacking the German heartland, reflected his moat mentality. So, perhaps unconsciously, did his decision to give Ulbricht what amounted to a veto by asking him when his zone would be ready to compete in a united Germany.[28] Stalin wanted other things at least as much as unity.

But Stalin also took a monumental risk. Above all else, he had long feared a link between the Western occupation zones of Germany and the power of capitalist America. And with good reason, for he knew that the Soviet Union could not match the combined strength of Germany and the United States.[29] Yet his and Molotov's diplomacy opened the door to precisely what he feared.

Molotov made more diplomatic blunders than he could afford. He passed up major opportunities to gain leverage over all of Germany when he rejected both Byrnes's and Marshall's proposals for a four-power treaty against German remilitarization. He constantly set the teeth of his diplomatic colleagues on edge, perhaps a smart and even essential tactic to boast about in Stalin's paranoic Kremlin but not a way to reach agreement.

Stalin and Molotov wanted more guarantees than any Western foreign minister could give. When Molotov told Byrnes that Germany had to have an "antifascist" government and added that he would not sign a peace treaty until such a government had functioned long enough to establish its credibility in Moscow, Byrnes did not need Kennan to tell him that Molotov would leave little to chance and nothing to German voters.

When Byrnes left the Council of Foreign Ministers for the last time, he told the Soviet foreign minister rather sadly that he had never been able to negotiate with him because he had never known what Molotov really wanted. Molotov did not reply, perhaps because he himself did not know.

After leaving office, Molotov said that it had been his task to "expand Soviet frontiers as far as possible" and that there could be no "peace-loving" Germany that was not on "the path of socialism."[30] If that was what Molotov truly wanted, he and Byrnes could never have reached agreement.

Stalin's occupation commanders deepened Germany's division when they rejected Clay's repeated efforts to merge two or three occupation zones. Had they accepted, and accepted quickly, Bevin and later Bidault would have been hard-put to resist joining. Virtually all of Germany would have had a central administration within one or two years at most. That reality would have given Stalin the influence he wanted but could have jeopardized Ulbricht's position. Sokolovsky apparently would not risk such a bargain.

Indeed, Stalin may have made his biggest mistake when he picked Walter Ulbricht as his man in Berlin. Ulbricht could do only half of what Stalin wanted. He could control the Soviet occupation zone. But Stalin had Zhukov and Sokolovsky to do that. Stalin needed an SED leader who could appeal to Germans outside the Soviet zone; Ulbricht could not. Neither could Grotewohl after Ulbricht had finished with him. Ulbricht's tactics and his manner made enemies for Stalin and for communism.

Ulbricht also pursued his own agenda. While Stalin wanted his occupation zone to offer a springboard to the West, Ulbricht wanted to seal it off. As Ulbricht's standing collapsed, he could stay in power only by keeping the Soviet zone under his own ever more burdensome absolute authority. As he did, other Germans turned away. Ulbricht seemed determined get his own domain even if Stalin might not get a united Germany.

By the end of 1947, Ulbricht had his wish. Germany would remain divided. He controlled the civilian apparatus in the Soviet zone. He had made his choice and Stalin could not change it.[31] Better a bird in hand, he thought, than two birds in the bush.

Stalin's policies in Germany defy explanation even after half a century. By the end of 1947, two and a half years after the greatest military victory in Russian history, Stalin had gained nothing more. Like Alexander I after 1814, Stalin had squandered a military triumph by incompetent diplomacy. Molotov has to take his share of the blame, but it was Stalin who set the tone.

Charles de Gaulle, the only Western leader who consistently wanted a divided Germany, got what he wanted although not as he had wanted it. He and Bidault could not separate the Rhineland and the Ruhr from Germany as they had wished, but the actual dividing lines served French purposes at least equally well. De Gaulle and Bidault could be confident that France would be safe, at least from their last enemy. France also received an absolute veto over Germany's future.

While de Gaulle had not helped to draw the occupation zones, he understood immediately that they offered him a heaven-sent way to keep Germany weak. That was why he vetoed every effort to merge any of the zones. For the same reason, under different circumstances, Bidault assured Marshall that the French zone would join Bizonia. Bidault had come to realize that Bizonia would divide, not unite, Germany. Although he reversed de Gaulle's policy, he held to the same strategic purpose.

Whereas Bidault had changed French policy without changing French strategy, Bevin changed British strategy. By 1946, he had decided that Britain could not make the grand European deal with Stalin that Churchill had wanted. Nor could Britain wait any longer in its once-cherished splendid isolation before deciding where to throw its weight to keep the European continent in balance. Instead, he saw that the only way to prevent Soviet domination of the entire continent would be to formalize Germany's division between East and West and to persuade the United States to keep a broad foothold on the continent. Bevin had developed a strategic vision for an American role in Europe long before the Americans themselves had.

Unlike de Gaulle, who wanted a divided Germany because he feared the Germans, Bevin wanted a divided Germany because he feared the Soviets. The result, however, was identical, and Britain's new western European system was to be formed around France, Great Britain itself and an American presence in a divided Germany.

Truman did not have a German policy when he took office. He did, however, have an occupation policy, JCS 1067, a modified version of the Morgenthau Plan.

The president studied his briefs and listened to his advisers and to his experience. All told him that he could not trust Stalin to negotiate an equitable arrangement for Germany and Europe. Like Bevin, although later, he chose a divided Germany because he saw no terms under which a united Germany could be safe from Stalin's domination. Byrnes's frustrations with Molotov in 1946 and 1947 made Truman agree with Kennan that he could not deal with Stalin. Under the circumstances, he felt that he could not withdraw U.S. forces from Europe.

Once Truman had decided to link up with London and to keep an American presence in Europe, he had a German policy. However, he then had to change his occupation policy. He had to abandon the Morgenthau Plan because he would need to build up the Western zones of Germany.

Molotov correctly asserted that Truman had not followed Roosevelt's line. But Truman could have replied that Stalin had not met Roosevelt's wartime expectations.

The four World War II victors had designed the occupation on the basis of several wrong assumptions. They had assumed that their interests would remain similar even after they had defeated Hitler. That proved untrue. They had assumed that the Germans would remain passive observers at their own occupation. Instead, the Germans began to express a clear preference for the democratic West. As they did, Stalin had to demand Western Allied guarantees that a united Germany would not turn against him.

The World War II victors also may have assumed that they could negotiate about Germany in a vacuum. But the talks they had about Germany's allies poisoned their diplomacy before they even began discussing Germany itself. The Cold War did not begin over Germany, although it came to center on Germany. The Cold War began over eastern Europe during the Soviet occupation of 1944–1945 and the East-West negotiations of 1946.

German division did not emerge full-blown from any master plan conceived in Moscow, London, Paris or Washington. It emerged from a process of incremental decision-making, where the logic of one action followed the logic of another with a mutual ratchet effect leading to a result that most had not expected.

Except for de Gaulle, none of the World War II victors at first wanted the division of Germany, and they finally chose it for different reasons. Bevin chose it to protect Europe from Stalin and to keep U.S. forces in Europe. Truman chose it to prevent Soviet domination of Europe and of Germany. Stalin chose it because Molotov could not negotiate an arrangement for real influence over Germany and perhaps over Europe. The four powers could not agree on how to unite Germany. But neither could they agree on how to divide Germany. Instead, they made separate decisions to keep whatever they had. None asked the Germans, who had forfeited their right to choose.

The armies that had entered Germany to conquer remained to occupy. They also remained to struggle, not against Germany but against each other.

FOUR

THE BERLIN AIRLIFT

ERNEST BEVIN CONTINUED TO SET THE PACE AND DIRECTION OF Western policy toward Germany after he and his colleagues had decided to adjourn the meeting of the Council of Foreign Ministers in London. He called a meeting of Western officials in London for February 1948 to decide on the next steps for Germany and Europe.[1] To make sure that other west European states would accept German economic recovery, Bevin invited the ambassadors of Belgium, Luxembourg and the Netherlands as well as the French and American ambassadors. He encouraged them to begin planning to make a western German state part of a European-American alliance system. Because nations still traumatized by German invasion and occupation needed time to reflect, Bevin scheduled the London meeting in two phases, from February 23 to March 6 and from April 20 to June 7, 1948.

The Western ambassadors had a common purpose but many questions. After some discussion, all agreed that German recovery held the key to European recovery. But Georges Bidault insisted that France still needed defense against Germany at least as much as against the Soviet Union. The ambassadors from the Benelux states shared that feeling. Bidault also said that he would not permit Western Germany to reassume control over the Ruhr. Nor would he permit Western Germany to be included in the Marshall Plan until London and Washington let France absorb the Saarland's economy. London and Washington accepted Bidault's terms. All then agreed to consider including the Western occupation zones into the Marshall Plan despite their reservations about Germany.

The ambassadors also began discussing a future government in Western Germany.[2] The French continued to balk at associating the French occupation zone with other zones but finally had to do so.[3] Once they agreed, the London meeting could conclude that western Europe would accept the western part of a divided Germany into whatever institutions it might develop.

When the first half of the London conference adjourned on March 6, Stalin decided to fire a shot across the bow by pressing on the West's most exposed point, Berlin. He called Marshal Sokolovsky and his political adviser Vladimir Semyonov to Moscow and told them to begin applying stricter control measures on the access routes to Berlin. Stalin had been considering such steps for some time and the London meeting provided a good occasion to try them. In addition, Molotov recommended a conference of east European states to press for another CFM meeting. Stalin agreed.[4]

Stalin ordered Sokolovsky to denounce the London results at the Allied Control Council in Berlin. Sokolovsky did so, accusing the Western powers of trying to decide matters that all four ACC powers should decide jointly. He charged that the West was tearing up the Potsdam agreement and burying the control council. He warned of dire consequences. One of Ulbricht's mouthpieces, the *Berliner Zeitung*, predicted that the "the day is not far off" when the Western occupation forces would have to leave Berlin.[5]

On March 31, 1948, Sokolovsky blocked military trains from traveling between the Western occupation zones and Berlin unless Soviet inspectors could verify all passengers and cargo. On the following day, he ordered that no trains could leave Berlin itself unless the Soviet Berlin Kommandatura office had granted permission. Those orders gave the Soviet authorities full control over all Allied military rail traffic in and out of the city.

General Lucius Clay found himself in a paradoxical position. He himself had not welcomed the London decisions because he still preferred a united to a divided Germany. But he would not accept any limits on U.S. authority in Germany and Berlin. He rejected Soviet demands to inspect the trains. Clay offered to give the Soviets full passenger lists and train manifests as a compromise. Sokolovsky rejected that offer. No Allied military trains moved to or from Berlin.

Clay faced not only Soviet pressure but hesitation at home. Secretary of State George Marshall did not want a crisis in Berlin. He had gone along with Bevin's drive for dividing Germany but had not yet decided to accept all the consequences. The U.S. Army also proved reluctant. Secretary of the Army Kenneth Royall questioned Clay's decision to reject Sokolovsky's demands. He urged compromise. He also proposed evacuating American dependents from Berlin. Clay refused to order evacuation but agreed to permit it if an entire family volunteered. He knew that none would. He warned Royall that the evacuation of American dependents would devastate morale in Berlin and that "when Berlin falls Western Germany will be next."[6]

Clay decided to test Soviet intentions by dispatching a train to go through the Soviet zone after carefully instructing its commander to resist all Soviet inspection demands. Clay hoped the Soviets would let the train through. But the Soviets, without actually blocking the train, shunted it to a dead-end siding. Clay, who had to withdraw it ignominiously several days later, concluded that "the Russians mean business."

Clay then ordered a small airlift to meet the immediate needs of the military garrisons. The airlift achieved its purpose, reaching the required capacity of about 100 tons within a few days. On April 10, less than a fortnight after Sokolovsky had issued his demands, he withdrew them; the so-called "baby blockade" had ended. Traffic continued relatively smoothly again, although the Soviets tried from time to time during the following weeks to pose new demands. Sokolovsky had given his warning. Clay had shown what he would do.

THE D-MARK AND THE BLOCKADE

Stalin and the Soviet leadership considered the "baby blockade" a success. Semyonov claimed that the control measures had damaged U.S. prestige and that Clay's airlift had proven futile. He said that the Soviets had discovered a weak spot in the Western position. He recommended further such pressures as appropriate and expressed his confidence that they would succeed. Other Soviets shared his view.

Walter Ulbricht urged Stalin to use this new-found tactic to expel the Western powers from Berlin. Ulbricht's adviser Wilhelm Pieck told Stalin on March 26, 1948, that the SED would be able to get more support in the Soviet occupation zone if the West was out of Berlin. Stalin replied: "Let's make a joint effort—perhaps we can kick them out." At that, Sokolovsky and Ulbricht began making plans to incorporate all of Berlin into the Soviet zone.[7]

The Western occupation commanders had been warned about a Soviet blockade. They had a report that at a Soviet military party in January 1948 drunken Soviet officers had bragged that they would blockade the city and expel the Allies by June. Clay and Colonel Frank Howley, the U.S. Commandant in Berlin, had questioned the report because relations with the Soviets then seemed good. But those relations deteriorated dramatically after Stalin removed the elected government in Czechoslovakia in February 1948 to impose a communist dictatorship.[8]

Howley saw the handwriting on the wall. He thought that the West's failure to break through the small blockade would encourage Stalin and Sokolovsky to find some reason to try again. He and his staff quietly began to build up food, medical and other emergency stocks for the Berliners as well as the occupiers. That modest buildup was to prove vital a few months later.

Tensions continued to rise along the access routes throughout the spring. Clay, like Howley, realized that it was only a matter of time before the Soviets tried to blockade civilian as well as military traffic to Berlin. In May, the Soviets promulgated new documentation requirements for military and civilian freight. In early June, they delayed and sometimes blocked civilian freight trains, cutting civilian freight cars off at random from trains already in the Soviet zone. Those cars were never seen again.

On June 7, the second phase of the six-power conference ended in London with plans for a West German state to be established on the following principles:

- The Western occupation zones of Germany would be fully associated with the Marshall Plan.
- A new international control authority for the Ruhr would integrate Ruhr production fully into the Marshall Plan.
- Prompt action would be taken to coordinate the economic policies of the three zones.
- A federal form of German government would be adopted for an eventual united German state and, until then, for the Western occupation zones.
- France, the United Kingdom and the United States would not fully withdraw their troops from Germany until the peace of Europe was secured.[9]

The London announcement marked a setback for Stalin. It meant that the Western Allies would remain in Germany, that they would exclude Moscow from the Ruhr, and that there would be no more reparations.

Sokolovsky denounced the London agreement in the ACC and intensified Berlin access harassment. On June 10, Soviet forces tried to remove locomotives and switching equipment from the U.S. sector of Berlin. On June 11, they stopped rail traffic between Berlin and western Germany for two days. On June 12, they stopped traffic on a highway bridge "for repairs." They began to stop a large percentage of rail cars by claiming "bad order" and they stopped most outgoing rail cargo from West Berlin, allowing only empty cars to return to the west. They meant to split the Berlin economy from the Western occupation zones.[10]

Stalin and the West had set the stage for a major clash. By refusing to treat Germany as an economic unit, Stalin had ignored Western rights in the Soviet zone. In London, the Western Allies had decided to ignore Soviet rights in their zones. Stalin would now challenge Western rights in Berlin.

On June 18, the Western occupation authorities made a key move toward reviving the German economy. They announced a currency reform to be effective on June 20 throughout their zones. In deference to Soviet sensibilities, after long discussions with Sokolovsky and his office, they did not extend it to Berlin. The reform was based on the new Deutsche Mark, the D-mark, against which limited quantities of old Reichsmarks could be exchanged at a ten-to-one ratio. The Western powers hoped that the new currency would put an end to inflation and to the black market. They had proposed a four-power currency reform early in 1948, but Sokolovsky had rejected it because the Western authorities wanted to have joint control over the currency to prevent the Soviets from printing at will as they had done with the Reichsmark.

At the same time, the West German civilian authorities under their economic chief, Ludwig Erhard, abolished many of the regulations that had been imposed on the German economy by the Nazis and by the occupiers. This defied Western as well as Soviet authority. Clay, whose advisers were angered to see many of their regulations abolished, called in Erhard to lecture him. He told Erhard that U.S. experts had warned that Erhard's policies would fail. Erhard, puffing on his ever-present cigar, replied laconically: "My experts tell me the same thing." Clay—who had long since learned to distrust experts— thereupon backed Erhard to the hilt.[11] The Western zones would go their own way economically.

The currency reform gave Sokolovsky the opening he wanted for a blockade. He excoriated the reform in next day's ACC meeting, saying that the Soviet government regarded currency reform for all of Germany as necessary and possible but that the Western reform risked splitting Germany. He added that all of Berlin belonged to the Soviet occupation zone. Ulbricht, going Sokolovsky one better, asserted that the currency reform had *already* split Germany.

On June 23, Sokolovsky and the Soviet occupation authorities introduced a currency reform of their own, applying it not only throughout the Soviet zone but throughout all of Berlin. The Western commandants agreed to let the Soviet currency circulate throughout Berlin if they could have some voice in its control. Alternatively, they offered to introduce the new D-mark into Berlin under quadripartite control. Sokolovsky would not accept either offer. The Western powers thereupon introduced the new D-mark to their sectors of Berlin, leaving the city with two competing currencies.

On June 24, the Soviets closed the rail and road routes linking West Berlin to the Western occupation zones. They blamed technical difficulties. Equally important, considering West Berlin's dependence on its hinterland, they blocked shipments and services coming to the western sectors from the Soviet zone, including food, coal and most electric power. They gradually tightened the stoppages ever further, so that by August the blockade on land and water was virtually complete.[12]

As Molotov had recommended, Stalin called a meeting of east European states in Warsaw. On the day after the blockade began, they issued the Warsaw declaration in reply to the London declaration. It included the following five demands:

- Four-power implementation of final German de-militarization.
- Four-power control over Ruhr heavy industry.
- Four-power agreement on a "provisional, democratic, peace-loving" government for all of Germany, composed of representatives of democratic organizations as well as of democratic parties in Germany.
- A peace treaty with Germany, in accordance with the Potsdam decisions, with all occupation forces to be withdrawn from Germany within a year after the conclusion of the treaty.
- The fulfillment of reparations.[13]

The Warsaw declaration expressed Stalin's full range of demands. Its categorical tone showed that Stalin and Ulbricht believed they held a strong position. They could squeeze West Berlin and appeal to German opinion by arguing that the Western powers wanted to divide Germany.

CLAY INVENTS STRATEGIC LIFT

The fate of West Berlin hung in the balance during the next few days. General Clay issued a statement that the United States would remain in the city, but he seemed isolated. Western newspapers reported that the Allies feared they could not supply Berlin by air and that they might have to leave the city to avoid imposing hardships on the Berliners. Many Western officials privately said that they could not hold the city. Soviet officials in Berlin voiced complete confidence that the Western Allies would be forced out.

The Berlin authorities and the Berliners themselves chose this moment to voice their views. Governing mayor Ernst Reuter called a mass meeting that was attended by 80,000 Berliners in the Olympic Stadium. He expressed the city's determination to hold out against the Soviets and Ulbricht no matter what hardships the West Berliners might have to endure. He called on the Western powers to support the beleaguered city and not to leave.

Reuter was in no mood to compromise when he was invited to Clay's office on the following day. He asserted that the Berliners would rather live in penury without coal and electricity than lose their freedom once again, this time to Stalin and Ulbricht instead of to Hitler. When Clay asked him directly whether the Berliners would continue to support an airlift even if it meant serious food and other shortages, Reuter replied that the Allies could count on the Berliners not to complain and not to undercut a policy of defiance.[14]

Reuter had said what Clay had wanted to hear. Clay had already decided that the United States could not in good conscience leave Berlin. Although he had once hoped to pull out U.S. forces from a united Germany in 1947, he realized after the London CFM that Germany would remain divided. In that case, he did not want to let Ulbricht have Berlin. He decided to supply the city with an airlift. He coordinated with the British military governor, General Robertson, who fully endorsed an airlift and ordered British aircraft to join it.

Clay called General Curtis LeMay, the commander of the U.S. Air Force in Europe, to ask if the air force could begin shipping coal, food, medicines and other supplies by air. LeMay said: "We can carry anything." Having already expected problems with the Soviets, he was ready to mobilize aircraft and to establish a system to ferry goods to Berlin from the Western zones.

Clay would have preferred to run an armored convoy up the Autobahn to Berlin from Helmstedt in western Germany. He had already gone to Frankfurt to set up a convoy and arranged for air cover. Believing that Stalin did not want a war and that the convoy would be able to get to Berlin through the Soviet zone, he confidently asserted that such a convoy would put an end to the blockade. But, although Clay had the authority to order a convoy as well as an airlift, he believed that he should not order it without asking Washington because it might provoke a confrontation with the Soviets.

The U.S. Army adamantly opposed the convoy. Senior officers and civilians feared escalation if Stalin instructed Soviet forces to block a convoy by force. Some officers said that they might consider sending such a column if it proceeded without ammunition, an option that Clay dismissed as ludicrous. Clay had to try the airlift although he had his own doubts whether it could supply Berlin's full needs.[15]

Neither the State Department nor the Pentagon wanted an airlift. On the first day of the blockade, they asked Clay to slow down the introduction of new currency (which had already been completed) and again urged him to begin evacuating American dependents (which Clay again refused to do). As occupation commander, Clay had full authority in Germany and would not take instructions from Washington or elsewhere.

Despite Clay's and Robertson's resolve, the airlift began excruciatingly slowly. On its first day, U.S. aircraft carried only 80 tons of supplies, well below the 2,500 tons believed to be the absolute minimum daily requirement to feed and take care of the city over the long term. Two days later, the British Royal Air Force joined the airlift by delivering 44 tons.

The first statement of support from any Western capital came out of London, not out of Washington. On June 26, Bevin announced that the British government intended to stay in Berlin and would not be forced out by the blockade. Bevin had favored an airlift from the beginning of Soviet stoppages. To show Stalin that the West would be able to protect its rights and interests, he requested that two squadrons of U.S. B-29 bombers, which had delivered the atomic bombs over Japan, be sent to England.

While Clay, Reuter and Bevin acted, Washington's doubts persisted. During a meeting held at the Pentagon on Sunday, June 27, to prepare for briefing Truman, senior defense officials considered a wide range of options including early withdrawal. None believed the airlift could supply the city's needs. Nonetheless, the meeting came to an important decision that went beyond Berlin itself. Responding to Bevin's invitation and fearing that the U.S. position was under threat throughout all of Europe, defense officials decided to send two squadrons of B-29 bombers to Germany and to station two squadrons in England. They did not send the aircraft equipped to carry atomic bombs, but the dispatch of strategic bombers to Europe showed that the U.S. government would be prepared to defend its forces and interests. When the B-29s arrived in Europe three weeks later, on what was termed a routine training mission, Europe for the first time came under the direct protection of the U.S. Strategic Air Command.

Truman would not even consider withdrawing from Berlin. Royall remonstrated that it might have to be considered, but Truman said that the United States was in Berlin "by right of an agreement" and that the Soviets had "no right to get us out by either direct or indirect pressure." He said: "We are going to stay. Period."[16] He thus joined Bevin in giving Clay and Robertson full support.

Bevin rejoiced at Truman's decision and spoke in even stronger terms three days later, telling the House of Commons:

> We recognize that, as a result of these decisions, a grave situation might arise. Should such a situation arise, we shall have to ask the House to face it. His Majesty's Government and our Western allies can see no alternative between that and surrender, and none of us can accept surrender.[17]

The Soviets and Ulbricht increased the pressure. The Soviet representative on the Kommandatura announced on July 1 that the Soviet Union would no longer participate in Kommandatura activities because the four-power government of Berlin no longer existed. Sokolovsky withdrew from the ACC, and Soviet soldiers pulled down the Soviet flag in front of the ACC building.[18]

Ulbricht simultaneously promulgated a new two-year economic plan that would put the Soviet zone on the path toward socialist economic development and would fully incorporate all sectors of Berlin, west as well as east. In announcing the plan at an SED central committee meeting on June 27, 1948, he said that it represented part of the class struggle against those who wanted to sabotage German development.[19]

Despite Truman's decision, the State Department and the Pentagon continued to have their doubts about remaining in Berlin. Several of Secretary Marshall's advisers, including Charles Bohlen and George Kennan, reportedly favored abandoning the city.[20] Kennan proposed negotiating with Moscow about the withdrawal of all foreign forces and the neutralization of Germany. Marshall himself tried to have Clay removed from Berlin, but former secretary of state James Byrnes protected Clay without telling him of Marshall's wish. Marshall's own statements on Berlin, especially at the beginning of the blockade, did not match either Truman's or Bevin's in their firmness and conviction.[21] France also hesitated, worrying about whether the West could remain in Berlin under pressure.[22]

Marshall decided in August 1948 to explore a possible diplomatic solution to the Berlin crisis. Although Bevin questioned the effort, he agreed at Marshall's personal request. The three Western Allies instructed their Moscow ambassadors to call on Stalin to ferret out his thinking. They found him the soul of reason, eager to end the crisis and to seek solutions for Germany as a whole. He insisted that Berlin could not be separated from the German problem and from the Ruhr and that all should be discussed. He returned to his wish for an all-German government and a peace treaty.[23] He apparently wanted to use the blockade to reopen the CFM on better terms.

Stalin told the Western ambassadors that the "technical difficulties" preventing access to Berlin would end if the assurance were given that the London decisions would be held in abeyance until the representatives of the four powers had met and had agreed on the most important aspects of the German problem. Such a meeting should discuss all the questions left open from the London Council of Foreign Ministers. Stalin insisted that the Soviets had introduced a new currency only because the West had forced them to do so. He added that he believed the Western powers wanted to compel the Soviets to establish a new government in their zone but "the Soviet government does not wish to do that."

Speaking as calmly as he had spoken to Marshall in Moscow little more than a year earlier, Stalin added that the Berlin currency problem could be solved. He agreed to accept four-power control of the Soviet currency circulating in Berlin.[24]

Acting on Stalin's words, the Western military governors tried during the following month to negotiate an agreement under which the Soviet zone currency would be used in Berlin under the control of a special commission of the four occupation powers. While they met daily with Sokolovsky during the first week of September, he never repeated Stalin's offer. He dismissed four-power control over any East Berlin or East German currency, rejecting a four-power finance commission that Stalin had appeared to accept. Sokolovsky also asked for restrictions on Allied use of the Berlin air corridors, which the Western military governors rejected.

Although Stalin had sounded moderate, he and Ulbricht must have felt confident that they could impose their will in Berlin. The airlift had begun to carry an average of over 2,000 tons a day by the end of August and had set a record of 3,100 tons on August 31, but the Soviets and Ulbricht could still expect the blockade to fail once the Berlin winter set in with its paralyzing ice, snow and fog.

Stalin felt emboldened when the Western ambassadors called on him. He thought it showed the West's fear that it would lose its position in Berlin. He planned to use the eastern currency circulating in Berlin to integrate the Berliners into the Soviet zone, believing that he had finally found the lever that would decide the German question in his favor.[25] At best, he would achieve a united Germany on his own terms, as expressed in the Warsaw declaration. At worst, he would get all of Berlin.

In the meantime, Ulbricht and Sokolovsky decided to end the anomaly of having a Berlin city government sitting in the Soviet sector in the old Berlin city hall with an SPD majority that sometimes carried out policies going against SED wishes. Ulbricht organized mobs that began besieging the city hall while Sokolovsky's soldiers stood by. During the first days of September, the mobs blocked the city assembly from the building and physically threatened Louise Schröder, a frail woman who served as acting governing mayor because Sokolovsky had never permitted Reuter to use his office in the Soviet sector.

After the mob action had continued for several days, preventing the city government from functioning and even from meeting, the Berlin assembly on September 6 decided to move to the Schöneberg district city hall in the British sector. That city hall became the seat of the governing mayor and of the West Berlin government.

On November 30, Ulbricht and the SED completed the split of the Berlin city administration by formally establishing a new city government in East Berlin. The Berlin assembly thereupon sponsored elections in the Western sectors on December 5. The SPD and Ernst Reuter won a majority. Berlin was to have separate administrations for the Soviet sector and for the Western sectors until 1990.

Reuter took charge of the West Berlin city administration, although it still remained under occupation. He despised the communists and the SED. He had long been a member of the KPD, having joined as a youth and having by 1921 become its secretary general. But he had resigned because he opposed Soviet domination of the party, and had then become a Social Democrat. While he was not a charismatic orator, his speeches carried great power through his obvious conviction and his long association with democratic causes in Germany and Berlin. His determination particularly influenced British policy because Bevin's Labour Party felt a socialist comradeship for the SPD.

Reuter believed, more than the occupiers, that Berlin did not need to be ashamed of its past. Most Berliners had never liked or supported Hitler although the city had become the capital of the Nazi Reich. Berlin remained a city of the Left, of socialist workers and of intellectuals, not of the extreme Right. Many Nazis, like many SED officials, had felt that Berliners remained too independent.[26] Reuter did not want West Berliners to have to endure yet another dictator.

Like Clay, Reuter understood logistics. He had served as transport and public utilities manager of Berlin during the 1920s, when the extensive public transportation system of the city had been built. He knew the system perfectly. He had smuggled out many of the plans and blueprints for the system well before the blockade because he expected the Soviets and Ulbricht to try to gain control over the city.

On September 9, as the Allies still negotiated with Moscow, Reuter called for a mass demonstration in front of the Reichstag and near the Brandenburg Gate to make it easy for East Berliners to attend. More than 300,000 persons came. Speaking boldly for a mayor of an occupied city, Reuter warned the West that it had to hold:

> We cannot be bartered, we cannot be negotiated, we cannot be sold. . . . Whoever would surrender this city, whoever would surrender the people of Berlin . . . would surrender himself.[27]

The airlift continued and expanded. Truman, again acting against the advice of the Pentagon and the State Department, ordered 66 C-54 transport planes of ten-ton capacity to join the airlift. Those aircraft gave the airlift the equipment it needed, for the lack of airspace and landing facilities placed a physical limit on the number of planes that could be landed in Berlin during any single day.

At the crucial White House meeting at which Clay asked for the C-54s, all senior State Department officials and military officers strongly opposed the request. Truman listened carefully and said nothing. When, after the meeting, a despondent Clay turned to say good-bye to him, the president said: "General, you will have your planes." He then instructed the reluctant U.S. Air Force to make the planes available. Clay returned to Berlin elated, certain for the first time that the airlift could succeed despite the weather. With the U.S. election coming up, Clay said that he would have voted for Truman to be president not just of the United States but of the world.[28]

New planes joined almost every week, either from far-flung U.S. Air Force bases or from the British Royal Air Force. To permit more landings, Berlin volunteer laborers built a new airport at Tegel in the French sector and three new runways at the Tempelhof and Gatow airports in the American and British sectors. The U.S. Air Force built a duplicate air corridor system in Montana to train pilots for the airlift. The Allies equipped the airlift with the latest radar and guidance systems to permit flights on even the foggiest days.

Clay and Reuter knew that the tide had turned. They had enough aircraft available and on the way to deliver at least the minimum that the residents of the Western sectors would need through the winter, including coal, food, and other essentials. Skeptics abounded, especially in Washington and to a lesser degree in Paris, but those who were on the ground in West Berlin had become firmly convinced that they would succeed.[29]

Sokolovsky tried to harass the airlift. In mid-September he warned the four-power Berlin Air Safety Center (BASC) that Soviet aircraft would conduct maneuvers over the Soviet zone, and that those maneuvers would take them through the air corridors in which the Airlift planes crossed the zone. Clay replied that the Soviet Union would be held responsible for the consequences of any accident. Soviet fighters occasionally came quite close to the slower cargo planes but they avoided accidents.[30]

By December, the airlift averaged over 4,500 tons of cargo a day, well above the minimum. By the end of February, after the worst flying months, it rose to an average 5,500 tons. Newer and heavier planes joined the airlift. By spring of 1949 the daily average went over 8,000 tons. Although life in the Western sectors remained cold and uncomfortable, with limited heating, electricity, and other amenities, the Berliners did not complain. The D-mark proved attractive enough to bring in a flow of black market goods from areas around West Berlin. East Berlin and East German families helped by taking packages to their relatives across the sector borders.

The airlift also carried out goods produced in West Berlin in order to integrate the city's economy into the Western zones despite the blockade. It also carried out refugees, who were arriving in West Berlin at the rate of almost 100 a day despite the blockade. Directed by an Anglo-American operations center commanded by American Major General William Tunner, the airlift functioned with model efficiency.

The airlift achieved its single largest lift on what became known as the "Easter Parade" because it occurred over a 24-hour period from noon Saturday, April 16, to noon on Easter Sunday, April 17, under perfect flying conditions. The airlift that day carried 12,941 tons in 1,398 flights, almost one a minute. It turned the tide definitively. Although the Allies did not repeat the demonstration, they had made their point. They could supply Berlin as long as necessary. Clay had shown the strategic use of peacetime airlift.

But the airlift carried more than food and coal. It carried a political message that the Western Allies would not abandon the city of Berlin. It also began to generate a powerful political appeal. Programs like "Operation Little Vittles," begun when U.S. pilot Gail Halvorsen dropped candy and chewing gum for Berlin children, or "Operation Santa Claus," which dropped Christmas presents, became wildly popular with young Berliners. A visit to the airports, and especially Tempelhof in the American sector, became a childhood treat. The airlift had created a lasting emotional bond between the West Berliners and their occupiers.

In the meantime, a Western counter-blockade had become ever more effective against the Soviet zone. Imposed by Clay and the other Western military governors as soon as Sokolovsky had imposed the Berlin blockade, and tightened considerably in January and February 1949, it stopped rail and water shipments from the Western zones or from West Berlin into the Soviet zone. Thus, it prevented the Soviet zone from obtaining the Ruhr steel, machinery and coking coal on which it had traditionally relied.

By the spring of 1949, the Soviet zone economy may have felt the effects of the counter-blockade at least as strongly as the West Berlin economy felt the effects of the blockade. East German factories had to lay off workers and shut down entire production lines because of missing supplies or components. The counter-blockade also damaged the Soviet economy itself, as many of the machine tools imported for the Soviet zone were actually destined for the Soviet Union.

STALIN ENDS THE BLOCKADE

On January 31, 1949, with the worst of the winter over, Reuter told Drew Middleton, a correspondent for *The New York Times:* "It's over. The Russians know they can't get Berlin by blockade. Soon they will start to find a way out."[31]

Stalin two weeks later, in an interview with another American journalist, listed his conditions for lifting the blockade. They did not include his earlier demand for the Western Allies to reverse the currency reform.

The State Department instructed its United Nations representative, Philip Jessup, to ask the Soviet representative, Jacob Malik, whether Stalin's omission had been deliberate. Jessup posed the question during an apparently casual conversation in the delegates' lounge. Malik, obviously caught by surprise, replied that he would get an answer.

On March 15, Malik invited Jessup to his office and told him that Stalin's omission was "not accidental." He offered to discuss lifting the blockade, provided that the counter-blockade would be lifted simultaneously and that the West would attend another session of the Council of Foreign Ministers to discuss the entire German problem including currency questions.

After six weeks of further talks, the four powers announced on May 5 that the blockade and counter-blockade would end on May 12 and that the CFM would convene eleven days later to discuss "questions relating to Germany." Although that CFM meeting, which lasted about a month, proved futile, it provided Stalin with a way to end the blockade.

Sokolovsky must have told Ulbricht by January that the blockade would be lifted, for Ulbricht changed his comments about Berlin significantly around that time. After having maintained for months that the whole city belonged to the Soviet zone, he said in a speech at the end of January that Berlin was not a city of the Soviet zone but the capital of Germany.[32]

Even after the blockade had ended on May 12, when the first Western train entered Berlin-Charlottenburg station, the Allies continued the airlift until September 30 to build up stockpiles. On that date, the 276,926th flight officially ended the airlift with a load of coal.[33]

The success of the airlift assured the Western position in Berlin. It also validated the Western financial position in the city. On March 20, 1949, the D-mark became the sole legal tender in the Western sectors, linking the city to the West German economy. The eastern currency, which had steadily declined in value and which West Berlin merchants had long refused to accept, could still circulate but could not be used for most transactions.

In total, the airlift had carried more than 2.3 million tons, less than a third of which was food. Almost two-thirds of all flights carried at least some coal. Altogether, 689 aircraft, 441 American and 248 British, had flown more than 124 million miles. Seventy-eight persons, almost half of them American, died as the result of crashes or by other accidental means. By its end, as the Berlin economy began to revive, the airlift took out 100 tons of manufactured goods for every 260 tons of material flown in. Thus the airlift kept West Berlin working as well as alive.[34]

The Berliners had made their own contribution to Allied policy debates. Their obvious preference for the West and their capacity to endure the hardships of the blockade made it impossible for any Western leader to consider abandoning the city. Even those Americans and others who had proposed withdrawal during the summer of 1948 changed their views by 1949. Howley said of the Berliners: "It was their Valley Forge. They bought their right as a people willing to suffer and die for democracy."[35]

To an extraordinary degree, four men decided the future of Berlin, Germany and the West. All four—Ernst Reuter, Ernest Bevin, Harry Truman and Lucius Clay—had to act against the doubts of others.

Reuter, who could not bear the thought of having the Berliners fall into Ulbricht's hands, committed Berlin to the West. Bevin supported Berlin at a time when most Britons still hated the Germans. Truman made the key decisions to send the aircraft against the advice of his senior staff. And Clay grasped the politics as well as the logistics of the Berlin airlift. When the four had finished, they had formed a strong bond between Berlin and the West.

On the other side, Stalin, Ulbricht and Sokolovsky misjudged the logistics as well as the politics of the blockade. Stalin tried to recover by calling for a CFM meeting, but the blockade and airlift had ended chances for a negotiated solution on terms acceptable to him. The blockade had also jeopardized Soviet prospects for a good relationship with a united Germany. Stalin had raised the struggle into the open and had failed. He would now have to face the prospect of a divided Germany.

FIVE

POLITICAL DIVISION

THE BERLIN BLOCKADE FURTHER CONVINCED PARTICIPANTS IN THE London meetings that they had to create a state in Western Germany. Many German political figures agreed. They saw no prospect for German unity in the near future. They would lose nothing by linking the Western zones, and they might gain security and prosperity.[1]

The Allies could thus proceed toward creating a West German government. But they still disagreed about the form it should take and about the authority they should give it.

Recognizing that they could not agree, the Western powers decided to see what the Germans themselves preferred. They invited the minister-presidents of their occupation zones to convene a constitutional assembly no later than September 1, 1948, in order to prepare a constitution for a new German government. The Allies reserved a veto right, but they would give the Germans a chance to offer ideas and to make concrete proposals. The Allies also agreed that they would draft an occupation statute to list the powers they would still reserve if a German constitution emerged.

ADENAUER FORMS THE FEDERAL REPUBLIC OF GERMANY

On July 1, 1948, three weeks after the end of the London conference and one week after the beginning of the blockade, the three Western military governors met in Frankfurt with the minister-presidents of the western German *Länder* (states) and presented them with three documents. Those papers, which came to be known as the "Frankfurt Documents," invited the minister-presidents to proceed toward the establishment of a West German state with a constitution to be drafted by a special convention beginning no later than September 1, 1948, and to be approved by a referendum. The documents also rearranged the borders of several German *Länder* and advised the Germans in general terms of the rights, especially in finance, defense and foreign affairs, that the occupiers would keep.[2]

The minister-presidents reacted soberly to the Allied proposal. They knew full well that it meant a divided Germany. Konrad Adenauer, a leading political figure in the British zone, complained that the Allies were trying to force the Germans to accept long-term Allied sovereignty over Germany by dividing the country. He speculated out loud, much to the Allies' anger, that the Germans should perhaps save their honor by rejecting the Allied invitation. In fact, the SPD did reject it at first.

But the pragmatists among the Germans prevailed. They argued that beggars could not be choosers. A country that had launched and lost a world war had to seize even an imperfect opportunity. After long and often painful deliberations, the minister-presidents agreed to accept the Allied invitation to create a western German state. But they also agreed among themselves that they would not write a permanent constitution but only a temporary document under which that state could function until sovereignty and unification came.

The Germans debated long and hard about the term they should use to describe the document. Having dismissed the word "constitution" because it implied permanence and suggested that the document governed an entire nation, they decided that they also disliked the word "administration" because it lacked legitimacy and would leave moral authority in occupation hands. Finally, they seized upon the concept of a *Grundgesetz* (Basic Law) as a formula that had moral authority but did not carry the meaning of "constitution." One of the Germans described the term as "heaven-sent."

In a covering note to the Allied powers, the SPD leader Carlo Schmid justified the importance of the concept of a "Basic Law" and tried to explain how reluctantly the West German minister-presidents faced the responsibility of speaking for the entire nation. He also tried to make the Allies understand that the minister-presidents could not accept political responsibility for dividing Germany if the Allies retained so much authority that the Germans had no freedom to act.

Clay reacted angrily to Schmid's letter, complaining that the Germans seemed to have forgotten who their friends were. He insisted that the Allies could accept no changes in the terms and in the language that they had offered to the Germans. He thought the Germans were trying to make the Allies take the full blame for forcing Germany either to remain under occupation or to accept division. The French commander, General Joseph-Pierre Koenig, felt that the German reaction had vindicated French doubts about offering the Germans any sovereignty at all.

But the British commander, Robertson, persuaded Clay and Koenig to let the process evolve. They agreed to urge the minister-presidents to review their position and to see if they could not find a compromise with Allied needs. Clay cited the Berlin airlift to show that he and the other occupation commanders wanted to help, not hurt, Germany's prospects. He warned the minister-presidents that they might themselves jeopardize Germany's and Berlin's best chance to win international support by rejecting an offer that had been tediously difficult to arrange.

Ernst Reuter sided with Clay, pleading with the minister-presidents to accept the Allied offer. He reminded them of Berlin's exposed and dangerous position. Pointing to Ulbricht's seizure of power in the Soviet zone and to the blockade, he said: "The division of Germany is not being decided here, for it has already taken place."[3] His words carried great weight, for he could detail what Sokolovsky and Ulbricht had done.

After long discussion, the minister-presidents agreed to accept many of the Allied concepts. But they remained firmly committed to the term "Basic Law" instead of "constitution." They also insisted that the document should be approved by the separate West German *Länder* governments instead of by referendum. They warned that a referendum campaign could give the extremists of the Right and Left a chance to direct German national feelings against the Western Allies and against those Germans trying to cooperate with them. They feared SED propaganda as well as the German conservative groups that had been expelled from Prussia and Silesia. After further debate of their own, the Allies accepted German views.

On September 1, the Germans set to work. A parliamentary council of 65 members met in Bonn to begin the drafting process. The minister-presidents had decided to hold the meeting in Bonn instead of in the Bizonia capital of Frankfurt because they wanted to avoid any sign that they accepted Germany's division. Frankfurt, because of its size and its tradition as one of the centers of the old Germanic Confederation, might be regarded as a potentially permanent capital for a new German state.

The parliamentary council reflected the strength of the German parties. The two most important groups, each having 27 votes, represented the Social Democratic Party and the joint parliamentary group of the *Christlich-Demokratische Union* (Christian Democratic Union, hereafter CDU) and its Bavarian sister party, the

Christlich-Soziale Union (Christian Social Union, hereafter CSU). Berlin had no formal members but sent five non-voting observers. Many representatives had worked in the anti-Nazi resistance.

The SPD wanted Carlo Schmid, a widely respected SPD leader and humanist political philosopher, to chair the principal drafting committee because the party wanted to make sure that the new Basic Law would respect the social rights as well as the political freedoms of the German electorate. Schmid, a brilliant and articulate man of great moral authority, was mainly responsible for the text that emerged.

With Schmid chosen as principal drafter, the CDU/CSU group received the consolation prize of the chairmanship of the convention. Konrad Adenauer assumed that post. As he may have recognized from the beginning, the chairmanship proved to be the more rewarding political if not legislative post. Adenauer became the spokesman for the proceedings, leaving his mark on the image of the convention as much as Schmid left his mark on the text.

Adenauer had already been an important figure in the Weimar Republic, having been lord mayor of Cologne from 1917 to 1933. He had modernized the city and its administration and had become one of the leaders of the Weimar Republic's Catholic *Zentrum* party. Hitler had removed him from office because Adenauer had ordered Nazi symbols removed from municipal buildings and spaces. The Nazis had twice imprisoned him during the Third Reich, a fact that raised Adenauer's stature even higher in postwar Germany. As a leading spokesman for German centrist conservatism, Adenauer naturally assumed a position of authority. He was to make the CDU/CSU into a national force.[4]

The victorious Allies did not find Adenauer accommodating. The British occupation authorities did not like him, in part because of his long opposition to German social democracy. They had removed him when he had resumed his post as lord mayor of Cologne after the war because he had refused to cut down city trees for firewood. But the American authorities supported him, although Clay never found him a particularly easy partner either.

If the Allies faced the ghosts of Versailles in dealing with postwar Germany, the Germans faced the ghosts of Weimar. They had learned from the bitter experience of the Weimar Republic and its paralysis and collapse before Hitler that perfect proportional representation combined with an excessively powerful chief of state could produce such a disaster as the destruction of German democracy and the promotion of a madman to power. They wanted at all costs to avoid repeating that catastrophe.

The members of the parliamentary council wrote three important features into the Basic Law:

First, they agreed that parties that could not win 5 percent of the total electorate or three direct mandates would not enter the new parliament, the Bundestag. This destroyed the incentive for ideologues or petty politicians to establish small parties that could paralyze a parliament or bring down a government merely to display their power or to promote their views.

Second, they required a "constructive vote of no confidence" to bring down a government. Under this provision, the parliament could not vote one government out of office without simultaneously electing another in its place. This provision forced the parties to accept responsibility for their actions and meant that Germany would not be without an effective government, as it often had been before Hitler. It made for a stable chancellorship without creating a dictatorship.

Third, they limited the powers of the chief of state, to the point where they even thought of dispensing with the office. They made certain that the chief of state could not name a government without parliamentary approval. They did not want another cabal of sclerotic conspirators and a senile field-marshal imposing a government that did not have a popular mandate, as Franz von Papen and a group of conservatives were able to do with Field Marshal Paul von Hindenburg to make Hitler chancellor in 1933.

Beyond correcting the mistakes of Weimar, however, the Germans wanted to make certain that no one would see their new state as permanent. They especially did not want to turn their backs on the Soviet zone or the Saar. Therefore, they wrote article 23, a provision that permitted easy admission for German *Länder* that were not founding members.

The convention created a government structure with strong federal elements. The *Länder* had significant powers, as did the cities and even the smaller localities. While London had favored greater central power and Paris had favored less, the final German text came closest to Washington's wishes—perhaps because Clay had asked a German political scientist, Carl Friedrich, who had emigrated to the United States and who had an understanding of federal systems, to serve as a consultant to the parliamentary council.[5]

But the Germans also had their own model, the constitution for a democratic and united Germany written by the German liberals and humanists and adopted at the Frankfurt assembly on March 28, 1849. They drew the basic structure of their institutions as well as their bill of rights from that model, often duplicating the exact language. They wanted to show that the Basic Law followed the German liberal tradition and had its roots in German history, not in Allied instructions. The federalist form of the Basic Law also fell into line with the historic German tradition of small self-governing states, rejecting the Bismarck/Weimar/Hitler centrist models.[6]

Even after the parliamentary council had approved the final draft on February 10, 1949, the Allies still voiced reservations, especially about the tax and budget powers the draft assumed for Germany and for the *Länder*. Once again, the two sides appeared irrevocably split.

At this point, a new personality entered the scene to assume a central role. The new French foreign minister, Robert Schuman, proved to be the kind of partner that Bevin had been seeking and that western Germany needed. Schuman had grown up in Alsace-Lorraine, an area of mixed French and German influence. He had served in the German army during World War I and spoke fluent German. He and Adenauer often spoke German together in order to understand each other clearly, although other French officials would have to await interpretation to know what their chief had said.

Schuman wanted a new Europe. He believed that France and Germany had both a historic obligation and a historic opportunity to create that Europe. He also believed that the future of both nations lay not in a Europe encrusted with old fears and hatreds but in new continental structures that they should build together.

When Schuman went to London in January 1949, he and Bevin ended many long-standing differences about Germany. They agreed that German civilians should begin governing West Germany, provided they respected Allied rights and interests. They agreed on a Ruhr regime that respected special French interests but did not disadvantage others. They disagreed on the precise structure of a future Europe, with Bevin maintaining traditional British distance from the continent. But they did agree that their nations and the Germans had to find a larger European framework to transcend hoary national rivalries.

Bevin and Schuman compromised on German federal structures. They agreed with the new U.S. secretary of state, Dean Acheson, to lift some restrictions on German industrial production and to stop the dismantling of West German industry that was provoking ever more violent worker protests. Finally, largely due to Schuman's wish to establish a new French relationship with Germany, they agreed to simplify the Allied occupation statute to reduce residual Allied powers. General Clay described his talks with Schuman in Paris to help draft the new occupation statute as the most satisfactory that he had ever had with a French official.[7]

With France now favoring rapid solutions to German problems, the Allies and the Germans could overcome their disagreements. Most important, the Allies concluded that they had to grant the new western German state enough authority to give it legitimacy and popular appeal. This meant that the Germans had to govern under their own documents and not under Allied prescriptions. Lengthy and indecipherable legal briefs prescribing Allied residual powers had to be scrapped in favor of clear formulas giving the new state genuine authority within justifiable limits. The Germans appreciated the simpler occupation statute and the replacement of the Allied occupation commanders through a new system of high commissioners.

During several days in April 1949, the three foreign ministers performed what Acheson termed "prodigies of agreement." They finished their work on the German Basic Law and on the Ruhr authority. They agreed to respect some of the more delicate compromises that the German parties had reached on the Basic Law so as not to make the German constitution into an Allied draft. And they also agreed that Philip Jessup should tell Jacob Malik that the preparations for a West German government would continue whether or not the Soviets ended the Berlin blockade. Bevin insisted that Stalin should not be permitted to delay Allied plans for Germany and Europe.[8]

Although Clay and the other military governors had agreed to a shorter and more limited occupation statute, the Western Allies still kept many powers. They retained ultimate control over foreign policy, reparations, industrial production and every kind of military activity. They could veto any West German legislation that conflicted with occupation policy. They also could reassume their full authority as occupying powers in case of an emergency, and they retained full power over Berlin. The latter formulas satisfied Schuman, who needed to be able to assure the French National Assembly that France could prevent Germany from again becoming a threat.

On May 8, 1949, the parliamentary council approved the Basic Law by an overwhelming majority of 53 to 12. Within the next 12 days, the necessary ten *Länder* parliaments ratified the text (only Bavaria refusing because it wanted more autonomy). So did the three Western military governors. On May 23, the Basic Law entered into force, creating the *Bundesrepublik Deutschland* (Federal Republic of Germany, hereafter FRG).

On August 14, the first West German elections took place. On September 15, the Bundestag, by a single vote, chose Adenauer as chancellor, a position he was to hold for 14 years. He won with the votes of the CDU/CSU, the liberal *Freie Demokratische Partei* (Free Democratic Party, hereafter FDP) and the conservative *Deutsche Partei*. On September 21, the new occupation statute entered into force and the Federal Republic of Germany began its existence as an independent state with limited sovereignty. Four years after the collapse of the Third Reich, the western Germans had a new political lease on life. They thus began to help decide their own fate. But they paid a high price: national unity.

Throughout much of the spring of 1949, even as the Allies and the Germans proceeded with plans for the Federal Republic, Acheson had not finally made up his mind about the division of Germany. He had studied and liked what had been described as "Plan A," a proposal by George Kennan to withdraw Western and Soviet forces from Germany and to aim for German unification. Clay, who had favored German unification until 1948, had changed his mind after the Berlin blockade and opposed Plan A. But Acheson still wanted to study it. He began to change his mind only when Bevin and Schuman argued strongly against a united Germany and especially against a withdrawal of U.S. forces.

Acheson finally decided in favor of a divided Germany after he spent some weeks with the new Soviet foreign minister, Andrei Vishinsky, at the Paris CFM meeting that had been scheduled at Stalin's request to end the Berlin blockade. Confronted with Molotov-style tactics, Acheson became the third American secretary of state in a row to conclude that the CFM could not reach agreement on Germany. As a sign of his conversion, the elegant patrician Acheson marched arm in arm with the rumpled Labourite Bevin into Vishinsky's office to be told that Moscow had just vetoed a proposal it had earlier supported for an Austrian peace treaty. Bevin suggested that they sing "Red Flag" together while they marched, "as a sign of solidarity, as we Labour blokes say."[9]

ULBRICHT FORMS THE
GERMAN DEMOCRATIC REPUBLIC

Before and during the Berlin blockade, Walter Ulbricht and Vassily Sokolovsky continued their drive to change the power structure of the Soviet zone. Those changes put Ulbricht's SED more thoroughly and more overtly in charge.

Private comments by senior SED functionaries in the summer of 1947 had already begun to predict the SED takeover of full authority over the Soviet zone's civilian administration. So had the increasing domination of the KPD within the SED itself. Political officers attached to the Soviet occupation issued similar predictions throughout late 1947.[10]

SED plans unfolded slowly, however, perhaps to protect Soviet relations with the Western Allies. Ulbricht told mid-level SED officials only on April 10, 1948, that there would be a visible change in the SED's role. He said that the SED had moved slowly to take over full authority because of its own ideological immaturity and because it first needed to establish an "anti-fascist democratic" order in the Soviet zone. With the completion of land reform and the national-ization of industry, the time had come for the SED officially to become a "state party." No longer would it be just another political movement; rather, it would take over the civilian arm of the Soviet zone administration. All other political groups and parties in that zone would now formally have to follow the SED lead, and the SED would henceforth carry out its full program.[11]

Outside events may have determined Ulbricht's and Sokolovsky's timing. Ulbricht spoke two months after the communist coup in Czechoslovakia and around the time that the Soviets readied for the Berlin blockade. He did not want disparate eastern German voices arguing against his policies at those times, especially if he was to take over West Berlin.

Ulbricht announced that the SED was no longer only the party of Karl Marx and Friedrich Engels, the German communist philosophers, but also the party of Vladimir Lenin and Josef Stalin, the architects of the Soviet communist model. He fully abandoned his earlier bargain with the SPD, renouncing the special "German" road that the SED had ostensibly chosen in 1946 and 1947 when Ulbricht still wanted to attract SPD members. To reinforce this point further, the SED on July 4, 1948, published a "Declaration about the Yugoslav Question" which fully supported Stalin's denunciation of Marshal Broz Tito of Yugoslavia as a renegade. The SED stated that the Soviet model represented "the only possible position for every socialist party."

Following a pattern widely practiced in eastern Europe, those who had argued for a distinctly German contribution to socialism recanted in public. Anton Ackermann, the most prominent SED author on ideological matters, dissociated himself from an earlier article in which he had advocated and predicted a unique German road. He denounced his own article, written at the beginning of 1946, for "giving room to anti-Bolshevism."[12] In its place, he and the entire SED now pledged themselves to the Soviet model for "the political rule of the working class as the precondition to socialism."[13]

To complete its full adoption of the Soviet model, the SED in September 1948 established a party control commission with appropriate branch organizations that would enforce ideological solidarity and purity within the party. The party purged recalcitrant members, mainly from the former SPD, who did not fully accept "the leading role of the Soviet Union and the Communist Party of the Soviet Union." Following earlier patterns, Sokolovsky had some of them arrested. Several prominent former SPD members fled to western Germany.

Under Ulbricht's and Sokolovsky's new system, the *Deutsche Wirtschaftskommission* fully assumed the role of proto-government for the Soviet zone, growing to a staff of more than 5,000 involved in every aspect of government. In 1948 and 1949 it took on the look of a government bureaucracy but remained under SED control. Ulbricht told SED officials who worried about dividing Germany that the DWK would make it easier for the Western occupation zones (and especially the Western sectors of Berlin) to join with the Soviet zone because they could adhere to the DWK structure.

This part of Ulbricht's prediction failed, however. The Sovietization of the SED and the creation of a Soviet zone administration dominated by the communist party further undercut Stalin's wish to attract support in the Western zones. Refugees from the eastern parties urged Western German political figures to avoid all contact and cooperation with the SED or with other Soviet zone parties. Once again, Ulbricht's moves for greater control in the Soviet zone sabotaged whatever efforts Stalin might still want to make to expand Soviet influence in the other zones.

Nonetheless, Ulbricht continued to build structures that would, he hoped, enable the SED to attract other German political organizations into common formations that the SED could dominate. He organized a first, then a second, and later a third *Deutscher Volkskongress* (German People's Congress) that claimed to reflect public opinion all over Germany. Ulbricht called the first congress in December 1947 to bring together over 1,000 delegates from all Soviet zone political parties and also from SED-dominated trade unions, youth organizations and cultural leagues. He called the second one in March 1948 to elect a "People's Council" that claimed to represent western as well as eastern German opinion by including some KPD members from the Western zones.

Once again, however, Ulbricht and Sokolovsky damaged their own cause in the Western zones. They forced the Soviet zone CDU to take part in the people's congress against the wishes of two of its most prominent and respected leaders, Jakob Kaiser and Ernst Lemmer. To show his anger, Ulbricht expelled both men from their CDU offices, whereupon they fled to West Berlin. Kaiser's and Lemmer's widely reported defection nullified any impact that Ulbricht's "congresses" might have had in western Germany. It cast the CDU in a heroic mold and helped Adenauer in the 1949 election. While Ulbricht might have intended that, for he might have preferred to face a CDU government that would be more likely to favor dividing Germany than an SPD government, it did not necessarily serve Stalin's purpose.

With the SED having taken total control of the Soviet zone's civilian administration by 1948, Ulbricht could begin to prepare for a separate state in eastern Germany. Working with Sokolovsky to expand the DWK and its functions, Ulbricht began to build an administration that could function as a national government.[14] He also announced the two-year economic plan that included all of Berlin in the Soviet zone economy.

Because of his confidence that the Berlin blockade would drive the Allies out of West Berlin, by mid-1948 Ulbricht began establishing the basis for a communist state that included all of Berlin. Ulbricht pulled out some of his original plans for a separate government for the Soviet zone. He had first urged those plans on Sokolovsky and the Soviet administration in August 1946, but Stalin had vetoed them and Ulbricht had put them away. By 1948, however, he could return to them with Sokolovsky's support.[15]

Also with an eye to an eastern German state, Sokolovsky and Ulbricht began establishing the foundation for a new German army in the Soviet zone. On July 3, 1948, Sokolovsky issued the order for a new police force, the *Kasernierte Volkspolizei* (People's Police in Barracks), an eastern German paramilitary organization housed in its own barracks and organized—as well as trained—like an army. By 1950, Ulbricht had expanded the *Kasernierte Volkspolizei* to a strength of over 50,000 men, the largest and best-armed military force in central Europe except for the occupying powers.

Stalin realized by the end of 1948, perhaps due to warnings from Semyonov, that Ulbricht was moving farther and faster than Stalin wanted. He also may have realized by then that the airlift might overcome the blockade, that he would not get Berlin and that he should try once more to negotiate German unity. Ulbricht's moves toward a separate communist authority in the Soviet zone could undercut Stalin's negotiators.

Stalin called Ulbricht and Pieck to Moscow and instructed them to reverse their policies, telling them that the situation in Germany was not like that in the people's democracies in eastern Europe. "There is no united state," he said, according to Pieck's notes of the conversation, "we are not on the threshold of power." He told them to work for unity and peace.

Stalin chided Ulbricht openly, deriding the Germans for fighting "like your ancestors, the Teutons, with an open visor." "That," Stalin said, "may be brave, but it is often very stupid." He said that it was foolish to talk about creating a socialist order in Germany, as the SED was doing, when the party had not yet gained power across all of Germany. First, he said, "one should work better."[16]

Stalin told Ulbricht and Pieck to return to the policies of 1945, to work for German unity and to stop talking about different forms of development in East and West. Socialism was not yet on the agenda. When Pieck dared to ask whether the SED could join the Cominform, Stalin dismissed the notion disdainfully. Pieck concluded that the way to socialism in Germany would follow a "zigzag" path.

Stalin removed Sokolovsky, who had encouraged and accepted Ulbricht's drive for a separate communist German state. But once again he did not remove Ulbricht himself. He may have felt that he needed Ulbricht in the impending struggle over Germany whatever the price. But the price was high. Stalin could tell Ulbricht to change his policies, but he could not reverse the effects of those policies on the thinking of other Germans.

Stalin's effort, therefore, came too late. Events continued to spiral out of his and Ulbricht's hands. The Western occupation zones were moving toward integration. Ulbricht and his SED were increasingly despised within the Soviet occupation zone itself. Ulbricht realized this enough to insist that the SED and other Soviet zone parties and organizations would run a unitary list in the elections for the third "people's congress" in May 1949. On such lists, the SED allocated the seats in the congress among various parties before the elections. The voters could only register their approval or disapproval of the entire slate rather than pick and choose among the parties.

But eastern German voters rebelled against Ulbricht. Almost 35 percent of the ballots came in as "nay" votes and another 7 per cent came in invalid. This constituted a strong popular rejection of the new Soviet road to socialism in Ulbricht's zone.

Stalin did not quickly accept the new reality of the Federal Republic of Germany. By September 1949, however, he had no other choice. The new West German Bundestag had been elected and Konrad Adenauer had become chancellor. The legendary KPD, the strongest prewar communist party in Europe, had won only 5.7 percent of the popular vote. It could no longer carry Stalin's hopes for a powerful voice throughout a united Germany. According to Pieck's notes, only then did Stalin approve having a government for the Soviet zone. He reluctantly accepted the constitution for the *Deutsche Demokratische Republik* (German Democratic Republic, hereafter DDR or GDR) that Ulbricht had drafted and that he had himself vetoed in 1946.

But Stalin insisted that the new government be described as the "Provisional Government of the German Democratic Republic." He also refused to specify its geographic area of authority, leaving open the possibility that it might one day include Berlin and might perhaps even rule over all of Germany. Under those constraints, and with Stalin's tepid congratulatory telegram, the new German Democratic Republic began its life on October 7, 1949.

Because Ulbricht wanted to avoid the embarrassment of yet another negative vote, he had the third "people's congress" transform itself into the new GDR lower house of parliament, the Volkskammer.[17] Under its unitary list, the SED and its mass organizations constituted a majority with 210 of the 330 seats in the Volkskammer. The remaining 120 places were assigned to the remnants of the eastern CDU and to smaller parties.

On October 11, the new Volkskammer and the East German *Länder* parliaments elected Pieck as president of the GDR. On the following day, the Volkskammer elected Grotewohl as premier of its first government. Ulbricht became first deputy premier. Partly following the model used in West Germany, the Soviet military administration dissolved itself on October 10, 1949, to be replaced by a Soviet Control Commission.[18]

Among other state organs, the GDR constitution created a *Ministerium für Staatssicherheit* (Ministry for State Security, hereafter MFS) responsible not to the premier's office but to the SED politburo. Thus Ulbricht rather than Grotewohl controlled the main enforcer of state authority, later to become better known as the Stasi.[19]

ACHESON AND THE NORTH ATLANTIC TREATY

Stalin's actions in eastern Europe continued to arouse Western public opinion and to influence Allied policies in western Europe and Germany during 1948 and 1949 as they had during the early postwar years. In the West, the coup against the democratic Czech government had an effect similar to that of Stalin's earlier occupation and domination of Poland. In each case, Stalin acted against a country that had gained widespread sympathy for having resisted Hitler and for having suffered under German occupation. Whatever Stalin's motives may have been, his actions cast the Soviet Union in the same mold as Nazi Germany.

The western Europeans felt real fear. If the communists could mount a coup in Prague, might they not do the same in Paris or Rome, where the communist parties were calling for general strikes to bring down the governments? And, if they did, could or would any other state help?

Ernest Bevin took the lead on Europe as he had on Germany. He proposed a new political and military alliance that would bind Europe and North America, suggesting that the new alliance be based on the 1947 Anglo-French Dunkirk Treaty. Georges Bidault agreed, saying that he did not want to have to lead a resistance movement again. They concluded that the new alliance should have a military component but wanted it mainly to help calm European public and political opinion by showing that communism could not march unchecked across the continent. Because the United States would be needed to help defend against the Soviet Union, Washington was invited to join.[20]

Bevin argued that the survival of the West would depend upon the establishment of some form of union, formal or informal, in western Europe, backed by the United States, Great Britain and the British dominions.[21] He had told Marshall right after the Czech coup that they should create a military alliance between the United States and western Europe. When Marshall demurred, Bevin in March 1948 invited the foreign ministers of France and the Benelux to join in a west European military pact, the Western Union (WEU). Like the Dunkirk Treaty, the WEU protected against Germany as well as against the Soviet Union in order to be acceptable in France and the Benelux states. But Bevin still wanted a transatlantic treaty.

American attitudes were shifting as well because of the Czech coup. On June 11, the U.S. Senate passed the Vandenberg Resolution urging President Truman to pursue "the progressive development of regional and other collective arrangements for individual and collective self-defense."

The process for creating a treaty across the northern Atlantic moved in ever-widening circles. After Bevin had promoted the initial discussions between Britain, France and the Benelux states, Canada and the United States had joined the talks during the summer of 1948. They held what they called "exploratory conversations on security" in Washington from July 6 to September 9, 1948, during the most uncertain period of the Berlin blockade. They concluded that they needed a military alliance to restore western European confidence.[22]

When these seven had agreed, they invited Denmark, Iceland, Italy, Norway and Portugal to join the discussions. All then signed the North Atlantic Treaty on April 4, 1949, creating the North Atlantic Treaty Organization (NATO).[23]

France once again insisted that any defense treaty protect against Germany as well as against the Soviet Union. Even the new foreign minister, Robert Schuman, wanted this, although he hoped to reconcile France and Germany. At his request, Washington agreed to plan for the defense of Europe along the Rhine, permitting the French government to join the treaty by stating in the National Assembly that the North Atlantic Treaty would protect all of French soil. Knowing that France could not separate the Rhineland from Germany, Schuman wanted transatlantic as well as European states to help protect it.

The North Atlantic Treaty called on the signatories to create a common defense system, an unprecedented step in European history. Field Marshal Bernard Montgomery of the United Kingdom, the victor at El Alamein and Britain's most distinguished soldier, chaired the military committee of NATO. But the alliance did not immediately appoint a supreme commander. Although many Western leaders felt afraid of Soviet military superiority in Europe, none saw NATO as primarily a military alliance. Instead, they saw it as a political structure that would give the West a greater sense of confidence. Each state still preferred to keep its own military forces under its own command.

The North Atlantic Treaty did not explicitly protect the new Federal Republic of Germany, which was not even invited to sign the treaty. Military plans provided for defense along the Rhine, as the French insisted, not along the Elbe or in Berlin.

Nonetheless, article six extended the protection of the treaty to the occupation forces of the signatories, thus covering the American, British and French forces in Germany and Berlin. This provision in effect protected West German territory, for any attack against West Germany would necessarily have attacked the occupation forces. The Soviets could not move into Berlin or any of the Western zones without coming into conflict with those occupation forces. Few expected a Soviet invasion, but the U.S. military began to make preliminary plans to protect American forces.[24]

Most important, as the Washington discussions recognized, the presence of U.S. occupation forces in Germany would involve the United States immediately in any hostilities that might break out in Europe. Those forces became the guarantors of the American commitment to western Europe, although they were organized and equipped only as occupation forces.

While the Federal Republic of Germany had not joined NATO, German territory held the key to the security of western Europe. With France and Italy potentially paralyzed by their powerful communist parties, with the Benelux states being too small for an effective defense and with Britain separated from the continent by the English Channel, West Germany began to emerge as the area where the initial defense of western Europe would have to be mounted.

But the formation of NATO did not necessarily mean the arming of Germany. In April 1949, Acheson told the Senate Foreign Relations Committee that "the disarmament and de-militarization of Germany must be complete and absolute."[25] The West German government declared its earnest determination "to prevent the recreation of armed forces of any kind."[26] It would not try to counter the *Kasernierte Volkspolizei.*

SIX

WAR IN ASIA, WARNING IN GERMANY

HARRY TRUMAN PROUDLY ANNOUNCED THE "FAIR DEAL" SOCIAL program at his inaugural ceremony on January 20, 1949. He wanted to concentrate American resources on such programs, not on the military, and to expand the American role abroad mainly through economic programs such as the Marshall Plan or "Point Four" development aid. He appointed a new secretary of defense, Louis Johnson, who aimed for a low defense budget. Other Western leaders shared Truman's wish, continuing to see any threat from Stalin in political more than military terms.

This picture began to change on August 29, 1949, when the Soviet Union conducted a successful test of an atomic device. That test dramatically altered the global strategic picture and especially the balance in Europe and in Germany. Until then, the U.S. nuclear monopoly balanced Soviet ground force superiority in Europe, making the new Atlantic treaty viable. Once Moscow could strike American forces and territory with an atomic bomb, Washington's ability to threaten atomic retaliation lost some credibility.

A few weeks later, on October 1, the Chinese communist forces under Mao Zedong won the Chinese civil war and established the People's Republic of China (PRC). Many Americans saw Mao's victory as a sign that communism would advance wherever it could. And they noted Mao's saying that "power grows out of the barrel of a gun."

Truman tried to reestablish the credibility of U.S. military force by announcing in January 1950 that the United States would produce a hydrogen bomb. He also ordered the State Department policy planning council to review national security needs.

Dean Acheson had already begun questioning George Kennan's argument that communism remained a political more than a military threat. In December 1949 Acheson appointed Paul Nitze to replace Kennan as head of the policy planning council. Under Nitze, a young but already respected strategist, the planning council responded to Truman's order with a new policy document numbered NSC 68.[1]

Nitze did not mince words. NSC 68 warned that the United States and its allies risked losing their security to an orchestrated threat from the communist world. To counter this threat, Nitze proposed a "rapid build-up of political, economic, and military strength in the free world." He particularly warned that the Soviet Union and its satellites could overrun Germany and western Europe quickly.

Nitze urged that such former enemies as West Germany and Japan help the Allied buildup by rearming. He dismissed any suggestion that Germany could be an island of neutrality in a divided world.

Nitze's arguments convinced Acheson, but Truman did not want to begin a major military buildup. He felt as uncomfortable about NSC 68 as he had earlier felt about Clark Clifford's paper. Truman ordered that NSC 68 be held in the strictest confidence and that all but a few copies be destroyed. The president also opposed rearming Germany.[2]

KIM IL SUNG LAUNCHES THE BUNDESWEHR

Events in Asia validated Nitze's arguments. Kim Il Sung, the communist dictator of North Korea, persuaded Stalin in April 1950 to let him unite the Korean peninsula by force. Stalin had long resisted Kim's wishes, but he changed his mind because of what he termed the "changed international situation" (perhaps the Soviet atomic bomb, Mao's victory or a speech by Acheson suggesting that the United States, having withdrawn its occupation forces from Korea, would establish its defense line between Korea and Japan).[3]

The North Korean invasion of South Korea on June 25, 1950, forced Truman to conclude that Nitze and Acheson might be right to fear a communist invasion of western Europe. Even if they were wrong, Truman had to be prepared. He was already being accused of having "lost" China and did not want to be accused of having lost Europe.

Walter Ulbricht wanted to use the Korean attack to convince all Germans of the imminent victory of communism. To make sure of that, he made an explicit link between Korea and Germany. At an SED conference in August 1950, he called for liquidation of the new West German government and cited the

North Korean attack as an example of how this might be done. He called on West Germans to get ready to support the Soviet Union.[4] Even before, on June 27, Soviet media cited Korea as a model for what might happen in Germany.[5]

West Germans and West Berliners feared an East German or Soviet attack. Those living in the border areas began to move or to prepare for flight. American occupation forces began more frequent alert exercises to reassure the German public as much as possible, although U.S. forces would have been vastly outnumbered in any conflict. West Germany lived in a state of dread that Stalin would decide to launch a third world war or at least to invade West Germany and perhaps hold portions of its territory hostage to compel talks on his terms.

On September 30, 1950, Truman ordered that NSC 68 be taken "as a statement of policy to be followed over the next four or five years and . . . that the implementing programs . . . be put into effect as rapidly as possible."[6] Truman also concluded that western Europe could not be defended without West German troops.[7] From the moment that Kim Il Sung's forces crossed the 38th parallel, Washington decided that it had to prepare for war in Europe and to use West Germany to help defend the continent as well as to help support the global buildup that NSC 68 had advocated. West Germany had to be converted from a defense liability into a defense asset.

But Acheson also knew that France would never accept having German troops in NATO without a unified command to control them. In September 1950, Acheson met with Schuman and Bevin in New York to argue for unified NATO forces under a supreme commander, probably General Dwight Eisenhower who had led Western Allied forces against Hitler. They agreed, not without some reluctance, that this should include a German force. But they did not go into detail about such a force.[8]

Stalin may not have foreseen the American and West European reaction when he agreed to let North Korea invade the South. The most recently released Soviet documents, like earlier evidence, suggest that he may have seen the effects of the invasion only in Asian terms.[9] If that was true, he had miscalculated once again.

Konrad Adenauer had already begun considering West German armament. In December of 1949, he had told the *Cleveland Plain Dealer* that the question of a German contribution to a European army might have to be considered "if the worst came to worst."[10] Although the interview provoked a violent controversy in West Germany, where an overwhelming majority opposed rearmament, Adenauer did not retract it.

General Hans Speidel, Field Marshal Erwin Rommel's former chief of staff and one of the German generals who came out of the war with their reputation untarnished by Nazism, began working with other senior German officers to propose counters to a Soviet threat. Speidel had earlier recommended German membership in NATO as well as a force of fifteen German divisions to be incorporated into a European army. Adenauer saw Speidel's memorandum in 1949 and may have been influenced by it.

Adenauer asked Speidel and several other generals to make specific proposals. In October 1950, after the Korean invasion and Ulbricht's threat, the generals and some staff officers proposed a force of about 500,000 with 12 highly mobile armored divisions. The generals believed that West German and other Western forces could hope to stop an attack short of the Rhine only if they could harass and counter-attack immediately along the entire West German frontier instead of permitting Soviet and East German forces to advance into the country.

Adenauer and the generals feared the growing power of the East German *Kasernierte Volkspolizei*. Combined with the GDR Ministry of State Security, it gave the GDR a powerful military and security force. If Stalin had North Korea invade South Korea, might he have East Germany invade West Germany as Ulbricht had hinted?

After the Korean invasion, Adenauer decided that West German armament was not only necessary but inevitable. He also wanted to use it to raise West Germany's status. He believed that the Allies would now want a West German army for the defense of the West as a whole, and he wanted the Allies to give the Federal Republic its sovereignty in exchange. He also wanted the West German army to help integrate Europe. He saw a German armed force in political as well as security terms.

Adenauer had already asserted his claim to equality on September 21, 1949, when he had presented his cabinet to the Western high commissioners. They had met at the Petersberg, a large resort hotel that loomed high above the Rhine just south of Bonn and which the Allies had taken over for their offices. Many Germans resented the Petersberg because it seemed to give the Allies a superior vantage point from which to supervise Bonn and Germany. The high commissioners had assembled on a large rug to receive Adenauer's cabinet. Obviously, they had intended for the Germans to stand next to the rug. But Adenauer defiantly stepped onto the rug with the high commissioners, showing that the new Federal Republic would be their equal. Having himself suffered under the Nazis and lost his wife to treatment she had suffered in a Nazi prison, he did not feel morally inferior.

Adenauer had constantly pressed for greater powers and fewer restrictions for the Federal Republic. Within weeks of that first meeting with the Allied high commissioners, the Federal Republic and the Allies had signed an agreement known as the Petersberg agreement that gave the Federal Republic consular authority and cut back Allied dismantling plans for German industry.

Now the prospect of German rearmament made Adenauer redouble his efforts to gain sovereignty. If there was to be a German army, it should not be an army of vassals or mercenaries. Adenauer's quest for full sovereignty became a lead topic in every conversation between the Germans and the Allies about military plans. And the Allies knew that they had to yield because Adenauer would not create a German army until he thought that it would be defending a German state, not foreign occupiers.[11]

Adenauer presented two memoranda to U.S. High Commissioner John J. Mc-Cloy on August 30, 1950, as McCloy was leaving for a meeting of the foreign ministers of the Western powers. The first memorandum offered a German contribution to a European army but rejected any notion of a separate West German force. The second called for the end of the occupation statute and for full German sovereignty and authority in foreign and domestic affairs.

Within weeks, Adenauer had received some of what he wanted. The three Allies agreed to a revision of the occupation statute and of the Petersberg agreement so that the Federal Republic could have its own foreign ministry and diplomatic service. They accepted a German military contribution within the NATO framework in principle. Truman also decided that the United States would increase the number of its forces in West Germany—an important requirement before France would approve German rearmament.

Kim Il Sung's attack on South Korea had another unexpected result. As American industry had to concentrate on armaments, which West German industry was not allowed to produce, the Germans entered an export boom in civilian goods that was to last for several years. The Korean war thus boosted the West German "economic miracle," reinforcing Adenauer's position and his policies.

MONNET, SCHUMAN AND
ADENAUER CREATE EUROPE

The prospect of German rearmament did not sit well in Paris. French citizens had suffered terribly during the German invasion and occupation. French public opinion could not accept having Germany rearmed and capable of launching its fourth invasion of France within eighty years.

By the early 1950s, France still had not found its definitive policy toward Germany. De Gaulle had pursued two concepts, the negative goal of dismembering

Germany and the positive one of cooperation within Europe. Bidault had first tried dismemberment but had to change course when no one agreed. France had then joined NATO to make certain that Britain and America remained committed to Europe to protect against Germany and the Soviet Union. But France still had to find a way to live with the new Federal Republic.

One Frenchman, Jean Monnet, had an answer. He had spent most of the war years in the United States as an international economist and had thought a great deal about the future of France and Europe. As early as 1944, he had told *Fortune* magazine that European states would have to yield sovereignty to some kind of European union. He had envisioned Germany, France and Great Britain as the key members of that union. After the war, he tried to find a way to put his ideas into reality. Like Bevin and Acheson, he looked for new solutions to old problems.[12]

Monnet found a ready listener in Robert Schuman, who recognized that France had to find its own solution for Germany if it was not be swept away by Anglo-Saxon proposals. In April 1949, Monnet had briefed Schuman on his idea for the integration of the French and German coal and steel industries into a European entity. That would make war between the two states impossible in practical terms. It would also advance the integration of Europe. Schuman, who understood the revolutionary implications of Monnet's proposal, persuaded the French cabinet to approve it with a minimum of debate. He announced it on May 9, 1950. He had already informed Adenauer, who only two months earlier had proposed the complete union of France and West Germany. Adenauer was so enthusiastic that he had to be restrained from making the announcement himself because it needed to come from France.

From then on, Monnet proceeded to establish the European Coal and Steel Community (ECSC), finding total support among German and American officials. Adenauer, with whom Monnet became friends for life, forced the hidebound German coal and steel producers of the Ruhr to give up their cartels and to operate under a supranational high authority. McCloy supported him strongly, for without U.S. pressure the Ruhr barons would not have yielded. But Great Britain, although invited and supportive, did not join. Bevin would not and could not commit Britain fully to Europe.

Paris had found its German policy. Signed on April 18, 1951, the treaty to establish the ECSC ended historic Franco-German hostility and gave form to de Gaulle's notion of Europe as the vessel for containing Germany. Instead of trying to weaken Germany, Paris gave both states a stake in cooperation. Monnet, Schuman and Adenauer perceived the ECSC not as an industrial agreement but as a profoundly moral act. They hoped that it would end the continent's internecine battles and lead to a new era.

A new German army presented a greater challenge to France than the Ruhr barons. The very thought enraged every French citizen, for too many had lost friends and relatives to German arms. France opposed German remilitarization as firmly as German unification.

But the French premier, René Pleven, knew that France could not alone resist the pressure for German armament. He also knew, as did his military, that a German army could help protect French territory against a potential Soviet attack. And Pleven, like Schuman, decided that the best strategy for France would be to join with a revived Germany instead of trying to prevent the inevitable.

On October 24, 1950, five months after Schuman made his ECSC proposal, Pleven announced a novel but complex plan for German armament within Europe. His plan would create a European Defense Community (EDC) in which Germans would serve as officers and soldiers but could neither hold senior commands nor establish major combat units of their own. Germans and others would have *groupements de combat*, combat groups of perhaps 5,000 soldiers each. Those units would combine to form divisions, with no single nation to have more than a single combat group in a division. No German would become a division commander. Nor would Germany be permitted to have certain types of armaments and capital ships. West Germany would not become a separate member of NATO.[13]

Pleven's plan won some support although many French and other military officers doubted its combat feasibility. Jean Monnet had conceived it as a military complement to the Schuman Plan. He wanted it to serve the same political purpose as the ECSC. By creating a European rather than a German army, the EDC gave the French government an opening to support German armament without suffering a violent backlash from French public opinion.

But the German people opposed German armament even more than the French people. Germans were sick of war, of fighting, of losing sons, brothers, fathers and husbands. They wanted no part of any army, German or European or whatever. Their favorite phrase became *"Ohne Mich"* (without me), to show that a European army would have no German soldiers. The Social Democrats flatly opposed German armament, in part because they feared that it would surrender any chance for unification. Adenauer's coalition partner, the Free Democratic Party, had grave reservations. The GDR tempted the West German public to give up the armament plans in exchange for such things as "all-German" committees that would improve relations within Germany, but Adenauer rejected them.

Adenauer tried to persuade Germans to take up arms by reminding them that they alone could stop an invading force before it reached the Rhine. He also said that German armament would help Germany regain its sovereignty. He made very clear to Germans as well as to the Western Allies that the Federal Republic would not contribute to the EDC as an occupied country.

German and Allied officials met almost continually after Pleven's announcement in order to develop military plans as well as the political assurances that France needed. Adenauer also used those meetings to press his demand that West Germany be treated as a sovereign ally. British officials generally accepted Adenauer's arguments. The Americans hesitated because they could more easily deploy forces in an occupied territory under American control than in a foreign land under foreign laws. The French remained consistently reserved but finally agreed to most of Adenauer's proposals.

Adenauer and the Allies established a process for building West German forces under the EDC. They agreed on rules for stationing foreign forces in a more sovereign West Germany, reducing Western occupation rights but leaving some intact. The Allies insisted, as in 1949, that they needed to reserve their authority on a settlement for Germany as a whole as well as their rights in Berlin. But they yielded powers in finance and other areas.

Like Adenauer, Pleven saw the EDC in political terms. He wanted to bind Germany with so many European links that it could never again be a threat to any nation. Together with the Schuman Plan, the EDC was to help establish an integrated western Europe in which Germany would be a strong element but not a dominant force.

One year after the ECSC treaty had been approved, Germany agreed to enter the EDC. This gave the EDC some prospects for a meaningful force. In exchange, the Allies agreed to end the occupation statute and to give the Federal Republic much of the sovereignty on which Adenauer had insisted. The treaty that Adenauer and the Allies signed in Bonn on May 26, 1952, became known as the *Deutschlandvertrag* (Germany Treaty) because it reconstituted Germany after the war. On the following day, Adenauer and the Allies signed the EDC treaty in Paris.

In exchange for these new rights, however, the Allies demanded German loyalty. The Americans and the British especially made it clear that they not only expected a German defense contribution but expected the Federal Republic to remain fully attached to the West. McCloy told Adenauer bluntly that the Allies would not abandon their powers "in order to see Germany take a neutral position."[14] The Federal Republic could not resume Bismarck's *Schaukelpolitik* (swing policy), playing East against West, if it counted on Western support and on respect for its new authority. There could not be another Rapallo agreement, the treaty that had established a special relationship between the German and Soviet outcast states in 1922.

In terms of the struggle over Germany, Adenauer had taken a crucial step. From 1952 on, the West saw the Federal Republic as an important military, economic and political ally. Adenauer had solidified West Germany's integration into European and Atlantic structures. Germany remained divided, but West Germany had won democracy and authority. Kim Il Sung had changed the map of Europe more than the map of Korea.

Ulbricht fully understood the importance of what had happened. On the day of the *Deutschlandvertrag*, he ordered a prohibited zone of 5 kilometers (3.1 miles) on the eastern side of the demarcation line with West Germany. That zone could be entered only with special permission by residents, pre-announced visitors, reliable civilian officials or military units. Along the border itself, East German border police units cleared a plowed strip 10 meters (about 33 feet) wide that became known as the *Todesstreifen*, the "death strip." The border police built watch-towers to provide line-of-sight fields of fire and constantly conducted armed patrols. No human could move in that strip or across it except under the threat of death.[15] West Germans might join western Europe but East Germans would not.

STALIN'S FINAL TRY

By the beginning of 1952, Stalin feared that the European Defense Community would come into being and that the inclusion of West German units would mean that Soviet troops would face German troops directly for the first time since 1945. Having those forces under European command did not soften that reality.

Stalin decided that he had to act quickly. He believed, as attested by several postwar documents, that "whoever supports German unity will also win the German people."[16] He decided to act on that conviction.

Stalin instructed Molotov, whom he had brought back as foreign minister, to prepare a proposal containing a new formula for German unification including the text of a peace treaty. He wanted the proposal to be made public and to attract attention and support in West Germany.[17] But the draft that Molotov and the foreign ministry staff sent to Stalin failed to meet his wishes. It repeated shopworn formulas and contained new and obviously unacceptable demands, such as the exclusion of the Ruhr from the ECSC and the extradition of Soviet refugees who had found asylum in West Germany.

Stalin ordered a new draft, which the foreign ministry, acting under his specific guidance, produced. It had several new ideas designed to attract the West Germans.

On March 10, 1952, Stalin surprised the West by offering Germans the unity they professed to seek. And he offered it with many details filled in and on better terms than before. But he also attached some new conditions. The Soviet deputy foreign minister, Andrei Gromyko, called the ambassadors of the three Western occupying powers into his office and gave them a note proposing the unification of Germany under the following terms:

- Germany was to be reestablished as a united state within the boundaries "established by the provisions of the Potsdam Conference."
- A single united German government was to play a role in the negotiation of the peace treaty.
- All occupation forces were to be withdrawn within one year following the date on which the treaty would go into effect.
- Democratic political parties and organizations were to have free activity.
- Germany was "not to enter into any kind of coalition or military alliance directed against any power which took part with its armed forces in the war against Germany."
- Germany was to have "its own national armed forces which are necessary for the defense of the country."
- Germany was to be permitted to manufacture munitions for its armed forces.
- Germany was to have full access to world markets.
- Former members of the German armed forces and of the Nazi party, except for convicted war criminals, could join in establishing a peaceful, democratic Germany.[18]

The Soviet note, which became known as the Stalin Note, created a sensation in Germany and in Allied capitals. Although Stalin had always shown an interest in German unity and although many Soviet diplomatic moves professed to seek German unity, Soviet policy had helped to divide the country. Stalin's move reversed everything that the West had come to believe about his German policy.

Stalin's note hinted at possibilities that would appeal to most Germans. Germany would be united. A German government would help negotiate the peace. Germany would have its own armed forces. Freedom would return through the unrestricted activity of political parties. Occupation forces, including the Soviet forces, would leave.

The note also contained some points, however, that many West Germans did not welcome. The German boundary would run at the Oder-Neisse line, a border that many Germans had not yet accepted. Germany could not join organizations ostensibly directed against any of its former enemies, a clause that Stalin might use to exclude Germany from a wide range of organizations that the West Germans wanted to join.

The language of the note lent itself to endless differences of interpretation. It demanded "free" political activity and denounced organizations "hostile" to any power that had fought against Germany. Depending on the interpretations of those words, a new united Germany could be independent or it could be tightly bound. Earlier talks with Soviet leaders and officials suggested that it would take a long time to reach agreement on the meaning and the application of those terms.

And who could agree on the forces that Germany would need to defend itself? The EDC talks had shown that the victims of Hitler's aggression wanted a small German army but that Germany might need a large one if it had to rely fully on its own forces. A German army large enough to hold back the Red Army would look terrifying to France, let alone Belgium or Holland. Those countries had found it difficult to accept German units under a European command. A German army under German command would be nightmarish.

Stalin's note, therefore, could slow down the process of West German integration into European and Atlantic institutions. In the meantime, Soviet armies would continue to stand at the Elbe with no comparable force to counter them. The Western Allies and Adenauer would have to reverse the policies they had followed since the Berlin Blockade and the Korean invasion.

But the Allies found it hard to reject Stalin's proposal. They had to find a way to continue their integration policies without appearing to reject what might really be a meaningful Soviet offer no matter how skeptical they were. They could not lose sight of public opinion or be responsible for keeping Germany divided without good reason [19]

Acheson believed that any talks with Moscow would be useless and would jeopardize the momentum for west European unity at a crucial time. He feared that Germany would fall under Stalin's influence if American troops had to withdraw across the Atlantic while Soviet forces remained on the German border. Moreover, he believed that the United States could never find as good a base for its strategically essential European forces as it could find in Germany. Therefore, he wanted to turn down Stalin's offer.

British foreign secretary Anthony Eden shared Acheson's fears. He also did not want to countenance the delay that any talks with Moscow would impose. But British public opinion had not yet fully accepted a European army. Some British diplomats still feared an integrated western Europe. The Stalin Note tempted them.[20]

Schuman and the French government saw the Stalin Note as highly dangerous. It could create a united and armed Germany, ostensibly neutral but subject to pressure from Soviet armies on its borders. To counteract that combination, France would have to maintain a huge military force that it could ill afford.

Stalin's note revived the French "Rapallo complex," the fear that Europe would again be dominated by Germany backed by Russia. Germany and the Soviet Union would marginalize France, Italy and the Benelux countries. Although Schuman trusted Adenauer, Paris could not help but wonder whether the chancellor or the German public might be tempted by such a proposition.

On March 17, Adenauer himself resolved the dilemma faced by the Western powers. He became the first Western leader to say openly and unambiguously that he rejected the ideas contained in the Stalin Note. Although Stalin had not sent his note to the Federal Republic, Adenauer wanted to state his views. He derided the note as a backhanded Soviet compliment to the Allied policy of integrating West Germany into the West. He thought that Stalin wanted to stop or at least delay that process. Privately, Adenauer told the Allies that he expected to be included in all Western discussions about a reply.

Recognizing the public appeal of Stalin's note, Adenauer suggested posing a number of questions that would ferret out the Soviet dictator's true purpose. He thought those questions would show that, as he believed, the note constituted a trap rather than an opportunity.

Only ten days before the note, on March 1, 1952, Adenauer had predicted to a CDU congress how Moscow would react to Western armament:

> When the West is stronger than Soviet Russia, then the time to negotiate with Soviet Russia is at hand. Then, on the one hand, the fear of Germany will be removed. Then one will also need to explain to Soviet Russia that it is impossible to keep half of Europe in slavery.[21]

But Adenauer thought that the conditions he foresaw had not yet come. He wanted to play for time. The Western Allies agreed. They did not even try to discuss the merits of Stalin's proposal with Moscow. Instead, they tried a tactical approach, focusing on some of the note's more ambiguous elements and especially on the processes it suggested. They asked how the all-German government would be formed. They also asked whether a united Germany would have to abstain from the Schuman Plan and other forms of economic integration as well as from military alliances. And they rejected Stalin's suggestion that East and West Germany negotiate a joint delegation.

The Allies demanded free elections to form the all-German government that Stalin suggested, an ostensibly unassailable condition that they knew Moscow could not accept after Ulbricht's electoral debacles. Going back to an earlier United Nations report on the difficulties of holding truly free elections in East Germany, they proposed that a U.N. commission visit there to examine current conditions for free elections. Stalin rejected that. He also avoided answering some of the more pointed Western questions.

The Stalin Note and the Allied reply led to an exchange of notes that lasted for six months. The Soviet Union sent four notes, beginning with the first on March 10 and continuing with others on April 9, May 24 and August 23. The Allies sent their replies on March 25, May 13, July 10 and September 23. Moscow did not even bother to reply to the last Allied note because by then the exchange had lost whatever purpose it might originally have served. Even as the notes were going back and forth, the Allies signed the *Deutschlandvertrag* and the EDC treaty.

By late spring, Stalin appeared to begin losing interest in the exchange of notes. The Soviet note delivered on May 24 differed in tone and style from the earlier ones. The foreign ministry had obviously drafted it. Later Soviet notes did not even reiterate some of the more dramatic proposals of the first one. Stalin had either changed his mind or had decided that the West would not reply positively. Eden informed his colleagues on May 28 that the West had won "the battle of the notes."[22]

Stalin would not accept Western terms and the West would not accept his. Acheson denounced Stalin's offer as a delaying tactic.[23] Neither Eden nor Schuman wanted to let Stalin dictate the organizations that West Germany could join.[24] When the follow-up Soviet notes argued that West German membership even in non-military organizations would put Bonn into the "aggressive North Atlantic bloc,"[25] the Western leaders saw their skepticism about Stalin's purpose vindicated. Adenauer felt even more strongly that such a condition would mean permanent instability in Europe.[26] All concluded that they were right to reject Stalin's offer.

Whatever its intent and merits may have been, the Stalin Note became a contentious issue in Germany. Some Germans saw it as an opening that might lead to German unification. Others saw it as a chance to keep Germany out of European bloc politics and out of another cycle of armament. A number of political analysts accused Adenauer of missing a golden opportunity. But that charge never attracted as much political as intellectual attention, in part because the West German SPD also mistrusted Stalin.

One German author, Rolf Steininger, pursued the subject, asserting that Adenauer had acted for narrow political gain because he was afraid that the SPD-minded voters in eastern Germany would remove him and the CDU from office. Two others, including Adenauer's biographer Hans-Peter Schwarz, rejected this claim, asserting that the Stalin Note was only a propaganda ploy and that western Europe could offer Germany an infinitely brighter future than Moscow.[27]

Adenauer might well have feared the note even more as a real offer than as a propaganda ploy. He favored German unification in the long run, but during the 1950s he did not want another united Germany playing an independent and potentially mischievous role in Europe and in the world. He believed that Germany in the postwar years needed democracy and stability more than it needed unity. He hoped that integration into western Europe would not only give Germany peace but would also strengthen the liberalizing forces within the country itself. Privately, he did not oppose the Oder-Neisse line as a border but said he would prefer to sign that with a free Poland.[28]

No Soviet or East German document released to date offers concrete evidence that Stalin was prepared to unite Germany and abandon the GDR during the 1950s, although many earlier documents attest to his wish for a united Germany. Nor does any document suggest that Stalin would negotiate German unification on terms more acceptable to the Western Allies and West German public opinion than those he had suggested in the late 1940s. Stalin had presumably accepted Voroshilov's wartime advice to make an occupation arrangement that would serve Soviet interests even without a peace treaty.

Stalin may perhaps have been sincere in wanting a united Germany on the terms he set forth in his note. But so many points were subject to interpretation that, like his postwar wish for a "democratic" Germany, one still cannot really know what he wanted. The Allies knew only that they had never been able to negotiate on Germany with Molotov and that they did not want to try again. Even if the Stalin Note presented an opportunity for German unification, they did not think that it presented an acceptable one.

If Stalin had wanted to achieve a mood of reconciliation leading to a successful negotiation, he did nothing in Moscow to further it. Kennan, who became U.S. Ambassador to Moscow in May of 1952, after the Stalin Note, reported facing a totally hostile environment. Soviet media denounced the United States and the West unremittingly. When the U.S. embassy delivered the American reply to the Stalin Note, Vishinsky acted as if he had expected and even wanted a negative answer.[29]

The Stalin Note did not resolve the basic dilemma that the Soviet premier had faced from the beginning. Stalin could achieve a united Germany only by letting the Germans make some of their own choices. But because Ulbricht kept hurting communism's reputation in Germany, any free choice would go against Stalin. One might legitimately wonder whether Ulbricht deliberately provoked the Allies and the West Germans. The more he did so, and the more he frightened German voters, the more guarantees Stalin would have to demand if communism was to have even a remote chance in a united Germany, and the harder it would be to negotiate a treaty.

Stalin could send any number of notes, but it was Ulbricht who determined the mood in which they were received and negotiated. And Stalin must have recognized by 1952 that a united and truly democratic Germany would not be as friendly to Moscow as he might have expected in 1945. He had to ask the Western occupiers to give him advance guarantees on future German policies and associations. Otherwise, a united Germany might well not serve Soviet interests.

Whatever Stalin may have intended, he did not stop Western integration. The Allies carried out their plans for the ECSC. The EDC faltered, however, as no French government dared even to present it to the National Assembly for a vote.

In the meantime, Ulbricht went ahead with his plans to solidify the separation of the GDR from West Germany economically and politically as well as physically. In July 1952, after receiving appropriate Soviet approval, the second SED conference decided on the "forced construction of socialism" and stepped up the collectivization of agriculture and socialization of industry. Ulbricht followed up by imposing higher work norms and quotas, promising to catch up with the West German standard of living by 1961.

BERIA AND THE BERLIN UPRISING

Ulbricht's efforts to increase East German production by accelerating socialization and raising work norms failed badly. East German production fell instead of rising. The GDR entered a deep recession.

By late 1952 and early 1953, the East German economy risked collapse. Refugees fled in rising numbers, well over 100,000 of them during the first four months of 1953. Ulbricht's decision to seal the boundary between East and West Germany with the "death strip" did not stop refugees from leaving through Berlin.

In the middle of the GDR crisis, on March 5, 1953, Radio Moscow announced that Josef Stalin had died. This news shook the global scene, opening new questions and perhaps new opportunities.

The new cast of Soviet leaders revealed little. Georgi Malenkov, the head of the party secretariat, appeared to emerge as the front man. But several other old and new faces, including Vyacheslav Molotov, Lavrenti Beria, Nikolai Bulganin and Nikita Khrushchev, shared in the new collective leadership.

In his oration at Stalin's funeral, Malenkov called for better relations with the West and for the peaceful settlement of disputes. The Soviet leadership gave instructions to end the war in Korea. But they did not agree on everything. Molotov favored continuing Stalin's foreign policy whereas Malenkov and especially Beria wanted to go in new directions.[30]

The new U.S. President, Dwight Eisenhower, wanted to try new peace initiatives. On April 11, 1953, he spoke of "a chance for peace" and offered to ease tensions between East and West. Although John Foster Dulles, Eisenhower's secretary of state, followed with a narrow interpretation of what the president had said, the United States was offering its hand to Moscow. Eisenhower listed progress toward German unification as one of his goals.[31]

Eisenhower's speech did not evoke the response he sought. Internal Soviet documents described it as "irritating and provocative," unworthy of a serious reply. Malenkov and Beria expressed some interest in exploring a few of Eisenhower's proposals, but Molotov dismissed them all. Dulles's speech drew an even more negative reaction. The new Soviet leaders had as much trouble as the West in setting on a new course. Molotov, apparently the most reluctant to explore new ideas, drafted some proposals for a German settlement, but they did not go as far as Stalin's had a year earlier.[32]

Winston Churchill, having returned as Britain's prime minister, had a very hopeful agenda. He decided to use his old friendship with Eisenhower to reach a grand European settlement with a united Germany at the center. Great Britain would resume its earlier role, settling major global issues with Moscow and Washington. He did not regard Paris or Bonn as equals.

On May 11, one month after Eisenhower's speech, Churchill offered his ideas. He proposed a summit of the Big Three to address the world's problems without any agenda. While he offered no specific plans, he said that the West had to respect Soviet security needs.[33]

France did not endorse Churchill's three-power summit, suggesting instead a four-power summit or, at least, a three-power Western meeting to prepare for a later talk with Moscow. Nor did Churchill win any support from Adenauer or from British foreign secretary Anthony Eden, who saw Churchill's effort as a self-serving gambit to stay in office. Moscow did not accept any of Churchill's ideas.[34]

Moscow did not offer new ideas of its own, especially about Germany. Recently released documents show that Soviet leaders still wanted to prevent the combination of German and American power that the EDC might represent and that Stalin had feared. But the Soviets also feared a united Germany unless it could be "neutralized" in their own meaning of the word. Moscow could not decide between a united or a divided Germany.[35] Nor could it decide on the conditions under which it wished to live with either.

The East German economic crisis brought matters to a head. In early April 1953, Ulbricht had to ask Moscow for massive aid infusions to prevent the total collapse of the East German economy and perhaps of the East German state.

The new Soviet leaders did not trust the information provided by Ulbricht and asked for a special report from a team of their own. That report blamed Ulbricht and the SED for creating the crisis. Its figures startled the Soviet leadership. Almost half a million persons had fled the GDR between the beginning of January 1951 and the end of April 1953. Moreover, 125,000 persons had been convicted in East Germany over the same period, largely for "economic crimes." Seven percent of East German arable land was not being tended because the farmers had fled.[36] The leaders of the Communist Party of the Soviet Union (CPSU) agreed on a secret paper strongly condemning Ulbricht for his policies and for the danger they posed to the survival of the GDR.[37]

Soviet complaints about Ulbricht and his policies ranged widely. The council of ministers charged that "the political and ideological work being carried out by the leadership of the SED is not adequate for the task of strengthening the German Democratic Republic." The Soviets listed a number of specific charges: Ulbricht had fomented fear among workers, farmers and youth, leading to record numbers of refugees. He had exacerbated "class conflict." He had applied "excessive and arbitrary criminal codes," engaged in the "artificial establishment of agricultural production cooperatives," and "committed serious errors . . . with regard to the clergy," engaging in "crude administrative methods and repression." The SED had not listened to Soviet suggestions to moderate its policies.[38]

Faced with this grim reality, the presidium of the Soviet council of ministers had an angry debate about Germany on May 27, 1953. Beria and Molotov differed sharply, with Beria arguing that the GDR had failed miserably and demonstrably. He wanted to remove those responsible for the failure, Ulbricht and Grotewohl. The Soviet Union had to try for German unification before it was too late. He favored a united Germany that would be governed by a coalition government recognizing Soviet as well as Western interests and perhaps playing a balancing role instead of becoming an American base against Moscow.[39]

To justify giving up the GDR, Beria argued, Moscow would insist that East Germany remain an autonomous province in a united Germany and that the new German government make large-scale payments to the Soviet Union for ten years. Germany would be neutralized. It could not join the EDC. It would not be a strategic threat and would be an economic asset. Soviet forces would, however, give up their occupation of the GDR.

Beria seemed an unlikely advocate of accommodation, for his hands were covered with blood. He had been in charge of Stalin's secret police and purges. He had overseen the slave labor camps, the Gulag. He had confined, tortured and often brutally executed millions of Russians and others. He had established the Soviet espionage networks and managed the Soviet atomic weapons program, Stalin's highest priority. His colleagues hated and feared him.

But Beria had a clear mind. From his seat in the KGB he saw the world with unvarnished realism. More than any other Soviet leader of his time, he believed that Moscow needed to shed some of its foreign burdens. He wanted a change of course on Germany, with some support from Malenkov. Nonetheless, according to the records now available, he never made his precise proposals clear. Nor do those records show the depth of his commitment. Khrushchev, wanting a divided Germany, may have altered the records later to justify his move against Beria and to eliminate even a chance at German unification.

Molotov rejected Beria's proposals on Germany although he recognized that something different had to be done there. He said that Moscow should continue building socialism in the GDR but not through Ulbricht's "forced construction of socialism." He argued that this would heal discontent and permit the GDR to survive. He still opposed German unification. Khrushchev supported Molotov, and Bulganin later joined them. All denounced Beria and, to a lesser extent, Malenkov. Because Beria could not defeat that kind of opposition, Germany would remain divided.

Although the presidium members decided to keep the GDR, they showed total disdain for Ulbricht. They decided that East Germany had to change course and change it fast. Virtually every presidium member criticized SED policies, with Malenkov and Beria going so far as to state that the East German regime could not survive without Soviet troops to prop it up. Malenkov denounced the SED's "gravely mistaken political line" and its "unacceptably simplistic and rash policies."[40]

The Soviet government distanced itself from Ulbricht and revived some of its occupation principles. It told the head of its control commission, Vladimir Semyonov, to make sure that the GDR government carried out the Potsdam agreement and to keep up ties with the Western high commissioners. Those instructions might have led to new four-power discussions about Germany if they had been pursued with Eisenhower and especially with Churchill. But Molotov still preferred division.[41]

On June 2, Malenkov signed a presidium decree that enunciated a "new course" in the GDR. On the same day, Walter Ulbricht and Otto Grotewohl appeared in Moscow. The Soviet leaders told them that the GDR had to change course immediately. They gave Ulbricht a paper recommending different policies. Ulbricht remonstrated. He tried to redraft the Soviet paper to moderate some of the instructions, but Beria threw the revision back at him with the charge that it was a "bad remake."

The Soviets told Ulbricht and Grotewohl to "change conditions in the GDR." They warned about a "catastrophe" if the SED did not act and act "quickly." Molotov told Ulbricht to make sure that all Germans could see the changes to be made.[42] Whether he liked it or not, Ulbricht had to follow Soviet instructions.

Ulbricht and Grotewohl returned to East Berlin and the SED politburo spent four days in rancorous debate. Semyonov attended the sessions and spoke frankly. When Rudolf Herrnstatt, the editor of the SED daily *Neues Deutschland*, warned that any basic policy shift would create confusion if the SED did not have fourteen days to prepare public opinion, Semyonov bluntly replied "in fourteen days you may not have a state any more."[43] With no options left, Ulbricht on June 9 issued a decree reversing the socialization program. The debate within the SED leadership had become so chaotic that one GDR minister complained "this is not a politburo, but a madhouse."[44]

The Soviets not only made Ulbricht change course, but they also began to look for new standard-bearers in East Germany. Semyonov encouraged a group of East German SED leaders who had long challenged Ulbricht's policies to come to the fore. Herrnstatt and Wilhelm Zaisser, the minister for state security (and thus linked to Beria) headed the group. They denounced Ulbricht for the gulf he had created between the SED and the East German people.

Confusion reigned in East Germany. While the regime recognized its mistakes, it did not reverse all its policies. Ulbricht did not retract the draconian work norms that had fomented most of the popular resentment. The workers, still angry, demanded that the norms be revoked. Rumors of a new Soviet policy and of new East German leaders spread like wildfire. Party officials, demoralized and uncertain, did not know what to say or do. On June 16, demonstrators began to appear on the streets of East Berlin and of other East German cities. Ulbricht, thinking he could handle any problems in Berlin, decided to send SED agitators to the other cities to calm the population.

On June 17, 1953, the cauldron erupted in East Berlin and throughout the GDR. East German workers, fed up with Ulbricht's demands, with their squalid living conditions and with continuing reparations to the Soviet Union, rebelled. Half a million workers went into the streets of over 400 cities all over East Germany, demanding free elections and, secondarily, German unification.

Having heard frequent broadcasts in favor of freedom and democracy from the American-sponsored *Radio im Amerikanischen Sektor*, better known as RIAS, the rebellious workers may even have expected some support from the West. But they got none. Like the Western governments, the RIAS staff had not expected, or prepared for, the uprising. West Berlin newspapers later denounced RIAS for not having reported fully on the uprising and for not even having changed its regular programming to inform Berliners and East Germans what was happening.[45]

Moscow also reacted in surprise. The Soviets had misjudged the intensity of East German anger at the SED. No Soviet leader thought that Germans would rebel. Stalin had laughed that the Germans would not cross a street unless the lights were green, and Lenin had predicted that Germans would not attack a railroad station without first buying platform passes. The Soviets also misjudged the scale of the uprising. Until the morning of June 17, Soviet officials thought that the East German police and armed forces could cope with any dissent. But they changed their minds during the day, especially when Ulbricht and his senior officials sought refuge at the Soviet headquarters in Karlshorst and had plainly lost their will or power to act. Soviet tanks then put down the rebellion mercilessly and effectively.[46]

The riots showed both the failure and the hollowness of Ulbricht's regime. Most of the rioters were the workers on whom the SED had built its claim to power. The SED froze in the face of the riots and would have been swept out of office without Soviet tanks—although the suspicion remains that Ulbricht in fact kept the high work norms because he thought they might lead to riots and to Soviet action.

After it had put down the uprising and obliged the SED to engage in a self-rectification campaign, Moscow directed the party in late June to reverse steps toward accelerated industrialization and socialization. For example, on June 24 Grotewohl denounced the same burdensome work norms that he had praised on May 28. Other East German leaders performed similar acts of contrition.[47]

Paradoxically, although the workers rose up against Ulbricht, they actually saved him. The uprising made it clear that rage against the SED ran so deep that German unification would destroy the Soviet position in central Europe. It showed that the East Germans would swing a united Germany against Moscow even more than the West Germans. It also warned against experiments within the GDR itself.

For the next two months, the new CPSU leadership could not decide what to do about Germany or about Ulbricht. While it did not endorse Ulbricht, it saw no good alternative. Finally, after discussions with Ulbricht and among themselves in July and August 1953, the CPSU leaders decided to keep and to support him, no matter what blunders he had made, and to preserve East Germany as a separate state. The Soviets could not risk more chaos. Talk of unification subsided.

The Western Allies reacted in confusion. Eisenhower and Dulles did nothing to help the East Berliners, although the United States remained legally sovereign throughout all of Berlin. In a later policy review, the U.S. government decided that West German integration into western Europe took priority in its German policy and that Washington had no acceptable way to weaken

Moscow's hold on the GDR. It concluded that "we must accustom the East Germans to a long-lasting struggle."[48]

Eisenhower decided even more firmly than before that he did not wish to meet with any Soviet leader. But Churchill kept pushing for East-West talks. He even tried to justify the Soviet repression as understandable and moderate under the circumstances. To appease Churchill, Dulles agreed to let the British propose a meeting of foreign ministers. Molotov accepted.[49]

Beria's hopes for a new German policy, like Beria himself, could not survive. His enemies could claim that his moves against Ulbricht had helped foment the uprising. The conservative Molotov had won back full control of foreign policy. Moreover, deepening opposition in the West toward a summit showed that no breakthrough on Germany would come. On June 26, other CPSU leaders charged Beria with "capitulationist behavior on the German Question," and he was subsequently executed. It was only on December 24, 1953, that *Pravda* reported his death.[50]

With Beria went the last postwar Soviet figure who might propose or favor unification. The failure of the Stalin Note and the perverse result of Soviet efforts to moderate Ulbricht's policies destroyed whatever chance there might have been for such a proposal from Moscow. Adenauer's massive victory over the SPD in the West German elections of September 1953 provided even more evidence that Moscow could not hope for support in either the western or eastern portion of a united Germany.

Right after his victory over Hitler, Stalin might have hoped for a united Germany that would support Moscow politically and economically. But eight years of Soviet occupation practices and Ulbricht's policies had destroyed whatever political base communism once had in Germany. With the workers themselves in revolt against the communist system and with all reputable East German political figures having fled, the Soviets understood that only the Red Army kept the SED in power. Under those circumstances, the Red Army had to remain. As the East Berliners complained, *"Der Ivan geht nie weg"* (Ivan will never leave).[51]

Ulbricht and Molotov had blocked Beria's plans as they had earlier frustrated Stalin's. And Ulbricht took full advantage of Khrushchev's and Molotov's support. He purged the SED of any remaining independent figures, including Zaisser and Herrnstatt. He promoted the communist youth leader Erich Honecker, who had supported him. He also imposed further belt-tightening. The latter, coming at the time of West Germany's "economic miracle," further deepened disgust with the SED regime.

Although Moscow and the Western Allies exchanged some desultory notes and further meeting proposals during the remainder of 1953, nothing was to come of them. Neither did anything come of the meeting of foreign ministers. The West did not want to risk jeopardizing the EDC vote in the French Assembly by even hinting that a united and neutral Germany might be in the offing. While Churchill continued to press for a summit with the Soviets, Eisenhower remained skeptical and both Adenauer and Eden made their opposition ever more clear.[52]

The Soviet leadership chose the course that Molotov and Khrushchev wanted—to keep Germany divided by force—although that course froze Moscow into a defensive political position. Moscow announced that the GDR had become a "sovereign state," closing the Soviet control commission and appointing a high commissioner in Germany, like the Western Allies. It even began an aid program to overcome the worst effects of Ulbricht's accelerated socialization. Moreover, Moscow lowered its reparations demands and ended them completely within two years. Once the CPSU had decided to keep the GDR, it had to stop trying to exploit it.

This did not mean, however, that Moscow had given up its long-term hopes for a united, socialist Germany. Ulbricht continued to speak of the GDR as a "socialist state in Germany," leaving open the door to ultimate unification of Germany under socialism. Separation was to be temporary, giving the GDR time to show its true worth as a model. If Marx's belief that workers would be alienated in a capitalist system held true, the socialist system and the GDR would ultimately prevail.

West Germany had its own model, a democratic capitalist system with a large social component. Erhard called it the "social market economy." Having revived the long German tradition of high-quality industrial production, it also brought into being an all-encompassing if costly social welfare system that expanded upon the model Bismarck had first introduced in the nineteenth century. The system was designed to show that a capitalist Germany could take better care of workers and of the needy than the GDR.

But after June 17 the West Germans could not expect Moscow to surrender the GDR either to the West or to its own people, no matter how attractive the Western model might be. Adenauer continued to integrate West Germany into Europe. The struggle over Germany would continue, with both sides having made the definitive decisions to keep their part of Germany.

Bertold Brecht, the Left-leaning German poet and playwright who lived in East Berlin, had the last word. Of the June 17 riots, he wrote: "The people have lost the confidence of the government. Why does the government not dissolve the people and elect a new one?"[53]

SEVEN

THE LINES HARDEN

WESTERN EFFORTS TO CREATE THE EUROPEAN DEFENSE COMMUNITY met with one delay after another because of French hesitation. Dulles exerted persistent pressure on the Europeans and especially on France, warning that the United States would make an "agonizing reappraisal" of its European policy if the French Assembly did not ratify EDC. This threat only inflamed the mood in Paris further. Eden, worried that EDC would fail, began to develop plans for that contingency.[1]

A new French premier, Pierre Mendès-France, decided that France could no longer postpone a decision. He brought EDC before the National Assembly, where it failed to survive a procedural motion on August 30, 1954. The end of the EDC plan compelled the Allies to look for another formula to bring West Germany into Western defense. Dulles, bitterly disappointed, nonetheless pledged that Washington would help its allies to find that formula.[2]

EDEN BRINGS WEST GERMANY INTO NATO

Anthony Eden became the man of the hour. He thought that the Brussels Treaty, which had established the Western European Union, could be transformed to bring West Germany into the Western military system and NATO. With Churchill's approval, he proceeded to test his idea.[3]

Eden met with a very friendly reception in Bonn. Adenauer continued to want West Germany to be fully in western Europe. While he preferred to have

German forces integrated into a European army, as in the EDC formula, he could agree to establish a separate German army under NATO and to accept some limitations to ease French fears. He definitely wanted Britain to join. Eden met an equally friendly reception in Rome.

Paris was a different story. Mendès-France said that the French public would not accept separate German forces in NATO without special safeguards. The French premier needed to be able to say that France would not find itself facing a German army alone.

To complicate Eden's efforts further, Dulles warned him that the U.S. Congress would agree to keep American troops in Europe only if the Europeans formed an integrated force and stopped playing the old European nationalist game. Although Dulles supported Eden and wanted his efforts to succeed, he faced a highly skeptical Congress.

On September 28, at a London conference of west European and north American foreign ministers, Eden made the same European commitment of British forces that Truman had made of U.S. forces after the Korean war. He promised a permanent British military presence on the European continent. He pledged that Great Britain would keep four divisions and a tactical air force in western Europe as long as the majority of the WEU states wished.

This British commitment, which France had sought since the end of World War I, changed not only the tone of the conference but the strategic picture in Europe. It pledged a strong British presence to balance the Germans, reassure the French and let the Americans know that they would not be the only outside power helping to defend the continent.

London's commitment convinced Mendès-France that he would have a chance to obtain National Assembly approval for a new treaty. It also convinced Adenauer that Germany would not have to defend itself alone. That enabled West Germany to renounce the right to manufacture atomic, bacteriological and chemical weapons as well as the right to produce guided missiles, large naval vessels and bombers.

But persuading the German people to arm remained an uphill battle. The U.S. Ambassador to Bonn, James B. Conant, found himself in the ironic position of having to urge West German armament after having despised the German military most of his adult life. He commented wryly that he secretly liked not having Germans want to rearm.[4]

On October 20, 1954, in Paris, the Allies signed the treaty that expanded the West European Union and made it part of NATO. The treaty also invited Germany into NATO. Most important from Adenauer's standpoint, it revised the *Deutschlandvertrag* one more time to end the occupation regime in Germany. It limited Allied residual authority to Berlin and to a peace settlement. It also provided the framework within which the Saar was to be returned to Germany on January 1, 1957, under the provisions of Article 23 of the Basic Law.

When the French assembly approved the Paris treaty on December 29, the struggle over Germany changed. West Germany became a military asset for the West and a full part of western Europe in military as well as economic terms. It had regained sovereignty with only a few limitations. Adenauer's integration policy had triumphed. With West Germany in the Atlantic system and East Germany in the Soviet security belt, the two Germanys stood at the fulcrum of the new strategic division of the world.

Dulles welcomed the new agreements. The Americans had reached their goal, a western European defense arrangement that included Germany and that provided the basis for an American presence.[5]

DIVIDED EUROPE

As the West tied the Federal Republic into NATO, Moscow tied the East German military into its own alliance system. The GDR joined the Warsaw Pact in May 1955, and the Soviet Union recognized the GDR's sovereignty in September. These steps followed logically on Khrushchev's and Molotov's 1953 decision to turn away from German unification as well as on Western steps to integrate West Germany into western Europe.

Futile efforts to deal with the German question continued. The Geneva summit of July 1955, the first meeting between Western and Soviet heads of government since Potsdam, tried to address the problem. Following on the heels of the Austrian State Treaty of May 1955, the summit seemed to promise at least some prospect for a serious discussion of German unification. The summit delegates, President Dwight Eisenhower, Prime Minister Anthony Eden, French Premier Edgar Faure and Soviet leaders Nikita Khrushchev and Nikolai Bulganin, issued a document stating that "The heads of government have agreed that the settlement of the German question and the reunification of Germany by free elections shall be carried out in conformity with the national interests of the German people and the interests of European security."[6]

Eisenhower and Dulles felt pleased that they had gained language providing for the unification of Germany by free elections, although it had been included in the context of Europe-wide security requirements demanded by the Soviet delegation and Moscow had also linked it with Bulganin's proposal for a 26-nation European security treaty. But the follow-up foreign ministers conference in October and November led nowhere, as the Soviets refused to consider any proposal for free elections.

On his return from Geneva, Khrushchev stopped in East Berlin. He reaffirmed his determination to keep Germany divided, announcing that henceforth there would be two German states. He added that there could no longer be any talk of German unification at the expense of the GDR. Unification, he insisted, could take place only through the creation of a European system of collective security and through direct contacts between the two Germanys.[7]

Adenauer periodically offered ideas for unification through private as well as public channels, but he insisted that he would not be a party to any agreement that led to an undemocratic united Germany. On March 19, 1958, he went so far as to make a secret proposal to the Soviet ambassador to delay unification while giving East Germany an "Austrian" neutral status for an interim period of ten years. Moscow would not, however, accept Adenauer's demand for free elections as part of any unification process.[8]

Ulbricht, like Khrushchev, insisted that unification could come about only through direct talks between East and West German authorities. He wanted equal status for the GDR and the Federal Republic. Premier Otto Grotewohl had proposed GDR-FRG meetings in a letter sent to Adenauer on January 15, 1951. Similar proposals followed over the years. East German leaders in 1953 proposed having the two Germanys meet and talk "over one table" (*"Deutsche an einen Tisch"*). On December 30, 1956, the SED newspaper *Neues Deutschland* proposed a confederation of the two German states. Adenauer rejected any and all such proposals, as he had the Stalin Note, because they would recognize the GDR and made no provisions for free elections.[9]

East and West continued to exchange notes about German unification, but those notes became stale with repetition. Moscow rejected plans that called for free elections and the West rejected plans for direct contacts between the Germanys as well as any proposals that made German neutrality a condition for unity. The West also rejected the Polish October 1957 Rapacki Plan which would have banned nuclear weapons from East and West Germany as well as from Poland and Czechoslovakia. Other diplomatic ventures faltered; the Soviet 1957–1958 proposals for another East-West summit did not even put Germany on the agenda, although the West wanted it there.[10]

East and West Germany kept up a mutually advantageous trade although they did not recognize each other officially. While East Germany wanted to call it "foreign trade," West Germany did not. To solve this problem, the two governments negotiated an accord known as the "Berlin Agreement" to govern what the West Germans termed *Interzonenhandel* (Interzonal Trade, hereafter IZT). Under the terms of that agreement, the two sides dealt with each other as "currency areas," with West Germany and West Berlin represented by an ostensibly private Berlin office called the *Treuhandstelle für Industrie und Handel* (Trustee Agency for Industry and Commerce) and East Germany represented by the GDR Ministry of Foreign Trade. Except for occasional interruptions caused by political crises, that system administered inner-German trade until the collapse of the GDR.

Over the years, the trade became increasingly important. It enabled the GDR to buy high-quality West German machine tools for East German and Soviet industry while paying with relatively low-technology exports such as coal and electrical power. West Germany offered a revolving credit system (termed the "swing") to facilitate GDR purchases. Although Adenauer did not like to support the GDR, he wanted to help the East German people to reach a decent standard of living. He realized that the Soviets would again violently put down any revolt provoked by disastrous living conditions.

To underline his conviction that the GDR did not represent the German people and even its own population, Adenauer and his allies insisted that only the Federal Republic had the right to represent the German people internationally. In December 1955, as the GDR sought to expand its own international contacts, Adenauer promulgated what became known as the Hallstein Doctrine (after the secretary of state in the German foreign office, Walter Hallstein). Under that doctrine, West Germany would regard it as an unfriendly act for any government other than the four World War II victors to establish relations with the GDR. This meant that Bonn would break relations with that government. It actually did with Yugoslavia. The doctrine effectively sealed off East Germany from most official contact with the non-communist world for most of two decades, although it did not prove easy to enforce and subjected the Federal Republic to a certain amount of blackmail from countries demanding West German aid in exchange for not recognizing the GDR.

Americans and Germans also began to establish closer relations in business and public life. The former U.S. High Commissioner, John J. McCloy, helped form an American private group, the American Council on Germany, to promote greater contact. In Germany, Eric Warburg, a banker who had fled the Nazis and returned to Hamburg after the war, helped form a partner organization, *Atlantik-Brücke* (Atlantic Bridge). Mrs. Eleanor Dulles, the sister of the secretary of state but a government official in her own right, spearheaded American campaigns to obtain greater support for West Berlin.

Adenauer might have been able to ignore the GDR, but he could not ignore the Soviet Union. Too many German prisoners of war still remained in Soviet hands after Moscow had stopped repatriation in 1950. Too many Germans were under Soviet domination. No German chancellor, especially one who wanted to keep foreign policy under his own control, would want to conduct his discussions with Moscow only through others. Nor could the Soviet Union ignore West Germany, which by the mid-1950s had become a rising European star while the GDR still reeled from the 1953 revolt.

Adenauer did not relish going to Moscow. But West Germany could not remain the only state that did not appear to embrace the "Spirit of Geneva" and peaceful coexistence in the more relaxed international atmosphere that followed the Geneva summit and the signing of the 1955 Austrian State Treaty, which provided for Austrian unity on condition of neutrality. When Bulganin and Khrushchev invited Adenauer to Moscow during the fall of 1955 to discuss the opening of diplomatic, cultural and economic relations, Adenauer accepted the invitation although he had turned down an earlier one. He knew that the Soviets wanted to talk mainly about trade, but he wanted to talk about prisoners. In order to show that he had other things than trade on his mind, he did not include Economics Minister Ludwig Erhard in his delegation.[11]

Adenauer and the Soviet leaders had no friendly chitchat. In bitterly disputatious talks, Khrushchev besmirched the Germans as followers of Nazism. Adenauer replied that it was Molotov who had signed the treaty with Hitler that had led to World War II through the 1939 invasion of Poland. Adenauer denounced the behavior of Soviet soldiers in Germany. Khrushchev replied in kind about German soldiers in the Soviet Union. Whenever Khrushchev talked about trade, Adenauer talked about prisoners of war. At one point, with the negotiations completely stalled, Adenauer instructed his pilot to file a return flight plan. That broke the deadlock, but Adenauer and Khrushchev needed several more days to establish diplomatic relations.

All topics of discussion proved contentious. But Adenauer achieved his purpose of bringing out at least some prisoners of war, although the numbers were disappointing. Out of over a million and a half German soldiers that were unaccounted for, Moscow released only 9,626 as well as about 20,000 civilians. Khrushchev in turn achieved his purpose of increasing trade. But neither of the men spoke of the "Spirit of Geneva." They had done what they needed to do, but each had swallowed a bitter pill.

By 1956, Khrushchev had reason to congratulate himself for having kept the GDR under control. Moscow's East European satellites suffered one crisis after another. First, Czechoslovakia had student protests. Then, in Poznan, Poland, a series of riots forced the Polish government to reverse some of its socialization policies before it could restore order. Finally, a full-fledged revolt broke out in Hungary during the fall of 1956. Only Soviet armored forces could reestablish

Hungary as a Soviet satellite. Hundreds of thousands of Hungarians fled to the West through neutral Austria.

Khrushchev could well have thought to himself that the Soviet bloc could survive such crises only with the GDR as a security zone between West and East. When he became premier in 1958 as well as party chief, Moscow's preference for a divided Germany became locked in stone.

THE STRATEGIC EQUATION

Stalin was lucky that he died in the first part of the decade, for he would not have liked what he would have seen in Germany after 1955. Moscow still controlled its old occupation zone and had the GDR for civilian administration, but the Soviet Union had no position in Germany or Europe as a whole. The KPD had sunk below five percent in West German election returns, and West Germany had become part of the Western strategic security system.

The United States, primarily a maritime power, needed reliable bases on the opposite shores of the great world oceans. It had found the ideal partner in West Germany. With a territory wide enough for major U.S. conventional and nuclear deployments, West Germany provided space for U.S. defense forces in Europe and joined Great Britain in becoming one of the most important European links in the American and Western strategic system. Even Stalin, who had dreaded the German-American link, could not have imagined its importance. The United States could station large numbers of ground forces and establish major air bases, enough to defend not only West Germany itself but all of western Europe and to give American power access to the Middle East, Africa and beyond.

The Federal Republic had started to become a military factor in its own right. Although West German public opinion continued to resist plans for a German army of 500,000, Adenauer had begun to build a force of a quarter million by the late 1950s. There was even talk of German nuclear delivery systems. Defense Minister Franz Josef Strauss suggested that Germany had the right to the same weapons as its major allies. While those allies seemed unlikely to give any German sole control over nuclear warheads, Moscow could not be sure.

For the immediate future, however, West Germany mainly relied on others, particularly the Americans, to defend it. To avoid having to match the numbers of Soviet and east European conventional forces, especially the large armored concentrations in East Germany, Washington deployed various nuclear weapons in western Europe and mainly in West Germany. They included nuclear bombs, nuclear artillery and in later years short- and medium-range missiles with nuclear warheads. Those weapons complicated Soviet tactics because they could prevent the massing of Soviet forces needed to break through German and other NATO defenses.

With the arrival of the American nuclear arsenal, an almost surreal dialogue developed between Bonn and its Western allies. Bonn wanted NATO nuclear weapons for deterrence. It hoped they would never be used, for every nuclear weapon could kill tens and perhaps hundreds of thousands of Germans. But Bonn had to plan for their use in order to deter the Soviets. And, to make certain that the Soviets were truly deterred, Bonn had to plan to have the weapons used in the first stages of a war. If they were used too late, Soviet forces would have the chance to overrun much of West Germany.

To deter effectively, Germany wanted NATO to prepare to use nuclear weapons first, before Moscow might use them. The "first use" doctrine, as it came to be called, made clear to Moscow that the West would use nuclear weapons at a time of its own choosing no matter what the Warsaw Pact forces might do. Although the Americans feared that any use of nuclear weapons in Europe might provoke a Soviet nuclear attack on the United States, they maintained the same first use principle. In a unique partnership of risk, West Germany and the United States had the most direct exposure to Soviet nuclear retaliation.

An equally surreal discussion developed over the best place to detonate the nuclear warheads. The "front line" between NATO and the Warsaw Pact ran through the middle of Germany. If nuclear weapons were used along that front line, both East and West Germany would be destroyed. NATO planners used to say "the shorter the missiles, the deader the Germans." German strategic planners therefore wanted NATO to have as many mid-range weapons as possible to aim as far east as possible, hitting Czech and Polish and perhaps even Soviet territory. Not only would this save German lives, but it also would increase the deterrent effect, for the Soviets and east Europeans would know of such plans and would think twice about attacking.

Deterrence, therefore, required planning for early use of nuclear weapons as far east as possible. Defense, and perhaps common sense, might suggest planning for later use. Neither the Germans nor any of their allies ever fully solved this dilemma. NATO planners rarely discussed it in public, except at the annual conferences of strategic planners convened by the International Institute for Strategic Studies or by the German strategic review, *Wehrkunde*, in Munich. But it remained the crucial dilemma of NATO strategy. So did the wish for "escalation control," with the West being able to choose what weapons to use when. While NATO planners did not want to reveal where they stored their nuclear weapons, they, as well as many Germans, knew that large numbers of warheads were in West Germany although not under West German control.

Moscow stationed nuclear weapons of its own in East Germany to supplement its conventional forces. At first, Soviet strategic planners concentrated on short-range nuclear missiles. Those did not directly threaten major European cities except in West Germany. But Khrushchev liked to remind his listeners that all of Europe would be at risk if the West began the nuclear exchange.

These were the devilishly difficult strategic and tactical questions that the West Germans and their allies attempted to answer in the mid-1950s and beyond. They represented real dilemmas for the West. But they represented even greater dilemmas for the East. On and under the soil of divided Germany and divided Europe lay enough nuclear material to blow all of Europe to the sky many times over. Ironically, if the struggle over Germany ever reached the military stage, Germany itself might not survive. But neither might those who had launched an attack.

Lord Ismay, secretary general of NATO, said that NATO served "to keep the Americans in, the Russians out, and the Germans down." But the Germans could not be kept down. Germany's partners, and especially the Americans, had to recognize the crucial importance of West Germany to NATO defenses and to the global interests of the United States.

THE SPLIT

After the mid-1950s, Germany and Europe remained militarily as well as politically divided between East and West. Two opposing military alliances faced each other, as did two opposing political, social and economic doctrines. The West had the North Atlantic Treaty Organization, linking western Europe and the north American continent. The East had the Warsaw Pact. The West also had a west European structure, the European Coal and Steel Community, soon to become the European Community, and the West European Union as the west European component of NATO. Moscow had the Council for Mutual Economic Assistance, the COMECON.

Stalin had failed. He had not been able to obtain a united and friendly Germany, either by force or by diplomacy. Lenin's dream of a firm link between the Russian and German proletariats remained a dream. Even with his 1952 note, Stalin never clearly decided whether he preferred a united Germany or a communist East Germany. This left the decision in the hands of others, whether Molotov's, Ulbricht's, or Adenauer's. And none of them held unity as a priority. Indeed, Adenauer continued to make clear that democracy and stability came first for him.[12]

Ulbricht, however, had succeeded. He had done so, paradoxically, by failing. His brand of communism in the Soviet zone had so alienated all Germans that

Stalin could not risk negotiating unification on terms that left any freedom of choice whatever. He had to negotiate an outcome, not a process. And opposition to Ulbricht in East Germany convinced Soviet leaders that he had to be kept in office by force. Ulbricht had been either very stupid or very smart. Moscow could not try for unification while he was around but had to keep him in place with his own Stasi state no matter how badly he managed it or how many fled. He could not claim legitimacy either by democracy or prosperity, but he could not be replaced.

Both West and East needed their parts of Germany. West Germany had become an important part of the Western system, providing the European continental pedestal of the great strategic arch across the Atlantic ocean. It had the largest and most prosperous economy in Europe. The D-mark, carefully managed by the Bundesbank, had become the most important world currency after the U.S. dollar. East Germany, in turn, had become the outer bastion of Moscow's east European strategic security belt. Its economy did not match West Germany's, but it provided Moscow and COMECON with some crucial necessities, including uranium from Wismut and machine tools from Saxony and Thuringia.

By 1956, Ulbricht's death strip separated eastern from western Germany, eastern from western Europe, and the Stalinist system from the Atlantic system. Few entered the death strip. Those who did, died.

Only one door remained open, the dividing line between the Western sectors and the Soviet sector of Berlin. It was here that the next test had to come.

The Airlift, August, 1948. Photo courtesy of Corbis-Bettmann.

Previous page: Winston Churchill, Josef Stalin and Franklin D. Roosevelt at Yalta, February, 1945. Photo courtesy of the Franklin D. Roosevelt Library.

Opposite page: Construction of the Berlin Wall, August, 1961. Photo courtesy of UPI/Corbis-Bettmann.

Tank Confrontation at Checkpoint Charlie, October, 1961. Photo courtesy of Corbis-Bettmann/UPI.

Opposite page: Ronald Reagan telling Mikhail Gorbachev to "tear down this Wall," June, 1987. Photo courtesy of the Ronald Reagan Library.

Overleaf: Dismantling the Wall, November, 1989. Photo courtesy of Corbis/Reuters.

EIGHT

THE BERLIN ULTIMATUM

ON OCTOBER 28, 1958, A GERMAN EMPLOYEE OF THE U.S. MISSION IN Berlin asked if she could see her American supervisor urgently. Highly agitated, she asked him whether the United States would take her and her family out of Berlin quickly if they were in danger because she worked for the Americans.

Asked to explain, she replied that Walter Ulbricht had said the previous day that the GDR would "neutralize" West Berlin. She had never heard Ulbricht say that before.

Whatever Ulbricht may have meant, she added, his words showed a more aggressive policy toward West Berlin. She and many others would be at risk if Ulbricht and the SED could "neutralize" West Berlin in their meaning of that word. After calming her fears, her boss alerted the U.S. State Department that Ulbricht had used a new word with ominous implications.[1]

The supervisor did not know that Ulbricht had long complained to Moscow about the open border to West Berlin. In 1957, he had asked a Warsaw Pact meeting to let him close the border. But Khrushchev and other east European leaders had turned him down because such an action would have undercut Khrushchev's public assertions that the East would soon overtake the West. Moreover, Khrushchev did not want to risk a nuclear confrontation over Berlin.[2]

But much had changed between 1957 and 1958. Soviet power and prestige had grown. Between May and August 1957, Moscow had begun testing intercontinental ballistic missiles (ICBMs). In October, the Soviet Union had created a sensation by launching two Sputnik satellites while the American space program literally sputtered on its launching pad. Khrushchev also had forged firm alliances with leaders of successful wars of liberation in the developing world.

Nevertheless, things had not changed for the better in the GDR. East German workers continued to flee in large numbers. By 1958, an estimated four million eastern Germans had fled to the West, with more than half (about 2.3 million) fleeing after the GDR had been founded.[3] Yuri Andropov, the head of the Soviet intelligence service and one of the most clear-sighted members of the Moscow establishment, warned the CPSU central committee that refugee flight from the GDR had reached a critical phase.[4] Soviet and East German officials met at least once a month to discuss it. Virtually all refugees crossed the sector border in Berlin. Ulbricht blamed the open border for his economic failures and told Khrushchev that something had to change.

KHRUSHCHEV SETS A DEADLINE

Once again, events in East Asia affected Germany. A sharp and highly dangerous confrontation between Beijing and Washington over the islands of Quemoy and Matsu off the shore of the People's Republic of China made Washington accept the division of China. Dulles admitted the existence of two Chinas as part of the bargain that ended the crisis. Ulbricht thought that Eisenhower and Dulles would accept two Germanys and two Berlins if they could accept two Chinas. He immediately called in the Soviet ambassador and told him that Germany had to be next on the agenda.[5] The neutralization of West Berlin led Ulbricht's wish list.

Khrushchev did not want another crisis on his periphery. He had urged restraint on China. But he agreed, under Ulbricht's pressure, to push for a complete division of Germany and for East Germany's protection from West Berlin influence. He wanted to get the problem out of the way quickly in order to concentrate on "peaceful coexistence" and a higher Soviet standard of living.

On November 10, two weeks after Ulbricht had called for neutralizing West Berlin, Khrushchev made a speech complaining that "the imperialists have turned the German question into an abiding source of international tension." He said the time had come for the signatories of the Potsdam Agreement "to give up the remnants of the occupation regime in Berlin."[6]

On November 27, Khrushchev sent a note to the Western occupation powers in firmer language and with a deadline. Accusing the Federal Republic of being like Hitler's Germany, he demanded a peace treaty with the two German states within six months.

Khrushchev reserved his most serious threat for West Berlin. He asserted that the West could not continue to keep its rights in Berlin long after violating the accords establishing those rights. He wrote that it was time to end the occupation regime in the city. If a peace treaty with both German states was not signed within six months, the Soviet Union would unilaterally transfer its authority in Berlin and over the access routes to the GDR. If the West did not accept GDR authority, the Soviet Union would defend the GDR. As for West Berlin, it was to become a "free city." Khrushchev described that as a concession because West Berlin sat on the territory of the GDR and should be a part of the GDR.[7]

Khrushchev had not yet decided on the exact treaty terms he would seek. Gromyko did not complete the Soviet treaty proposals until the end of 1958. He then prepared two drafts. One was for both Germanys and was to be signed by the four occupation powers. It provided for the partial withdrawal of foreign troops. This, Gromyko explained, "would be effectively tantamount to a collapse of NATO." After adding that "the Western powers and the FRG obviously will not agree with our proposals," Gromyko offered a second option: a draft for a separate treaty with Ulbricht. But he added that this should be used only after "the possibilities of political struggle with the whole of Germany will be sufficiently exhausted." This suggested that he and Khrushchev planned to use the new campaign as much for its political effect in West Germany and West Berlin as for a treaty itself.[8]

Ulbricht wanted quick action. He looked at the balance of power around Berlin. Khrushchev and he had overwhelming superiority. They controlled the access routes to Berlin and had more forces in the immediate vicinity. Soviet and East German troops could overrun the Western garrisons in West Berlin within a day. Ulbricht wanted direct action to challenge the Western Allies. He repeatedly told Khrushchev and others that West Berlin sat on East German soil and should be incorporated into the GDR.[9]

Khrushchev had to remain more cautious. Well aware of the Western weakness in Berlin, he also had to look over the horizon. He did not want a showdown with America. Although he talked as if he had nuclear superiority, he knew that he did not. He wanted to negotiate, hoping to use the prestige generated by Soviet space achievements to intimidate the West. Ulbricht might not care about the crises he might provoke, but Khrushchev did.[10]

Khrushchev did, however, hope to use the Berlin issue for a wider purpose. He wanted not only to change the Berlin situation but to divide the Western Allies, to split NATO at the English Channel, and to humiliate the United States so that it would be forced to withdraw its forces from Germany and continental Europe. West Germany would then have to turn to Moscow. Khrushchev thus had to win demonstrably and quickly. That would leave the Soviet Union with a European dominance that Russia had never enjoyed. It would give Khrushchev a chance to renew the old link between Russia and

Germany. It would dramatically alter the balance of power in the world, fully exploiting Moscow's advantage in space. Khrushchev wanted to win by pressure and negotiations what Ulbricht wanted to win by direct action.

Khrushchev also had to think about China. With the Sino-Soviet split having moved into open polemics after 1956, Khrushchev could not afford to appear less ideologically committed than Mao. But he also could not afford to put himself into a corner in which he would have to risk nuclear war. When Mao referred to the United States as a "paper tiger," Khrushchev reminded him that the paper tiger had nuclear teeth.

Khrushchev may have wanted to solve his Berlin and German problem by negotiations, but his demands were so far-reaching that the West would not yield unless he could bring overwhelming psychological pressure to bear. He had to generate an aura of invincibility and hope that the West would be sufficiently awed to yield.

Whatever the differences between Khrushchev and Ulbricht, by the end of 1958 they had decided to move. They had launched a dramatic venture that would bring the struggle over Germany to a new level of intensity. The woman at the U.S. Mission had seen only the first sign.

THE ALLIES DEBATE

Khrushchev's speech and note threw the West into disarray. Different Western leaders reacted differently. Each had his own specific interests and his own attitudes about the world, about the Soviet Union, about Europe and about Germany. Each had his private and sometimes not so private doubts about the others.[11]

Khrushchev had hit the leaders of the West at a sensitive moment. Eisenhower, close to retirement, wanted a strong position in Berlin but also would have liked a diplomatic success. Dulles believed in holding firm but did not want war. De Gaulle had returned to power only in 1958 and had to concentrate on trying to end the rebellion against French rule in Algeria. British Prime Minister Harold Macmillan wanted to regain Britain's old stature as one of the Big Three. Adenauer believed that the West held a strong position but feared that his allies might yield.

To complicate matters further, a Berlin challenge could take almost any form. Soviet or East German forces could directly block access to Berlin, which Western leaders regarded as unlikely. East German police could suddenly appear at rail or road control points, taking over duties previously carried out by Soviet soldiers. Soviet officials helping to staff the Berlin Air Safety Center (BASC) could walk off the job and refuse to guarantee the safety of Allied and civilian air flights through the corridors.

The Allies could agree on what to do if their rights were directly challenged. They found it harder to agree on how to deal with what they called "salami slices," or challenges that did not appear to warrant major crisis reactions. Such "salami slices," which might only alter procedures and might appear to affect Western rights only marginally, could over time take away a whole salami, an entire body of Western rights and Berlin needs. East German police replacing Soviet soldiers without blocking access amounted to a "salami slice," difficult to challenge but perhaps only a precursor of more to follow if one did not react promptly.

Eisenhower believed that U.S. nuclear superiority would keep Khrushchev from bringing the Berlin issue to a head. He remembered having supported General Lucius Clay's 1948 recommendation that force be used to break the Berlin blockade, and he saw no real change in the global balance since that time.[12] But he also believed that elements of the Berlin situation had become anachronistic. He did not want the Allies to rely only on what he termed "obsolete" agreements.[13]

Eisenhower also believed that the United States needed a solid anchor and major presence in Germany to support its European and global strategy. He did not want to do anything that would jeopardize Adenauer's position. Nor did he want to boost the GDR. But he did not want to risk war over something that the American people could not understand, such as a "salami slice."

Dulles felt that the United States could not lose Berlin without jeopardizing many other positions. When Khrushchev sent Anastas Mikoyan to Washington in January 1959 to learn the U.S. reaction to his note, Dulles told the CPSU leader in unmistakable terms that the situation would become extremely serious if Khrushchev chose to challenge Allied rights.[14] But, being a lawyer, Dulles sometimes approached issues in a way that the Germans regarded as legalistic. He believed that the Western Allies could accept East German personnel at the checkpoints as "agents" of the Soviet Union without recognizing the GDR. Dulles provoked a firestorm of protest in Germany, especially from Adenauer, when he said this during a press conference after Khrushchev's speech.

Adenauer and Berlin governing mayor Willy Brandt expressed deep shock over Dulles's "agency" theory. Adenauer told U.S. Ambassador David Bruce that any allied dealings with East Germans would imply recognition of the GDR. He also sent Ambassador Wilhelm Grewe to express the chancellor's concern to Dulles.[23]

More than any other Western leader, Macmillan wanted to negotiate a Berlin and German settlement. When he visited Khrushchev in Moscow in February–

March 1959, he concluded that the Western states should make concessions to avoid the risk of war.[15] He believed, as Churchill had in the early 1950s, that he had to guide U.S. policy and that talks on Germany would revive Great Britain's role as global arbiter. He thought that rejuvenating Britain's direct wartime links with Moscow and Washington would advance British interests more than the Atlantic and European structures erected by Ernest Bevin and Anthony Eden.

Macmillan thought Germany should remain divided for a long time and that the Allies should deal with East Germany. He thought the GDR had the right to stop the refugee exodus, and that Western rights in Berlin were "flimsy" and should be adjusted to new realities.[16] England, he warned, would not support a war fought over such a trivial matter as who stamped passports.[17]

Macmillan thought Eisenhower incompetent and inept.[18] Eisenhower and Dulles returned the compliment. Eisenhower found Macmillan "highly emotional" during a meeting on March 20, 1959, during which Macmillan constantly reiterated that eight atomic bombs could kill 20 to 30 million Englishmen. Macmillan broke off the meeting because he felt he could no longer discuss the issue.[19]

Macmillan reserved his sharpest quills for Adenauer, whose continental European orientation he disliked. In his memoirs, he complained that Adenauer had "sold his soul" to the French. He freely admitted that he had slept through much of Adenauer's presentation during a meeting between the four major Western leaders.[20] Whereas he kept his barbs about Eisenhower private until he published his memoirs, Macmillan derided Adenauer frequently and openly. Adenauer, who had an acid tongue of his own, replied by accusing Macmillan of flabby thinking and of wanting to sell out Germany to promote British interests.

De Gaulle remained unbending throughout the Berlin crisis. He saw no reason why the West should take Khrushchev's threats seriously. He thought it undignified to negotiate "just because Mr. Khrushchev has whistled" and said that "if we accept the Russian *diktat*, the Western alliance is finished."[21] To de Gaulle, the Soviet Union under Khrushchev was just another power which had permitted its grasp to exceed its reach and which would have to retreat.

De Gaulle felt that Khrushchev was asking for more than he could expect to receive. Comparing Khrushchev's demands with Western positions, he concluded that the two sides were too far apart to agree unless either capitulated. He saw no reason for the West to capitulate and no likelihood for Khrushchev to do so. The crisis would, therefore, peter out one day. De Gaulle thought negotiations more dangerous than stalemate because they would generate strong pressures for the West to make concessions. Nonetheless, de Gaulle often followed U.S. policy while making clear that he did not agree with it. He argued that he had to accept U.S. views in certain crises because the United States had the nuclear deterrent and France did not have it yet.[22]

De Gaulle supported Adenauer and insisted throughout the entire Berlin crisis that any decisions regarding the future of Germany had to be made by the Germans themselves and not by the former occupiers. He warned that any move to usurp German sovereignty would renew the German sense of betrayal that had helped destroy the Weimar Republic and bring Hitler to power. De Gaulle sharply limited the subjects on which the Allies could be prepared to negotiate and even to consult without full German concurrence. Wanting to build a strong Franco-German link for the future of Europe, de Gaulle worked especially hard to convince Adenauer that France was on his side.

Adenauer faced the most difficult problem. Having won the return of German sovereignty in 1954–1955 by agreeing to establish a new German army, he now found himself facing a political and diplomatic assault against the one part of Germany that had not regained sovereignty, Berlin. Worse than that, he saw that Khrushchev wanted to use Berlin as a lever to negotiate about Germany as a whole. And, because the talks would ostensibly deal only with Berlin, Khrushchev could conduct them with the Western occupation powers without West Germany. Adenauer would be excluded from negotiations about his own country. Khrushchev's tactic put Adenauer on the defensive, forced to remind his allies that Germany was no longer under occupation and was not to be bargained when that was exactly what they were under pressure to do.

Adenauer bitterly resented this situation. He believed that the future of Germany was at stake during the Berlin crisis. He also feared for German democracy because an unfavorable settlement would fuel a conservative reaction that could return the German Right to power. Germany must have a voice in its own fate, he insisted, if German democracy was to survive. But among the Allies only de Gaulle had the sense of history to understand and support Adenauer's argument.

The leaders of the West thus had their differences even as Khrushchev and Ulbricht did. As they moved toward a crisis over Berlin, all parties had to manage their disagreements with their friends as well as with their foes.

EISENHOWER TRIES SUMMITRY

The Western Allies could still hold together after Khrushchev's speech and note. In December 1958, they joined in a NATO declaration rejecting Soviet demands and insisting that "no state has the right to withdraw unilaterally from international engagements." The United States and West Germany sent equally firm replies to Khrushchev's letter. Khrushchev replied by sending Gromyko's first draft for a peace treaty to all states that had fought against Germany.[24]

Although it became clear that they did not follow a common line, especially after Macmillan's visit to Moscow, the Western foreign ministers invited Gromyko to a meeting of the four occupation powers in Geneva in May 1959. They hoped that the meeting would persuade Khrushchev to lift his ultimatum. The conference lasted until August, with Dulles's successor Christian Herter representing the United States after Dulles had died.

The Western powers tried to meet some of Khrushchev's demands by proposing an interim Berlin agreement that would include a ceiling on Western forces and would curtail some Berlin activities, such as the radio stations that specifically targeted East German audiences. Allied proposals would have begun giving Moscow and the GDR some voice in West Berlin, a concession many Berliners saw as a highly dangerous step toward neutralization. But in exchange the Allies demanded that Moscow continue to recognize Western occupation rights in Berlin. Gromyko rejected the proposals, insisting on abolition of Western rights.[25]

This foreign ministers' conference represented a significant departure from earlier meetings, however, in allowing for German participation. The four principals sat at a round table and the two German delegations sat at separate rectangular tables placed at a carefully calculated distance of two inches away from the main table. The German delegates could not address the meeting unless invited by one of the principals. This rather awkward formula, which Adenauer resented bitterly because it implied equal status for the GDR, reflected the growing awareness among the victorious powers that they could no longer reach agreement on Germany without German consent and presence.[26] But it kept the Germans in a subordinate role, seated at what the West Germans disparagingly (and angrily) called a *Katzentisch* (cat's table), reminiscent of the tables at which cats sat in some German children's fables.

As the foreign ministers' conference droned on, Eisenhower realized that he would not be able to point to any progress on which to base a four-power summit. Still wanting to meet with the Soviet leader, he issued a personal invitation for Khrushchev to visit the United States. Khrushchev accepted quickly and met with Eisenhower at the president's retreat at Camp David in September 1959. The two men reached no conclusions regarding Germany or Berlin but were able to establish a friendly atmosphere. Macmillan first denounced Eisenhower's invitation to Khrushchev as stupid and naive, but later concluded that it did help to defuse the Berlin crisis.[27]

The conference of foreign ministers and his visit to the United States persuaded and enabled Khrushchev to annul the six-month deadline for a Berlin treaty. He could say to Ulbricht and others that he had made progress. The ultimatum yielded to a much longer and more imprecise deadline of a year or more. Ulbricht did not like the delay, but had no choice in the matter.

The tone of Allied contingency planning, as leaked to the American press, may also have helped to convince Khrushchev to postpone a crisis. The contingency plans, which included military actions to break any Soviet or GDR interference with access to Berlin, must have made Khrushchev realize that any confrontation along the access routes posed a severe risk.[28] They must have also made Khrushchev hesitate about turning over access controls to Ulbricht, for he knew that Ulbricht might take risks.

Recent revelations by the former Soviet ambassador in Washington, Anatoly Dobrynin, show that Khrushchev did not want war with the United States and would do all he could to avoid it. Instead, he would bluff as long as possible to gain concessions from the West but would recoil from actual hostilities. Khrushchev even told Dobrynin that war with the United States was inadmissible.[29]

To advance Western consultations, de Gaulle invited Eisenhower and Macmillan to Paris in December 1959, with Adenauer to join later. This enabled de Gaulle to capture the initiative without appearing to act under the pressure of Khrushchev's ultimatum. De Gaulle then invited the Allied leaders and Khrushchev to a summit to be held in Paris on May 16, 1960. All accepted.

Khrushchev must have begun to ask himself whether he had been smart to accept. By the end of 1959 he had realized that the West would not alter its basic position on Berlin but offer only cosmetic concessions. Intelligence reports warned him that the United States would support Adenauer. Eisenhower had even told a press conference in February 1960 that he would ask for more liberal legislation about sharing nuclear secrets, a clear sign that the United States was preparing to give Bonn some access to nuclear weapons. When de Gaulle told Khrushchev during the Soviet leader's pre-summit visit to Paris that he saw no reason to sign a German peace treaty, Khrushchev realized that he would not achieve a breakthrough on Germany or Berlin without inordinate risk.[30]

Ulbricht pressed Khrushchev hard during early 1960. He complained that no peace treaty had been signed eighteen months after the ultimatum and that the refugee flow was increasing. Beijing leaders mocked Khrushchev's willingness to delay a treaty after first demanding one. Although they were privately urging Khrushchev to be cautious on Berlin, they criticized him elsewhere for having talked so loud and then having to back down.[31]

Khrushchev knew that he could not reach an agreement in Paris giving him what he wanted in Berlin. He thus seized the chance to leave Paris after an

American U-2 spy plane was shot down over Soviet territory only days before the planned summit and Eisenhower refused to apologize for the overflight. If Khrushchev had remained in Paris, he would have been forced to admit that he could not obtain a new four-power agreement and would have had to sign a separate treaty with East Germany. The resulting crisis would have helped Vice President Richard Nixon—whom Khrushchev detested—in the November presidential election against John Kennedy. Thus the Paris summit never met, to Eisenhower's disappointment, Macmillan's frustration, and Adenauer's relief.

The plans for the summit did, however, give de Gaulle another chance to woo Adenauer. Just before the abortive meeting, de Gaulle promised the chancellor that he would defend German interests and would inform Adenauer of the results.[32]

Khrushchev had a harder chore with his German ally when he stopped in East Berlin on his way home to Moscow. Ulbricht angrily said it was time to act, unilaterally if necessary, and that Khrushchev should take revenge for the U-2 humiliation by signing the German peace treaty then and there and confronting the West over Berlin. A Soviet diplomat informed Moscow that "at least seventy percent" of SED activists were in a "fighting mood" and wanted to storm West Berlin—although with Soviet troops in the vanguard. The SED also briefed Soviet officials about its plans for "purification" of West Berlin after a peace treaty had been signed.[33]

Khrushchev assured Ulbricht that he had not given up on the separate treaty but that he could not sign one right after the abortive summit without being accused of having broken up the meeting to have an excuse to sign the treaty. He also assured Ulbricht that they would have a better chance for progress on Berlin with a new American president. Khrushchev made a speech to SED activists to calm them down, but without solving Ulbricht's basic problem.[34]

Ulbricht undercut his own argument with Khrushchev, however, when he asked Moscow for more economic support and especially when he asked Khrushchev to provide contingency aid in case West Germany used economic sanctions to retaliate against East German moves against West Berlin. Only then did Khrushchev realize how badly the East German economy was doing and how deeply it depended on the West. Khrushchev told Ulbricht that he could offer no more aid. For the first time, Khrushchev saw how much the Soviet Union risked economically as well as militarily by a Berlin confrontation.[35]

When Ulbricht went to Moscow a month later with more proposals for Soviet steps against West Berlin, Khrushchev told him that under no circumstances would Soviet troops move into the city. Instead, he envisioned "gradually crowding out" the Western powers without war. He reiterated his pledge to sign a separate peace treaty at the appropriate moment while warning Ulbricht not to act unilaterally. Ulbricht had to postpone his plans.[36] Two years after his pledge to neutralize West Berlin, neither he nor Khrushchev had gained much.

The situation in East Germany continued to deteriorate. Refugees left at an ever-faster pace as Ulbricht's latest socialization program took hold and as his bombast against West Berlin frightened the people. Khrushchev and Ulbricht could only hope that the new American president would prove more ready to deal than the old. They eagerly awaited the inauguration of John F. Kennedy.

NINE

THE WALL

WHEN JOHN F. KENNEDY BECAME PRESIDENT IN JANUARY 1961, HE wanted to devise a more coherent strategy toward Berlin because he feared that a confrontation over the city could lead to nuclear war. He did not like the way Eisenhower had mixed firm statements of principle with deliberately fomented ambiguity to keep Khrushchev at bay. Kennedy wanted detailed positions.

Kennedy and his advisers worried constantly about escalation, fearing that minor incidents could become major crises if either side tried to overpower or outbluff the other. Kennedy thought that only precision and restraint could preserve peace.[1] He wanted to apply those principles to Berlin.

Truman and Eisenhower believed that Hitler had started World War II because he had thought that his enemies were weak and not ready to act. They strengthened and united the West to avoid having Moscow repeat Hitler's mistake. But Kennedy and his advisers looked more closely at the events that had led to World War I. They believed that a sequence of mutually threatening mobilization plans and actions had gotten out of hand and escalated into war in 1914.[2] They thought that U.S. policy should strive to avoid such misunderstandings.

Kennedy's attitude, however, contained a contradiction of its own. Throughout his campaign he had committed himself to reestablishing U.S. military superiority and to a more assertive defense and foreign policy. His advisers now feared that he might have talked too boldly and perhaps threateningly. Kennedy wanted Khrushchev to understand exactly what he would do and what he would not do. In his inaugural address he had spoken expansively about America "bearing any burden," but he had not intended this "burden" to include any needless risks over Berlin.

Kennedy did not look forward to crises. He had no experience in handling them. Although he promised to reassert American leadership, he did not want the kinds of confrontations that might result from it. He thought that Khrushchev would be reasonable because he would also fear war by miscalculation. Kennedy wanted to negotiate compromises on Berlin, Germany and elsewhere.

The new president surrounded himself with experts on the Soviet Union. They saw Germany and Berlin as problems in Soviet-American relations, not as separate U.S. interests in their own right. Charles Bohlen, one of the most re-spected Soviet experts, thus became a principal adviser on Berlin. In 1948, he had reportedly recommended ceding all of the city to the Soviets instead of try-ing to break the blockade.[3] McGeorge Bundy, the national security adviser, knew England better than the European continent and looked more to Harold Macmillan than to other Western leaders for advice.

Kennedy's foreign policy team did not include a senior expert on Germany. Dean Rusk, the secretary of state, wrote in his memoirs that Berlin had been as much a bone in his throat as in Khrushchev's.[4] Rusk had spent three years at Ox-ford University and had a profound dislike of "continentals." He had served in Asia during World War II and found that part of the world more congenial than Europe.[5] Foy Kohler, another expert on the Soviet Union, became the assistant secretary of state for European affairs, dealing with Berlin and Germany in the Soviet context. None of these men had been involved in the transatlantic bargain of 1954–1955 that had armed West Germany within NATO in exchange for sovereignty and protection.

Kennedy's advisers could brief him about the Soviet Union and about Asia but not about Germany, the nascent European movement or France. They drew him into talks with Moscow. They also drew him inexorably into Asia, first into Laos and later into Vietnam. But they felt no commitment to Berlin.

Kennedy used the British as unofficial advisers. Macmillan developed a warm and almost fatherly relationship with the young president. David Ormsby-Gore, who became British ambassador in Washington after Kennedy's inaugura-tion, had known Kennedy from the days when both were at school in London. A man of wit, charm and erudition, infinitely better suited to the Kennedy White House than the earnest and sometimes pedantic German ambassador Wilhelm Grewe, he frequently joined Kennedy family outings. Members of the adminis-tration sometimes referred to him as their "tutor."[6] Ormsby-Gore, like Macmil-lan himself, pressed consistently for a negotiated compromise on Berlin to improve ties with Moscow. Macmillan's fear of nuclear war over Berlin influ-enced Kennedy far more than it had influenced Eisenhower.

Trying to devise a new approach to Berlin and Germany, Kennedy wanted especially to know which U.S. interests were worth the risk of war. The words "miscalculation" and "escalation" became the touchstones. Any policy option had to avoid those two hazards.

Kennedy and his advisers decided that only three U.S. interests in Berlin were worth the risk of nuclear war: the Allied presence in West Berlin; Allied access to West Berlin on land and by air; and the freedom and viability of West Berlin itself. They termed those the "three essentials." The president decided that the United States would vigorously resist any Soviet action against those "essentials" but would not resist Soviet actions against any other element of the Allied position.

Kennedy's attitude toward Adenauer helped shape his attitude toward Berlin and Germany. The president had already written that "the age of Adenauer is over" and that the chancellor was a shadow of the past.[7] He believed that Adenauer had been too friendly with Eisenhower and Dulles and that he had favored Nixon in the U.S. presidential election. Kennedy found Adenauer old, unimaginative and excessively prone to recall agreements that he had made with Kennedy's predecessors. The president also complained that Grewe "gets on my nerves."[8]

But Kennedy did not only belittle Adenauer himself. He and Rusk frequently questioned the democratic and peaceful instincts of their German allies. At the end of November 1961, Kennedy gave an interview in which he said that he did not like the idea of a German finger on the nuclear trigger.[9] These words shocked Adenauer, who had held a friendly and apparently successful meeting with the president only weeks before the interview. In a letter to Khrushchev, Kennedy wrote that he noted "a spirit of nationalism and tension" in Germany, a comment that must have boosted Khrushchev's hope to make his own deal with Adenauer.[10]

Kennedy also abandoned the demand for Germany unification that had been a part of U.S. policy since the 1940s. He did not regard it as practical. Macmillan made him question whether it was even desirable. But Kennedy's view created immense problems for Adenauer. Although the chancellor knew that unification was unlikely in the near term, he needed to espouse it and needed Allied support for it to protect himself against charges from the German Right that he had abandoned German interests in his alliance with the West. Adenauer had told Kennedy this, but the president had not understood it.

Kennedy frustrated Adenauer by keeping West Germany out of Allied contingency planning about Berlin and Germany. During their first meeting in April 1961, Adenauer had asked Kennedy to include Germany in those consultations. He continued to ask. Kennedy ignored the requests but did not openly reject them. He invited the Germans to join only after the Berlin Wall had been built.

KENNEDY'S TRIAL BY FIRE

Because of his interest in relations with Moscow, the president wanted an early meeting with Khrushchev. He thought that it would provide a good opening for the kind of wide-ranging dialogue he wanted. Kennedy hoped to establish a broad agenda within which the two leaders could move toward the "peaceful co-existence" that Khrushchev claimed to espouse and that Kennedy sought. His advisers had told him that Khrushchev was tough but would be ready to deal.

Kennedy sent a personal note to Khrushchev on February 22, barely a month into his presidency, to propose a summit meeting. Although Khrushchev had earlier advised the president's brother and Attorney General Robert Kennedy (through an undercover Soviet channel that Khrushchev had opened) that he would like to meet with the new president as soon as possible, the Soviet leader did not reply to Kennedy for over two months. Kennedy's embarrassment over the failed Bay of Pigs invasion of Cuba in April 1961 may have made Khrushchev decide to take his time. He finally replied in May, by which time the Soviet Union had sent the first human into space, had seen its friends advance in Laos, and had watched Kennedy stumble in Cuba. Khrushchev must have believed that the delay had helped him.

The summit itself was set almost immediately, for June 4, in Vienna. Given the short notice, neither Kennedy nor Khrushchev could prepare themselves thoroughly on all possible agenda items, or take the time to find areas of possible agreement.

Nor could the Western Allies coordinate their views about Berlin and Germany before the meeting. A NATO foreign ministers' meeting of May 8 to 10 broke down in confusion because of differences between American and British views on the one hand and Germans views on the other. British foreign secretary Lord Home pressed the German foreign minister, Heinrich von Brentano, to tell the group what concessions Germany was prepared to make. Dean Rusk asked whether the West Berliners really would be prepared to endure another blockade merely for the sake of freedom. When von Brentano in turn asked for American contingency plans regarding a Berlin crisis and reiterated Adenauer's request to be included in Washington consultations, Rusk said that the United States had no fixed views on any Berlin subject. When Khrushchev reiterated his threat against Berlin a few days later, the Allies had not agreed how to react.[11]

The Vienna meeting with Khrushchev staggered Kennedy. His experts had told him that Khrushchev would want to negotiate about Berlin and that there would "probably be considerable flexibility" in the premier's position. But Khrushchev showed no interest in compromise. He treated Kennedy much more brutally

than he had treated Eisenhower at Geneva or at Camp David, bullying and be-
rating the president loudly and persistently throughout the meeting. Contrary to
the experts' predictions, he sounded especially threatening about Berlin.

Khrushchev reiterated that he would sign a peace treaty with East Germany
and warned that Western resistance would mean "there will be war." He exuded
raw power and oozed contempt, insisting that communism was the wave of the
future. Never before had a Soviet leader so openly threatened a U.S. president.
Never again was one to do so.

Well before the summit, Kennedy had been briefed that the United States
retained overwhelming superiority in missiles and other nuclear armament. But
he was not sure if Khrushchev knew it, and he decided not to put Khrushchev in
a corner by using the information. As Khrushchev's tactics showed no fear of
confrontation or war, Kennedy and his staff began to worry even more about the
danger of war by miscalculation.[12]

But Kennedy's warnings about "miscalculation" did not frighten the Russian, who screamed that the very word made him ill. Kennedy was threatening
him and he would not be threatened. He circled the president, wagging his finger angrily. He ended with a threat that he would act in Berlin, signing the treaty
with the GDR and ending Western rights. Kennedy did not say how he would
react, merely observing that "it will be a cold winter."[13]

In a statement that was not recorded in the official Soviet or American tran-
scripts because it was too provocative but that was reported later by Soviet participants, Khrushchev told Kennedy that, if the United States wanted to unleash
a war, let it be now before more terrible weapons were developed.[14]

The Americans, like the Soviets, showed their derision for the interests of
their German allies during the meeting. U.S. ambassador Lewellyn Thompson
told Khrushchev that the Americans would much rather deal with the Soviets
about central Europe than "leave it to the Germans." He added that "I refuse to
believe that your Germans are any better than ours," to which Khrushchev
replied "let's shake on that."[15]

U.S. political leaders and journalists concluded that the Vienna summit
had been a disaster for the president. Kennedy himself told his advisers that
Khrushchev "just beat hell out of me."[16] He spent days in contemplation and
near seclusion, trying to absorb the impact of what Khrushchev had said and
done to him. Rusk, who had urged Kennedy not to go to a summit that had
not been properly prepared, wrote that Kennedy had been sobered and
shaken.

George Kennan and other Soviet experts on Kennedy's staff privately criticized the president, saying that he should have contradicted Khrushchev's ideological statement about the superiority of communism. But those very same

advisers had not prepared him for this eventuality. They had led him to expect something very different from what he encountered.[17]

When Kennedy stopped in Britain on his way home from Vienna, he was still so shocked that he did not follow his original plan for a conference with Macmillan and the foreign office staff but instead talked privately with the prime minister at great length. Macmillan, who described Kennedy as "stunned" by the "almost brutal frankness and confidence" of the Soviet leader, used this meeting to press his own views on the shaken president. He presented what he called the "underlying realities" of Berlin, writing in his journal that he was glad to do that privately to avoid being accused of being "yellow" or afraid. He warned in urgent terms about the danger of nuclear war over Berlin.[18] Such words, coming after his tough meeting with Khrushchev, must have had a profound effect on Kennedy.

If Kennedy saw the summit as a disaster, Khrushchev claimed it to be a triumph, but, oddly, made that claim on the basis of an alleged meeting of minds that Kennedy certainly had not noticed. The Soviet premier left Vienna with a call for "the peaceful solution of controversial questions by means of negotiations." This left some questions as to what he might actually have wanted to achieve. When he first returned to Moscow, the Soviet press trumpeted the summit as a victory for the policy of "peace" as if some real agreements had been reached. It spoke of a new "Spirit of Vienna" and termed the meeting a "good beginning."[19]

But Khrushchev soon returned to threats, first against West Germany and then against the United States and the West as a whole. On June 9, within days after the summit, the Soviet press agency TASS published the full text of a threatening note that Khrushchev had given to Kennedy in Vienna. This came as a surprise to Rusk, who thought that the Soviet Union would have kept the note secret to make negotiations easier.

In his radio and television report on the summit, Khrushchev made no bones about his determination to change the situation in Berlin. Obviously emboldened, he reiterated his six-month deadline for the first time since 1959. He warned that "times have changed" and that the Soviet Union "has the means to defend its interests."

One of Khrushchev's staff, Fjodor Burlaski, told a Western journalist that Khrushchev had decided that Kennedy was "too young" and "too intellectual" to be able to make hard decisions. Khrushchev had seen Kennedy's restraint as a sign of weakness.[20] If some in Moscow still feared a clash over Berlin, Khrushchev could now assure them that Kennedy was not likely to react dangerously. Whatever Ulbricht or Khrushchev might do would not lead to war.[21]

But Khrushchev had not really helped himself at Vienna. He did not need to bully Kennedy if he wanted peaceful coexistence and wanted to concentrate Soviet resources on economic growth. He needed to negotiate with Kennedy, who had come to Vienna for that purpose. Instead, Khrushchev's boorish style and tactics had left Kennedy so convinced of impending crisis that he raised his defense budget by $7 billion, called up thousands of reserves, and lengthened the period of service in U.S. forces. Yuri Andropov complained that Khrushchev's behavior had mainly helped the U.S. military-industrial complex, forcing Kennedy into an arms race that the Soviet Union could not afford.[22]

Khrushchev knew the risk he was taking but chose to take it. Ten days before the summit, he had convened a special session of the CPSU politburo at which he had outlined his plan to exert as much pressure as possible on Kennedy. The only politburo member to advise against such tactics was Anastas Mikoyan, who had met with Eisenhower and Dulles earlier and thus understood the depth of the U.S. commitment to Berlin. Mikoyan thought that a friendly attitude would lead to a constructive dialogue that would improve Soviet-American relations. But Khrushchev dismissed Mikoyan's advice.[23]

Ulbricht viewed the summit as a triumph. Having long favored action over negotiations, he now believed firmly that Washington would not block moves against Berlin. Within a week after the meeting, Ulbricht made a speech asserting firmly that the West had no rights in any part of Berlin, East or West. He claimed that the GDR frontier lay on the Elbe River and that "the territory of West Berlin forms part of the territory of the GDR."

Ulbricht gave his own definition of what he envisioned for West Berlin when he demanded neutralization:

> The free city of West Berlin, after the conclusion of the peace treaty, will not be disturbed either by occupation forces or by agents' centers, or by radio stations of the organizers of the Cold War, or by other measures which might serve the preparation of war. That is to say, West Berlin must not be used . . . against the interests of the GDR and the socialist states . . . West Berlin is truly to be a neutral city.[24]

Ulbricht's ebullience over the Vienna outcome burst forth at a press conference on June 15, right after the summit. In reply to a question about refugee flight, he dismissed any suggestion that he would try to block refugees at the sector border between East and West Berlin, saying specifically that "we will not build a wall."

This statement was later widely interpreted as a sign of duplicity, with Ulbricht allegedly saying one thing while planning another. But it was actually the opposite. At that point, Ulbricht must have believed that he could solve the

Berlin problem, including the outflow of refugees, by converting West Berlin into his kind of neutral city. Such a city would not permit refugees to pass through it on their way to West Germany; it might not even accept them in the first place. Berlin would not need a wall through its middle. Ulbricht much preferred a wall between West Berlin and West Germany to a wall along the sector border.

Khrushchev and the Soviet military, like Ulbricht, followed up the summit with their own preparations for a test of strength with the West. On June 21, a date of immense symbolic importance because it was the anniversary of Hitler's attack on the Soviet Union, Khrushchev appeared at a Moscow rally in his World War II lieutenant general's uniform. A Soviet marshal told the rally that only Soviet troops were in Berlin by right of arms. Soviet forces had given the Western Allies their occupation sectors after the end of the war and therefore had a legitimate claim to the city as a whole.

Accurately, if perhaps uncharitably, Rusk said that the Germans were "nervous as cats" and "biting their fingernails."[25]

ULBRICHT GETS HIS WALL

Even before Khrushchev and Kennedy met in Vienna, Walter Ulbricht had again demanded that Khrushchev permit him to seal off the flow of refugees.[26] On March 30, 1961, he had told a meeting of the Warsaw Pact in Moscow that it might be necessary to close the sector border with barriers of some kind, perhaps with barbed wire, if there were no other solution to the Berlin problem.

But Ulbricht had met with the same widespread skepticism that he had encountered in 1957. Khrushchev had criticized the proposal as premature. And the Hungarian delegation had warned that such an action would sully the reputation of the entire Warsaw Pact. Ulbricht could only get consent to make full and secret preparations to study what might need to be done to stop the flow of refugees. The Soviet embassy had even warned Khrushchev that Ulbricht had become so impatient that he did not seem to understand that sealing the sector border would complicate negotiations for a German peace treaty.[27]

As the summer advanced, Ulbricht put Khrushchev into an increasingly uncomfortable situation. He urged prompt action to stop the refuge flow by blocking air traffic out of West Berlin. To show Khrushchev that the Allies would not react, he began to harass Autobahn traffic to Berlin over the summer. But he hurt his own cause. The sharp tone of the Allied protests persuaded Khrushchev that he was not ready for that kind of confrontation.

The Soviet premier increasingly wondered whether he could trust Ulbricht to control the access routes. By giving Ulbricht that authority, Khrushchev would give him leverage over relations with the West. The impatient SED leader could create a crisis at his own choosing, whether it suited Khrushchev or not, and Khrushchev would have to back him or appear weak before the Chinese and others. Khrushchev feared that Ulbricht could put the entire Soviet empire at risk.[28]

De Gaulle's analysis was bearing fruit. Faced with the risk of nuclear war, Khrushchev hesitated. As Ulbricht became more assertive, Khrushchev became more cautious. He faced the risk of a war that the Soviet Union could not win and the risk of yielding one of the most sensitive levers of political pressure to a man whose judgment he increasingly questioned. The Soviet military also became anxious about Ulbricht.

Ulbricht's pressures already created realities that complicated both Khrushchev's and Kennedy's decisions. The threatening tone of his June 15 press conference had caused an overnight surge in the refugee flow, fueling what the Germans named *Torschlusspanik*, a frantic race by East Germans to get to the West before the exits closed forever. More than 100,000 East Germans had fled during the first six months of 1961, with 20,000 fleeing in June alone. In July, 30,000 left. Planes flying out the air corridors from Berlin to West Germany were so full of refugees that extra flights had to be added.

Three American statements helped Khrushchev find a way out of his dilemma.

The first statement came from Kennedy himself, when on July 25 he told the press his "three essentials": the freedom of West Berlin, Allied rights in West Berlin, and Western access to West Berlin. Kennedy spoke in a firm and determined tone, making clear that the United States would defend those rights and that he would take steps to increase U.S. military readiness. But the president said nothing about the wider occupation rights over all of Berlin that the Allies had reserved in the *Deutschlandvertrag*.

The second statement came from William Fulbright, chairman of the U.S. Senate Foreign Relations Committee. On July 30, he said publicly that he did not understand why the East Germans did not simply close their borders to stop the refugee flow. He added that they had the right to do so at any time "without violating any treaty."[29]

The third, a week later, came again from Kennedy, when he refused to distance himself from Fulbright's remarks when asked about them during a press conference.

Ulbricht reacted immediately. On July 31, citing Fulbright's statement to show that the United States would not help the refugees, he asked Khrushchev to close the air corridors between Berlin and West Germany because they carried refugees. Khrushchev refused. Instead, he and Ulbricht agreed that Ulbricht could put a wall around West Berlin. Khrushchev said that Soviet forces would not be involved so that they could not be accused of violating their agreements on Berlin.

Khrushchev also told Ulbricht to get the approval of the Warsaw Pact states. At a secret session from August 3 to 5, Ulbricht made a long plea running over fifty pages. He argued that the West German government was blocking Kennedy's and Macmillan's efforts to negotiate a peace settlement for Germany. He warned that the Federal Republic was trying to acquire nuclear weapons to use against the Warsaw Pact states. As part of this policy, he argued, West Germany was trying to undermine the existence of the GDR by sending agents, recruiting spies and trying to generate popular resistance. He added that these "aggressive measures" had already harmed the GDR and had to be stopped.

Although Ulbricht talked about blocking the sector borders, he insisted that it was the problem of West Berlin as a whole that needed to be solved. He added that a wall would only be a step toward a peace treaty and would not be an end in itself; only a treaty would fully solve the Berlin problem.

Ulbricht revealed far-reaching ambitions toward West Berlin. He told the Warsaw Pact leaders that the GDR should have "full control" over all traffic to and from the city, including air as well as surface traffic and Allied military as well as German civilian travelers. He added that all air traffic should be forced to use the East German airfield at Schönefeld just south of Berlin, so that all passengers and air cargo would have to pass across GDR territory and could be checked (and perhaps stopped) by East German officials.

But Ulbricht also promised the Warsaw Pact some benefits. He said that the existence of West Berlin compelled GDR economic planners to keep East German living standards higher than they should be. Once the city had been neutralized, the East German economy could concentrate more on Warsaw Pact and COMECON needs than on its own.[30]

The Warsaw Pact states, and Khrushchev himself, thereupon gave their consent to a wall. But Khrushchev insisted that Ulbricht had to proceed gradually, first using barbed wire to block access. He was to begin building a wall only if the Western powers had not reacted after several days. Khrushchev, mistrustful of his ally and anxious to avoid a nuclear showdown, warned that Ulbricht was to act with care and that he was not to advance "one millimeter" beyond what the meeting had authorized.

Khrushchev wanted one additional assurance from Ulbricht. Although he now believed that the United States would not react, he still worried about the reaction of the East Berliners. Khrushchev asked whether the East German police could contain a possible uprising. He did not want to have to use Soviet tanks as in 1953. Ulbricht returned to Berlin to discuss this problem with security officials. Three days later, back in Moscow, he said that it could be done. He argued that Fulbright's and Kennedy's statements made it clear that the East German police would be able to close the border undisturbed by any Western reaction which might provoke problems in East Berlin.[31]

Khrushchev thus did not give Ulbricht what he wanted most: permission to stop the refugees from leaving on the access routes from West Berlin. That would have begun the process of neutralizing West Berlin without a wall. Instead, he let Ulbricht seal off East Berlin. But he refused to use Soviet forces for that purpose, for he did not want to commit Soviet prestige in case the Allies reacted and the move failed.

Khrushchev had picked the right course. On August 5, the British, French and U.S. foreign ministers met secretly in Paris to decide about how to react to a possible Soviet move on Berlin. They agreed that any steps by Khrushchev and Ulbricht in East Berlin would be defensive in nature and would not be worth blocking at what they thought would be the risk of a war. Within three weeks, Khrushchev had received a full report on the meeting.[32]

To keep control over Ulbricht and the Berlin situation, Khrushchev sent Marshal Ivan Konev to assume command of Soviet forces in East Germany. Konev, whose rough manner had earned him the nickname "the tank," had repeatedly beaten Nazi troops during World War II. He had won the battle for Prague and had helped to conquer Berlin. He was known to despise Germans, and he told those who welcomed him in Berlin that he had come to take charge.[33]

Konev and his fellow Soviet officers showed their contempt for the East Germans at a party that he gave for Allied occupation liaison officers at the Soviet army headquarters in Zössen-Wunsdorf shortly after his arrival. As the drinks and the toasts in Russian, English and French flowed freely, Konev turned to Ivan Yakubovsky, the Soviet general he was replacing as commander, and asked, "And how do they say a toast in this country, General?" Yakubovsky replied, "Why, this is the way they say it here," and he made yet another loud toast in Russian to show who was in charge in the GDR. Konev and the other Soviet officers roared with laughter.[34]

All this did not bother Ulbricht, if he even heard of it. Now he had the authority he had long sought. He called together the forces needed to seal off West Berlin. He did not trust East Berlin police or border guards to string the wire but ordered special units sent in from Saxony to make sure that the police would carry out their orders. The Saxons would feel no loyalty to Berliners and would not be sure exactly where they were or what precisely they were doing. The Berliners called the Saxons the "fifth occupying power." Ulbricht instructed the Stasi to coordinate the effort. To keep it secret, he gave the operation a code name.

That code name was "Rose."

THE ALLIES THANK ULBRICHT

Shortly after midnight on Sunday, August 13, 1961, Walter Ulbricht's Saxon police began unrolling barbed wire along the sector border between East and West Berlin and along the border between West Berlin and East Germany. They also closed and sealed the access gates at rail and subway stations, making it impossible for East Berliners and East Germans to get on trains bound for West Berlin. No Soviet forces took part although they were on alert and had some patrols driving around the city to keep an eye on the operation.

Simultaneously, the GDR published a decree announcing the closing of the borders and listing the East-West Berlin sector border crossing points still open for West Berliners, West Germans, and non-Germans. The decree stressed that the closing would not affect Allied rights because Allied personnel could still enter East Berlin. The measures would protect the GDR against West German and West Berlin smugglers, spies and subversives. A supporting Warsaw Pact statement also stressed that arrangements governing Allied access would not change.

East Berliners and East Germans who had waited for that day to flee stood at the crossing points and the subway stations, weeping disconsolately. Some could still escape by leaping across barriers or by finding a way through old houses along the sector border, but the police sealed those routes as fast as they could find them. Erich Honecker supervised the operation personally. Later in the day, Ulbricht visited some of the police and congratulated them for "defending the Republic."

As the day progressed, crowds of East and West Berliners assembled on both sides of the border. East German police, often in armored cars equipped with water cannons, pushed the East Berliners back. West Berlin police also tried to prevent crowds from getting too close to the barbed-wire barriers. They feared West Berliner moves against the barriers, perhaps leading to riots and casualties in possibly violent confrontations with East German police.[35] Brandt returned from a trip in West Germany to try to keep control over the situation. The Western military and diplomatic missions in West Berlin sent urgent cables to their capitals to inform them of what was happening and to urge some type of response.

Even as these desperate scenes unfolded in Berlin, the U.S. embassy in Bonn and the administration in Washington greeted the frantic news reports and messages with glacial calm. The duty officer at the Bonn embassy did not bother to tell the ambassador, Walter Dowling, about the cables. Dowling learned of the crisis in Berlin only after he had left his residence to throw out the first ball at a little-league baseball game. To show a studiedly calm reaction, he threw out the ball and went to his office only after the game had started.

Washington reacted with equal and perhaps even more deliberate nonchalance. Kohler told the State Department duty officers who called him at home that he would not come to the office. Instead, he said that they should "play it cool and not be rushed into making rash statements." He added that "the East Germans have done us a favor."[36]

Rusk did the same, as he had already decided that no action could or should be taken. He squelched the protest note that the Allied missions in Berlin had hastily drafted, stating that any U.S. reaction would come from Washington. Shamefaced American officials in Berlin had to tell their British and French colleagues as well as Brandt that the United States would accept Ulbricht's action without even a protest.

Rusk thought that the East German actions presented no threat to peace. He did not know how very cautiously Khrushchev had approved Ulbricht's actions and that an Allied reaction would have stopped the East Germans from going further. Instead, he feared that any reaction would lead to escalation. He warned that "if you take that first step by military means, then you must think of the second, third, and fourth steps." Therefore, he preferred to do and say nothing.[37]

Rusk told Kennedy, who was spending the weekend sailing at Hyannis, that the Soviet forces had not moved and only the East Germans were taking action to build the border barriers. He cited the Warsaw Pact statement guaranteeing Allied access. Thus, he said, any Allied reaction might even be provocative. He urged that the U.S. government release a statement pointing out that the East German actions were aimed at their own residents and not at the Allies. He thought the West should try to take propaganda advantage of this demonstrated failure of the communist system.

Rusk and Kennedy concluded that Khrushchev's decision to seal the border against refugees actually eased the Berlin crisis because Moscow had solved its most urgent problem within the city itself, not by trying to cut the access routes as the Allies had feared. Kennedy said to his assistant Kenneth O'Donnell that the East German action was "not a very nice solution but . . . a hell of a lot better than a war."[38] Rusk and other Kennedy advisers believed that the border seal-off meant the end of the Berlin crisis because it would stop the refugee flow. Kennedy thought the same.[39]

The American reaction played into Ulbricht's hands. As soon as he had begun stringing the barbed wire, he had launched a whispering campaign in West Berlin suggesting that the Americans had been informed in advance of the sector closing and had agreed to it. The accommodating U.S. response appeared to confirm those rumors and gave the impression that the Allies were scheming with Ulbricht against their friends and against refugees. Ulbricht could not have asked for an Allied response more likely to destroy West Berlin confidence.

Brandt, who had thought that Kennedy supported Berlin and the Berliners, wrote to the president in despair. He pleaded for some reaction and even proposed that West Berlin be made into a three-power city. The letter angered Kennedy, who dismissed it as a political trick aimed at the upcoming German elections and who thought it presumptuous for Brandt to address him as "friend." His reply, distant and cool, rejected three-power status for West Berlin.[40]

But other voices began to press in on Kennedy. Marguerite Higgins, a veteran *Herald Tribune* reporter, contacted General Lucius Clay in New York and they agreed to tell Kennedy that more than refugee flight was at stake. She then visited Hyannis to warn Kennedy that he could not afford to ignore what had happened. She urged prompt and dramatic action.

At the German desk in the State Department, those who feared the impact that the East German measures would have on West Berlin and Germany protested furiously and vociferously. Their dismay reached others who could get to Kennedy directly. Clay wrote separately to General Maxwell D. Taylor, Kennedy's military adviser, to warn privately that the Berlin situation was very serious and to offer his services.

The most important direct admonition to Kennedy came from Edward R. Murrow, a distinguished reporter who had become the director of the U.S. Information Agency. He happened to be in Berlin on August 13. After traveling around the city and meeting with numerous Berlin officials and others, he sent a personal cable directly to Kennedy telling the president that Ulbricht was aiming not only at the East Germans but at the faith that West Berliners and West Germans had in the Americans. He warned of a crisis of confidence that could destroy not only the Allied position in Berlin but the U.S. position throughout western Europe. He ended by saying that "what is in danger of being destroyed here is that perishable quality called hope."[41]

Murrow's cable had a profound effect on Kennedy. While the president and his advisers could dismiss the attitude of the U.S. Mission in Berlin as a symptom of "clientitis" and "localitis," Kennedy held Murrow in the highest esteem. Moreover, the American press echoed the theme. Many editorials all over the

West criticized the Allies and especially Kennedy. Richard Nixon accused him of indecision. Kennedy realized that he faced a political crisis at home and in Europe as well as in Berlin.

Kennedy chose to underscore the American commitment to West Berlin no matter what happened on the sector border. He decided to send Vice President Lyndon Johnson and General Clay to Berlin to show that he was fully prepared to protect the freedom of West Berlin even if he could not prevent Ulbricht and Khrushchev from stopping the refugee flow. He even accepted Clay's suggestion to order the simultaneous arrival in West Berlin of a U.S. battle group from West Germany, although Kennedy's Soviet experts bitterly opposed the suggestion as being too provocative. Clay found then, as he was often to find later, that Kennedy supported action on Berlin even when his advisers did not.[42]

Johnson's visit on August 20 proved a huge success. He drew large crowds of Berliners, especially because Clay, the hero of the Berlin Airlift, accompanied him. The arrival of the U.S. army battle group, personally met by the vice president, reinforced Kennedy's message. Ulbricht ordered East German troops and police to seal off the Autobahn that day so that no East German could approach the battle group to ask for asylum or to show support.

Johnson's visit left a bitter taste, however, in the mouth of Konrad Adenauer. When the vice president stopped in Bonn before flying to Berlin, Adenauer asked to accompany Johnson and Clay to Berlin. His presence would underscore the fact that Berlin, while not a part of the Federal Republic, was a legitimate German interest. But Johnson, on the advice of the White House staff, did not allow the chancellor to join him. The official explanation was that the United States did not want to take sides in the election campaign between Adenauer and Brandt, but Adenauer and many other Germans suspected that the White House feared offending Khrushchev. Adenauer never forgot the slight, which helped to poison his relations with Kennedy.[43]

Other Allied governments also held back. Macmillan, who was shooting grouse in Scotland on August 13, wrote in his journal that "there is nothing illegal in the East Germans stopping the flow of refugees." He thought the GDR had been compelled to act, and added that sealing the sector border was "not (I believe) a breach of any of our agreements."[44] Britain did, however, send three armored cars and some soldiers with the U.S. battle group in response to Kennedy's personal plea to Macmillan.

France made no military gestures of any kind, not sending even a token group of reinforcements to Berlin. Instead, Paris reprimanded the French commandant for having sent troops to the sector border. Many French officials even felt a sense of relief that the Soviets and East Germans had merely closed the sector borders instead of challenging Allied access rights to Berlin.

And de Gaulle had insisted from the beginning that the United States had the principal responsibility for military action. If Washington did not move, Paris would not. More important, Kennedy's acquiescence in Ulbricht's action served de Gaulle's strategic objective of protecting German interests against the Anglo-Saxons and not against the East.

The events of August 13 did not end the debates among the Allies. Macmillan argued even more strongly for negotiations with Khrushchev. De Gaulle maintained his aloof opposition, warning Kennedy in a personal letter on three specific points: first, that the opening of negotiations under pressure would be seen as "a prelude to the abandonment . . . of Berlin, and as a sort of notice of our surrender"; second, that the Soviet Union would follow by making arrangements with "a number of our allies of today" (an obvious reference to de Gaulle's constant fear of a Soviet deal with West Germany); and, third, that France would not join in talks "which are in fact demanded by Moscow." He concluded, however, by giving Kennedy the opening that the president wanted, stating that the United States was of course free to explore the possibility of negotiations if it chose.[45] De Gaulle was setting a trap for Kennedy; any such exploration would destroy Adenauer's confidence in the United States and force him to turn to Paris.

Adenauer, whose representatives had begun to be included in the Allied consultations after the Wall had been built, opposed negotiations. He knew that the West had no strategic objectives and he feared that Kennedy would be hounded into concessions. He also believed that Khrushchev would make Kennedy and Macmillan ignore the interests of the Federal Republic by promising a deal on Berlin.

Adenauer asked Rusk to assure him that Kennedy regarded the 1954 Paris Agreements as the basis of U.S. policy. Rusk pointedly refused to give that assurance. This upset Adenauer, who concluded that Washington wanted to join London in treating Germany as a defeated vassal instead of as a sovereign ally.[46]

After hearing Allied views, Kennedy decided to negotiate with Khrushchev. He believed that he had shored up the American position and Berlin morale sufficiently by sending the battle group. He also decided to ask General Clay to return to Berlin as his personal representative in the city.

Khrushchev had a clear idea of American policy by then. His ambassador in Belgrade had asked George Kennan, whom Kennedy had sent as U.S. ambassador to Yugoslavia, whether the United States would agree to recognize two German states. Kennan, known to be close to the White House, said that this appeared "reasonable."[47] That reply showed Khrushchev that Kennedy would make concessions on Germany to have peace in Berlin.

Khrushchev had gained a respite by letting Ulbricht close the border. They had stopped the refugee flow. They now needed to find the combination of pressure and diplomacy that would make Kennedy surrender the "three essentials." Having sealed East Berlin, Khrushchev and Ulbricht began their attack on West Berlin.

TEN

THE BATTLE FOR WEST BERLIN

GENERAL LUCIUS CLAY ARRIVED IN BERLIN AS PRESIDENT KENNEDY'S personal representative on September 19, 1961. Brandt called on the Berliners to line the streets to greet a friend. Along the wide avenue that bears his name and along the crowded Kurfürstendamm, they welcomed the man who had saved them once and might save them again. Their cheers reflected both their hopes and their fears.

The Berliners wondered whether Clay could produce yet another miracle. He knew no better than they, but he knew they were counting on him to try. He also knew that he would have to move fast to maintain the momentum of his arrival.[1]

Clay understood that Ulbricht wanted not only to seal off East Berlin but to neutralize West Berlin. Contrary to Washington's thinking, he feared that August 13 had begun, not ended, the battle for Berlin. As he told Kennedy, he expected Ulbricht to keep up the pressure.[2] West Berliners' morale would make the difference. So would the city's prospects as seen from abroad. During the weeks after August 13, young persons had begun to leave West Berlin in large numbers, and the level of investment had crumbled. Clay needed to reverse that.

Ulbricht had taken advantage of Allied hesitation. Within three days after his original edict closing the sector border, his forces began building the Wall, as the Warsaw Pact had authorized him to do if there was no Allied reaction to the barbed wire. A week after that, on August 23, he reduced the number of crossing points through the Wall. He shut off all traffic through the Brandenburg Gate and let foreign persons and vehicles enter East Berlin through only one crossing point, the one where Friedrichstrasse crossed the Wall and the border between the Soviet and U.S. sectors. To show his power and Allied impotence, he forced the theoretically sovereign Allies to use that single entry point, making British and French cars detour through the center of the city in order to enter East Berlin. The Friedrichstrasse crossing became known as Checkpoint Charlie, being so designated in a U.S. military naming system that labeled the two Autobahn checkpoints on the way to Berlin as Alpha and Bravo.

Ulbricht then issued a further decree instructing West Berliners to remain 100 meters (328 feet) away from the Wall. Violators would be shot. Thus he began to show that his writ ran into West Berlin and that people living near the border had better watch their step.

The Wall had solved Ulbricht's refugee problem. Fewer and fewer persons could still find a way to the West. Ulbricht had taken a step toward neutralizing West Berlin, but, as he had told the Warsaw Pact, he needed to do more. He needed to raise ever greater doubts about the commitment of the Allies and especially of the Americans. As his police shot and killed those still desperate enough to try to flee, and as the Allies did nothing, West Berliners should begin to recognize who was in charge.

Ulbricht wrote to Khrushchev on September 16 that "the enemy took fewer counter-measures than were to be expected" and that "GDR state authority has risen in public consciousness." He specifically suggested that Khrushchev instruct the Soviet occupation authorities in East Germany to reject any Western protests to any actions that the GDR or Moscow might take in Berlin or, better yet, to refuse even to accept Western protests. He also suggested some steps against the access routes.[3]

Khrushchev, whose ambassador in East Berlin had reacted angrily to the East German decree naming Friedrichstrasse as the only foreign crossing point (presumably because he believed that no German should be telling any occupier what to do), wrote back on September 28. He expressed pleasure that August 13 had gone so well but added that the most important next step should be a peace treaty and that Ulbricht should do nothing to jeopardize it.[4]

CLAY MAKES HIS MOVE

Clay looked about urgently for ways to counter Ulbricht, and the first chance came within days after his arrival. On September 21, despite Khrushchev's injunction to Ulbricht, East German Volkspolizei (Vopos, or People's Police) began harassing U.S. and other Allied personnel traveling along the Autobahn to Berlin, especially U.S. military who were not in uniform but were in clearly marked occupation vehicles. The Vopos stopped cars, made the Americans get out, threatened them and refused to let them proceed. They sometimes interrogated or held them for hours. Other travelers, including Berliners, saw how the Vopos could bully Americans.

Clay immediately ordered U.S. radio-equipped "courtesy patrols" and "flag tours" to travel back and forth along the Autobahn every hour or so to help any Americans stopped by the Vopos. The Soviets protested but did not block the patrols. Later, when the Soviets did attempt to block the patrols, Clay replaced them with convoys of U.S. military vehicles that traveled back and forth at random hours several times a day.

The courtesy patrols and convoys made East German harassment more precarious and virtually eliminated it within days. The patrols may even have been tacitly welcomed by the Soviets in East Berlin because of their private concerns about Ulbricht and their discomfort at having any German moves against any occupation power.[5]

Clay also ordered U.S. forces in Berlin to patrol the U.S. sector border facing the Wall so that Ulbricht could not carry out his threat to shoot West Berliners. The patrols were to show themselves openly and frequently. Moreover, if East German guards harassed any U.S. vehicle in East Berlin, Clay instructed U.S. soldiers to delay a Soviet car in West Berlin. Marshal Konev, who wanted freedom of movement for his own soldiers and had no affection for the GDR, told Ulbricht to stop the East Berlin harassment.

Clay's next chance came over Steinstücken, a tiny community that had been assigned to Berlin when the city's administrative borders had been drawn in the nineteenth century although it actually lay about 100 meters (328 feet) away from the main body of the city. It consisted of several hundred square meters of land with only a handful of houses and inhabitants.

Steinstücken became the site of Clay's and Ulbricht's first open confrontation by chance. An East German refugee whose intended escape to West Berlin had been blocked by the new border controls had fled to safety in the little exclave. Vopos threatened to enter Steinstücken to bring him out although Steinstücken was U.S. occupation territory.

Clay believed that neither the U.S. government nor Kennedy himself could live down the humiliation of having the GDR seize a refugee who had sought American protection. When the U.S. military hesitated to get the refugee out for fear of escalation, Clay ordered a helicopter for his personal use and instructed the pilot to land him at Steinstücken accompanied only by his civilian assistant. Having learned that no resident had a television set, he brought one with him as a gift. He remained in Steinstücken less than an hour and then flew the refugee out to West Berlin. East German border guards trained their guns on the helicopter in a show of force but did not dare shoot at an American military craft.[6]

Clay cabled Kennedy to tell the president what he had done. Knowing that White House advisers would criticize his action as provocative, he ended his cable with the sentence "I am not afraid of escalation." He wanted to begin to influence Kennedy's tactical thinking.

The Berliners reacted predictably to Clay's actions and especially to his flight to Steinstücken, cheering wildly the next time he appeared in public. Kennedy also probably understood, although his advisers pilloried Clay and Macmillan complained. De Gaulle said nothing.

Clay had drawn his own conclusions about Soviet attitudes. He did not fear that Khrushchev would escalate over Berlin. Contrary to Kennedy's advisers, Clay shared de Gaulle's conviction that the Soviet leader did not want a war. Having been on the president's foreign intelligence advisory board, he knew that U.S. military power remained comfortably ahead of Moscow's. He also believed that Khrushchev knew that he could not risk a war. He thought the United States need not fear Khrushchev's bluff.

Clay believed that any Allied reaction would make Khrushchev uneasy. Therefore, he wanted the Allies to become unpredictable. Before Clay had arrived in Berlin, Khrushchev and Ulbricht could be certain that the Allies would respond to any new harassment or to any further infringement of their rights merely with a protest note, if at all. They had no reason to stop. But if Khrushchev had to expect the unexpected, he would hesitate. Clay believed that Khrushchev feared escalation at least as much as Kennedy did. If Khrushchev believed that he and Ulbricht could control the temperature of the Berlin crisis, he would keep it bubbling. But if Khrushchev feared it boiling over, he would turn off the heat. Thus, two could play at escalation.

To end the Berlin crisis, Clay had to make it unpredictable and potentially dangerous enough for Khrushchev and Konev to clamp down on Ulbricht. Khrushchev hoped to create as unstable a situation as possible, manipulating the West Berliners to flee the city because they had lost their confidence in the U.S. and also making the Allies negotiate the withdrawal of their troops. Clay thought that uncertainty about Allied reactions would make the Soviet leader think twice and finally decide to leave the city alone.

Clay believed that with solid support he could cope with any confrontation that Khrushchev or Ulbricht might provoke, and that he could do it in Berlin itself. He thought that a Berlin confrontation would not lead to a nuclear showdown, and that Khrushchev would never provoke such a showdown anyway unless he felt certain that Kennedy would yield.

Kennedy's advisers, and especially his experts on the Soviet Union, fought this analysis. They told Kennedy that Khrushchev meant exactly what he said and would pay no heed to what the West did. They warned that Clay's tactics would lead to a nuclear confrontation and that Kennedy would have to back down because Khrushchev would not. Clay saw such talk as self-defeating capitulation before the fact.

Clay also knew the Soviet military better than perhaps any other American, having worked with them closely in Berlin during the occupation. He had spent more time actually talking and dealing with Soviet officials than Kennedy's experts had. He knew that the Soviets did not like to take pointless risks. He also knew that the Soviets, and particularly the military, had nothing but scorn for Ulbricht.

Documents released by the Soviet government after German unification have confirmed Clay's analysis. They show that the Soviet military frequently protested to senior GDR officials about the behavior of East German guards and about GDR instructions to those guards. Marshal Konev complained to Ulbricht himself about the number of times that Vopos had fired during incidents along the sector border. Konev said that he had noted thirty-one instances of "disorderly firing" by East German guards that might create "undesirable serious consequences." He said that he and he alone would give orders along the sector borders.

The Soviets constantly worried about the potential for rash actions by trigger-happy Vopos. Soviet defense minister Marshal Rodion Malinovsky in mid-October wanted Khrushchev to tell Ulbricht not to take any further measures without consulting with Moscow. After watching Clay in action, he feared that any incident would only serve the purposes of the Americans.

Andrei Gromyko still hoped to negotiate a treaty that would get the Allies out of Berlin. He feared that Ulbricht's behavior would inflame Western opinion and make negotiations impossible. Gromyko and Malinovsky also warned Khrushchev of the possible effects of further East German plans to restrict Allied travel between West and East Berlin. They wanted Ulbricht to establish procedures under which a Soviet officer would be called immediately in the event of any incident involving Western occupation personnel. Specifically, they did not want East German officers to demand identification of Allied military personnel in civilian clothing and did not want Ulbricht to start any crisis without first consulting Soviet officials. He was to "halt such actions of the police and GDR authorities which create tensions not corresponding with the requirements of the moment." Khrushchev repeated some of those concerns in a letter to Honecker, who replied that the GDR would set any such measures aside. But Ulbricht had his own plans.[7]

In his first full report to Kennedy on October 18, 1961, Clay cabled that the United States had to react sharply to Ulbricht's maneuvers if it wanted to keep up the German confidence which was essential to the survival of West Berlin. He added that escalation "works both ways" and that occasionally it would be necessary to take some risk by using force to bring the Soviets out of hiding, but he assured the president that U.S. forces would then withdraw because they had achieved their purpose. He noted differences between Ulbricht's and Khrushchev's approaches. He warned that failure to make U.S. views known early in any minor incident would risk having the East Germans or perhaps even the Soviets next try something major.

Clay hinted that he might resign if Kennedy did not back him. He warned that consistent U.S. failure to act would erode confidence so deeply that it would have been useless to send him to Berlin. Kennedy would be seen as responsible for any Western failure to act as long as he kept Clay in Berlin. The general concluded that "I can be of no real service if it is deemed wise to be extremely cautious in Berlin."[8]

TANKS AT CHECKPOINT CHARLIE

Clay's next and most dramatic chance to show that two could play at escalation came over an incident that Moscow did not authorize and almost certainly did not welcome. It went directly against Khrushchev's, Gromyko's and Malinovsky's advice to Ulbricht. It came on a Sunday evening, October 22, as Allan Lightner, the chief of the U.S. Mission in Berlin, wanted to pass through Checkpoint Charlie to attend the opera in East Berlin.

The twenty-second Soviet communist party congress had begun meeting six days earlier, on October 16, in Moscow. On October 17, Khrushchev had given a speech in which he had drawn back from the brink over Berlin. He had not reiterated the December 31 deadline for the signature of the long heralded German peace treaty. Trying to establish his own foreign affairs doctrine against Mao Zedong's, he stressed "peaceful coexistence." Ulbricht, also at the congress, had been surprised and had reacted angrily. In his own speech to the congress three days later he had asserted that the peace treaty was "a task of the utmost urgency."[9]

To anger Ulbricht further, the congress had supported Khrushchev against Frol Kozlov, secretary of the CPSU central committee, who favored more confrontational policies against the United States as well as closer links with China. The support from the congress had given Khrushchev a freer hand to take his time in negotiating a Berlin settlement and a nuclear test ban treaty.[10] He could continue to exert pressure but without a deadline.

Ulbricht wanted action. He thought that he could move on his own and that the West would not react. Khrushchev wanted to negotiate a neutral West Berlin; Ulbricht wanted to create it. He decided to frighten the Berliners by showing U.S. impotence, and he chose to act even before senior Soviet officials had returned to Berlin from the Moscow congress.

Thus the East German police stopped Lightner and asked for his identification documents as he tried to go through Checkpoint Charlie. Lightner, following long-standing instructions, said that he was a member of the U.S. occupation authority, as shown by his U.S. Mission license plate. He refused to show identification and, in accordance with the usual practice, demanded to see a Soviet officer. The East German guards refused, as they normally did at first before letting the U.S. official pass after a brief delay. The Soviets had not authorized East German guards to stop Allied personnel for long periods of time.

On that evening, however, Ulbricht had given different instructions. The East German guards did not let Lightner pass. Clay and the U.S. Commandant in Berlin, Major General Albert Watson, went to the American operations center in West Berlin. Clay sent a squad of American soldiers to the checkpoint, ready to escort Lightner through if necessary.

The Soviets had not been expecting a crisis, especially one initiated by their ally. The Soviet political adviser had not even returned from Moscow, so his deputy hurried to the scene. He protested to U.S. political adviser Howard Trivers (who also had just arrived) about Lightner's behavior and about the U.S. soldiers. Trivers asked what the East Germans would do if the car proceeded under escort. The Soviet official said, "They have their orders."

Clay then ordered the U.S. soldiers to escort Lightner's car through the checkpoint. The East Germans drew back and the car proceeded. It went in and out several times to make the point. Several more American cars went through that evening and were not blocked.[11] The Soviet official told an American officer at the checkpoint that the incident had been a "mistake."[12]

Ulbricht decided the escalate the confrontation and to compel Khrushchev to support him. On Monday morning, the GDR published a decree stating that henceforth all foreigners, except those dressed in Allied military uniforms, would have to show identification to the East German police. The SED paper *Neues Deutschland* carried the decree, which had probably been prepared in advance of the incident, along with the charge that the American action was a serious "border provocation." Khrushchev could no longer stand aside without making himself or his ally lose face.

Washington criticized Clay's action. Kennedy himself objected that Lightner had not been sent to Berlin to go to the opera. But Clay cabled Washington that he intended to meet the East German action firmly and that U.S. personnel had to show their faces in East Berlin to avoid ceding the city entirely to Ulbricht. He also reiterated his message of October 18 that such incidents could have a serious effect in West Berlin if not firmly met.

Next, Clay launched a probe. On the morning of October 25, the U.S. Mission sent a car to Checkpoint Charlie with two soldiers dressed in civilian clothes. They were, as expected, stopped by East German guards. When Trivers again appeared to insist on a Soviet officer, the new Soviet political adviser himself came to the checkpoint to tell Trivers that the East German guards were behaving properly and that the American cars had to follow East German regulations. Khrushchev had decided to support Ulbricht.

Clay then mounted a bigger show of force, bringing up ten tanks to a short distance from the checkpoint. Once again, a squad of U.S. soldiers escorted the American car in and out. The Soviet officer walked over into West Berlin to see the U.S. tanks. He then warned Trivers that "we have tanks too."

The arrival of U.S. tanks, some equipped with bulldozer blades, alarmed the Soviet military. They knew that no East German had authority to stop the tanks if they were to enter East Berlin. Just north of Checkpoint Charlie, the Berlin "Mitte" government district, which had become part of the Soviet sector, formed a salient only twenty blocks wide toward the Brandenburg Gate, with parts of West Berlin to the north and south of it. The tanks could easily proceed straight through it, pushing any obstacles aside with their bulldozer blades. They would thus cut off all major East German ministry buildings, as well as SED and Stasi headquarters, from the rest of East Berlin. The Soviets either had to block the tanks themselves or authorize the East Germans to do so. And they knew that having Ulbricht confront U.S. tanks would add to the unpredictability of an already explosive situation.

Clay saw a chance to bring Moscow into the open. On the next afternoon, he had an American car repeat the test. Once again, the East German police blocked the car. Once again, the U.S. military escorted it through the checkpoint and the U.S. tanks moved close to the checkpoint. By now, however, the Soviets had begun to take precautions of their own. Rather than authorize Ulbricht to block the U.S. tanks, Konev had sent ten Soviet tanks to an empty lot in East Berlin several blocks from the checkpoint. Although the tank crews covered their insignia with mud to suggest that the tanks were East German, U.S. soldiers monitoring their turret radios knew that they were Soviet. So did American reporters, who had gathered as the tension grew.

Clay welcomed the arrival of the Soviet tanks but wanted to bring them farther into the open. He repeated the test. Once again the East Germans blocked the U.S. car. Once again, the U.S. military walked the car through the checkpoint. But simultaneously Clay also brought the tanks right up to the checkpoint. In response, the Soviet tanks rumbled out of their lot and came up to the checkpoint themselves. As there were more Soviet tanks than American, Clay ordered more tanks brought to the checkpoint. And, from late afternoon through the evening, with lights glaring on all sides and camera flashbulbs popping, the Soviet and American tanks facing each other provided some of the most dramatic photographs of the Cold War.

Clay had done what he wanted. He immediately issued a press release greeting the arrival of the Soviet tanks as a sign that the Soviets had finally assumed their responsibilities and had shown that they and not the East Germans were really in charge in East Berlin. He felt relieved that Konev had sent the Soviet tanks. They eliminated any chance that Ulbricht might provoke a real crisis.

But Washington, Paris and London heard frighteningly alarmist reports. Press stories conveyed a fear of imminent war that was not felt in Berlin. Macmillan expressed shock to Kennedy. And Kennedy's own advisers, again worrying about war by escalation or miscalculation, urged Kennedy to call off the confrontation.

Kennedy called Clay in Berlin, reaching him at the U.S. operations center. When Clay said, "Hello, Mr. President," the center fell silent. Kennedy asked about the situation. Clay told him that the Soviets had matched the American tank force, tank for tank. This showed that Moscow wanted no trouble, for Konev could easily have brought up many more tanks than the Americans could muster.

Clay added that he saw the Soviet tank deployment as a sign that the Soviets did not trust Ulbricht and wanted to take over when the risks grew too high. Kennedy urged Clay and his colleagues not to lose their nerve. Clay replied that he and the others in the operations center had not lost their own nerve but wondered if those in Washington had lost theirs. Kennedy, who had by then received Clay's October 18 cable and understood what the general was doing, replied, "I've got a lot of people here that have, but I haven't."[13]

The confrontation did not last long. By half past ten the following morning, the Soviet tanks began withdrawing. Clay instructed the U.S. tanks to retreat as well. In an elaborately artful minuet, the Soviet tanks first pulled back about ten yards. The U.S. tanks matched that pull-back. A few more pull-backs followed.

Within half an hour, all tanks had left the checkpoint. They had stood face to face for sixteen hours.

Clay felt that the U.S. tanks had done what he had told Kennedy in his cable and that Soviet behavior had proven his point. He had not expected or intended the face-off to last. But he had wanted to draw the Soviets to the checkpoint to stop them from hiding behind Ulbricht and to make them assume their responsibilities. They had done it, pulling Ulbricht's chestnuts out of the fire but also inflicting a deep humiliation on the GDR.

The Checkpoint Charlie confrontation proved to be one of the decisive moments in the struggle over Germany. It boosted the morale of the Berliners because it showed that the Allies and especially the United States would not continue to yield to East German pressure. It also destroyed the image of the GDR as a sovereign force that could deal on an equal basis with the Western occupation powers. Soviet tanks had to come and save Ulbricht only a few blocks from his own office.

Khrushchev and Konev could not have welcomed the incident. They did not want to risk war to enhance Ulbricht's claim to sovereignty over Soviet occupation territory in East Berlin. They agreed with Clay's wish to whisk the East German genie back into its bottle. Having seen what Ulbricht would do on his own, Khrushchev subsequently kept him under stricter control. The level and frequency of East German harassment eased, and no more East German efforts to impose new controls followed.

Clay regarded the confrontation as a success because it showed that the Allies would not desert West Berlin. By that winter and through the following spring, investment again flowed into West Berlin and people stopped leaving. This gave the city an essential shot in the arm and put an end to Ulbricht's hope that West Berlin could be neutralized by direct action. Clay also hoped that the demonstration had shown Kennedy that he did not need to let his advisers paralyze him.

On the other hand, Ulbricht had achieved at least one objective. To avoid another confrontation, Kennedy ordered U.S. official civilians to stop going into East Berlin in official vehicles. A number of his advisers suggested that the United States follow the British procedure of having their civilian personnel show identification to the Vopos even in official cars. Clay recommended strongly against this because he feared that it would set a precedent for East Germans to control Allied traffic on the Autobahn. Kennedy again supported Clay.

Kennedy must have drawn some important conclusions by November 1961. He had repeatedly heard that the United States had to avoid any confrontation with Moscow because the Soviets would always escalate to the point of war. But at Checkpoint Charlie, as elsewhere in and around West Berlin, the opposite had happened. In fact, the Soviet tanks had come on the scene to avoid the kind of miscalculation that Kennedy feared. Kennedy, who had begun to develop his own ideas about how to deal with Moscow, may have seen things that helped him later.[14]

Kennedy showed his appreciation to Clay himself. When Clay returned to Washington in late November for consultation, the president drew him aside and thanked him for what he had done and how he had done it. Under Secretary of State Chester Bowles sent Clay a cable transmitting the president's congratulations.[15] Rusk said nothing.

But Kennedy's advisers spent the next several weeks reassuring Soviet officials that Clay had acted improperly and without authorization. Macmillan sent his highest-ranking official in West Berlin to the Soviet embassy in East Berlin to inform Moscow that Clay had lost authority and would soon be removed.[16]

Khrushchev wrote later that he had ordered the tank withdrawal as a step toward peace. Moving forward would have meant war. To watch and to manage the situation, he wrote, he had been in constant touch with Konev and Malinovsky. He did not mention Ulbricht.[17]

But Ulbricht sent a letter asking Khrushchev for even more steps against the Allies. Ulbricht's letter, dated October 30 (after the Checkpoint Charlie confrontation) but perhaps written earlier, called for "stronger pressure" against the Allied position in Berlin. He wanted urgent completion of the GDR flight control safety center to replace the four-power Berlin Air Safety Center, and he asked Khrushchev to instruct Soviet flight controllers to walk out of the Allied center so as to compel Allied flights to register their flight plans with the GDR safety center. The flights would then be directed to Schönefeld. Ulbricht wanted the Soviet Union to insist on the immediate suspension of U.S. "courtesy patrols" on the Autobahn. He also wanted all East German legislation to apply automatically in East Berlin.[18]

In retrospect, Ulbricht's proposals appear illogical in timing and in substance. They went against Soviet even more than against Western interests. Moscow would not be better served by an East German air safety center than by its own, and its occupation rights in East Berlin also remained an important asset. There is no record of what Khrushchev replied, if indeed he replied at all. The letter thus served mainly to document Ulbricht's frustration over the twenty-second CPSU congress and over Checkpoint Charlie. But it also showed Ulbricht's own weak spots, for he again wrote that the situation in Berlin jeopardized fulfillment of East German economic plans while admitting that some of the steps he wanted to take might provoke a damaging West German economic embargo.[19]

The Checkpoint Charlie confrontation, although taking place at the sector border, helped win a key phase of the battle for West Berlin. Some Western diplomats criticized Clay, but he had actually kept open for negotiations an outcome that Ulbricht and perhaps Khrushchev had wanted to settle by force.

Checkpoint Charlie also showed Khrushchev the limits of the possible in Berlin itself. It showed him that he had better manage a confrontation with the United States himself rather than let others manage it, and that Berlin might not be the best spot for such a confrontation. London's and Washington's reactions may also have persuaded him that other spots might be more promising.

KENNEDY PROBES

By December 1961, the situation in West Berlin had begun to stabilize. The worst was over. But Kennedy and his advisers still feared war over Berlin. They also continued to harbor deep suspicions about their German ally. McGeorge Bundy warned Kennedy before a visit by Konrad Adenauer against the risks of "increasing nationalism and militarism" in Germany. He urged Kennedy to tell Adenauer that the U.S. government would propose major concessions to end the Soviet threat to Berlin. But Kennedy did not want to alert the chancellor. He decided that he would wait for the results of the soundings that he planned in Moscow before telling either Adenauer or de Gaulle what he was doing.

Although Kennedy and Macmillan wanted to reach an agreement with Khrushchev, they had no room left to bargain on Berlin itself. Kennedy did not want to concede on his "three essentials," and Ulbricht had taken everything else. Kennedy had nothing to offer except concessions on Germany. He and Macmillan talked about recognizing the GDR and the Oder-Neisse line.

Kennedy did not want to tell Adenauer that he planned to negotiate about Germany. He told the chancellor only that the United States would continue to pursue negotiations, and he assured the chancellor that he would firmly uphold the freedom of West Berlin as well as access to the city. He asked Adenauer to use his influence to persuade de Gaulle to join the diplomatic consultations. Adenauer made no commitments about de Gaulle. But, having heard rumors about London's and Washington's diplomatic plans, he warned Kennedy that talks had to be limited to Berlin itself and should not include Germany or European security issues.[20]

Macmillan had a hard sell in his simultaneous meeting with de Gaulle in Sussex. The president of France flatly refused to take part in any negotiations on Berlin or Germany. He said that the Allies had to avoid any actions that would make the Germans feel betrayed. He also described Soviet proposals as unacceptable. Macmillan complained to Kennedy that de Gaulle was merely trying to get credit for being a good friend of Germany, leaving the Americans and the British to bear the brunt of German anger.[21]

Kennedy and Macmillan believed that recognizing the status quo in divided Germany and divided Berlin would stabilize Europe. Adenauer and de Gaulle feared that doing so would destabilize Europe. They thought Khrushchev and especially Ulbricht would use recognition as a lever for further demands.

Khrushchev, well aware of Allied disagreements and German-American tensions, tried to see if he could take advantage of the situation to make a separate agreement with Adenauer. He told the German ambassador in Moscow that he wanted to improve relations with Bonn, saying that he would regard a reconciliation of the German and Russian peoples as his crowning work in foreign policy. On December 22, 1961, Khrushchev asked for German-Soviet talks on Berlin. But Adenauer rejected Khrushchev's advances.[22] He still did not want to repeat Bismarck's policy of maneuver between Russia and the West.

Kennedy recognized that he was trying a dangerous move behind an ally's back. To avoid betraying the letter of his promise to Adenauer, he described the offers that he wanted to make to Khrushchev as "probes."[23]

Probes or not, the U.S. proposals went beyond anything that any Western leader had ever suggested to Moscow. Kennedy offered to recognize the Oder-Neisse line and the GDR as well as to accept the Soviet demand that Germany be united through discussions between two equal German governments. Kennedy also offered to negotiate a nuclear-free zone in central Europe, which would have removed the U.S. weapons defending West Germany.

De Gaulle got wind of the American ideas and tried to call a halt. On January 14, 1962, he wrote Kennedy to warn him that the proposals "might result in the neutralization of West Germany." He proposed periodic summit meetings between France, Great Britain, and the United States. Kennedy, who may not have understood what neutralization of West Germany would do to America's global power position, rejected de Gaulle's suggestion.[24]

In February 1962, frustrated that Khrushchev had not replied to his initial "probes," Kennedy offered more. He wrote to the Soviet premier that the United States would accept a role for the GDR in controlling access to West Berlin, offering for the first time to negotiate on one of his three "essentials." He added a proposal for an international access authority that would have equal numbers of Western and Eastern members and would include Sweden, Austria and Switzerland as neutrals. He said that it would "respect the sovereignty of the GDR." To sweeten the bargain, he accepted the long-standing Soviet proposal for a non-aggression pact between NATO and the Warsaw Pact.[25]

When Khrushchev ignored these proposals as well, Kennedy tried a new approach. In early March, he offered a "principles paper" that proposed mixed West and East German technical commissions and new agreements on non-diffusion of nuclear weapons. He asked Rusk to make these proposals to Gromyko, but not to put them into writing as they "might shock our allies if presented without prior consultation." On March 25, 1962, as he presented the new ideas to the Soviets, assistant secretary of state Foy Kohler went out of his way to point out that the American proposals accepted important Soviet positions and even Soviet language. Kennedy also wrote to Khrushchev that he would "take great pleasure" in a trip to Moscow if an agreement could be reached.[26]

Kennedy was practicing smorgasbord diplomacy, putting one offer after another on the table to see which Khrushchev would select. He was also practicing occupation diplomacy, ignoring all that had happened in Europe and across the Atlantic between 1945 and 1960 and starting all over to negotiate a postwar German settlement and access arrangements for Berlin.

Kennedy said nothing about any of this to Adenauer, the man who had helped create most of the realities Kennedy chose to ignore. He even wrote to Adenauer that the United States did not favor any special military status for any country in western Europe, "especially the Federal Republic," a sentence that must have amazed the chancellor, who had certainly read press reports about Rusk's offer of a nuclear-free zone in central Europe.[27] Kennedy's "probes" made clear why Rusk had said he did not honor the 1954 agreement giving West Germany its sovereignty.

But Khrushchev, Gromyko and Ulbricht overplayed their hand. If Khrushchev had accepted Kennedy's "probes," the Soviet Union would have been able to undo fifteen years of North Atlantic and West European diplomacy. It would have faced a much weaker American strategic base in Europe. West Berlin would have become a "neutral" city within a few years because Ulbricht could have virtually determined who could travel. But Ulbricht rejected even the offer for an international access authority instructed to respect his sovereignty. He wanted sole control. He insisted that the Allies withdraw from Berlin before he would even negotiate.[28]

Kennedy and his advisers failed to realize the complexity of Khrushchev's situation, which made American and Soviet negotiators talk past each other.

While Khrushchev wanted the GDR to gain recognition, he did not want Ulbricht to have real power. Kennedy continually offered formulas that would have given Ulbricht both, and that would, over time, have divided Germany cleanly along the Elbe. But Kennedy's concessions helped Ulbricht more than Khrushchev wanted. Khrushchev valued his occupation authority and mistrusted Ulbricht at least as much as Kennedy mistrusted Adenauer. Khrushchev and Ulbricht both wanted the United States out of Berlin, but Khrushchev did not want Ulbricht to have as much power as Kennedy was prepared to grant him. He wanted to exercise control himself. Kennedy offered concessions that Ulbricht spurned in a fit of pride but that went in the wrong directions for Khrushchev.

Whatever his reasons, Khrushchev reacted with the same contempt for Kennedy that he had shown in early 1961. He either did not reply or, when he did, demanded more. He wrote that he would accept the international access authority only if it included the withdrawal of U.S. forces from West Berlin, asking Kennedy to give up one and perhaps two of his "essentials" immediately. The only logical explanation is that he wanted to humiliate Kennedy so badly that he could undercut the U.S. position in Europe and force Adenauer finally to turn to Moscow.

Thus, instead of negotiating, Khrushchev applied more pressure. He did it in the Allied air corridors, the most sensitive possible arena, but which he might have chosen because he, and not Ulbricht, controlled it directly. Beginning on February 7, 1962, the Soviet controllers at the Berlin Air Safety Center began to reserve for Soviet flights the most frequently used altitudes within the air corridors.[29] This tactic had the potential to stop Allied aircraft from using those altitudes and to crimp air traffic to Berlin severely.

The Soviets followed with other efforts to harass air traffic. They refused to guarantee the safety of Allied flights, opening up the risk of catastrophic insurance claims in case of accident. They periodically dropped metallic chaff in the corridors to confuse radar and radio signals and to raise the risk that Allied aircraft would either stray out of the corridors or hit each other by accident.

But the Allies could not afford to yield the air corridors; air travel was the one thing they could not surrender. The Allies continued to fly at the altitudes that the Soviets attempted to block. General Clay himself flew to a ceremony in Bremen through one of the reserved corridors. Although Soviet aircraft buzzed his plane, it stayed on course. Berliners flew through the corridors as if everything were normal, treating the Soviet "reservations" and threats as another form of Kremlin chicanery. They relished the opportunity to show that they would not be bluffed. Khrushchev had to stop the air harassment because he did not dare to shoot down an Allied aircraft.

By April, Kennedy had grown grew ever more concerned about the air corridors and Berlin in general. He decided to move from "probes" to actual negotiations. For that, however, he had to consult or at least inform all those concerned, in particular Adenauer. On April 11, therefore, Kennedy decided to give the "principles paper" to Ambassador Grewe and tell him to obtain Adenauer's approval within twenty-four hours. When Grewe protested that this amounted to an ultimatum, the White House stretched the deadline to forty-eight hours.

Adenauer reacted furiously to the ultimatum as well as to the proposed terms for negotiations. He thought that Kennedy had preemptively accepted virtually all Soviet demands, including those from the 1950s for German neutrality. But the president had not even asked for German unification, which Moscow had often offered in exchange for neutrality. Adenauer believed that an agreement on the basis proposed by Kennedy would destroy the West German government and NATO.

The chancellor felt that Kennedy had betrayed their November agreement. He informed the president on April 14 that he objected strongly to the U.S. proposals. He noted that the proposals dealt not only with Berlin, where the United States still had occupation rights, but with Germany itself, over which Washington no longer had the authority to negotiate. He charged that the U.S. proposals exceeded any concessions ever put forward by any Western government and that he would not join in them or support them.

Adenauer insisted that the United States could not ignore a sovereign ally on matters central to that nation's security. He noted that Kennedy offered one concession after another without asking anything in return, and demanded a pause in the "probes." Kennedy and Adenauer had reached total deadlock.

Within days, the deadlock became a crisis of confidence. The American "principles paper" appeared in the German press and in the *New York Times*. Kennedy and Rusk, enraged, accused Adenauer of leaking the paper to undercut U.S. negotiators. Adenauer flatly rejected the charge.

Whether Adenauer had leaked the paper or not, the public exposure of Kennedy's offers served the chancellor's purpose. The proposals to recognize the GDR and to transfer American rights to a neutral international access authority generated such an uproar in the United States, in NATO and in Berlin that Kennedy had to withdraw them. Many commentators criticized the very notion of offering compromise proposals in the midst of Soviet air harassment. Berliners complained that the same Americans who condemned the Germans for not resisting Hitler now demanded that they bow to another dictator.

In the clear light of day and in cold print, Kennedy's diplomacy looked more like Neville Chamberlain's appeasement of Hitler in 1938 than like the spirit of King Arthur and the Knights of Camelot that Kennedy wanted to evoke. The "principles paper" went by the board as soon as it was subjected to press and public scrutiny. On May 16, Kennedy wrote to Adenauer and suggested that relations return to where they had been in November. Adenauer, having won his point and torpedoed the negotiations, agreed.

With the end of the harassment in the air corridors and the end of the "probes," Clay left Berlin. He had already begun to question his usefulness there by February of 1962, for he felt that he had done what Kennedy had asked him to do. He had helped restore the confidence of the Berliners and had made Khrushchev realize that Ulbricht had to be kept under control.

Clay had then written to Kennedy and asked to leave, writing the letter in longhand and sending it by postal channels because he did not want it distributed through the bureaucracy. Kennedy had sent General Taylor to ask Clay to stay until the air corridor harassments were over and until the negotiations were either successful or demonstrably futile. Clay had agreed.

Clay had not liked what he had been able to learn about the "probes" and felt that he should have been consulted. Although he had expected Khrushchev to ask for more than Kennedy could offer, he knew the pressure that Macmillan and others were putting on the president. Clay feared that he would either have to defend an agreement that he regarded as dangerous or to denounce it and cause a panic in Berlin.[30] Once the air incidents had stopped, Clay saw no reason to remain. Neither, apparently, did Konev, who left Berlin at about the same time.

As his last official act, Clay spoke at Brandt's request before a May Day rally of 750,000 Berliners. He told them that he would leave the following day because his job was done, but he promised to return if Berlin ever needed him again.

With the "probes" and their contents discredited, the Allies never resumed diplomacy on the same terms. Khrushchev, Gromyko and Ulbricht had missed a major chance for a favorable Berlin arrangement. It became clear only some months later that they may have done so because they hoped for an even greater and quicker triumph.

KHRUSHCHEV'S END RUN TO CUBA

Khrushchev had eased his pressures on Berlin in the spring of 1962 not because he or Ulbricht had given up their aim to control the city but because the Soviet leader had decided to move the confrontation into a different and distant arena. He had to wait until he had reached a stronger position in case of escalation.

In the artificial calm of the summer, Berlin suffered a human tragedy that disgraced the United States in the eyes of the Berliners almost as much as the Wall itself had done. On August 17, a young East German, Peter Fechter, tried to climb over the Wall about 100 meters (328 feet) to the east of Checkpoint Charlie. As he climbed, East German guards shot him repeatedly. He fell back, badly wounded, onto East Berlin territory but within sight of several West Berlin apartment buildings and within earshot of the checkpoint's American guards. He could not get up and lay on the ground crying for help.

As Fechter lay bleeding, it would have been an easy matter for an American military ambulance from the checkpoint to enter East Berlin—as it could do under occupation rules—to give him first aid. But U.S. Commandant Watson, fearing the risk of escalation, asked higher headquarters for instructions and did not order the ambulance to help Fechter. After about two hours, during which the Vopos refused to help him, Fechter bled to death.

The young man's death sent a shockwave through West Berlin and West Germany. Many saw his death as a symbol of the moral swamp into which the West had sunk itself and its sense of decency. The fear that had paralyzed those who could have saved Fechter's life became to many Berliners and many Americans as much a sign of inhumanity as the Wall itself.

Enraged and frustrated, crowds of young Berliners began stoning both American and Soviet cars. They particularly targeted the buses that brought Soviet guards to the Red Army war memorial in the Tiergarten several hundred meters west of the Brandenburg gate. The Soviets reacted by driving the guards into West Berlin in armored personnel carriers, violating the unwritten understanding that for years had kept the occupiers from sending combat vehicles into each other's sectors without invitation. The Western commandants protested to the Soviet commandant but did not try to block the armored cars. Clay, living in New York but well aware of Berlin's codes of conduct, advised Kennedy that the Allies should immediately stop the armored vehicles at the sector border, but the president did not act.

Disgusted, Clay informed General Taylor as well as Adenauer and Brandt that he no longer held U.S. government status because he wanted to be free to speak his mind. He also warned that Kennedy's inaction would lead to a loss in prestige and respect "that is to be recovered only by renewed determination involving greater risks."[31]

Within days, as quickly as the crisis had arisen, it ended. Just as they had earlier stopped trying to harass air traffic, the Soviets stopped sending armored cars into West Berlin and resumed busing their guards to the memorial. They also abolished the office of Soviet commandant, signaling that they no longer adhered to the Berlin occupation regime.[32]

The Soviets stopped diplomatic exchanges as well, rejecting a Western proposal for a special committee of deputy foreign ministers to try once again to negotiate a Berlin settlement. They said that it seemed pointless to repeat well-established positions, a statement that must have surprised and perhaps amused those who had dealt with Soviet diplomats over the years.

Instead, Soviet officials began telling Western diplomats that they believed the spring discussions had settled most issues. They said that they had decided to accept the concessions Kennedy had offered in the "probes," but they still offered nothing in exchange. They told Allied governments that only the nationality of the troops in West Berlin remained to be settled, and that those should be United Nations forces rather than Allied forces.

Soviet officials added that they did not want to resolve the Berlin matter until November, after the U.S. congressional elections. In the meantime, they observed generously, they would let Kennedy concentrate on the election campaign. White House counsel Theodore Sorensen had asked Khrushchev through Dobrynin to exercise restraint prior to the election to avoid helping the Republicans.[33] Khrushchev could say that he was complying with Kennedy's request.

Khrushchev told U.S. Interior Secretary Stuart Udall in Moscow that he would freeze the Berlin question until November "out of respect for your president." But he warned that he would not allow U.S. forces to remain in Berlin and that the Soviet Union would make sure that Kennedy solved the problem: "We will put him in a situation where it is necessary to solve it." He also warned that de Gaulle, like Adenauer, would have to "get wise in a hurry" for "war in this day and age means no Paris and no France."[34]

Gromyko concentrated on Berlin when he met with Kennedy on October 18, 1962, although the meeting became notorious because he denied the presence of Soviet offensive weapons in Cuba. In firm and unyielding language, he offered Kennedy no concessions on Berlin, warning that West Berlin represented "a rotten tooth which must be pulled out" and adding forcefully that Western troops would have to leave.

Gromyko proposed that the United Nations play a role in the free city of West Berlin. He also told Kennedy that Khrushchev would come to the United Nations in November and hoped to meet with the president then to settle the Berlin matter. Seeming confident of a Berlin solution soon after the U.S. election, he said that the Western presence in Berlin was the only difference remaining between U.S. and Soviet views. Kennedy replied that he would be glad to meet with Khrushchev, but that Berlin involved other states as well.[35]

Other evidence of Khrushchev and Gromyko's intent began to appear. In May, U.S. intelligence officials noticed that the Soviets had begun to lay long pipelines from east to west across the GDR with fewer attempts at camouflage than usual. Such pipelines, designed to carry fuel, normally preceded large-scale Soviet troop maneuvers and deployments. This time, they ended near two highly strategic points on the inner-German border, the city of Magdeburg opposite the British Army of the Rhine and the Fulda Gap opposite the U.S. Seventh Army. An American military intelligence officer in Berlin said: "If their purpose is to persuade us they are preparing to jump off, this is how I think the Soviets would go about it." By the first week of October, major Soviet deployments to those areas began. The Red Army obviously planned to mass forces very visibly along the West German border by November.[36]

The purpose of the pipelines and of Soviet restraint during the spring and summer became evident on October 22, when Kennedy publicly revealed that the Soviet Union was in the process of deploying offensive missiles in Cuba and insisted that Khrushchev remove them. Khrushchev apparently had decided that the Berlin crisis could be solved by moving the confrontation from Europe to a point from which he could directly threaten U.S. territory.

By the spring of 1962, Khrushchev must have sensed deep frustration about Berlin. Clay had stopped Ulbricht from winning by direct action in the city itself. And Adenauer had blocked Kennedy's "probes" before Kennedy had offered to withdraw U.S. forces from Berlin—the most essential part of making West Berlin a "neutral" city.

By the end of April, Khrushchev must also have realized that he could not stop Allied and civilian aircraft in the Berlin air corridors without shooting some down. And he could not let the GDR control and perhaps block Allied traffic on the land routes without giving Ulbricht more power than he could trust him to use. All such steps could be highly risky in the face of American strategic superiority. To gain real leverage in Berlin, Khrushchev needed to change the strategic balance in his favor quickly and decisively.

With missiles based in Cuba, Khrushchev could neutralize U.S. strategic superiority. And Soviet forces massed along the West German border would add a highly immediate threat to British and American as well as German forces.

Although the literature about the Cuban missile crisis has generally focused on the island itself, with most authors accepting Khrushchev's claim that he installed the missiles to protect Cuba itself, the missile deployment becomes more logical when perceived in the context of Berlin.

Khrushchev knew, as Kennedy did, that missiles stationed in Cuba could reach Washington. Those missiles, against which the United States had no defense, would have made any president hesitate before launching U.S. missiles or bombers. They would also have made any president think twice before provoking a confrontation over Berlin. Khrushchev himself told the SED congress in January 1963 that the missiles would have compelled American leaders "to make a more sober assessment of objective reality."

Rusk also saw the link between Berlin and Cuba. The State Department cabled several major U.S. embassies on October 24 that the U.S. Government believed the Soviet missiles were "probably primarily geared to showdown on Berlin," with the timing so arranged that Khrushchev would be arriving at the United Nations in New York just as the missiles were completely installed and ready to fire.[37] Kennedy himself informed Macmillan during the Cuban crisis that "Khrushchev's main intention may be to increase his chances at Berlin."[38] And Rusk later said that Khrushchev's main purpose in deploying the missiles was "to liquidate the occupation regime in West Berlin."[39]

In Kennedy's National Security Council Executive Committee (Ex Comm) deliberations during the Cuban crisis, many remarks focused on the risk that Khrushchev might hold Berlin hostage in the Cuban confrontation. A number of Ex Comm members expressed concern that Khrushchev might retaliate in Berlin for the U.S. blockade around Cuba. All could see the similarities in the situation, where both the Soviet Union and the United States could theoretically block the other's access to an exposed position. This suggested U.S. caution.[40]

But Berlin also imposed certain obligations. Kennedy would have to take firm action against the Soviet missiles in Cuba if he wanted his commitment to Berlin to be credible. If Kennedy yielded on Cuba, Khrushchev would move against Berlin. Having made Kennedy retreat over Cuba, he might expect the president to retreat over Berlin. And a Soviet military move against Berlin would precipitate a general war. Several Ex Comm members said that Kennedy had to act firmly in Cuba to keep his credibility in Berlin.[41]

Some Ex Comm members appear to have considered whether they might try trading off either Berlin or U.S. forces stationed there for the missiles in Cuba or for some other purpose, although they recognized that doing so raised some difficult questions. McGeorge Bundy observed: "If we could trade off Berlin, and not have it our fault . . ."[42] But Kennedy said that the United States could not avoid responsibility for the loss of Berlin.[43]

If Khrushchev had wanted only to defend Cuba, he could have sent Soviet troops and anti-aircraft missiles. The ballistic missiles pointed at Washington did not serve a defensive purpose. Instead, as Dobrynin later wrote, Khrushchev wanted to change the global balance of forces in a way that would serve him on Berlin. But Khrushchev and other Soviet officials never revealed this to Fidel Castro or other Cuban officials.[44]

Recently published Soviet papers on the Cuban missile crisis record the talk between Castro and Mikoyan after the crisis, when Mikoyan was trying to make Castro accept Khrushchev's decision to withdraw the missiles. Even in that conversation Mikoyan never replied directly to Castro's anguished request for an honest explanation of the deployment.[45] But the Cuban leader himself told the French correspondent Claude Julien that Khrushchev had earlier told him the missiles would "reinforce socialism on the international scale."[46]

Khrushchev may have gained the impression in Vienna that Kennedy could be intimidated in direct confrontation even if he reacted firmly outside the frame of that confrontation. He may also have interpreted Kennedy's "probes" as evidence that the president could be pressured to yield on Berlin. Unable to make headway in Berlin itself, he might have decided that the only way to get U.S. forces out of Berlin was to apply the most direct pressure on Kennedy. Missiles in Cuba offered the answer. Khrushchev must have had his plan and his purpose for the missiles in mind when he told Udall that he would put Kennedy "in a situation where it is necessary to solve" the Berlin question.

Khrushchev also realized that he would have to exert more pressure on Adenauer and de Gaulle. The pipelines being built across East Germany, like the initial troop deployments at the border, offer a clue to Khrushchev's intentions. The Soviet leader knew that Adenauer opposed concessions that Kennedy and Macmillan wanted to make. But Adenauer might well become more accommodating if large Soviet forces stood on his borders and Soviet missiles were deployed in Cuba. He might decide to favor compromise. If one takes Khrushchev's remarks to Udall at face value, Khrushchev wanted to threaten France as well. De Gaulle had not yet developed the French nuclear *force de frappe*.

Gromyko himself offered an important piece of evidence. Stopping in East Berlin on his way back from meeting with Kennedy in Washington, he made a speech demanding very firmly that U.S. forces leave Berlin. Obviously, he expected Kennedy to yield under the pressure of Soviet missiles in Cuba. Although the president had revealed the missile construction in Cuba almost forty hours earlier, Gromyko had not yet returned to Moscow and he either had not yet realized or had not yet been told that Khrushchev might be the one to retreat. Gromyko became the last Soviet official to demand American withdrawal in such an uncompromising tone.[47]

The timing of the pipeline construction in East Germany indicates that Khrushchev and the Soviet military began their strategic preparations in spring of 1962. The decision may have been made at the CPSU presidium meeting between April 22 and 25, 1962, and announced to the Cubans at a meeting with their ambassador in Moscow on May 5.[48] That would also coincide with the Soviet decisions to suspend the air corridor harassment in the spring and to stop sending their monument guards into West Berlin in armored cars, as well as with their refusal to engage in any exchanges about Berlin after the spring. Khrushchev thought he would be in a better position by November and wanted no distractions before then.

Some uncertainty remains about what Khrushchev might have demanded if he had been able to make his missiles fully operational. His and Gromyko's remarks suggest that he planned at least to invite the U.N. General Assembly in November 1962 to send U.N. forces to replace the Western forces in West Berlin. With the threat of nuclear war hanging over Washington and the world, this demand might have seemed reasonable. Kennedy would have been hard put to argue for his "essentials." Khrushchev would have achieved a "neutral" West Berlin. He might have also hoped to try for an entirely new settlement on Germany as a whole, neutralizing West Germany as well as West Berlin and realizing Lenin's dream of a direct link with Germany.

Khrushchev had launched a gamble of historic proportions. If it had worked, he would have been well on his way to splitting the Western alliance. He would have won a major and perhaps decisive battle in the struggle over Germany, and he would have firmly established his authority within the communist world against the Chinese challenge.

Khrushchev had made a massive blunder, however, by wanting to threaten the United States directly. He had moved the crisis from Berlin, where he had a local advantage, to the Caribbean, where Kennedy had one. He also had changed the politics of the situation. Kennedy could make some concessions on Berlin and Germany without paying too high a price in the United States. He could not do the same on Cuba, especially on the eve of a U.S. congressional election.

Berliners immediately understood what the Cuban crisis meant for them, even before it had been resolved. They did not fear any Khrushchev moves against Berlin to balance the American moves against Cuba. They believed that Khrushchev would not dare to have two simultaneous crises. Gromyko admitted as much when he wondered before the Supreme Soviet in January of 1963 "how the whole matter might have developed if yet another crisis in central Europe had been added to the critical events around Cuba."[49] As soon as the Cuban crisis began, many Berliners predicted to their American friends that Kennedy's determination on Cuba meant the end of the Berlin crisis as well. Kennedy himself understood the connection, for during the crisis he called General Clay as a consultant.

Kennedy's tactics in the Cuban missile crisis made Khrushchev's defeat all the more complete and thus helped to end the Soviet threat to Berlin. For, while

Kennedy made a secret concession, he demanded that Khrushchev retreat in public. Robert Kennedy told Dobrynin that the United States would withdraw U.S. missiles from Turkey after Khrushchev withdrew his missiles from Cuba, but he added that the president insisted on secrecy. Robert Kennedy said, in Dobrynin's words, that if the missiles in Turkey represented "the only obstacle to a settlement," then "the president saw no insurmountable difficulties."[50] Kennedy said that the missiles could leave Turkey in four to five months (as indeed they did).

The president wanted secrecy for several reasons. He feared a nasty debate in NATO if the United States made that kind of concession without first discussing it in the NATO Council. He also feared domestic consequences. Even Robert Kennedy worried about those; he made it clear to Dobrynin that one reason he insisted on confidentiality was that he himself might in the future wish to run for president and could not win if it was known that he had made this kind of concession to Moscow.[51]

Kennedy's friends and associates maintained the secrecy even more zealously than the Kennedys themselves. Presidential counsel Theodore Sorensen edited Robert Kennedy's memoirs of the Cuban missile crisis, *Thirteen Days*, after Robert had died, and in the process altered the thinly veiled admission that a deal on the Turkish missiles had been made and that the United States had demanded secrecy for that deal.[52]

Kennedy's insistence on secrecy turned a partial bargain into a triumph. Khrushchev could have portrayed his pull-out of missiles from Cuba as less than a total defeat if he could have announced that the United States had agreed in turn to withdraw missiles from Turkey. But the president would have none of that. Robert Kennedy even told Dobrynin that he would not exchange any documents on the deal.

The total victory that Kennedy could thus claim in Cuba had a dramatic effect in Berlin. Khrushchev's and Ulbricht's threats had lost credibility, and West Berlin no longer needed to fear neutralization.

The Cuban outcome changed the tone and the terms of the talks about Berlin and Germany. The Soviet Union dropped all deadlines for a German peace treaty. Mikoyan made that clear in his meeting with Rusk on November 30, 1962, on his way back from Cuba. Mikoyan had not even mentioned Berlin during his meeting with the president a day earlier.

The Cuban crisis also had an effect on U.S. and Soviet negotiating styles. Kennedy and Macmillan had continued to make compromise proposals for a Berlin settlement during the summer of 1962, even after Kennedy had promised Adenauer that he would no longer do so. But U.S. negotiators dropped their occasionally pleading tone after Cuba.

Khrushchev, in turn, acted less assertively. He wrote to Kennedy on December 11 that only one question—the U.S. troop presence in Berlin—remained to be settled, and he promised rather meekly that a Berlin agreement would lead to an improvement in Soviet-American relations. He made no threats. But Kennedy told Macmillan only a few days later that he wondered whether it had not been a mistake always to treat the Soviet leaders "with consideration and courtesy." He remarked that the Soviets had been given ample opportunity to settle the Berlin question over the past year and should no longer ask for the removal of Western troops.[53]

Kennedy also acted against something of great interest to Khrushchev: a Soviet physical presence in West Berlin. The Soviets had long owned a large building on Lietzenburgerstrasse in the British sector at the edge of the U.S. sector. It had housed their trade mission in Germany before World War II. Near the end of the Berlin crisis, they tried to refurbish it to use it as a consular office, a cultural center and a major installation in West Berlin. They had hired an architect, had constructed a sizable auditorium, and had planned a large public ceremony to move into the building. It would be a citadel of influence and would give credence to Khrushchev's claim that West Berlin had become a four-power city, especially after the end of the Kommandatura. Macmillan wanted to let Khrushchev proceed, but Kennedy learned of Soviet plans and said that he wanted them stopped. He persuaded Macmillan to block them, removing an important element of Moscow's West Berlin presence.[54]

In a later White House staff meeting, Kennedy even said that he saw no useful purpose in continuing a dialogue with Moscow if the Soviets did not make meaningful proposals. His Soviet expert Lewellyn Thompson reiterated his earlier view that the West had to talk with Moscow to prevent a Berlin crisis, but Kennedy was not listening any longer.[55] Cuba had reinforced the Checkpoint Charlie lesson. It showed that Khrushchev also feared escalation, and Kennedy no longer dreaded it as he had.

As a further sign of Kennedy's hardening attitude, he took the Berlin and Germany negotiations away from the Soviet experts on his staff and turned them fully over to Rusk. The secretary of state, under stiffer instructions from Kennedy, conducted those talks with Gromyko and Dobrynin in a much firmer style than the Soviets had experienced before. Rusk objected when Gromyko asserted that the concessions offered in the U.S. "probes" of the previous spring, especially the "principles paper," had actually been agreed to. When Gromyko said that Moscow had rights in West Berlin, Rusk raised what he termed "reciprocity," Western rights in East Berlin. This drew a frustrated rejoinder from Gromyko, but he left the subject and did not return to it.[56]

The Soviets occasionally reverted to earlier positions. For example, they raised objections to Adenauer's "provocative" presence in Berlin when President Kennedy visited there in June 1963. Kennedy dismissed those objections, reversing his 1961 decision to keep Adenauer off Johnson's flight to Berlin. Adenauer even rode in the same car with Kennedy and Brandt during the Berlin motorcade.[57]

Khrushchev had correctly foreseen that his missile deployment in Cuba would decide the Berlin crisis. But he had not expected to lose the confrontation that he had prepared. In the distant waters of the Caribbean, the West had won a signal victory in the struggle over Germany.

ELEVEN

DE GAULLE MOVES IN

THE BERLIN CRISIS HELPED TO DETERMINE THE FUTURE STRUCTURE of Europe and the role that Germany was to play in it and in the world.

Western Europe was shaping its future during the years of the crisis. In particular, Great Britain was negotiating for membership in the European Economic Community (EEC). Harold Macmillan wanted Britain to join so as to avoid being isolated from the continent's booming economy. John Kennedy supported Macmillan's efforts because he thought British membership would strengthen EEC links with the United States.

Charles de Gaulle harbored virulent suspicions about British intentions. He thought that the British and the Americans, whom he termed the "Anglo-Saxons," did not share the traditions, attitudes or interests of the continental European states. Pressing the EEC to drive a hard bargain with Macmillan, he wanted to make certain that Britain would be forced to relinquish its traditional Commonwealth links if it wanted to join Europe. Many EEC states disagreed with de Gaulle, believing that British membership could be good for the EEC and for Europe.

Konrad Adenauer had the swing vote. If he supported British membership, he would isolate de Gaulle and Britain could enter. If Adenauer supported de Gaulle, Macmillan had no chance.

De Gaulle and Adenauer did not have the same approach to Europe. De Gaulle spoke in myths; Adenauer dreaded myths. De Gaulle was romantic; Adenauer was practical. De Gaulle worshiped the nation; Adenauer despised the nation. De Gaulle wanted a Europe directed by its leading states; Adenauer wanted a Europe that would transcend states. De Gaulle saw the Atlantic and the Channel as moats; Adenauer saw them as bridges. All they had in common was the absolute determination to build a Europe different from the past, and to build it together.

The Berlin crisis reconciled whatever differences they had because it convinced both men that they could rely only on each other. De Gaulle consciously wooed Adenauer, stressing that France alone protected the interests of the Europeans. The chancellor proved unable and unwilling to resist, especially because the evidence proved de Gaulle's point.[1]

ADENAUER THANKS DE GAULLE

Adenauer and de Gaulle had met for the first time in the fall of 1958 at de Gaulle's home at Colombey-les-Deux-Églises, shortly after de Gaulle's return to power and right before Khrushchev's first ultimatum. De Gaulle had made Adenauer feel at ease and welcome. He had also convinced Adenauer that, for the first time in centuries, France would not try to weaken Germany. Two years later, at the French chateau of Rambouillet near Paris, de Gaulle had told Adenauer his concept of Europe and had proposed a strong Franco-German link as the foundation for the continent.

In May 1962, de Gaulle spoke of "solidarity between Germany and France." In July, during a visit by Adenauer to France, de Gaulle hailed the chancellor as the man who had led Germany to freedom, prosperity and respectability. French and German troops marched side by side at Mourmelon in an act of reconciliation that only de Gaulle could command. In September, de Gaulle visited Germany for what the French were to call the first visit to Germany by a French head of state in a millennium, since 921. De Gaulle spoke partly in German, a gesture that was especially successful—as the French ambassador in Washington, Hervé Alphand, told Rusk.

To cap the point, during a speech in Hamburg de Gaulle called the Germans "a great people."[2] Coming in sharp contrast to consistent savaging from Washington and London, de Gaulle's words had a powerful human as well as political effect.

But de Gaulle did more than speak kind words. He helped Adenauer to steer through the labyrinth of the Berlin Wall crisis and of Kennedy's "probes." He briefed Adenauer from time to time on new proposals being discussed between Washington, London and Paris. He cast himself as the protector of German security and German interests. By resisting the British and American tendency to suggest ever more sweeping concessions to Khrushchev, de Gaulle put the chancellor in his debt. Much to the annoyance of Kennedy and Rusk, de Gaulle did not offer Berlin or Germany the kind of military protection that U.S. and British forces did, but he honored German sovereignty and he offered respect to a leader who appreciated it.

De Gaulle had his own solution to the German question: a solid and unbreakable link between Paris and Bonn. That link would form the central element of a new continental Europe independent of both America and the Soviet Union (although intended ultimately to include a revived Russia). With that link firmly in place, Europe could reestablish itself and recover its greatness.

With Kennedy and his advisers concentrating on Asia and the Soviet Union, the president did not have a clear vision of or for Europe until July 1962. Then he sketched out what he called a "Grand Design" of a new European-American partnership that would include the United States, Great Britain and the continent in a single structure. He put England at the center of his "Grand Design," echoing Macmillan's and rejecting de Gaulle's ideas.

Kennedy failed to see the threat that de Gaulle represented. Nor did he realize that the general's tactics had begun to carry the day in Bonn. Although many of Adenauer's ministers supported Kennedy's European concept more than de Gaulle's, and although Adenauer had himself tried to associate Great Britain with European integration in the early 1950s, the chancellor had decided by 1962 that Great Britain had an occupation mentality toward Germany and that Kennedy had bought into it.

Kennedy wanted Adenauer to support British membership in the EEC. In remarkably threatening messages, Rusk warned Adenauer that the United States expected him to support Great Britain and that there would be "grave consequences" for Bonn if West Germany should help France to make British entry "unreasonably difficult."[3] Rusk used harsher language with Adenauer than he ever used with any other U.S. ally (or with Khrushchev), defeating his own purpose by validating de Gaulle's contention that the Anglo-Saxons looked down on the continent.

Kennedy's own cabinet sabotaged his policies. First, Rusk alienated Adenauer. Then, Secretary of Defense Robert McNamara unilaterally abrogated an Anglo-American nuclear missile program, "Skybolt," on which Great Britain and Macmillan had hung their long-term nuclear deterrent plans. To repair the damage, Kennedy met with Macmillan in Bermuda just before Christmas, 1962, and agreed to provide Polaris-type nuclear missiles for Great Britain. But they did not brief NATO, de Gaulle or Adenauer. Nothing could have better suited de Gaulle's purpose. On January 14, 1963, he announced that he would veto British entry to the EEC.

Eight days later, de Gaulle and Adenauer signed the Elysée Treaty for Franco-German cooperation. Adenauer agreed to the treaty in order to lay the foundations for a European peace before he retired. Having personally seen their nations try to destroy each other twice in half a century, the two old men wanted to set those nations on a new and unalterable course.

Kennedy and all of Washington reacted as if they had been hit by a clap of thunder. Only a week before the signing of the Elysée treaty, the United States had invited Adenauer to have Germany join in a new nuclear multilateral force, the MLF, that was to link the nuclear defense of the United States and continental Europe. Adenauer had agreed, perhaps in part to soften the impact of his impending accord with de Gaulle. Now, Adenauer had helped sabotage Kennedy's design for Europe.

The Franco-German treaty, coming on the heels of de Gaulle's veto against Britain in the EEC, meant that de Gaulle was winning the competition for Germany and was deciding the shape of Europe. Adenauer remembered who had treated Germany as an ally and as a sovereign state, and he would not fight de Gaulle for the sake of Macmillan.

The Bundestag, however, did not agree with Adenauer. Most of its members welcomed a close link to France but did not want to jeopardize either the American or the British connection. When the Bundestag approved the Elysée treaty, it added a preamble underlining the importance of all German alliances, especially that between Europe and the United States. It also expressed support for the integration of NATO forces and for British membership in the EEC. While ratifying the agreement with France, it reaffirmed the ties with others and especially with the United States.

But the Bundestag could not reverse Adenauer's decision. The chancellor had to forgive what Kennedy had said, especially after the Cuban missile crisis. Kennedy had grown in stature and had protected West Berlin. Moreover, the United States remained West Germany's main strategic ally. But Adenauer did not have to forgive or forget what Macmillan had said and done.

KENNEDY BECOMES A BERLINER

Kennedy went to Berlin on June 26, 1963, facing a grave dilemma. He realized that de Gaulle had developed a friendship with Adenauer and was using it to shape a Europe very different from the one that Kennedy had envisioned. He also realized that he still needed to talk with Khrushchev on arms control and other matters. He needed to appeal to the Germans and the Berliners enough to counter de Gaulle, while still keeping the door open for talks with Moscow.

Kennedy planned to make two speeches in Berlin: A public address at the West Berlin city hall in Schöneberg, and an academic lecture at the Free University. He planned to use the speeches to outline U.S. policy in the European and global context. He wanted to praise the Berliners for their courageous stand but to speak in terms that Khrushchev would regard as accommodating. A memorandum from the German desk in the State Department had suggested a careful middle course that balanced both purposes, warning the president to avoid sounding "overtly provocative" while still dealing with what it termed the "political and emotional requirements" of the visit.

But Kennedy and his advisers had not reckoned on the Berliners themselves. Although Clay had told them to expect an enormous reception, they had not prepared themselves for the overwhelming mass of delirious humanity that engulfed the presidential motorcade from the moment that Kennedy's party left the Tegel airport.

The Berliners greeted Kennedy very differently from the way they would have greeted him in the fall of 1961 or the spring of 1962. By 1963, he was the hero of the Cuban missile crisis and the man who had saved West Berlin. Over two million came to cheer him along his thirty-five-mile route. Over three-quarters of a million overflowed the square in front of the city hall to hear and applaud his speech.

The throngs of cheering Berliners began to impact on Kennedy and his entourage as their cars and buses advanced slowly through the throngs. Although members of the White House staff initially snickered at the Berliners who had gathered at the exits of the airport, saying that such crowds had undoubtedly also cheered the Nazis and that Germans would do anything for a parade, the unbridled acclaim from the vast hordes of people gradually made them realize that this reception differed from anything they had ever experienced.

Kennedy, a politician from head to foot, reacted to the power of the crowd. He realized that he could not follow the rather dull text that had been drafted for his speech at the city hall. Instead, he had to make a political statement. He began redrafting in his mind and asked others to help. He rewrote even more after he had stood on an observation post facing the Wall and had noticed some East Berlin women surreptitiously waving their kerchiefs at him while trying not to be noticed by armed Vopos. For the first time, Kennedy saw the Wall and the Ulbricht regime in human terms.

Kennedy's city hall speech, as he changed it, lost its balanced tone. It rang as a paean to freedom and to those brave enough to defend it. Following de Gaulle's model, he wanted to say some words in German, which he had practiced before his trip. He even trumped de Gaulle, capturing not only the imagination but also the unique role of the Berliners when he hailed their pride in being able to say *"Ich bin ein Berliner."* Praising the spirit of the Berliners and their determination to resist the tyranny all around them, he challenged all people to come to Berlin to see the contrast between the free and the communist worlds.[4]

Sorensen and Bundy looked on uncomfortably. They did not like Kennedy's speech.[5] They did not think its tone would promote negotiations with the Kremlin. But Kennedy felt that he had seized the moment. He understood better than they the kind of language that he needed to use. He also may have understood there, even more than he had ever learned from letters and talks with Clay, that the United States should regard the attitude of the Berliners as an asset.

Kennedy's briefing papers had warned him that he should use his visit to Germany not only to keep the door to Moscow open but also to undercut the growing influence of de Gaulle. To do the latter, Kennedy had to say things that his staff had not planned or advocated.[6]

In one brief visit, and in one speech, Kennedy turned around his policy toward Germany and Berlin. He and his advisers had once seen Germany and Berlin as inert pieces to be fitted into a new global structure to be negotiated with Khrushchev. They had tried hard to build that structure, but Khrushchev had rebuffed them despite his talk of "peaceful coexistence." Seeing West Germany slip into the Gaullist camp, and seeing the spirit of the Berliners, Kennedy proclaimed his new policy in dramatic terms. When he had finished, he had created a new bond.

Kennedy gave a formal policy speech later that same day at the Free University of Berlin.[7] In the part of that speech addressing Khrushchev, Kennedy stressed the importance of negotiations. He also warned his audience that they, like he, would have to deal with Moscow.

Even in the Free University speech, however, Kennedy used words he had not used before. He advocated German unification for the first time, although he warned that it would not be "either quick or easy." He said that unification would require patience and a readiness to deal with "realities as they actually are and not as we wish they were." Against the realities of "the police state regime" in East Germany, he summoned "the realities of Western strength, the realities of Western commitment, the realities of Germany as a nation and a people."

The speeches marked Kennedy's final reconciliation with the paradox of Berlin and Germany as simultaneous problems and assets. His speech at the Schöneberg city hall marked his final liberation from his fear about offending the Soviets. For the first time, he fully committed himself to the American and Western position in Germany and Berlin. By the ringing tenor of his speech he reinforced and extended both that position and that commitment.

Kennedy's speeches also showed that he no longer saw Berlin and Germany only in the context of Soviet-American relations. He had come to understand that the U.S. presence in Germany constituted a political and strategic prize instead of a hazard. Unlike the early days of his presidency, when he and Rusk had wanted Berlin to go away, he had returned to Germany as the cornerstone of any American policy in Europe. Having watched Khrushchev and de Gaulle struggle over Germany, Kennedy for the first time understood the stakes.

Kennedy's speech at the Schöneberg city hall was to become part of the legend of Berlin and of Kennedy himself. No other Kennedy speech, except perhaps his inaugural address, is cited as often. From that speech forward, America and Berlin became bonded more firmly than they had been even after the blockade or Checkpoint Charlie. After Kennedy was assassinated, the bond took on a mythical quality that his successors could not ignore and that they dared not abandon.

Kennedy's full commitment to Berlin ended whatever hopes Ulbricht or Khrushchev might still have had to push or negotiate American forces out. No American president could back away from the words that Kennedy had spoken. It did not matter that he had not begun his presidency with that commitment. It mattered only that he ended it that way.

As Kennedy and his euphoric entourage flew away from Berlin, he told Sorensen, "we'll never have another day like this, as long as we live."[8]

WINNERS, LOSERS, AND TWICE DIVIDED EUROPE

The Berlin Wall crisis changed the struggle over Germany. It ended whatever hope had remained for early German unification. It also marked one of the main turning points in the Cold War through its two classic confrontations at Checkpoint Charlie and Cuba.

The crisis ended on an unresolved chord. The Wall had completed the separation of the German people, but West Berlin with its Western garrisons remained an island in East Germany. No single leader had achieved all that he had wanted. Nonetheless, winners and losers did emerge, and the Berlin outcome was to shape the future for them as well as for Germany and Europe.

Charles de Gaulle emerged as the biggest winner. He had correctly predicted that Khrushchev would neither negotiate nor fight. Germany had been divided, as he privately wished, but he bore no responsibility for dividing it. Britain had been barred from Europe, as he also wished, with German concurrence. Adenauer had balanced his reliance on the United States with reliance on France. By supporting Adenauer, de Gaulle forged a Franco-German link that tied West Germany firmly to the future of the European Community and the European

Union. He outmaneuvered Kennedy in the competition for Europe and Germany while Kennedy focused on a deal with Moscow. And he would not have been human if he had not relished the thought that he had finally destroyed the notion that the Big Three could decide the fate of Europe and Germany.

De Gaulle's vision of Europe as a continental entity, excluding England and America, made important progress and—at least for a time—won German support. It was to remain a powerful vision that would return again and again as Europe rebuilt itself during the remainder of the century.

Kennedy stumbled at the beginning of the Berlin crisis but recovered at the end. Initially intimidated by the risks of confrontation, escalation and miscalculation, he permitted the Wall to be built without even a murmur. But he proved a quick study. He learned that managed and controlled confrontations could be good policy and good politics. He used in Cuba the tactics he had watched in Berlin.

Kennedy permitted himself to be enticed by the wistful notion that the superpowers could establish in 1961 the stable world order that they had failed to build in 1945. He understood by 1963 that this could not be done, especially because Khrushchev did not make a reliable partner for that kind of agreement. At the end, therefore, Kennedy returned to the transatlantic architecture of Bevin, Truman, Acheson and Eisenhower. And he understood, as they had, that such an order needed a sovereign West Germany. But he permitted de Gaulle's continental concept to gain a strong foothold which it never again relinquished.

Ulbricht moved in the opposite direction from Kennedy, starting well but ending badly. By blocking the refugee flow, he solved his immediate problem, But he could neither stabilize his regime nor obtain the border he wanted. And he left a legacy of mistrust in Moscow.

Ulbricht's policy with respect to West Berlin proved disastrous. Far from "neutralizing" West Berlin as he had announced in 1958, he attached it more firmly than ever to the West. And Ulbricht knew, better than anyone, that he would never be totally secure as long as West Berlin remained independent in the middle of his state. He had built perfect fences but he knew that he would need something more.

Khrushchev had started the Berlin crisis but had increasingly shown that he did not really know what he wanted. He won East Berlin for Ulbricht but nothing for himself. He undermined his own hope for "peaceful coexistence." As Henry Kissinger later wrote, Khrushchev knew how to begin a crisis but not how to end one.[9]

Khrushchev and Gromyko proved poor negotiators. Their tactics, like Molotov's, put others on the defensive but gained no agreement. Eisenhower could not deal with them even when he was ready to do so. At Vienna, Kennedy wanted to make an accommodation on Berlin. In 1962 he virtually begged Khrushchev to accept terms that accommodated most Soviet views and even used Soviet language. But Khrushchev kept asking for more than Kennedy could give. He wanted to negotiate only after the Cuban confrontation, but by then Kennedy had lost all incentive to make a deal on Berlin. Khrushchev got the divided Germany he wanted, but he ended up as trapped behind the GDR as Stalin had been. Peaceful coexistence became a dead letter.

Khrushchev's periodic efforts to talk separately with Adenauer showed that he may have wanted to entice Germany back to a neutral course between East and West. Among the occupation leaders, de Gaulle alone understood the trap that Khrushchev had set. But Adenauer also understood it and avoided it.

Macmillan proved the greatest loser. Through his influence over Kennedy, Macmillan dominated Western policy on Berlin and Germany during most of 1961 and 1962. But he looked to the past, not the future. He tried to reverse Ernest Bevin's and Anthony Eden's work and go back to Churchill.

When the Berlin Wall crisis had ended in 1962, British policy had lost credibility in Germany and over much of Europe. Dreaming of a bygone global role for Britain, Macmillan made Germany accept de Gaulle's definition of the continent.

London was never to recover its once strong voice in German affairs. British troops remained in Germany, as Eden had arranged, but Macmillan surrendered a political presence on the continent. Although Britain was to enter the EEC by 1973, it missed the chance to do it at an early stage with the continent still in flux.

The Wall, therefore, divided Europe not only along the East-West border but also along the Channel. It drew two lines. One ran between the democratic and the communist systems; the other ran between the continent and Great Britain.

The Wall also served as a wake-up call for West German leaders. The Allied reaction showed the West Germans that their friends would defend NATO and their own interests, protecting West Germany and West Berlin even at considerable risk to themselves, but that they would not go beyond those interests to defend specifically German concerns.

Adenauer understood this as he stood on the tarmac at Bonn to watch Johnson fly to Berlin. Brandt understood it as he watched the Allied reaction to the Wall and as he heard Kennedy's speech at the Free University. Unification might have returned in American rhetoric but not in American policy. The Germans themselves would have to find the way to end or ease their country's division.[10]

The Wall and the "probes" dispute dropped the German question into German hands. The West Germans could rejoice in that, for it meant that the struggle over Germany would no longer be decided over their heads or without them. The occupation would truly be over. But it also meant that they would themselves now have to address the German question and shape their country's future. To do this, they would have to come to terms with their history since Bismarck's creation of the German Reich in 1871. They would also have to decide upon their real strategic, political and human priorities, and they would have to accept responsibility for those decisions at home and abroad.

TWELVE

THE POISONED CHALICE

PRESIDENT JOHN KENNEDY'S BERLIN SPEECHES HAD TOLD THE Germans on both sides of the Wall what the United States would and would not do. The United States would defend the freedom and viability of West Berlin and would defend West Germany. But no longer would Kennedy negotiate with Soviet premier Khrushchev about Berlin or the German question. And he would not go out of his way to try to unify Germany.

Chancellor Konrad Adenauer could relax. He would not be asked to approve any more unappetizing peace packages under unacceptable deadlines. He and Germany would be left alone.

But Adenauer could not take too much satisfaction either. The German question had not roiled West German politics for years because the occupation powers bore the sole responsibility for it. Now, the Germans would have to take that responsibility. They would have to make the difficult decisions about their future, and they would have to deal with the results, at home and abroad.

Kennedy had given the Federal Republic a poisoned chalice, a gift that might look tempting but that could be deadly. Or, as the Germans themselves might say, *Der Schwarze Peter* (as in a card game, the "Old Maid") had come to Bonn. The Germans would now have to address a problem that had baffled the Council of Foreign Ministers and many others. They might have to propose concessions that they had condemned others for considering. And they would have to face the arguments that were sure to follow.

Moreover, Germany was now fully divided, as it had not been before the Wall. The country had been split not only in political and military terms but in human terms. And the Wall might give Walter Ulbricht time to consolidate his rule and to keep Germany divided for a long time to come. Those who wanted to keep the German nation united would have to act fast.

GERMANS FACE THE GERMAN QUESTION

Bonn's allies had done as much as they would do. Neither they nor the Soviets could win the struggle over Germany, either by force or by diplomacy. They would now back off. They could accept the status quo, imperfect as it might be.

But West Germany could not accept the status quo. The Federal Republic's commitment to unification remained in its Basic Law and in its politics. West German politicians had to try for unification or at least appear to be trying.

Adenauer continued to try to neutralize the GDR. After 1958, he had periodically renewed his invitation to Nikita Khrushchev to negotiate an Austrian solution for the GDR. Under his proposals, East Germany would be neutralized like Austria and would have a democratic regime to improve the lives of its people. Later, perhaps in five or ten years, free elections would decide Germany's fate. Khrushchev neither accepted nor rejected the offers. Nor did he appear to have mentioned them to Ulbricht.[1] He kept them in reserve, perhaps hoping one day to use them to make his own deal and split West Germany from its allies.

Adenauer limited his own options. He would not deal with the GDR. He rejected Ulbricht's often-reiterated proposals to negotiate a German "confederation" based on the equal status of the GDR and the Federal Republic. Nor would he authorize any reply to messages that GDR officials sent to West German officials. Adenauer had established democracy and respectability in West Germany, putting an end to nefarious elements of Bismarck's legacy; someone else would have to establish unity across all of Germany.

The German policy that Adenauer bequeathed to his successor, Ludwig Erhard, held the German question in abeyance. He did not leave a plan. And, by constantly reiterating his own views, he placed strict limits on what Erhard could do.

Even if Washington would not negotiate for Germany, it still reserved the right to comment on German efforts. In September 1963, U.S. Ambassador George McGhee complained that Adenauer had not briefed him on his offers to Khrushchev.[2] Later, McGhee warned about the risks entailed in talks that Berlin Governing Mayor Willy Brandt wanted to open with the GDR (this topic is discussed more fully later).[3] Paradoxically, President Lyndon Johnson complained that West Germany did not pursue relaxation of tensions hard enough.[4]

Despite these constraints, the West German foreign minister, Gerhard Schröder, wanted to try to relax tensions in Europe and to expand West German influence to the East. In 1963, he began systematically to negotiate trade treaties and to exchange trade missions with east European states. He enlarged the West German presence and created better relations but did not violate the Hallstein Doctrine because he did not establish diplomatic ties. Between March of 1963, when he was still in Adenauer's cabinet, and March of 1964, when Erhard had become chancellor, Schröder had agreed to exchange trade missions with Poland, Hungary, Bulgaria and Romania. Only Czechoslovakia rejected Schröder's offers because of conflicting claims surrounding Hitler's invasion of Czechoslovakia and the Czech expulsion of Germans after World War II.

Ulbricht saw Schröder's policies as dangerous. He feared that West Germany could undercut east European support for the GDR. He protested vigorously to his allies, denouncing the trade missions as "Trojan horses."

Schröder won no support at home either. CSU leader Franz Josef Strauss said that the trade missions risked subverting the Hallstein Doctrine. He blocked talks with Czechoslovakia because many refugees in Bavaria had fled from there and wanted compensation for their property. Erhard did not back Schröder firmly, and the foreign minister found himself hemmed in on all sides. He had to end his efforts for contacts with eastern Europe.

American strategic policy further limited Schröder's dealings with the East. While Kennedy wanted West Germany to improve its relations with Moscow, he promoted a strategic plan that would have given West Germany the theoretical authority to help direct NATO nuclear weapons against Soviet territory. The Multilateral Force (MLF) that he had offered Adenauer provided for NATO submarines and surface vessels manned by multinational forces including West Germans. Such a force could have fired 200 Polaris and other missiles against east European and Soviet territory, giving NATO a powerful regional deterrent against a Soviet attack in central Europe.

Erhard followed Adenauer in accepting the U.S. plan, despite many personal misgivings. It would not give Bonn authority to launch nuclear weapons but would give it a voice. The MLF could help West Germany because it might reduce the risk that NATO would have to launch immediate nuclear defensive strikes along the inner-German border, killing countless Germans to destroy attacking Soviet forces. But Strauss and German strategists feared that a deterrent at sea would be less credible than one on land because it could take its time to retaliate. It might undercut the "first strike" concept, letting Soviet forces overrun West Germany before reacting. But the West German defense community had become so disturbed by the diverse strategic ruminations emanating from

Washington that Bonn was disposed to accept even an imperfect plan that had some substance. The Germans worried about Defense Secretary McNamara's concept of "flexible response." They feared that West Germany would be defended with conventional weapons alone, not enough of a deterrent to hold back the Soviets. The MLF seemed to offer at least some deterrent.

Erhard wanted to cooperate with Washington on defense. He poisoned his relations with de Gaulle by accepting the MLF proposal instead of a French plan for a European nuclear deterrent.[5] Even the SPD, after an exceptionally divisive internal debate, accepted the MLF. Helmut Schmidt, the SPD's main defense expert, argued strongly for it.

Khrushchev objected fiercely. NATO missiles at sea could reach much farther into the Soviet Union than the short-range missiles stationed in Germany. Soviet territory would be at risk in a European conflict, even if American territory was not. Nor did Khrushchev want to have Germans learning nuclear weapons technology and management. To the Soviets, MLF represented a strategic German threat. Khrushchev and Ulbricht harped on the MLF to claim that "revanchists" in Bonn were planning to start a world war.

In late 1964, Johnson and McNamara suddenly canceled the MLF, embarrassing Erhard and enraging Schmidt, who complained that the United States had proven "inconsistent and unreliable." Most German defense experts also resented the sudden U.S. reversal, although they welcomed the permanent German membership in the newly formed NATO Nuclear Planning Group that Washington and NATO offered as an alternative to the MLF.[6]

American decisions first to initiate and then to cancel the MLF reinforced the belief held by many West Germans that they had to look out for themselves more than before. They increasingly began to search for a more autonomous foreign policy.

Against this background, Khrushchev launched another personal venture in the diplomacy of Germany. In March 1964 he let it be known that he would like to visit the FRG. He sent his son-in-law Alexei Adzhubei, then the editor of the Moscow newspaper *Izvestia*, to Germany to prepare the visit. Adzhubei said that Khrushchev definitely wanted to improve German-Soviet relations; he even intimated that his father-in-law might be prepared to contemplate German unification.[7]

Khrushchev never explained why he wanted to visit. With the Soviet economy entering what was to prove a long decline, he may well have wanted more German investments and credits. He had announced in late 1963 that the Soviet Union needed to produce and to import more chemicals, especially fertilizers and pesticides. In March 1964, he announced the purchase of a chemical herbicide plant from Krupp. Adzhubei met with leaders of such German industrial giants as Krupp, Thyssen and Hoechst.

Ulbricht reacted angrily to Khrushchev's plans. To show that Moscow did not need to sell its soul for West German chemicals, he announced a major program to expand East German chemical production. He also began a vicious propaganda campaign against the Federal Republic, singling out as "fascist" the very enterprises that Adzhubei had visited.

Ulbricht went even further to distance himself from Khrushchev. He had long meetings in East Berlin with two conservative Soviet defense officials, Defense Minister Rodian Malinovsky and Marshal Andrei Grechko. He had the SED newspaper *Neues Deutschland* publish articles denouncing "the traitor, Beria" for having tried to make a deal with West Germany. He also had the newspaper instruct Khrushchev that he should not make any deals with Erhard until after the latter had signed an agreement fully recognizing the GDR. When Ulbricht visited Moscow in June 1964 to sign the Treaty of Friendship and Cooperation that Khrushchev offered him as a sop for having failed to achieve the separate peace treaty, he openly distanced himself from a number of the Soviet leader's remarks.

By mid-1964, Ulbricht and Khrushchev had fallen out completely. Ulbricht already despised Khrushchev for failing to carry out his pledges on Berlin. He now had more complaints. He may also have known that Khrushchev's enemies planned to move. For no matter how angry he might have been, he would never have defied the Soviet leader so openly if he had not thought that Khrushchev's days were numbered.

Khrushchev in turn must have disliked Ulbricht intensely. Ulbricht had pushed him into the Berlin crisis but then had to be bailed out at Checkpoint Charlie. The Wall had humiliated the communist system as a whole. Three years after it had been built, Ulbricht's GDR could show some economic progress but could still not produce all that Khrushchev wanted.

Right after Khrushchev had signed his treaty with Ulbricht, the West German government announced that the Soviet premier would visit West Germany in 1965. It also announced that the agenda would be open-ended, meaning that Khrushchev would be prepared to discuss the German question.

On the night of October 14–15, 1964, however, Khrushchev was deposed. His successor, Leonid Brezhnev, quickly made statements supporting Ulbricht more firmly than Khrushchev had done. The statements implied that those who had deposed Khrushchev had done so at least in part to block his latest German venture, whatever it might have been. But, if Brezhnev had helped Ulbricht, it was not out of any firm personal sympathy for the GDR or any strong views on Germany. A Soviet diplomat wrote that Brezhnev had been picked because he was the CPSU leader most ready to carry out the wishes of the senior Kremlin collective, not because he had opinions of his own.[8]

Khrushchev had come full circle. He had helped to crush Beria by accusing him of planning German unification. He had chosen to deepen Germany's division with the Wall. At the end, he had again hinted at German unification. Yet he still faced the same dilemma Stalin had faced: how to have influence over all of Germany while preserving the Soviet protectorate in eastern Germany. He could not solve it any better than Stalin.

Khrushchev's fall humiliated Erhard. On October 15, the chancellor had told the Bundestag that he planned to offer a new German unification plan to Khrushchev in Bonn. Later it became clear that the Soviet leader had already been deposed by the time Erhard spoke.

To add insult to injury, in early 1965 the new Soviet Premier, Alexei Kosygin, rejected Erhard's invitation to visit Bonn. After that, the stagnation in Erhard's German and foreign policy became a running sore. Erhard himself could perhaps not be blamed. Adenauer had left him on a dead-end street, and his allies had made it worse. But he had failed to put forward new ideas at a time when Germany was groping for them.

With no German settlement on the horizon, Willy Brandt decided to try some steps in Berlin itself to ease at least some burdens of the Wall. He wanted to help West and East Berlin families meet during the Christmas and New Year season, if it could be done without excessive political cost.

In late 1961, after the Wall had gone up, Brandt had informally asked East German authorities to make it possible for families separated by the Wall to get together at Christmas. He had followed up through various contacts in East Berlin, but had received no response for two years. Efforts to bring families together, even in emergencies, failed. Ulbricht showed no interest.[9]

Suddenly, on December 5, 1963, Brandt got a message from the GDR Council of Ministers offering to talk about passes for West Berliners to meet relatives in East Berlin during the upcoming Christmas and New Year season. Brandt immediately agreed. The Allies gave their approval. Erhard also concurred, but only at the last moment due to objections from some CDU/CSU members.

A series of hurried negotiations ensued. As Brandt had to avoid substantiating Ulbricht's claim that West Berlin was a separate sovereign state, the negotiations proved extremely complicated, involving hundreds of meetings in East and West Berlin and producing such complex legal and procedural circumlocutions that few persons could understand them. But Ulbricht finally accepted formulas that did not make the agreement an inter-state document. To skirt the most sensitive political issues, the negotiators devised the face-saving formula that "both sides have established that it is impossible to reach agreement on joint definitions of *localities, authorities, and official posts*" (*Oerter, Behörden, und Amtsbezeichnungen*). Each side could use the terminology it wished.[10]

West Berliners wanted far more passes than anyone had expected. They lined up for six to eight hours in the cold to apply. The East German authorities had prepared for about 30,000 visitors. They got almost 800,000, who made over 1.2 million visits because some came several times. Although officially the West Berliners could meet only East Berlin family members, other relatives came from all over East Germany. Brandt hailed the reunions as a humanitarian triumph, estimating that over 4 million people had seen each other over Christmas and the New Year. Ulbricht also had reason to be pleased because of the fees that the GDR received for the passes and the funds that the West Berliners spent in the East.

The West Berlin administration and the GDR reached similar agreements over the next three years, for Christmas 1964, Easter and Pentecost 1965, Christmas and the New Year 1965–1966 and Easter and Pentecost 1966. They also reached agreements covering visits for emergency family situations. After mid-1966, however, Ulbricht stopped the agreements. He no longer accepted the face-saving clause that skirted irreconcilable debates about terminology, perhaps because he wanted full recognition immediately or because he thought he could do better with a new government that might emerge in Bonn.

East German documents later revealed that SED leaders argued fiercely about the pass agreement. Some objected that the face-saving formula failed to recognize GDR sovereignty over East Berlin. Ulbricht called five meetings of the SED politburo over five days. At one point, the politburo had decided to reject the formula and had prepared a press release announcing the collapse of the talks. At the last moment, however, Ulbricht decided to go ahead. Although the documents do not reveal Soviet views, Ulbricht could not have acted without Soviet consent.[11]

Ulbricht did not always get Soviet support for openings to the West. In February 1966, he proposed speaker exchanges between leaders of the SED and the SPD, with SED leaders to speak in West Germany and SPD leaders in East Germany. Brandt and the SPD readily accepted and designated their speakers. A series of letters detailing the arrangements followed. At the end of June, however, when everything appeared to have been agreed, the SED suddenly drew back and canceled the arrangement.

Ulbricht blamed the West German Bundestag for not having passed legislation that would give SED officials the full immunity they needed against charges that they played a role in refugee killings at the Wall.

But it later became known that the Soviet ambassador in East Berlin, Pyotr Abrasimov, had blocked the exchange. He informed other diplomats in East Berlin curtly that "the meetings will not take place." The Soviets evidently still mistrusted Germans, including their own. Abrasimov later told Brandt in a private talk that the Soviets did not like direct meetings between SED and SPD leaders: "Who knows what might be said behind closed doors?"[12]

THREE MEN AND A PREGNANT PHRASE

As Erhard floundered, the Social Democrats saw their chance. If the Allies and the CDU had given up on the German question, they wanted to try. Even small steps unworthy of great power attention, like Christmas passes, meant something.

Three men in particular—Willy Brandt, Egon Bahr, and Herbert Wehner—knew what they wanted to do.

Brandt believed that the new generation of Germans owed it to themselves and to history to come forward with new ideas. He took President Kennedy's message seriously and personally. If the ice age of the Cold War could be ended, Germans had to help define the next phase.

Brandt spun visions where others might craft policies. He could conceive new solutions for old problems and evoke them in terms that would inspire support. As his obvious sincerity gave him a hold over his listeners, even jaded diplomats, he could lead by conviction and by the sheer force of his ideals.

Brandt's priorities differed from both Bismarck's and Adenauer's. Bismarck had chosen German unity without democracy. Adenauer had chosen democracy and had been ready to postpone unity. Brandt wanted to try for both. He thought he could find the right policy.

Like Adenauer, Brandt condemned Bismarck, mainly for having pursued cynical *Staatsraison*, reason of state, instead of any kind of ideals. Brandt loathed the meticulous calculation of interests, objectives, concessions and counter-concessions, tactics and counter-tactics, artifice and counter-artifice, that he saw as the fabric of conventional diplomatic discourse. He pursued diplomacy with conviction and intuition, sure that his open demeanor could achieve more than the carefully calibrated maneuvers of others.

Brandt feared that Germans could lose their sense of being one people if the physical division remained in place too long. He did not want the German sense of nation to atrophy. Whereas Adenauer saw unity as a distant commitment, to be sought only in secure, stable negotiations, Brandt saw it as an urgent human need. He also thought he could maneuver better terms than Adenauer had been offered.[13]

Brandt had chosen Egon Bahr to bring the vision to reality, to find the words to articulate Brandt's ideals and the processes to implement Brandt's concepts. As a radio reporter, Bahr understood the value of the right word at the right time. He could make things happen, inventing diplomatic formulas and sequences that others could not imagine. Strategically tenacious yet tactically inventive, he could bob and weave through any diplomatic minefield that Brandt wanted him to cross.

Although Bahr shared Brandt's fundamental goals, he could not command loyalty like Brandt. Many, especially foreigners, distrusted him, finding him too quick and almost excessively articulate. They thought that he manipulated language to persuade rather than to inform. With Brandt's credibility behind him, however, Bahr could achieve Brandt's objectives even if he could never carry political responsibility.

While supporting Brandt's fundamental purpose, Bahr always operated at the outer edge of his authority. He sometimes left Brandt to justify actions that might have been unexpected. Most leaders would have fired Bahr many times over, but Brandt understood his value and protected him.

Herbert Wehner served as the practical and often ruthless politician who made things work. He had long since given up visions for reality. He lacked Brandt's charm, charisma and flair. He also lacked Bahr's capacity for verbal prestidigitation. But he could manage the SPD and control its direction better than the other two. Although not on the front pages as much as they, he was in many ways the most important of the three. He shared with Brandt, Bahr and Adenauer a powerful commitment to make this German democracy stronger and more enduring than the last. He also wanted to show that the Social Democrats could carry out the responsibility of governing the Federal Republic.

Wehner bore within himself the anguished frustrations and contradictions of the German Left: fury at the German communists and socialists for having failed to work together to stop Hitler when he could have still been stopped; disgust that the East German SPD had accepted Ulbricht's and Stalin's dictate to join in the management of yet another German police state; contempt for the comfortable German middle class; hatred of the struttingly self-important Prussian aristocracy that had taken Germany into World War I and had not opposed the Nazi dictatorship. He sometimes erupted volcanically out of a deep-seated rage, leaving others stunned at his anger.

Out of Wehner's fury rose a towering conviction that the Left could not afford again to be outmaneuvered either by the machinations of others or by its own passion for purity. Having fought against the Nazis on behalf of the Comintern from exile in Prague, Sweden and elsewhere, and having seen friends, comrades and family members imprisoned and butchered by Hitler, he had no patience for small talk or small men.

With the possible exception of Konrad Adenauer, Wehner possessed the keenest political mind in postwar Germany. As a former member of the German Communist Party, a former agent of Stalin's, and an avowed Marxist, he understood politics and he understood power. He realized that the German electorate would no longer tolerate extremism and would not again abandon the center for radical experiments. He also recognized that the German worker did not wish to abandon the prosperity and safety of western Europe and the NATO alliance. He, therefore, more than Brandt or Bahr, forced the SPD to forego leftist intellectual sloganeering and to move toward the center of the political spectrum.

Like other Comintern fighters, Wehner had many skeletons in his closet. No one knew what he said to the Soviets, with whom he had maintained direct contact throughout most of the postwar era. Many suspected him of double-dealing. He had few friends. Few dared to talk to him; fewer dared oppose him.

The three men did not act alone. Other SPD figures, such as Helmut Schmidt, realized that they could not keep the party in the wilderness. But Wehner, with Brandt's support, drove a new policy through the party. First, he organized the 1959 SPD party congress to adopt a new program, which became known as the Godesberger Program and which officially abandoned Marxism as the ideological foundation for the party's domestic policies. The following year he told the Bundestag that the SPD accepted the basic principles of Adenauer's pro-Western foreign policy. Coupled with Brandt's resistance to Khrushchev and Ulbricht in Berlin, Wehner's speech moved the SPD away from Kurt Schumacher's old charge that Adenauer was the "chancellor of the allies" and let the party compete in the mainstream of German public opinion. When Erhard faltered, they were ready to take responsibility.

Brandt found the chance to articulate his vision in July 1963 in a speech at the Evangelical Academy at Tutzing in Bavaria. He formulated his proposals in very human terms, speaking of the pain of German division, of the families split by the Wall and the death strip. He added that force and tension would not bring Germans together again. Such policies only hardened the lines and hurt the people more. Germans had to try new ideas and new approaches in dealing with enemies as well as friends.

In this spirit, Brandt drew several conclusions that were to become the foundations of SPD and later West German policy:

- Reunification is a foreign policy problem that can be solved only with the Soviet Union, not without and not against it.

- It is a path with many steps and many stations.
- The despicable regime in East Germany cannot be destroyed; one must work with it as well.
- Discontent and confrontation will not destroy that regime, but some steps might improve conditions in East Germany.
- These thoughts are uncomfortable and go against our deepest feelings, but they are unavoidable.[14]

Brandt also reminded his audience that June 1953 had shown how the Soviet Union would defend its interests. It would be pointless to expect a violent East German uprising to accomplish anything useful. Instead, Moscow had to see some advantages in change.

Under other circumstances, Brandt's speech might have led to what he wished: a wide-ranging debate and sobering discussion about German division and hopes for German unity. But Bahr, perhaps unwittingly, became the real star at Tutzing. For he trumped Brandt's speech, which he had helped to write, with a phrase of his own.

Bahr had put the phrase *"Wandel durch Annäherung"* into the text of his speech. A friend made it the title. Brandt, perhaps unthinkingly, approved it before Bahr used it. He did not grasp its full meaning and fascination until after the speech.

Like many German phrases, *Wandel durch Annäherung* cannot be translated into English without sacrificing its delicate shadings. Translated directly, as it usually is, it means "change through mutual approach," or, with the customary French word, "change through rapprochement." But the content goes far deeper and can be better expressed as "transformation through mutual accommodation." It implies that parties or states engaged in conciliation might be profoundly if unwittingly altered in the process. It hints that a higher degree of accommodation might produce a higher degree of transformation.

The phrase *Wandel durch Annäherung* was to haunt German political debate. It hinted that the SED regime might change by contact with the West. But it also hinted that the West might change as well. It could thus be construed as positive or negative, aggressive or accommodationist, idealistic or realistic. Who and what was to change or to be transformed, and how? What did Bahr mean specifically? Would Ulbricht's dictatorship become more humane if it were recognized? Would the SED tolerate dissent?

And what if change came in the West, not in the East? Would the West lose its unity, its determination and perhaps its own sense of right? And what might "accommodation" mean in the context of the German question? Formal mutual recognition, anathema to most West Germans? Or East German acquiescence to something less?

Bahr's words glinted in mid-air, demanding and yet defying explanation, evoking either glorious or ruinous possibilities. Brandt later said that he came to dislike the words intensely because they suggested that the democracies might change toward the Soviet totalitarian system, which he did not believe or want. But neither he nor Bahr could wish the words away.

Most important, Bahr's phrase suggested that the mere fact of accommodation might be more important than the terms of that accommodation, for any accommodation might initiate a process of change which could lead in unforeseeable but perhaps desirable directions. Bonn might do well to sign even flawed accords, as even those could perhaps transform Ulbricht's regime and come to have a greater value than might first appear.

Bahr had wanted the East German leadership to know what he and Brandt would say. Two days before the Tutzing speeches, an official from Bahr's office went to East Berlin to present the texts. SED press and propaganda officials analyzed them with great care and some skepticism. They welcomed the notion that the SPD would review German policy toward the GDR but noticed that the speeches did not promise full recognition. They said the speeches did not truly meet GDR needs or wishes.[15]

East Germany's foreign minister, Otto Winzer, saw the danger in Bahr's phrase. He denounced it as *Aggression auf Filzlatschen* (aggression in felt slippers). The GDR could not accept any kind of transformation without risking its very existence. *Wandel durch Annäherung* could mean that the GDR would lose in the long run more than it might appear to have gained in the short run.

As the debate roared on, Bahr found himself engulfed in a firestorm of analysis, criticism and cautious approval. Brandt, ever charitable, supported Bahr and accepted the phrase even if it had stolen his own thunder. But he scolded Bahr for having sent the speech with its pregnant title over the newswires. He also warned that Bahr had begun the debate too early. Wehner grumbled that Bahr talked too much.

With summer coming on, the SPD leaders scattered in various directions for their vacations. But they had left behind them a policy clearly articulated by Willy Brandt and an explanation ambiguously articulated by Egon Bahr. They had also left West Germany's electorate and its allies with a sense that the SPD would look at the German question in a new way.

KIESINGER MANAGES THE TRANSITION

If West German voters had indeed tired of Erhard, they did not show it in October 1965. They returned Erhard and his CDU/CSU as well as the coalition partner FDP to power. Erhard, long in Adenauer's shadow, had won a national election on his own.

But Erhard's victory rang hollow. His coalition received fewer seats than Adenauer's had won at his peak. And the government had run out of ideas. Moreover, despite Erhard's renown as the author of Germany's economic miracle, the economy had begun to slow.

Erhard and Schröder tried to launch a new diplomatic initiative, sending a "peace note" on March 25, 1966, to friend and foe alike (except to the GDR). The peace note represented a landmark departure for West Germany. With the MLF out of the way, Bonn could renounce nuclear weapons to try to ease East-West tensions. But the note said little new, and only Bonn's allies expressed any interest. Brezhnev and Ulbricht thought they could get better terms by waiting.[16]

Wherever he turned, Erhard found more problems than solutions. Lyndon Johnson, whom Erhard met several times in Texas and Washington, undercut him, insisting that West Germany had to help in Vietnam or at least to pay offset costs for U.S. forces stationed in Germany. Johnson and McNamara thought that those forces defended West Germany and that Germans should pay for them. They did not see them as part of America's global strategic architecture.

Erhard used his final visit to Washington in late September 1966 to ask for more time to make the payments. The U.S. Ambassador in Bonn, George McGhee, a personal friend of Johnson's, pleaded with the president to give Erhard that time. He reminded Johnson that Erhard had turned away from Adenauer's French connection and was America's most reliable friend in Europe. But Johnson and McNamara insisted on full compliance with their demands and made no concessions whatsoever to Erhard.[17] Johnson even damaged Erhard's German policy by publicly and forcibly stating that general East-West détente should precede any solution of the German question. Erhard, deeply shocked, had no place left to turn.

Erhard also lost the support of the Free Democratic Party. Walter Scheel, the rising star of the FDP; Ralf Dahrendorf, its principal intellectual; and Hans-Dietrich Genscher all wanted a more active Ostpolitik and especially a new inner-German policy. When Erhard said that he would have to raise taxes to meet Johnson's demands, FDP leader Erich Mende also abandoned him.

The CDU/CSU, full of men who saw themselves as potential chancellors in Erhard's place, agreed to form a grand coalition with the SPD under a new CDU chancellor. That chancellor proved to be Kurt Georg Kiesinger, the minister-president of Baden-Württemberg, who had left Bonn some years earlier in disgust at the petty politicking of the capital.

On December 1, 1966, Kiesinger became chancellor. Brandt, leading the SPD into the grand coalition, became foreign minister. Wehner became minister for all-German affairs, and Bahr became planning chief in the foreign office.

Kiesinger concentrated more of his energy on economic than on foreign policy. But he pledged to do all he could to improve relations with the Soviet Union and with east European states. He began by establishing diplomatic relations with Romania in January 1967 and with Yugoslavia a year later. As both of those states already had relations with the GDR, Kiesinger in effect abandoned the Hallstein Doctrine.

Kiesinger had little success improving relations with Moscow. Although he tried some conciliatory gestures, the Soviet invasion of Czechoslovakia in August 1968 reinforced the aversion of most CDU/CSU members toward the Soviet Union. Kiesinger did not press for further openings.

The new chancellor tried to be more flexible about inner-German relations, changing both the tone and the terminology toward the GDR. He began to refer to the GDR as "the other part of Germany," a relatively neutral formula that avoided both the pejorative "Soviet occupation zone" and the official "German Democratic Republic." He promised to do all that he could to avoid deepening the split between East and West Germany, specifically pledging to try to improve economic and human contacts. Warning that this might entail meetings with East German officials, he said such meetings would not imply recognition of "a second German state."[18]

Five months after his inauguration, Kiesinger announced before the Bundestag a list of specific ideas for better relations between East and West Germany. He proposed easier arrangements for travel, Berlin passes, money and medicine transfers, family reunion, trade, postal and telephone contacts, sports matches, cultural exchanges and the like.

Kiesinger even took part in an exchange of letters with East German premier Willi Stoph. Stoph had begun the exchange in May 1967 with a letter proposing a formal treaty to normalize relations between the two German states and also asking for funds to compensate the GDR for alleged West German sabotage of the East German economy. Kiesinger replied by rejecting what he termed Stoph's "all-or-nothing approach" and suggesting instead a whole range of steps that would make life easier for Germans on both sides. Stoph in turn submitted a draft text of a treaty. Kiesinger rejected that, although Brandt and Wehner showed some interest in negotiating.

Although the Kiesinger-Stoph letters changed nothing, they did offer a measure of recognition. Kiesinger addressed Stoph as "Chairman of the Council of Ministers" while not adding the other half of Stoph's title "of the German Democratic Republic." Even that half-title, however, unleashed bitter debate within the CDU/CSU.[19]

To show the importance that he attached to the German question, Kiesinger in March 1968 issued the first of what were to become annual reports on the State of the Nation in Divided Germany, written in Wehner's ministry. He tried to frame new proposals and new ideas. He even said that he would meet personally with Stoph if such a meeting would lead to a successful negotiation.[20] But Stoph and Ulbricht insisted that there could be no progress unless and until the Federal Republic formally recognized the GDR.

Brandt wanted to go farther and faster than Kiesinger, pulling the coalition forward into new policies. If he could not do so, he at least wanted to have a case to present to the voters in the elections scheduled for 1969. Brandt therefore moved as far forward as he could within the limits of CDU/CSU/SPD coalition policy.

Brandt began talking with the Soviet ambassadors in Germany, Semyon Tsarapkin in Bonn and Pyotr Abrasimov in East Berlin. The two invited Brandt to meet, hoping to learn what he might do if he became chancellor. Although generally noncommittal, they said that Brezhnev wanted to improve Moscow's relations with West Germany. They must also have informed Brezhnev that Brandt planned to make dramatic moves toward Moscow if he became chancellor. Brezhnev in turn instructed Gromyko to meet with Brandt when both were in New York and to say that Moscow did not see the West Germans as "the eternal enemy."

Trying publicly to reinforce his private promises for better relations with the East, Brandt told an SPD convention in March 1968 that it was time for West Germany to recognize the Oder-Neisse line as the border with Poland. When Kiesinger objected that such a statement went beyond coalition policy, Brandt replied that he was a party leader as well as foreign minister and that he had the right to speak his mind at party meetings.[21]

Brandt nonetheless tried to remain within the broad outlines of Western policy. He believed that Germany could not have a private détente, but he also believed that global détente could not succeed without Germany.

Fortunately for Brandt, other NATO governments were then also searching for new ideas and for some kind of détente. When Brandt in 1967 advocated a new NATO approach to Moscow, he found himself pushing on an open door. Belgian foreign minister Pierre Harmel prepared a NATO report urging a combination of vigorous East-West diplomacy and continued military readiness.

Brandt also got some encouragement when he briefed the new American president, Richard Nixon, in 1969. But Brandt worried because Nixon warned against "selective" détente. He realized that Washington wanted to keep German détente policy from getting too far ahead of U.S. thinking.[22]

Despite Kiesinger's differences with Brandt, Bonn's policy toward Moscow began to shift. Kiesinger accepted the Non-Proliferation Treaty and foreswore nuclear weapons. He said that he would make the declarations which Moscow wanted renouncing the use of force. He thus changed German policy on several points.

But Kiesinger could not fully accept Brandt's ideas. Although he had few partisan instincts and generally exercised patience with his coalition partner, he increasingly called Brandt on the carpet. Sometimes he did it privately, as when he complained to Brandt about his remarks regarding the Oder-Neisse line. At other times he did it publicly, as in speeches at CDU meetings.

Bahr particularly irritated Kiesinger. Bahr used his press contacts to signal some of the directions in which he and Brandt would have liked to go if permitted. For example, he leaked that he believed Kiesinger would have been more successful with Stoph if he had addressed the GDR premier by his full title. Kiesinger resented such leaks, denouncing Bahr privately as "a really dangerous man." But Brandt, as usual, protected Bahr.[23]

Kiesinger knew, as did others in the CDU/CSU, that many Germans wanted to bring an end to the most inhumane effects of Germany's division. He wanted to offer some hope for change. But Kiesinger could not negotiate with himself. He had to find an East German partner who would talk on his terms. And Ulbricht did not want to talk without first getting full and formal recognition.

When Leonid Brezhnev and Alexei Kosygin had first come to power in Moscow, Ulbricht could fully justify his policies to them. He could report that the Wall had helped the East German economy by stopping the flight of valuable workers. The East German growth rate rose between 1961 and 1963. But Ulbricht could not maintain the momentum. The GDR began to stagnate again by 1965 and 1966. The growth rate fell, as did the balance of payments, and the GDR failed to meet its own investment plans. Ulbricht's economic planning director, Erich Apel, committed suicide because East German growth could not keep up the pace needed to meet Soviet economic demands and its own needs.[24] Brezhnev did not help when Ulbricht asked for more economic aid, although Stoph told the Soviets that "we have no substantial reserves."[25]

But Brezhnev continued to support Ulbricht on international political matters. Ulbricht protested vigorously in Bucharest after Romania had established diplomatic relations with Bonn. Brezhnev helped Ulbricht by calling a special conference of east European governments to censure the Romanian government (which had also sided with China in the Sino-Soviet dispute). At that meeting, the east European states promised, under pressure from Ulbricht, not to improve relations with the Federal Republic unless Bonn fully recognized the GDR. Brezhnev himself went to an SED congress in April 1967 to show his support. He said: "Bonn has extended its hand to the socialist countries of Europe. But there is a rock clutched in that hand."[26]

Ulbricht increasingly barred openings toward West Germany. He not only refused to renew the holiday transit pass agreement in 1966 unless Kiesinger first recognized the GDR,[27] but he also criticized the SPD for joining the conservative parties in the grand coalition. While he sent East German officials to discuss technical arrangements with West Germany, such as train schedules, he permitted no other contact.[28]

Going further, Ulbricht took a number of steps to establish the GDR more solidly as a separate state and to enhance its authority toward East and West: He promulgated a new citizenship law in 1967, with East Germans no longer citizens of "Germany" but of the "German Democratic Republic." He established a new penal code, creating a system of justice independent of the old German code and separate from that of West Germany. Beginning in 1968, he insisted that West Germans visiting East Germany or passing through East German territory on the way to Berlin had to carry passports and obtain visas.

To crown these steps, Ulbricht decreed a new constitution for the GDR on April 6, 1968. That constitution defined the GDR as a "socialist state of the German nation," a new political and societal entity distinct from any previous state in Germany or in the world. It still spoke of the German nation, holding the door open for unification on socialist terms, but stressed that the GDR would protect and advance its own social system.[29]

Ulbricht defined the new East German state, community and society in ways that set him apart as an original Marxist-Leninist thinker. He issued a new ideological doctrine for the GDR, proclaiming that East German socialism had established a new model different from the Soviet one.

By elaborating a new ideology and new model, Ulbricht wanted to show that German unification had to come on a socialist basis if at all. He also wanted to advance the GDR as the ideological equal of the Soviet Union. Ulbricht spoke proudly of his "new order of society" as a singular achievement of the GDR. His state could not be traded away or treated like some petty acquisition.

But Ulbricht's new model of society failed to win over the East German population. When Ulbricht offered a referendum on the new constitution, perhaps counting on the usual 99 percent support that SED candidates could expect under his electoral system, the constitution received only 94.5 percent approval and only 90 percent in East Berlin. In Ulbricht's police state, such a shortfall amounted to rejection. The results showed that despite the Wall—or because of it—the GDR had not gained legitimacy.

Nor could Ulbricht fully control his Soviet allies. He reacted furiously when Abrasimov told him about a meeting with Brandt on June 18, 1968. He protested this kind of contact, especially as Abrasimov nominally served as ambassador to the GDR, not to West Germany. But Abrasimov reminded Ulbricht that the Soviet ambassador in East Berlin had retained the residual authority of the Soviet high commissioner for Germany and that he could deal with inner-German issues.

This did not reassure Ulbricht, for it showed that the Soviets might still try to negotiate the future of Germany with Brandt and the SPD. When Abrasimov told Ulbricht that he had explored with Brandt the possibility of an Ulbricht-Brandt meeting, Ulbricht told the ambassador in clear terms that such a task did not fall within the ambassador's competence. He then ended the meeting.[30]

Ulbricht also had to work hard to help keep eastern Europe under control. When Alexander Dubcek assumed power in Prague and began preaching "socialism with a human face," Ulbricht insisted sooner and more forcefully than any other Moscow ally that the Soviet Union and the Warsaw Pact states had to intervene to restore order.[31] He sent East German forces to participate in the Warsaw Pact invasion of Czechoslovakia in August 1968, although they played a relatively minor role. No Czech regime wanted to owe its existence to any German forces, socialist or not.

After the Warsaw Pact invasion of Czechoslovakia, *Pravda* on September 26 announced what became known as the "Brezhnev Doctrine." In an editorial addressing the "international obligations of the socialist states," it asserted that "in a class society . . . the rules and norms of the law are subordinate to the class struggle . . ." It added that the socialist states would not accept either the export or the import of "counter-revolution" and that Moscow thus retained the right and the duty to intervene whenever the nature of any regime was under threat. Ulbricht supported the Brezhnev Doctrine for it meant that he would have Soviet satellites east and south of the GDR.

But Ulbricht may not have had his own SED house fully in order. Erich Honecker, his designated successor, did not fully join Ulbricht's declaration of ideological equality with Moscow. Honecker repeatedly went out of his way to underscore the GDR's indebtedness toward Moscow and its dependence on the Soviet state and Soviet ideology. He said that any course that the GDR might follow had to be taken in "firm union" with Moscow, for the GDR had to profit from the Soviet Union's "progressive example."[32]

Ulbricht was swimming against a tide far more powerful than himself. Brezhnev and Kosygin had to concentrate much more on problems on their eastern border with China than on their western border with Germany. Mao Zedong had quarreled sharply with Khrushchev and had not been able to find a meeting of the minds with Brezhnev and Kosygin although he had sent his ablest negotiator, Premier Zhou Enlai, to Moscow in October 1964. By 1965, Sino-Soviet polemics had resumed. Relations continued to deteriorate as the Sino-Soviet conflict evolved from the competition of the 1950's toward an increasingly bitter confrontation.

If Brezhnev saw conflict on his eastern border, he saw opportunity on his western border. Nixon used his inaugural address on January 20, 1969, to proclaim the end of the "era of confrontation" and the beginning of the "era of negotiation." Henry Kissinger, Nixon's assistant for national security, told Soviet Ambassador Anatoly Dobrynin that the new president wanted a new type of relationship with the Soviet Union and wanted to reach major agreements. But Nixon and Kissinger introduced the concept of "linkage," indicating that Washington would not negotiate on subjects that Moscow wanted to discuss—such as arms control—unless it could also talk about topics that the West wanted to discuss—such as Berlin.

A few weeks after Nixon's inauguration, the Sino-Soviet confrontation turned into a shooting war at one of the disputed points along the Ussuri River between the Soviet Maritime Provinces and Chinese Manchuria. On March 2 and 15, thousands of Soviet and Chinese soldiers clashed in two border incidents with hundreds of casualties. Although both the Soviet Union and China pulled back to avoid further incidents, Brezhnev and Kosygin—as well as the Soviet military—must have recognized that they could not afford simultaneous crises along the German and Chinese borders.

Nixon's, Brandt's and Kissinger's policies and remarks, combined with the clashes on the Ussuri, offered new openings and compulsions for Soviet diplomacy on the German question. If Brezhnev and Kosygin pursued those openings, Moscow would have a chance to stabilize the situation in Europe. Soviet influence in Germany and Europe would grow. If necessary, Soviet forces could be deployed from Europe to Asia. Beijing would be isolated.

In this context, Brezhnev and Kosygin had to rein in Walter Ulbricht, who had just renewed his demand for full recognition and who had again harassed and temporarily blocked civilian access to Berlin when the West German parliamentary assembly met at the Reichstag to elect a new federal president. Kissinger complained about Ulbricht's capricious behavior. The new Soviet leaders, even more than Khrushchev before them, decided that they could not permit Ulbricht to control inner-German relations or to provoke East-West crises at will. Soviet diplomats in Bonn approached each of the major West German political parties to say that they were prepared to work toward better relations.

Ulbricht had violent arguments with Soviet leaders during his visit to Moscow in April 1969. The debate, which continued in the Soviet and East German press for weeks after Ulbricht's return from the Soviet capital, concerned the relations between the communist and socialist parties in Germany. The Soviet press asserted, as Brezhnev undoubtedly did with Ulbricht, that the German communists had erred by failing to cooperate with the socialists against Hitler during the Weimar era. By implication, Ulbricht and the SED should now be prepared to cooperate with the SPD and Willy Brandt. Ulbricht's press openly opposed the Soviet argument.

Vladimir Semyonov, the veteran Soviet expert on Germany who had become Soviet deputy foreign minister, went to East Berlin in July to tell Ulbricht that Brezhnev and Kosygin would improve relations with the SPD and would do what they could to support that party in the upcoming West German election. Semyonov told Ulbricht to change his policy toward the SPD. In the meantime, FDP leaders had also visited Moscow and won Soviet support.

Semyonov upset Ulbricht even more, however, when he said that Moscow had agreed with Nixon and other Allied leaders to discuss improvements regarding the situation in and around Berlin. He said that it would be good to preserve peace and quiet around Berlin during those discussions. Ulbricht was not to harass the access routes or to direct other pressures against West Berlin.[33]

Ulbricht argued strenuously with Semyonov. He did not want to deal with the SPD or any West German party until the West had given him full recognition and acknowledged his control over Berlin access. He did not want to hear that the Soviets would henceforth exercise their Berlin rights directly, but he had no choice.[34]

The Polish government also fell into line with the new Soviet view. In May, shortly after a visit to East Berlin, Premier Wladislaw Gomulka announced that Poland would welcome normal relations with West Germany as soon as Bonn recognized the Oder-Neisse border. Thus the Kremlin leaders signaled Brandt that they would pave the way for Ostpolitik, a new German opening toward the East.

The West German election of September 1969 turned on Ostpolitik. Kiesinger charged that Brandt, if he came to power, would make too many concessions to Brezhnev and Ulbricht. Brandt in turn accused the CDU/CSU of ignoring realities and of forfeiting any chance for progress.[35]

Kiesinger led the CDU/CSU to what appeared to be a victory. The CDU/CSU won enough seats to remain the largest grouping in the Bundestag. But the SPD jumped from 202 to 224 seats. If it was joined by the FDP, which had lost substantially but remained in the Bundestag, it would have a narrow majority. Brandt proposed to FDP leader Walter Scheel that they form a coalition. Scheel agreed, for he shared Brandt's views on Ostpolitik and on inner-German policy.

Kiesinger had managed the transition from one German policy to another honorably. Although he disapproved of many of Brandt's ideas and actions, he had initiated a major shift in West German policy without fomenting a crisis within the country or within the Western alliance. He had changed some of Adenauer's policies but had maintained the principles of democracy and reliability. He had gone as far as he could. Now Brandt would have his turn.

Brandt knew the limits. He could not end the division of the German state. But he could perhaps ease the division of the German nation. At least, he would try. As all eyes turned toward the new team in Bonn, he made no secret of his wish to test new ideas. And others made no secret of their readiness to listen.

THIRTEEN

DÉTENTE IN MOSCOW

WILLY BRANDT'S DESIRE TO NEGOTIATE DREW WIDESPREAD SUPPORT and interest. In Washington, President Richard Nixon favored negotiations on Germany and instructed Henry Kissinger to pass this message not only to Anatoly Dobrynin but also to a Soviet intelligence contact who would report it to Yuri Andropov, the head of the KGB Soviet intelligence service and himself interested in détente. This meant that it would reach Leonid Brezhnev directly instead of getting lost or distorted in Andrei Gromyko's foreign ministry.[1]

In Moscow, Brezhnev and many of his colleagues also clearly favored new approaches. When Kissinger had complained about Walter Ulbricht's harassment of the Berlin access routes, Dobrynin had replied that Moscow would do its utmost to calm the situation.[2] Ulbricht might be unhappy, but he could not block Moscow and Washington.

NIXON AND BRANDT OPEN DOORS

Nixon's insistence on diplomatic linkage became a key element in the diplomacy of détente for Washington, Moscow and Bonn. It came to serve Brandt well, for Moscow had to make progress with Bonn if it wanted to make progress with Washington. But linkage could also present problems, for Bonn could not move much faster than the other two partners in the trio.

Nixon believed that the key to superpower relations lay in arms control. No American or Soviet leader could count on a real relaxation of tensions as long as both engaged in an uncontrolled arms race. And the key to any meaningful system of arms control lay in an agreement on the most destructive weapons of all, the intercontinental ballistic missiles (ICBMs) with nuclear warheads, through the Strategic Arms Limitation Talks (SALT).

The Soviets agreed to open SALT on November 17, 1969, in Helsinki. The opening sessions revealed prospects for constructive negotiations but also showed that they would take a long time, perhaps years, and would require careful management on both sides.[3]

Nixon had remembered Berlin. Having visited the city officially or privately many times, having crossed the Wall and talked with East Berliners as well as West Berliners, he understood the tensions in the city. He recognized that trouble could erupt at any moment either by a shooting at the Wall or by East German harassment on the access routes. He also understood that the city aroused powerful emotions and that any Berlin crisis would destroy the political atmosphere essential to détente. When he went to Berlin for a working visit on February 27, 1969, barely a month after his inauguration, he proposed four-power talks about the city. After reaffirming the U.S. commitment, he said that Berlin should become a place for "negotiation . . . and reconciliation," not coercion.

Nixon formally offered to negotiate about Berlin in a March 26 letter to Soviet premier Alexei Kosygin. At his suggestion, the American, British, French and German governments then began intense consultations in Bonn to prepare for negotiations. Nixon wanted no "probes" behind anybody's back. The consultations forum became known as the Bonn Group.

Soviet views on Berlin and Germany remained guarded. Like Nixon, Brezhnev wanted no crises in or around Berlin.[4] He did not want his foreign policy disrupted by incidents on the access routes, especially while he had clashes with China on his mind. But he had kept the Berlin negotiations on the back burner during 1969 until Brandt had become chancellor and he could see what Brandt would do.

Even before Brandt assumed office, Abrasimov had told one of Brandt's associates that Moscow would like to discuss a number of subjects: West German adherence to the Nuclear Non-Proliferation Treaty, a renunciation of force and better inner-German relations. Abrasimov also promised that the Soviet Union would prevent incidents around Berlin and on the access routes if Brandt would refrain from provocations and would begin to engage in a serious dialogue.[5]

The ambassador's remarks posed Brandt and his new government an immediate challenge when they came into office. Brandt needed to show Moscow that the new German government was serious. But he did not want to give anything away before negotiations began, especially because his allies had their own views on many topics.

Brandt decided that he would address inner-German relations, a relatively exclusive German domain. He wanted to improve those relations. But he had to avoid saying anything that Ulbricht could use to stimulate a world-wide wave of recognition for the GDR. Otherwise, Brandt would have suffered a major defeat during the first weeks of his chancellorship.[6]

In his government declaration of October 28, Brandt followed the pattern outlined by Abrasimov, saying that:

- his government would sign the Non-Proliferation Treaty (it did so on November 28).
- his government would resume talks on a treaty for the renunciation of force (those talks did resume shortly thereafter).
- there were "two states" on German soil, the closest that the FRG had ever come to recognizing the GDR. But he added that his government would not extend full recognition.
- Germans, like others, had the right to self-determination.[7]

Beyond those specific points, Brandt tried to evoke a new spirit and to show that he wanted to look at old problems in new ways. He said that he wanted better relations with Poland and Czechoslovakia, adding that he would negotiate with Poland about everything. Brandt thus indicated that he would accept the Oder-Neisse border.

Brandt's remarks about the GDR reflected his dilemma. He needed to assure Brezhnev that West Germany would not try to subvert the East German regime because that regime anchored the Soviet security belt in Europe. He would not challenge the European status quo and the Brezhnev Doctrine. But, while he would deal with Ulbricht as necessary, he would not offer full legal recognition to the GDR. Doing so would violate the Basic Law and generate a firestorm of criticism in West Germany. Brandt had to hope that Moscow wanted security for itself more than recognition for Ulbricht.

Brandt's speech also showed that he had given up German unity as a policy but had kept it as a goal. He signaled that he would not press for early unification. But he also showed that he had not given up the long-term dream of bringing the German nation together under one roof. Brandt knew that Ulbricht would not accept that bargain, but he hoped that Brezhnev and his colleagues would.

Brandt wrote to Kosygin, offering more details than were in his speech. He wrote that his government was ready to sign renunciation of force treaties with the Soviet Union, Poland and the GDR. He also wrote that he would hope to begin talks with the Soviet government soon and would like to sign mutually advantageous agreements within a reasonable time.[8]

Brandt wanted linkage even more than Nixon wanted it. German détente needed four components: three separate West German treaties with Moscow, Warsaw and the GDR respectively, and an agreement on Berlin that Brandt could not negotiate but in which he had a major stake. He could not get those agreements without a new climate in East-West relations. Given his narrow majority in the Bundestag, Brandt could not survive an East-West crisis.

Ulbricht had his survival at stake as much as Brandt did. He needed to show his sovereignty and to get others to accept it. He wanted to be the main negotiator on Berlin with the Allies, and he wanted to get full recognition from Brandt. If Moscow took over the Berlin talks, Ulbricht would not get the results he wanted. But Brandt had sent his main signals to Brezhnev and Kosygin, not to him. Ulbricht could not help but worry that Bonn, Moscow and Washington might try to force something unpleasant down his throat.

To make certain that he remained at the center, Ulbricht on December 17 sent a letter directly to the West German president, Gustav Heinemann, to propose immediate state-to-state negotiations between the FRG and the GDR as well as mutual diplomatic relations.

Ulbricht's office alerted the West German presidency that the letter would be delivered. But Brandt had the letter delivered to the chancellery instead. After reading it, he concluded that the letter offered nothing new. He also concluded that Ulbricht was obviously anxious to signal Brezhnev that he wanted a leading role in the impending round of diplomacy.

Brandt replied himself, avoiding the political trap of a letter from the West German head of state. And he replied to his nominal equal, GDR premier Willi Stoph. He used Stoph's full title, as Kiesinger had not done, to show that he would offer a measure of recognition. He wrote that he was ready to open talks between "our two states." But he added that all topics had to be open for discussion, including "practical steps to ease the lives of persons living in divided Germany." Brandt's letter was designed for Soviet as well as East German eyes. He wanted to show Moscow that he would talk to the GDR even if he would not recognize the regime formally.

Brezhnev made his personal interest clear to Brandt by introducing a top-level direct channel into Soviet-German diplomacy.

On Friday, December 21, as Egon Bahr made ready to leave his office for the long Christmas weekend, a visitor from Moscow asked to see him. He agreed, slightly annoyed at the delay but always ready to see a Russian.

Bahr's annoyance grew as the visitor rather diffidently offered him a small plastic Christmas tree as a greeting and muttered some anodyne comments about the importance of good relations. Bahr was about to thank the visitor and ask him to leave when the Russian mentioned Brandt's letter to Kosygin, a letter that was known to only four persons in Bonn and presumably not to many more in Moscow. The visitor added that Moscow would be prepared to negotiate seriously with Brandt. He said that he had been sent by Yuri Andropov to serve as a direct personal channel for Brandt and Bahr to the highest levels of the Soviet government, and said that he would be in touch again.

Bahr felt elated. He understood now that the Soviets took the new German government very seriously. He also understood that Brandt and he would not have to pay undue attention to letters from Ulbricht.[9]

Ulbricht accepted, perhaps under Brezhnev's pressure, a proposal by Brandt for an exchange of visits between the heads of the two German governments without formal recognition. Brandt met Stoph in the East German city of Erfurt on March 19, 1970, and Stoph went to West Germany to meet Brandt in Kassel on May 21.

The meetings between Brandt and Stoph, and especially the one in East Germany, must have confirmed Ulbricht's worst fears. Brandt's presence generated an outpouring of genuine popular enthusiasm unprecedented in the GDR. He could barely make his way along the streets from the Erfurt train station to the hotel where he and Stoph were to meet. From the moment of his arrival, thousands of East Germans lined the streets shouting "Willy! Willy!" at the top of their lungs. To make certain that nobody thought they were shouting for Willi Stoph, many held up signs bearing a large "Y" in the center. Crowds of East Germans pushed through police lines to be close to Brandt.

Brandt had to go out of his way to calm the demonstrators and avoid chaos. Once he managed to get to his hotel, he went to the window to greet the demonstrators and to urge them to control themselves. In his own words:

> I reminded myself that this was not the first time that I had visited a Germany devoid of freedom . . . I was moved, but I had to consider the fate of these people. I would be back in Bonn next day; they would not . . . I made a gesture urging restraint, and my point was taken. The crowd fell silent. Turning away with a heavy heart, I noticed that many of my aides had tears in their eyes.[10]

The talks themselves produced nothing. Stoph demanded full and immediate recognition and joint applications for membership in the United Nations. He also demanded full compensation for DM 100 billion that West German policies allegedly had cost the citizens of East Germany before the Wall had been built. Brandt rejected both demands.

The meeting in Kassel proved equally fruitless. In a twenty-point paper, Brandt offered various formulas short of full recognition. He proposed an East German–West German treaty to govern future relations and offered to establish permanent representations between East and West Germany. He urged respect for the four-power status of Berlin and for the links that had been established between West Berlin and West Germany. He proposed greater freedom of movement. Stoph replied that the GDR would negotiate only one thing, a treaty for full diplomatic recognition, and gave Brandt a draft. Brandt would not negotiate on that and the two men parted.

The exchange of visits led to no progress in relations between the two Germanys. Officials from the two were not to meet again until October 1970.

But the exchange of visits had placed a complex obligation on the Soviets and on Brandt if they wanted détente. The demonstrations in Erfurt had shown that Bonn and Moscow had to deal directly with each other even on matters concerning East Germany. Clearly, the Wall had not stabilized Ulbricht's regime. If the Soviet Union wanted a deal with Brandt, Moscow would have to negotiate for the GDR, for Ulbricht could not afford to yield on anything. And any major concessions that Brandt made directly to Ulbricht would discredit Brandt's government and offend the East Germans who had demonstrated for him.

Moscow and Bonn faced a paradox in détente: They would have to work together to preserve the GDR for the sake of European stability and Soviet security even if it had no political legitimacy and could show no flexibility. They would have to bring Ulbricht along. And the GDR would have to be given something, even if not what Ulbricht wanted. But it need not be given very much.

First, however, Brandt had to find out if Brezhnev, Kosygin and Polish prime minister Wladislaw Gomulka would let Ulbricht slow them down.

EGON, LEO AND SLAVA

Even while Brandt and Stoph were meeting, the real diplomacy proceeded elsewhere. True to his government declaration and to his letter to Kosygin, Brandt moved quickly to begin talks with the Soviet government. The new foreign minister, Walter Scheel, told Soviet ambassador Semyon Tsarapkin that the Germans wanted to resolve existing disagreements and contribute to peace in Europe. The German government followed up with a note proposing to start talks in Moscow as soon as convenient.

But those Moscow talks began badly. In three conversations with the German ambassador, Helmut Allardt, Andrei Gromyko followed his time-honored tactic of presenting long lists of preconditions and unacceptable demands without even a hint of flexibility. He repeated well-known Soviet positions uncompromisingly. He denounced the ideas that Brandt had presented in his government declaration as unrealistic and unproductive. West Germany had to recognize the GDR fully and immediately, he said. Bonn had to renounce force completely and unconditionally and had to make a formal declaration giving up any expectations for reunification. If and when Germany had a new policy, Gromyko said, he would be happy to hear of it. Otherwise, he added, he did not want to waste his time.

Gromyko did suggest that Moscow took the Germans seriously by spending an unusually long time with the German ambassador. This created a sensation among foreign diplomats in Moscow but also aroused suspicion, for Gromyko never bothered with Western ambassadors. The Moscow diplomatic corps could not understand why Gromyko would have three separate talks with Allardt without breaking new ground. Germany's allies wondered what they were not being told.

Brandt for his part could not believe Allardt when he returned to report on his talks and to present his conclusion that nothing could be achieved. Brandt and Scheel refused to conclude that Moscow had sent misleading signals for the past several years. Nor could they accept the notion that the Soviet government would reject the chance for a better relationship so quickly and so totally, even allowing for Gromyko's pugilistic style.[11]

Brandt decided that Bahr should go to Moscow. The German government could not risk sending Scheel and having its foreign minister humiliated on his very first foreign trip. Bahr, being lower on the ladder, could be sacrificed. Equally important, Andropov had made a point of contacting Bahr. The Soviets might be ready to talk to him. They might think he would give them better access to Brandt.

Bahr flew to Moscow on January 30, 1970, before Brandt and Stoph had met at Erfurt. He thus undertook the task for which he had been preparing himself since the Berlin Wall had convinced him that Germans themselves had to begin negotiating about their country. In Moscow, he began a series of talks with Gromyko that were to last a total of fifty-five hours. He also had frequent meetings with Andropov's personal messengers, who went by the code names of "Leo" and "Slava." They were instructed to keep Brezhnev and Andropov informed about Bahr's side of the talks in case Gromyko did not tell them the full story. They were also there to solve any problems that might arise.[12]

When Bahr arrived in Moscow, Leo came to tell him to be patient; although the Soviets had not wanted to postpone his visit they could not really get down to business yet. They needed more time to develop their positions. But they also needed to hear German ideas. Gromyko would listen but would have nothing new to say.

Leo's message proved correct. Gromyko tried to gain time by treating Bahr as he had treated Allardt. He produced a list of eighteen totally uncompromising demands formulated in language that he must have known to be unacceptable. He asserted, for example, that Bonn had to sign a treaty for the renunciation of force, had to recognize the European status quo and all existing European borders, had to sign the Non-Proliferation Treaty immediately, had to recognize the GDR formally, had to stop all activities in West Berlin and had to recognize West Berlin as a separate political entity. He added, for good measure, that Bonn had to take all these steps before negotiations could even begin.

Bahr feared that Gromyko's demands could pose a major political risk for Brandt. If Gromyko's attitude was to become known, Brandt would be totally discredited—especially after the conciliatory tone of his government declaration. Gromyko's game could help only the opponents of détente.

But, unlike an ambassador, Bahr could conduct a free-flowing exchange without having to ask for guidance. Although he had to keep Brandt himself informed of his talks, and although he had to return to Bonn several times for consultations, he could manage the talks largely on his own. He also knew that he could go around Gromyko to Andropov and perhaps Brezhnev if necessary.

Bahr thus replied to Gromyko by suggesting that he and the foreign minister deal with realities, not slogans. Bonn would renounce the use of force. Brandt recognized that this meant accepting the status quo in Europe. One did not need to argue over words. Turning Gromyko's argument around, Bahr said that Germany's signature on a treaty to renounce force would in itself mean that Germany accepted all borders. After all, borders could be changed only by force. If a renunciation of force did not mean an acceptance of borders, what else could it mean? What more could anyone ask?

Bahr added that Brandt could not legally recognize the GDR, whether he wished to do so or not. Recognition would require amending the German Basic Law, which would require a two-thirds Bundestag majority that Brandt did not command. Moreover, recognition of German borders with Poland, like recognition of the GDR, would have to be part of a peace treaty. Thus, it required the agreement of the Western Allies, which they would not give without counter-concessions.

Instead, Bahr suggested, it would be best if Gromyko and he concentrated their efforts on the things that they could do together without involving others, and also on the things that were realistically possible.

Bahr also turned around Gromyko's argument regarding Berlin. Saying that he accepted Gromyko's suggestion that the status quo in Europe should not be changed, he argued that the status quo in and around Berlin should not be changed either. That would mean a mutual acceptance of the present realities, including West German links with West Berlin. Bonn would accept realities, but Moscow would have to do the same. Neither the Allies nor the Bundestag would accept any arrangement that worsened the present situation. In particular, Bahr warned, the Allies would not accept any accord on Berlin negotiated between Moscow and Bonn.

Bahr quickly proved correct on this last point. As soon as reports of his talks with Gromyko reached the Allies, the latter decided that only the victors of World War II should hold discussions about Berlin. They told this to Abrasimov, who immediately agreed. Within days, Berlin disappeared from the Gromyko-Bahr agenda.

In response to Bahr and prodded by Brezhnev, Gromyko began an intense discussion about the core items on the Soviet-German agenda. But Bahr had not adequately reckoned with Gromyko's methodical and persistently confrontational manner. Nor had he reckoned with Moscow's interest in orchestrating a full range of simultaneous talks with Washington, Bonn and East Berlin. The talks often seemed to drag on pointlessly.

Leo and Slava encouraged Bahr to stay the course. From time to time they briefed him on Soviet thinking, including the information that the Bahr-Gromyko talks had provoked the most intense politburo discussion about Germany in years. They urged him to remember that "opponents" in the Soviet leadership needed to be brought along and could not be hurried. Leo, who had served the KGB on Germany for many years, proved an expert guide as well as counselor for Bahr.

Leo and Slava could be very helpful. Once, when the talks had been stuck for days, Leo asked Bahr what was holding up progress. When Bahr told him that it concerned an obscure, almost scholasticist point of language, Andropov called Brezhnev to tell him where the problem lay. Brezhnev called Gromyko and told him to settle the problem and to go faster.[13]

To confirm that Moscow took Germany seriously, Kosygin himself invited Bahr for a conversation. The talk revealed nothing new but may have been necessary for internal Soviet reasons. It did, however, lead to the release to West Germany of 192 ethnic Germans whom Bahr hurriedly listed as humanitarian cases after Kosygin asked what he could do for Bahr.

The Kosygin meeting also revealed the tensions between Moscow and Ulbricht. Leo told Bahr that "the man with the beard" (Ulbricht) had gone into a tantrum and tried to block Bahr's appointment with Kosygin, but Kosygin went ahead anyway, although it was a close call. He told Bahr that Ulbricht had not briefed Moscow about his and other GDR letters to the West Germans. Leo also told Bahr of other instances where Moscow had not honored Ulbricht's requests. Ulbricht, Stoph and Erich Honecker had even visited Brezhnev personally once to ask him not to sign an agreement with West Germany, but Brezhnev still wanted to sign it.[14]

Ulbricht had made his opposition clear well in advance of West German–Soviet talks. In a long meeting with Gromyko on February 24, 1970, he had said that he wanted the Soviet Union to insist on formal West German recognition of the GDR and of all GDR borders (which would, in his mind, have included the sector border in Berlin and the Wall). Ulbricht complained that Moscow was not asking enough and dismissed Kremlin worries about the stability of Brandt's government if détente failed. He feared that Moscow would ignore GDR interests for a deal with Bonn.[15]

Bahr's talks with Gromyko, while lengthy, did achieve something important and unprecedented in Germany's postwar history that counted almost as much as immediate results: Bahr and Gromyko had met as equals. Brezhnev, Kosygin and Gromyko no longer pretended that they could ignore West Germany as Khrushchev had tried to do, negotiating above its head with the Americans and other Allies. And, as Leo had said, Moscow had conducted the most serious review of its German policy in years, if not decades.

Gromyko's readiness to meet with Bahr as often and as long as he did showed an important change in the order of things. Western ambassadors in Moscow wondered what it might mean. The French ambassador, Roger Seydoux de Clausonne, told Bahr that the political landscape of Europe had shifted.[16]

But Brandt had to think about the talks going on between Moscow and Washington as well as about Bahr's talks. If Bahr and Gromyko failed to agree, Brezhnev and Gromyko might well decide to concentrate their negotiations with the West fully on the United States. That would again leave the Germans in limbo. Although Brandt knew that Brezhnev and Andropov wanted to improve Soviet links with Bonn, he could not be sure that the two men could persuade the CPSU conservatives to make concessions on both the SALT and the German fronts. Brandt could not permit Bahr's talks to drag on too long or to strain the Soviet domestic debate too much.

Gromyko and Bahr made their crucial breakthrough in May 1970, before Brandt and Stoph met at Kassel. By May 22, when Bahr returned to Bonn for the third time, he could produce a twenty-point paper summarizing the basic principles on which it appeared a German-Soviet treaty could be based.

Of Bahr's twenty points, the first four were the most important:

- The Federal Republic and the Soviet Union regard international détente as an important foreign policy goal. They are determined to achieve normalization of the situation in Europe. For that purpose, they will act on the basis of the present situation and the development of peaceful relations with all European states.

- They will solve disputes through peaceful means. In accordance with Article 2 of the United Nations Charter, they will avoid any threat or use of force in matters that affect European security or their bilateral relations.
- They agree that peace in Europe can be preserved only if present borders are not challenged, and they undertake to respect the territorial integrity of all European states in their present borders. They declare that they have no territorial claims against any party and will not raise them in future. They regard all European borders as inviolable, including the Oder-Neisse line, which constitutes the western border of Poland, and the border between the Federal Republic of Germany and the German Democratic Republic.
- The treaty between the Federal Republic and the Soviet Union does not affect earlier bilateral or multilateral obligations incurred by either party.[17]

Even a cursory reading of the four points revealed that they would quickly become controversial in West Germany if they became widely known, officially or by a leak. They accepted a reality that West Germany could not change but that every previous West German government had pledged to change. Any West German commitment to respect European borders—especially the Oder-Neisse line—meant that the Federal Republic gave up any claim to German land that had become part of Poland and the Soviet Union, including Silesia, Prussia and Königsberg. It also meant that West Germany would accept the reality of the GDR. But no West German government had ever formally accepted the Oder-Neisse line. And the Basic Law had committed the Federal Republic to a united Germany.

Although Bahr had told Gromyko in their first conversation that the German government could not officially renounce what had been German territory, the twenty points came perilously close to doing precisely that. They could legitimately be so interpreted.

Brandt knew that the twenty points would present a problem. The CDU/CSU would argue that Bahr had negotiated an agreement that was incompatible with the Basic Law, that gave away historic German lands and that jeopardized Germany's deepest national interests. To try to help contain this problem before the paper became public, Brandt asked a committee of state secretaries, the ranking officials of the German government below the cabinet ministers, to evaluate the constitutionality of Bahr's points.

The committee, which included the state secretaries of the foreign ministry and the justice ministry, concluded that the treaty would not be incompatible with the Basic Law if it was accompanied by a document that reasserted West Germany's continuing interest in unification and in Berlin. That decision helped Brandt and Bahr, for it at least did not charge them with having acted unconstitutionally. But it meant that Brandt would have to ask Gromyko to accept an explanatory letter, and Gromyko had already objected to that when Bahr had warned him of the possibility.

Bahr's twenty points raised two even more serious questions, questions that concerned not only West Germany but its Western allies and especially the three Western powers that had a continuing responsibility for Germany and Berlin.

First, could such a far-reaching agreement have any validity if the three Western victors of World War II had not helped negotiate it? A treaty based on Bahr's points would address some matters that could properly have been in a final German peace treaty. Yet Bahr's treaty would be signed by only one of the four victorious powers, the Soviet Union. West Germany's principal allies would be excluded from an important agreement signed with West Germany's principal enemy.

Second, could the points be interpreted to mean that one of the realities West Germany accepted was that of East German control over East Berlin? The GDR claimed that its border ran along the Wall, and West Germany was pledging to respect all borders.

These two issues touched directly on Allied rights and responsibilities. West Germany had no authority to negotiate a peace treaty. And it certainly had no authority to give away East Berlin, although the Allies had already gone a long way toward doing that when they had accepted the Wall.

Bahr knew as well as anyone that his twenty points would disturb West Germany's friends. He had tried to deal with that by telling Gromyko that the Soviet Union had to recognize the limits of any negotiations with the Federal Republic. Acting under Brandt's careful guidance, Bahr had told Gromyko on May 12 that the German-Soviet agreement could not stand alone but would have to be part of a totality of negotiations. Among those would have to be an agreement regulating the situation in Berlin. But Gromyko had replied that it was too late for Bahr to make that kind of argument. If Bahr wanted an agreement, he could not change its terms at the last minute.

Bahr's twenty points showed both the strengths and the weaknesses of West Germany's new situation. Bahr had not come back from Moscow empty-handed. Gromyko had promised a new relationship and a new policy that would ease tensions and could make life easier for many Germans. More important, Gromyko had abandoned some traditional Soviet demands, including some that he had firmly listed to Allardt. Like Bahr, Gromyko had accepted reality. But Bahr had surrendered points that earlier German governments had protected. Bonn could still not deal on a truly equal basis with the World War II victors. While West Germany might be ever more important, it was not fully sovereign yet.

As the state secretaries had concluded, the agreement that Bahr had reached with Gromyko could not stand on its own. It needed interpretation to be compatible with the Basic Law and with the interests of Bonn's allies. Brandt would have to send Scheel to conduct a final set of negotiations with Gromyko in July 1970.[18]

Scheel wanted to go to Moscow to conclude the negotiations with Gromyko. He thought that he could help Brandt by showing that the entire German government and not only Bahr had negotiated with Moscow. Bahr's reputation as a manipulator and backstage operator could jeopardize Bundestag approval for the treaty. Scheel would give more authority and credibility.

To complicate Brandt's situation, the German tabloid *Quick* on July 1 printed Bahr's twenty-point paper. The paper aroused a storm of controversy and opposition. If Gromyko now chose to complicate the talks, he could cost Brandt the chancellorship. Gromyko even had reason to be angry, because Scheel's wish to talk further meant that Brandt wanted to improve on the terms that Bahr had negotiated.

But Gromyko could not dismiss Scheel out of hand. If Brandt's government fell because of the breakdown of his détente policy, no West German government would dare to negotiate with Moscow for at least a decade. The situation in Europe would remain tense and costly. Détente with Washington might also suffer. Moscow might be left with no viable diplomatic opening toward Germany, Europe, China or America. Gromyko had to deal with Scheel whether he liked it or not.

Moreover, Moscow needed economic and technological links with West Germany. And the treaty also represented the kind of legitimation of the European order that Moscow had long sought, even if it did not comply with Moscow's wishes on every point.[19] Brezhnev needed a positive result as much as Scheel did.

Gromyko did not make it easy for Scheel. He complained heatedly and at length about Scheel's demands to improve the terms of Bahr's agreement. His talks with Scheel lasted more than a dozen hours over an entire week. Scheel even had to take a page out of Adenauer's 1955 book and order his aircraft to pick him up to return to Bonn. Finally, Gromyko invited Scheel to his dacha for a long informal talk clearly intended to produce results. During the talk, he gave

Scheel a piece of paper containing a Soviet "proposal" that Scheel had himself offered earlier and that took care of both German and Soviet needs.

Leo and Slava, working behind the scenes with Andropov, had arranged the maneuver. They did not even tell Scheel about it because Brandt did not want the foreign office to begin using the Andropov channel and perhaps talking about it.[20] Andropov himself had told Leo that "without West Germany, we cannot get out of our present situation." He had also said that "we must build our house in Europe, and that cannot be done without Germany."[21]

Scheel concluded the treaty with Gromyko on August 7, 1970. Moscow had made major concessions, dropping its demand for West Germany's formal recognition of the GDR and of European boundaries while accepting the West German presence in Berlin and its membership in NATO. In exchange, Bonn had recognized the permanent loss of historic German territories, if in language that Brandt could defend more easily in the Bundestag than Bahr's original draft. On August 12, Brandt and Kosygin signed the Moscow Treaty, the first of the four major elements of German détente policy.

Scheel had persuaded Gromyko to let the German delegation hand over an explanatory letter when the Moscow Treaty was signed and to have this letter called *Brief über die deutsche Einheit* (Letter on German Unity). The letter reaffirmed the German wish for reunification, complying with the recommendation of the committee of state secretaries. By agreeing to accept the letter, Gromyko once more showed that Moscow would make significant compromises to reach an agreement with Bonn.

Gromyko said that he would not acknowledge receipt of the letter officially. Instead, he would be like the monkey who would "see no evil, hear no evil, and speak no evil." But Mikhail Gorbachev said later, at the time of the German unification negotiations of 1990, that accepting the letter had committed the Soviet government to German unification.[22]

During the informal reception after the treaty signing, Gromyko told Valentin Falin, one of Moscow's leading experts on Germany, to tell Brandt that the SPD should now change its name from *Sozialdemokratische Partei Deutschlands* (Social Democratic Party of Germany) to *Sozialdemokratische Partei Westdeutschlands* (Social Democratic Party of West Germany), for Brandt had recognized the division of Germany. Falin nodded but did not tell Brandt. Falin noticed that Gromyko, evidently miffed at Falin's failure to deliver his message, himself went over to talk to Brandt. From the look of pure stupefaction on Brandt's face, Falin surmised that Gromyko had indeed made his suggestion.[23] Gromyko had still not understood that Brandt had not given up German unity but was only looking for another route.

Willy Brandt believed that the first step toward German unity would be to renounce it as a policy while keeping it open as a prospect. West German diplomacy would no longer be tied to insistence on unification. But the hope for unification would undercut the legitimacy of the GDR. Ulbricht, who fully recognized Brandt's purpose, saw Soviet acceptance of the letter as a major mistake and as an act of betrayal.[24]

Ulbricht showed his disgust the following week, when he boycotted a Moscow meeting to which Brezhnev invited all east European government and communist party leaders to brief them on his treaty with Brandt. Brezhnev stated that he had won a number of important West German concessions, including the recognition of all borders. He said that the treaty would add to tensions within the NATO alliance and that he had specifically asked Brandt how the chancellor felt about "the yoke that the Americans have placed around your neck." He added that he thought it useful to work with social democratic parties despite the "irreconcilable differences" that still existed between communism and socialism.[25]

In separate meeting with GDR officials, Brezhnev warned against letting the GDR get too close to West Germany. He said that he thought it important for East Germany to expand its economic contacts within the Warsaw Pact rather than to increase its dependence on West German credits. He said that Poland should be the next state to negotiate with Brandt, and he vetoed a third Brandt-Stoph meeting that Ulbricht had proposed. Brezhnev clearly wanted to keep contacts with Bonn in his own hands.[26] Like Khrushchev, he would try to get a measure of recognition for the GDR but he would not grant Ulbricht real authority.

As his détente talks proceeded, Brandt tried an additional and novel route to gain influence in Moscow and eastern Europe. A Hamburg industrialist and friend of Brandt's, Kurt Körber, began using a forum his foundation had created, the Bergedorfer Gesprächskreis, to hold informal meetings between West German, Soviet and eastern European intellectuals, journalists and political figures. The meetings permitted wide-ranging but noncommittal discussions on all aspects of West German relations with the East. They also began developing personal contacts and better mutual understanding. Brandt wanted to use the meetings to create a cooperative climate between West Germans and those with whom they were opening new relationships. He also hoped they would influence policy.[27]

Brandt wanted to develop support among American journalists and intellectuals as well. In 1972, the twenty-fifth anniversary of Secretary of State George

Marshall's speech announcing the Marshall Plan, he created and endowed the German Marshall Fund of the United States. He also used Karl Kaiser, a prominent German professor, and Theo Sommer, then editor of *Die Zeit*, to explain his policies informally to the Washington bureaucracy and to their wide contacts throughout the United States.

The Allies did have reservations about German policy and about the Moscow treaty. They had watched the extended German talks in Moscow with some concern, especially because they thought that Bahr never told them everything. They saw the final text as a possible threat to Allied rights, not only because the Federal Republic signed a treaty with only one of the occupation powers but also because the treaty implied a settlement of some of the basic issues of the German question.

The Allies feared that Moscow could use the German-Soviet treaty to show that Allied rights no longer extended to East Germany and East Berlin. They urged Scheel to obtain a Soviet statement to the effect that the treaty would not alter Allied rights and responsibilities. The British ambassador in Moscow called on Scheel late in the evening before the scheduled signing ceremony to ask the Germans not to sign the treaty.

Brandt rejected the British request. He thought the British were trying to use the German government to win a Soviet concession in 1970 on a matter that the Allies had themselves surrendered in 1961. Brandt, still smoldering about the Allies' mute acceptance of the Berlin Wall, felt that London seemed more anxious to protect Allied legal rights than German human rights. Brandt wanted to create realities, not legalities.

But Bonn did support Allied views on linkage. Scheel repeatedly told Gromyko what he did not want to hear: that Bonn could not formally ratify the German-Soviet treaty until the occupation powers had reached a satisfactory agreement on Berlin.

Gromyko understood, and told Scheel, that a normalization of the situation around West Berlin was in the interests of both states. Three months later, on the fourteenth hole of the golf course at Kronberg Castle near Frankfurt, Gromyko even acknowledged to Scheel that the Bundestag could not be expected to endorse the German-Soviet treaty until a Berlin agreement had been signed. Gromyko did not like linkage but had decided to accept it.

Gromyko did not, of course, have the final word. Yuli Kvitsinsky, one of Moscow's rising diplomatic experts on Germany, reported later that Gromyko did not agree with the treaty that he had himself negotiated. Kvitsinsky wrote that Brezhnev and Andropov had wanted it and told Gromyko to get it done. Bahr reported the same thing, saying later that he could never have concluded the treaty without Leo and Slava helping. But, once the treaty had been signed, Gromyko hailed it as a major achievement of Soviet diplomacy.[28]

Moscow sought German economic cooperation throughout the entire process of the German-Soviet talks. Brezhnev and Kosygin repeatedly told Brandt and other West Germans about the immense significance to both countries of economic cooperation in the past and in the future. They recalled how the first Soviet experts on Germany had dreamed of combining Russian raw materials and German manufacturing genius.[29]

Moscow and Bonn concluded a series of trade agreements after the Moscow Treaty. Bonn promised and delivered high-technology and high-quality finished goods from large-diameter pipe to machine tools, items the Soviet Union could not produce and the United States would not sell. Bonn also offered credits. In return, Germany obtained raw materials at competitive and sometimes highly advantageous prices.[30] Trade between West Germany and the Soviet Union more than quadrupled between 1969 and 1975, to a level of $4 billion, and German exports to the Soviet Union rose at almost twice that rate, to a total of $2.8 billion.[31]

German-Soviet economic relations fomented more Washington-Bonn discord than political relations. To help persuade Bonn to sign the Nuclear Non-Proliferation Treaty, Moscow offered Germany rock-bottom prices for enriched uranium for peaceful purposes. The United States, which had held the monopoly on supplying fissionable materials to West Germany, protested. But U.S. suppliers could not match the Soviet price. The Germans justified the deal on economic grounds although all knew its political significance.[32]

BRANDT KNEELS IN WARSAW

Brandt opened negotiations with Poland in February of 1970. As part of the Soviets' own linkage, Kosygin would not have signed the Moscow Treaty if West Germany had not begun improving relations with Poland. But Brandt wanted reconciliation with Poland for his own reasons as well.

Brandt faced some of the most wrenching moments of his life during the negotiations with Poland. The Poles, whose country had over the centuries fallen victim to German, Russian, Austrian, French, Swedish and other invasions, had been traumatized by history. Their borders had often been treated as callously as the matches that Churchill had used to show Poland being shifted to the West at Teheran. They needed and deserved firm security guarantees, especially from Germany.

Hitler's invasion and occupation of Poland had written one of the most darkly evil chapters of Nazi history. The Holocaust had shown its cruelest face in Poland. The concentration camps, the bestial enslavement, torture and killing of the innocent and of the helpless, and the destruction of the Warsaw Ghetto had left an ineradicable legacy of pain. Brandt had to recognize that pain and had to show that he recognized it, if Poland was ever to have confidence in a new Germany.

Some Germans could make a case against Poland. When the Yalta accords had shifted Poland westward, millions of Germans had been expelled unceremoniously, with millions also killed in the process. Many of the refugees opposed any agreement with Warsaw that did not restore the homes their families had owned for generations or that did not offer at least some hope for Polish compensation. Stalin may have made a mistake when he had shifted Poland's borders, but he had also—perhaps deliberately—made Polish-German reconciliation almost impossible. Brandt had to consider politics in Germany as well as pain in Poland.

Brandt therefore had to handle the Warsaw negotiations with the utmost sensitivity. He decided to start by giving the appropriate guarantees to Moscow and Warsaw, immediately offering language to recognize the Oder-Neisse line: "The Federal Republic of Germany and the People's Republic of Poland state . . . that the existing boundary, the course of which is laid down in Chapter IX of the decisions of the Potsdam Conference . . . shall constitute the western State frontier of Poland."[33]

Brandt nonetheless reiterated the long-held West German view that the final decision on all German borders had to await a general peace settlement and that his decision would not bind any future German government in its negotiations for a peace treaty. But he had, in effect, yielded the territories that Stalin had claimed for Poland at Teheran and Yalta.

Brandt justified his decision unflinchingly when he returned to Bonn, insisting that he had given away nothing that Hitler had not lost earlier. He added that Germany could not have good relations with states whose borders it challenged. In his memoirs and in conversation, he said that he had never forgotten the words of Ernst Reuter that "we cannot expect the Poles to accept a country on wheels."[34]

Brandt's visit to Warsaw produced the most memorable moment of the détente years, a photograph of the Chancellor of the Federal Republic of Germany falling to his knees before the monument to the victims of the Warsaw Ghetto. Brandt said afterward that he had knelt spontaneously because no words—not even a prayer—could adequately convey the grief and sorrow that he felt as he stood before the memorial to so much suffering. He told Bahr afterwards that he believed that laying a wreath, as he had done, was just not enough. The act conveyed the depth of Brandt's commitment to reconciliation. It became one of the images that marked his era and his person.

On December 7, 1970, four months after the Moscow Treaty, Brandt and the Polish prime minister, Josef Cyrankiewicz, signed the Warsaw Treaty, the second of the four major steps in détente over Germany.

From that date, the German question and the struggle over Germany assumed a different shape in two fundamental ways. First, by renouncing its former territories east of the Oder-Neisse, Bonn could begin a more active policy toward the East. Second, the Federal Republic assumed the mantle of the true government of Germany although its writ ran only in West Germany. Both Moscow and Warsaw had asked Bonn to take a stand on a border that did not even touch West Germany but ran between Poland and the GDR. Those requests reflected the widespread perception, even in the states that recognized and supported the GDR, that the Federal Republic represented the true voice of the German people.

With the Soviet and Polish treaties, the Brandt government had completed the initial phases of Ostpolitik. Now the time had come to deal with Berlin and the German Democratic Republic.

ONCE AGAIN, KEYSTONE BERLIN

When all was said and done, the struggle over Germany and even the entire Cold War revolved around Berlin. At times, events in Berlin shaped East-West relations as a whole. At other times, outside events shaped what would happen in Berlin.

Brandt, Brezhnev and Nixon knew that a true détente had to include Berlin. East-West relations as well as inner-German relations could not improve if West Berlin remained under siege. The city and its access routes had to be brought into détente.

Although Berlin had calmed down since the Wall crisis, its situation had never truly stabilized. All parties had too much at stake there. The West German government and West German political leaders did all they could to use and to try to expand the city's links with the Federal Republic. They established a growing number of government offices and ministries in Berlin. They held West German government meetings there, including periodic Bundestag meetings and sessions of various Bundestag committees. They held the Bundesversammlung, which elected the federal president of Germany, in Berlin. The

Allies occasionally questioned such practices but permitted them because they added to the viability of West Berlin and to its links with the West.

Ulbricht and the SED tried consistently to keep West Berlin under pressure and to complicate life for West Berliners and for those doing business there. Ulbricht wanted to discourage Western investment so as to force the economy and the population to wither away or to depend more on East Germany. He also wanted to show that the future of Berlin lay with the GDR.

The East German bureaucracy exercised all its imagination to devise ever more ingenious means to harass travelers to West Berlin, especially at times when West German government organizations held meetings there. They increased tolls dramatically (up to ten-fold) without warning. They left border traffic lights on red for hours. Vopos forced drivers to buy East German license plates for a trip to Berlin, or they conducted interminably meticulous searches of cars, persons and luggage. They randomly confiscated written material as subversive propaganda or as intelligence documents.[35] Such measures discouraged road and rail travel to West Berlin and made people wonder if they wanted to live and raise a family there.

The Allies, and especially the United States, did all they could to show their solidarity with West Berlin and with the Berliners themselves. They countered Ulbricht's efforts by reasserting their interest and commitment, and they continued to exercise their right to visit East Berlin. West Germany poured money into West Berlin, subsidizing its economy and culture while legislating incentives for West Germans to live and invest there. In addition, as West Berlin had no draft, many young West German conscientious objectors moved there.

All parties had honed the skill of protest writing and countering to a fine art. They knew the Berlin jargon by heart and could produce statements at the drop of a hat. Some statements, such as those that protested shootings at the Wall, had real meaning to those who wrote them. Although none changed the situation, they had a purpose. As long as West Berlin was free, as long as the West rejected Ulbricht's claim to the city and resisted his pressures, Germany was not definitively divided.

The Berlin problem resembled a World War I battlefield. It had been fought over many times. All knew the strategically sensitive points that might provoke a violent counter-attack. All knew, or thought they knew, the other side's contingency plans. All knew they could not win except at unacceptable cost. But they did not dare to lose. With the prestige of all parties fully engaged, with emotions on all sides having run high for over two decades, the Berlin question could not be solved in a day or perhaps even in a year. Diplomats had learned that, as on a World War I battlefield, they could be safer by remaining in the trenches than by moving forward to try for a breakthrough.

Events in or around Berlin could shake Europe. Every crisis over Berlin provoked a challenge to the very concept of East-West accommodation. This gave Walter Ulbricht real power. Whenever he chose to block traffic on the Berlin Autobahn or to create any other problem, all parties had to return to Cold War rhetoric, Cold War policies and Cold War politics. All would be hostage to any incident, no matter how trivial. Ulbricht could make or break détente at will.

The Allies had long coordinated their responses to Ulbricht through the Bonn Group, a forum that included the three Western occupation powers and the Federal Republic. With détente in the air, they now needed the Bonn Group to coordinate their views and their papers for East-West talks. By using the Bonn Group they involved West Germany, which had a major political and psychological interest in Berlin although it had no sovereignty there and could not participate in four-power talks about the city.

On August 7, 1969, before the Brandt government had come into office, the three Western powers had followed up Nixon's letter to Kosygin with an invitation for talks regarding the situation in Berlin and the access routes. They added that they had been informed that Bonn would be prepared to compromise about West German activities in Berlin.

The Soviet reply included an expression of interest and the ritual list of preconditions. A virtually simultaneous Soviet message to the West German government also said that Moscow was ready to talk but listed even more preconditions.

Having committed themselves to talks, the Western powers and the Soviet Union had to address the following three principal issues:

- *The area and the extent of four-power occupation rights.* The Allies asserted that all of Berlin remained under the Allied occupation regime established at Potsdam and that neither West Germany nor East Germany had any rights over any part of the city. The Soviet Union asserted that it had yielded sovereignty over East Berlin to the GDR. The Allies said that Moscow had no authority to transfer sovereignty unilaterally to the GDR. Moscow added that only West Berlin remained under the occupation regime and that it was now under the control of all four powers, not only the Western three. Thus, the four did not agree even about the area to be negotiated in the quadripartite talks, with the Allies defining it as "Berlin" and the Soviets defining it as "Westberlin" or "Berlin (West)."
- *The rights of access to West Berlin from the West.* The Allies said that all access to all parts of Berlin was implicitly part of the original occupation

arrangements and was to remain free from any controls except those exercised by the World War II Allies themselves. If any members of the three occupation powers met with any hindrance traveling either to West Berlin from West Germany or to East Berlin from West Berlin, Moscow should remove the hindrance. Civilian traffic also should be free. The Soviets were prepared to grant certain transit privileges to Western military traffic but said that civilian traffic to Berlin (West) was subject to control by the GDR and could proceed only with East German agreement. They sometimes added that Allied civilian traffic was also subject to GDR control but did not really push that argument. Moscow also said that the right of access and all conditions of access had to be negotiated with the GDR. The Allies said that the right of access, and especially that of their own forces and personnel, had emerged out of the victory over the German Reich and was unchallengeable. They would discuss the modalities only with another victor, the Soviet Union.

- *The ties between West Berlin and West Germany.* The Soviet Union, while insisting that East Berlin was part of the GDR, insisted with equal determination that West Berlin could not be part of West Germany and could have no ties of any kind to West Germany. Moscow further asserted that all West German activities in the city should cease and that all West German offices should be closed. The Allies insisted that they had the right to permit the introduction of West German offices and functions into West Berlin.

Behind the entire Berlin debate and the negotiations lay one central question: Who had and who would have authority to do what? If the Allies and the Federal Republic could obtain an agreement conceding their full authority over West Berlin and over access, they would have assured the long-term stability and viability of West Berlin. If the GDR emerged with that authority, Ulbricht would have won the right to throttle the city at whatever pace he chose.

Although East-West negotiators could perhaps compromise on specific points, they could not divide authority. That dilemma had defeated all earlier efforts to negotiate a Berlin agreement; it now faced the negotiators trying to institute détente.

All parties to the Berlin conflict understood the importance of this issue and had steeled themselves to face it. Each wanted to handle it in the most advantageous framework. Brandt wanted to press Moscow to acknowledge Western authority by using overall German-Soviet relations as a lever. Kissinger preferred to deal with it in the wider context of Soviet relations with the United States and the West as a whole. Ulbricht did not want it linked to any other topic because he did not want to be subject to outside pressures. The Soviets also wanted to divorce it from other matters but knew that they might not be able to. The quadripartite negotiators would have to determine whether Berlin matters would be handled locally, as Ulbricht wanted, or globally, where the West was stronger.

The main parties to the Berlin talks soon developed private channels to make certain that the negotiations did not get caught up in bureaucratic delays. Nixon and Kissinger chose the American ambassador in Bonn, Kenneth Rush, a lawyer-industrialist who was a personal friend of Nixon's. The U.S. role had become so important to Berlin that a strong American personality had to play a central part.

Brezhnev chose Valentin Falin, who became Soviet ambassador in Bonn. Abrasimov, the Soviet ambassador in East Berlin, remained the official negotiator, but Falin had special links to Gromyko and Brezhnev regarding Berlin.

Brandt again chose Bahr. Although Bonn did not officially take part in the Berlin talks, Brandt wanted a close friend to follow the talks and express Bonn views. Bahr soon had a visit from Leo and Slava, who would be his direct contacts to Andropov. The KGB chief did not trust Gromyko on Berlin any more than on other matters.[36] Bahr also opened a direct channel to Kissinger.

Rush, Falin, Kissinger and Bahr formed the crucial diplomatic network behind the curtain of the official talks. Other players, including British and French and most American officials, met and spoke in front of the curtain. But the private network guided events.

In addition, Bahr had contact with Michael Kohl, a state secretary in the East German premier's office, with whom he discussed the preparations for a bilateral treaty between East and West Germany that was unofficially linked to progress on Berlin. Brandt had overruled Allied objections to a dialogue between Bahr and Kohl in order to be able to speed up the pace of détente with the GDR and Moscow. Bahr may not have been grateful for he found Kohl so unyielding that he told friends that Gromyko seemed like a playboy by comparison. Kohl, hearing this, felt immensely pleased.[37]

The mechanics of the Berlin talks became almost grotesquely complicated at times, especially when some of the official negotiators were told to change their positions but did not know that something had been worked out by the negotiators behind the curtain. This irritated American professional diplomats more than others because they disagreed strongly with some of the compromises. Nixon sometimes had to intervene personally to keep the negotiations on track.

Neither the Soviet nor the Western occupiers felt in a hurry to reach agreement on Berlin. They met only six times between the fall of 1969 and the spring of

1970 and recessed completely during the summer of 1970. They then resumed at the relatively leisurely pace of one meeting every third or fourth week. Brandt wanted sessions around the clock, but neither the Allies nor the Soviets would negotiate at that pace.[38] Brandt and his détente would have to wait.

Nonetheless, the signing of the Moscow Treaty gave a boost to the Berlin talks. At the next session, on September 30, 1970, the Berlin negotiators exchanged their first papers. The papers showed their differences but, for the first time, did not try to dramatize them.

The Western paper proposed easier access to West Berlin and a greater West German presence in the city. It proposed sealing shipments to West Berlin to avoid GDR inspections, paying all tolls in a lump sum to avoid delays, and establishing an international authority to mediate complaints but not to manage the access routes. It also proposed including a "Berlin Clause" in transactions between West Germany on the one hand and the Soviet Union and its east European allies on the other, treating West Berlin as part of the Federal Republic.

Departing from Gromyko's usual style, the Soviet paper on Berlin offered a potentially promising approach. Like the Western paper, it spoke of "uninhibited access." Contrary to traditional Soviet papers, it did not reject out of hand any economic, social or cultural links between West Berlin and West Germany. But the Soviet draft still called for a separate West Berlin entity and forbade political ties with the Federal Republic. The Soviets also wanted all Western intelligence and broadcasting activities in the city to cease. More troubling, the Soviets asserted that the four-power status for all of Berlin should now apply to West Berlin only.

From that first exchange, the Berlin negotiators began sorting out separate issues and searching for solutions. Given the importance of the subject and West German pressure for urgent progress, the discussions quickly reached the political level. Nixon discussed Berlin with Gromyko and found the foreign minister much more conciliatory than usual. Gromyko said that East-West differences over the legal status of Berlin did not need to prevent agreement on practical issues regarding the future of the city. In separate meetings with British and French foreign ministers, Gromyko delivered the same encouraging message. The Soviets appeared to be well on the road toward a compromise on Berlin that would get the Moscow Treaty ratified in Bonn.

A worried Walter Ulbricht chose this moment to step in. Making one of his increasingly rare television appearances in mid-November 1970, he insisted that the GDR had to conduct any talks regarding access to West Berlin and that he would conduct such talks only with West Berlin authorities. For good measure, Ulbricht added that *all* West German activities in the city should cease.

Ulbricht made his point to the Kremlin as well, and apparently with some success. At the next Berlin four-power meeting, Abrasimov partially supported Ulbricht by endorsing Ulbricht's demands that the GDR instead of Moscow negotiate about access to West Berlin and that West Germany should end its presence in West Berlin. Within a few days, Michael Kohl invited Bahr to hold talks on "mutual transit problems."

That was too much for the West. Neither Brandt nor the Allies would tolerate having Berlin access, especially that of the Western military, under Ulbricht's control or even on his diplomatic agenda. Brandt told Bahr to reject any discussion of access. But Ulbricht did not give up easily. He reinforced his point by harassing and delaying traffic to Berlin.

That, in turn, was too much for Moscow. Gromyko went to East Berlin to press Ulbricht. When that failed to produce results, senior officials from the Soviet Union and all east European states went to Berlin for an unprecedented push to tell Ulbricht that he should not jeopardize the prospects for global détente. Brezhnev himself went to East Berlin, accompanied by Kosygin and Marshal Andrei Grechko. As if to emphasize that Moscow would not abandon the GDR but that it reserved the right to control the East-West dialogue, Brezhnev said during a speech on November 30 that Moscow would take "the *legitimate* interests and sovereign rights of the GDR" (emphasis added) into account. This statement showed that Soviet support for the GDR was not unlimited, for Moscow would plainly decide which GDR interests were "legitimate" and which were not.

Ulbricht was not playing a lone hand. Although Brezhnev, Kosygin and Andropov might want him to make concessions over Berlin, Ulbricht could find senior figures in the CPSU who did not fully support Brezhnev's policies. Petro Shelest, the Ukrainian communist party chief, opposed the Kremlin's handling of détente. So, perhaps, did some high-ranking Soviet military officers.[39] Ulbricht knew that Brezhnev had to get the authority of the upcoming CPSU congress to conduct détente, and he must have reasoned that Brezhnev did not have absolute control over that congress. At the very least, Ulbricht did not want basic decisions about the GDR and Berlin made before there was a chance for a full debate at the congress. In the meantime, the Berlin negotiations could wait, unless Brandt and the Allies would accept GDR views.

The Allies ignored Ulbricht and raised all issues directly with Moscow. On February 5, 1971, they presented a draft proposal on Berlin, stressing their wish for "practical improvements." They wanted two things in particular.

First, they wanted a firm Soviet commitment in writing that all access to and from West Berlin would be free of interference. They wanted detailed rules governing access, in order to end the spurious "interpretations" that had permitted the Soviets and especially the East Germans to block or harass traffic in the past.

Second, the Allies wanted detailed arrangements that would improve the lives of West Berliners, such as easier availability of permits to visit East Berlin, additional crossing points through the Wall, and some minor exchanges of territory around West Berlin to smooth out the borders. The Allies also suggested that East and West Berlin authorities negotiate about passes that would permit West Berliners to enter East Berlin.

In exchange, the Allies offered a firm commitment limiting West Germany's role in West Berlin. They pledged that West Berlin would "continue not to be a constituent part" of the FRG and that West Germany would lower its profile in West Berlin, especially curtailing its "demonstrative presence." But West Germany was to continue to represent West Berlin abroad, and West German economic, social and cultural links with the city were to remain in place.

The Berlin talks treaded water pending the twenty-fourth CPSU congress. The Allies hoped that their offer would show the congress that they wanted to find a reasonable solution. But the Soviet government could say nothing new before the congress. And the East Germans continued to harass traffic on the access routes, pressing both the West and Moscow.

The CPSU congress, which met in Moscow between March 30 and April 5, 1971, finally made the necessary decisions to give new impetus to détente and to the quadripartite talks on Berlin. In his speech to the congress on opening day, Brezhnev announced a program designed to advance the world-wide "struggle for peace." The congress fully supported him, endorsing not only the Moscow Treaty and the Berlin negotiations but also the SALT talks with the United States and the impending negotiations for Mutual and Balanced Force Reductions (MBFR) in Europe. It supported Brezhnev's opening toward the West and called for cooperation instead of confrontation with the United States and West Germany. It thus put an end to Ulbricht's hope that Brezhnev would have to change course. But Brezhnev still had to deal with his recalcitrant satellite.

FOURTEEN

DÉTENTE IN GERMANY

WALTER ULBRICHT HAD REACHED HIS SEVENTY-SEVENTH BIRTHDAY when Willy Brandt and Leonid Brezhnev began their negotiations. After a lifetime of service to Marxism-Leninism, including twenty-five years in East Berlin, he could look back on a long record of dedication and achievement. He had known Lenin and had served Stalin, Khrushchev and lastly Brezhnev. He had controlled and Sovietized East Germany for Moscow, organizing the SED and forcing collectivization and socialization. He could deservedly claim the rank and reverence due a senior communist figure.

Ulbricht even claimed his own distinct contribution to Marxism-Leninism. He had created what he termed "a new socialist system" in East Germany, frequently claiming that the GDR was the model *Arbeiter- und Bauern-Staat* (worker and peasant state). He believed that the expansion of communism in Europe depended on the kind of strong and ideologically pure GDR that he had built.

But Ulbricht's time had come. Whatever loyal service he might have rendered, he could not manage East Germany as Brezhnev wanted.

ODD MAN OUT

Ulbricht had failed to deliver the kind of economic performance that Moscow expected and needed. His callous implementation of the socialist transformation had fomented confusion, opposition and production shortfalls. He had provoked the flight of essential people, including engineers, doctors and technicians as well as the workers and peasants he purported to represent. The Wall helped return the GDR to growth, but only briefly. By 1970, East Germany was deeply in debt not only to West Germany but to a number of east European states and to the Soviet Union itself. Soviet officials criticized Ulbricht's economic policies harshly,[1] with Brezhnev himself joining that criticism in 1970.[2] Moscow no longer accepted Ulbricht's tired explanation that West German sabotage caused his problems.

During 1969 and 1970, Ulbricht had tried to counter Moscow's burgeoning trade with West Germany by launching another ambitious economic program that promised to overtake the West and to create a new "developed societal system of socialism" in the 1970s. But that program, clearly intended to make links with the West unnecessary, had failed disastrously by early 1971. When Ulbricht went to the Soviet party congress, he had to ask for more aid. His failure reinforced Brezhnev's determination to expand economic links with West Germany, if necessary at Ulbricht's expense.[3]

Ulbricht had fought Brezhnev on détente. From the moment of his arrival in Berlin in 1945, and even against Stalin's wishes, Ulbricht had done everything possible to separate East Germany from West Germany. He had opposed the meetings between Stoph and Brandt before West German de jure recognition of the GDR. Brezhnev had overruled him.[4] He resented having Brandt tell Stoph in Kassel that he could not reply to a question from Stoph until he had heard the results of Bahr's talks with Gromyko.[5]

Most of all, Ulbricht had opposed four-power negotiations about Berlin as a whole. After all, East Berlin was Ulbricht's capital, sheltered from Western intervention by the Wall and not to be discussed by others, certainly not between Moscow and Bonn. If anyone was to talk to West Germany and to the Allies about any part of Berlin, it should be Ulbricht himself.

But Brezhnev no longer had any choice. He had to pursue a variation of some of Stalin's old ideas, seeking contact and influence in West Germany. Brezhnev regarded the Federal Republic as the "true" Germany.[6] He thought that the future of Europe and of the Soviet Union had to be negotiated with Bonn. He would not surrender the GDR, but he wanted Ulbricht to get into line. Ulbricht made his reservations clear.[7] He felt that any weakening in Soviet support for GDR authority would amount to surrender, whether Brezhnev intended it or not.

Ulbricht had earned the enmity of many of his senior SED colleagues. A majority of the SED politburo disliked him. They hoped that Brezhnev would depose him and they pleaded with Abrasimov to make it happen. Citing Ulbricht's "difficult personality" and "irrational ideas,"[8] they complained about his mistakes, about his Stalinism and about his unscrupulous handling of people.[9] Abrasimov criticized Ulbricht in his own reports to Moscow, and briefed Erich Honecker instead of Ulbricht on Gromyko's negotiations with Bahr.[10]

Honecker led the opposition to Ulbricht. Although Ulbricht had advanced Honecker's career and anointed him as successor, Honecker had begun to undercut Ulbricht systematically during the late 1960s. He had formed his own links with Brezhnev and other Soviet leaders and had distanced himself from those Ulbricht policies that he knew Brezhnev disliked—such as Ulbricht's claim to a unique SED contribution to Marxism-Leninism. He did not fully support Ulbricht's insistence on full West German recognition and would remain silent when Ulbricht expounded such views to Soviet officials. Honecker had built the Wall but wanted to keep some lines open to West Germany. He feared that the GDR would atrophy without West German contact, although that contact had to be carefully managed.

In mid-1970, Honecker had pressed Brezhnev to force Ulbricht to resign. Brezhnev, while agreeing, had said that Ulbricht could not simply be "shoved aside." Brezhnev made clear that he himself would keep control.[11] He added, however, that Ulbricht could not expect to govern without Soviet approval: "After all, we have troops in your country."[12]

Confronting Honecker's demands, the Soviet leadership split. A few remained loyal to Ulbricht, but some important figures wanted him out. Andropov, for example, wanted an opening to Bonn and would readily sacrifice Ulbricht, especially as his own intelligence reports confirmed Ulbricht's increasing isolation in the SED.[13] But Brezhnev hesitated, although he did not like Ulbricht, whom he had long found arrogant and with whom he had experienced several unpleasant encounters.[14] The ever cautious Brezhnev did not want to replace Ulbricht or agree to his replacement unless the CPSU had incontrovertible evidence that the SED itself really wanted him to retire.[15] Thereupon, a majority of SED politburo members wrote to Brezhnev in January 1971 to ask him to remove Ulbricht.[16]

Brezhnev and his colleagues must have made the decision to replace Ulbricht with Honecker during the twenty-fourth congress around the beginning of April 1971. Within days after the congress, Soviet press releases upgraded Honecker's status.

Honecker then made sure that Ulbricht understood what he was to do. He visited Ulbricht at the latter's retreat in Dölln, accompanied by a detachment of the private guard force for senior GDR officials. Brandishing machine pistols, the guards surrounded Ulbricht's compound and blocked all entrances and exits. When the guards had taken their posts, Honecker went in and, after a conversation of an hour and a half, gained Ulbricht's agreement to leave office.[17]

Ulbricht formally resigned at an SED central committee meeting on May 3, 1971, announcing that "there is no prescription against advancing years." The central committee anointed Honecker as SED first secretary.

Honecker followed up with some further blunt measures to reduce Ulbricht's stature. He forced Ulbricht into a humiliating "rectification of errors" at an SED politburo meeting in October, 1971, as if Ulbricht had been a minor intellectual dissident. After Ulbricht suffered a heart attack and was removed even further from political responsibility, Honecker assigned spies to report on his activities. When Ulbricht died on August 1, 1973, Honecker's interior minister and closest political ally, Erich Mielke, sent security officers to pick up 255 boxes of Ulbricht's personal files from his home.[18]

On May 18, 1971, two weeks after he had succeeded Ulbricht, Honecker and a delegation of senior GDR officials made a pilgrimage to Moscow. Not surprisingly, Honecker accepted the basic directions of Brezhnev's détente policy. He specifically said that he wanted the quadripartite Berlin negotiations to conclude quickly. The SED abandoned its assertion that West Berlin was on GDR territory. Instead, it termed West Berlin a city with "a special political status." That position conformed with Soviet, Allied and West German views even if it did not use the same language.

The communiqué published after Honecker's Moscow talks said that the GDR approved "the peace program adopted by the 24th party congress" and regarded it as "an expression of the two countries' common aims and interests." The communiqué added that the two parties had expressed their views on the quadripartite Berlin negotiations and had agreed that "an understanding on this question" would remove the basis for arguments. This language showed that Moscow and East Berlin did not yet agree fully on Berlin but that they were at least on common ground. It also showed that Honecker would make a positive contribution to the quadripartite negotiations and to détente.[19] He would not undercut Brezhnev's policies.

To make the transition complete and to show that he would not create any problems, Honecker told Brezhnev: "The GDR is our common child. It is the result of the Soviet victory in the Great Patriotic War against Hitler's fascism. We will never forget that."[20]

Those fine words did not impress all Soviet officials. Yuli Kvitsinsky, then minister at the Soviet embassy in East Berlin, noted that Honecker and his closest colleagues had backgrounds significantly more worrisome than Ulbricht's. They had not spent the war years in Moscow, as Ulbricht had. Nor had they done their postwar planning in Molotov's foreign ministry. Most had spent the war years in Hitler's concentration camps. They might have a somewhat more nationalist standpoint, a greater tendency to see things from a German perspective and less sense of loyalty to Moscow.[21]

But all that was for the distant future. In the meantime, the negotiators had work to do and a new freedom to do it.

WRAPPING UP THE BERLIN ACCORD

Ulbricht's removal did indeed break the deadlock. Within a week after Honecker's visit to Moscow, Abrasimov accepted the basic Western prescription for the Berlin quadripartite talks. He told Allied delegates that he would help draft a text that would concentrate on "practical improvements" in Berlin while avoiding questions about status. That formula offered the only route to an agreement and marked the end of Ulbricht's influence and of GDR demands for control over Berlin. Given Abrasimov's sometimes stormy relationship with Ulbricht, the ambassador had good reason to feel pleased. He no longer spoke of East German control over the access routes but of "contractual arrangements with the interested parties."[22]

The four powers concluded the first draft of an agreement in three days of intense negotiation in June. But problems remained. Although Abrasimov accepted Soviet responsibility for keeping transit between West Berlin and West Germany open for West Germans and West Berliners as well as for Allied personnel, he did not accept the general principle of freedom of movement. And, although he no longer insisted that West German institutions in West Berlin had to be removed, he did not accept all existing links between West Germany and West Berlin. Moreover, many details still had to be ironed out.

The SED fell into line with the new Soviet position at its own eighth congress in mid-June. Honecker hailed the talks on Berlin and wished them success, which Ulbricht had never done. The congress abandoned Ulbricht's long-held insistence on formal recognition of the GDR. Honecker also found support in the party for greater contacts with the West. Ulbricht himself pleaded illness and did not attend.

The negotiations then picked up more speed, perhaps because President Nixon announced in July that Kissinger had visited Beijing and that he himself would visit China in 1972. The negotiators scheduled a marathon session beginning on August 10 to bring the talks to a successful conclusion. They reached basic agreement within a week. The Western delegates later learned that Gromyko had secretly gone to East Berlin to supervise the final Soviet position personally. They had noticed that Abrasimov periodically left the meeting and had wondered why.[23]

By August 23, the four ambassadors scheduled a "final" session at Rush's residence in West Berlin. There they initialed the draft text after wrapping up some details, including approval for a Soviet consulate general in West Berlin at the old Lietzenburgerstrasse building that Khrushchev had wanted to use in 1963. Many West Berliners and some U.S. officials objected to Soviet plans, fearing that a consulate general might reinforce the Soviet claim that West Berlin had become a four-power city. Nixon himself made the final decision. He did so at Brandt's request and on the basis of a Soviet commitment not to use the building as a political or diplomatic headquarters.[24] With that agreement, the West as a whole had put into place the third element of Brandt's détente on Germany.

The Berlin quadripartite agreement dealt with the three main elements of the Berlin question, finessing issues that could not be solved and finding compromise solutions wherever possible:

- *The area and the extent of four-power occupation rights.* The parties agreed to disagree, using such malleable terms as "the relevant area" to avoid defining whether the agreement covered only West Berlin or all of Berlin.
- *The rights of access to Berlin from the West.* The West won important concessions, including specific pledges that transit traffic would be "unimpeded." This was probably the item that most disturbed Ulbricht, for he had long wanted authority over access in order to gain control over West Berlin.
- *Ties between West Berlin and the Federal Republic.* West Germany won an important basic concession, for the agreement permitted existing ties to be "maintained and developed." In exchange, Bonn had to promise to exercise discretion and not to abuse those ties by such demonstrative exercises as the election of the federal president in Berlin. It also had to recognize that West Berlin continued not to be "a constituent part of the Federal Republic." Moscow made an important concession by permitting West Germany to represent West Berlin abroad, except in security matters that remained within Allied competence, and also by recognizing West German passports for West Berliners. Bahr felt particularly pleased about this Soviet concession because he had won it after the Americans had told him that he should give it up for lost. Once again, Leo, Slava and Andropov helped Bahr. In return, Moscow could place the consulate general in West Berlin.[25]

Abrasimov made an additional concession by agreeing to permit West Berliners to visit East Berlin and the GDR under arrangements to be negotiated between the West Berlin administration and the GDR. Brandt regarded this as a fundamental objective and an important gain for West Berliners. By endorsing such a right in the quadripartite agreement itself, Moscow limited the GDR's capacity to block it.

Politically, the West gained more than the East from the negotiations because West Germany could continue to exercise some role in West Berlin. But Brandt wanted mainly to open more contact within the German nation across the Wall. He and Brezhnev—as well as the Western powers—also had a common interest in making certain that the Berlin question could no longer disrupt East-West relations at inconvenient moments.

The Western occupation powers achieved their greatest gains in the crucial area of authority. The Soviet Union took responsibility for traffic on the access routes across East German territory. East German personnel had less leeway to harass although they remained at the checkpoints. The Allies had to scale back West Germany's presence and activities in Berlin, but this did not disturb them unduly because they felt the West German presence had over time exceeded their own original intent. The four occupation powers essentially decided that they wanted to manage the Berlin situation themselves.

Brandt endorsed the agreement within two days. His spokesman said that the agreement "preserves the interests of West Germany and Berlin," representing a major contribution to easing tension in the center of Europe.

Sticky problems emerged, however, in the German text of the agreement. Because the nominal negotiators of the Berlin agreement were the victors of World War II, German was not an official language of the negotiations or of the agreement. But the German words would color the Bundestag debate about Ostpolitik as a whole and also would provide the definitive context for any separate implementing agreements that the two Germanys had to negotiate. Therefore, the German text took on importance beyond a technical translation. The choice of one or another German word would convey one or another interpretation about the status of Berlin and therefore perhaps about Germany as a whole. A major argument was over the choice of the word *Bindungen* or *Verbindungen* to define the links between West Berlin and West Germany, with the West Germans preferring *Bindungen* and the East Germans the somewhat weaker *Verbindungen*.

The language differences took time to be reconciled. Hans-Otto Bräutigam, the diplomat who was later to become the West German representative in East Berlin, carried on the main talks with the GDR about these problems, but Brandt also asked Bahr to become involved on some of the more sensitive decisions.[26]

The translation problem again illustrated the ambiguous role that the Germans played in the Berlin negotiations. Although West Germany did not officially take part in the talks, Brandt had to make sure that West German public and political opinion accepted the text. He would have to carry out many of its provisions and would have to talk with the GDR. He wanted to resolve the language differences while his Western friends could help out if necessary.

In the text of the agreement itself, the passage that most pleased the Allies was the formula for the relationship between West Berlin and West Germany. For months, the West would not accept the Soviet concept or vice versa. Bahr finally asked the German foreign office to find a formula, which they did although Brandt and Rush changed it somewhat. The phrase that Berlin "remains not a constituent part" of the Federal Republic was technically correct because Berlin had never been part of West Germany. But the word "remains," accepted by Gromyko and Falin, implied Soviet acceptance of the institutions that the Federal Republic had established in West Berlin since 1949.[27]

The quadripartite agreement and Ulbricht's departure gave West Berlin a shot in the arm. The city no longer had to worry about its main tormentor and about the chicanery that had discouraged many who might have wished to live there.

THE WEST COORDINATES

Although the Western states never had the intramural confrontations that marked Ulbricht's relationship with Brezhnev, they had their differences. Washington agreed with Brandt's wish to complete the Berlin agreement before he would submit the Moscow Treaty to the Bundestag, recognizing that Brezhnev would thus be under pressure to reach a Berlin agreement. But the American government, always interested in supporting Poland, did not welcome Brandt's decision to delay approval for the Polish treaty until Berlin had been settled.[28] Nixon and Kissinger also thought that Brandt at times wanted to move too fast, letting Gromyko take advantage of him. Brandt in turn felt that the Allies and especially the Americans did not work fast enough. He wanted a true momentum for détente.

Brandt reluctantly recognized that the Allies would not always do as he wanted. He also recognized, as earlier in his career, that the Western powers reserved the last word on Berlin for themselves. But, while he occasionally complained of this, he also welcomed it. Washington could resist Soviet pressure better than Bonn, especially after the opening to Beijing. He did not feel ready to take on Moscow directly across the full range of the German question. At the beginning of 1971, Brandt said in public that "the Four Powers have, and will retain, competence for Germany as a whole and for Berlin."[29] But he also thought that Germany had its own special interest in Berlin because a Berlin settlement would open a new window for German diplomacy to the East.[30]

Brandt took a backseat to no one in terms of his close cooperation and friendship with America.[31] He never had the type of disagreements with Nixon that Ulbricht had with Brezhnev. He believed that his policies had helped the United States and that he actually had reinforced the American position in Europe rather than weakened it.[32] But coordination did not move smoothly at first. Washington remained a problem for Brandt until late 1971, when he thought the U.S. government began to accept and appreciate what he had achieved for the alliance as a whole.[33]

Brandt expected détente to help erode the Soviet empire. He believed that the GDR and the other east European regimes could never be stabilized as long as people could travel freely. Curiously, he and Ulbricht agreed on this. Brandt later believed that history had proven him correct.[34]

Kissinger and Bahr developed a close although somewhat guarded working relationship on Berlin. The two had known each other for years before they had both assumed key offices. They often differed on East-West questions, but they needed to work together to get a Berlin accord. They saw each other at the Bildeberg Conference in early 1971, when the Berlin negotiations were in deadlock, and exchanged ideas about how best to break it.

Bahr told Kissinger, as he had told the Soviets and others, that it was a mistake to approach the Berlin talks on a legal basis. Instead, the Americans should look for practical solutions without trying to reach an impossible meeting of the minds on status and other legal matters.

Kissinger accepted Bahr's approach and suggested a White House meeting among himself, Bahr and Rush. At that meeting, the three agreed to set up a separate channel among themselves, in effect bypassing the regular Allied Bonn Group consultations. Bahr-Kissinger contacts became very close after April 1971, when Bahr went to Washington to make a special plea for the Allies to accept the presence of the Soviet consulate general in Berlin (not coincidentally, perhaps, just after Moscow had agreed to accept a West German consulate general in Leningrad).

Kissinger still feared that the Germans would go too far too fast. He did not think that they could jeopardize Soviet-American priorities but worried that they might permit their old yearning for the East to get in the way of the broad interests of the Western alliance.[35] He also feared that Gromyko's passion for petty tactical maneuvering might tempt him to try to take advantage of even slight divergences between Bonn and Washington. He was glad to have his own line to Brezhnev (as was Bahr).[36]

Kissinger saw Berlin as only one part, albeit an important one, of U.S. global strategy. It did not rank as high on his priority list as on Brandt's, and he sometimes delayed the Berlin talks to avoid having to ask Moscow for a concession on Berlin when he had something that he regarded as more important to negotiate on another subject. Bahr sometimes resented Kissinger's delays because he understood their meaning. But he later said that he did not recall any delays that were dangerous to the future of the Berlin agreement, and his own memoirs speak warmly of his work with Kissinger.[37]

The meeting among Kissinger, Bahr and Rush set in train the most intensive period of German-American diplomatic coordination before the 1990 talks on unification. Bahr recalls sending messages to Kissinger and receiving answers within hours, as if they were each sitting at telex machines. He felt that he and Kissinger were in very close contact. Kissinger often accepted Bahr's suggestions, as he believed that the Americans should not stand in the way of German proposals unless such proposals were truly unwise. The Americans and the Germans, and especially Kissinger and Bahr, thus became intimate partners in détente.

Falin joined on the Soviet side, but Bahr still kept and used the special KGB channel through Leo and Slava to Andropov. Bahr wrote later that this channel solved countless problems for him.[38]

The trilateral back channel offered indispensable flexibility but risked confusion and misunderstanding. The principals constantly had to remember what was in the front channel and what was in the back channel and whom to tell what. Fortunately, the French and British ambassadors did not try to prove their mettle by raising questions about how some "solutions" might miraculously appear before them.

France wanted to use the talks on Berlin primarily to endorse four-power responsibility. As in the past, Paris also wanted to use Berlin to draw Germany closer to the European Community. London, which was to join the EC in 1973, shared the general French approach and would support American and German efforts if they remained within broad Berlin arrangements. Although the British and French participants in the Bonn Group occasionally raised questions, they would go along with American and German suggestions if they did not violate their notion of four-power rights.

Western coordination, like Eastern coordination, represented a constant challenge. But Bonn and the Allies all wanted détente and could solve any problems that arose. The West had no Walter Ulbricht to remove.

THE TWO GERMANYS

Within weeks after the CPSU congress and Walter Ulbricht's resignation, Leonid Brezhnev invited Willy Brandt to join him at his vacation retreat in Oreanda on the Crimean Peninsula. The visit took place in mid-September, less than two weeks after the four powers had signed the Berlin agreement.[39]

Before Brandt's visit to Oreanda, Kissinger had visited Beijing again. Although neither Brezhnev nor Brandt spoke of that, it made a difference in their relationship. Once Beijing and Washington began to talk, Moscow needed a major partner along the western borders of the Soviet system. The Oreanda meeting gave West Germany that role.

Brezhnev made clear that he regarded Brandt as a major figure. Using the credit that he had gained by his earlier concessions, he asked Brandt to support his proposal for a Conference on Security and Cooperation in Europe (CSCE). Brandt agreed, thereafter arguing strongly for CSCE in Washington. Brandt also agreed to let the German Communist Party (KPD) again take part in West German politics although it had earlier been banned because of some of its provocative tactics.

Brezhnev permitted Brandt and the German delegation to come in a Luftwaffe aircraft, the first time a West German military plane had landed at a Soviet airport. Brezhnev stood on the tarmac by himself. He invited Brandt and his colleagues to round after round of toasts at the airport lounge, making Brandt wonder whether the Soviet leader was trying to drink him and his delegation under the table.[40]

Brezhnev and Brandt kept up a friendly manner during the entire meeting, skirting difficult issues while trying mainly to establish a positive mood. Brezhnev spoke glowingly of trade and of future cooperation between West Germany and the Soviet Union. He cited the importance of German-Soviet friendship for the peace of the world and the well-being of both countries.

Brezhnev warned Brandt very sternly, however, that the Bundestag had to pass the Moscow and Warsaw treaties if it did not wish to set back German-Soviet relations "for decades." He also warned that the Berlin agreements and related implementing accords would be null and void if the Moscow Treaty was not approved. Brandt in turn tried to impress on Brezhnev that Soviet and especially GDR behavior would have an impact on the Bundestag vote and thus on the future of the treaties.

Brandt later expressed some concern in his memoirs about Brezhnev's imprecision at Oreanda on military matters. Brezhnev seemed to have no sense for the European military balance when he spoke of Soviet force deployments. Nor did he seem to appreciate the hazard that such deployments might pose to détente. As Khrushchev once had boasted that Moscow was producing missiles "like sausages," Brezhnev now boasted that Moscow was producing nuclear submarines "like sausages."[41]

Brezhnev's comments may have reflected the results of the CPSU congress. Although he could persuade the congress to support détente, he had to compromise

with the generals. Military spokesmen at the congress stressed the growing importance of nuclear weapons in Europe, insisting on a continued Soviet buildup on the
continent. And the Soviet military budget rose for the sixth consecutive year since
Brezhnev had assumed power. Moscow's détente policy might operate in diplomacy
and in trade, but not in the military field.[42] Brandt found some of Brezhnev's comments worrisome, fearing such attitudes could jeopardize German political support
for détente, but he did not perceive their full meaning until some years later.[43]

Despite this ominous undertone, the Oreanda meeting put the new Soviet-
German relationship on a firmer footing. Both Brandt and Brezhnev wanted the
world to know that Europe had changed between 1961 and 1971.

Against this positive background, the time had come to put the fourth and final
piece into the mosaic of détente over Germany. East and West Germany now
had to conclude the agreement that would govern their relations with each
other.

Negotiations between East and West Germany had at one time seemed the
main sticking point in East-West détente. By 1971, however, with the Moscow
and Warsaw treaties in place, with Ulbricht out of the way and with Berlin issues
settled, Moscow and Bonn had taken care of the most difficult inner-German
questions in other contexts.

Nonetheless, the German-German negotiations proved to be wearisome
and difficult. While Honecker proved more accommodating than Ulbricht
would have been, he still needed to reinforce the authority of the GDR as much
as possible. And Brandt for his part could not abandon any basic West German
position without having to answer to the West German constitutional court and
to the opposition in the Bundestag.[44]

Brandt wanted to use the talks to expand contacts between the East and
West German people and to keep the German question open. Honecker had to
be more careful. He also wanted contact, but only under his own control. He
still needed to upgrade and protect the GDR even if he did not insist on formal
recognition. And both found that they had to deal simultaneously with such
basic issues as the form of mutual diplomatic contacts and with such practical
matters as travel regulations and other day-by-day frictions, with each solution
affecting all others.

Brandt and Honecker knew that Brezhnev would be the final arbiter. He
would decide what the GDR would have to yield and what it would have to receive. And they also knew that he wanted compromise. Like Brandt, he wanted
to keep the German question open, because that gave Moscow the greatest
leverage. Like Honecker, he wanted to make certain that the GDR remained
stable.

Linkage remained Brezhnev's main concern in these talks as in the others. The Moscow Treaty, the Berlin agreement, and even the Warsaw Treaty depended on a Brandt-Honecker success. Thus, when Bahr and Michael Kohl began their most intensive talks, those leading toward a basic agreement on inner-German relations, they were effectively putting the final stone into an arch that not only they but their principal allies wanted built. They met almost continually for two months. Herbert Wehner, minister for all-German affairs, sent West Germany's most imaginative and able expert on inner-German questions, Jürgen Weichert, to support Bahr.

Brezhnev pressed Honecker to make concessions. He compelled Honecker to accept travel arrangements for which Honecker—who had begun to realize that West Germany would pay good money for political concessions—thought he could have received up to DM 3 billion from Bonn. When Honecker complained that such arrangements meant "the practically full opening of our state frontier to West Berliners" and that they would impose "considerable ideological burdens," Brezhnev did not yield. Honecker argued against Brandt's references to unification, but he had to accept Brezhnev's decision that the Berlin agreement and the treaty between the two Germanys would go forward in order to get the Moscow Treaty ratified.[45]

Brezhnev made certain that West Germany would not have to recognize the GDR de jure and that the two states would exchange only "permanent missions" instead of embassies. He also decided that Bonn had the right to negotiate for Berlin transit across East Germany, with West Berlin having to negotiate only for West Berliners' access to East Berlin. Brezhnev could not be expected to do more.

Brandt also made several important concessions. Most important, he made a speech acknowledging the existence of two German states. This followed his earlier decision to put a formal end to the Hallstein Doctrine, thus allowing a wide range of GDR diplomatic contacts across the world. He also agreed that both German states should enter the United Nations, a move that reinforced the GDR's global status. Brandt opened doors that other West Germans had kept closed.

The negotiators agreed once again to set aside the sticky legal issues that they could not resolve. Brandt still insisted, however, on a preamble clause asserting that the agreement would not prejudice fundamental questions, "including the national question." The matter of four-power rights was settled by a clause that the treaty would not affect "the bilateral and multilateral international treaties and agreements concluded by . . . or relating to" both the GDR and the Federal Republic. Each clause represented a fundamental concession, but by 1972 the die had been cast and the negotiators wanted reasons to agree, not to quarrel.

Bahr and Kohl initialed the Basic Treaty on November 8, 1972. It was signed on December 21, 1972, a Christmas present to those who had been separated for over ten years. As with the Moscow Treaty, the West German delegation presented the "Letter on German Unity" at the signature ceremony to make clear that the treaty did not put an end to West Germany's commitment to unification.

The Basic Treaty and the accompanying agreements between East and West Germany had greater practical effect in Germany itself than any other détente accord because they applied to many of the details of Berlin travel and of inner-German relations. The sheer number of agreements and associated documents that were to follow established a wide web of contacts between the two Germanys and their residents although the Wall remained in place.

The agreements included texts on transit traffic between West Berlin and West Germany as well as a substantial body of agreements between West Berlin and the GDR about West Berliner visits to East Berlin. The various agreements between Bonn and West Berlin on one side and the GDR on the other substantially facilitated travel between East and West in Germany. Within months, millions of persons took advantage of the new provisions and the number grew in later years. The agreements also made it easier to send mail and to make phone calls.[46] Willy Brandt had created further openings in the Wall even if he could not tear it down.

Honecker had an attitude almost opposite to Ulbricht's and, of course, also different from Brandt's. Whereas Ulbricht had wanted *Abgrenzung*, keeping firm barriers between the two Germanys, he had still nurtured a long-term vision of a Germany united under his concept of socialism when the time was ripe. Honecker had relaxed the separation between the Germanys but did not expect or want a future united Germany. He saw the GDR as a permanent entity. Honecker opened GDR borders as much as he dared and as much as Brezhnev insisted, but did not think that such openings would lead to German unity. Brandt, on the other hand, hoped that one day they would do so, and that in the meantime they would keep alive the concept of a German nation. The Allies agreed with his tactics, although they later proved to have divergent ideas about where those tactics should lead.

FIFTEEN

BRANDT'S BRIEF TRIUMPH

WILLY BRANDT'S MOST ANXIOUS MOMENTS STILL LAY AHEAD. THE CDU/CSU opposition under Rainer Barzel chose to denounce Brandt's Ostpolitik and to try to bring the chancellor down when his treaties came to the Bundestag for approval. Barzel thought that he had enough defections from Brandt's own coalition to have a sufficient if razor-thin majority against Brandt.[1]

Barzel, the CDU/CSU parliamentary leader and chancellor candidate, knew better than to attack Ostpolitik directly. More than four out of every five Germans supported it. Moreover, Brezhnev's form of linkage meant that Berliners would pay the price if Ostpolitik failed. Barzel tried to overcome this dilemma by arguing that he did not oppose Ostpolitik in itself but wanted better terms. Barzel had plans for several CDU/CSU officials to fly to Moscow on the day after the Bundestag vote to make a new agreement with Brezhnev. He pointed out that the Soviet Union had not specifically acknowledged either the German right to self-determination or the role of the European Economic Community in economic and political relations.

The debate on the eastern treaties, as the Moscow and Warsaw treaties became known collectively, began on February 25, 1972. To help Brandt, Brezhnev made a point of personally acknowledging both the German right to self-determination and the EEC role. But the Soviet government also opened a personal contact with Barzel, recognizing that he might win and that Moscow might have to deal with him.

THE BUNDESTAG MYSTERY

Both sides maneuvered for votes. Barzel had some defectors from Brandt's coalition. Brandt in turn gained some votes from the opposition. On April 24, Barzel submitted a "constructive vote of no confidence" motion to the Bundestag. Under the West German Basic Law, such a motion allowed a vote of no confidence in an incumbent government but also immediately had to replace that government with a new one (under Barzel's motion, his own). This provision had been written into the Basic Law to prevent votes of no confidence that would leave the country with no government, as it had often been left during the Weimar Republic.

Brandt denounced the motion as immoral, as a sleazy maneuver to give Barzel an office that he could not hope to win through a popular vote. He pointed out that public opinion polls showed widespread support for his policies and especially for the eastern treaties.

Whatever the merits of Brandt's arguments, most political analysts saw him as a certain loser. Barzel could allegedly count on just enough ballots (249) to give him the necessary absolute majority. The German trade unions, anticipating Brandt's defeat, planned a general strike. Although such CDU Bundestag moderates as Richard von Weizsäcker opposed Barzel's tactics, they could not prevent a vote. Ostpolitik appeared doomed.

But Barzel's motion failed. It received only 247 votes, two short of the needed 249. Some CDU/CSU deputies apparently had voted for Brandt, but in a secret ballot nobody knew who. Some might have voted for him because they believed in détente; others might have been bribed. Rumors of large payments floated around Bonn, with some defectors from the CDU/CSU said to have received DM 50,000 or more to vote for Brandt. Wehner, a grizzled veteran of many battles on the streets and in the parliament, said that "people were paid." In 1980, he said that only two persons knew how the whole thing had been managed: "I was one, and the other is no longer in the parliament."[2]

Much of the speculation concentrated on the Soviet role. Just before the vote, the Soviet government took additional steps, including the release of many ethnic Germans, to show détente in a good light. Soviet money allegedly flowed. Leo and Slava appeared in Bahr's office with a briefcase containing DM 200,000, enough—they hoped—to buy four Bundestag votes. Markus Wolf, the East German spymaster, asserted after unification that the GDR had paid a CDU Bundestag member DM 50,000 for a vote.[3] Whatever may have happened, Brandt emerged triumphant. Barzel ended as a ruined figure, never again to play a leading role.

With the constructive vote of no confidence out of the way, the Bundestag ratified the eastern treaties on May 17, 1972. Brandt took advantage of the popular support for Ostpolitik to call early elections in November. He used not only the Moscow and Warsaw treaties but the agreements with the GDR as evidence that he had successfully reopened the German question and had eased the human burden of division. The West German electorate returned him with a larger, more comfortable, majority, endorsing the policy of détente and the opening to the East. With that victory, Brandt and the course of West German policy appeared firmly in place.

Détente continued. After the Basic Treaty with the GDR, West Germany signed the Prague Treaty with Czechoslovakia on December 11, 1973. It voided the Munich agreement of 1938 which had given the Sudetenland and other ethnic German areas in Czechoslovakia to Hitler. It added that both states declared their border inviolable and raised the existing trade missions to embassy status. Moscow and West Germany signed a far-reaching agreement on economic, industrial and cultural cooperation. The Conference on Security and Cooperation in Europe opened in July 1973 with the United States and Canada as full members in part because of German insistence. Three months later the MBFR talks opened in Vienna. In July 1973, the West German constitutional court decided that the Basic Treaty between the two Germanys did not violate Bonn's Basic Law.

Brandt could savor his triumph, but not for long. He was to be hit from an unexpected quarter.

HONECKER AND THE FALL OF BRANDT

Brandt's accomplishments assured him a permanent place in history but not in the chancellery. He had to leave office on May 6, 1974, following the arrest of Günter Guillaume, one of his closest aides. Guillaume confessed that he was a colonel in GDR intelligence and that he had spied on Brandt almost from the day that Brandt had entered the chancellery.

Brandt thus suffered a major embarrassment and had no choice but to resign. Helmut Schmidt, his defense minister, succeeded him. Schmidt continued Brandt's détente policy, changing its style if not its substance.

Brandt need not have fallen from office because of Guillaume. The West German security services had shadowed Guillaume for some time before they arrested him. They could have warned Brandt to remove Guillaume from the chancellery. But Hans-Dietrich Genscher, the interior minister responsible for the security services, apparently did not deliver the warning with full force.

Honecker could have withdrawn Guillaume from Brandt's office earlier. Well before his arrest, Guillaume had alerted GDR spymaster Wolf that the West German security services had begun following him and his wife. Wolf had in turn informed GDR interior minister Erich Mielke that the West Germans had learned of Guillaume's activities. Mielke, being the closest of Honecker's advisers, certainly told him immediately. More likely, he did not need to. In eastern Europe, communist party leaders knew who and where their top spies were. An agent in the chancellor's office represented a political risk as well as an intelligence opportunity. And Guillaume should normally have been pulled out as soon as he began to be shadowed. But Honecker did not recall Guillaume, although he had plenty of time to do so.[4]

Many German politicians, East and West, had reason to seek Brandt's removal from office: Helmut Schmidt, Brandt's likely successor; Genscher, who could play an important role as foreign minister under Schmidt; and Wehner, who believed that Brandt did not have the patience to manage government successfully on a day-by-day basis after the high-wire triumph of Ostpolitik and who might have feared that the SPD would lose the next election if Brandt remained in office. Wehner persuaded Brandt to resign after Guillaume had confessed.[5]

Most probably, however, Honecker himself played the most important role in forcing Brandt out. If he had recalled Guillaume immediately after the spy had first been suspected, Guillaume would not have been arrested. He could have easily disappeared back into East Germany. Whereas his departure might have provoked some attention and controversy, there would not have been a major scandal. Brandt would have been spared the level of embarrassment that could remove him from office.

Honecker professed to regard Brandt's departure as a great loss, but he also must have recognized that Brandt posed a greater danger to him and to the GDR than any other West German leader. Brandt had reached cult status among East Germans, evoking far more trust than any East German official, including Honecker. He could—if he so chose—say or do things that could threaten any such official. He could and did negotiate for the East German people against their own government. It was widely known that he had not given up on unification. He also had a close personal relationship with Brezhnev, being almost certainly more influential in Moscow than Honecker.

From Honecker's viewpoint, therefore, Brandt represented a threat. Brandt's departure solved some of Honecker's problems with his own people and with Moscow. No other West German could arouse the same emotions in East Germany as Brandt, or appeal as effectively to Brezhnev over Honecker's head.

In his memoirs, Wolf offered some superficially plausible explanations (such as routinely dispatched birthday cards) for Guillaume's discovery by the West

German counter-intelligence services. But he did not explain why other top East German spies, some of whom worked in extremely sensitive and carefully monitored settings in the West German intelligence services or at NATO headquarters, eluded discovery until after unification.

Honecker might well have instructed GDR intelligence services through Mielke to leave clues that would let the West Germans "discover" Guillaume. At the very least, he alone must have decided to leave the agent in place so as to cause the greatest possible political damage to Brandt and to enable his spy to "confess" after being arrested.

And Guillaume's swift and full confession must in itself warrant suspicion. A professional spy would not have made such a confession without instructions. After all, Guillaume could count on being traded back to the GDR after a brief and not too unpleasant stay in the most high-class West German security facility. Why should he have confessed?

Honecker told Brandt ten years later during a meeting in East Berlin that he had known nothing about Guillaume until he had read about the spy scandal in the newspapers. He said that he blamed "our people" and would have said "throw the man out!" if he had known about him. Brandt remained skeptical in his memoirs, reporting Honecker's denial of complicity and adding "whatever one may think of that."[6]

Honecker's removal of Ulbricht had shown that he could deal mercilessly with persons who stood in his way. Bringing about Brandt's fall would have not given him a single twinge of remorse. Once it had been accomplished, Honecker could better control the pace and direction of inner-German détente.

If Honecker engineered or at least permitted Brandt's fall, Brezhnev certainly did not. Brandt's resignation left him in shock. He could not understand the reason for it and raged at Honecker for having put an agent in the chancellery. He wondered out loud why Honecker had not considered Soviet interests. It must also have bothered him to have had Honecker monitor Soviet contacts with Brandt through Guillaume. Brezhnev thought that there should have been no East German spies in Brandt's office once he himself began dealing to Brandt.

Whatever Brezhnev may have believed about Honecker's complicity, the Guillaume incident left a deep personal animosity between the two men.[7] Brezhnev complained about it to a senior SED official, Horst Sindermann. Perhaps in reply, Honecker on May 20, 1974, wrote a letter apparently addressed to the CPSU leadership as a whole. He justified Guillaume's presence in the chancellery, arguing that the GDR had to hold its own against West German intelligence services, which spent DM 220 million to spy on the GDR and other socialist states. He pointed out that the West Germans did not spend that money "in order to study the life habits of butterflies."[8]

Honecker added that SPD/FDP coalition leaders had decided to remove Brandt even before the Guillaume affair because they did not believe that he could govern effectively. He spoke warmly of Schmidt as Brandt's successor, saying that Schmidt would carry on détente successfully. He expressed some concern about Schmidt's support for the Western alliance and NATO in his first policy address, but he downplayed the new chancellor's remarks about the importance for détente of keeping a military balance in Europe. Whereas Honecker wrote that one could not expect "particular affection" from a Schmidt or a Brandt government, his letter clearly showed that he felt comfortable about the change in Bonn.[9]

Brezhnev returned to the subject on June 17, in a personal talk with Honecker. He hailed Brandt's achievements, saying that one had "to pay tribute" to Brandt for having "taken the risk" of conducting an Ostpolitik that permitted the socialist states to achieve recognition of principles (such as the inviolability of borders and GDR recognition) which they had sought for thirty years. He added that "we all, including the GDR, gained from that policy." The East German minutes of the meeting reflect Brezhnev's displeasure but record no Honecker reply.[10]

TURNING THE CORNER

Willy Brandt's triumph, while brief, had an enduring effect. His détente policy changed the struggle over Germany, reversing the trends of the 1950s and especially of the 1960s toward a fully divided Germany. It forced the German question open again.

With that policy, Brandt answered the challenges posed by Kennedy and Johnson when they decided that they would no longer negotiate on the German question. Brandt showed that the Germans could begin to do it themselves. They needed help, but they could play.

Because Brandt could not act alone, the détente negotiations brought Washington and Moscow back into European diplomacy, compelling both—as well as Britain and France—to look again at the German question and at their own roles. Nixon and Kissinger, despite periodic squabbles with Paris, reinforced the arch over the Atlantic that Kennedy and Johnson had weakened. And Brezhnev, through CSCE and his dealings with Germany, began developing the pan-European range of interests that Stalin had sometimes articulated but never pursued and that Khrushchev had neglected.

The "practical solutions" that Brandt devised could not solve political problems. In fact, they were accepted precisely because they did not claim even to address those problems. They certainly could not solve the fundamentals of anything as complex as the German question. But they were to have powerful effects over time.

Nor could Brandt unify Germany. He gave no overt sign of wanting to do so while in office. As he had planned, he would make unification possible in the long run by giving it up in the short run. Brezhnev could accept the risk of future change because he saw no risk of immediate change. Détente could point the German question in new directions only because no one knew where those new directions might lead.

Brandt also solved an intricate diplomatic puzzle by having each piece of German détente fall into place at the right time and in the right square. There could be no inner-German treaty without a Moscow treaty. There could be no Moscow treaty without a Warsaw treaty. Nothing would hold without a Berlin agreement. That, in turn, made the Moscow agreement acceptable at home.

Brandt did not succeed without cost. He had to make major concessions, concessions that almost brought down his government. He dealt with the GDR, which his predecessors had not done. He gave up old German lands. He negotiated with Brezhnev barely a year after Soviet tanks had suppressed the democratic awakening in Prague and Brezhnev had pronounced the Brezhnev Doctrine.

But these concessions, significant as they were, faded beside Brandt's accomplishments. In an important step for German democracy, he accepted Germany's losses in World War II instead of blaming others for having imposed them. He opened doors that had long been closed, easing the pain of human division. He turned the wheel—not a full turn, but away from the course on which others had set it. What he yielded in the present was not as important as what he hoped to gain in the future.

Brandt showed the East German people that they were not forgotten. His visit to Erfurt left a deep and lasting impression. The East Germans recognized the limits to his power as well as he did and perhaps better. But they saw that he understood them better than their own government. They appreciated what he did because they knew that he went as far as was possible and wise. He became their spokesman.

Brandt thus brought something politically important—a new and influential German role—in part because he spoke for all Germans. For the first time since the end of World War II, a West German chancellor had sat down on an almost equal basis with the top leaders of the Soviet Union, the United States and the other states that had defeated Hitler. Unlike Hitler, who had tried to revise the Versailles treaty by threats and ultimately by war, Brandt used persuasion, diplomacy and the new German record as his instruments to begin revising Yalta.

Brandt followed Adenauer as the night must follow the day. Adenauer had concentrated on the Federal Republic's links in the West. Brandt, working from that base, concentrated on the Federal Republic's links in the East. He began to convince the governments and peoples of eastern Europe and of the Soviet Union that it might be possible to have some confidence in Germany's future policies. He accepted totalitarian regimes as partners, but he believed that dé-tente would weaken all dictators over time by removing the external threat they invoked to justify their repression.

Germany's return to senior-level diplomacy, with Allied and Soviet concur-rence, began the process of undermining the Europe of Yalta. Brandt reached the halfway house to German rehabilitation after the humiliation at Versailles, the horror of Hitler and the capitulation at Reims. But it could not be the last stop, for him or for the Allies.

SIXTEEN

BREZHNEV ALTERS THE BARGAIN

HELMUT SCHMIDT AND ERICH HONECKER HAD BECOME THE LEADERS of West and East Germany by the middle of 1974. They had profoundly different political credos, but they resembled each other in many ways. Both saw the world in pragmatic terms, although Schmidt had a wider vision of Europe and the Atlantic. Priding themselves on their managerial skills, both had carried out difficult tasks. And both wanted inner-German relations to continue to improve. Each felt that he could manage his respective state better than his predecessor. Honecker owed his job to Leonid Brezhnev. Schmidt may well have owed his job to Honecker.

The two men would have to work in an unprecedented setting. Détente had not ended the struggle over Germany but had made it more subtle if less confrontational. It had taken some of the heat out of the German question but had not solved it. The two Germanys would have to coexist within an ambiguous mix of mutual competition and cooperation.

With the Germans having assumed day-by-day management of German matters, Schmidt and Honecker saw a good chance to advance inner-German relations. But East and West Germany had incompatible philosophies and existed in opposing alliance systems. Others still watched them closely. They would have to respect the limits to what they could do.

Schmidt and Honecker wanted different things from inner-German relations. Schmidt, like Willy Brandt, wanted easier contacts at the human level, making life less burdensome for German families divided by the Wall. He wanted to keep Berlin stable as well as prosperous. Honecker wanted better relations at the state level and wanted West German trade and credits. Both men would have to find a way to serve their separate interests without giving up too much.

Schmidt and Honecker also had different long-term purposes. Schmidt wanted relations between East and West Germany to narrow the gulf between the two states and to keep the German question open. Honecker wanted to consolidate his regime and to keep the Germanys divided. But he also needed money.

SCHMIDT AND HONECKER TAKE OVER

The Basic Treaty between East and West Germany served as the blueprint for Schmidt's and Honecker's work. It allowed for better relations between the two states in a number of practical areas within a mutually acceptable political framework and provided for further agreements on different specific matters. But it also set some limits on political accommodation.[1]

To help define those limits, Honecker decided to write a new constitution that redefined the GDR. Whereas Ulbricht's 1968 constitution had called the GDR "a socialist state of the German nation," leaving unification open—although only on the basis of the East German model, Honecker foreclosed unification. His constitution of October 7, 1974, called the GDR "a socialist state of workers and farmers" with no reference to the German nation as a whole.[2] Honecker wanted to make clear that the GDR now functioned on its own and did not expect unification on any basis.

Nonetheless, East and West Germany followed up the Basic Treaty with further agreements on the detailed terms of their relationship. The two states either established joint commissions or designated one or another set of ministries to reach and to carry out such agreements. One by one, they worked out accords on trade, payments, travel, border demarcation, health, the environment, sports and cultural exchanges, energy transfer and other specific topics, linking the two states in myriad ways without appearing to narrow the differences between them.

East and West Germany also established mutual representations. On June 6, 1974, they opened what they called *Ständige Vertretungen* (permanent representations) in Bonn and East Berlin respectively. Both joined the United Nations. France and Great Britain opened embassies in East Berlin in 1973; the United States did so in September 1974.

Although the two Germanys did not exchange formal recognition in diplomatic terms, they developed what one observer called a "far-reaching identity of interests" that had its own existence independent of general East-West relations.[3]

Schmidt could certainly state that West German policy had paid off in human terms. West German statistics showed significantly expanded contacts during the 1970s:

- The number of visitors from West Germany and West Berlin to East Germany and East Berlin more than doubled to 8 million.
- The number of telephone calls from West to East rose from 1 million to 17 million.
- Cars traveling from West Germany to East Germany and East Berlin rose from 83,000 in 1970 to 860,000 in 1979.
- Cars traveling from West Berlin into East Germany and East Berlin rose from 408,000 in 1970 to 840,000 in 1979.
- Cargo shipments from West Germany and West Berlin into East Germany and East Berlin rose from 1,107,500 tons in 1970 to 3,191,000 tons in 1979.
- Every year, several hundred thousand East Germans were able to travel and even to emigrate to West Germany and West Berlin to meet special humanitarian needs. Most of them were elderly, whose pensions the GDR was happy to save, but some were not. From the standpoint of inner-German relations, each visitor and even each telephone call helped maintain the unity of the German nation.[4]
- The GDR also released between 1,000 and 1,500 political prisoners per year to West Germany, with Bonn paying an average of DM 50,000 for each during the 1970s.[5]

Traffic between West Germany and West Berlin moved relatively smoothly. The Soviets kept control over Allied military traffic, not permitting East German officials to interfere any more. East German controls over civilian traffic eased, although GDR police occasionally delayed traffic to protest one or another West German official meeting in West Berlin. Capricious East German interference with traffic, like arbitrary arrests on the access routes, declined. As a result, the number of land travelers between West Germany and West Berlin rose steadily from 8 million in 1968 to 18 million in 1979. Air travel declined somewhat, from 4 million in 1968 to 3 million in 1979, a sign of confidence in the safety of the land routes.[6]

West German money became the steady lubricant of the inner-German relationship. After lengthy talks during 1973 and 1974, the two Germanys agreed to increase the "swing" credit, further helping the GDR to cover deficits in its trade with West Germany. The GDR also insisted that West German and West Berlin visitors exchange at least DM 20 on any visit to East Germany and DM

10 on a visit to East Berlin, thus compelling each visitor to contribute to GDR hard-currency reserves.

The Federal Republic poured money into the GDR, agreeing between 1974 and 1978 to pay more than DM 2 billion to rebuild and maintain East German roads between West Germany and Berlin as well as major parts of the Autobahn ring around Berlin and of a major East-West canal. West Germany paid for a new highway between Hamburg and Berlin. It also agreed to pay hundreds of millions of D-marks to cover the transit fees that the East German authorities wanted to charge individual Westerners entering East Germany and East Berlin.

Schmidt justified these expenditures during a Bundestag speech as steps toward "human and political improvements."[7] With GDR economic growth continuing to lag, Schmidt believed that West Germany had to subsidize East Germany for the sake of the East German people, even though the West German economy faced problems of its own due to the "oil shocks" of 1973. The inflow of funds from West Germany permitted Honecker to ease some of Ulbricht's austerity measures by increasing both vacation time and minimum wages during the 1970s.

Despite mutual good intentions, the differences between the two systems still generated countless frictions. In 1975 and 1976 the GDR expelled two West German reporters, *Der Spiegel* correspondent Jörg Mettke and West German television reporter Lothar Loewe, who had become a respected and frequently watched personality in East Germany. Both were denounced for inaccurate reporting, with Loewe being accused of "gross defamation of the people and the government of the GDR" for his reports about the situation in the border area. After West German officials retaliated by delaying the signing of some trade agreements, Honecker decided to admit some new correspondents.

After 1975, Honecker's regime clashed increasingly with its writers, intellectuals and church leaders. It expelled composer and cabaret singer Rolf Biermann in 1976, and then exerted intense political pressure on twelve writers and artists who protested the expulsion. When one hundred more artists joined the protest, the regime cracked down by imprisoning some and expelling others to West Germany. Like Ulbricht, Honecker could not tolerate free expression.[8]

East German border controls remained a constant irritant. Schmidt, like other Germans East and West, regarded the Wall and the death strip as abominations. The Federal Republic repeatedly protested shootings and arrests along the border. After the deaths of an East German soldier who was trying to escape, of a West German visitor and of an Italian truck driver, Foreign Minister Genscher at the 1976 United Nations General Assembly publicly demanded an end to such killings. Although Schmidt persuaded Honecker to have the police act less brutally in the border area, shootings did not stop entirely.

East German international ambitions also proved an irritant. Despite its economic and financial woes, East Germany kept up aid and training programs in Africa which again raised the old question of whether the GDR could claim to represent Germany abroad. Honecker launched major aid programs in Algeria, Angola, Ethiopia, Libya and Mozambique. A total of 3,000 East German technicians went to those states. Some joined in military as well as economic aid programs. Honecker and other East German leaders visited several African states.[9]

Schmidt and Honecker kept their personal relations on an even keel. They met cordially at the concluding session of the Conference on Security and Cooperation in Europe in Helsinki on July 30 and August 1, 1975, as their delegations sat next to each other in alphabetical order. They had a long private meeting to talk about family unification and the improvement of travel arrangements. The two could regard their bilateral détente as a success.

Brezhnev began to wonder if Honecker might be letting Schmidt have too much of a success. Like Nikita Khrushchev, he had an ambivalent attitude toward the GDR and its contacts with the West. He wanted the GDR to gain recognition in order to help stabilize the regime, but he did not want it to get too autonomous, to exert independent authority, or—in particular—to grow too close to West Germany and perhaps dependent upon it. While he wanted good inner-German contacts for the advantages they could bring, he worried that the Germanys might get too close to each other and he tried to make certain that he did not lose control.

Thus, after he had pushed East Germany into closer relations with West Germany, the Soviet leader began to fret about the implications of those relations. Brezhnev worried particularly about rising GDR debt toward West Germany. He heard that the total had risen to DM 10 billion by 1974. He warned Honecker: "We must not permit them to strangle us by the throat. We must be able to breathe freely." Honecker challenged Brezhnev's figures, saying the debt was about half that amount. He also pointed out that machinery imports from West Germany helped the GDR to produce the goods that the Soviet Union needed. He informed Brezhnev that, despite the large debt to West Germany, the GDR had net reserves of DM 2 billion.[10]

Brezhnev's ambivalence persisted. In October 1975 he expressed his concern about the number of West German visitors to the GDR, although he and the CPSU continued to approve inner-German agreements as well as proposals for West Germany to pay for road and rail construction in the GDR. He warned about the impact of 40,000 West German cars on some small East German cities: "Ideology comes with the automobile."[11] He apparently worried more than Honecker about *Wandel durch Annäherung*.

BREZHNEV ENTERS THE GRAY AREA

Schmidt wanted to continue Ostpolitik in his own style. He dropped Egon Bahr from his government to concentrate power in his own hands and in the foreign office under Genscher. Schmidt did keep the special channel through Leo and Slava but did not use them much because he thought that he could get to Brezhnev himself without being blocked by Gromyko.[12] To show that the new government would abandon Brandt's visionary approach in favor of a more pragmatic policy, Genscher spoke of *realistische Entspannungspolitik* (realistic détente policy).[13]

Brezhnev and Schmidt met five times during Schmidt's chancellorship: in Moscow, from October 28 to 31, 1974; in Helsinki, on August 1, 1975; in Bonn, from May 4 to 7, 1978; in Moscow, from June 30 to July 1, 1980; and in Bonn, from November 22 to 24, 1981. But Brezhnev never felt as warmly toward Schmidt as toward Brandt. Schmidt had been in the Wehrmacht whereas Brandt had fought against Hitler in the resistance. Brezhnev had occasionally called Brandt "comrade," a term he never used toward Schmidt. Nonetheless, he and Schmidt developed a good working relationship. Beyond them, hundreds of Soviet officials frequently met with West German officials and business leaders at all levels. They also continued to meet in the Bergedorfer Gesprächskreis, with Schmidt himself sometimes joining in.

Brezhnev and Schmidt continued to expand German-Soviet trade. West Germany agreed to sell specialized equipment for the Soviet natural gas industry as well as 9,000 heavy trucks that the Soviet Union could not produce. Germany and the Soviet Union signed a ten-year agreement for economic cooperation, giving Moscow German technical support as well as additional credits. For the first time since before World War II, Moscow had access to high-quality Western capital goods and know-how. Détente was paying off.

Schmidt also gained some influence over Soviet policy. Three days before his October, 1974, summit with Brezhnev, the GDR accepted a West German demand to lower the currency exchange requirement for West German visitors. It obviously did so under Soviet pressure intended to please Schmidt.

Schmidt's détente policy, like Brandt's, included relations with eastern European states as well as with Moscow. Schmidt believed that Germany should act as a bridge between East and West in Europe, and he did all he could to carry out that role. During 1974 and 1975, his government signed trade and other economic agreements with every east European state except Albania. The agreements exchanged West German industrial goods, financed by West German bank credits guaranteed by the West German government, for east European raw materials or farm products. They also established joint commissions to solve any problems that might arise. Hungary and especially Poland received very favorable trade and credit arrangements. By the late 1970s, Schmidt had established good working relationships with almost all east European states.

Schmidt did more in eastern Europe than consolidate the openings that Schröder had initiated and that Brandt had developed. He began to establish good personal links with a number of east European leaders and further changed the attitudes of many east Europeans toward Germany and all things German. By encouraging trade and travel, Schmidt developed a level of personal contact between West Germans and east Europeans that had not existed since before World War I. Many east Europeans found West Germany a much more congenial and reliable partner than the GDR. They also began to gain more confidence in West Germany.

Schmidt's positive appraisal of détente began to give way to uncertainty and even anxiety in 1976 and 1977, however, when Brezhnev altered the bargain that he had appeared to make with Brandt. Having gained an opening to the West—and especially to West Germany—through diplomacy and accommodation, Brezhnev began to act as if the Soviet Union might try to achieve military domination over West Germany and even over all of western Europe.

In the middle 1970s, Moscow began to deploy in Europe a new and potentially ominous nuclear missile delivery system that came to be known in the West by the name SS-20 (the Soviets labeled it RSD-10). The SS-20 launcher, which could fire three missiles with nuclear warheads as far as 5,500 kilometers (over 3,000 miles), represented a dramatic shift in the relatively stable European balance of forces. It could threaten every state in western Europe. It was especially threatening to the Federal Republic, not only because West Germany was the closest target but also because Bonn's deterrence and defense strategy relied on NATO's ability to balance Soviet troop numbers with Western nuclear weapons.[14]

European détente had functioned under the unwritten assumption that both sides would respect the fundamentals of the European military balance. Each side had introduced new weapons systems from time to time, but those did not disturb the fundamental equation. East and West were even trying to negotiate force reductions through the MBFR talks, which Schmidt considered very important and tried to advance.

As Schmidt saw the European balance, Warsaw Pact ground forces (58 divisions and 19,000 main battle tanks) outnumbered NATO's (28 divisions and 6,500 tanks). In the 1970s as in the 1950s, Soviet and Warsaw Pact forces theoretically could advance far into West Germany and perhaps beyond unless they were deterred by the threat of NATO nuclear weapons in Europe.

The American strategic arsenal had once provided a protective cover for NATO, but that cover had progressively deteriorated over the years as Moscow had expanded its own intercontinental missile arsenal. U.S. superiority was less overwhelming than it had been in 1962, when Khrushchev had been forced to retreat over Cuba and Berlin, and Moscow had an advantage in some areas. West Germany could no longer rely on U.S. strategic superiority to deter a Soviet attack in central Europe.

Given NATO's inferiority in conventional forces and the decline in America's strategic superiority, West Germany had to rely on the European nuclear balance for deterrence. That balance had somewhat favored the West since the 1950s, compensating for NATO's conventional shortfall. The Soviet Union had about 500 medium-range obsolescent SS-4 and SS-5 nuclear missiles, but Western military experts thought them to be so inaccurate that 82 U.S. missiles (Lance and Pershing I) in Europe could more than compensate. Both sides also had rough parity in their nuclear bombers stationed in Europe, with the new Soviet "backfire" bombers matching the American F-111 fighter-bombers that often were called "forward-based systems" (FBS).

The arrival of the SS-20 launchers meant that Moscow could back up its European troop and tank superiority with overwhelming European nuclear superiority. With the intercontinental balance tilting from Washington toward Moscow, Schmidt feared that western Germany and western Europe lay exposed.

Because SS-20 launchers were mobile and could be easily hidden in east European forests, they could not be attacked. The threat to launch the SS-20 missiles against west European capitals and major military bases thus could paralyze the alliance and prevent NATO from using its nuclear weapons to stop Soviet forces before they overran West Germany.[15] NATO would be significantly weaker than the Warsaw Pact in what Schmidt termed the "gray area" between the intercontinental and conventional armaments levels. Moscow could, if it wished, plan the invasion and destruction of West Germany virtually at will unless NATO could deploy weapons powerful enough to have a deterrent effect. Although a Soviet invasion seemed unlikely, the Soviets appeared to be aiming for the chance to exert much greater political pressure on western Europe in general and on the Federal Republic in particular.

Brezhnev's reasons for deploying the SS-20 launcher system remain a mystery to this day. Moscow may indeed have wanted political domination through military superiority, as Schmidt feared. Or the Soviet military may have intended nothing more than a normal weapons upgrade, especially as the SS-20 missile was easily at hand because it had originally been designed as one stage of an intercontinental missile that Moscow had never deployed. Brezhnev may have wanted new missiles to reinforce the Brezhnev Doctrine, in defensive rather than offensive terms. He might have even been forced to accept deployment against his better judgment because of pressure from the Soviet military in the Soviet Defense Council.[16] The Soviet military may have even intended the SS-20 primarily against China and not western Europe.

Brezhnev and the Soviet military may have thought in terms of a global buildup, not in terms of Europe alone, for the SS-20 appeared as part of a series of Soviet strategic moves that launched a much more active and purposeful global presence. In a sweeping statement, Defense Minister Marshal Andrei Grechko had said in 1974 that: "At the present stage the historic function of the Soviet armed forces is not restricted merely to the function of defending our motherland and other socialist countries." Instead, he said, the Soviet military were to support "the national liberation struggle" and to resist imperialist aggression "in whatever distant region of our planet it may appear."[17]

Soviet ambitions reached well beyond Europe during the 1970s. Moscow sent weapons and advisers to almost a dozen African countries and to several central American countries. The Soviet Union also began a major naval buildup, directly threatening America's global strategic position. Whatever Soviet thinking may have been, it went well beyond what Stalin had envisioned during the 1940s as the reach of Soviet might. Brezhnev certainly wanted to use détente to improve economic support from West Germany, but apparently he did not intend to use détente for the wider economic purpose of easing the burden of defense on the Soviet economy. The SS-20 showed that Moscow might be seeking military superiority in Europe as well as elsewhere.

The SS-20 thus rang alarms bells among strategic thinkers in Europe and especially in Germany. The deployment could not help but attract Schmidt's attention. Whatever Brezhnev's purpose, Soviet deployments challenged the military balance on which German détente had been founded. And Schmidt, although prepared to accept a measure of Soviet influence through diplomatic and economic exchanges, did not want West Germany to fall victim to Soviet military pressure.

Schmidt also had to think of his position in the SPD. Willy Brandt had earned enormous popularity through Ostpolitik. The West Germans appreciated the greater sense of stability as well as the relaxation of tensions around Berlin. But Schmidt feared that a new arms race or a new global confrontation would kill détente and hurt the SPD. He had to persuade Brezhnev to stop deploying the SS-20, and he had to do it soon.

Schmidt warned the Soviet embassy in Bonn several times during the mid-1970s that Moscow should stop deploying the SS-20. Later, he tried to discuss the subject with Brezhnev during their meeting in Bonn in May 1978. Schmidt asked the Soviet leader and Gromyko directly to stop the SS-20 deployment. But Brezhnev appeared to lack either the will or the power to act. He did not reply to the chancellor. During most of the summit he appeared feeble and almost senile, sometimes unable to get up or to stand without help. He often had to be propped up from behind. Schmidt wondered whether Brezhnev had lost control of his government to the military. Brezhnev did agree to sign a declaration in which he and Schmidt pledged not to strive for military superiority, but the continued SS-20 deployments made a mockery of that pledge.

Even if Brezhnev might have introduced the SS-20 into Europe without intending to threaten Germany or wanting to damage détente, he must have known by the mid-1970s and certainly by 1978 that such a system put relations with West Germany at risk. If he still permitted further deployment, he had either lost all power to control the military or he had decided that the missile's strategic value outweighed its political cost.

Gromyko told his staff on his return to Moscow in 1978 that the SS-20 problem had been solved. He and the Soviet general staff rejected out of hand Schmidt's suggestion that the SS-20 launchers be withdrawn behind the Ural Mountains. Gromyko, whose position appeared much stronger than before, warned Schmidt privately not to spread too much excitement about the missiles. He showed no readiness to compromise. Schmidt even thought that Gromyko had hardened Brezhnev's positions throughout the summit.[18]

Schmidt had read Gromyko correctly. The foreign minister dismissed Schmidt's wish to negotiate about the missiles as "impudent." When Soviet ambassador Falin reported Schmidt's worries about the SS-20, Gromyko accused Falin of dramatizing the issue and warned that such reporting might jeopardize the ambassador's career. He did not pass Falin's reports to Brezhnev, leaving the Soviet leader in the dark about the intensity of Schmidt's concerns. Gromyko reportedly hoped to use the SS-20 to pressure Bonn out of NATO without yielding on either the German question or Berlin.[19] Schmidt could count on no help from him.

With the deployment of the SS-20, the nature of the struggle over Germany reverted to what it had been during the mid-1960s. Brezhnev had, either intentionally or unintentionally, taken the German question out of German hands and put it back into the realm of the great powers. West Germany could not compensate for such a major shift in the European balance. The Americans would have to do it. And Schmidt hoped they would act before the Soviets had an insurmountable advantage and before détente cracked under the weight of the new missiles.

But the Americans presented problems of their own for Schmidt.

THE DREAMER AND THE *MACHER*

Schmidt and U.S. President Jimmy Carter had the most consistently difficult relationship of any chancellor and president during the Cold War. Schmidt found Carter confusing and unpredictable, and called Carter a *Schwärmer* (dreamer). He himself gloried in his reputation as a *Macher*, a person who makes things happen and gets things done. Carter did not like Schmidt, thinking that the chancellor treated him arrogantly and rudely.

Schmidt particularly disliked Carter's habit of listening alternatively to his secretary of state, Cyrus Vance, who wanted good relations with Moscow based on significant arms reductions, and to his national security adviser, Zbigniew Brzezinski, who mistrusted the Soviet Union and who often acted as if détente in Germany had never happened or should never have happened. Schmidt himself wanted good relations with Moscow but also wanted a strong defense. Schmidt thus confused Carter, who thought those policies incompatible, and he also made sure that at least one or another of Carter's senior advisers would at any time disagree with German policy.[20]

Vance muted his differences with Schmidt. In his memoirs, he described Schmidt as "an outstanding statesman" for whom he had profound respect. He understood Schmidt's efforts to work with Honecker and Brezhnev even when Soviet-American détente lagged.[21]

Brzezinski, on the other hand, highlighted his differences with Schmidt, putting the chancellor in an untenable position. Although West Germany by the 1970s had become more influential than before, it still needed U.S. protection in NATO to remain independent from Soviet power. Schmidt did not want to distance himself openly from the United States, but he and Brzezinski fought an almost constant battle.

Brzezinski and Schmidt had a bruising encounter at the 1977 London economic summit when both thought the other had been insulting. Brzezinski called Schmidt "Helmut" and thought that Schmidt had bristled. Brzezinski concluded that Schmidt did not regard the national security adviser as his first-name equal. Matters got no better in the future.

Schmidt had almost equally poisonous relations with Carter himself. Schmidt's schoolmasterly style, his air of intellectual superiority and his acid tongue ruined his relations with the president. Carter told his staff early in his term that Schmidt had been obnoxious to him. Relations between the two men deteriorated from then on.

Schmidt made matters worse by his penchant for uttering a choleric stream of invective about every foreign or German politician who did not completely suit him at any given moment. He frequently pilloried Carter in his talks with others. Genscher and some of Schmidt's personal staff tried but failed to stop this habit. Some Americans in Bonn made it their business to send often false or exaggerated reports of such remarks to Brzezinski, who passed them on to the president.

Carter could accept some of these comments and Schmidt's professorially delivered lectures, but not when they went on constantly. Although Schmidt blamed his disagreements with Carter mainly on Brzezinski's influence, believing that Brzezinski's Polish origins made him suspicious of both Germany and the Soviet Union and particularly suspicious when Germans and Soviets got together, Schmidt himself bore considerable responsibility.

But Schmidt did not only dislike Carter and Brzezinski; he also feared them. Germany and the SPD would pay the price if Carter and Brzezinski ruined détente. Schmidt needed good relations with Moscow as well as with Washington.[22] Some of Schmidt's friends expressed the hope that Washington would understand and accept Bonn's "balancing act."[23] Vance did, but Brzezinski did not.

Schmidt tried to contribute to better Soviet-American understanding. Having long suspected that Gromyko opposed détente, Schmidt suggested that Carter go around Gromyko and Ambassador Dobrynin. The Germans had learned the advantages of dealing directly with Brezhnev, and Schmidt felt he could give Carter useful advice. At Brezhnev's request, Schmidt offered himself as intermediary in Soviet-American matters. But Carter and especially Brzezinski found this offer presumptuous. They had become used to Dobrynin and had come to trust him, as had many Washingtonians. Although Carter in 1977 wondered out loud to Schmidt why the Soviets did not seem to understand his policies, he did not realize that he might have a bad channel to Moscow. He did not share German skepticism about Dobrynin and Gromyko.[24]

Schmidt and Carter had almost opposite appraisals of CSCE. As Schmidt had helped to broker the treaty and had fought to get Moscow to accept American and Canadian membership, he had some stake in its success and sometimes felt responsible for carrying forward its principles. But Schmidt wanted to use great care in applying the treaty clauses that advanced human rights. This led to constant criticism from Brzezinski and Carter, who wanted to launch a major campaign for human rights in the Soviet Union. Schmidt warned Carter against meeting with Soviet dissidents. He doubted the wisdom of Carter's formal recognition of China (a breakthrough that Brzezinski regarded as a personal triumph on a par with Kissinger's secret visit to Beijing), for he feared it would jeopardize U.S. relations with Moscow. Carter and especially Brzezinski dismissed Schmidt's advice.

Brzezinski thought that the chancellor was going too far in accommodating Moscow, especially when Schmidt argued that Radio Free Europe should be removed from its Munich headquarters. Brzezinski often described Germany as "Finlandized," a term of opprobrium that sounded more sophisticated than "neutralized" but that meant the same thing.

Schmidt's greatest anger at Carter arose out of a potential U.S. weapon, the Enhanced Radiation Weapon (ERW), that came to be known as the neutron bomb. The weapon, designed to stop Soviet tank attacks, directed most of its energy into radiation and thus could kill crews and soldiers even inside tanks and armored personnel carriers without expending energy on destroying the vehicles themselves. A small neutron weapon, detonated above ground level, could stop more Soviet tanks with less collateral blast damage than a normal nuclear warhead. But the American newspapers that first revealed the weapon to the public in June 1977 (after the U.S. Congress had released a classified briefing) denounced it as "the ideal capitalist weapon" because it could kill people without destroying property. Liberal groups in the Democratic Party opposed the weapon from the start.

The neutron bomb had to be deployed in West Germany if it was to be deployed at all, as it could theoretically stop a Soviet armored and mechanized infantry attack in Europe. But many SPD members, like Democrats, opposed the weapon. Its purported military advantages carried a major political price. Bahr denounced it as a *Perversion des Denkens* (perversion of thinking). Free Democrats in Schmidt's coalition also opposed deployment in Germany.

Carter wanted to overcome Democratic Party opposition by shifting responsibility for the bomb to Schmidt and other Europeans. He said that the United States would produce the weapon only if the Europeans would deploy it. Schmidt did not want to bear responsibility for a nuclear weapon because Germany had formally renounced such weapons and could not control them. Soviet propaganda called the neutron bomb a risk to détente. When Schmidt said that he would agree to deploy the weapon only if other European NATO states did, Brzezinski cited this to Carter as further evidence of Soviet influence over Schmidt.

Schmidt finally did agree to deploy the neutron bomb because other NATO states also agreed. But he paid a high price within the SPD. Wehner, Brandt and other SPD members feared the threat that the new weapons posed to relations with Moscow. Schmidt could persuade the SPD to accept the weapon only by committing his full prestige. He made strong personal pleas to the Bundestag and to his party, asserting that NATO needed the neutron bomb to help balance Soviet tank superiority in Europe.[25]

After Schmidt had made this commitment in March 1978, Carter changed his mind and decided to cancel production. He himself had moral reservations about the bomb. He and Brzezinski blamed Schmidt, claiming that the chancellor and other Europeans had not fully committed to deployment although Schmidt thought he had. Vance nobly took a share of the blame, saying that he and Brzezinski had neither understood nor warned the Europeans that the president might change his mind.

Schmidt felt so betrayed by Carter that he could not contain his rage. He thought that the president had lured him into a political trap and had then run away, leaving him to deal with the mess in his party and with Moscow. *Die Zeit*, a weekly close to Schmidt and to the SPD, labeled Carter's decision *Ein Lehrstück der Verworrenheit* (a masterpiece of muddle-headedness).[26]

In the midst of their neutron bomb debate, Carter and Schmidt had to begin coordinating a response to the SS-20.

Schmidt had tried to alert the NATO Nuclear Planning Group in 1976 and early 1977 to the SS-20's strategic and political implications for what he termed the "Euro-strategic" balance. His defense planning chief, Walther Stützle, alerted the U.S. government directly through the U.S. embassy in Bonn. Stützle said that the only conceivable reason for the SS-20 deployment was "blackmail" against Germany and Europe. He added that the Soviet Union appeared indifferent to any warnings on the subject, reinforcing Schmidt's concern.[27]

Washington paid no attention. Schmidt even asked Carter and Brzezinski personally at the London economic summit in mid-1977 to talk to Moscow in order to try to limit the deployment of the SS-20 in Europe. But Carter did not want to complicate the difficult SALT II negotiations by raising a new category of weapons, especially because he did not want to negotiate about NATO nuclear weapons in Europe at that time. Schmidt thought that Carter paid attention only to missiles that could hit America and not to those that could destroy Germany and Europe.[28]

Totally frustrated, Schmidt went public, using a speech at the International Institute of Strategic Studies on October 28, 1977, to alert the West openly about the new threat. He warned that the intercontinental nuclear parity negotiated under SALT made any imbalance in Europe highly dangerous. He concluded that NATO "must make available the means to support its present strategy, which is still the right one, and to prevent any developments that would undermine the basis of that strategy."[29]

Schmidt's speech reverberated around Washington. Carter had not wanted to face the SS-20 problem at that time. The Pentagon had developed some new missiles of its own for Europe, but Carter had not agreed to deploy them. The Congress, however, began displaying interest. Schmidt's public admonition, obviously aimed at the president, put Carter on the spot. He and the U.S. government had to find a way to recreate the European balance either though a new U.S. system or, as Schmidt preferred, through negotiations.

Having lost confidence in the United States, Schmidt followed Adenauer's example in turning to France. He did so even more on economic than on strategic matters. He cultivated particularly good relations with the French president, Valéry Giscard d'Estaing, who regarded Carter with disdain. Paris and Bonn formed a common bond against Carter's economic policies and especially against Carter's "benign neglect" of the U.S. dollar. Like Adenauer, Schmidt leaned toward a continental system when he could no longer count on the transatlantic system.

Schmidt coordinated economic and political policies closely with Giscard. In 1975, the two had originated the informal summits among leading industrial states that were to become the Group of Seven (G-7). They, like other leaders of the European Community, concluded that Washington could no longer keep the global economic system stable. They decided in 1978–1979 to create a new European Monetary System to preserve a European zone of stability within the global economic chaos that they feared. French influence, which had fallen in Germany during the late 1960s because of de Gaulle's excessive demands on Erhard and his second veto of British membership in the European Community, rose to new heights. Talk of a "Paris-Bonn" axis surfaced with renewed vigor.[30]

Schmidt also developed good relations with British prime minister Margaret Thatcher after she took office on May 4, 1979. She argued firmly for a decision to counter the SS-20 missiles by placing new NATO missiles into Britain and Europe. At Schmidt's request, she agreed to station more missiles than originally planned on British soil so as to ease the chancellor's domestic problems. If she thought Schmidt was "Finlandized," she did not show it.[31]

Brezhnev and Gromyko had not taken advantage of détente to strengthen a pan-European alternative to Washington's transatlantic concept. During the 1970s, Brezhnev had perhaps the best chance of any Soviet leader since Stalin to gain influence across all of Germany. If he had not deployed the SS-20, or if he had told Schmidt during their 1978 Bonn summit that he would delay production and deployment, he would have won a much more important victory in Germany than any weapons system might give him. Instead, he and particularly Gromyko forced Schmidt to a higher level of nuclear deterrence and thus back to Carter, for even after détente the United States remained the ultimate guardian of West German military security. Schmidt had no other alternative, despite the intense dislike between himself and Carter. And Carter had to act if he wanted to maintain America's strategic position.

Carter also came under ever-increasing pressure at home. Paul Nitze, who had maintained his interest in strategic matters, formed the Committee on the Present Danger to warn about Moscow's global military buildup and its foreign adventures. The committee stated that Washington had to counter Moscow's efforts to upset the strategic power balance. Nitze, as in his NSC 68 paper three decades earlier, warned very specifically about dangerous trends toward Soviet dominance over Europe. Growing Soviet penetration into Africa and Central America, as well as extensive Soviet naval construction, also alarmed many other Americans and created a mood for more defense spending and for a much firmer stand toward Moscow. Carter, himself increasingly troubled by Soviet policies, followed that mood.[32]

With Carter and Schmidt leading the way, the NATO Council decided on December 12, 1979, to deploy a total of 572 new intermediate-range nuclear force (INF) missiles in Europe. Of that total, 108 were to be Pershing II (P-II) ballistic missiles with a range of about 1,500 kilometers (930 miles) that could reach targets close to Moscow from launch sites in West Germany. The other 464 were to be ground-launched cruise missiles (GLCMs), slower but able to fly below the Soviet radar defense system. NATO added what it termed a "dual" track, offering to negotiate with Moscow about the SS-20 and its own new INF systems. Also, on Schmidt's suggestion, NATO agreed to withdraw 1,000 nuclear warheads from German soil.

The NATO decision exposed Moscow to an unprecedented threat. Although the Pershing II could nominally not quite reach Moscow from West Germany, Soviets officials believed that it actually could. Even if it did not have that range by 1979, they thought it would certainly have it by 1985. The antiballistic defense system around Moscow had not been designed to protect against attack from German territory. The warheads would, of course, be under U.S. control, as Schmidt had insisted, but Germany had agreed to station them.

The Federal Republic would have the major role in the new INF deployment. Although four other NATO members—Great Britain, Italy, Belgium and the Netherlands—had joined Germany in agreeing to deploy the GLCMs, Germany alone would have the Pershing II. West Germany, Moscow's partner in détente, would now station weapons that could reach the Soviet capital in a few minutes. Gromyko later told Honecker that he had shown Schmidt a map with the areas that the INF weapons could reach but that Schmidt had wondered whether they really had such a long range.[33]

The deployment on German soil of a weapon that could sooner or later destroy Moscow would change the strategic picture dramatically. West Germany had suddenly become an even more dangerous nuclear threat than it might have been under the defunct MLF proposal. America and Germany, working together within NATO, appeared to hold Moscow itself at risk. Stalin's worst fears had come back even more tellingly to haunt Brezhnev and Gromyko.

Schmidt still hoped that détente could survive. He saw the INF deployment as part of détente because he thought it would reconstitute an essential balance and thus maintain stability. But two weeks after the NATO decision, on December 27, 1979, Soviet forces marched into Afghanistan to prevent the overthrow of a communist regime that had seized power in Kabul in April 1978. The attack marked the first foreign invasion by the Red Army since Czechoslovakia in 1968 and the first Soviet military takeover of a non-communist state since the 1940s. It meant the end of détente.

The invasion shook Washington and other Western capitals. None had expected it. Carter said that it taught him more about communism than he had ever known before.[34] As Western opinion shifted, Carter, Schmidt and other Western leaders had to stake out positions that would meet the new sense of alarm.

THE END OF SCHMIDT

Détente had lasted almost exactly ten years, from 1969 to 1979. It had served Europe and Germany well. But the distant invasion of Afghanistan, following upon the SS-20 and the NATO dual-track decision, destroyed it. Once again, events in Asia had an impact in Germany.

In Moscow, NATO's INF decision devastated the leadership. They could not agree on how to react. Brezhnev himself wanted to negotiate. But Gromyko, probably misled by what had happened on the neutron bomb, believed that public pressure would stop the NATO deployment without Moscow having to make any concessions. He announced during a visit to Bonn on November 25, 1979, that a Western decision to deploy missiles would remove any basis for negotiations on the SS-20. Two months later, as he prepared to brief the Warsaw Pact states on the Soviet position, he asked Leo (whom he had learned of) to find out how his firm stand had affected Schmidt's views.

Leo brought bad news. Schmidt could not and would not change his mind. If Moscow continued to deploy the SS-20, NATO would deploy the Pershing II and the GLCM. Bahr, although personally opposed to the NATO decision, supported Schmidt in his talks with Leo. He added that the time for negotiations was running out. But, even after Leo passed this news, Gromyko still hoped that Moscow could count on the SPD to scuttle the deployment. Swearing that Moscow would build two missiles for every one built by the West, he told Brezhnev that he wanted to punish West Germany by breaking off all détente relationships. Brezhnev rejected that, reminding Gromyko that the Soviet Union needed West German trade and credits.[35]

Nonetheless, Brezhnev decided that inner-German détente had to be slowed. Having already become worried about East German dependence on West German trade and credits, he objected to a Honecker agreement to visit Schmidt in Kassel at a time that would come just before NATO's INF decision. He and Gromyko told Honecker not to take the trip, with Gromyko explaining that West Germany was using its détente policy in order "softly, slowly, and as flexibly as possible, to undermine the GDR."[36] In 1980, he again prevented Honecker from visiting West Germany.

Yuri Andropov, frustrated by the risks that Soviet policy posed to détente with Germany, privately denounced Gromyko. He asked sarcastically what had happened to Soviet diplomacy when it set Moscow on simultaneous collision courses against both Europe and America. He had been warning Brezhnev for some time that the Soviet system had become inefficient and corrupt, but the Soviet leader had not wanted to hear him. Andropov consoled himself with his hopes for future reforms and with the quiet conversations he held with Mikhail Gorbachev, the rising CPSU figure whom he discreetly supported. He hoped that the Soviet system could hold together until those reforms.

Upon emerging from the politburo meeting at which the decision to invade Afghanistan was made, Andropov immediately recognized that he had to alert Schmidt. He knew that the chancellor would lose whatever confidence he still had in the Soviet leadership if he first learned about the invasion from the press. He sent Leo and Slava to Germany to brief Schmidt and Bahr around Christmas, 1979, only days before the invasion. Bahr could not believe what Leo told him about Soviet invasion plans and asked if Moscow had gone totally mad. He added, as did Schmidt, that the invasion of Afghanistan made any further East-West talks pointless.

Nonetheless, as Andropov had hoped, Schmidt and Bahr appreciated being briefed about the invasion in advance. They felt that it showed Soviet confidence in Germany and a wish to try to prevent a total collapse of Ostpolitik. Bahr also remarked that he and Schmidt had been disappointed that Washington had not briefed Schmidt as Moscow had. Bahr learned on a later Washington visit that U.S. intelligence had tracked Soviet force deployments closely for weeks before the invasion, but the Americans either had decided not to alert Schmidt or had not even thought of it.[37]

American foreign policy changed in 1980, even before a new president had been elected. Carter, who had entered office by denouncing "the inordinate fear of communism," began raising the defense budget. Brzezinski took command of

U.S. foreign policy and became secretary of state in all but name. Vance resigned. Carter withdrew the SALT II treaty, which he and Brezhnev had signed in Vienna on June 16, 1979, from consideration by the U.S. Senate. He began looking for steps that he and America's allies might take to push Soviet forces out of Afghanistan or at least to punish Moscow for the invasion.

Carter's new policies once again brought him into conflict with Schmidt, who did not want to go as far to isolate and punish Moscow as Carter now wanted to go. Schmidt still hoped to preserve a measure of détente in Europe and to keep the kinds of human benefits that détente had brought. He also faced a very different kind of domestic dilemma. He believed that he could defeat the CDU/CSU candidate, Franz Josef Strauss, in the upcoming elections for a new Bundestag and thus for the chancellorship, but feared losing control of the SPD if he abandoned détente.

During most of 1980, therefore, Carter and Schmidt went in different directions. Schmidt did not match Carter's economic sanctions against the Soviet Union. He did persuade the West German Olympic Committee to join the U.S. boycott of the Moscow Olympics, but Carter complained that Schmidt had not done so firmly enough. Schmidt felt embittered that German athletes had missed their chances to win medals in Moscow for what he saw as a ploy to help Carter's reelection campaign.[38]

At first, Schmidt still had some hopes for dealing with Brezhnev. He tried to make a breakthrough during his visit to Moscow in June-July, 1980. Carter had objected to the trip because Brzezinski had told him that Schmidt would take Germany into neutrality. He even wrote a letter to Schmidt warning him not to abandon the NATO decision. But Schmidt went nonetheless.

Schmidt believed that he actually did make a breakthrough in Moscow. Over several days, he met not only with Brezhnev but with the entire politburo and several top Soviet military leaders including Marshal Nikolai Ogarkov and Marshal Dimitri Ustinov. He warned all of them that the SS-20 threatened Germany (to which Ustinov replied "That is correct!") and that only a diplomatic solution could forestall Western deployment. Brezhnev, who appeared to agree more than the others, told Schmidt that they were ready to negotiate. Schmidt immediately informed Carter, who did not welcome the chancellor's help because he could see no reason to talk to Moscow at that time. Schmidt returned to Bonn as angry about his allies as they were about him.[39] He saw détente at risk, with himself trapped between Washington and Moscow. And Carter's policies did not help him in the campaign, as Ronald Reagan won the election in November 1980.

Carter's relations with Schmidt often matched Kennedy's with Adenauer. Like Kennedy, Carter wanted to make a deal with Moscow and did not want to be distracted by German issues. This worked better for Carter than Kennedy at first, largely because the Germans handled most problems themselves. But it broke down when Brezhnev launched the SS-20 challenge and aimed for domination over Germany much as Khrushchev had. Then Carter had to protect the American position in Germany and Europe. Unlike Kennedy, he could not turn around in time. As he ended his presidency, he left the SS-20 problem and INF deployment plans in Schmidt's and Reagan's hands.

Schmidt's last meeting with Brezhnev, in Bonn in November 1981, served little purpose, with the chancellor as frail politically as the Soviet leader had become physically. Schmidt warned Brezhnev that the Soviets should not expect the "peace" movement to stop NATO from deploying the INF weapons if negotiations failed. But he could see that control of Soviet foreign policy had passed from Brezhnev to Gromyko and that the foreign minister would not negotiate an agreement.[40]

The German and Soviet leaders could at least continue to improve mutual economic links despite the collapse of détente. The twenty-five-year "framework agreement" for economic cooperation that Schmidt had proposed in 1978 produced some results. But détente continued by momentum more than by conviction. Neither Schmidt nor Brezhnev dared abandon it, but neither retained any illusions that they could continue the kind of relationship that Brandt and Brezhnev had envisioned when they had met in 1971.

In the hardened global climate, Schmidt even found it difficult to sustain inner-German détente, especially after Brezhnev had vetoed Honecker's visits to West Germany in 1979 and 1980 as well as a visit by Schmidt to the GDR in 1980. To keep up some high-level contact, Honecker sent SED politburo member and economic chief Günter Mittag to Bonn. The SED gave the Soviets only a carefully edited report on Mittag's talks with top West German officials, reinforcing Soviet suspicions that the Germans dealt with each other behind the Kremlin's back.[41]

Schmidt did finally get to the GDR on December 11 and 12, 1981, when he visited Honecker's hunting lodge on Lake Werbellinsee. Neither man expected much to come out of the talks, and little did. The East German record of the conversations, again perhaps edited for Soviet consumption, revealed no breakthroughs. Schmidt and Honecker talked in broad and noncommittal terms about the world, saying nothing new or startling. They discussed various problems in inner-German relations, such as the minimum exchange requirement, passes, Autobahn construction and the like. They made some progress on some of those topics. Both wanted to continue a decent relationship even if they did not take many concrete steps.[42]

Schmidt tried to use his trip to mingle with the East German people as Brandt had done at Erfurt, visiting the small town of Güstrow near Werbellinsee. But Schmidt met more police than ordinary citizens. As Honecker had calculated back in 1974, Schmidt had neither Brandt's charisma nor his emotional rapport with the East German people. Nonetheless, the SED leader took no chances. The police discouraged people from showing themselves. Honecker made sure that there would not be another Erfurt.

Honecker and Schmidt could not successfully insulate inner-German links from the new ice age into which the Cold War was passing. Even as they met, martial law was proclaimed in Poland to suppress the trade union Solidarity. Schmidt seriously considered breaking off his meeting and returning immediately to Bonn but failed to do so, raising questions as to whether he regarded human rights in Poland to be as important as human rights in East Germany.

East German documents later revealed that Honecker had played a role in Polish events. Honecker opposed Solidarity and urged Brezhnev to move against it. The East German army made all necessary preparations to intervene in Poland. Schmidt found himself in East Germany on the very day of General Wojciech Jaruzelski's proclamation of martial law. Schmidt's failure to leave East Germany as a sign of protest against the military dictatorship in Poland further confirmed Brzezinski's opinion of him. It also made many Germans wonder whether they were paying too high a price for détente.[43]

The world had turned against Schmidt. He put a brave face on Ronald Reagan's 1980 election, although he feared that Reagan might try to push him even harder against détente than Carter had. He went to see Reagan immediately after the election to establish a personal relationship and was pleased to learn that Reagan was friendly toward Germany, but he still worried that the new president's policies would not please the SPD. Schmidt appreciated Reagan's assurance that he would at some point begin negotiating with Moscow about the SS-20, although Schmidt would have welcomed immediate talks. Schmidt announced that he liked Reagan "very much."[44]

Bonn could not have a leader whose policies differed from those of all the countries that had an interest in Germany. Brezhnev had adopted a conservative policy during the mid-1970s. Britain had turned to conservatism in May 1979, the United States in November 1980, and France—at least in foreign affairs—in May 1981. The policies initiated by Brandt could not continue. Schmidt had become the odd man out. West Germany itself risked being out of step.

Schmidt ended as Erhard had, without reliable friends in East or West or in his own party. Like Erhard, Schmidt could rejoice in a national election victory, this one in his September 1980 defeat of Strauss. But under that result lay a warning to Schmidt, for the left wing of the SPD raised its Bundestag membership from sixteen to sixty. They disagreed with the chancellor on Ostpolitik and on the decision to deploy new missiles in West Germany as well as on domestic economic policy. From then on, Schmidt lived on borrowed time.

Two years later, an SPD party congress handed Schmidt a serious defeat by insisting on economic policies that Genscher and the FDP would not accept. Schmidt called for a Bundestag constructive vote of no confidence that would either reinforce his authority or permit him to withdraw with a measure of dignity.

As expected, Schmidt lost the vote. On October 1, 1982, the Bundestag chose CDU/CSU leader Helmut Kohl to succeed him as chancellor. Seven weeks later, Kohl went to Washington for easy and relaxed conversations with Reagan. The German press and German political circles rejoiced that the tensions of the Schmidt-Carter era had gone and that the leaders of the United States and of West Germany appeared to enjoy congenial political views and a warm relationship. In March 1983, Kohl won election with the FDP as his partner against a deeply divided SPD.

Following Brandt's example, Kohl wanted to have informal contacts with American academics and intellectuals. He established his own links to them in order to supplement the contacts that Germans had developed with France and Britain through the European Community. He endowed three "centers of excellence" for German and European studies at three top American universities (Harvard, Georgetown and the University of California at Los Angeles). He used Werner Weidenfeld, a prolific author and respected professor, to select those centers and to travel frequently to the United States as head of a special office for German-American coordination.

Détente had not failed because of Schmidt, although he paid the highest immediate political price. It had failed because of Brezhnev and the SS-20. The Soviet leader and his colleagues had not understood that détente brought not only benefits but also mutual dependencies and obligations. Brezhnev and especially Gromyko had not given enough thought to German public opinion, to the political backlash against a military buildup, or to Schmidt himself. They had vindicated Brzezinski's, not Schmidt's, predictions. They would now have to deal with the results.

But détente had left a mark. It might not have provided a solution to the German question, but all parties to the struggle over Germany had seen possibilities other than confrontation. No matter what might happen, the future would not be like the past. Andropov's angry reaction to the Afghanistan invasion showed that some Kremlin leaders might want to look for other options than the SS-20.

The struggle over Germany would again intensify. But it would take a different form and have a different context from the past. And all the protagonists would know that they could open other doors if they so chose.

SEVENTEEN

MOSCOW UNDER PRESSURE

RONALD REAGAN HAD TWO SECURITY GOALS WHEN HE BECAME president: first, to strengthen U.S. nuclear and conventional weaponry across the board; second, and to some paradoxically, to neutralize and ultimately to eliminate nuclear weapons. He had rarely voiced the second goal in public and few had believed him when he had said it.

Within months of his inauguration, Reagan raised the defense budget dramatically. He resurrected several weapons programs canceled by Jimmy Carter, including the neutron bomb and the B-1 bomber. He appointed an energetic young secretary of the navy, John Lehman, who pledged to build a 600-ship fleet that would overwhelm Soviet efforts to take over the oceans. Reagan countered Soviet support for revolutionary movements and states in Africa and Latin America, increasing support to anti-communist governments and movements around the world. He helped Afghan rebels fight against Soviet forces by sending them missiles to destroy Soviet tanks and helicopters.

Seeing the Soviet threat on a global scale and planning to meet it on a global scale, Reagan announced the most wide-ranging challenge to the Soviet system that any Western leader had articulated since Harry Truman in the Truman Doctrine.[1] He did not foreswear diplomacy but wanted to use it as an adjunct to other actions.

REAGAN AND KOHL DEPLOY THE EURO-MISSILES

Reagan planned especially to meet Moscow's challenge in Europe. He had inherited NATO's 1979 commitment to deploy the Pershing II and the cruise missile. He had also inherited the commitment to try for an arms control agreement that would make the deployment unnecessary. Although Reagan did not expect Moscow to negotiate seriously, he agreed to begin the talks before the end of November 1981 in Geneva.

Eager to deal with Reagan, Yuri Andropov tried several times in 1981 to establish a direct KGB line to the White House. But Secretary of State Al Haig blocked the link, having seen (and helped) Nixon and Kissinger circumvent another secretary of state. Andropov later established a direct channel through the U.S. negotiator to the CSCE, Max Kampelman, but Kampelman let Dobrynin know and Gromyko closed the channel immediately. This prevented any informal exchange of ideas that might have avoided INF deployment and might have helped develop a wide-ranging Soviet-American dialogue.[2]

The INF negotiations began in Geneva as agreed, with Paul Nitze and Yuli Kvitsinsky as the American and Soviet negotiators. Nitze had attracted Reagan's attention because of his role in the Committee on the Present Danger. Kvitsinsky, who had served in both West and East Germany, was one of the rising stars of the Soviet diplomatic profession. As he lacked experience in arms control talks, he may have been chosen mainly for his knowledge of Germany. He told Nitze early in the talks that the Americans "have no right to be in Europe at all," suggesting that he had not been instructed to compromise.[3]

Reagan and other NATO leaders faced strong opposition from peace groups, anti-nuclear groups, some churches and many others who wanted to stop the arms race. To help meet that opposition, Reagan and his allies proposed what became known as the "zero option," under which NATO would forego deployment of any and all new INF missiles if the Soviet Union would agree to destroy the SS-20 launchers already deployed and to forego future deployments of new theater nuclear weapons in Europe. This proposal helped defuse at least part of the European opposition, although some critics saw it as unattainable and disingenuous. Gromyko showed no interest in it.

Richard Perle, the assistant secretary of defense for international security affairs, had proposed the zero option for strategic reasons. He thought that NATO would either have the missiles it wanted or the Soviet Union would have to give up a powerful new weapon. He hoped the proposal would have some public appeal because of the "zero" target. Schmidt also favored the zero option. Perle and Reagan expected the Soviets to resist giving up the SS-20 and to accept the zero option only very reluctantly if at all.

Nitze felt under time pressure. Schmidt had told him that he had to show real progress before the end of 1982 to avoid a chaos of protests and demonstrations in Germany. At Nitze's suggestion, he and Kvitsinsky conferred informally.

By mid-July of 1982, during a long walk in the Jura Mountains near Geneva, the two worked out what became known as "the walk in the woods" formula.

The formula appeared to give each side what it wanted most. NATO would give up the Pershing II ballistic missiles but would deploy 75 cruise missile launchers that might carry 225 missiles with one nuclear warhead on each. The Soviet Union would cut the number of its SS-20 launchers to 75 with 225 warheads. The ballistic missile threat to Moscow from West Germany would disappear, but the West would keep some modern deterrent weapons. Moscow would lower the threat to NATO. Nitze saw it as an honorable and achievable compromise and believed it might ease the threat of demonstrations in Germany.

The "walk in the woods" plan failed in Washington by September 1982, as neither Reagan nor Perle approved it. It also failed in Moscow, where Gromyko still expected the protest movement to prevent any missile deployments in Germany. At a politburo meeting, with Kvitsinsky present, Brezhnev read a statement prepared by Gromyko to turn down the proposal.[4]

At the end of September, the new Secretary of State George Shultz reiterated the zero option to Gromyko in New York. The next day, Nitze reiterated it in Geneva. Only then did Kvitsinsky tell him that Moscow had not accepted the "walk in the woods" formula either. He repeated Soviet insistence that NATO deploy no new weapons in Europe and threatened to abort the talks if NATO did. He added for good measure that Gromyko had firmly instructed him not to engage in any more informal talks or walks.[5]

In November 1982, Brezhnev died. Andropov became secretary general of the Soviet communist party but was already too ill to effect some of the changes he had earlier envisaged. He retained Gromyko as foreign minister.

As the INF talks droned on, Reagan kept Moscow under pressure. He described the Soviet Union in highly critical terms, stating, for example, on March 8, 1983, that the Soviet Union was "the focus of evil in the modern world." In the same speech, he termed it an "evil empire." He also wrote an epitaph for communism, labeling it "a sad, bizarre chapter in human history whose last pages are even now being written."[6]

Two weeks later, on March 23, Reagan launched what was to become his most dramatic and most controversial defense program, the Strategic Defense Initiative (SDI). With high hopes for new space-age technology, Reagan wanted the SDI program to design and deploy a system that would protect American territory against ballistic missiles. The program went directly against the principle of mutual assured destruction (MAD) which had dictated American deterrence theory since the 1960s and which had been enshrined in the Nixon-Brezhnev arms limitation agreements.

Under MAD, Soviet-American nuclear deterrence depended on each side's ability to absorb a nuclear attack and still destroy the country that had launched the first strike. It rested on the combination of two treaties that respectively limited the number of each side's offensive missiles (the SALT treaty) and of each side's defensive systems (the ABM treaty). Washington had never deployed any defensive systems, although Moscow had deployed one around Moscow.

Some American critics derided the SDI concept as "star wars," asserting that it risked de-stabilizing a workable balance for the sake of an unrealistic pipe-dream, but it had important strategic effects. It deeply worried Soviet defense planners who could not hope to match the technological fixes that the program envisioned. It also made a mockery of the post-Cuba Soviet buildup and challenged the Soviet strategic concept in which Moscow had invested massively.

The Reagan program, and especially INF and SDI, constituted an existential threat to the Soviet system. Many Soviet leaders recoiled at the thought of having to finance an entirely new strategic architecture with a shrinking economy, an obsolete industrial base, and the costly burden of the Afghan war.[7]

Reagan's SDI plan thus led to a "dramatic metamorphosis" in Soviet behavior, according to Reagan's assistant for national security affairs, Robert McFarlane. He recalled that between April and October 1983 the KGB resumed its efforts to establish a direct channel to the White House—presumably under Andropov's orders. But Gromyko continued to block it.[8]

Whether such a channel might have helped or not remains a question. Reagan did not pursue what might have been a chance to meet with Brezhnev because he wanted to get a credible military buildup under way before having talks with Moscow. Moreover, Reagan saw his views of the Soviet Union confirmed when a Soviet jet fighter on September 1, 1983, shot down a civilian Korean Airlines 747 jetliner that had mistakenly strayed over Soviet airspace. An American member of Congress and sixty other Americans died. American intelligence agencies had heard radio broadcasts proving that the Soviet pilot and his supervisors on the ground knew that he was firing on a civilian airliner. Reagan bitterly denounced Moscow for the attack, especially when the Soviet government failed even to express regret.

With the Geneva talks deadlocked and with East-West relations impaired, NATO continued with INF deployment plans. François Mitterrand, France's new president, told the Bundestag in January 1983 that France remained fully committed. Margaret Thatcher expressed the same view during her visit to Bonn in November. As often before détente, the West and the Soviet Union stood face to face in Germany.

Andropov hoped to develop a new opening toward Bonn if he could not do it toward Washington. He met with Kohl in Moscow during the Brezhnev funeral ceremonies and tried to establish cordial relations. In December 1982, he tried to make a new INF offer that would have permitted some Pershing II deployment but reduced missile numbers on both sides. It raised the prospect of an interim agreement. But neither Gromyko nor the Soviet military liked those terms. After further consultation, Andropov had to return to Gromyko's formula that Moscow would deploy two missiles for every one deployed by NATO.[9]

Andropov liked Kohl. He told Leo that he had found Kohl energetic and intelligent and that he hoped to carry on with Kohl the dialogue that Brezhnev had begun with Brandt. Shortly thereafter, however, Andropov entered the hospital. He never recovered. Leo and Slava despaired as the channel to Bonn came to a close. Bahr watched sadly as his two friends, their heroic moments behind them, sank back into the faceless morass of the Soviet bureaucracy.[10]

Unable to decide on a new policy, Moscow chose to frighten the German public about the missiles. Soviet propaganda thundered that "for the first time in postwar history, a military threat again stems from German soil against the Soviet people."[11] The Soviet government threatened to aim Soviet nuclear missiles at West Germany, an empty threat because West Germans had long known that they were targets.[12]

The German peace movement committed itself to blocking the INF deployment, promising a *heisser Sommer* and a *heisser Herbst* (a hot summer and a hot autumn). It made good on that promise with violent attacks against U.S. military installations. Protesters assaulted an American military headquarters in Frankfurt, detonated a pipe bomb at a U.S. base in Berlin, and staged demonstrations at many U.S. installations. A car explosion outside the U.S. Air Force base at Ramstein blew out almost 600 windows and injured twenty-two Americans. Protesters overturned and burned American cars in Wiesbaden.

As a planned high point of the demonstrations during the week of October 15–22, 1983, over 300,000 protesters assembled in Bonn and other cities throughout West Germany and in West Berlin. Willy Brandt spoke to the crowd in Bonn.[13] It became clear that NATO would never have been able to place any new missile systems in Germany if Moscow had not first deployed the SS-20.

The SPD used whatever signals it could get from Moscow as arguments against the missiles. In mid-November, it proposed a new strategy for European defense, with a special SPD congress voting to discard all nuclear weapons under "alternative strategies." Only Schmidt spoke in favor of the INF deployment. The party veered as far to the left as it had been before Wehner and Brandt had put together the Godesberg program.[14] But a few days later, on November 22, 1983, the Bundestag voted to accept deployment of the INF missiles.

On the following day, Kvitsinsky suspended the Geneva INF negotiations. Gromyko's hope of preventing INF deployment through the protest movement had come to naught. In a few more days, the Pershing II and the cruise missiles began arriving in the Federal Republic. Protests continued but were not strong enough to block deployment.

Kvitsinsky's move to end the Geneva talks right after the Bundestag vote showed Moscow's fear of the Pershing II. Whereas Kvitsinsky had first threatened to suspend the talks when any INF weapons arrived in Europe, he did not do so after some cruise missiles reached their bases in Great Britain. He walked out only when the P-II began to arrive in Germany.

Moscow faced opposition to its own deployments. Honecker did not want more SS-20 launchers and certainly did not want two missiles on his soil for every one in West Germany. Gromyko persuaded him to accept the "countermeasures," but only after Czechoslovakia agreed. Honecker, like Schmidt, did not want to be the only one with more missiles. He finally agreed to accept them only after a Warsaw Pact meeting held in East Berlin to exert additional pressure on the GDR.[15]

When Moscow then did station additional missiles in East Germany, Honecker said that these "unavoidable" deployments "have caused no celebration in our country," an astonishing statement for a Soviet ally to make. *Neues Deutschland* even printed a letter from a Lutheran priest in East Germany expressing horror at "answering evil with evil." The East German organizations that the SED had created to protest missiles in West Germany also began to show their opposition to missiles in East Germany. So did churches in East Germany, overtly supporting opposition groups for the first time in years and forming a link that was to become increasingly important.

Honecker, who had said earlier that war in the nuclear age could not be considered the continuation of politics by other means, called for "a coalition of reason" between the two Germanys as East-West relations buckled around them. Kohl agreed, with both men speaking of a "German community of responsibility."[16] *Neues Deutschland* did not report some *Pravda* attacks on West German policy and instead announced after an SED politburo meeting that dialogue and cooperation with Bonn were more important than ever.[17] The SPD's *Wandel durch Annäherung* might be achieving some of its predicted "transformation through accommodation," although it could not stop the missile deployment in either East or West Germany.

Reagan could not have hoped for a German partner better than Kohl. The chancellor had long appreciated the help that the United States had given Germany after the war. He liked to tell his American friends that he had worn a pair of trousers from a CARE aid package on his first date with his wife. He maintained warm and close contact with U.S. officials and felt a genuine appreciation for the United States. He sent his sons to American universities and pursued particularly close cooperation with Washington during his long chancellorship.

Kohl had a different style from Schmidt. He did not glisten with the kind of steely arrogance for which Schmidt had been both admired and condemned. He worked effectively behind the scenes, seeking consensus rather than debate. Whereas Schmidt saw all issues intellectually, Kohl saw them politically. He had learned to listen to political vibrations at the local level. He would tread carefully and slowly until he saw an opening and would then pounce with an agility that belied his lumbering manner and understated style. He had a sense of Rhineland conviviality and Rhineland pride, like Adenauer, believing that Germans had not regained their sovereignty in order to be lectured by the occupation powers and especially by the Soviets. This made him a cordial but occasionally difficult partner for Moscow and a good partner for the West.

By accepting the Pershing II, Kohl had reaffirmed the transatlantic partnership with the United States that Adenauer had first established in 1955. But he had reaffirmed it with weapons that totally changed the European strategic equation, the dynamic of escalation and the German role. For the first time, a missile fired from a non-nuclear country in Europe could destroy the capital of a superpower.[18]

Kohl also enjoyed a much more relaxed personal relationship with Reagan than Schmidt had ever developed with Carter. He radiated cordiality during his first visit to Washington in November 1982. Kohl and Reagan chose to ignore any problems on the agenda and to accentuate the positive. Kohl suggested that Reagan meet with Andropov but did not attempt to act as a middleman. He stressed that he wanted Germany to remain America's greatest friend on the European continent. If Gromyko had counted on having the protesters split Kohl from Washington, he had badly misjudged his man.[19]

But Kohl deeply resented being excluded from the fortieth anniversary celebration of the Allied landings on the beaches of Normandy on June 21, 1944. He wanted to be invited as a gesture of reconciliation for Germans who had suffered under Hitler and resisted the Nazis. To ease Kohl's resentment, Mitterrand invited him several months later to a joint visit of the great World War I battlefield at Verdun. There, on September 22, 1984, Kohl and Mitterrand stood hand in hand at a field on which a million Germans and Frenchmen had slaughtered each other.

Kohl wanted a similar gesture with Reagan to generate a mood of reconciliation between Germans and Americans. Reagan agreed and accepted an invitation from Kohl to visit a German military cemetery at Bitburg, near Kohl's home in Rheinland-Pfalz, in November 1984.

The Bitburg visit turned into a public relations disaster because the military cemetery also contained the graves of many Waffen-SS veterans, troops that had normally volunteered or been especially recruited to join Nazi elite fighting units. The German government had not reviewed the records or visited the sites in advance. During a White House advance inspection visit, the American press noticed the SS graves under the snow. Jewish groups found the visit offensive. Kohl insisted on going through with it, warning that his government would fall if Reagan did not join him at the cemetery. Some Germans pointed out that the Waffen-SS had made up fighting units and had not supervised concentration camps like the Himmler-SS, but Americans found this a distinction without a difference. Reagan held to his plans to visit the cemetery, but he also visited the concentration camp at Bergen-Belsen to show that he had not forgotten the Holocaust.[20]

Kohl also supported Reagan on SDI despite strong and repeated Soviet objections.[21] The Soviets published a diplomatic note warning Bonn about the "dangers" of collaborating on the SDI project.[22] Moscow issued similar warnings at every possible occasion in Germany and elsewhere.

Kohl's defense minister, Manfred Wörner, a strategic expert who favored close cooperation with the United States, supported SDI. Genscher, eager not to offend Moscow further, privately opposed it. Kohl appointed his chancellery foreign affairs adviser and close collaborator Horst Teltschik to devise a German position. Teltschik visited Washington and reviewed the strategic, political and technological implications of SDI.

After careful study, and under challenge from the SPD, Kohl on March 27, 1985, issued a government statement cautiously endorsing SDI.[23] The statement concluded that, under certain conditions, SDI could strengthen strategic stability. It also stressed the potential importance of SDI technological research, not only for its strategic implications but for its potential peaceful uses for German as well as other firms. West German business wanted to have a part in any SDI-funded research.

Because of Genscher, Kohl could not support SDI as fully as he wished in an official government paper. But Teltschik had told him of the importance that Reagan attached to SDI, and Kohl spoke out more positively on his own. In several public statements, in the Bundestag and at the *Wehrkunde* meeting in Munich in February 1985, Kohl said that he and his government supported SDI because West Germany could not oppose a project so important to the United States and to an American president. He added that both superpowers conducted research on strategic defense and the United States had the full right to do so. He expressed an interest in having Germany participate in SDI research and even conjectured that SDI could lead to a new and more stable strategic order based on a mix of offensive and defensive systems.[24] With that, despite Soviet warnings, Kohl again put West Germany fully on Reagan's side.

Gromyko tried again during Genscher's visit to Moscow in March 1985, right after the Bundestag debate. He warned that German participation in the SDI project would make West Germany "an accomplice in the violation of the treaty on anti-ballistic missile defenses."[25] But Kohl still went ahead, urging West German firms to join in the program. They did, winning more than DM 100 million in SDI research contracts.[26] Kohl tried also to please the French by committing West Germany to participate in EUREKA, a French-led European research program intended to match the SDI technological leap.

Although NATO had successfully carried out the INF deployment, Reagan himself still had not given up on his idea of reducing nuclear weapons. On January 16, 1984, he tried to ease the confrontation with Moscow by proposing wide-ranging East-West talks on arms control and other matters. Andropov, under pressure from the Soviet bureaucracy, formally rejected the proposal by letter twelve days later, but he added that Moscow would accept deep cuts in intercontinental and European missiles "even to the point of ridding Europe entirely of medium range and tactical nuclear weapons." Reagan wrote a note to McFarlane saying "let's take him up on that."[27]

Within weeks, on February 9, Andropov died. But he had left an important legacy. He had helped to bring about détente with Willy Brandt through the KGB channel of Leo and Slava, and he had prevented relations from collapsing completely during the INF deployment. By the end, he had done everything possible to ensure that Mikhail Gorbachev would be, if not his immediate successor, at least the next one in line.[28]

Andropov's actual successor, Konstantin Chernenko, was so feeble that he could barely finish reading his inaugural speech. Within thirteen months, he also died. Reagan had tried to exchange letters with him but had received only bureaucratic replies. Reagan complained: "I can't get down to business with Soviet leaders. They keep dying on me."[29]

THE MAN FROM DIXON AND
THE MAN FROM STAVROPOL

Mikhail Gorbachev, the new general secretary of the CPSU, resembled Ronald Reagan in some ways. Like Reagan, he wanted to reduce the role of central government. Like Reagan, and unlike previous Soviet leaders, he had made his career mainly outside the capital city and outside the temples of the central bureaucracy. He had worked in his native city of Stavropol in the Caucasus, trying as the local CPSU leader to make the local economic and social system function. He complained about lack of new ideas from Moscow and about rigid central planning that stifled local initiative and wrapped everything in red tape. His travels abroad had shaken his faith in the Soviet system, as he had seen how well others lived compared to the misery of the people in his Stavropol territory. Even after he had moved to Moscow, his politburo responsibilities for agriculture had made him sympathize with farmers instead of with bureaucrats.[30]

Gorbachev believed that Brezhnev's immobility had deepened the stagnation of the Soviet system. He had seen how Brezhnev's predilection for accommodating every element in the Kremlin bureaucracy had bankrupted the Soviet Union. He hated watching the military budget rise at twice the pace of the Soviet gross domestic product and complained that Soviet factories produced good tanks but junk tractors.

Gorbachev listened to Gromyko's and Ustinov's optimistic briefings on Afghanistan in disgust. He admired Andropov for trying to reverse an increasingly desperate situation. He had exchanged ideas with the older man from time to time in Stavropol and elsewhere, although Andropov warned that too many such meetings would raise suspicions in the Kremlin cabal. Gorbachev would now have to do what Andropov could not.

Gorbachev looked out on a very different world from the one that had greeted Brezhnev. China under Deng Xiaoping was privatizing and modernizing its agriculture and boosting productivity. Most of the world was introducing new technologies that the Soviet Union could not match. The Soviet military had suffered a humiliating defeat by proxy when the Israeli air force and air defenses in 1982 totally outclassed the Syrians who had relied on Soviet training and equipment.[31] Mitterrand had been astonished to hear Gorbachev say that Soviet agriculture had not functioned properly since 1917, and even more astonished to hear him say that his job as general secretary would be "to take out the garbage."[32]

As Reagan wanted to change the United States, Gorbachev wanted to change the Soviet Union. But, whereas Reagan wanted primarily to overcome the collapse of U.S. international prestige, Gorbachev wanted to concentrate on Soviet domestic needs.

Gorbachev thought that the people of the Soviet Union had reached the end of their strength, if not of their patience. He saw that Soviet domestic problems could not be solved without changing Soviet foreign policy and cutting the military budget. He wanted domestic needs to determine security policy instead of the other way around, and he felt that he had to act fast if he was really to help the people. Like Reagan, Gorbachev was a man in a hurry.

Gorbachev's first act in foreign affairs reflected his wish for quick action. He removed Gromyko from the foreign ministry, elevating him to the Soviet presidency and replacing him with an old friend, Eduard Shevardnadze. Gorbachev knew that Gromyko could not and would not carry out the kind of high-speed, high-impact diplomacy that Gorbachev believed the Soviet Union needed.

The Soviet leader could hardly have found a foreign minister more different from Gromyko than Shevardnadze. A Georgian, Shevardnadze had risen through party ranks to be the minister of the interior and later the secretary of the communist party for Georgia, where he had cleaned out corruption. As Georgia bordered on Stavropol, Gorbachev had watched Shevardnadze and had become impressed by his realistic and creative approach to problems. Shevardnadze might know nothing about foreign affairs, but he knew what Soviet priorities had to be. For the first time since World War II, the Soviet Union had a foreign minister who was not seeking tests of will and who wanted to solve problems rather than invent them.

Gorbachev felt that he could only reduce his defense budget by reaching an accommodation with the United States. To that end, he and Reagan began a regular correspondence and ultimately had five summit meetings over three years. Although they did not specifically discuss the German question at any of those summits, the meetings left a deep imprint on the German question by reviving détente and by solving several arms control issues including the Euro-missiles.[33]

Gorbachev wanted to use his meetings with Reagan to block SDI and to have the INF missiles removed from Europe, for those two weapons systems disturbed him and other Soviet leaders the most.

Before he met with Reagan, Gorbachev had met with Margaret Thatcher and François Mitterrand. He had spoken to both of them about a "common European home," a formula that they found intriguing and attractive although they did not know all its implications. He had told them that he wanted true "peaceful coexistence," not merely a new form of class struggle, and had hinted that he wanted to negotiate real cuts in military arsenals. Thatcher had told Reagan that she liked Gorbachev and that one could do business with him.

Reagan himself found Gorbachev a good partner. Before their first formal negotiation, which took place in Geneva from November 19 to 21, 1985, he invited Gorbachev for a private fireside chat, hoping to develop good personal chemistry. He told Gorbachev that they had both come from small towns (himself from Dixon, Illinois) and that they had never been expected to amount to much and yet now had a chance to change history together. They agreed that they should try. Reagan invited Gorbachev to Washington and Gorbachev invited Reagan to Moscow. Their first talk gave them a mutual confidence that survived the disagreements which occasionally followed. Unlike Nixon and Brezhnev, Reagan and Gorbachev met in summits that had not been fully prepared by their staffs. If they had not wanted to find agreement and if they had not trusted each other, that habit could have led to the same kind of disaster that had befallen Kennedy and Khrushchev in Vienna.

Even before the Geneva summit, Gorbachev had told George Shultz that he wanted Reagan to stop the SDI program or at least to confine research to the laboratory. But Reagan in Geneva reiterated his commitment to SDI. Suggesting other arms control ideas, he gave Gorbachev a paper prepared by Paul Nitze that proposed a 50 percent reduction in strategic weapons and an interim reduction in INF missiles. Gorbachev replied that he could not accept any cuts in offensive weapons as long as a potential defensive system like SDI loomed on the horizon. The Geneva summit thus did not reduce weapons, but it did produce a mutual understanding to keep trying.

Gorbachev had domestic priorities on his mind. Three months after the Geneva summit, between February 25 and March 6, 1986, he won the support of the twenty-seventh CPSU congress for his program of Perestroika (restructuring). He informed the congress that Soviet foreign policy "must contribute to the domestic development of the country" and insisted that the Soviet Union had to begin looking for security through diplomacy instead of through military power alone. The congress majority agreed.

Gorbachev invited Reagan to what he termed a "preliminary meeting" to be held in Reykjavik, Iceland, between October 10 and 12, 1986. They carried the discussion of nuclear weapons to levels that unsettled many Europeans—including Germans.

At Reykjavik, after two days of intense and highly personal discussion, Gorbachev and Reagan tentatively agreed that they wanted to eliminate all their nuclear missiles and nuclear weapons over time. But Gorbachev made clear throughout the discussion and especially at the end that Reagan also had to limit SDI research to the laboratory. The president would not accept that condition, which he thought would kill the program. The other proposals, including a virtually total elimination of INF missiles, fell by the wayside because of SDI. Reagan also declined Gorbachev's efforts to scrap strategic arms quickly, for that would have left Moscow well ahead in non-strategic weapons.[34]

Nonetheless, even the tentative INF agreement represented a breakthrough. Under that agreement, NATO and the Soviet Union would have given up mid-range nuclear missiles in Europe. NATO would have destroyed all Pershing II and cruise missiles and the Soviet Union would have destroyed all SS-20 launchers in Europe. The agreement would have ended the SS-20 threat to western Europe and the Pershing II threat to Moscow but would have left NATO at a significant disadvantage because the Soviets had more troops, more tanks and more short-range missiles.

West European governments and military staffs, including the Germans, felt considerable relief that Reagan and Gorbachev did not finalize their deal on nuclear weapons. Helmut Kohl said privately that Reagan had gone too far, having stripped West Germany's defenses of their mid-range deterrent while doing nothing about either the short-range or the conventional imbalance. After having first complained that Reagan did not show enough flexibility on arms control, many Europeans thought the president had gone too fast without consulting them.[35]

Gorbachev and Reagan did not give up. Gorbachev decided that the next step should be to try to cut INF weapons by de-coupling them from the SDI roadblock. A series of negotiations between Shevardnadze and Shultz, with the latter working in close consultations with Thatcher, Kohl and other NATO leaders, removed all the remaining obstacles and produced an INF accord.

The INF agreement had not one but two zero options. The first eliminated all Soviet SS-20 and all NATO Pershing II and cruise missiles. The second eliminated all nuclear missiles with ranges between 500 and 1,000 kilometers (310 and 620 miles). The Soviet Union had several hundred of these weapons, known under the acronym SRINF (Shorter-Range Intermediate Nuclear Forces). NATO had none but reserved the right to build up to Soviet levels. Rather than debate about how many weapons each should keep, Gorbachev and Reagan decided to eliminate the weapons as a class. This still left both sides with tactical nuclear weapons, especially important to NATO because they could counter the Soviet superiority in conventional forces. Both East and West could feel more secure, although the reliance on short-range weapons left the Germans uneasy because the warheads would land on or near German soil.

Gorbachev and Reagan signed the INF treaty in Washington on December 8, 1987. The treaty led to the destruction of 1,846 Soviet missiles and 846 NATO missiles within three years. It marked the first time that the two superpowers actually reduced the number of nuclear weapons, not merely capped them, and also the first time that they had jointly agreed to eliminate a whole class of armaments.

The INF treaty ended the Soviet drive for military domination over Europe and Germany, ten years and two months after Helmut Schmidt had alerted the world to the SS-20 threat. It signaled the shift in Soviet policy from the later

Brezhnev era back to the pan-European accommodation that Brezhnev had wanted earlier. Henceforth, the Soviet Union would use diplomacy rather than missiles for influence. The Red Army still had conventional superiority, but the departure of the SS-20 made Soviet forces much less dominant. And the struggle over Germany returned to the bargaining table and to the realms of diplomatic, political and economic influence.

Gorbachev also received an unplanned boost in authority from a young German. A nineteen-year-old student from Hamburg, Mathias Rust, flew his single-engine aircraft from Helsinki to Moscow in order to give Gorbachev a twenty-page plan for global nuclear disarmament. The gigantic Soviet radar and air defense system bristling with every form of anti-aircraft weaponry failed to detect him. He landed jauntily in Red Square and began asking how to get into the Kremlin to deliver his message. Much to his surprise, he found himself under arrest.

As the Soviet military reeled in disgrace for having allowed a propeller-driven aircraft to fly undetected all the way to the Soviet capital, Gorbachev moved with lightning speed. He fired the Soviet defense minister and replaced him with General Dimitri Yazov, who had endorsed Perestroika. Other senior military officers also had to resign. With Marshal Sergei Akhromeyev—who had opposed the invasion of Afghanistan—remaining as chief of staff of the Soviet armed forces, Gorbachev for the first time had his own allies in place at the top of the Soviet defense establishment. Gorbachev kept Rust in jail for over a year, but many Westerners thought that the Soviet leader should actually have given Rust a medal of appreciation instead.

Gorbachev still had further to go. Having begun to withdraw Soviet forces from Afghanistan in mid-1988, he decided to begin withdrawing Soviet forces from Europe as well. At the United Nations General Assembly on December 7, 1988, he announced that the Soviet Union by 1991 would unilaterally withdraw and disband six tank divisions in the GDR, Czechoslovakia and Hungary. Moscow would withdraw such offensive personnel and equipment as assault-landing troops and bridging equipment, leaving in place only purely defensive units and equipment. It would remove a total of 50,000 troops, 10,000 tanks, 8,500 artillery systems and 800 combat aircraft from all Warsaw Pact countries and from the contiguous areas of the Soviet Union. Those who might have worried that the INF treaty would permit Soviet forces to overrun Europe could see Soviet military superiority melt before their eyes.

Gorbachev's new cuts provoked genuine debates among Gorbachev, Shevardnadze and the military. Akhromeyev resigned on the day of Gorbachev's announcement. The military recognized, as did Gorbachev, that cuts on this order would end Moscow's control over eastern Europe. They knew what this would mean for the governments that Moscow had installed and kept in power. But Gorbachev could point to the worsening Soviet economy to show that the state had simply run out of resources.

Gorbachev used his visit to New York to tell the United Nations that Perestroika would save communism as Franklin Roosevelt's "New Deal" had saved capitalism. Meeting over lunch with Reagan and President-elect George Bush, he summarized his policy in remarks addressed specifically to Bush:

> You'll see soon enough that I'm not doing this for show and I'm not doing this to undermine you or to surprise you or to take advantage of you. I'm doing this because I need to. I'm doing this because there's a revolution taking place in my country. I started it. And they all applauded me when I started it in 1986 and now they don't like it so much, but it's going to be a revolution nonetheless.[36]

Bush, after some initial hesitation, decided to take advantage of Gorbachev's troop reductions for a breakthrough in the long-deadlocked negotiations for troop cuts in Europe. At the NATO summit meeting of May 29–30, 1989, Bush persuaded the alliance to accept and to announce a series of new proposals for troop, tank and aircraft reductions.

The combination of the INF treaty and of Gorbachev's and Bush's proposals changed the dynamics of the German question. After the difficult days of the SS-20 and the 1979 NATO decision, East-West relations had changed in fundamental ways. That new atmosphere would affect the German question as it did everything else, although no one could predict exactly how.

Before leaving office, Reagan himself had pointed to one change he wanted to see in Germany. When he visited the Berlin Wall for the second time on June 12, 1987, Reagan said at the Brandenburg Gate: "Mr. Gorbachev, open this gate. Mr. Gorbachev, tear down this wall." Although many commentators dismissed the speech as an empty propaganda gesture, Reagan meant it seriously and thought that Gorbachev might do it. Reagan recalled his remarks during speeches and broadcasts after returning to the United States. He also repeated almost the same words to Gorbachev in private when they met in Moscow at the end of May 1988. Removing the Berlin Wall would symbolize the Soviet Union's determination to return to "the broader community of nations," he said."[37]

With those remarks, Reagan reversed Kennedy's policy of accepting the Wall while denouncing it. Kennedy and his advisers had even welcomed the Wall because it promised to stabilize the Soviet imperium. But Reagan wanted to end that imperium and thought that Gorbachev wanted to do the same.

GORBACHEV REVERSES HIS ALLIANCES

Mikhail Gorbachev did not want to deal with Helmut Kohl at first. Like many other Soviet officials, he had admired Willy Brandt and he leaned toward the SPD. Kohl had deployed the INF missiles in Germany, had supported SDI, and had done everything possible to support Ronald Reagan and NATO. Although he had not opposed Ostpolitik during the 1970s, he had never committed to it as fully as Brandt. With some opinion polls showing that the SPD might well return to power in 1987, Gorbachev saw no reason to be friendly to Kohl. Soviet propaganda consistently attacked Kohl during 1985 and 1986, especially when Kohl said that German unification remained on the diplomatic agenda.[38]

When foreign leaders assembled in Moscow for Chernenko's funeral, Gorbachev as the new CPSU general secretary met at length with Thatcher, Mitterrand and Bush. He met Kohl only at the very end in a generally cold tone and with little Soviet press coverage compared to what *Pravda* had given the others. The Kremlin assigned Kohl to a house outside the center of Moscow while housing other foreign figures more comfortably within the center of the city. Gorbachev did not even bother to reply when Kohl invited him to visit West Germany. Later in 1985, he had a friendly and well-reported meeting with Willy Brandt in Moscow. The SPD promised to be a better partner than Kohl, urging the Soviet leader not to support Kohl by inviting him to Moscow or by going to Bonn.[39] Gorbachev even prevented Honecker from visiting Bonn in 1985 and 1986 because the visit might help Kohl win votes.[40]

Gorbachev did meet with Genscher when the foreign minister went to Moscow, perhaps because he thought that Genscher might well keep his post even if the SPD won the election. But he would not meet with a German Bundestag delegation headed by a CDU member. And the Soviet press did not report a meeting between Kohl and Shevardnadze at the United Nations in New York in October 1985. Whereas Gorbachev did send Kvitsinsky to Bonn to replace Ambassador Semyonov, whose imperious manner had offended many Germans, he made no other gestures to court Germany while awaiting what he thought would be an SPD victory.

Kohl did not court Gorbachev either. In a *Newsweek* interview on October, 26, 1986, he likened Gorbachev's expertise in public relations to that of Nazi propaganda chief Joseph Goebbels. Kohl later said that he had been quoted out of context, but he refused to make a personal apology to Gorbachev although he expressed his regret over the incident. He probably believed that tweaking Gorbachev's nose a little might help him with some conservative German voters.

As it turned out, Kohl won the election in January 1987 by a wide margin and returned to power with the same CDU/CSU/FDP coalition. At about the same time, Soviet economic statistics showed even greater failings than earlier feared. Gorbachev, speaking of "crisis phenomena" in the Soviet Union, realized he would need a lot of help for Perestroika.

Gorbachev and Kohl both knew that only the Federal Republic could provide the economic support that Moscow needed. And Gorbachev knew that he would have to deal with Kohl if he wanted to have any funds from West Germany. Within weeks of Kohl's reelection, therefore, Gorbachev instructed Kvitsinsky to state in an interview that Moscow wished to end the "lull" in relations with West Germany.[41]

For a start, Gorbachev reinvigorated a working group originally established by Andropov to examine Soviet Cold War policy toward Germany. Next, Gorbachev sent a number of senior experts on Germany to visit Bonn during the first few months of 1987. Copying Brezhnev's tactics with Brandt in 1969, they said that Gorbachev awaited Kohl's Ostpolitik with great interest; some even hinted that Moscow might not oppose unification. A senior Soviet diplomatic expert on Germany, Nikolai Portugalov, said that East and West Germans all belonged to one German nation, a remark quickly "corrected" but obviously intended to leave some doors open if Bonn reacted properly.[42]

Genscher warmed more quickly to Gorbachev's overtures than Kohl. Speaking at the World Economic Forum in Davos, Switzerland, in January 1987, Genscher said that it would be a mistake "of historic proportions" if the West did not take advantage of Gorbachev's more positive attitude. He said the West should not wait for Gorbachev to "deliver" but that it should "take him at his word."[43] Kohl, in contrast, said that it was good to hear nice words but that he would like to see "deeds" as well.[44] He did not want wishful thinking but a "realistic" détente. Teltschik, echoing Kohl's thinking while keeping all options open for the chancellor, said in Davos that "new opportunities are in the offing" without committing the chancellor further.[45]

To begin a dialogue with the Federal Republic without inviting Kohl to Moscow immediately, Gorbachev decided to invite West Germany's president, Richard von Weizsäcker, for a visit in July 1987. Gorbachev outlined his plans for Perestroika and talked about better relations with the West. He made clear to von Weizsäcker that his wish to reform the Soviet Union had led him to take a new look at Germany. Von Weizsäcker saw that Gorbachev's needs and outlook opened new and far-reaching opportunities.

Kvitsinsky had told Gorbachev that an invitation to von Weizsäcker would have an impact in Bonn, and it did. The new German president, inaugurated on May 23, 1984, had brought to his office an important personal authority as a former businessman, lay church leader and governing mayor of Berlin. He not only elevated the presidency but helped change the image of Germany and the Germans.

In the most widely quoted speech by any German in the postwar era, von Weizsäcker had spoken somberly of "remembrance, sorrow and reconciliation" on May 8, 1985, the fortieth anniversary of the German surrender. He had recalled the Hitler years with bitterness, lamenting the loss of life of the Jews in the concentration camps, of the conquered peoples (including the Russians), of the Germans themselves, of soldiers and of civilians. Denouncing the horrors of the Hitler dictatorship, he had said that they could and should never be forgotten. He had praised the quiet heroism of the women who had held the nation together and helped rebuild it. He had thanked other nations for giving Germany a chance for a new beginning after the war, and had urged friendship with the people of the Soviet Union.[46] For many former enemies, von Weizsäcker represented a new Germany, one that Russians and east Europeans could trust. Gorbachev welcomed him in that spirit, seeing that he could deal with Bonn even after the SPD had lost.

But Gorbachev gave little away on the German question. He brushed aside von Weizsäcker's first reference to German hopes for unification. When the German returned to the theme, Gorbachev said that only history could decide those questions and "nobody knows what might happen in a hundred years." He smiled when von Weizsäcker asked if he knew what might happen in fifty years.[47]

To continue his drive for better Soviet-German relations, Gorbachev invited Franz Josef Strauss to Moscow at the end of 1987. Strauss, who had met with Brezhnev in Bonn in 1978, followed Mathias Rust by flying himself to Moscow. Having filed a flight plan, he had a three-hour private talk with Gorbachev instead of being jailed. They arranged for some business contracts between Soviet and Bavarian firms, but Gorbachev mainly wanted to make sure that conservative Germans would support better relations. He later invited Lothar Späth, the CDU premier of Baden-Württemberg.[48]

Gorbachev also asked Soviet officials for ideas on new Soviet policies toward Germany. But this provoked angry reactions. At a meeting in early 1989, sponsored by the international division of the CPSU, Valentin Falin erupted in rage when Vyacheslav Dashichev, a German expert at the Moscow Institute for East European and Foreign Policy Studies, said that Moscow should free itself of the burden of keeping Europe divided.[49] Gorbachev must have begun to realize, if he had not realized it before, that he was embarking on a journey with an uncertain destination over a road seeded with land mines.

Gorbachev clearly had some preparations to do at home if he wanted to win CPSU support for a new foreign policy in general and a new German policy in particular. Therefore, he scheduled the nineteenth nationwide CPSU conference in July 1988 to discuss the connection between domestic and foreign policy. He urged CPSU members to recognize that the Soviet Union would need foreign help for its economic restructuring. To underline the importance that he had begun to attach to Germany in the context of Perestroika, Gorbachev invited Kvitsinsky to speak at the meeting. The ambassador used his speech to stress the importance of a reformist approach to foreign policy.

To gain support from the conservatives who might oppose Gorbachev's policies, Kvitsinsky warned that the Soviet Union risked losing its place in the world if it did not match the competition posed by western Europe and especially by the integration of the European Economic Community (EEC).[50] If the Soviet Union wanted to solve its domestic problems, it would need a new foreign policy in line with its resources. It would also need to work with existing European institutions, including NATO and the EEC, and might see some advantage in that.[51]

Earlier, Kvitsinsky had told a German newspaper that the Soviet Union did not object to West Germany's NATO membership because "the more firmly the Federal Republic is imbedded in the Western alliances, the more stable are the European frontiers."[52] Such controversial ideas sustained the debate about what Gorbachev might want to achieve with Bonn.

The resolution published by the nineteenth CPSU conference specifically stated that foreign policy should "increasingly contribute to releasing the country's resources for peaceful construction," that it should be closely tied to "the democratization of society," and that it should open "broad opportunities for mutually beneficial cooperation and diverse democratic ties with the rest of the world." Defense had to be subject to "qualitative parameters" and had to adhere strictly to the party's doctrine.[53] Reversing long-standing Soviet priorities, the resolution committed Soviet resources primarily to domestic needs. It did not pillory West Germany as many past CPSU documents had done.

Kohl still refused to visit Moscow unless Gorbachev made a firm commitment to visit Bonn. He said that he would not be summoned like some lackey and then humiliated as Erhard had been when Kosygin had rejected his invitation. Shevardnadze had to go to Bonn to tell Kohl that Gorbachev genuinely wished to improve relations. They then arranged twin visits, with Kohl first to visit Moscow and Gorbachev later to visit Bonn.

More than three years after Gorbachev had taken office, Helmut Kohl arrived in Moscow for a formal visit on October 24, 1988. He traveled like a potentate of old, bringing with him the largest delegation that any postwar German chancellor had taken anywhere. Five ministers accompanied him. So did the chairman of the Deutsche Bank, more than seventy of Germany's most important business figures, and hundreds of journalists. Nothing could have better shown the impetus that both leaders wanted to give to a new and different relationship. And nothing could have better shown that the Federal Republic would use its economic power for political gain. Kohl could rightly say "the ice is broken." Gorbachev spoke of a "great change of course."[54]

Gorbachev and Kohl used their summit to give Soviet-German relations a genuine new start. They or their ministers signed a host of economic and cultural agreements, and they gave their personal blessing to the signature of countless contracts between private German firms and Soviet ministries or firms. They pointed with pride to the sharp growth shown in German-Soviet trade as well as to more than fifty joint ventures agreed or in process.[55]

Kohl and Gorbachev agreed to help each other on multilateral problems. That pledge fell more heavily on Kohl, for he had to persuade the United States to ease restrictions on trade with Moscow. He also had to persuade NATO to speed up the talks on reducing conventional weapons in Europe. But Kohl also asked Gorbachev to help, saying that Soviet troop superiority represented "the main obstacle to European security." This remark may have helped to encourage Gorbachev to make the troop cuts he announced at the United Nations in December 1988. Commentators in Moscow stressed that Gorbachev regarded this troop reduction specifically as a concession to Germany and presumably as a gesture of thanks for the financial support that Kohl had given to Perestroika.

Kohl and Gorbachev spoke their minds openly during their meetings. Kohl raised German unification, telling his host that all Germans wanted to live in one land. He expressed his appreciation for past agreements but said that he wanted even more progress. Gorbachev encouraged Kohl by suggesting that further agreements with and about Germany might follow. But he also took care to point out that the Soviet Union shared "a common social system and common socialist aspirations" with the GDR.

In June 1989, Gorbachev visited West Germany. He found hordes of screaming Gorbomaniacs and the greatest European outpouring of adulation for any Russian ruler since Czar Alexander's triumphal entry into Paris after the defeat of Napoleon. Even Gorbachev himself seemed at times to be taken aback by the shouts of "Gorby, Gorby," although he helped encourage them by kissing every baby within reach.[56] He could certainly sense the widespread German wish to end the Cold War and the militarization of Europe, as well as the German hope to end the division of their country.

Gorbachev in turn proved himself the world's greatest master of the politics of promise. In a joint declaration, he and Kohl endorsed self-determination for all peoples and the right of nations to choose their own political systems. Germans could legitimately conclude that the declaration opened a door to unification. Gorbachev also accepted, upon Kohl's insistence, a place for the United States and Canada in the "common European home." He said that West Germany and the Soviet Union should build the European home together, and he spoke of the possibility of "two German apartments with lots of doors between them" in that home. He traveled widely around Germany, visiting high-technology centers like Stuttgart and industrial cities like Dortmund as well as Bonn. Everywhere, he spoke in glowing terms of future Soviet-German economic and political cooperation, and he invited Germans to invest in the Soviet Union.

When asked about the Wall at a news conference, Gorbachev came close to saying what his audience wanted to hear without giving much away:

> Nothing is everlasting . . . The Wall sprang up in a specific situation . . . The GDR decided to use its sovereign rights and the Wall may disappear when the conditions that gave rise to it cease to apply. I do not see a big problem here.[57]

When asked about German unification, he said that "I think everything is possible" but that "time itself must deal with it."[58]

Beyond their joint political declaration in Bonn, Kohl and Gorbachev reached agreements on trade, investment and other matters that could help Perestroika. Gorbachev agreed to buy 300,000 Siemens computers. He promised to encourage more Soviet-German joint business ventures, although West German firms already led the world in such ventures. With German and Soviet firms having already used up half of a DM 3 billion credit that German banks had established at the end of 1988, Kohl promised that there would be more to come. And German business opened 85 places for Soviet managers to study German entrepreneurial techniques. Kohl and Gorbachev also signed a dozen further agreements, providing among other things for a "hot line" between Bonn and Moscow to avoid potential misunderstandings in any military emergencies.[59] Gorbachev noted that Kohl would agree to limit NATO nuclear missiles stationed in West Germany as part of a comprehensive European troop cut.[60]

When Kohl and Gorbachev had finished, they had changed West German–Soviet relations as profoundly as Brandt had done with détente. They had lifted those relations to what they themselves termed a "new quality" of genuine cooperation. Gorbachev had to send Shevardnadze to East Berlin to explain to Honecker what he was doing.

Gorbachev's thinking on European issues, including the German question, NATO and the U.S. role, had evolved quickly during 1987 and 1988. Two informal Soviet-German meetings showed this evolution. In the first one, an early 1988 meeting sponsored by the Bergedorfer Gesprächskreis before Kohl's visit to Moscow, several Soviet officials said that United States could not be a legitimate member of Gorbachev's "common European home." The German participants, including Volker Rühe and Egon Bahr, insisted on the United States and Canada as members. Falin unequivocally rejected such a "special role" for the United States in Europe. He said that the Germans had to choose between Gorbachev's new European home and their old home, suggesting that Gorbachev's pan-European concept was incompatible with West Germany's role in the transatlantic security system and in NATO. One Russian suggested an independent European defense system, inviting the Germans to withdraw from NATO.[61]

In December 1988, at a later meeting of the Bergedorfer Gesprächskreis, Soviet officials said that an American role in Europe would not only be possible but necessary. The Soviet statements, made by central committee member Vadim Zagladin and others, constituted Moscow's strongest endorsement for an American presence in the "European home." Privately, Soviet officials told the Germans that Gorbachev himself had endorsed an American and Canadian place in Europe. The Germans felt that they—and Kohl himself—had helped change the Soviet position and that this meant that Gorbachev took Germany and its transatlantic commitments seriously.[62]

Between 1987 and 1989, Gorbachev conducted a reversal of alliances. Its full dimensions became apparent only gradually. The Soviet Union gave up its reliance on the SED apparatus as Moscow's main instrument in Germany. Instead, Gorbachev made a new unspoken but important alliance with Helmut Kohl and West Germany.

Gorbachev acted because the Soviet Union's needs had changed. A close military alliance with the GDR could help Moscow so long as the CPSU saw security in military terms. But now Gorbachev needed the West German economy more than he needed East German territory and troops. If Moscow wanted a fortress of east European states, it needed the GDR. But if Moscow wanted to concentrate on improving its economy, the GDR had long since shown that it could not help. Ulbricht and Honecker had failed to deliver. Gorbachev would look elsewhere.

THE "COALITION OF REASON"

Even as the struggle over Germany continued between East and West, a more quiet but equally important contest went on between the two Germanys. The first phase had ended with détente, when West Germany had given up its claim to be the only German state and East Germany had given up its drive for legal recognition as a full and separate entity. After that, both knew that Germany would be divided for some time and they entered a phase of mutual cooperation and competition, with Bonn and East Berlin having increasingly close relations marked by an undertone of mutual testing to see which system could best combine political legitimacy and economic prosperity. In this phase of their particular struggle, the two Germanys wanted to deal with each other no matter what happened between East and West, while of course keeping up their guard.

Thus relations between the two Germanys took on a life of their own, almost independent of Soviet or Western policies and attitudes. After 1981, the two states sheltered their direct links from the tensions in East-West relations going on around them. The advent of Chancellor Kohl, once seen as an opponent of inner-German détente, did not disrupt cooperation. Instead, Kohl looked for further improvement. Although he spoke of German unification more than Brandt and Schmidt, he made clear that he saw it as a distant rather than an immediate goal. For the moment, Kohl concentrated on improving the lives of those behind the Wall.

By the 1980s, inner-German trade had risen to almost 10 percent of all East German trade, although it accounted for less than 2 percent of West German trade. East Germany needed that trade as well as the credits that helped finance it. West Germany in turn wanted to use the trade and especially the credits to promote ever more contacts across the Wall.[63]

To make certain that inner-German relations moved smoothly, Kohl and Honecker agreed to establish a confidential channel directly between their offices. Honecker used Alexander Schalck-Golodkowski, a veteran intelligence officer and one of his closest advisers. Kohl used Philipp Jenninger and later Wolfgang Schäuble, successive heads of his chancellery office. The East and West German officials met over thirty times during the 1980s, alternating between East Berlin (generally in Schalck-Golodkowski's home) and Bonn (mostly in Schäuble's home or office).[64]

Working closely with Kohl, Honecker took many different steps to maintain good inner-German relations. Even before the INF deployment, as protests erupted all over West Germany, the GDR agreed to improve inner-German postal and telephone service and to remove limits on the number of parcels that any East German could receive from the West. The GDR also agreed to let

Bonn improve the cable link from West Germany to West Berlin. In exchange, West Germany agreed to make an annual "service compensation" payment of DM 200 million. Internally, the GDR used West German help to improve cable television service to cities like Dresden that could not be reached by normal broadcasts from the West, reportedly because SED functionaries did not like to be assigned to cities without Western television. Gromyko could prevent Honecker from visiting West Germany because of the impending missile deployment, but he could not block other contacts.[65]

West Germany helped Honecker's economy. In June 1983, Bonn guaranteed a bank credit of DM 1 billion for the GDR. Franz Josef Strauss arranged the credit, in part because it meant business for Bavaria but also because he thought that more contact between East and West Germany would ultimately force a change in the GDR. Schalck (as Schalck-Golodkowski was commonly known) helped persuade Strauss by letting him see—but not keep—top secret figures on the GDR's desperate financial situation.[66] Honecker's economic expert, Günter Mittag, later said that the survival of the GDR "stood on a knife's edge" at that point.[67] To thank Strauss, whom he later also met at the Werbellinsee, Honecker promised that the GDR would dismantle the 60,000 automatic scatter-gun firing devices that sprayed bullets in all directions whenever their sensors noticed any approach to the border between East and West Germany.[68]

Honecker did not carry out the threat he had once made that West German deployment of the INF missiles would lead to an "ice age" in inner-German relations. Instead, he made very clear that after the deployment he would try to keep things going as before. Unlike any Soviet official, he said that "we are in favor of limiting the damage as far as possible."[69] During the INF deployment, Honecker even defended the importance of contacts with the Western world. *Neues Deutschland* editorialized that socialist states had to maintain what it called "normal economic relations" with Western states.[70]

Within months after the INF deployment, Honecker and Kohl had a friendly two-hour talk in Moscow on the occasion of Andropov's funeral. They dealt successfully with sensitive issues, with Honecker permitting some East Germans camped at the West German mission in East Berlin to leave for West Germany.[71] They later announced that Honecker had accepted Kohl's invitation to visit West Germany in September 1984.

Throughout the summer and fall months of 1984, Bonn and the GDR planned detailed programs for Honecker in Bonn and elsewhere. As part of the broad improvement in relations, they announced a West German guarantee for another major bank credit of DM 950 million to the GDR.

But Moscow had continued to worry about Honecker's mounting debt to West Germany, and by 1984 had become genuinely alarmed. One CPSU politburo member revealed later that, "at every meting with Honecker the Soviet party leaders—Brezhnev, Andropov, Chernenko, Gorbachev—warned of the great danger of indebtedness to the West." As early as 1979, when he had come to the GDR's thirtieth anniversary celebration, Brezhnev had pounded his fist on the table and accused Honecker of leading the GDR into bankruptcy. Honecker had pretended to take these remarks seriously and promised to reduce the debt, but he had not done so.[72]

Moscow thus did not like the further DM 950 million credit. On August 2, 1984, ten days after the loan announcement, a *Pravda* editorial criticized Bonn for trying to undermine the foundations of the socialist system with such credits. But *Pravda* was really addressing Honecker, telling him that he should not have sought or accepted the loan.

It could thus not have come as a great surprise when Moscow once again put its foot down against Honecker's planned visit to West Germany. Gromyko, fully in charge of Soviet foreign policy after Andropov's death, urged Honecker to cancel the visit. But Honecker did not give up easily. Chernenko and Gromyko had to invite him to a special meeting in Moscow to press him not to go.

In a brutally frank Kremlin meeting on August 17, 1984, Honecker used the traditional East German prestige argument to justify his visit. He pointed to improved status for the GDR. He also pointed to the influence it would give the GDR in West Germany. But the old arguments did not work in a new situation. Soviet leaders worried too much about the growing West German influence over East Germany.

Gromyko had assembled the top Soviet figures to bring Honecker to heel, including Ustinov and Gorbachev. The latter, by then clearly identified as the next CPSU general secretary, seemed the most reasonable of the Soviet leaders. He offered detailed arguments why Honecker should not go to Bonn but added that relations between Moscow and the GDR needed to be repaired to full harmony.

Chernenko concluded by telling Honecker that "we Soviet communists would react positively if in the circumstances that have arisen you were to cancel the visit." Honecker had to yield. *Neues Deutschland* used the excuse that West Germany had been making "revanchist statements," but Schalck told Jenninger that Soviet pressure had prevented the visit.[73] A Western diplomat commented: "Everybody in eastern Europe has limited sovereignty, but some people have sovereignty that is more limited than others."[74]

Honecker did not let himself be deterred fully. Whereas he had to accept Chernenko's and Gromyko's veto on his visit to Bonn, he did not have to do everything that Moscow wanted. By the end of 1984, he dismantled the automatic firing devices all along the inner-German border, although several hundred thousand mines still dotted about one third of the death strip. He permitted a record number of East Germans, over 40,000, to emigrate in 1984. And 2.4 million West Germans and West Berliners visited East Germany and East Berlin. Following up these steps, Honecker sent Mittag to Bonn in his own place to give Kohl the next list of GDR needs.[75]

West Germany continued to make funds available to East Germany, raising the "swing" credit for interzonal trade from DM 650 million to DM 800 million. West German officials, including Kohl, continued talking with Mittag to arrange less direct forms of support for the GDR as well. In exchange, East Germany removed all the mines along the border and permitted further emigration. Honecker also agreed to include West Berlin in a technical and scientific agreement that the GDR signed with the Federal Republic. This revolutionary move, which was the culmination of eighteen years of West German effort to include West Berlin in such inner-German accords, reversed Walter Ulbricht's policies of the 1960s and showed how West German credits paid political dividends.

The GDR also reacted with remarkable aplomb to Kohl's decision to support SDI. Even as Moscow excoriated Reagan for pursuing SDI and Kohl for supporting him, the GDR said little. *Neues Deutschland* observed magisterially that "it is obvious that this ominous step runs the risk of making relations between West Germany and the socialist states more difficult."[76] Those words hardly amounted to a denunciation and they certainly could not be described as a call to arms.

Over two dozen East and West German cities formed city partnerships. Like-minded towns such as the ports of Bremen and Rostock, historic centers like Trier and Weimar, or major Elbe cities like Hamburg and Dresden became partners. The partnership agreements enabled city officials as well as some others to meet and to discuss common problems, opening East Germany ever further to West German ideas and influence.[77]

Tens of thousands of East Germans and East Berliners had been permitted to visit West Germany and West Berlin every year for urgent family reasons during the early 1980s. In 1987, the number of such visits increased to over 1.2 million, then reached 3 million in 1988. With the number of pensioners also traveling to the West, over 5 million East German visits to West Germany took place during 1988. The pace continued during 1989. Kohl pointed to these figures with satisfaction.

Not all aspects of inner-German relations moved smoothly, however. Kohl complained in January 1987 about East German violations of human rights. He said that the GDR held 2,000 political prisoners in jails and in concentration camps. The GDR protested, especially about the term "concentration camps" which recalled Hitler.[78] Honecker rejected an invitation to attend a West Berlin ceremony on Berlin's 750th anniversary because West German officials would also attend.[79] Although the GDR had promised to "humanize" the border regime, incidents offensive to West German and general Western public opinion continued to occur. East German arrests and shootings along the border, including along the Wall in Berlin, still aroused angry West German protests whenever they happened and once led Kohl to cancel a visit by Mittag.[80] But West as well as East German officials played down such disputes and insisted that inner-German relations would continue on a steady course.

Erich Honecker finally had his own chance to visit West Germany in September 1987, after a number of cancellations forced by Moscow. Although the visit was only labeled as "official," Kohl treated it like a state visit. He met several times with Honecker, as did von Weizsäcker and many other leading West German political and government figures. The East and West German flags flew next to each other, and both anthems were played. Honecker went not only to Bonn but to such centers of West German industry as the Ruhr and Bavaria. He also made a sentimental journey to his native Saarland, visiting the graves of his parents and meeting with a sister whom he had not seen since his arrest by the Nazis in December 1935.[81]

Honecker's visit gave him a personal sense of vindication and gave the GDR a modest boost in its status, but it produced no breakthroughs. Honecker's talks dealt with the familiar inner-German agenda. Kohl went outside that agenda to say publicly that he wanted German unification, although he knew that he risked an angry reaction from Honecker. But Honecker countered unexcitedly by talking about "realities." He had said earlier in 1987 that "it is as impossible to unite socialism and capitalism as it is to unite fire and water."[82]

Honecker and his West German hosts pledged continued cooperation on a wide range of issues. In the joint communiqué issued at the end of the visit, they promised to use their influence within their respective alliances toward "relaxing tensions and ensuring peace."

Although Honecker's visit produced nothing sensational, it represented a new departure in inner-German relations. The Federal Republic gave the GDR a practical level of recognition that it had never given before. Honecker basked in that recognition. But no one had any illusions that anything basic had changed. And Kohl, who had been unenthusiastic about the visit but regarded it as essential, made no effort to schedule a return trip although Honecker invited him personally.

Honecker's base began crumbling under him even as he appeared to triumph. During the 1970s, the East German economy had begun admitting its problems in official statistics showing a declining growth rate. By the 1980s, it suffered severe but unacknowledged shortages in basic commodities, including food. It did not abandon its traditional emphasis on machinery production, for Soviet planners always needed more East German machine tools, but exports of industrial products to the West fell. The East German economy could not keep up with technological progress in the European Community, Japan or the United States. It could not even expand interzonal trade with West Germany as much as it wanted because it had nothing more to sell.[83]

During the first years of the 1980s, the GDR's small deficits in inner-German trade could be covered within the "swing" and with some special credits. But in 1984 the GDR suffered a deficit of DM 1.3 billion when inner-German trade peaked at over DM 7 billion. Although Mittag cut back valuable West German machinery imports, he could not end or even limit the deficit.[84]

As the 1980s advanced, the East German economy could no longer produce enough exports for Moscow or for West Germany. The Soviet Union, with its own failing economy, could no longer subsidize oil, gas and raw material exports. The GDR thus had to rely on its own inefficient and pestiferous brown coal. And it desperately needed ever larger infusions of West German credits. Glowing statistics led foreign scholars to rank the GDR as the world's eleventh-largest industrial economy, but the statistics did not fool anyone living and working in East Germany.[85]

A 1990 Deutsche Bank survey showed that productivity in East Germany averaged less than half that in West Germany on a sector basis. But the economists who wrote the survey later said that on second look East German productivity probably averaged only a third of West Germany's.[86]

The GDR incurred expenditures that it could not afford. Much of the money or credit that came from the Federal Republic supported a costly range of GDR intelligence and political operations in West Germany itself and beyond. The SED in 1983 established a special office, the *Bereich Kommerzielle Koordinierung* (Commercial Coordination Office, hereafter KoKo) to manage transactions with the West under the aegis of intelligence chief Erich Mielke. To head KoKo and to make certain that it followed intelligence and SED directives rather than economic considerations, Honecker appointed Schalck-Golodkowski.[87]

Schalck ran the account primarily for SED and intelligence purposes. Every year, tens of millions of D-marks supported GDR spy operations and the KPD in West Germany. Although Schalck knew how badly the GDR needed Western money, he instructed East German trade representatives in West Germany and in foreign countries to give their top priority to intelligence work, mainly for the Stasi, and not to trade.

Schalck also supervised the funds that West Germany paid the GDR to release persons to the West. East Germany sold human beings more successfully than any other item, using ransom as its most profitable trade. Schalck collected for the release of East Germans imprisoned for one reason or another, those who had friends and relatives in the West and those who attracted some attention and interest. Either private West Germans or the West German government paid. Under Mielke's direction, and using the East Berlin lawyer Wolfgang Vogel as intermediary to the West, Schalck arranged the releases and kept track of the names and of the funds.

The ransom business proved so profitable because the average price for releases from East Germany rose progressively over the years, from thousands of DM to tens of thousands and often more. Schalck had the ideal seller's market. Only the Stasi could free the people whom others wanted released. Ransom payments to the GDR rose from DM 38 million in 1964 to DM 387 million in 1984, with Schalck placing the funds in a number of foreign banks in Vienna, Geneva, Zurich, Copenhagen, Luxembourg and Lugano.[88]

When Schalck closed the accounts upon German unification, he calculated that West Germany had paid a total of DM 3.5 billion in ransom money between 1963 and 1989, from the time Konrad Adenauer had initiated the payments to the collapse of the GDR. In exchange, East Germany had released 33,755 prisoners and had permitted about 250,000 family reunions. It had used the ransom funds for international political and intelligence operations and to purchase luxury goods, such as Western limousines, for the private use of senior SED functionaries.[89] It had not used the funds to help pay off the debt that worried the Soviets.

West German money worked its influence on the GDR. The SED would never have permitted East Germans to travel had West Germany not offered subsidies in exchange. The SED would not have permitted Western cars to enter the GDR if Bonn had not paid for the privilege. Whatever Brandt, Schmidt or Kohl might want, Honecker would present a bill. And West Germany would pay, usually asking for nothing more than such seemingly innocent concessions as an easing of travel restrictions, reductions in travel fees or some specific releases.

No reliable total has ever been calculated for the amount with which West Germany subsidized East Germany. Official payments outside the Interzonal Trade arrangements had risen to about DM 25 to 30 billion by 1988, averaging DM 2 billion a year from 1975 to 1988. Private funds sent by West Germans to the East may have amounted to at least the same figure, with one estimate indicating that the packages and gifts sent or carried from West to East Germany over the years had a value of DM 20 billion and that private money transfers amounted to another DM 10 billion. Over forty years, public and private subsidies may have totaled between DM 75 billion and 100 billion. Economic and political analysts have wondered whether these funds helped the GDR by keeping its economy functioning despite its inefficiencies or whether they hurt the GDR by permitting it to avoid the reforms that might have helped it to succeed on its own. They have also asked whether West Germany did the right thing by subsidizing some improvement in conditions for East Germans or whether it should have refused to support the GDR in hope that the system would collapse. To date, there is no clear answer.[90]

The SED further handicapped the East German economy by the resources that it committed to the Stasi. By the late 1980s, full-time Stasi employees had risen to 85,000, with another 200,000 paid spies and perhaps 1 to 2 million informers. The Stasi opened about 5 percent of all East German mail and routinely monitored all telephone calls and any other means of communication. It kept files on 6 million out of 16 million East Germans, perhaps half of the adult population, as well as on 2 million out of 60 million West Germans and on countless foreign visitors. The Stasi grew to twice the size of Hitler's Gestapo secret police but monitored a population only one-fifth as large. It also attracted universal hatred. All East Germans knew that any meeting or event that they might attend would include a sizable number of Stasi informants even if it had no conceivable political purpose. East Germans never said anything meaningful to any person they did not know and trust.[91]

Informal estimates on the length of Stasi files ranged up to 160 kilometers (100 miles) of carefully collected and sorted material.[92] No one has reliably calculated the proportion of East German gross domestic product spent on police and intelligence operations.

The West German SPD, having originated Ostpolitik under Brandt, tried to continue it even while out of office. During much of the 1980s, it conducted its own inner-German policy separate from Kohl's. The SPD policy, spearheaded by Bahr himself, departed radically from the SPD's Bad Godesberg program and largely accepted the SED view of European and German issues. It also accepted many SED proposals in a semi-official manner as if the SPD represented some alternative West German government or a government in waiting.[93]

Bahr and many younger SPD members endorsed East German formulas for what they termed "common security" between East and West Germany and for a "European peace order." Andreas von Bülow, one of the party's defense experts, committed himself and the SPD to superpower disengagement from Central Europe by the year 2000. Abandoning Brandt's traditionally firm commitment to the Western alliance, the new SPD generation actively considered and sometimes advocated splitting West Germany from NATO.

In 1985 and 1986, the SPD and the SED produced the kinds of documents that governments would normally negotiate, such as a treaty proposal for a "chemical-weapon-free-zone in Europe" and for a "nuclear-weapon-free-corridor." Later, after the SPD had lost the 1987 elections, it and the SED produced a joint proposal for a "zone of trust and security" in Europe. Just before Honecker's visit to Bonn, they produced a joint paper on "common security" which advocated not only security cooperation but environmental protection and the furtherance of human rights. The latter points must have appeared bizarre to the East German population, whose environment and human rights had been systematically destroyed by the SED itself.

As Soviet and East German documents later showed, the SED often consulted the CPSU and the Soviet government about its discussions with the SPD, making certain that its positions accorded with Soviet policy. Gorbachev could not be blamed for waiting until after the 1987 election to turn to Kohl, for an SPD victory would have brought to power a party that appeared fully ready to accept Soviet views on foreign and security issues.

The German social democratic political philosopher Richard Löwenthal distanced himself from the trend. He wrote that there was, in a large part of the young generation, "a loss of understanding that the conflict with the Soviet Union is not only a conflict between two great powers and their associates but also a conflict between freedom and tyranny."[94] But Bahr and the SPD persisted.

Bahr's *Wandel durch Annäherung* had worked both ways, leading to transformation through accommodation within the SPD itself. It might have made East Germany more susceptible to West German influence, but it also changed SPD policy and drew the West German Social Democratic apparatus closer to SED thinking than it had been even at the height of détente. Only in the East German elections of March 1990 was the SPD to learn how the East German people themselves felt about all this.

The SPD-SED papers did not represent the main work of inner-German relations. The West German and East German governments were doing that work themselves, and they were doing it on the basis of principles very different from the propaganda exercises in which the SED still engaged. They were doing it on the basis of a mutual acceptance of realities. Gorbachev and Kohl dealt on that same basis. Yet Kohl and his government, like Reagan, remained committed to changing those realities.

EIGHTEEN

BURSTING THROUGH THE WALL

AS THE ICE BEGAN TO CRACK BETWEEN THE SUPERPOWERS AND between the two German states, it also began to crack in eastern Europe. Mikhail Gorbachev provided an opening, but the principal impetus came from the people themselves.

In June 1979, Pope John Paul II paid a visit to his native Poland. As he spoke and celebrated mass in one Polish city after another, he summoned an older and higher loyalty than that of the communist state. Without overtly challenging that state, his speeches de-legitimized it. One scholar wrote that the Pope's visit to Poland marked the "beginning of the end" for communist domination of those trapped behind the Wall and the Iron Curtain.[1]

The free Polish trade union Solidarity came to life a year after the Pope's visit. Although suppressed under martial law, it became a form of underground government, just as the resistance to Nazism had become the underground government in many countries under German occupation during World War II.

Gorbachev made clear that he would accept change in the Soviet satellite system. In September 1986, the Soviet Union signed the Stockholm agreement promising to refrain from the threat or use of force in its relations with any state, regardless of that state's political system.

Gorbachev made his point even more clearly in a speech to the Council of Europe in Strasbourg in July 1989, when he said that the social and political order of European countries was "entirely a matter for the peoples themselves and of their choosing." He excluded the possibility of using force within the "common European home," either "by one alliance against another, within alliances, or anywhere else."[2] In effect, he told the leaders of the satellite regimes to make their peace with their own people for the Red Army would not keep them in power.

Gorbachev did not want to keep the Brezhnev Doctrine. Kremlin spokesman Gennady Gerasimov called Gorbachev's philosophy "the Sinatra Doctrine," after Frank Sinatra's song "I Did It My Way." Gorbachev understood that the Red Army could hold the land but could not hold the people. And holding the land had become prohibitively expensive.

THE HUNGARIAN GATE

The Hungarians joined the Poles in leading the way toward democracy. They did it by honoring the memory of Imre Nagy, who had led the Hungarian revolution of 1956 and who had been hanged by the Soviets and their Hungarian satraps after having been released from the Yugoslav embassy in Budapest against a promise of immunity. He had been buried in an unmarked grave. On June 16, 1989, a crowd of 200,000 honored his memory in Budapest with a memorial ceremony and a reburial, at his family's request, in the same plot where the Soviets had buried him.[3] The burial led the way to talks between the Hungarian government and the opposition, culminating in the proclamation of a Hungarian republic on October 23, 1989.

As part of the process of liberalization, Hungary signed the United Nations Convention and Protocol on Refugees, an important symbolic gesture because the refugees fleeing the Red Army's 1956 invasion of Hungary had given a powerful impetus to the development of the global refugee system.

With Hungary and Poland liberalizing, East Germans who wanted to flee to the West began to see those countries as potential way-stations. They could get GDR exit visas for eastern Europe even when they could not get them for western Europe. Once they had reached a liberalizing east European state, they could go to the West German embassy in the capital and ask for permission to travel to the Federal Republic. By August 1989, almost 200 East Germans had moved into the West German embassy in Budapest. The West German embassy gave them passports, as Bonn considered all Germans, whether living in East or West Germany, to be German citizens. Hungary then permitted them to leave for West Germany under escort by the International Red Cross, honoring its new commitment to the Refugee Convention.

Hungary provided a route to West Germany for many more East Germans than for those in the West German embassy. The Hungarian government on May 2, 1989, began to dismantle the barbed-wire border barrier that had prevented flight to Austria since 1956. The government had neither expected nor planned for the mass exodus of East Germans that followed. But it did nothing to stop them, even after the GDR reminded Budapest that in 1969 the two governments had mutually agreed to enforce each other's travel restrictions.

East German would-be refugees did not waste time, driving to Hungary by the tens of thousands. When the Hungarian government at first did not let them enter Austria through regular border crossing points, the refugees abandoned their boxy little Trabant cars in any convenient wooded area near the border and continued on foot. Once in Austria, they went to the West German embassy in Vienna to get West German passports.

As the exodus continued, the West German government asked Hungary to permit the East Germans to leave through the established border checkpoints. The Hungarian government, wanting to prevent the Hungarian woods from becoming a dumping ground for Trabants, agreed. It also received an unrestricted credit, reputedly on the order of DM 1 billion, as a gesture of appreciation from Bonn. And the Austrian government helped by granting an entry visa to any East German who appeared at any border checkpoint.

The GDR protested that Hungary was "betraying socialism." It wanted to call a meeting of the Warsaw Pact foreign ministers to press the Hungarians to block the exodus, but Gorbachev and Shevardnadze prevented the meeting because they objected to open arguments between socialist states. The GDR complained but could not deny that it had itself sold exit permits for D-marks. Hungary probably received less money per refugee than Schalck-Golodkowski had.

Many East Germans went to the West German embassy in Prague. That embassy, a palatial residence built in Prague's glory days and surrounded by a large walled garden, became the haven for thousands. They walked around the outside wall until they found a convenient and unguarded spot and then helped each other into the embassy compound. Many had children with them. They strained the embassy food and sanitation facilities to the breaking point but would not leave unless they were promised a safe exit to West Germany. The situation within the embassy compound quickly became unbearable.

As the crisis at the Prague embassy deepened by the end of September 1989, the West German foreign minister, Hans-Dietrich Genscher, and the East German foreign minister, Oskar Fischer, met at the United Nations and worked out a plan for the East German squatters to proceed to West Germany. But Fischer stipulated that they travel in sealed trains back into East Germany, through the Dresden station, and only then to West Germany. Honecker wanted to be able to claim that the GDR had expelled the refugees of its own sovereign will. His decision to permit their departure provoked a crisis in the SED politburo, with some members objecting that the refugees should not be allowed to leave, but Honecker wanted to solve the embarrassment before the impending fortieth anniversary celebration of the GDR.

Genscher, who regarded the agreement as a triumph, went to Prague on September 30 to announce it personally to the crowd crammed into the embassy grounds. In what he termed the most moving moment of his career, he received enthusiastic applause. Genscher had himself been a refugee from Halle in East Germany. Before then, he had been one of the last Wehrmacht soldiers to cross the Elbe River to the west in front of the advancing Red Army. He must have felt a pang of recognition when the refugees surged around to thank him.

Some citizens of Prague, in honor of the refugees, painted an abandoned Trabant car in imitation gold and placed it on blocks into one of the squares of the old city. The "Golden Trabi" became a symbol of East German flight and of Czech readiness to help.

But Honecker and the SED remained angry. As soon as the trains had filled, Honecker ordered the Czech border closed. East Germans could no longer travel even to their neighboring socialist states.

The SED had been forced to swallow some bitter pills. By the time of the GDR anniversary, about 10,000 East Germans had fled to the West through the West German embassy in Budapest, another 5,000 through the embassy in Warsaw, and 15,000 through the embassy in Prague.[4] Over a hundred thousand had fled through the Hungarian woods or along Hungarian roads to Austria. East Germany could not afford to lose them, for most were young and had good prospects wherever they might settle.

Kohl urged Honecker to introduce reforms that would persuade people to stay in East Germany, while warning that West Germany would accept all refugees.[5] But the SED could not make decisions. Honecker fell gravely ill, requiring a major operation that took him out of action for six weeks in August-September and that left him visibly weakened. Mittag had already suffered through several operations. The SED reacted to all refugee flight by claiming Western plots against the GDR. Even in its most confidential meetings, the politburo did not dare to discuss the root causes of the exodus.[6]

As Honecker and the SED were soon to learn, however, those East Germans who chose to remain in the GDR would prove even more troublesome than those who chose to leave.

KURT MASUR, THE *KAPELLMEISTER* OF LEIPZIG

The first overt sign of trouble in East Germany itself had seemed quite innocuous and had long preceded the mass flight through eastern Europe. It came in the form of a few hundred teenagers who had assembled on the eastern side of the Wall to hear a rock concert being given on June 7, 1987, near the Reichstag building in West Berlin. As the rock fans listened, cheered and danced, the Stasi and border police moved in to disperse them and to arrest some for listening to western music.

The scene repeated itself the following two evenings as the concerts continued. But the fans on the eastern side grew more numerous and the police more determined to punish them. The fans threw stones at the police and shouted "*Mauer weg!*" ("Away with the Wall!") and "*Wir wollen Gorbatschow*" ("We want Gorbachev"). The police beat up and arrested dozens. Western journalists who could look over the Wall reported on the arrests, giving everyone in East Germany a chance to know about them because almost all watched West Berlin or West German news. Anger at the regime mounted, but nothing happened immediately.

The next incident came five months later, when the Stasi ransacked the ecology library that had been established in the East Berlin Zionskirche (Church of Zion). They confiscated or destroyed all materials that reported on the poisonous environment around East German industrial sites as well as any papers with proposals to improve the environment in East Germany. The Stasi arrested several ecologists associated with the library or the church, taking them away on the spot. Once again, the East German police acted openly before the eyes of West German journalists who happened to be visiting the library. They provoked angry articles in the West German press; more important, they virtually challenged East German church leaders to defy the regime.

Two months later, in January 1988, several small East German human rights advocacy groups petitioned to join the annual East Berlin memorial ceremony to the communist martyrs Rosa Luxemburg and Karl Liebknecht, who had been assassinated by German reactionary goon squads on January 17, 1919. The human rights groups asked if they could put up banners bearing two of Luxemburg's most famous quotes: "Freedom is always the freedom of those who think differently" and "If you do not move, you do not feel your chains."[7]

The Stasi again reacted with cold ferocity. The police threatened the petitioners, forcing about 150 of them to promise not to come to the demonstration. They arrested some at home early on January 17 and arrested others on their way to the demonstration. They arrested and beat up others when they tried to unfurl their banners. Altogether, the Stasi and the police arrested more than a hundred, threatened some with six months jail sentences and finally expelled many would-be demonstrators as well as their supporters to West Germany.

The Stasi might have hoped that a stiff reaction would solve the problem, but it did not. By 1988, having heard the new message coming out of the Soviet Union, East Germans would no longer accept the kind of repression that had become the GDR norm. In particular, East German church leaders who had tried to make their peace with the regime felt guilty for having stood by in silence while others suffered the crudest forms of police brutality.

Manfred Stolpe, the president of the Berlin evangelical church assembly, complained to the Stasi and warned that churches would help the activists. Pastors said openly that churches should not continue to submit.[8] One pastor, Rainer Eppelmann, created the Samaritan Church especially to protect human rights activists. Thereafter, churches in East Berlin became havens for dissidents, letting their facilities be used by applicants for emigration and by increasingly widespread but still discreet East German resistance groups.

The movement spread to Dresden, where thousands of persons assembled in several churches on February 13, 1988, in support of those arrested in East Berlin. After services, they marched quietly along the streets of the city center, carrying candles and placards. The police moved against the demonstrators but, in response to requests from church authorities, did not act as brutally as in East Berlin. Hans Modrow, the reform-minded SED secretary for Dresden, told the police to exercise moderation. The Dresden SED sent some of the protesters quietly to West Germany, especially if they had applied for emigration, and released others without further action. This restrained reaction avoided a potential crisis but did not solve the basic problem of ever-widening dissidence.[9]

Throughout the remainder of 1988 and much of 1989, the resistance movement smoldered and spread beneath the surface of GDR politics. Churches became sites for clandestine prayer meetings promoting human rights. Activists began discussing new political groupings that would advance human rights and would undo the ecological damage that the SED had done. Whereas many East German dissidents applied for emigration, others vowed to stay and to work for change within East Germany itself. They argued that the time had come for the GDR to establish legitimacy at home rather than to search for it abroad.[10]

Gorbachev's two guiding principles presented grave problems for the SED regime and for Honecker. Perestroika demanded efficient and effective economic management. If it were to be applied to the GDR, it would require a dramatic shift in economic direction and performance.

Gorbachev's second principle, Glasnost, could wreak even greater havoc. Usually translated as "openness," Glasnost called for frank discussion. It should have been translated as "honesty," telling those truths that everyone knew but no one dared to mention. The Russian author Alexander Solzhenitsyn had written that communism could not survive the truth, and that dictum applied more in the GDR than in any other state.

To the East German dissidents, Glasnost would mean frank talk about the surveillance and the repression that all experienced but did not speak of in the open. It would mean a real dialogue between the SED and those it ruled, requiring honest debate about the Wall and about why so many people were trying so hard to leave East Germany. It would entail a total revision of the GDR's unwritten rules of behavior.

Honecker believed that he had good reason to resist Gorbachev's ideas. He did not feel ashamed of the GDR. The East German standard of living was well above the Soviet standard. So was East Germany's general infrastructure. The GDR provided some of the most modern products and most reliable machine tools available in the Soviet bloc, as well as optics for the Soviet space program. Although East German products could not compete in Asia and western Europe, they had served the Soviet system adequately before Gorbachev came along.

Gorbachev wanted to change the Soviet Union quickly, but Honecker felt in no hurry to change the GDR. And he made his views clear to the Soviet leader. Honecker's principal ideologist, Kurt Hager, asked rhetorically in April 1987: "If your neighbor chose to repaper the walls of his house, would you feel obliged to do the same?"[11] If Gorbachev wanted to practice new slogans and new ideas, he should feel free to do so. But Honecker would not follow him. He saw no need for Perestroika and could not tolerate even the notion of Glasnost.

But the East German writer Stefan Heym replied to Hager by stating on western television: "This is not about wallpaper. It is about the ghosts in the basement, about the skeletons in the closet, and about the grimy muck that must be exposed to the light."[12]

Honecker could reject Gorbachev's ideas but could not suppress them. Occasionally, Soviet articles disregarded GDR sensitivities. The Moscow journal *Literaturnaia Gazeta* wrote in July 1988 that there was no such thing as a "GDR" or "FRG" or "West-Berlin" nationality, only a "German" nationality. This drew a sharp protest from Honecker to the Soviet ambassador in East Berlin.

Glasnost's worst offense against the GDR came in the Soviet *Sputnik* magazine in November 1988, with an article denouncing the German communist party for its hostility to the SPD during the Weimar Republic. The article recalled that, under Stalin's orders, the German communists fought the socialists and refused to cooperate with them to form a united Left that could have blocked Hitler from reaching power. Honecker resented the article not only because it was true but because it ripped at old lesions that the SED had tried to heal or to conceal. He denounced the *Sputnik* article as "*Gequäcke wildgewordener Spiesser*" ("demented gibberish"). The GDR sent a sharply worded protest to the Soviet embassy, and *Neues Deutschland* published an editorial denouncing "the distortion of historical reality."[13] Honecker then banned *Sputnik* from the GDR.

Honecker could complain all he liked, but Gorbachev had begun to understand the reality of the GDR better than most East German leaders. He had
once conceived of the GDR as a possible economic bridge between East and
West, but had slowly come to realize that Honecker had not told him the truth
about the East German economy and might not even know it himself. Gorbachev suggested that Honecker bring the reformer Modrow into the SED
politburo. He saw Modrow, a personal friend, as a potential successor to Honecker. But Honecker turned him down flatly.[14]

The Soviets invited former East German spy chief Markus Wolf to Moscow,
hoping that he knew what was really happening in the GDR. Several of
Moscow's best German experts asked him about the state of the economy. Wolf,
who had left the spy game and harbored political ambitions of his own, wanted
to level with Gorbachev. He told the Soviets that the GDR had external debts of
at least DM 40 billion and could not repay them without lowering the East German standard of living by 25 or 30 percent. When he saw the report on Wolf's
statements, Gorbachev concluded that Honecker and the bankrupt GDR could
not be a bridge to anywhere. He saw that he had no alternative to Kohl.[15]

On January 17, 1989, the seventieth anniversary of the assassination of the communist martyrs Luxemburg and Liebknecht provoked the next overt East German crisis. As in 1988, human rights activists wanted to display their own
banners and placards during the celebration. Again, as in 1988, the SED objected. Over 100 protesters demonstrated. And again, the Stasi and the police reacted harshly. But this time, the dissidents did not retreat to churches and private
meetings as they had before. Instead, they began to promote their ideas widely
within East Germany.

During the course of 1989, the dissidents began to form new political
groupings, an illegal action in the GDR. First came New Forum, headed by such
long-time activists as writer Bärbel Bohley and professor Jens Reich. Others followed, named Democracy Now, Democratic Awakening, Social Democrats, Initiative Peace and Human Rights, the Greens, the United Left and the like.
Although some had names similar to West German political parties, they insisted on their own separate identity. None had more than one or two hundred
members, at least at first.

The new groups proclaimed an idealistic humanism that reminded many observers of those Germans who had tried and failed to launch a democratic German revolution in 1848 and 1849. Reich, for example, told a Washington seminar
in the spring of 1990 that a visit to the democratic West represented a dream he
had never expected to realize. But idealism did not prevent the new groups from
organizing effectively and expressing themselves forcefully. New Forum's public

appeal challenged "the disturbed relationship between the state and society" and warned that the time was ripe for change.[16] The groups also cooperated closely enough with each other and with the churches to create a nascent political force.

The new political groups drew their strength from the dissatisfaction and resentment seething throughout East German society. Even if none had any immediate chance of challenging the SED, they began a process of political discussion and association that struck at the very core of the artificial construct that Ulbricht had designed and built. The churches and the new opposition groups even had the courage to denounce the results of the GDR local elections in May 1989, in which the SED had claimed its usual 98.77 percent of the vote. They also denounced the SED for endorsing the Chinese repression at Beijing's Tienanmen Square.

Popular resistance came to a full boil in October 1989 as the trains carrying East German refugees from Prague passed through East Germany on their way to West Germany. Several thousand East Germans converged on the Dresden station to try to stow away on the trains. But the trains did not come when first expected. The mood turned ugly as a police voice over a loudspeaker told everyone to leave the station. The crowd chanted "We want out." The police emptied the platforms with their truncheons. This enraged the people, many of whom had brought their children.

The next night even more people, perhaps 10,000, crowded around the station. Desperate to leave, they threw stones at the police who would not let them near the tracks. Again, the police cleared the station, arresting hundreds of persons. Police and demonstrators clashed several times over the following days and nights. The police continued making arrests, raising the level of popular anger higher. Word of these events, broadcast on West German radio and television, reached everywhere in East Germany.

By Sunday, October 8, Dresden crackled with tension. Demonstrations continued most of the afternoon and evening. The police arrested demonstrators and others by the hundreds. They threatened more arrests. At this point, however, some Dresden church leaders intervened and arranged for the demonstrators to choose twenty representatives to negotiate with the SED. The demonstrators talked to Modrow, who tried once again to reduce tensions and open a real dialogue. But the demonstrations had left their mark. SED officials and church leaders realized that dissension in East Germany had risen to the boiling point and that massive violence might lie ahead if no one prevented it.

To add to the suspense, Gorbachev himself arrived in East Berlin for the fortieth anniversary celebration of the GDR on October 6 and 7. Honecker wanted to use Gorbachev to reinforce the authority of the SED.

Gorbachev did not like the way Honecker had rejected Modrow and continued to reject reform. He also disliked some of the links that had been established between the GDR and Soviet conservatives.[17] His statements at the official anniversary ceremony showed restraint. He did not try to undercut or contradict Honecker's triumphalist recital of GDR accomplishments. Instead, he used his official speech to stress the importance of change in the socialist system, saying only that questions that concerned the GDR had to be settled in Berlin rather than in Moscow. But all observers reported that he and Honecker barely spoke to each other at the ceremony or at other public meetings.

Gorbachev threw the fat onto the fire during a brief exchange with the press the following day at an East German wreath-laying ceremony honoring the victims of fascism. He observed almost in passing that "life punishes those who come too late." Although Gorbachev later insisted, in his memoirs and elsewhere, that this phrase reflected his fear that he himself could not reform the Soviet Union as fast as necessary, all East Germans heard it as a slap at Honecker for resisting change. The sentence coursed like lightning through Berlin and East Germany, especially as it was repeated and debated endlessly on West German radio and television. Everyone saw it as an open rebuke to Honecker and the SED. It convinced the East German opposition that Gorbachev sympathized with their cause.

Gorbachev privately urged his hosts to act. In a small meeting with the most senior SED and Soviet officials, he asked Honecker what the GDR would do to improve its economy. The SED leader repeated his usual claims about East German successes and prospects. Gorbachev, making his impatience and disapproval clear, expressed his wish for far-reaching reforms. He reiterated his remark that history would punish those who came too late. Even during the meeting, the police were dispersing a demonstration in East Berlin and the crowd was responding "*Gorby, hilf uns*" ("Gorby, help us").

That evening Honecker hosted an elegant dinner in East Berlin's Palace of the Republic to celebrate the regime's forty years of existence. Waiters passed trays laden with food and drinks. Musicians played. Officials and diplomats spoke quietly and earnestly. But they could not keep their concentration as shouts of "*Freiheit*" and "Gorby" penetrated through the windows from demonstrations that still continued near the center of the city. Finally, using water cannons and truncheons, the police forced the demonstrators away. A guest at the reception wrote that he felt as if he was on the *Titanic* at five minutes after midnight. He thought that the *Götterdämmerung*—the end—of the SED regime had come.[18] He did not know that many East German cities, including Leipzig, Dresden, Halle, Erfurt and Potsdam, had seen similar demonstrations that evening in reaction to official anniversary celebrations.

Leipzig, the largest city in East Germany, became the largest center of dissent. The SED had for forty years used the city to hawk East German progress and products to the world at what had been for centuries one of Germany's biggest annual fairs. Those fairs had shown the Leipzigers how royally the SED treated foreigners and, in comparison, how shabbily it treated them. The contrast helped to underline the mendacity of the regime.

For some months during the summer and fall of 1989, ever larger crowds had attended Monday night services for peace at the Nikolaikirche (Church of St. Nicholas) in the old center of Leipzig. They had begun to walk through the streets together after those services, carrying candles and praying for peace and freedom. A particularly large march was scheduled for the night of Monday, October 9, 1989.

Honecker decided that any demonstrations that evening would be put down by force. The police authorities, expecting violence, distributed extra blood plasma to their medical units. Companies of regular and mobile police as well as additional militia units and Stasi units stood ready to repeat Tienanmen Square in central Europe. With the Chinese vice premier visiting Honecker in Berlin, the Chinese model for solving political problems through shootings and arrests loomed over the proceedings.

SED leaders told the police that they should be prepared to use firearms if truncheons did not suffice for crowd control. And the police jammed the march route to make certain that they would come into direct confrontation with the anticipated marchers. To help the police, several elite East German military units, including a paratroop company from an air attack regiment and a motorized guard battalion, went on battle alert.

The East German police and army knew, however, that they were on their own. During his visit to East Berlin, Gorbachev had learned of the impending clash and had issued strict orders forbidding any Red Army action against any demonstrators. One person present at his meeting with the Soviet army commander said that Gorbachev's orders were "like iron."[19]

At this moment, as the course of East German history veered toward mass repression, a powerful figure arose from the sidelines. Kurt Masur, the bearded, barrel-chested *Kapellmeister* (conductor) of the Leipzig *Gewandhaus* orchestra (and later conductor of the New York and London philharmonic orchestras), had been appalled by earlier East German police brutality against peaceful demonstrators and had complained about it on West German television. Seeing the possibility of a bloodbath, he chose to step in.

Masur called the local Soviet army commander. He asked about Soviet intentions and learned that the Red Army would stay in its barracks. But he learned from the East German army commander that his forces were on alert. He then called a pastor, an influential cabaret artist and three local SED party officials to propose a joint appeal for calm. He made it clear that he would issue his own appeal if they did not join him.

The three SED officials telephoned Egon Krenz, a senior SED politburo member and Honecker's putative successor, to ask SED headquarters to approve the appeal. Krenz went to Honecker but got no clearance. Instead, Honecker said that he had great plans for Krenz but now wondered if Krenz was up to them. He said Krenz should do what he wished but that the politburo would react appropriately. Perplexed and intimidated, Krenz delayed replying to Leipzig until evening.[20]

In the meantime, Leipzig SED officials decided on their own that they had to join Masur's appeal. All of Leipzig revered its orchestra and its conductor. The local SED leaders could not stand up against him. By the time they heard from Krenz, approving the appeal, they had already agreed to it themselves.

Masur's appeal stated that "all of us need an open exchange of opinion." It asked all Leipzigers to act with calm and reason in order to make a "peaceful dialogue" possible.[21] He thus warned the Stasi and the police not to start any trouble. To make sure that the appeal became widely known, Masur arranged to have it read on the radio and in the main churches, including the Nikolaikirche. He also asked the East German police commander to pull back his forces from the route that the marchers would take and to inform the police of the appeal. Like the SED officials, the police commander could not turn down the *Kapellmeister.*

Masur's message and person carried the day. That evening, after church services, the hitherto largest crowd of Leipzig demonstrators assembled for a candlelight march through the city center. Seventy thousand strong, they flowed slowly through the dark streets of the old city to the main square, singing hymns as they marched. In an unstated armistice, the police and army drew back and did not try to stop the march or to harass the marchers. From time to time the crowd shouted *"wir sind das Volk"* ("we are the people") or "Gorby, Gorby." When they had finished, they had changed the face of East Germany. They had shown that the authorities had to respect the power of the assembled people.

The SED politburo met in emergency session on October 10 and 11. Its members realized that the SED needed either to change course or to conduct a mass repression without Soviet support and with no guarantee of success. The economic planning staff told them for the first time the size of the GDR external debt and its prospective burden on the people in future years. Staggered by the combination of political resistance and economic failure, the politburo members demanded action. Honecker agreed to a declaration that promised "necessary new measures" and called on East Germans not to flee to the West but to remain to help build the future. It said that "socialism needs everybody." But it provided no specifics and instead asked for fresh ideas. After forty years in power, the SED did not know what to do or to promise next.

Demonstrations continued throughout virtually every city in East Germany. On October 16, over 100,000 persons assembled after the Nikolaikirche service. Another 10,000 met before the city hall in Dresden. The Stasi reported ever more open criticism of the SED, increasingly from long-time party members and from industrial workers as well as from intellectuals.

By the time of the next politburo meeting on October 17, Egon Krenz had acted. Working with politburo members Willi Stoph, Günter Schabowski and even Honecker's friend Erich Mielke, he had outlined a plan for Honecker's departure. As the SED chief opened the politburo meeting and wanted to proceed to the agenda, Stoph interrupted to say that they should first discuss the removal of the party general secretary. Honecker, stunned and stony-faced, agreed. He called on one politburo member after another, beginning with the ones he thought most likely to support him. All told him that it was time for him to go.

Like Ulbricht before him, Honecker tried some maneuvers to evade the issue, but even his closest friends refused to be deterred. Mielke threatened to reveal how Honecker had denounced his associates to the Nazis while in prison, warning that he would open the files that he kept in a "red safe" in his office. When Honecker asked for a vote, it went twenty-five to zero against him. At the end of the meeting, he agreed to resign "for reasons of health." He concurred in Krenz as his successor.[22]

Krenz wanted to use his new-found authority to guide the SED and the GDR through the crisis, but he could not shed his old skin. On October 18, he made a televised appeal pledging change and promising to "seize the initiative" for a political and ideological offensive. But he also said that he would continue to build socialism and not to surrender "the achievements of the GDR." Asserting that the SED represented the people and could make any needed changes, he said that he would not talk on an equal basis to the new political groups. He thus made it clear that he would change little if anything and that the SED would keep its claim to be the leading party. The reform plans that he mentioned, such as authorizing East Germans to travel again to Hungary, excited no response.[23] Reform groups like New Forum dismissed the speech as they continued to gain new members by the thousands. Recalling Krenz's visit to Beijing at the time of the Tienanmen repression, they called him "Krenz Hsiaoping."

The East German people continued to take to the streets. On Monday, October 23, over 300,000 marched in Leipzig to demand real reforms and true democracy. Similar demonstrations occurred everywhere as the people began to show anger. Krenz thought that he might be able to get a major economic aid package from Bonn, but Kohl said that he would give nothing unless the GDR introduced far-reaching reforms, including free elections.[24]

Krenz knew that Gorbachev had disliked Honecker's frozen policies and attitudes and wanted to persuade the Soviet leader that he would be the right man to lead the GDR through this crisis and to work with the Soviet Union. He flew to Moscow on November 1 and told Gorbachev that he would abandon Honecker's policies, which he himself described as "short-sighted and wrong," and that he wanted close relations with Moscow.[25] Although Gorbachev met with Krenz, he must have been disappointed that the SED had not picked Modrow to succeed Honecker. [26]

Gorbachev told Krenz to make real reforms quickly and warned that the popular demonstrations showed that the situation could pick up speed dramatically. Krenz would have to make the kinds of changes that would "draw all citizens into the process." Gorbachev went out of his way to reassure Krenz that the Soviet Union would not permit German unification. Moscow, he said, favored maintaining the "realities of the post-war period, including the existence of two German states." Unification would be "extremely explosive."

Krenz and Gorbachev also discussed the disastrous state of the East German economy. Gorbachev cited the secret briefing which showed GDR bankruptcy and told Krenz that the SED would have to be honest with the East German people, especially if the people were asked to accept a severe cut in living standards. If the SED told the truth, people might cooperate. If it did not, they would not.

As it turned out, Gorbachev and Krenz talked past each other. The career SED functionary could not even begin to grasp Gorbachev's concept about the relationship between a communist party and society. He expressed agreement with Gorbachev but he did not understand the Soviet leader's real meaning. He flew away from Moscow encouraged but unenlightened.

Krenz had no idea how to deal with the spreading crisis. He thought that he could still reverse the trend without making more than minor adjustments in SED and GDR policies. He and his colleagues did not realize that they faced a real revolution, a revolution against their work, against their party, against their state, and against themselves.

THE HATED STONES

On the day after Krenz returned, almost a million demonstrators converged on the Alexanderplatz in the center of East Berlin for the largest gathering ever held in the city.[27] Speaker after speaker reiterated the same reform and freedom themes that other rallies had addressed all over East Germany. They also demanded the right to travel.

The rally in Berlin shifted the priorities of the East German revolution. The East Berliners had a very specific and very intense grievance, the Wall. Like other East Germans, they wanted freedom of expression, basic human rights and real elections. But the Wall topped their agenda. From the moment they began to demonstrate in earnest, the East German government had to address freedom to travel more urgently than anything else.

The Wall burned like a festering sore in the minds of most East Berliners. It confined them in a prison. Even if some could leave, they could do so only on special occasions and with special permission. And most could never leave. The Wall prevented them from going west to see family and friends. It barred the little excursions that city dwellers anywhere else could take. They could not see movies or rock bands half a mile away. They could not take their children to the old Berlin zoo, which happened to be in West Berlin, or to see the popular West Berlin soccer team. They could not take a stroll along West Berlin avenues or in West Berlin parks. Not a day passed without a sense of frustration and, for many, a sense of pain. Some carried placards that said "Long Live the October Revolution— 1989"; others said "*Mauer weg!*"

Krenz tried to relieve the pressure by easing travel in several directions. He opened the borders to Czechoslovakia again. The Czech government, after discussions with Bonn, then opened the border to West Germany. Within a week, 25,000 East Germans fled by that route while another 50,000 escaped via Hungary. New Forum demanded passports and exit permits for all East German citizens to go wherever they might wish.

Unable to prevent ever larger and more frequent demonstrations, Stoph's government formally resigned although its ministers remained in office until a new government could be appointed. Several SED politburo members also resigned, but Krenz remained as general secretary.

Krenz tried to save himself and to keep at least some authority for the SED. In another address to the GDR, he promised to conduct a true reform policy. He denounced Honecker for "political arrogance" and abuse of power, explaining that the politburo decided to remove him because he would not initiate reforms. But Krenz did not impress the East Germans. Another 50,000 East Berliners, including many SED members, demonstrated that same evening, denouncing Krenz for not having gone far enough in his speech.

Christa Wolf, the East German author and human rights activist, began to worry about the number of persons fleeing the GDR. She and Bärbel Bohley appealed for people to remain. Bohley said that she would not leave because "the land belongs to us, not to the government."

But it became increasingly clear that even those who wanted to remain in the GDR would do so only if they were guaranteed the right to leave and to return whenever they wished.[28] Krenz and the SED decided that they had to accommodate the demand for travel, not only in order to respond to the demonstrators but to placate an angry Czech government which wanted Prague no longer to be a rest stop for East German refugees.

Late on Thursday morning, November 9, the GDR ministries for interior and state security finished drafting the text of a law that would ease travel regulations. The new law provided that East Germans could apply for private trips abroad without offering any explanation (such as family reunion) and that the applications would be approved quickly in all but exceptional cases. Travelers could use any border crossing to West Germany or to West Berlin and could receive permits for repeated trips. The legislation was to go into effect the following day, November 10.[29]

The draft next went to Krenz, who was presiding over a meeting of the SED central committee. Krenz glanced at it and liked it. He hoped it would ease the pressure from the streets and would offer a breathing spell for the SED. During an afternoon break in the proceedings, he read the text quickly to the remaining politburo members in the hall and to other central committee members. He got immediate approval.

Late in the afternoon Krenz gave the text to Günter Schabowski, the politburo member and press spokesman, and hurriedly asked him to announce the new law, saying "*Das wird ein Knüller für uns*" ("that'll be a real hit for us"). He did not brief Schabowski on the details of the law or explain that it was not to enter into force until the following day. Schabowski, who had not attended the meeting, did not have time to glance at the text before going into his daily briefing for the German and international press. As usual, most of the briefing concentrated on the situation in the GDR and on the demonstrations.

At the end of the briefing, an Italian journalist asked Schabowski whether the GDR had passed a new travel law yet. Schabowski said that it had done so, permitting East Germans to travel freely. Pressed for details, he scratched around among his papers and found the text. He read it out loud, reiterating that the new law would make it possible for East Germans to travel out of the country at any time and through any border point. He did not stress that people would have to apply for exit permits before they could leave.[30]

The journalists concluded that the GDR would now let people travel freely. Schabowski, no better informed than they, agreed. Tom Brokaw of NBC News asked if this meant the Wall was open. Schabowski said "yes." Asked about the timing of the new rules, Schabowski gave a disorganized reply, which, however, included the key word "*sofort*" ("immediately"). He wondered briefly if anybody had notified the Soviet embassy, for the Soviet occupation authorities remained theoretically responsible for the sector borders. Then, exhausted from the strain of the week's events and not realizing that he had dropped a bombshell, he went home for dinner and a rest.[31]

Although Schabowski did not make his announcement until after 7:00 P.M., both the East and West German evening news broadcasts carried reports based on it. Western media reported excitedly that East Germans could now travel to the West at will. One news service reported that the Wall would open that same evening. East Berliners did not hear the official text, only the news. They did not understand exactly what the new rules might mean, but throughout the evening more and more of them decided to go to the Wall to find out. West Berliners, equally curious, also moved toward the Wall by the thousands. So did western radio and television crews and print reporters.

Such border checkpoints as Bornholmerstrasse and Invalidenstrasse, located north of the center of Berlin and near large East Berlin worker housing complexes, began drawing large crowds. They also drew traffic jams of abandoned or blocked Trabants radiating out as far as ten blocks in all directions. The workers, well versed in the language of the GDR bureaucracy, shouted at the guards in an authoritative tone that they had heard the announcement from SED politburo member Schabowski and now wanted to get through as he had said. The guards had received no authorization to let anyone pass, but knew better than to ignore anything that a politburo member had said.

The guards called their headquarters for guidance, but East German ministries had no instructions either. The GDR caretaker government, in total disarray, had not yet officially promulgated the SED decision. Some border police commanders, not on the scene, proposed pushing the crowds back several hundred meters. The guards said that could not be done, and that they could not ask people to come back the next day because Schabowski had said the border would open immediately. The guards were armed only with their service revolvers and a few machine pistols. They had more guns stored nearby, but feared that the crowd would horse-whip them with their own weapons if they began firing. Reinforcements could not get through the streets jammed with abandoned cars and shouting people.

No guard wanted to be the last "hero of socialism." They all knew that West Germany kept a list of border guards who had fired at refugees. Many had their own private doubts about the regime; some had even joined in resistance marches. All had witnessed the fraying of SED authority, and they were not about to go down fighting.

Around 10:30 P.M., the guards at Bornholmerstrasse let the loudest and most obnoxious demonstrators through. They thought they did it cleverly by stamping exit visas on the workers' identification cards, in effect expelling them as unwanted. But they had not reckoned with western television and radio.

When the "expelled" workers burst into West Berlin, television reporters who had massed around the checkpoint grabbed some to ask what had happened. The workers shouted that they had gotten out and were free to go where they wanted. No one asked to check their identification cards to see that they had been expelled. Brokaw and others announced that the GDR was letting people leave. Within minutes, that news hit every apartment in central Berlin and every home in the GDR. Others wanted to follow those who had gone through.

As the crowds grew larger by the minute, the guards feared for their own safety with people shouting at them and pressing around them ever more insistently and impatiently. Around 11:30 P.M., the guards at Bornholmerstrasse and Invalidenstrasse checkpoints began letting everyone through without even bothering to check or stamp passports or identification cards. They reported to their headquarters that "we are flooded, we have to open up," and "we are being overrun." By midnight, about 20,000 East Berliners had raced out at Bornholmerstrasse alone.[32] Other checkpoints followed suit.

Thousands of West Berliners stood waiting on the other side of the checkpoints. The governing mayor, Walter Momper, himself went out to welcome the East Berliners. Then, as the crowds mingled and confusion spread, some of the younger West Berliners ran into East Berlin. The Western city commandants had to be called out of a dinner at the U.S. commandant's home to instruct West Berlin guards to let West Berliners through. All guards at one checkpoint after another threw up their hands and let everybody go in both directions.

By two minutes after midnight, according to official GDR reports, all checkpoints along the entire border between East and West Berlin had been opened. Even Checkpoint Charlie, officially reserved for foreign visitors, had to let East Berliners out because rebellious throngs of East and West Berliners blocked the checkpoint and the police were afraid that the Soviets or Western occupation powers would protest that they could not get through. In scenes of indescribable chaos, some were shouting "Let us out!" and others "Let us in!" as the guards stood dazed and paralyzed.

East German state authority had ceased to exist along the Wall. Krenz later said that he had personally given instructions that there should be no shooting at the border and that people should be let through. This may be correct; the instructions that finally did reach the checkpoints told the guards to avoid any provocation. But some SED central committee members reported seeing Krenz walking in a daze through the corridors of the central committee building late in the evening not knowing what to do.

Only the Brandenburg Gate remained closed, for it had no crossing point. There the Wall consisted of two parallel lines of concrete slabs laid flat to a height and width of about three meters (almost ten feet) on the western side of the gate. As the proudest part of Walter Ulbricht's *Schutzwall* (protective barrier), it had been officially defined as the key fortification that prevented Western tanks from attacking East Berlin through the Brandenburg Gate. On that night it represented much too tempting a target.

By midnight, hundreds of young Berliners began converging on the gate from opposite directions. The East Berlin police, as uninformed there as elsewhere, tried at first to keep the East Berliners back from the gate and from the Wall itself. They could not, however, stop the West Berliners from coming right up to the concrete barrier and shouting encouragement. Hundreds of East Berliners broke through the police cordon, saying that they wanted only to walk through the gate without even going into West Berlin. Although some of the guards made lame efforts to hose down the crowds on both sides, others permitted them to go up to the Wall. One East Berlin woman in a wheelchair had herself pushed through the gate.

Once at the concrete barriers, the young pulled themselves and each other up. As a final touch, some used the empty water hoses of the police as climbing ropes. Carrying their ever-present boom boxes, they danced on the Wall in the garish glare of the searchlights intended to prevent refugees from scrambling across in the dark. To add rhythm to the dance, some hammered away at the concrete barriers for souvenirs. The police could not clear the area around the Brandenburg Gate until 4:30 in the morning.

Berlin had never seen such a night of cheers and tears. Few slept. Once the East Berliners got into West Berlin, they called friends and relatives. If they had brought a car through the Wall or could get a taxi, they went to the Kurfürstendamm or to the homes of people they knew. Or they merely drove around West Berlin to see in person what they had viewed on television.

Many did not join the party until the early hours of the morning. Some did nothing more than dance and race around aimlessly and joyously for the sheer pleasure of being out. Those who had not seen each other for years embraced and wept. Many visited family and friends in homes they had never seen, or hugged young relatives whom they had never met before.

Only during the course of the following day did the East German government and the SED grasp the full meaning of what had happened. They kept issuing decrees announcing where and when people should apply for exit permits. They even managed to issue some for persons who wanted to leave without risking expulsion. But only a few paid any attention. Krenz understood that they could never close the Wall again without risking an explosion that would destroy the regime, and he let people continue to go where they wished.

In fact, the police opened more crossing points as East Berlin factories and offices operated with skeleton staffs. Everyone had gone to West Berlin. They received DM 100 as "welcoming money" from the West Berlin government and walked or drove around West Berlin to shop and to visit and to look.

By the weekend, millions had gone not only from East Berlin but from all over East Germany. They too wanted mainly to see people and sights they had not seen for a long time if ever. They bought things they could never buy at home. None could afford the luxury goods on the Kurfürstendamm, and most bought only a few items to show where they had been and what they had done. Grandmothers stood before fruit kiosks in the markets, weeping uncontrollably at the thought that they could finally bring bananas and pineapples home to their grandchildren.

After a generation, the Berliners had forced the Wall to yield. All the feelings pent up for almost thirty years burst forth. And everyone, from the highest world leaders to the East German workers holding their nieces and nephews for the first time, knew that nothing would ever be the same again.

WHY THE REVOLT?

The Western occupation powers had decided during the early 1960s that the Germans themselves should deal with the German question. They thus made West Germany responsible for finding—and accepting—a solution on their behalf.

This seemed like a sensible policy. The basic European framework held. Germany remained divided, giving the United States and the Soviet Union the bases they wanted in Europe and giving France, Great Britain and other European states no reason to worry about a German revival. No one needed to find a way through the central European diplomatic labyrinth or face the political and emotional nightmares that the German question could arouse.

Although the Germans had not yet learned how to take charge of their own destiny during the 1960s, they began increasingly to do so during the 1970s and 1980s. West Germany, the stronger partner, learned its lesson well. It embraced East Germany, appearing to support it but actually overwhelming it by giving its people a sense for the world beyond the SED. The GDR felt safe behind the

Wall, but the physical *Abgrenzung* that Ulbricht had achieved actually reinforced the yearning for unity in East Germany.

On November 9, 1989, the East Germans acted: not the government, but the people. They burst through the Wall. Exasperated by forty-five years of communism after twelve years of Nazism, they decided that they had known enough dictatorship. They seized control of the struggle over Germany, taking charge in ways that the occupation powers had not expected or wanted. They tore the German question open again.

Few thought this could or would happen. The GDR had acted the part of a solid communist state so well that the breach of the Wall surprised even the most sophisticated observers. George Kennan wrote in early 1989 that he expected Germany to remain divided and the Wall to remain in place for quite some time yet.[33] He had not realized that his own containment policy had worked. Egon Bahr expected the same.[34] One American expert on East Germany wrote about "the perils of success" for the GDR in 1989, even as it was about to collapse.[35] Some West German visitors to the GDR praised the material and even the political progress that they thought they saw.[36] Only Vernon Walters, the U.S. Ambassador to Germany in 1989, openly predicted that the GDR could not survive the end of the Brezhnev Doctrine.[37] And Schabowski observed in retrospect that a system which collapsed as soon as its people could travel freely would deserve whatever fate it suffered.[38]

In the SED's meticulously constructed realm of falsehood, outsiders could not see—or could choose not to see—what the regime wanted to conceal. They could not see the vast open-pit brown coal mines gouged hundreds of feet into the earth, nor the black soot nor the asthmatic and deformed children for miles around. They could not see, or they could choose to ignore, the crumbling facades of what had once been handsome buildings. They could not, or would not, see the corroded plumbing that obliged everyone living above the ground floor to go down to common toilets and common baths in the basement. They did not have to stand in line for hours to buy the simplest necessities for their families; nor did they have to wait fifteen years for a car or ten years for a telephone or three years for a refrigerator (if they were deemed loyal enough to have them at all). Visitors could say that material conditions had improved, but they did not make the invidious comparisons with West Germany that the East Germans made. They did not try to look behind the facade that they were shown. And they did not hear the workers say, "We pretend to work and they pretend to pay us."

Foreigners did not have to endure the pervasive suffocation. They could not imagine how it felt to hear incessant SED propaganda while watching a free German society only a border away. They could not understand how workers felt to see training programs and universities reserved for the children of the party and state elite, or how it felt to be constantly confronted with a corrupt and callous bureaucracy. They could not know how young people felt when they could not choose their jobs or careers or even their music and when their lives were governed by a Stasi *Gesellschaftliche Beurteilung* (political evaluation) file that they could not even see. Foreigners could joke about surveillance but did not have to fear it.

Most important, foreigners did not have to worry about whether they could leave. They did not face the prospect of having their children and their children's children live under the SED. They could not understand the hatred of the Wall because they could cross it. They could not grasp the passionate demand for fresh air, a demand that would finally sweep away not only the divided Germany but also the divided Europe fashioned at Yalta.

Even Gorbachev did not expect the system to fall. He, like other outsiders, did not foresee that the East Germans would ultimately revolt against an accumulation of hypocrisy and suppression. Like other outsiders, he did not realize how much the SED had become a stranger in its own land, demanding constant sacrifice, unquestioning obedience and a vow of silence in exchange for petty and selective favors. The East German people would no longer accept that. They wanted the same democracy that the West Germans had. They would no longer wear a political and economic hairshirt. In pent-up anger and deep frustration, they chose revolt.

A revolt. A German revolt, long considered an oxymoron in East and West. A peaceful revolt, derided by Lenin. A new kind of revolt, not like those of 1953 or 1956 or 1968. The only kind of revolt that could succeed against tanks and teargas.

The marchers in Leipzig rebelled with every step they took. All knew that the SED had endorsed the Chinese repression at Tienanmen Square. All knew and feared the risks they faced. And yet they came and they lit candles and they prayed and they sang and they walked. They may not have felt like rebels, but that is what they were. The candle-bearers in Leipzig and the rock fans in Berlin shared a common purpose with those who wanted to break through the Wall. Together, they brought about a revolution.

The East Germans perceived the Wall as the French revolutionaries of 1789 had perceived the Bastille, as both the main instrument and the main symbol of the regime. The hated stones had to go. Many had pushed against those stones all their lives, with their thoughts if not with their arms. Their obsession finally made the Wall a liability instead of an asset for the SED. Krenz understood this, but too late. He hoped that a new travel law would permit the GDR to survive, but the law brought down the regime instead of saving it.

During the night of November 9, 1989, the East Berliners wrote as sure an end to the old order as the Parisians had done 200 years and four months before. And, like those Parisians, they did not know and did not really care what would come next.

NINETEEN

PUTTING GERMANY TOGETHER AGAIN

THE BERLINERS WHO DANCED AND CHEERED ON THE WALL STIRRED up not only dust and mortar. They also stirred up the ancient fears of Germany and of the *Furor Teutonicus*, fears that had never been far below the surface even among Germany's allies during the Cold War. Like a dark monster crawling from its tomb, the image of a powerful and potentially dominant Germany arose again before the chancelleries and peoples of Europe and the world.

Germans, defeated and divided, had been under some control. Now they might escape from that control. They might unite. They might cut the ties they had established with those they had needed. And they might try once again to rule over others. The long peace might end.

Different countries felt these fears to different degrees. Those closest to Germany, often those with the most painful memories, felt them most intensely. Those farther away felt them less. But all knew that they faced a new situation and that they would have to find new ways to protect their interests and, some feared, perhaps their borders.

At first, none knew what to do. Should the occupiers try to regain control of Germany? But how? And at what cost? Should Germans be permitted to unite if they wished? If so, on what terms? Should others unite against the Germans? Or should they tighten their links to Germany and hope for the best?

KOHL TAKES CONTROL

The most immediate attention focused on East Germany. What, if anything, could and should be done there? The GDR faced an existential crisis. The breach of the Wall had shattered its authority. Hans Modrow, who became GDR premier on November 13, 1989, would have to reestablish that authority. If he could not, Gorbachev might have to. Otherwise, West Germany might absorb the GDR.

The destruction of the Wall thus set off a battle for control over East Germany among Modrow, Mikhail Gorbachev and Helmut Kohl. The winner would hold the key to the future of Germany and of Europe.

Gorbachev faced the most difficult decisions. He had to evaluate the situation carefully before he moved. His predecessors had passed the administration of East Germany to the SED in 1949. They had intended the GDR to compete with the Federal Republic. That had now failed. The GDR had never established a sense of identity, and West German influence had grown over the years. The GDR had been forced to permit more travel and more openings to the West in order to get West German credits. Honecker had paid a high price for the "coalition of reason." Could and should that policy now be reversed for a return to *Abgrenzung?*

Gorbachev had wanted Perestroika in East Germany because he thought that a reformed GDR could compete more effectively with the West. He had wanted Honecker out. But he had not expected the GDR to collapse. Now, the SED had let Moscow's strategic barrier at the Wall crumble without even telling Gorbachev in advance. And neither the SED nor Gorbachev had prepared any plans to deal with that contingency.

Although Gorbachev had congratulated Egon Krenz for permitting open travel and had not tried to tell him to close the Wall again, he feared that the breakout could lead to chaos in Berlin. He did not want to be forced to call on Soviet forces to restore order. On November 10, when he heard that the governing mayor of Berlin had called a rally in front of the West Berlin city hall and that Brandt and Kohl were to speak there, Gorbachev wanted to warn them not to say anything that might incite disorder.[1] His ambassador in Bonn, Yuli Kvitsinsky, had reached Brandt in advance but could not reach Kohl because the chancellor had interrupted a trip to Poland in order to fly to Berlin and was still on an American military aircraft from Hamburg when Kvitsinsky tried to reach him. Kvitsinsky could only get Gorbachev's message to Horst Teltschik, who went with Kohl to the city hall, and he could only reach Teltschik as the chancellor was about to speak.

Kvitsinsky told Teltschik that Gorbachev had received intelligence reports about potential riots in Berlin and feared trouble. Teltschik said that the situation remained very calm and that Gorbachev had no reason for concern. He added that those who started such rumors probably had sinister motives.

Teltschik then passed a note to Kohl, but Kohl needed it no more than Brandt. Both spoke in measured terms, welcoming the end of the Wall but not trying to provoke any action by the crowd.

Nonetheless, both Brandt and Kohl said some things that Gorbachev could not like. They specifically pointed out that the breach of the Wall had opened prospects for German unification. Brandt said that nothing would ever again be as it had been, and he added: *"Jetzt wächst zusammen was zusammengehört"* ("what belongs together is now growing together").[2] Whereas this did not incite the chaos that Gorbachev feared, it did make Brandt's expectations and preferences very clear. Kohl spoke along the same lines, although without any such specific phrase.

During the following weeks, Gorbachev tried several steps in order to regain some control over the situation in East Germany. He pinned his main longer-term hopes on Modrow, a personal friend who wanted to carry out an East German Perestroika.

As a first step, however, Gorbachev sent Valentin Falin, who had become head of the international department of the CPSU, to visit Berlin, study the situation, and make recommendations. Falin consulted with Soviet military and civilian officials as well as with East German leaders.

Falin wanted to establish a crisis staff and recommended that the Soviet Union close the Wall again, using as many as 1 million troops if necessary to reassert control over its occupation zone.[3] Gorbachev recoiled. He feared a bloodbath in East Germany and the end of Perestroika as the world returned to the darkest days of the Cold War. Gorbachev would not use force unless he had to. Falin later denied making such draconian proposals. He complained that Gorbachev put some of his recommendations into a private safe without reading them because the Soviet leader knew they would go far beyond anything he wanted even to consider.[4]

Whatever Falin may have recommended, a fierce debate over German policy erupted in Moscow. Shevardnadze later told Teltschik that the debate went on until the end of January, with some senior military officers wanting to intervene massively while others did not. Shevardnadze confirmed that Falin had recommended intervention.[5]

Some Soviet officials thought that they might be able to use West German interest in the GDR to get West Germany out of NATO, to get a confederation of the two German states and perhaps to get more German funds. Some wanted to make an arrangement with the SPD for new European security structures that would replace NATO and the Warsaw Pact. Kvitsinsky, fearing that the GDR might not survive an open border, urged Gorbachev immediately to propose a confederation of the two German states in order to stay ahead of events. But

Gorbachev, caught between conflicting expert views and still hoping for Mod-row's success, did not want to write off the GDR so quickly. He had also had a telephone conversation with Kohl in which the two had agreed on the impor-tance of "stability." But Gorbachev had understood this to mean that Kohl would not try to unite Germany, whereas Kohl had understood it to mean that German unification should not lead to European instability.[6]

Kohl wanted to work out an accommodation with Moscow over East Ger-many. He tried several times to see Gorbachev between November 1989 and January 1990. But once again Gorbachev did not want to see him. Kvitsinsky told Teltschik in January 1990 that Gorbachev had canceled all foreign appoint-ments. Although a number of other foreign and domestic crises might have forced Gorbachev to stay in Moscow, the German problem clearly ranked at or near the top. He did not want to meet with Kohl until he knew what to say.[7] He feared the Soviet military, telling Mitterrand in December that "In case of Ger-man unification, there will be a two-line announcement that a Soviet marshal has taken my place."[8]

Trying various maneuvers, Gorbachev accepted Falin's less drastic recom-mendation that the Soviet ambassador in East Berlin call a meeting of the four World War II powers in the old Allied Control Council headquarters in Berlin. Those ambassadors retained the residual authority of the former occupation commanders and high commissioners. Gorbachev proposed that they discuss how best to deal with the new situation in Germany.

Margaret Thatcher and François Mitterrand wanted to accept Gorbachev's invitation; George Bush did not. In order to placate his allies, Bush agreed to send his ambassador but limited the agenda to an old proposal for improving Berlin's status as an international conference and visitor center. When Soviet ambassador Vyacheslav Kochemasov proposed regular meetings of the four am-bassadors to deal with the German question, American ambassador Vernon Walters persuaded his British and French colleagues to reject that suggestion on the spot.

Bush refused to send Walters or anyone else to any further quadripartite meetings. Walters himself, disgusted by the Soviet effort to recapture the au-thority that the Allied occupiers had held forty years earlier, described a picture taken of the four ambassadors after their meeting as "the worst photograph I have ever seen."[9] Kohl and Genscher did not even want the meeting held, agree-ing to it only after Bush and his secretary of state James Baker had assured them that nothing would happen there.[10]

Soviet officials continued to ask for four-power sessions, requesting them six times within three weeks. Shevardnadze himself asked twice, but Bush and Baker rejected every request.[11] Gorbachev himself tried another tack in January, asking

Bush and Baker to agree to a four-power foreign ministers' meeting. When Baker asked Kohl about it, Kohl said that "we do not need four midwives." Bush then turned down Gorbachev's suggestion. Like Kohl, he saw no reason to go back to a format that had failed even when Germany was still under occupation and that now risked delaying a process that seemed to be moving on its own.[12]

Bush himself had long favored German unification. He had already begun to see it coming in 1988 and had it in mind when he proposed at Mainz in the spring of 1989 that Germany and the United States should be "partners in leadership." After the breakdown of the Wall, he had expected that unification would come sooner rather than later.[13] To confirm his thoughts, he had invited former secretary of state Henry Kissinger to meet with him in Washington. Kissinger told Bush that German unification had become "inevitable" and that the United States should not obstruct it. Kissinger warned that a "two-Germany" policy would be "disastrous" and that any failure to support Kohl and unification would give Gorbachev a golden opportunity to make his own arrangement with Kohl and to destroy NATO.[14]

Moscow did indeed test the waters for a direct agreement with Kohl. Nikolai Portugalov, one of Falin's associates, asked Teltschik on November 21 if Kohl might be ready to make an agreement with Moscow for German unification through a confederation. Portugalov stressed that Soviet officials wanted to keep the pace of change in Germany under control. Perhaps hinting at another exclusive German-Soviet deal like the Rapallo Treaty of 1922, he said that the Soviet Union could offer a more favorable peace treaty than those offered by others and especially by London and Paris.[15] He offered a number of options and asked for a German reaction.

Portugalov got the opposite of what he had wanted. Teltschik, who later wrote that he had been "electrified" by Portugalov's approach, did not recommend that Kohl make a deal directly with Moscow. Instead, he saw Portugalov's visit as the first sign that Moscow might accept German unification. He recommended that Kohl move quickly to establish his own terms for unity, as Kohl did.[16]

Gorbachev wanted to use Modrow and some SED reforms to revive GDR authority. He invited Modrow to Moscow in early December. But the meeting could not have encouraged Gorbachev. Modrow, a decent but limited man, was well beyond his depth. He needed cash and domestic credibility, not a show of Soviet support. Gorbachev could give him neither.

Not wanting to use Soviet forces, Gorbachev could only hope that Modrow might succeed. He himself had nothing to offer. He even had to instruct Kvitsinsky to ask Kohl for emergency food relief to prevent mass starvation in the Soviet Union itself. Kohl granted the food gladly, sending hundreds of thousands of tons of meat, but it went without saying that he expected something in return.

Ignoring Kvitsinsky's recommendation, Gorbachev encouraged Modrow to try to seize the initiative on the German question by proposing an inner-German *Vertragsgemeinschaft*, a "treaty community" under which the two Germanys would remain separate states but would expand their ties through a wide range of agreements. In a tough talk with Genscher on December 5, Gorbachev said categorically that unification was "not on the agenda." He insisted that the GDR would remain independent and a member of the Warsaw Pact.[17]

Modrow tried hard to get his government accepted. He had the GDR constitution changed to abolish the "leading role" of the SED. He forced Krenz to resign as head of state and chairman of the national defense council. He tried to polish the image of the Stasi, first giving it a new name (with the unfortunate acronym NASI) and then trying to limit its functions. The SED also changed its name, to *Partei des Demokratischen Sozialismus* (Party of Democratic Socialism, hereafter PDS), hoping to sound like the old SPD which it had obliterated.

Trying to widen his political base, Modrow began a series of meetings with East German opposition groups. Those meetings, called "the Round Table" because all members had an equal voice, tried to make decisions about the future of the GDR. They briefly became the nominal source of political authority in East Germany. They scheduled elections for a new East German parliament, the Volkskammer, for May 6, 1990, giving Modrow six months to show the people a new face and giving the opposition groups time to organize.

But the Round Table proved unable to summon forth a new mood between the East German authorities and the people. It did not force Modrow to clean out the entire SED politburo or the East German government and thus had to work through a universally despised GDR/SED bureaucracy. It soon became ineffective.

Even a reformer could not legitimize the GDR. The SED apparatus, firmly opposed to change, did not follow Modrow's instructions. Almost 60,000 persons left East Germany during December with even more (estimates ran as high as 100,000) leaving in January. The East German economy suffered a steep decline as factories had to stop or slow their work. Modrow's futile campaigns for more production made him sound like his predecessors. The government ground to a halt for lack of funds, direction or support.

The East German people did not believe that Modrow introduced reforms as fast as he should. Having been forced to live in austerity, they were shocked by revelations about SED corruption and about the luxurious lifestyles of senior SED figures. They watched in disgust as the discredited government apparatus clung to its positions and privileges. They began using the D-mark instead of the East German Mark for many commercial and personal transactions and for any services not contracted with the state. More important, they began looking to Bonn, not East Berlin, for political authority.

By December, more and more banners at East German demonstrations proclaimed "*Deutschland einig Vaterland*" ("Germany, united fatherland") or "*Wir sind ein Volk*" ("We are one people") instead of the earlier "*Wir sind das Volk*" ("We are the people"). Marchers increasingly shouted for one Germany. While Modrow touted a "treaty association" with West Germany, the people began calling for unification.

Modrow's moment of truth came during a meeting with Kohl in Dresden on December 19, 1989. The two men had a long talk which reflected Modrow's increasingly desperate political and economic situation and led to nothing. After their talk, they walked together to the ruins of the bombed-out Frauenkirche for a public meeting and a speech by the chancellor. Tens of thousands along their route waved West German flags and shouted for unification. A crowd of 200,000 greeted Kohl enthusiastically. Although, as Teltschik reported, most of them listened to Kohl's speech thoughtfully and quietly rather than with unbridled enthusiasm, the very size of the rally showed their interest in West Germany. Kohl tried to avoid arousing hopes for early unity, stressing that Germans needed to show self-control and patience. He ended his speech with a somber "God bless our German fatherland." The crowd, deeply moved, responded with calls for German unity. Modrow, who had gone to watch the rally on television, was forgotten. Kohl concluded that unification could come much faster than he had expected and that dealing with Modrow would be useless.[18]

The same thing happened on December 22, when Kohl and Modrow jointly presided over a ceremony in Berlin for the opening of a pedestrian crossing through the Brandenburg Gate. The occasion turned into another humiliation for Modrow as the crowd paid attention only to the chancellor.

By Christmas, 1989, officials of the West German government found that the GDR no longer functioned. The West Berlin city government even had to take over garbage collection in East Berlin. East German officials attended meetings and negotiated agreements but could not carry them out. On January 15, 1990, thousands of East Berliners stormed and sacked Stasi headquarters. SED and GDR government authority broke down completely. On January 28, the Round Table had to move forward the parliamentary elections from May 6 to March 18 because no one could pretend to govern any longer. Modrow had to plead for West German funds even as he insisted that there could be no unification.

As Modrow faltered, foreign and domestic pressures upon Gorbachev grew faster and stronger than he had expected, especially as the Moscow debate intensified.

A speech that Shevardnadze made to the European Parliament on December 19, 1989, reflected the state of the Moscow debate. Shevardnadze wanted to hint at the possibility of German unification but to make clear that Moscow needed some assurances about what unification would mean. He posed a number of questions reflecting the issues under debate. How might German unity affect the stability of Europe? Would Germany accept established borders? What would happen to European military structures? What about non-German military forces on German soil? And how could the Helsinki process and CSCE continue? Would a German peace settlement be part of a new European framework?[19] Shevardnadze's questions showed that the CPSU debate had become so fluid that he could not pose Moscow's wishes as clear conditions but could only indicate where Moscow would need some answers.

By the end of January, Gorbachev had to make a decision. Soviet forces in East Germany suffered severe morale problems because they no longer understood their mission. Mitterrand and especially Thatcher feared a rush to German unification and pressed Gorbachev to prevent it because they could not openly oppose it themselves. Gorbachev's advisers complained that West Germany's European allies wanted Moscow to play the heavy by blocking unification but that they would not support him if he did.[20] And it became eminently clear that Modrow could not hold the GDR together.

By January 26, 1990, Gorbachev decided that he had to act. He convened a meeting to discuss Soviet policy toward Germany. The usual debate flared between Falin, who still wanted to preserve the GDR, and Gorbachev's adviser Anatoly Chernyayev, who wanted to make a deal that would guarantee lasting friendship with a united Germany. Some others among Gorbachev's advisers, like Alexander Yakovlev, also favored unification although they hoped that it could be negotiated with the SPD. Shevardnadze tried to take a middle position, pointing out that the GDR no longer functioned but that "one should not give everything to Kohl." Chernyayev favored an early agreement while Moscow still had some leverage and the GDR had not imploded completely.

Gorbachev decided that Chernyayev had analyzed the situation correctly. Modrow and the "new" GDR had not established a political base for keeping an independent East Germany. Nor could they ever do it. And the SPD was not in power in Bonn.[21] Once again, Gorbachev had no choice but to deal with Kohl.

Kohl had slowly but surely begun to dictate the agenda and to guide relations between the two Germanys. But he had to move carefully. Even if he could increasingly determine the course of events, he needed to watch his pace. The Germans had come some distance since 1945, when they had forfeited the right to decide their own future. But, even four decades after the war, they had not regained full authority over their own fate.

Kohl had two audiences, the East German people and the outside world. The former wanted him to promise early unification with freedom and prosperity. But Kohl's international audience did not want the ugly domineering German of old. Foreign leaders watched him closely, ready to launch a barrage of criticism at the first sign of hasty or reckless action.

The East German people understood and accepted Kohl's delicate situation. Most of them desperately yearned for change, wanting to move faster than outsiders would allow. But they had developed enough political sophistication to act with restraint. They already had some of the advantages of unity, being able to buy at least some West German goods and enjoying the kinds of freedoms they had not known in decades. They gave Kohl time to seize the moment without provoking a crisis with the Allies or others. Kohl, who had a veteran politician's understanding for popular attitudes and for the art of the possible, could feel confident that the situation would evolve in his favor if he did not push it.

Kohl made his first overt move on November 28, after Teltschik's meeting with Portugalov. Speaking to the Bundestag, he outlined a program for Germany's future, proposing the following ten points:

1. To institute measures to ease travel between East and West Germany.
2. To expand technical cooperation with the GDR, as in environmental protection, railroads, communications.
3. To expand economic aid to the GDR if the GDR changed its political and economic system irreversibly, meaning truly free elections with no SED monopoly on power.
4. To establish a "treaty community" with the GDR to cooperate on common problems.
5. To proceed, after free elections in the GDR. to develop "confederative structures" between the two German states leading eventually to a federal system for all of Germany through a policy of "small steps."
6. To embed the process of inner-German relations "in the all-European process and in East-West relations."
7. To encourage the European Community to open itself to a democratic GDR and "other democratic countries in central and south-eastern Europe."
8. To speed up the development of the CSCE, perhaps including new institutions for East-West economic and environmental cooperation.
9. To support rapid progress in arms control.
10. To strive for a "peace order" that would allow German unification as one state without disrupting existing arrangements, and that would take into

consideration the interests of all parties concerned so as to guarantee peace and stability in Europe.[22]

Kohl dealt very carefully with the most sensitive issues. Refusing to define unification in a way that might provoke a reaction, he said that "nobody today knows what a reunited Germany will ultimately look like." He paid lip service to the "treaty community" and to "confederative structures" (not to a "confederation"), leaving all options open. But he added that "I am sure that unity will come if the people in Germany want it."

Kohl set German unity as his goal, not only because he wanted it but also because he did not want other Germans to attack him for failing to pursue it. Yet he had to make sure that unity threatened no other state enough to provoke too much resistance too soon. He wanted to fix a goal but to keep the timetable and the course flexible.

In his speech, Kohl combined clarity and obfuscation. He gave the East German public an objective, one that he hoped would reduce the numbers moving to West Germany every day. He also gave his coalition partners, the CSU and the FDP, a general plan for the future. Although he subsumed other proposals, he suggested no specific steps that others could block. He issued a broad pledge, not a detailed plan.

Kohl did not consult with anyone except Teltschik before issuing his ten-point plan. He knew that even his most loyal foreign supporter, George Bush, would want to offer suggestions that he might not be able to accept. He also knew that the other former occupiers would resent any German proposal because they still formally reserved their right to solve the German question.

Kohl knew which occupier would support him and which would not. He had given instructions that the speech should go to Bush even as he read it to the Bundestag. Teltschik then briefed the ambassadors of the other occupation powers after Kohl had read the speech. Kohl followed up by speaking to Bush for half an hour the next day, urging the president to use his upcoming summit with Gorbachev at Malta to support Kohl's plan. Bush agreed.

Kohl also had to keep his domestic friends and foes at bay. He did not tell Genscher about the ten points because he knew that the foreign minister had a breakfast meeting with the press that same morning and might announce the essence of the ten points as his own program. He also feared that Genscher might offer amendments to water down the thrust of the proposal.

Having issued his plan, Kohl used the next months to line up German and foreign support. He felt under some pressure, for a number of observers predicted that half a million East Germans would move to West Germany if they saw no prospect for early unity.[23] His ten points had gained a little time, but he needed to do more.

Kohl began to exercise growing influence in East Germany by establishing political groups to represent CDU interests there and to win East German support for his ten-point plan. The East German CDU and FDP withdrew from their forced alliance with the SED and began to open links to the West German parties. They used West German political funds to reorganize and strengthen themselves in the GDR and began calling for a social market economy along West German lines as well as for German unity.

Internationally, Kohl tried mainly to make other leaders feel that he recognized their concerns even as he kept the agenda in his own hands. He consistently rejected any and all efforts to return to a four-power format, but he listened carefully to suggestions from any of the former occupation powers even when he disagreed. He paid less attention to others, relying on Genscher to parry those who hoped that they could bargain about Germany's future. For example, when the Italian foreign minister, Giulio Andreotti, proposed a peace conference (in which Italy would sit among the victors) and asked Genscher to brief him about the state of play on Germany, Genscher—who recalled that Italy and Andreotti had opposed German unification—curtly told him "you are not a part of the game."[24]

Kohl seized the opportunities offered at a NATO summit on December 4 and a European Council meeting on December 8 to stress the German commitment to existing institutions and to the interests of Germany's allies and partners. Both meetings began with considerable skepticism about German unification and showed that even at the end Kohl had not won over all the doubters. They also showed the importance of American help, as U.S. support for unification led some of those doubters to support Kohl. After long private discussions, NATO and EC leaders voiced their initial if still tentative approval for German unification.

Kohl realized that he had to put on a show of cooperation with Modrow even as the GDR crumbled, and he thus had a lengthy talk with the GDR premier at the time of their meeting in Dresden on December 19. But the talk must not have satisfied Modrow. He warned against the risk of instability in East Germany and asked Kohl for a "contribution" of DM 15 billion. He complained that the discussion about unification had become unrealistic. Kohl agreed only to inner-German financial negotiations, rejecting Modrow's unilateral demands. His finance minister, Theo Waigel, then led the West German delegation to talks that opened on January 12, 1990. Kohl and Waigel did not promise specific aid levels but pledged support for the GDR in general terms. They did so to stem refugee flight and to show Gorbachev that Kohl would deal with Modrow, not because they saw any reason to prop up the GDR.

Gorbachev had realized even before his January 26 meeting that his gamble on Modrow was failing. He must have felt bitterly disappointed that even Modrow, his main hope for the GDR, could not credibly establish himself. Vadim Zagladin, one of Gorbachev's foreign policy advisers, had already told West German development minister Jürgen Warnke on January 18 that the Soviets saw German unification as inevitable.[25] When Modrow came to Moscow for a second visit on January 30, 1990, Gorbachev told him to abandon his "treaty association" proposal in favor of the gradual development of a German "confederation." Once Modrow made that proposal in public after returning to East Berlin, Kohl knew that Gorbachev had written off the GDR.

It remained for Gorbachev himself to clarify the Soviet stand directly to Kohl. To do that, he invited Kohl to visit Moscow at the beginning of February. Coincidentally, James Baker had visited Moscow just before Kohl and had brought Gorbachev a message from George Bush strongly urging German unification. Before leaving Moscow, Baker sent Kohl an upbeat report on his meeting with Gorbachev. Bush also sent Kohl a letter of his own, advising the chancellor that the president favored a united Germany. Kohl thus knew that he had strong U.S. support.

Gorbachev told Kohl in their private meeting that the Soviet Union, the GDR and the Federal Republic now agreed about unity and about the right of the German people to strive for it. The Germans had to decide for themselves what kind of state they wanted and how they wanted to get it. The people of East and West Germany had already shown that they had learned the lessons of history and that war would no longer come from German soil. Gorbachev added that border questions needed to be solved, for he regarded them as fundamental.

Gorbachev reminded Kohl that the GDR had made certain economic commitments to the Soviet Union and that those needed to be fulfilled if Perestroika was to succeed. He also said that, while the German people could choose to unite, they still had to negotiate the conditions for unity.[26] He then said that he accepted Kohl's invitation for another visit to Germany and looked forward to a meeting at the chancellor's home in the Palatinate.

Teltschik, who participated in the private meeting along with Chernyayev, reported that Kohl broke open the champagne for the German delegation on their way home from Moscow. They had achieved the breakthrough that they had wanted: Gorbachev had agreed to German unification. Within a few days, Modrow accepted Kohl's invitation to negotiate economic and monetary union.[27]

With Modrow's days numbered, the March 18 election became crucial to the future of the GDR. The East German CDU and its allies tried to appeal to what they hoped would be the wishes of the East German people for unity. They called for rapid unification by absorbing the East German *Länder* into the Federal Republic under Article 23 of the Basic Law. That article, written precisely for this purpose, had already been used to bring the Saarland back into Germany. In contrast, the East German SPD and its allies called for a much longer route which would use Article 146. Under that provision, East and West Germany would first negotiate for a new constitution and would then go through some form of confederation before uniting. The SPD wanted to use this process to transfer East German social legislation to the new united Germany.

Kohl campaigned hard in East Germany, holding a number of huge electoral rallies and often addressing several hundred thousand people at a time. He promised that unification would bring *"blühende Landschaften"* (flourishing landscapes) to East Germany. The polls, nonetheless, still showed the SPD—which had been the majority party in eastern Germany before World War II—with a substantial lead. If it won, Kohl could not be sure of setting the agenda and the drive for unification would slow.

But the SPD had made a strategic mistake. Except for Brandt, who became the lone SPD figure urging unity, party leaders showed no enthusiasm for unification.[28] Some SPD spokesmen, including the West German chancellor candidate, Oskar Lafontaine, even said that it might be best for the two Germanys to go their separate ways for quite a while longer. And many East Germans thought that the SPD had become too cozy with the SED in issuing their joint declarations during the 1980s.

To the surprise of many observers, the CDU won decisively on March 18. Firmly wishing unification, the East Germans gave the CDU and its allies 48 percent of the votes and 193 seats in a new Volkskammer. The SPD won only 22 percent and the PDS 16 percent. East German CDU leader Lothar de Maizière became the new premier of the GDR. He chose to govern in coalition with the East German SPD in order to have the widest possible political base for the negotiations on German unity. This continued to give the SPD some influence.

The original East German resistance groups won virtually no support in the elections. They had ideas and ideals, but they could not organize politically. They wanted reform rather than unification and they could not compromise with each other for a common program that could win widespread support.[29] Although they had led the revolution against the GDR and the SED, they were to play more of an intellectual than a political role in the new Germany that was to follow.

Gorbachev could read the election returns as well as anyone. He recognized that Kohl had won the battle for East Germany. The Soviet army might have been able to regain control but at repellent cost. The people of East Germany wanted unity and would follow Kohl.

Gorbachev now had to find a way to trade the GDR to Helmut Kohl at the highest possible price. Kohl later said that Gorbachev might not have liked the ten points but could not stop them. Kohl had seized what he termed "*Das Gesetz des Handelns*" (control of the situation).[30] In a relaxed mood, he told Baker that "everybody is confused except myself."[31]

THE OCCUPATION POWERS
SET CONFLICTING TERMS

No matter how much the East German people may have wanted unification, they could not bring it about by themselves. They could make their wishes clear and count on Kohl to support them. But the four occupation powers would, if they insisted, have the last word. And they could set the terms.

Washington led the way in urging German unification. Robert Zoellick, counselor at the State Department and Baker's closest adviser, had already written to Baker in mid-1989 that the United States should take the lead on the issue. Bush became the first leader of any occupation power to advocate a united Germany. He told a journalist on September 18, 1989, that he did not "fear" German unity. He added that he did not accept the notion that German unification might be detrimental to European peace. At the end of November, after the breach of the Wall, he told another journalist that "the people of Germany" should decide this matter.[32]

But Bush and Baker did not want to jeopardize Gorbachev's position. As Bush prepared for his December summit with the Soviet leader in Malta, he decided that he would not try to force the pace of unification. He said at the Malta meeting that he had not wanted to "complicate" Gorbachev's life and added: "That's why I have not jumped up and down on the Berlin Wall." Gorbachev said that he had noted that and had appreciated it. Bush also added, however, that he believed that the Soviet Union should accept the changes going on in Germany. Gorbachev, still in the midst of a brutal debate at home, did not challenge Bush, who concluded that the Soviet leader might agree to unification on terms that Bush would consider acceptable.[33]

Bush also believed that the United States had clear interests in the outcome of the unification process. Preparing for the NATO council meeting immediately after the Malta summit, he decided to include the following four points on Germany in his NATO statement:

1. Self-determination must be pursued without prejudice to the outcome.
2. Unification should occur in the context of Germany's continued commitment to NATO and the European Community and with due regard to the roles and responsibilities of the four Allied powers.
3. Moves toward unification must be peaceful, gradual, and part of a step-by-step process.
4. NATO should reiterate its support for the principles of the CSCE Helsinki Final Act with respect to borders.[34]

Bush's four points addressed two issues that Kohl had not listed in his ten points: that united Germany be a NATO member and that Germany had to make a commitment to respect existing borders. Bush wanted to address those points because he saw them as central to U.S. interests. Germany's continuing NATO membership would include a united Germany in a transatlantic structure that would make it unnecessary for Germany to develop an independent deterrent. And a commitment to the inviolability of European borders would reassure Poland that a united Germany would not challenge the Oder-Neisse line. Bush wanted his four points to provide some cover for Kohl's ten points but to go beyond them as well.

Bush especially believed that only a secure and united Germany solidly anchored in Western organizations would provide lasting stability for eastern Europe and over all of Europe. He also wished to protect the global strategic position that the United States and the West as a whole had gained in Europe through NATO and through American forces and bases in Germany. Bush favored German unity but not at the expense of the American and Western position in Europe. He would not agree to a neutral Germany wandering between two worlds any more than most of his predecessors or most Germans.

Bush reiterated his interest in NATO during a meeting with Mitterrand in December. He insisted that Germany's transatlantic relationships should be given at least as much weight as the European Community and CSCE relationships that Mitterrand espoused. He added that he wanted U.S. forces to remain in Europe as part of NATO forces. Baker reinforced the importance of NATO during a speech in Berlin on December 11.[35]

Before Kohl met with Gorbachev in February 1990, Bush sent Kohl a letter listing the main American objectives in a way that would support Kohl but also remind him of American interests: first, Germans should have the right to express their own choice; second, a united Germany should remain in NATO although a "special military status" might be acceptable for the former GDR; and, third, U.S. forces should remain in Germany although Soviet forces should leave.[36]

Once again, as with the four points, Bush wanted German unity but something else as well. He did not want Kohl to sign a Rapallo-style agreement in Moscow. Although he did not know why Gorbachev had invited Kohl, he had to fear that the Soviet leader might offer unity at the expense of Germany's existing commitments to the West. Although Bush believed that Kohl probably would reject such an offer, he feared that the German public—and especially the East Germans—might find it hard to resist. Bush needed to make clear that the United States and the West as a whole had a wider interest than German unity. No matter how confident he might be that Kohl agreed with that, Bush wanted to reinforce the message before Kohl met with Gorbachev.[37]

Bush and Baker also tried to design the format under which German unity should be negotiated. Bush thought that the four-power format that Gorbachev, Mitterrand and especially Thatcher favored had become obsolete. Nor did he want an unwieldy conference of all thirty-five CSCE members, fearing that it would delay unification and let every minor European state make petty claims.

Bush and Baker decided to propose a formula that would give each of the main interested parties a voice in the future of Germany without excessive complications. Zoellick suggested a Two-plus-Four format under which the two Germanys would decide internal unification matters and the four occupation powers would deal with the external aspects. Baker liked this format because it would enable the stronger West Germans to direct the internal aspects of unification and to set a fast pace without too much interference from London, Moscow or Paris. But it would still ensure that the four occupation powers had the ultimate authority on such key points as the future of Germany's alliance systems. Baker added the condition that the East German member of the "two" had to be freely elected. He wanted thus to postpone the four-power talks until the SED had been removed and Kohl had found time to build a German consensus.[38]

Gorbachev had no personal commitment to the division of Germany. Although he had lost his father in World War II, he had not suffered from any personally bitter occupation experience through Germans. While visiting Germany in 1975, he had not defended German division as a Soviet interest in his talks with Germans. He had said that Stalin had not wanted to divide Germany but that the West had forced the division upon him.

Privately, Gorbachev had come to believe that West German attitudes were changing for the better. He had particularly noted a large anti-fascist demonstration during his visit.[39] He had then told one of his junior aides that the day would come when Germany would be reunited. His foreign policy adviser Chernyayev said that Gorbachev had long had an intuitive belief that the unification of Germany was "inevitable."[40]

Gorbachev saw no reason for Moscow to keep costly troop concentrations in the GDR and eastern Europe. He wrote in his memoirs that Soviet numerical superiority offered no strategic advantage because NATO used it to justify its nuclear weapons.[41] If he wanted to devote Soviet resources to real prosperity for his people, Gorbachev had to put an end to the central European confrontation.

Eduard Shevardnadze had also long envisioned German unification. As early as 1986, he had told some of the foreign ministry German experts that the German problem would need to be dealt with in the near future, adding that he did not believe the German nation could be divided forever "through ideology, weapons and reinforced concrete."[42]

But Gorbachev could not accept unconditional German unification. The questions that Shevardnadze had posed before the European Parliament reflected very real Soviet security concerns. Like Bush, Gorbachev wanted a stable Europe, which he had chosen to call the "common European home." A united Germany would have to contribute to stability. It would have to accept its borders and especially the Oder-Neisse line. Gorbachev would not tolerate having a revanchist German government begin a new march to the East. That would force him to build another military barrier, but closer to home.

Gorbachev believed that the European alliance systems formed a part of European stability with Germany divided between them. If Germany was to be united, some equally stable system had to be devised. Gorbachev had not decided on the best formula, but he first favored drawing Germany out of NATO and into another arrangement. Whatever that might be, Gorbachev wanted to keep Germany in CSCE.

The Soviet leader said that the Soviet Union would not accept a united Germany in NATO. Zagladin told White House aide Condoleezza Rice in December 1989: "There used to be two Germanys—one was ours and one was yours. Now there will be one and you want it to be yours. That would be an unacceptable strategic shift in the balance of power."[43]

At other times, Gorbachev appeared to be playing with the "united and neutral" formula that Moscow had advanced on occasion during and after the 1950s. He asked Marshal Sergei Akhromeyev to develop plans for pulling Soviet forces out of Germany in conjunction with the withdrawal of all foreign forces.[44]

But Gorbachev needed German help for his programs at home. Perestroika needed money. He could get some by reversing domestic priorities, cutting the military budget and especially ending the foreign wars and interventions that Brezhnev had begun or at least permitted. He would, however, also need aid from Germany, and he thought that Kohl would recognize that such aid had to be part of any bargain for German unity. Recalling how quickly Kohl had sent food, Gorbachev must have thought the Soviet Union could work with the chancellor.

Gorbachev and Shevardnadze often confused Westerners. Shevardnadze sometimes made totally unacceptable demands when the more conservative Soviet military and civilian officials held the upper hand in Moscow. Perhaps he mainly wanted to show them that the West would not accept such ideas.[45] Gorbachev then abandoned those same demands as his own position in Moscow strengthened. The Supreme Soviet's February 1990 decision to increase the powers of the Soviet presidency strengthened his hand. So did his later victory at the twenty-eighth CPSU congress in July of that year.

Gorbachev wanted to drive a hard bargain with Germany but also wanted a good future relationship. Those objectives could and did conflict. Perhaps because of his own ambivalence, he permitted the Moscow debate to persist. Some senior Soviet officials later complained about Gorbachev's concessions. They did not realize that in the end he decided to give priority not to the negotiating points but to a relationship with a future Germany and with a stable Europe.

Mitterrand, like most French citizens, had always opposed German unification. He had, of course, supported the idea in his public remarks over the years because he did not believe it would happen and he wanted to say things that the Germans liked to hear. Only in late 1989, as the East German exodus took on dramatic proportions, did he begin to believe that the Germanys might actually unite.

In an October 18 meeting of the French council of ministers, where sentiment for and against unification ranged widely, Mitterrand spoke realistically: "France cannot stop reunification. We cannot fight a war to prevent it." He made a point of saying that he did not fear it. He insisted, however, that unification should come by democratic and peaceful means.[46]

Mitterrand did not see any reason for German unification right after the Wall came down. He made no secret of his wish to have the GDR reform instead of being absorbed by West Germany. Therefore, he objected strongly in private to Kohl's ten points, especially because Kohl did not consult him, raging, "I shall never forget this."[47] He even suspected that Kohl secretly stimulated East German calls for unification so as to be able to claim that he had to respond to popular sentiment. But he stifled his irritation while waiting to see what would happen.

Mitterrand in turn irritated Kohl when he went to the GDR and met with Modrow on December 20 after having earlier turned down an invitation from Kohl to visit Berlin. Mitterrand also visited Kiev, where he made a speech opposing German unification. He invited Gorbachev to join him in the GDR, where a joint appearance by the two men would have signaled strong support for the German status quo. Mitterrand also asked Gorbachev to join him in block-ing German unity. Gorbachev rejected both invitations.[48]

Meeting with Kohl during the Strasbourg European summit December 8 to 9, 1989, Mitterrand sketched out a bargain: He would accept a united Germany if Kohl would support a more integrated European Community. Mitterrand in-sisted on deepening and strengthening the EC to build a European Union framework that could contain a united Germany.[49] He wanted to relieve wide-spread French fears of having to face Germany all alone.[50]

Mitterrand later told Bush that the European and German unification processes had to move like a team of horses: "If the two horses do not run at the same pace, an accident happens."[51] Like Bush, Mitterrand also wanted Germany to recognize European borders and particularly the Oder-Neisse line.

For the new European Union, Mitterrand insisted on European monetary and financial union and on the replacement of national currencies by a new Eu-ropean currency, the Euro. Mitterrand believed that the German central bank, the Bundesbank, had long used the strength of the D-mark to set monetary policy for all of Europe without giving any non-Germans a voice. France had barely tolerated this while Germany had been divided. The power of a united Germany would make it unacceptable. Mitterrand wanted France to play a lead-ing role in shaping European monetary policy through a new European central bank with a strong French presence.

Kohl accepted Mitterrand's bargain with pleasure because he himself be-lieved in European integration. Moreover, he had little choice. Ever since 1945, France had played a key role on Germany. If Mitterrand opposed German unifi-cation, he could block it or could at least set intolerable terms. Kohl could not afford that. Although Bush would help Kohl, he could not create German unity by himself.

As Kohl accepted Mitterrand's conditions and as the pressures for German unification grew, by February 1990 Mitterrand realized that German unity would arrive that year or soon thereafter. During a press interview on February 9, French foreign minister Roland Dumas said that "German unification is at our doorstep."[52]

Margaret Thatcher had a complicated relationship with Helmut Kohl, especially as German unification came on the agenda. She, Kohl and Ronald Reagan had begun the 1980s in total harmony on INF deployment. She had joined Kohl in supporting SDI and in working closely with Reagan on NATO matters. During a visit to Berlin, she had predicted that the Wall would crack and that liberty would arise on the other side. Once she had even gone out of her way to visit Kohl in the Rhineland, an experience that she had apparently enjoyed except when Kohl had asked her to savor such local specialties as Rhineland sausage and pig's stomach. And the two had made an honest effort to develop a good relationship.

But Thatcher often found Kohl closer to France than to Great Britain, particularly on European Community matters. Kohl consulted much more frequently and closely with Mitterrand than with her. Thatcher's strongly ingrained opposition to the European Community put her constantly at odds with Mitterrand and increasingly at odds with Kohl. She did not quite trust Kohl on Europe, suspecting that he wanted to convert a European Germany into a German Europe. During much of the 1980s, despite efforts on both sides to improve relations, Britain remained as distant from German issues and from the struggle for influence in Germany as it had been during the 1960s and 1970s.[53]

Thatcher opposed German unification from the moment it first appeared on the horizon. She told Gorbachev in September 1989 of her apprehensions about Germany. After the Wall came down, she wanted to form a united front with Gorbachev and Mitterrand to block unification. She feared for Gorbachev's future in case of German unification, and she always believed that his position and the freedom of eastern Europe mattered more than German unity. Unification should wait fifteen years, she thought.[54]

When Kohl called Thatcher after the Wall breakthrough, she advised him to keep in touch with Gorbachev and to take the Soviet leader's needs into consideration. She complained privately that she did not like the way Kohl was "busily raising" expectations. She also called Bush to tell him that she opposed German unification and that genuine democracy in East Germany should take priority.[55]

Unlike Bush, Mitterrand or Gorbachev himself, Thatcher did not list a clear set of conditions for German unification. She did pursue the traditional British aim of a European continental balance of power. She feared a neutral Germany, maneuvering between East and West, and insisted that a united Germany had to remain in NATO. She advanced inconsistent views, following Winston Churchill and Harold Macmillan in wanting to negotiate about Germany among the Big Three, joining Ernest Bevin and Anthony Eden in wanting Germany to anchor NATO, but also wanting Kohl to meet Gorbachev's needs although she did not want a Russo-German link like Bismarck's "Reinsurance Treaty" with the Czars or the 1922 Rapallo treaty. Out of this mix, she did not establish her priorities so clearly that Kohl had to adjust. And Kohl must have found her a little condescending when she advised him that "the real task of German statesmanship . . . is to strengthen and deepen the post-1945 traditions of German democracy."[56]

Thatcher never appears to have appreciated the power of East German popular pressures for unification. Bush often ignored her.[57] But she helped him in an important way. Her insistence that a united Germany had to remain in NATO made Gorbachev realize that the West would not yield on that point.

Thatcher's talks with Mitterrand about Germany and Europe took on a surreal quality. She asked Mitterrand to help stop unification, saying that she feared that Germany would try to take back the lands east of the Oder-Neisse and would also try to take over Czechoslovakia. She once shouted at Mitterrand about Kohl: "We must stop him! He wants everything!"[58] She added that Kohl was a liar. Mitterrand realized that he could not involve her in building the new European Union in which he hoped to contain the new Germany. And he observed coldly to an aide that Thatcher was "alone" and that she would have to sign the agreement to unify Germany just like everyone else.[59]

As the reality of German unification drew closer, Thatcher began to shift some of her statements but not her attitudes. Her foreign secretary, Douglas Hurd, appears to have played a role in this.[60] Although Thatcher gave such a fiercely anti-German press interview in the spring of 1990 that Kohl refused to share a car with her in Cambridge, England, after she had met him at the airport, she softened during that same meeting and congratulated Kohl for the successful elections in the GDR as well as for his determination to keep a united Germany in NATO. After further talks, Kohl told the British press that "Margaret Thatcher is a wonderful woman."[61]

Whatever her personal qualities, Thatcher could not persuade either Mitterrand, Bush or Gorbachev to shape their policies on Germany to please her. She mainly articulated a set of attitudes. The "Iron Lady," whose power of conviction and personality had changed Great Britain fundamentally during one decade, followed all too many other British prime ministers in failing to play the principal role in the struggle for Germany that British influence and British interests might have suggested and perhaps required.

Thus, as the real negotiations on German unification began, the four former occupying powers agreed on some matters but disagreed on others. Surprisingly, if with varying degrees of enthusiasm or reluctance, all were prepared to contemplate German unification. But all insisted that unification had to contribute to European stability rather than to upset the balance. All demanded unequivocally that Germany recognize the Oder-Neisse line as the permanent boundary with Poland. And Mitterrand had a specific bargain to pursue on European Union, including European Monetary Union.

But the four powers differed on whether a united Germany should be a member of NATO. Gorbachev did not want it but Bush and Thatcher did. So did Mitterrand, if less strongly. Therefore, the Two-plus-Four negotiators would have to resolve that issue if Germany was to be united.

The negotiators would also have to find a way to fit a united Germany into a Europe that had itself evolved over the decades. The Europe of 1989 when the Wall was pierced bore little resemblance to the Europe of 1961 when the Wall was built. The European Community had grown to twelve members instead of six. And the CSCE, which had not even existed in 1961, had become an important institution by 1990.

When the East Berliners burst through the Wall, they were leaving not only East Berlin and East Germany to enter West Berlin and West Germany. They were leaving COMECON and the Warsaw Pact to enter the European Community and NATO. As they raced forward, they tilted the balance of the entire continent. Negotiations on German unity had to take far more than Germany itself into account.

TWO PLUS FOUR MAKES FIVE

Bush had at first questioned the Two-plus-Four negotiating format that Baker and Zoellick had devised, fearing that it would give Moscow too much chance to block progress. But he agreed to accept the idea because he saw the advantage of including all the states that had a legitimate role to play. He particularly liked having the "Two" come before the "Four," giving the German states—and especially Kohl—the initiative.[62] Bush did not want an interminable peace conference, preferring to let Europe sign on through the CSCE.

Baker took the Two-plus-Four proposal to Moscow in his February visit, stopping briefly in Ireland for a meeting with French foreign minister Roland Dumas. He persuaded Dumas to accept the format. Shevardnadze and Gorbachev accepted it as well, as it resembled a formula for negotiations by "The Six" that Chernyayev had proposed and that Gorbachev had already approved. Baker's office also briefed the British foreign secretary, Douglas Hurd, who accepted the proposal but told Baker that he would prefer "four plus zero," excluding the Germans.[63] The Soviets, like the French and the British, usually preferred to call it either "Four plus Two" or "The Six" because they wanted the four occupation powers to retain the initiative as well as the final authority. Those favoring a peace conference agreed to a CSCE summit as a substitute.[64]

But things were not going as smoothly as Bush and Kohl might have hoped. Although Baker and Shevardnadze agreed on a format for negotiations about Germany, they did not see eye to eye on the terms for a settlement. Shevardnadze accepted a united Germany in principle but wanted a neutral and demilitarized Germany, not a NATO member. Many of his positions appeared to come out of the Soviet lexicon of the 1950s, as if old bureaucrats had resurrected old files and old ideas. Baker, who knew that Washington had rejected such ideas when Moscow had been stronger, could not believe that Shevardnadze advanced them seriously. He said that Washington would not accept a German solution on that basis.

Baker's conversation with Gorbachev went better. The Soviet leader said that "there is nothing terrifying in the prospect of a united Germany." He added that France or Britain might worry about who would be the major player in Europe. But the Soviet Union—like the United States—could take care of itself: "We are big countries and have our own weight." Gorbachev did not even appear to shrink from the idea of Germany in NATO, seeming ready at least to consider Baker's suggestion that a German army under NATO command might better promote European stability than a German army under national command.[65]

Nonetheless, Gorbachev warned that the Soviet public still saw Germany as a potential enemy and that Washington as well as Bonn had to proceed with care. German nationalism, if permitted to have its own way, could ignite Russian nationalism. He added that he had not made final decisions on some matters regarding NATO and Germany. Baker concluded that Gorbachev seemed more flexible than any other senior Soviet official and appeared to have a different view of the long-term Soviet interest, but that a lot of work remained to be done.

Once consensus on the Two-plus-Four or The Six format had been reached, the process leading to German unification became a primer on the methods of late twentieth century diplomacy. It particularly showed that national leaders and foreign ministers did not like to let others conduct important talks. They wanted to contact each other directly on Germany, as they had become used to doing on other matters.

The leaders negotiated almost continually, by telephone and during mutual visits. Some, like Bush and Kohl, met repeatedly in many settings. The foreign ministers often talked in so-called "pull-away" meetings at the edges of conferences that ostensibly had little or nothing to do with Germany. They met on almost every continent and rarely dealt through what used to be called diplomatic channels. They worked at breakneck speed, relying on their harried staffs to try to keep a running record of what they had discussed and agreed with whom.

Whereas the Two-plus-Four structure served as the formal diplomatic setting, it was not the most important. It became a forum for bureaucratic setpieces and for necessary legal and procedural discussions while the breakthroughs came elsewhere. Once the senior players had reached the main agreements, however, the Two-plus-Four structure proved ideal for drafting treaty texts and for solving complex issues that the principals had ignored.

The first official Two-plus-Four meeting took place at the working level of foreign office political directors on March 14, 1990, just before the East German elections. It set the schedule and the agenda for the talks. The meeting left both the Americans and the Germans frustrated at the gaps between Western views despite their pre-meeting consultations. The American and German delegations felt that they needed to move quickly because they feared a military coup against Gorbachev. In contrast, London wanted a formal peace treaty requiring lengthy negotiations and Paris did not want to threaten the Soviets by showing too much Western coordination.[66]

Moscow and East Berlin had coordinated better. They agreed that they favored a slow process for unification. They did not want West Germany to absorb the GDR quickly under Article 23 of the Basic Law. Instead, they favored the slow Article 146 process. The first Two-plus-Four meeting hardly promised the speed that Bonn and Washington wanted.

But Bush and Kohl did not worry too much. They had decided even before the first meeting that they did not want serious talks until after the East German elections took the SED and Modrow out of the talks.[67] They succeeded. By the time of the first foreign ministers' Two-plus-Four meeting on May 5, 1990, the situation in Germany had changed radically. The CDU had won the elections in the GDR and had formed a government under Premier Lothar de Maizière.

Nonetheless, although the two German delegations now sounded more coordinated than before, the new GDR government did not completely meet Kohl's wishes. Markus Meckel, de Maizière's foreign minister, belonged to the SPD. He often consulted more closely with the SPD in West Germany than with his own premier. Although he could not change the East German pressure for unification, he sometimes pulled the GDR closer to Soviet positions (as on German NATO membership) than de Maizière or Kohl wanted. This posed some problems until the SPD left the East German coalition by mid-year.

Nor did the CDU victory in East Germany have a perceptible impact on Soviet Two-plus-Four positions. Senior military officers and career foreign ministry diplomats decided to use the first ministerial meeting to reiterate their views in the most unambiguous terms. Shevardnadze, perhaps reluctantly, accepted their guidance. His Two-plus-Four speech on May 5 sounded harsher than any Soviet statement for months. He said that there could be no NATO membership for a united Germany. Moreover, others would have to watch Germany carefully and should place restraints on German domestic politics to block any rise of Nazism. A new CSCE center "on the prevention of nuclear danger" should be located in Germany to monitor "the military-strategic situation in Germany." A peace treaty should confirm the legality of all measures that the occupation powers (and especially Moscow) had imposed over the years. That could mean that eastern Germany would retain its socialist system while western Germany kept its social market economy.

Shevardnadze also set forth a new notion designed to undercut Kohl's successful tactics over the past six months. He proposed splitting the negotiations on the internal and external aspects of German unity. If the Germanys wanted to unite, they could do so whenever they liked. But the agreement governing the external aspects of German unification, including those topics that Shevardnadze had just raised, would be negotiated later. Until then, the country would remain in limbo. Kohl might take over the GDR but could not prevent Moscow from placing the newly united Germany under an onerous supervisory regime. Moscow's terms on the external conditions of German unification had hardened even as Gorbachev had accepted unification itself.[68]

Shevardnadze's comments went beyond Germany. He said that the West had to transform NATO. If Germany wished to be a NATO member, Shevardnadze said, the alliance would have to change. He did not make that remark casually but repeated it privately to Baker in the most urgent terms. And a Soviet diplomat and expert on Germany, Igor Maximychev, made the same comment a few weeks later to an American observer at a conference in Potsdam, adding that Gorbachev needed changes in NATO for domestic political reasons.[69]

Shevardnadze was plainly trying to grope for a solution on NATO. He and Gorbachev could see some advantages in having American forces in Europe, although he did not expect them to stay more than five or ten years because he felt that the next generation of Germans would not want them. But NATO had too many unpleasant associations for the Soviets. Shevardnadze told Baker, "Frankly, we don't know the answer to that problem."[70]

Thus, the first Two-plus-Four meeting ended in a deadlock surrounded by uncertainties. Baker would not accept separate timetables for the internal and external aspects of German unification. The Western foreign ministers refused to establish monitoring stations in Germany. The six agreed on only one thing: that the Polish border question needed to be resolved through a German guarantee of the Oder-Neisse border. Everything else remained fluid and open.

After the meeting, the Western foreign ministers disagreed on a reply to Shevardnadze. Genscher wanted at least to consider the Soviet proposal for separate timetables so as to strengthen Gorbachev's position at home. But Baker and Hurd feared that extended negotiations about the external conditions of German unification would provoke a crisis of confidence between Germany and the Allies. Baker asked Kohl for help. Kohl, who disagreed with Genscher's view, supported Baker and Hurd. Genscher finally yielded. Hurd added that Britain would even consider abandoning its own occupation rights unilaterally if France and the United States would agree. That would leave Moscow isolated as the only state still claiming occupation rights.

The Western leaders also began considering Shevardnadze's message about NATO. They realized that Gorbachev had widened the focus from talks on Germany to negotiations on European security as a whole. He and Shevardnadze wanted to revise the European equation by removing a threat that Moscow had feared since 1955. If the West would agree to do that, Gorbachev would remove the threat that the GDR and Soviet forces had represented for the West. Bush, Kohl and others would have to decide if they would accept a deal on Europe in the context of a negotiation about Germany.

Bush and Baker knew that foreign ministry position papers never represented the last word in any negotiation. They decided to learn real Soviet thinking during Gorbachev's next visit to the United States, slated for the end of May.[71]

During the talks in Washington and Camp David, Gorbachev and Shevardnadze focused most of their attention on American aid and trade. Gorbachev in particular wanted to change Soviet-American relations, stating that "the confrontation we got into after World War II wasted our time and energy." He told Bush at the beginning of their first talk that a Soviet-American trade agreement was essential to Perestroika. Shevardnadze went even further, telling Baker in the strongest possible terms that Gorbachev needed the trade agreement to justify his policy of cooperation with the West. Bush and Baker made no promises, noting that pressures which the Soviet government was exerting against Lithuanian independence generated revulsion in the U.S. Congress.

The Bush-Gorbachev discussion on Germany concentrated on the prospects for German membership in NATO. Gorbachev began by explaining that it would be best for Germany to join both NATO and the Warsaw Pact for a long transition period. But this proposal cut no ice with the Americans. Instead, Bush and Baker reiterated that Germany should remain in NATO.

Bush's arguments began along familiar lines. A Germany anchored in two alliances or completely loose from either could shift its weight with more dangerous effect than a Germany tightly linked to NATO. Moreover, NATO provided for an American presence that could help to stabilize Germany and Europe.

Gorbachev conceded that the American presence could be stabilizing. But he then stressed the point that Shevardnadze had made in Bonn: NATO had to change. He could not ignore the feelings of the Soviet people. Perhaps NATO and the Warsaw Pact could turn more into political structures, and friendly relations could replace military confrontation.

Bush pointed out that the CSCE treaty gave any member the right to choose the alliance that it wished to join. He said that he believed a united Germany should also have that right, and asked if this was not so. Gorbachev nodded and said that this was indeed true.

To nail down the point, Bush persisted: "I'm gratified that you and I seem to agree that nations can choose their own alliances." Gorbachev replied: "So we will put it this way. The United States and the Soviet Union are in favor of Germany deciding herself in which alliance she would like to participate."[72] Bush added that the United States preferred German membership in NATO but would respect any choice that Germany made, even a different one. Gorbachev appeared to agree to this.

Because both the Americans and the Soviets knew very well that a united Germany would choose NATO, everyone concluded that Gorbachev had agreed to that choice. In Gorbachev's own record of the meeting, he recalled that he himself had raised the CSCE provision that Germany could choose its own alliance.[73]

Zoellick described the next scene as "one of the most extraordinary" that he had ever seen. Many of Gorbachev's advisers, largely career foreign ministry and defense officials, showed in their faces and their body language that they wanted to distance themselves from Gorbachev's views. Akhromeyev gestured angrily as he spoke to Falin, who seemed equally upset. Bush recalled later that the Soviet delegation seemed virtually in "open rebellion" against Gorbachev.

Some of this visible dissent emerged in the meeting. Falin tried to argue against the very statement that Gorbachev had just made. Even Shevardnadze at first refused to engage in discussions among foreign ministers that the Americans proposed to implement the agreement. He obviously did not want to shoulder responsibility for it. But Gorbachev, although disturbed at his colleagues' reactions, did not withdraw his assent to Bush's interpretation of the CSCE treaty.[74]

Gorbachev's delegation later had a lively discussion on the South Lawn of the White House. Several foreign and defense ministry officials accused Chernyayev of having persuaded Gorbachev to accept German NATO membership. He replied that Gorbachev had agreed to it spontaneously. But all had been surprised, for Gorbachev had told Mitterrand as late as May 15 that he would never accept a united Germany in NATO.[75]

Gorbachev spent much of his next meeting with Bush concentrating on the trade agreement. He and Shevardnadze once more made the importance of the agreement very clear. Bush believed that he had to make a concession to Gorbachev on the trade agreement to compensate for the Soviet leader's concession on German membership in NATO. After consulting with Congress, Bush concluded that he could go ahead with the agreement. He told Gorbachev, who reacted with great pleasure.

Before leaving Washington, Gorbachev's staff and he himself had approved Bush's announcement that the two had agreed to let united Germany choose its alliance system. But Gorbachev told the press that "it is not here that the German question will be resolved."[76] He still had a deal to make with Kohl.

Gorbachev's decision to permit Germany to choose its alliance system came as such a surprise that it took some time to sink in. Even Kohl did not grasp what had happened when Bush first called to tell him of it, and he had to be briefed in detail.

Bush and Baker understood, however, that now they would have to honor Gorbachev's condition for German NATO membership. Gorbachev could still change his mind. To prevent that, they would have to change NATO.

After the breakthrough in Washington, the next Two-plus-Four meetings seemed to exist in a different world. Although they accomplished some useful technical and drafting work on secondary points, they largely rehashed old arguments.

The working-level meeting that was held on June 9 in East Berlin concentrated on defining the borders of a united Germany. The political directors agreed that Germany would comprise "the territory of the Federal Republic of Germany, the German Democratic Republic, and the whole of Berlin."[77] This made clear that united Germany would make no territorial claims on Poland. The two German delegations further agreed that they would renounce any territorial claims that they might have against any country. They also promised that they would renew this pledge in a binding treaty with Poland and would repeal any parts of the Basic Law (such as Articles 23 and 146) that provided for the adherence of any earlier German territories to the Federal Republic.

The Bundestag and the Volkskammer followed this agreement with a joint declaration on June 21 recognizing the Oder-Neisse border with Poland as final. The Polish government welcomed the declaration and withdrew its demand for a border treaty before German unification.

The next foreign ministers' Two-plus-Four meeting, held in East Berlin on June 22, went on as if nothing had happened since the Bonn meeting seven weeks earlier. It began with two positive steps. The foreign ministers jointly attended the removal of the Checkpoint Charlie control booth on Friedrichstrasse, and they approved the working-level agreement on Germany's borders. But then the meeting degenerated into a bitter exchange of words and papers as the Soviet foreign ministry staff tried to get control of a negotiation that had gone badly awry for them.[78]

Shevardnadze presented a Soviet draft proposal for a four-power treaty on Germany. The draft, carefully coordinated by Yuli Kvitsinsky, who had by then returned to Moscow as deputy foreign minister after his service in Bonn, reiterated much of the earlier Soviet position. It tried to find a firm foothold from which the Soviet Union could take a stand against Kohl's speedy absorption of the GDR and could challenge what Kvitsinsky denounced as the West's inclination to act as if Moscow no longer mattered in decisions on Germany. Kvitsinsky later wrote that the delegation had to try "to achieve an optimal result in a game in which we had lost one trump after another."[79]

The Soviet draft stipulated that four-power rights and responsibilities would remain in force after German unification. The four powers would continue to monitor German behavior—especially any Nazi activities—and would hold a conference in 1992 to decide whether German performance justified the termination of four-power rights. Even if Germany became united, its territory would remain divided between NATO and the Warsaw Pact.

To underline the bureaucrats' determination to maintain Soviet positions, the new proposal stipulated that troops of the occupation powers could remain in Germany for five years after unification. But occupation forces would be withdrawn from Berlin, leaving West Berliners with no protection against the Soviet troops remaining in eastern Germany. The forces of united Germany would be limited to 200,000 or 250,000. And Germany would not only have to accept a ban on nuclear, biological and chemical weapons, but it would have to withdraw from decision-making on such weapons. This meant that Germany would have to leave the NATO Nuclear Planning Group. To make sure all this work could be done in time for the proposed fall CSCE summit, Shevardnadze suggested Two-plus-Four meetings in continuous session.

Genscher told Baker privately that the Soviet proposal amounted to "window dressing." As Shevardnadze certainly expected, all the Western ministers denounced it as unacceptable and unrealistic. While Kvitsinsky's efforts might have laudably reflected Soviet bureaucratic views, Western ministers treated them as museum pieces.

After the Two-plus-Four meeting, Baker had a long private exchange with Shevardnadze. He expressed shock at what the minister had said in the meeting. He stated that, as Shevardnadze knew, Bush wanted to improve relations with Moscow, trying to get a trade agreement through a recalcitrant Congress. But a collapse of the negotiations on Germany would reverse all that had been done, he warned.

Shevardnadze replied strangely and almost painfully. Defending the Soviet position as an accommodation to "our domestic situation," he said that the mood in the Soviet Union was not good and had to be taken into account. He added that a lot would depend on the outcome of the London NATO summit, and that the Soviet papers did not represent the final Soviet position. But he pleaded for help: "We are facing a crisis situation, a political crisis as well as an economic crisis, and it is not easy to convince our people today of what we are doing." Warning that there was "tremendous" opposition, he insisted that the Soviet people needed to see that they faced no threat from Germany, the United States or NATO. He stressed again the importance of the NATO summit and also recalled the Soviet need for economic aid. Baker realized that Soviet views on Germany would depend on Western actions on other matters.

As the Soviet delegation flew back to Moscow, Shevardnadze took out of his briefcase the position paper that he had presented at the meeting. He gave it to Kvitsinsky, who had not joined in the talk with Baker. He asked: "What, out of this paper, will probably be left?" Kvitsinsky, who was intelligent enough to know that he and others were erecting elaborate sand castles in the face of an on-rushing tide, did not reply.[80]

The West German government also had trouble coordinating its positions, for Kohl and Genscher had different approaches. Kohl wanted united Germany to be completely in NATO and wanted German forces to be able to operate throughout all of Germany. At first, Genscher did not insist on a united Germany in NATO, hinting on occasion that both NATO and the Warsaw Pact should be dissolved in favor of an all-European collective security system. Bush, Thatcher and Mitterrand would have rejected that out of hand, as would other NATO members.

Some White House officials reacted with particular concern to Genscher's statements. They noted that he did not mention NATO in speeches that he made in March of 1990, speaking only of German unification in the context of the European Community, the CSCE and the "common European home," or in what he alternately called "a pan-European peaceful order" or a "peaceful European order from the Atlantic to the Urals." They felt that he stressed Europe as a security arena separate from the Atlantic alliance and that he often spoke of "new peace structures" in ways that suggested that he wanted to abolish such older structures as NATO. He spoke about Germany as a NATO member only when he came to the United States in April.[81]

Genscher believed that German unification had to pass through a very narrow window that might close at any moment. He feared for Gorbachev's future and wanted to arrange the earliest possible compromise to get through the window and to help protect Gorbachev. Kohl also saw the narrow window but felt that he could help Gorbachev on the economic front without making concessions on Germany's alliance systems. He also believed that Bonn had to stay close to the United States, for Bush supported unification more than any other leader.[82]

Kohl and Teltschik distrusted Genscher. In his meetings with Gorbachev, Kohl often had only Teltschik and Chernyayev present, to avoid having to include Genscher in the talks. Teltschik complained that Genscher did not send Kohl the records of five important meetings with Shevardnadze. When Teltschik asked for the records, Genscher said that he had briefed Kohl separately (which the chancellor denied). Kohl also learned that Genscher had once told Shevardnadze in Bonn that the chancellor was not available to meet Shevardnadze although Kohl wanted a meeting.[83]

Kohl could not challenge his foreign minister openly because Genscher's ideas might run closer to German—and especially East German—opinion than his own. If Germans had to choose between NATO and unification, the majority might opt for unification. Kohl did not want that kind of debate. Like Adenauer, he dreaded having a neutral Germany that might constantly have to wonder what side to take in a Europe of shifting and competing alliances. He thought Germany needed NATO for internal as well as external stability.

The contrast between Kohl's and Genscher's views worried their allies. A number of Americans, troubled by Genscher's statements, began briefing Kohl about positions Genscher had taken in the Two-plus-Four meetings to learn if the Chancellor agreed, which often he did not. They wanted to make sure that the German attitude toward NATO had not changed.

Some Americans feared that Genscher either did not understand or did not accept the wider Western interest in NATO. Genscher may have thought that NATO had been established to protect Germany. But Bush, like most of his predecessors, saw NATO as an essential element in the American and Allied strategic position across the whole world. Many other countries, from Canada to Turkey, also had a stake in the alliance. Germany had not even been a founding member. Bush would agree to change NATO to help Gorbachev accept a deal on Germany, but he would not abolish it. And he thought that Genscher had no authority to talk about disbanding the alliance. Bush's national security adviser, Brent Scowcroft, disliked Genscher's talk of a "third way," fearing that Genscher was playing a dangerous game and perhaps misleading Gorbachev. The White House also fretted about what it termed a "poisonous relationship" between Kohl and Genscher. But Baker and his staff trusted Genscher more than the White House did and thought that the foreign minister's differences with Kohl could be kept under control.[84]

French officials also worried about Genscher and Kohl. Mitterrand's assistant Jacques Attali did not like Genscher's readiness to toy with disbanding the European alliance systems. He felt that Genscher consistently distanced himself from Kohl's positions, trying to veer closer to Soviet views, and he noted that Genscher even criticized Kohl during an EC foreign ministers' meeting. Attali wondered how Kohl and Genscher could continue working together.[85]

In his memoirs, Genscher complained that some of his views had been taken out of context by his opponents in Bonn, who had also planted newspaper leaks to embarrass him and to make him look like an appeaser. He wrote that he had needed to give Soviet leaders, and especially Shevardnadze, some leeway so that they could survive against the encrusted military and foreign office staffs. Although he had chosen to do this, he wrote, he had never diverged from NATO interests. If NATO were to be dissolved, it would happen only much later and in a very different Europe.[86]

As the diplomatic dialogue evolved, the Soviets never tried to take advantage of Genscher's differences with Kohl. Gorbachev and Shevardnadze had much larger objectives and did not want to waste time on gambits. Gorbachev in particular wanted to deal with the head of the German government, not with ministers. And other Soviet officials had conflicting purposes, trying either to reestablish the occupation of the 1940s or to return to Bismarck's Europe of the 1880s.

While the four powers took their time debating the external aspects of German unification, the internal processes raced ahead. Those processes forced the pace of the international negotiators and sometimes made their words and their work virtually meaningless.

By May, East and West Berliners began the full demolition of the Berlin Wall. During the same month, on May 6, the CDU scored another major victory at the polls, winning the first free local elections in East Germany with 34 percent of the votes against 21.3 percent for the SPD and 14.6 percent for the PDS. A week after that, Kohl announced that the CDU/CSU and the FDP wanted national elections throughout all of Germany before the end of 1990.

The inner-German process widened continuously. A growing number of East-West German commissions began meeting ever more frequently. And the two German states carried on two basic negotiations that were to set the framework for their common state.

First, in spring, 1990, the two Germanys conducted talks on monetary and financial union. Kohl knew that he could prevent a mass exodus of workers and migrants from East Germany only by helping the East German people to get the D-mark. Signs in East Germany read: *"Kommt die D-mark, bleiben wir; kommt sie nicht, geh'n wir zu Ihr"* ("If the D-mark comes, we stay; if it does not come, we go to it"). But merging two currencies proved harder than expected.[87]

Kohl chose Hans Tietmeyer, former state secretary in the Finance Ministry who had recently joined the Bundesbank governing board (and who later became Bundesbank president), to conduct the negotiations. Tietmeyer found the task highly delicate. While Modrow had been in power, he had wanted financial aid and a Bundesbank guarantee for the East German Mark without any West German controls. Kohl and the Bundesbank would not agree to either. De Maizière reversed Modrow's position, wanting to abolish the East Mark and introduce the D-mark. But he also wanted an exchange rate of one East German Mark for one D-mark at a time when the black market rate was four to one. Pushed by the SPD, de Maizière also wanted to negotiate social as well as economic and monetary union. He wanted East German social benefits to be paid in West German currency, although East German benefits exceeded West German benefits and could be financed only by printing money and depreciating the currency as the GDR had done.

The negotiations proved wide-ranging. For example, the GDR recognized only limited private property rights, preferring state property. But West Germans and foreigners would not invest in the GDR if they could not own private property. And East German firms had such low productivity levels and such high subsidies that they could not compete internationally at an even exchange rate. The East German hidden unemployment rate, that of persons who held jobs but did not produce, ran at 25 to 30 percent of the work force.

The compromises needed to reach agreement favored the West Germans, who had the stronger currency and negotiators with more experience in financial matters. But the West Germans had to make a number of political concessions. They had to permit an exchange rate that overvalued the East German Mark at one to one (for assets below DM 6,000), thus jeopardizing the future of East German industrial and agricultural production. They also had to fund a number of expensive GDR social programs and labor regulations that the GDR itself had never fully funded. To help support unification, Bonn promised the GDR financial support of DM 22 billion in 1990 and DM 35 billion in 1991. On June 16, the West German government and *Länder* established a "German unity" fund of DM 115 billion, with 95 billion to be raised on the financial markets.

On June 18, East and West Germany signed the treaty establishing a monetary, economic and social union to come into effect on July 1. De Maizière described the treaty as the birth of a social market economy for the East German *Länder*. Kohl termed it "the birth of a free and united Germany."

The two Germanys also agreed that the East German *Treuhandanstalt* (Trustee Agency) established in early 1990 to take over GDR state property would sell all East German firms to private bidders. It did so over a period of two years, selling 22,000 small businesses and service agencies (restaurants, travel agencies, etc.) as well as 32,000 parcels of real estate, primarily to East Germans.

But it favored West German buyers over foreigners and East Germans in its sales of 14,000 large properties, such as manufacturing plants.[88] Although many foreign companies wanted to invest and produce in eastern Germany, the *Treuhandanstalt* sold virtually all productive assets to West Germans.

By making itself a privileged auction house for West German buyers, the *Treuhandanstalt* helped to doom East German growth after unification. Many West German firms bought East German firms only to get cheap reserve capacity, tax write-offs or real estate. Most did not expect to produce there until their West German facilities could no longer satisfy demand, although they often presented elaborate production plans in order to get *Treuhandanstalt* approval for their applications. As German growth slowed in the 1991–1992 recession, many West German firms let their newly purchased East German facilities lie fallow. West German firms built more shops and malls than production plants in eastern Germany. The main West German investment consisted of DM 500 billion in government-financed infrastructure, such as roads, railroads or public buildings and facilities, creating short-term public sector employment but no long-term production.

The eastern German economy thus suffered from an overvalued currency, from the collapse of inefficient industries and ecologically disastrous work-sites, and from a conservative West German business culture that did not get production going quickly.[89] After July 1, 1990, when the financial and monetary agreement came into force, eastern Germany entered a depression from which it was not to recover fully even a decade after unification. While the amount of goods produced in eastern Germany climbed back in seven years to its level before unification, the greater efficiency of western production systems left an unemployment rate of about 20 percent. Many of the unemployed were in their forties and fifties and could not find new jobs.[90]

Inner-German negotiations for political union also proceeded, with the West German delegation headed by Wolfgang Schäuble, who had become Interior Minister. The negotiations proved harder than expected, in part because of different social systems. East German women had more generous social benefits and child care programs as well as greater abortion rights than West German women. On the other hand, West Germany had more strictly enforced environmental regulations and its own mass of social legislation. The SPD wanted to transfer many East German social programs to West Germany, complicating Schäuble's task because the CDU/CSU would not accept them. The negotiators found compromise solutions under deadline pressures, but almost every compromise raised the cost of unification.[91]

As the negotiations drew on, the West Germans increasingly absorbed East German functions and dominated East German politics. They had to pay the bills and knew more about political and bureaucratic management techniques. They had more power and more authority. The East Germans tended to follow them. The two German partners in the Two-plus-Four process began speaking more and more with one voice, especially after the SPD had left the East German government. The Two-plus-Four progressively became One-plus-Four.[92]

As if to underline their determination to establish a new beginning, the members of the new East German Volkskammer invited the West German Bundestag to a joint ceremony in an East Berlin theater to celebrate the anniversary of the June 17, 1953, uprising against Walter Ulbricht.

By July of 1990 the German and the international processes for unification were proceeding on dangerously unsynchronized paths. Internally, Germany had to all intents and purposes become one economic and political entity. High expectations abounded, especially in East Germany. But the external aspects of unification lagged despite the agreement on the Oder-Neisse line. Shevardnadze and Gorbachev had given the Soviet bureaucracy a chance to pronounce its views, confusing the West and delaying the talks.

If Bush, Gorbachev and Kohl wanted to avoid a crisis, they would have to bring the two processes back into line with each other. And they would have to do it quickly to forestall total collapse of the entire East German system and a mass exodus to the Federal Republic.

BUSH AND WÖRNER CHANGE NATO

Even before the Two-plus-Four meetings had begun, Kohl and Teltschik had known that they would need to show Gorbachev that united Germany would not be a threat but an asset. They decided to devise a German package of incentives to offer Gorbachev outside the Two-plus-Four setting. Kohl felt that he could never hope to meet the hoary demands of the Soviet bureaucracy before the refugee flow had exploded. But, if he hoped to skirt those demands, he would have to fulfill Gorbachev's legitimate political, security and economic requirements enough to win over the Soviet leader and help him to neutralize the Soviet opposition.

During an April 1990 brain-storming session between Teltschik and some German experts on the Soviet Union, one expert, Boris Meissner, suggested that Kohl offer a bilateral treaty of friendship to Gorbachev. Such a treaty could give Gorbachev the political and security guarantees that might help him justify German unification to himself and others. Mainly, it could offer the solid prospect of a fruitful long-term partnership.[93] For centuries, Russian leaders had wanted a separate German connection. Gorbachev's "common European home" needed one.

Teltschik briefed Kohl on Meissner's suggestion, and on April 23, the chancellor formally proposed such a treaty to Kvitsinsky, who was at that point still in Bonn. Kohl said that he wanted to raise relations between the two states to a new level by a political treaty and a new economic agreement. The political treaty would include a non-aggression clause. He added that he had discussed the treaty proposal with President Bush, who had fully supported it.

Kvitsinsky said that he thought Gorbachev would accept the proposal. He added that he himself welcomed it because he had hoped to use his tenure in Bonn to return to the Bismarck tradition of close German-Russian relations. Kohl disavowed that suggestion, saying that he did not plan to conduct a nineteenth century balance-of-power policy like Bismarck's. He thought Germany could cooperate better with Moscow when it was firmly integrated into the West—including NATO—than when it was on its own. He added that he wanted to think not of the past but the future.[94]

As Teltschik and Kvitsinsky had expected, Gorbachev and Shevardnadze embraced the proposal, saying that it would have "an enormous significance" for the two states and for Europe as a whole.[95] Although the terms of the treaty were not to be negotiated until later, Teltschik believed that even the offer had a decisive impact, persuading Gorbachev that the Soviet Union would have good relations with the new united Germany.[96] For Gorbachev, it meant that Kohl would put a definitive end to the hostilities that had marred Russo-German relations for a hundred years and that had helped to turn both states into armed camps.

Kohl also gave Gorbachev real help for Perestroika. When Shevardnadze asked Kohl for credits in early May, Kohl acted immediately. He asked Hilmar Kopper and Wolfgang Röller, the heads of the Deutsche Bank and of the Dresdner Bank, to join Teltschik on a secret mission to Moscow to learn Soviet needs.

Soviet premier Nikolai Ryzhkov and Shevardnadze explained to Teltschik and the bankers that they needed credits to get the Soviet Union through a transition period between the collapse of the centrally directed economy and the birth of the new Perestroika system. They warned that Gorbachev's ability to continue his foreign policy depended on the success of Perestroika. They then asked for two things: first, between 1.5 and 2 billion rubles (then about $1 to $1.4 billion) in short-term credits to meet immediate payment obligations; second, between 10 and 15 billion rubles in long-term credits to be repaid in ten to fifteen years after a five-year grace period.

Teltschik replied that Kohl would be disposed to help in every possible way but that it should be understood that the Germans would regard such credits as part of a wider arrangement that would include a German settlement. Shevard-nadze accepted this condition.[97]

Gorbachev met with Teltschik and the bankers the same afternoon, reiterating Ryzhkov's points and stressing his confidence that Perestroika would succeed. He said that any agreement had to convince the Soviet people that they had not lost the peace for which they had sacrificed so many lives. He added that he hoped to welcome Kohl during July not only in Moscow but also in his home region of the Caucasus. When Teltschik reported the talks to Kohl, the chancellor said that he would do everything possible to help Gorbachev by giving German government guarantees for the credits.

Kohl helped the Soviet Union further by supporting its credit wishes in other meetings. He spoke on behalf of Gorbachev at the European Community summit in Dublin at the end of April 1990, gaining some support. He also pleaded in favor of aid for Perestroika at the summit of the G-7 industrial nations in Houston on July 9 to 11. He failed to win immediate financial support for Gorbachev because of Thatcher's firm opposition and Japanese hesitation. Bush also did not want to commit American aid without more economic reforms in Moscow. Nonetheless, Bush joined Kohl in persuading the G-7 to agree to an urgent study of Soviet needs. Kohl could tell Gorbachev that he had done all he could to support Perestroika.[98]

One major hurdle still lay ahead: Bush and Kohl had to change NATO itself if they wanted both German unity and German NATO membership. Gorbachev had abandoned the Brezhnev doctrine. He had changed Soviet priorities with Perestroika and had removed the threat to West Berlin and western Europe. If Bush and Kohl wanted more, they had to show that Gorbachev's policies paid off for the Soviet Union and not just for the West.

That was easier said than done. NATO doctrine and strategy, such as forward defense and the first use of nuclear weapons, shaped the defense plans of every NATO member. Such plans would not normally change overnight. The alliance had already begun to consider revising them in response to shifts in Soviet policies. But NATO had its own bureaucracies and they normally would expect a lead time of a year or two for thorough staffing before making any adjustment in NATO strategy.[99] That was not fast enough to help Bush, Kohl or Gorbachev. Bush in May had called for a NATO summit and now had to use it.

Manfred Wörner, the secretary general of NATO, wanted to help. He had been the first German appointed to the NATO post. Although never close to Kohl, he knew what mattered for Germany and for the alliance.

Bush had known and respected Wörner as a strategist for several years. He invited the secretary general to Camp David, where Wörner strongly supported

NATO membership for a united Germany. Wörner warned that the Allies would make a historic mistake if they again permitted Germany to wander freely between alliances. Doing so would open "the old Pandora's box of competition and rivalry in Europe," destroying decades of organization-building and jeopardizing the peace that the continent had finally achieved.[100]

But Wörner urged Bush and Baker to take a personal hand in the NATO proceedings if they wanted to circumvent the NATO and national bureaucracies to get results. He pointed out that the process leading up to the NATO summit still lacked a sense of urgency, although some NATO members—including the Americans—already billed that summit as "the most significant reappraisal of the alliance's role since the 1960s."

Bush and Baker reacted immediately, with Bush taking personal charge of summit preparations. He directed the White House and state and defense departments to generate new proposals that would fundamentally change alliance doctrine. Bush's national security staff told all concerned that they needed to focus on "the primary strategic objective" of having a united Germany in NATO and that they needed to act fast.

Bush knew that Gorbachev and all east European leaders needed a new NATO doctrine to respond to their own efforts. On June 6, the Warsaw Pact leaders had met in Moscow and promised "to review the character, functions and activities of the Warsaw Treaty." They would begin to transform the pact from a Soviet-controlled hierarchy into "a treaty of sovereign states with equal rights, formed on a democratic basis." NATO foreign ministers had replied the next day when they had met in Turnberry, Scotland, and issued a declaration extending "the hand of friendship and cooperation" to the Warsaw Pact. But these noble words had to lead to concrete plans.

Under pressure from Bush, U.S. officials drafted a NATO summit declaration that would include a solemn non-aggression commitment which Moscow had sought for decades, a proposal for Warsaw Pact countries to send permanent liaison missions to NATO headquarters, several major arms reduction proposals and a decision to make nuclear weapons "weapons of last resort." It would also modify the "flexible response" doctrine to reduce NATO's reliance on nuclear weapons.

Bush approved the draft and on June 21 sent it to Kohl, Mitterrand, Thatcher, Wörner and the Italian prime minister. He wrote that the occasion demanded urgent review of these proposals by national leaders at the NATO summit, not the usual long-term studies by NATO or national staffs. Declaring that "we are at a pivotal moment" for helping the new democratic leaders of eastern Europe, he added that "this NATO summit is likely to fix the image of what our alliance stands for during this period of historic change." He also arranged to have the ideas in the proposal shown privately to Shevardnadze, who expressed positive interest.[101]

Kohl and Teltschik heartily welcomed Bush's letter. And Mitterrand, after talking to Kohl, informed Bush that he liked the American draft although he had reservations about changing NATO doctrine on nuclear weapons. But Thatcher questioned the implications of such a dramatic change in NATO strategy and wondered whether east European governments, "so recently our bitter foes," should be admitted to NATO headquarters. After talking to Thatcher, Wörner warned Baker that the U.S. government needed to show "considerable toughness and determination" to make the summit a success.

Bush decided to send the draft declaration to all NATO heads of government on July 2, only three days before the beginning of the London summit. He hoped that this would give the leaders time enough to read the document and reflect on it but not enough to send it to their bureaucracies for the kind of detailed study that would delay the process. Wörner helped once again by making Bush's draft the summit's working document and asking heads of government to review it personally.

Bush's move paid off. The summit approved the document's positive tone, although a number of national leaders, especially Thatcher and Mitterrand, still expressed doubts about specific parts and insisted on some changes. NATO extended the hand of friendship to the Soviet Union, invited the Soviet Union and east European states to "establish regular diplomatic liaison with NATO" and made nuclear weapons "truly weapons of last resort." Without completely shelving the "first use" principle, the Allies changed both the "forward defense" and "flexible response" concepts that envisioned the early use of nuclear weapons against east European and Soviet territory.

Bush and Kohl could hope that Gorbachev would see that NATO no longer represented a threat to the Soviet Union and that it would be safe to permit a united Germany to be a member of the alliance. More important, Gorbachev could show that his policies would permit Moscow to devote more resources to the domestic economy and to reform.

Wörner himself traveled to Moscow right after the NATO summit to brief Gorbachev and to invite Gorbachev to visit NATO headquarters. Gorbachev accepted.

Bush wanted to get the NATO declaration to Gorbachev as soon as possible. On the way home from London on *Air Force One*, he cabled a personal message to Gorbachev enclosing the text of the NATO declaration and telling the Soviet leader that he had worked for that declaration with Gorbachev "importantly in mind." He said that the NATO declaration promised alliance transformation "in every aspect of its work and especially of its relationship with the

Soviet Union." Chernyayev, who had come out of the CPSU congress to receive Bush's letter from an American diplomat, told the American that "this is truly an important letter."[102]

The twenty-eighth CPSU congress had begun before the NATO summit and continued beyond it. It would became the turning point for the Soviet Union and also for Germany. Over the long run it contributed to the collapse of the Soviet Union, as the party would split and a rising CPSU leader, Boris Yeltsin, would pull Russia out of the union. But in the near term it proved a victory for Gorbachev and his reform policies. The conservatives could not defeat him. He won a politburo with a majority of new faces supporting his policies. He won even greater freedom from the party bureaucracy, being elected directly as general secretary of the CPSU by an overwhelming majority. This vote, combined with the special powers that the Supreme Soviet had granted him in February, gave Gorbachev full executive authority. Moreover, Gorbachev could use the new NATO declaration to argue that he had achieved a major foreign policy triumph by ending the NATO threat to the Soviet Union. Many Soviet people, wanting peace, welcomed that.[103]

The conservatives in the congress denounced Shevardnadze ceaselessly for the policy on Germany.[104] At one point, citing the possibility of German NATO membership, Gorbachev's critic Yegor Ligachev shouted, "How can we permit this?"[105] But the military and the conservatives could not muster enough votes to force Gorbachev to change his policies, and Ligachev suffered a humiliating personal defeat when he opposed Gorbachev's candidate as deputy general secretary.[106]

Shevardnadze replied to his critics without yielding on a single point. He told the congress that the Soviet Union had lost eastern Europe not when it had launched Perestroika but when it had destroyed support for its own cause with the invasions of Hungary in 1956, Czechoslovakia in 1968 and Afghanistan in 1979. He denied any "deal" to give the GDR to Bonn, arguing that East Germans would and should decide their own fate. Asserting that it would be "catastrophic" to use Soviet forces to try to reestablish control over East Germany, he added that the Soviet Union could not afford to continue foreign and defense policies that cost 25 percent of its gross domestic product.[107]

Gorbachev later said that the congress helped him to decide that the time had come to settle the German question in order to concentrate on domestic matters. He felt that he could have confidence that Kohl and the new Germany would help to stabilize Europe while he transformed the Soviet economy.[108]

Kohl arrived in Moscow on July 14 with Teltschik and Genscher and with what he hoped would be the package that Gorbachev needed. He used his first private meeting with Gorbachev to talk about the new spirit in East-West relations shown at the NATO summit, at the European Community summit in Dublin, and at the G-7 meeting in Houston. He said that all these meetings showed Western readiness to support Perestroika.

Gorbachev thanked Kohl for his support and gave him a draft for the new German-Soviet treaty. He added that all signs pointed toward the dissolution of four-power rights in Germany and that a united Germany would have full sovereignty.

Gorbachev added that Germany could certainly remain in NATO if it wished but that NATO structures could not expand across former GDR territory while Soviet forces remained. Special arrangements would have to be made to cover the departure and the funding of those forces. Gorbachev added that united Germany would need to carry out the obligations assumed by the GDR in almost 400 agreements with the Soviet Union. He then broke the Two-plus-Four deadlock, saying that he would not insist on an interval between German unification and German sovereignty.[109]

As Gorbachev and Kohl flew toward Gorbachev's home base at Archyz in the Caucasus, the Soviet leader recalled a talk between himself and Shevardnadze in 1979, after the Soviet invasion of Afghanistan. It was then, he told Kohl, that the two men had agreed that they would have to try to save the Soviet Union. On that day, they had conceived Perestroika to end the suffering of the Soviet people.

In their talks at Archyz, Kohl and Gorbachev agreed that their impending treaty should become a cornerstone for a new European architecture. They agreed that Germany could join NATO but that the Two-plus-Four agreement would state only that a fully sovereign Germany could choose its alliance system.

Gorbachev and Kohl went into considerable detail about military forces in East Germany. They agreed that Soviet forces would withdraw over four years, a compromise between Gorbachev's five-year and Kohl's three-year proposal. Kohl agreed to assume the costs of the Soviet forces during the transition. The two confirmed that NATO structures would not enter East German territory while Soviet forces remained but that some West German forces not under NATO command could enter. A sovereign Germany could decide in due course whether NATO was to cover that territory. But Gorbachev added that he assumed Germany would not take steps that would jeopardize Soviet security and that no NATO nuclear weapons would be stationed there. Kohl and Gorbachev agreed that Western occupation forces in Berlin could remain as long as Soviet forces remained in eastern Germany.

Kohl proposed, and Gorbachev accepted, that the German army be reduced to 370,000. Kohl justified that figure, well above earlier Soviet proposals, by saying that he did not want to repeat the Weimar experience of having a small professional army outside the mainstream of society. A larger force would make certain that at least some German soldiers would be draftees, thus integrating the army into the life of the nation as a whole. Gorbachev accepted the argument and repeated his insistence, which Kohl accepted, that united Germany renounce nuclear, chemical and biological weapons.[110]

Kohl and the German delegation rejoiced in what some called "the miracle of Archyz." Gorbachev also expressed satisfaction. He had settled the German question not in Washington with Bush but in Moscow with Kohl. He wrote in his memoirs that "a democratic and politically stable and economically healthy Germany which accepts its own borders will become one of the most important elements of the European and international order."[111] Kohl wanted a united Germany. Gorbachev wanted a new European order. At Archyz they made an accord that served them both.

MOSCOW AND BERLIN: A NEW RAPALLO?

Gorbachev had the good fortune of having Shevardnadze at his side. The foreign minister could let his Western colleagues know how to solve problems even as he held the line. Gorbachev could then make the deal. No one else had any executive role, although Gorbachev had to weigh many pressures. As one Soviet official told his Western colleagues, "All decisions were taken out of Politburo hands."[112]

The West could get an agreement if it followed Shevardnadze's suggestions. Shevardnadze told Baker that Gorbachev would have found it difficult to permit a united Germany in NATO without the London NATO declaration. He said, "You made an effort to take into account all our problems and our concerns, and that is what made so much possible."[113]

After the summit at Archyz, the Two-plus-Four meeting held a day later in Paris moved quickly. Genscher briefed on the Soviet-German accords, which others endorsed. The Polish foreign minister, Krzysztof Skubiszewski, attended part of the meeting, as earlier agreed. He expressed satisfaction with the German border guarantees. He and Genscher said that Germany and Poland would sign a border treaty after German unification, thus laying the Polish question to rest. The final treaty, signed in Warsaw on November 14, 1990, recognized the Oder-Neisse border and pledged both parties to respect it.[114] Gorbachev did as he had promised. Once he had reached an agreement with Kohl, he changed Soviet instructions for the Two-plus-Four meeting to remove Soviet insistence on a time lag between the internal and external aspects of German unification, although he had not changed those instructions after his May agreement with Bush.

Before all parties could sign the final Two-plus-Four accords, however, the Germans still needed to settle two remaining matters with the Soviets, the terms of their bilateral treaty and the money that Germany would pay to help Soviet troops return home from Germany.

Kvitsinsky proved as good as his word. The draft that he prepared for the German-Soviet treaty clearly recalled the special Russo-German relationship of the Bismarck era that he had mentioned to Kohl. It included a number of clauses establishing security relations. Each party was to avoid any measures that could jeopardize the other's security, would refuse to support any act of aggression against the territory of the other, and would not make its territory available for acts against the other. Kohl said that his government would study the draft. Bonn did not reply until six weeks later, on August 28.[115]

The German counter-proposal, drafted by the foreign office, did not directly meet the main Soviet points. It played down security issues, ignoring the specific Soviet proposals and substituting broad commitments to renounce the use of force while supporting the United Nations Charter and the CSCE final act. That did not satisfy Gorbachev, who wanted more specific promises. Kvitsinsky and Genscher's political director, Dieter Kastrup, thereupon began marathon negotiations that removed some of the more far-reaching commitments proposed in the Soviet draft but still gave Moscow terms which Bonn would have preferred not to concede.

The final "Treaty on Good Neighborliness, Partnership and Cooperation" stated that "if one of the two states should become the target of aggression, the other side will give the aggressor no military aid or other support." (The official German text reads: *"Sollte eine der beiden Seiten zum Gegenstand eines Angriffs werden, so wird die andere Seite dem Angreifer keine militärische Hilfe oder sonstigen Beistand leisten."*)[116] That commitment did raise some questions. It could mean that German forces would not join or support a NATO engagement of controversial origin, NATO action that responded to a Soviet action elsewhere or NATO engagement in a conflict that Moscow interpreted as provoked by a NATO member. Mitterrand refused to sign a similar agreement when Gorbachev asked him.[117]

Kohl believed, however, that the treaty did not violate Germany's NATO commitments because NATO would never attack the Soviet Union. To reassure Germany's NATO allies, the treaty contained a clause stating that it would "not affect rights or obligations arising from existing bilateral and multilateral agreements which the two sides have concluded with other states." The German foreign office also pointed out that neither the United States, Great Britain nor France formally objected to the terms of the treaty.

The treaty established other mutual commitments. It provided for annual or semi-annual consultations by a number of senior officials, including defense ministers, and contained many provisions for economic cooperation and for other forms of contact, from environmental to cultural. It pledged Germany to help the Soviet Union develop relations with organizations of which Germany was a member, improving Moscow's links with the European Union, the Organization for Economic Cooperation and Development (OECD), and others. The treaty was to be valid for twenty years.

The treaty established an important new link. With its many security and economic clauses, it created a new relationship within the center of Europe. It gave Germany some ties to Moscow that went well beyond those of any other Western state. But Kohl could justify it as a necessary step toward unification and continued German membership in NATO.

The treaty did not constitute a "new Rapallo," as some termed it. Nor did it match the "Reinsurance Treaty" that Bismarck had signed with Russia to provide for mutual neutrality in cases where some other European states went to war. The new treaty's neutrality provision dealt with unlikely, even wildly improbable, contingencies—much more improbable than those covered by earlier treaties between Berlin and St. Petersburg or Moscow. It did not take Germany out of NATO. And Bonn pointed out that its NATO membership never included a commitment to attack the Soviet Union, although Moscow often claimed that it did.

But the new treaty, like the Reinsurance Treaty, established a diplomatic connection that created a political association more than a legal obligation. It opened doors and provided a basis for mutual understanding and confidence. Most important, it could lead Germany to look both ways on occasion. Gorbachev and Kvitsinsky certainly hoped that Germany would do so more frequently over the years. Otherwise, Gorbachev would have never attached to it the importance that he so obviously did.

And the new German-Soviet connection also gave Germany a privileged relationship with the Soviet Union. Bush was worried enough to place a forty-five-minute telephone call to Gorbachev a few days after Archyz, as if to remind the Soviet leader of Washington's primary role in the Western alliance.[118]

Kohl may have felt relieved about the German-Soviet treaty, but he still faced last-minute Soviet demands for funds and credits. Gorbachev asked Bonn to contribute major sums to help support Soviet forces in East Germany and their return to the Soviet Union. He even issued several ultimatums, threatening ei-

ther not to begin withdrawing Soviet forces or to extend the withdrawal schedule from four to seven years if Bonn did not help enough. The Germans realized
that the Soviet military had decided to dig in their heels. The Red Army had to
receive compensation for its costs in Germany and at home as well as for the humiliation of its withdrawal.[119]

The Soviets demanded funds for taking care of their forces in eastern Germany, for returning them to the Soviet Union, for retraining them and for building 72,000 new housing units, offices and schools for them at home. Moscow
also wanted to be paid for the bases left behind. The total sum, DM 36 billion,
represented far more than the 8 billion that Kohl had planned to pay.

When Kohl called Gorbachev to try to reduce the amount, Gorbachev
proved more obdurate than he had been on any of the other issues they had
discussed. He said the situation was "alarming" and Kohl's offer totally inadequate. It would prevent Moscow from signing the Two-plus-Four treaty. He
said that he was fighting "many battles" with the military and with budget officials and needed the funds. Kohl finally had to pay DM 12 billion and extend
an interest-free credit of DM 3 billion. Bonn literally bought East Germany's
liberation from Soviet forces. Once the funds had been approved, the agreement on a Soviet force withdrawal by the end of 1994 could be signed on September 27, 1990. Together with earlier commitments, Bonn had granted
Moscow a total of DM 60 billion in aid and credits for the Two-plus-Four
accord.[120]

One last question remained, however: the military status of the former
GDR. All Two-plus-Four states had agreed that non-German NATO forces
could not be permanently stationed in that territory right on the border of eastern Europe. But several NATO members, and especially the United States, did
not want to be prevented from having their forces deploy or maneuver there.
Bush wanted and expected Poland to join NATO and did not want to have a special military regime in the middle of the alliance. He and others wanted NATO
forces to have the right to be deployed there, perhaps for some time, even if they
were not permanently stationed there. All began arguing about how to interpret
"deploying" and "stationing" forces.

The Soviets and the NATO states finally decided to leave it up to the German government to decide "any questions with respect to the application" of the
word "deployed" and to decide them in "a reasonable and responsible way."
Kohl and his successors could judge how long a force of what size could remain
in eastern Germany, a remarkable sign of Gorbachev's confidence that the Germans would not permit a major NATO buildup to threaten eastern Europe from
German soil. The accord became an "agreed minute" to the treaty on German
unification.

From the resolution of that dispute, the process of moving toward German unification picked up speed.

On September 12, 1990, the Two-plus-Four meetings concluded in Moscow with the signature of the treaty governing the unification of Germany.[121]

A week later, on September 18, Mitterrand and Kohl met for the eightieth time in their long association and issued a common declaration pledging ever closer cooperation as well as a further commitment to European integration.

Two weeks after that, on October 1 and 2, in New York and Berlin, the four occupation powers gave up their residual rights in Berlin and Germany, closing down the Kommandatura four-power occupation authority in Berlin. On the next day, October 3, Richard von Weizsäcker, Helmut Kohl and Lothar de Maizière presided over ceremonies in Berlin marking the unification of Germany.

The Berlin ceremonies ended the Cold War. As Yalta had put Germany under occupation and divided it, Berlin brought back sovereignty and unity.

On November 9, Gorbachev visited Bonn to sign the new German-Soviet treaty with Kohl. That treaty became the first international agreement to be signed by the new united Germany.

From November 19 to 21, at their summit in Paris, CSCE members signed the "Charter of Paris for a New Europe" and a treaty reducing and limiting conventional forces in Europe.[122]

On June 17, 1991, Germany and Poland signed a treaty of "good neighborhood and friendly cooperation."[123] That treaty, signed fifty-two years after Hitler's invasion of Poland and fifty years after his invasion of the Soviet Union, completed the series of agreements formally ending World War II and the Cold War.

Those three agreements gave Gorbachev what he had wanted, the promise of a friendly and peaceful Germany and of a more stable Europe, a combination which he hoped would permit him to concentrate on Soviet domestic needs.

In December of the same year, Mitterrand received his end of the bargain, when all European Union members agreed at Maastricht in the Netherlands on the text of a treaty to establish the European Union and a new European monetary regime based on the Euro. European Union members signed the treaty on February 7, 1992.[124]

On the basis of this architecture of diplomacy, the World War II Allies ended the Cold War and united Germany. They also established a web of relationships into which the new Germany was to fit.

TWENTY

THE NEW GERMAN QUESTION

A BERLINER WHO WALKS ABOUT 2 KILOMETERS (1.3 MILES) FROM THE *Siegessäule* (Victory Column) in Berlin to the Brandenburg Gate can learn a lot about the history of Europe during the nineteenth and twentieth centuries as well as about true peace and security.

Around the *Siegessäule*, which was erected to commemorate the Prussian victory over France in 1870–1871, pose heroic statues of the Prussian and later German leaders who won that war, including Chancellor Otto von Bismarck and the chiefs of the Prussian General Staff. That victory gave Germany forty years of armed peace but no real security. France came back to win World War I and to impose the treaty of Versailles. But France, in turn, found no real peace and security. Hitler attacked and conquered France within less than a generation. That did not bring Hitler or Germany security either, as evidenced by the memorial to Hitler's victims that now covers the rubble of his chancellery. To the left, in apparent contrast, the walker can see the proud monument that the Red Army built after it had conquered Berlin. But that also proved an empty victory, as the Soviets were forced to leave Berlin and go home to bankruptcy. Finally, as he or she gets near the Brandenburg Gate, the Berliner walks over the site of the Wall, Walter Ulbricht's futile victory over his own people.

The center of Berlin thus recalls many hollow "victories" that brought no true security to Germany or central Europe. Each war led to the next, and each in turn was justified as an act of necessary retribution. All they brought was one armistice after another. To break the cycle of violence and to find true peace, the states would have had to seek reconciliation, but they had learned to think only of victory.

The victorious Allies faced that same security dilemma after World War II. They wanted to leave a legacy of peace, but at first still thought mainly in terms of victory. Their plans began to change, however, as the situation changed in Germany and as relations between the World War II Allies themselves deteriorated.

COLD WAR LEGACIES

During and after the war, the Allies had first wanted a permanently weak and truncated Germany, whether through Franklin Roosevelt's Morgenthau Plan or through Charles de Gaulle's plans for German dismemberment and for control over the west bank of the Rhine. Only Josef Stalin thought of a united Germany, at least at first, one that would have a communist or at least leftist government and be the Soviet Union's friend. He thought of reconciliation.

But expectations changed after the early months of the occupation and the initial sessions of the Council of Foreign Ministers. Western leaders began to think that they would have to establish or encourage a stronger Germany that could help protect the West as a whole.

General Lucius Clay began the process in Germany itself, by starting to build a democratic and federalist state in the west, although he still hoped for a united Germany. James Byrnes and George Marshall supported the new Germany with their speeches at Stuttgart and at Harvard University. They helped to lay the political and economic foundations of the Federal Republic.

Ernest Bevin became the first Western leader to begin reshaping Allied policy on the wider European level. He decided that Germany had to be divided between East and West, at least temporarily, to tie the Western occupation zones to western Europe and to create a balance of power with the Soviet Union. He kept the United States engaged in Europe.

Georges Bidault turned French policy away from de Gaulle's dismemberment plans and accepted division along the occupation lines to keep both Great Britain and the United States engaged on the continent. Jean Monnet and Robert Schuman then began designing a West European framework into which West Germany was to fit.

Stalin had ordered radical social and economic changes in the Soviet occupation zone as a model for all Germans. But the model failed to work and it had no appeal, in part because Ulbricht preferred to establish the communist system solidly and brutally in his zone before risking unification, and in part because Stalin's own armies had destroyed whatever mood of reconciliation might have existed. Stalin had to ask for a mortgage on united Germany in exchange for his occupation zone.

When these divergent aims clashed in the currency reform and the Berlin blockade of 1948–1949, the Western occupiers formalized Germany's division and began creating a transatlantic defense system. Many West Germans opposed division but saw little choice except to draw up the Basic Law. With that, the Western Allies formally surrendered plans to keep Germany defeated and supine. Paradoxically, the West then wanted the reconciliation with Germany that Stalin had originally wanted but had forfeited.

By 1950, Stalin realized that his original plan had unraveled. He may have considered military action in Europe, using Korea as a model. Then the Korean war went awry, blocking whatever plans he may have had. Moreover, the war convinced Dean Acheson that he had to accept Paul Nitze's NSC-68 proposal for a West German force as part of NATO. This deepened the Allied commitment to West Germany and further changed the prospects for Germany's Cold War legacy.

At that point, the Germans themselves began to shape that legacy. Walter Ulbricht chose communism and SED control for East Germany. Konrad Adenauer chose democracy and credibility as his priorities for West Germany. Each wanted his state to serve as the model for united Germany. Ulbricht hoped the Berlin Wall would help his model succeed by giving him control over all of Berlin, but he failed. Instead, Konrad Adenauer and Charles de Gaulle used the Wall to link the Federal Republic with France and with the European Community.

By the 1960s, therefore, the Germans and the occupiers had sealed the division of Germany and had begun building a German legacy very different from what the occupiers had first planned. They had even begun rebuilding German military forces.

Not all German leaders accepted the prospect of a Germany divided until either democracy or communism prevailed. Willy Brandt, for one, thought that reconciliation would promote unification. Kneeling before the Warsaw Ghetto memorial, he reopened the door to a united German nation, if not to a united German state, by beginning to show Poles, Russians and others that Germans could be trusted because they had broken with the past.

After Brandt's détente, the legacy of World War II and of the Cold War appeared sealed. Germany would be split, half democratic and half communist. European stability and reconciliation would be built on the basis of a divided German state.

Leonid Brezhnev's SS-20 deployment during the 1970s altered the prospects for Germany and Europe by destroying the continent's military balance and thus

Brandt's hope for a stable peace. Helmut Schmidt, while successful in expanding West Germany's global economic role, had to abandon East-West détente.

The Western response to Brezhnev, conceived and led by Ronald Reagan, brought on the collapse of the Soviet Union. Some saw the U.S. military buildup as the cause of Western victory.[1] They were right in part; that buildup, and especially SDI, showed the futility of Moscow's global ambitions and the impotence of Soviet technology.[2] Soviet Marshal Sergei Akhromeyev told U.S. Ambassador Vernon Walters that Reagan's refusal to give up SDI at Reykjavik had made him realize that Moscow had to change course.[3]

Helmut Kohl supported Reagan, challenging not only the Soviet SS-20 but also Moscow's wish to dominate Europe by a combination of détente and military superiority. He turned back Soviet efforts to revise the European military balance as Reagan turned back Soviet efforts to revise the global balance. But the Soviet system faced an even graver challenge when Pope John Paul II supported the dissident movement in Poland.[4]

Then, having pushed the Soviet Union by their military buildup, Reagan and Kohl turned to diplomacy to stabilize the continent on a new balance. In the process, they laid the foundation for a Cold War legacy of reconciliation for Germany and Europe.

Mikhail Gorbachev embraced and helped to build the legacy of reconciliation. Once he and Reagan had reached a broad East-West understanding and once Poland and Hungary had become democratic states, East Germany's SED system could not survive. The East German people then broke through the Wall, putting an end to the Soviet imperium in central Europe.

At that point, George Bush and Helmut Kohl seized the moment for a German unification that would bring a new relationship between East and West. To do that, Kohl had to offer reassurance in all directions, whether in Europe or across the Atlantic. François Mitterrand received the Maastricht treaty, European Union and the Euro. Bush received Germany in NATO. And even Margaret Thatcher, whose German policy risked becoming, in the words of one British scholar, an "unambiguous failure,"[5] at the last moment saw that a united Germany could help to protect the balance on the European continent.

Gorbachev did what Stalin, Khrushchev and Brezhnev could not bring themselves to do. He decided that Soviet influence over all of Germany and into western Europe mattered more than dominance over eastern Germany and eastern Europe. Under him, Soviet policy finally came full circle to Stalin's original wish after almost fifty years, although with a very different ideological thrust.

Above all else, Kohl and other Germans wanted to correct Bismarck's domestic and foreign policy mistakes. They wanted to leave a legacy of a democratic, not an authoritarian, German state, a state that would not carry the seeds of its own destruction. They wanted a Germany that would be surrounded by friendly rather than vengeful neighbors. Building on both Adenauer's and Brandt's policies, Kohl could then open the door to a new link with Moscow to reassure Mikhail Gorbachev and to reconcile the Soviet Union and Russia to German unification. That link meant that German unification was no longer a zero-sum game which the West would win and the East would lose, for the new united Germany would be a friend to both.

Kohl became the new Bismarck, creator of a united Germany. But he did it without imposing a victory or disrupting European stability. Like Reagan, he followed a military buildup with a diplomacy of reconciliation. In Horst Teltschik, he found his own Henry Kissinger.

Between them, the leaders of the occupation powers and the Germans created a Cold War German legacy very different from what their predecessors had expected or wanted in 1945 or even in 1970. Gorbachev could say at the signature of the Bonn-Moscow treaty in 1990 that "a new vision of the world triumphs."[6] And Shevardnadze could ask rhetorically: "From the beginning we asked what would better represent our interests, a divided, embittered and potentially explosive . . . or a united democratic Germany, one that takes its place among other sovereign masters of their fate."[7]

Gorbachev created the "common European home" he wanted. He ended the division of the continent. In exchange, he received a Soviet voice in western Europe. He could not hold the Soviet Union together for many reasons that went far beyond the settlement in Germany. But, through the NATO Permanent Joint Council, Russia later received what amounted to significant influence and a role in NATO's political decisions. Like Peter the Great, Gorbachev brought Russia into Europe and to its historical role on the continent.

The Germans and the occupiers thus left a stable Cold War legacy for Germany and Europe. Instead of an imposed peace or a surrender by either side, they left an architecture accepted by a united and democratic Germany and by its neighbors. They also left a Germany integrated into the West but with a close tie to Russia. To their eternal credit, they brought off a historic European revolution without a shot being fired.

But the leaders sometimes found themselves cast as followers to the Berliners and the German people—especially the East Germans. The people did not accept division even when governments did, and they kept the German question open after many political leaders and experts had pronounced it closed. They made the 1989 German revolution succeed after the failures of 1848 and 1953.

The Cold War, as the essential incubator of a new Germany, took the place of the peace conference planned for the Council of Foreign Ministers. But the protagonists bargained by military threat and counter-threat as well as by political pressure more than by traditional diplomacy. At the end, each of the four victors of World War II received what it needed although in a form that it might not have expected or accepted at the beginning. Each obtained security and stability. The Cold War made possible a better settlement in 1990 than any that could have been negotiated in 1947 or 1948. It left a legacy of mutual understanding and a prospect for peace.

The Cold War also helped the Germans. It gave them the chance to create a democratic state. It gave them time to digest and to accept the losses of World War II, in part by giving them new lives and new missions. It gave them a chance for reconciliation with themselves and with their neighbors. And Germany was united from its liberalizing and modernizing West, as Konrad Adenauer had wanted, not from its autocratic East.

The Cold War struggle over Germany, unstable and uncertain as it was at times, may have laid the foundations for a stable central European balance. It left a democratic Germany anchored in a number of treaty systems and at peace with all its neighbors. And the great conflict that had ravaged Europe since 1914 ended after two wars separated by a fragile armistice and followed by a long and bristling standoff. As Shevardnadze had said, everybody had to win.

But the world as a whole and especially the participants in the Cold War struggle over Germany had to bear immense costs. The money spent on keeping the military balance could have been better spent on postwar rebuilding. The regimes imposed on tens of millions of East Europeans and East Germans delayed peace and democracy. And no one could begin to calculate the burden in lives lost or ruined, in disruption, in pain, in separation and in anxiety.

Lothar de Maizière later recalled Gorbachev's thoughts on this as the principals relaxed in Moscow on September 12, 1990, after signing the treaty on Germany.[8] He reminded the Soviet leader of his remark in Berlin about life punishing those who come too late. Gorbachev replied: "Well, did we not all come too late?"

THE "BERLIN REPUBLIC"

On September 27, 1998, eight years after unification, Germany dropped the pilot. The German electorate voted Helmut Kohl and his party out of office, giving the CDU/CSU its lowest percentage of the vote since the founding of the

Federal Republic. Kohl had been chancellor for sixteen years, too long for most Germans and particularly for those in eastern Germany, who believed that he had not fulfilled the promises about "flourishing landscapes" that he had made before unification.

Gerhard Schröder of the SPD became chancellor with the support of the environmentalist *Grüne* (Green) party. But he brought not only a new political combination into government; he also brought a generational change. For the first time, the Federal Republic installed a chancellor and a cabinet of men and women who, largely in their forties and fifties, did not remember the Nazis, World War II or the penury of the postwar era.

Kohl had spoken of the *"Gnade der späten Geburt,"* the "blessing of a late birth," for those who had been spared the most bitter experiences of German history and had known only democracy and prosperity. If Gorbachev complained of having come too late, many Germans of the older generation felt that they had come too early.

Schröder's voters live in a Germany that has never existed before. The new Germany is a modern European country. It has different borders from historical German states or associations as well as a different social system and a different view of the world from any earlier united German state.

Unlike Bismarck's Reich or the Weimar Republic, the new Germany has no gerontocracy of the Left or Right and no vast body of rancorous dispossessed. It has no obvious enemies but is a full part of a continent-wide Europe and of a wider North Atlantic community. It has some hope—if no guarantee—for lasting prosperity and uninterrupted peace. Germans of every earlier generation since the Age of Charlemagne would have dismissed such a combination of expectations as inconceivable and perhaps as signs of delirium.

The Germany of today is not the bombastic Germany of the Hohenzollerns, the humiliated Germany of Weimar, or the murderous Germany of the Nazis. Over the course of fifty years, the West Germans and their allies brought forth a democracy that the East Germans were eager to join and that all want to preserve.

United Germany is also a different creature from West Germany. It has different boundaries, different neighbors, different interests, different priorities, different politics and a different weight. It will, and even must, pursue policies that will be different from West Germany's, and it will have a greater consciousness of its own independent role and interests than West Germany had. Although it may have the same official name as West Germany, it is not the same entity.

The politics of united Germany do not follow those of the former West Germany. With the addition of the traditionally Protestant and social democratic states that made up much of the former East Germany, the predominantly

Catholic states of the Rhineland and Bavaria no longer set the tone of German politics as they did in West Germany. The former communists have come back in eastern Germany as they have in some eastern European states. German fringe groups of the Right and Left draw more foreign attention than similar groups in other countries, but most Germans reject them.

In 1999, the Federal Republic moved its capital from Bonn to Berlin. The new Germany is now often called the Berlin Republic to distinguish it from the 1919–1933 Weimar Republic and from the 1949–1999 Bonn Republic.

In many ways, the Federal Republic of Germany has become what might be termed a "normal" state. It must no longer conduct a fight for survival, deliberately risking annihilation to deter a possible attack. It has a capital city that ranks as a world city, like Paris or London.

Germany went through a normal democratic change of government in 1998. For the first time since 1949, foreign or military matters did not dominate the election. Germans did not have to vote for or against the Atlantic alliance, for or against détente with Moscow or for or against new missile deployments. They voted on pocketbook issues, making their decisions as most normal electorates do.

This new electoral mandate will dictate the priorities of the new German government and, if luck holds, its successors. The government will want to concentrate on home issues, on solving economic problems such as unemployment and structural reform, on finding a way to integrate immigrants and refugees, on problems of welfare and social justice and on keeping Germany prosperous in an age of global economic uncertainty. Foreign policy will have a lower priority and will also have to reflect domestic attitudes. Germans will worry more about jobs than about war, even if they cannot completely forget about the latter.

With the end of the Cold War and the unification of Germany, Germans can be more self-confident and more conscious of their own needs and wishes than before. They need not fear that others will abandon them. And many do not believe that they need always to atone for Germany's past. Schröder did not, among his first official acts, participate either in a French commemoration of the eightieth anniversary of the World War I armistice or in a ceremony at the Warsaw Ghetto.

Schröder's attitude is neither new nor unique. Willy Brandt used to say that the day would come when a German would not make an automatic apology every time he or she entered a room.[9] Many younger Germans feel, as Schröder does, that they want to be normal and to be treated that way. They believe that the Federal Republic has been a responsible partner of the West for fifty years and has contributed to Western security, Western prosperity and Western success. They want others to think and talk of those fifty years, not only of the twelve years of Nazism. They know of Nazi crimes and brutalities and want to attone for them, but they do not see them as part of their own lives.

Germany is not a fully normal state, however, and it does not have a fully normal history. The Germans did not attain national unity until 1871, well after France, Great Britain, and even Italy. They attained democracy only in 1919, when they established the Weimar Republic, but that democracy was saddled with the burden of accepting the German defeat in World War I, with the Versailles Treaty and with a constitution that encouraged the proliferation of radical parties. It failed disastrously when some of its politicians decided to make Hitler chancellor because they thought they could control him in office.

Nor has Germany had what might be termed normal foreign relations. German diplomacy never had the moral tone or the allegedly moral ambitions of other states. Bismarck's *Staatsraison*, or "reason of state," appeared brutally cynical. Emperor Wilhelm II's megalomaniacal posturings led to Germany's isolation and to World War I. Germany's treaties with Russia and the Soviet Union, such as Bismarck's "Reinsurance Treaty," the Rapallo Treaty, or the Molotov-Ribbentrop Pact of 1939 that led to the Nazi invasion of Poland and to World War II, often seemed to serve insidious purposes. German diplomacy earned a reputation for cunning and craftiness.

Hitler's ascendancy and Hitler's policies added to the somber side of German history. The raving and ranting, the invasions, the Holocaust, the innumerable dead across much of the world, remain part of the German legacy and, while they may have happened in the past, still affect current reality.

All West German governments during the Cold War tried constantly and consciously to follow policies that would move away from the grim parts of German history, whether from Bismarck's diplomacy, Weimar's paralysis, or any part of Hitler's legacy. They looked backward as well as forward, wanting to make certain that the Federal Republic took a completely new and different road from past German regimes.

For the Berlin Republic as for the Bonn Republic, yesterday and today merge in ways that are different from other countries. And each generation of Germans needs to determine how it can best come to terms with the past and with those who remember it and who share in it. The Cold War changed but could not eradicate that legacy. It remains a grinding burden for all Germans to carry, whether they feel responsible for it or not.

Today's Germany has a new foreign policy, one very different from West Germany's policy during the Cold War. It wants to keep things as they are. From 1949 to 1990, successive West German governments wanted to change the European order, seeking a united Germany and a Soviet retreat. In 1990, Bonn got both. The German government now wants no more change and especially no upheaval. For the first time in its history, Germany has no enemies on its borders. For a state that has more European neighbors than any other, that brings a freedom that no German leader has enjoyed in centuries. But it also brings obligations, and the Berlin Republic will find itself with a more prominent international role whether it wants it or not.

The new united Germany harbors no wish for military adventures. Like France after the wars of Louis XIV and Napoleon, when many erroneously thought it had a perennial lust for conquest, Germany wants peace.

German relations with Europe represent domestic as well as foreign policy. The European Union is now an integral part of German economic administration. Many economic regulations are now EU regulations, not only German regulations. Unless the global or the European monetary system breaks down, Germans will lose their beloved D-mark by 2002 and will adopt the new European currency, the Euro. They also will need to help decide how the European Union is to evolve. Although European Union expansion to the East will cost Germany more than any other EU member, Germany will still try to bring it about because it wants to be surrounded by neighbors fully integrated into Europe.

The Berlin Republic remains a key member of NATO as well as of the European Union. The NATO commander-in-chief still commands German forces in case of war. Some NATO deterrence systems, including nuclear, remain in Germany although the Cold War is over. Germans will need to decide over time what role they wish to play within the NATO context. They will also need to decide what NATO deterrence systems should remain on German soil.

Germany cannot afford a divided Europe. Germany, more than any other state, must have a Europe united from the Atlantic to the Urals. Having twice as many European states to its east than to its west, it needs to extend stability in all directions. Germany will keep its links to the West, but must direct more of its energies and resources to its east.

More specifically, Germany must be a bridge between NATO and Russia. When NATO invited Poland, Hungary and the Czech Republic to become members, Kohl brokered the arrangement under which Boris Yeltsin accepted NATO expansion. Kohl also helped negotiate the agreement that gave Russia its voice in NATO through the Permanent Joint Council. With Russia stumbling politically and economically, only Germany can make the European arrangements that can continue the long peace. And Germany will try harder than any other state to keep lines open to Moscow as Schröder is doing.

Whatever else may result from the NATO campaign against Serb forces in the province of Kosovo, that campaign has become a watershed for Europe, for the NATO alliance, and especially for Germany.

The campaign gave German forces a combat role for the first time since 1945. The campaign's humanitarian purpose made it not only possible but even necessary for the Federal Republic to begin to wean itself from its reticence to use force. Comparing Serbia's "ethnic cleansing" of Albanians in Kosovo to Hitler's extermination campaign against Jews, German Chancellor Gerhard Schröder and foreign minister Joschka Fischer said that the Germans had a particular responsibility to act. German Tornado aircraft joined the bombing campaign against Serb forces, with the German Luftwaffe engaged for the first time since World War II, although Germany will not send ground troops.

In addition, around 5,000 German troops went to Macedonia to help protect and care for refugees from Kosovo. The German forces committed to peace-keeping in Bosnia remained at their posts, giving Germany a significant share of the international presence in the former Yugoslavia. German forces joined the United Nations peace-keeping force in Kosovo and were given a sector of their own. Germany also accepted more refugees from Kosovo than any other state.

But the Germans played a more important role in diplomacy than in combat. Fischer made a peace proposal accepted by the European Union and by the Group of Eight (the G-7 plus Russia). Some American officials, however, expressed reservations about it, because Washington wanted to lead in peace-making in Kosovo as well as in combat.

Schröder also made a direct effort to keep Russia involved in Kosovo diplomacy, especially because Moscow had broken its NATO link in anger at the NATO campaign against Serbia. While he coordinated his actions with other NATO members, Schröder decided to send Fischer's secretary of state, Wolfgang Ischinger, to Moscow to present the German plan in order to show his determination to heal the break with Moscow. The Germans thought they had a better understanding for the Russians than Washington, especially as the Americans tended at first to dismiss a Soviet role. Schröder and Fischer also thought the Balkans could not be stabilized without Moscow. German President Roman Herzog attended a meeting of heads of state from the countries of eastern Europe and the former Soviet Union, giving additional weight to a proposal by Schröder for a Marshall Plan for the region.

Germany will also play a key role in the new European effort to develop a special foreign and security identity for the Western European Union within NATO. The Kosovo operation convinced all European countries, but especially

Britain, France and Germany, that Europe must develop its own security role in military and diplomatic strategy. The American advantage in military technology helped Washington to dominate not only combat operations but also policy, making the Europeans realize that they had to develop their own technology and pool their resources better than in the past.

The Germans continually stress that they do not want a power position and do not want to revive the old German Empire's ambitions or policies. Right after German unification, Wolfgang Bergsdorf, a member of Helmut Kohl's domestic political brain trust, published an article detailing the differences between Bismarck's united Germany of 1871 and Kohl's united Germany of 1991. Rudolf Scharping, Schröder's defense minister, has consistently stressed the humanitarian purpose of German military engagement. During and after his visit to Moscow, Ischinger made clear that he was not pursuing a special German road but was acting on behalf of the entire NATO alliance as well as on behalf of the European Union. Germany will have a new Ostpolitik, but Schröder and his successors will want to avoid repeating Bismarck's *Schaukelpolitik* as much as Adenauer or Brandt did. There will be no separate German road. Nonetheless, there will be a distinct German lane.[10]

For the moment, however, the Germans want to concentrate on themselves. The Germans helped to revise Yalta and they helped win the Cold War. Now they want to forget the old realities and the old needs and concentrate on the new.

Germans would like to suspend history. They do not want to repeat it. They would like to live their lives indefinitely in the euphoria of peace and of the prosperity that West Germans came to enjoy and that all now want to share. They know that such a wish is unrealistic, but it captures the stability they want for themselves and for generations yet to come. They will choose as friends those who can best contribute to that purpose.

THE EUROPE OF BERLIN

The unification of Germany brought together a continent as well as a nation. And it began building the foundation for a new Europe, the Europe of Berlin.

Europe has gone through four phases of history since the dawn of the European state system and is now entering a fifth:

- First came the Europe of Westphalia, created by the Treaty of Westphalia of 1648 and ended by the Napoleonic wars around 1800.

- Second came the Europe of Vienna, created by the Congress of Vienna in 1815 and ended by World War I.
- Third came the Europe of Versailles, created by the Versailles Treaty of 1919 and ended by Hitler's invasion of Poland in 1939.
- Fourth came the Europe of Yalta, created by the Yalta agreement of 1945 and ended when the East Berliners broke through the Wall in 1989.
- The fifth phase, still in its formative process, will be the Europe of Berlin. It must be named for Berlin because it began with the breach of the Berlin Wall and because it will be marked by the slow but steady rise of Berlin to become the center of a Europe that stretches from the Atlantic Ocean to the Ural Mountains.

Europe is uniting again after almost a century of war and division. It is now easier to travel across Europe than at any time since 1914. Government officials, business leaders, artists, athletes and others are almost constantly in motion back and forth. Capital investment flows across the continent mainly from west to east. Workers and refugees flow from east to west. Trade in both directions is rising. Europe must now be seen as a continent in the process of recreating itself.

The new Europe can and should improve on the Europe that Sir Edward Grey knew and lamented in 1914, for that Europe had active hatreds and unalterable rivalries across its center. The new Europe has none, although some of the old fractures around the periphery, as in the Balkans, have again erupted and have strained European peace and European cohesion.

Europe needs to be fully united. It cannot be stable and peaceful as long as it remains half rich and half poor. Powerful forces, mainly economic and sentimental, have always pulled the continent together. Equally powerful forces, mainly political and strategic, have always pulled it apart. Now, the former forces can prevail, although political and economic crises could still disrupt and even reverse the process.

Some Western organizations have begun stretching across the continent, having started when NATO admitted the Czech Republic, Hungary and Poland in April 1999. Such expansion carries risks. Russia has objected, with Gorbachev asserting that the United States promised that it would not move NATO further east if he united Germany. The Soviet military have also complained and the Soviet government has delayed ratification of some arms control agreements because of NATO enlargement. Moscow's attitude will slow future NATO expansion, whereas the expansion of the European Union will be slowed by the sheer cost of bringing West European subsidy practices into eastern Europe.

Neither the West European institutions nor the Russians appear to realize, however, that NATO and EU expansion across the continent will change those institutions at least as much as it enlarges them. Moreover, as those institutions stretch to the east, they also move the European center to the east.

NATO and the European Union will change. NATO will have to revise some of its strategic doctrines, and the EU will have to revise some of its integration policies. Organizations created for a divided Europe cannot function in a united Europe. As Europe changes, they must change. As they do, western Europe will become less distinct from its eastern neighbors.

The expansion of West European institutions, like the general unification of the continent, will change the nature of Europe. NATO and the EU may keep their offices in Brussels, but they must move their thinking elsewhere. They must see things as the European center sees them. Brussels could be the center of western Europe; it cannot be the center of a full Europe. It can administer the European Union, but it cannot bring together an entire continent.

If the European institutions cannot change, or if they cannot expand, Germany itself will build the links between the two halves of the continent. It may want to do so anyway, to make sure that it can set the terms for new East-West relations.

Chancellor Schröder quickly recognized the special German interest in a Europe with no dividing lines. Within months after becoming chancellor, he said that Germany can and must play a special role across central and eastern Europe, for historical and more recent reasons—including the role that Czechoslovakia, Hungary and Poland played in helping Germans regain their freedom. He said that Germany would be an 'honest broker" in improving relations across Europe, including Russia, and that he wanted Germany to be a partner for Russia. He has spent special delegations to the Baltic republics and other eastern European states to widen contacts. He has stressed that this will not be a *Deutscher Sonderweg* (a special German road) in the Bismarckian sense but a German policy that should help all of Europe.

German business has been opening up new avenues to the east. German trade and investment in central and eastern Europe exceeds that of other western European states combined. Germany will finance new high-speed trains and superhighways that will link Berlin to Warsaw and beyond, to Minsk, Kiev and Moscow, and along the Baltic to St. Petersburg.

As powerful forces draw Europe together, they will coalesce the continent around Berlin.

Berlin is the geographic center of Europe. If one takes a map of Europe and draws one line from Paris to Moscow and another line from Stockholm to Rome, the two lines intersect remarkably close to the Brandenburg Gate. That gate, like the city of Berlin, stands at the central point between western and eastern as well as between northern and southern Europe. Berlin will be the world capital located most directly between east and west, north and south, no longer at the periphery but at the center of the continent. It is the only city that is part of western, central and eastern Europe at the same time.

People, businesses and influence will gravitate toward Berlin. The German government will sit there. The city will not regain its nineteenth-century status as a major center of heavy industry, but that kind of industry will not matter as much in the future as it did in the past. Instead Berlin will become a central point for high-technology investment, culture, tourism, politics and conferencing, some of the vital activities of the future. Like any great city, it can offer a variety of images to different viewers.

Berlin will become a communications center in a communications age, a multicultural center in a multicultural age. It will also have an East-West perspective that other major cities will not enjoy. This will not happen quickly, because the city acquired a touch of provincialism during the long years of the Cold War. But events will begin to cluster around it, as will people. It will resume its role as the most dynamic of German cities, carrying out those functions that will dominate the new economics and the new spirit of Europe. As Germany's capital, Berlin will draw Germany as well as Europe around itself.

As a reconstituted and rehabilitated Germany can return to its traditional role as what the Germans call *Das Land der Mitte*, Berlin can return to its traditional role as *Die Stadt der Mitte*. But it will be in the middle of a continent, not in the middle of a state. It will serve as the central link between different parts of Europe. If there is to be European stability, Berlin and Germany must be at its center.

Berlin and Germany will not dominate Europe, and they must not try. They can exert influence not by force, as they wanted to do before, but by other means. They must be involved in everything that happens east or west of them and particularly in anything that happens between the eastern and western halves of Europe. They will have a voice, not perhaps always pivotal but always heard, and they may be able to hope that others will not fear a German role but welcome it.

From its narrow role as the capital of the Reich, and from its even narrower role as a principal arena of the Cold War, Berlin can find a wider role as the center of a renewed continent. If it can do so, the Europe of Berlin can be a better Europe than any Europe of the past.

ANOTHER GERMAN-AMERICAN CENTURY?

When Raymond Aron, the French historian and political scientist, walked through the ruins of Berlin in 1945, he is reported to have said, "This could have been Germany's century."

In a sense, of course, it was, although not as any rational German might have wished. Germany remained at the center of world events throughout much of the century, either fighting against others or having others fighting over it.

One could also say, as publisher Henry Luce and many others have, that the twentieth century was America's century. The United States shaped the global polity and the global economy. It spearheaded the founding of the United Nations, the World Bank, the International Monetary Fund, major alliances such as NATO and other institutions. It also sparked a whole new global sentiment for humanitarian issues, such as the international human rights and refugee movements. Simultaneously, it led the world in science, technology, and many forms of industry, and it did so even beyond the end of the century.

Most accurately, one could say that the twentieth century was the German-American century, for each state played a crucial role not only in the world but in the other's fate. Germany brought America into the world and kept it there. Germany drew America into World War I, then into some of the global institutions that emerged in the middle 1920s, and into World War II. It, more than any other state, made the United States supplant Great Britain in its global role. After winning two wars against Germany, the United States then joined with West Germany and others to win the Cold War.

The United States in turn had the greatest influence on Germany. It helped to defeat Germany in two world wars, helped create and defend West Germany during the Cold War and helped to form the Germany that emerged from the Cold War. If Germany influenced America's destiny during the twentieth century, the United States more than returned the compliment.

The two states cooperated intimately during the Cold War itself. West Germany became a principal supporter of many of the global institutions that Washington had created, especially those with financial and strategic responsibilities. The D-mark became the second world currency after the dollar. The Bundesbank became the world's second most influential central bank. And Germany became the world's second largest trading nation. Washington and New York may have designed and founded the current global system, but the system could not have functioned effectively if West Germany had not joined and supported it. Nor could the United States have assumed its global strategic role if it had not had an alliance with West Germany and American military bases there.

West Germany fitted comfortably into Western strategic and financial structures and helped to give them their world-wide reach. It cooperated with Paris and Washington to found the global governing board, the Group of

Seven. It had a secure and respected role at the core of the global system, participating with growing weight in major international strategic and financial decisions.

The twenty-first century will not belong to any single nation or to any pair of nations. Too many major states are rising to global power and eminence. China, India, a revived Russia, a reinvigorated Japan, a more integrated European Union, will all have something to say. So will two other victors of World War II, the United Kingdom and France, as will the developing world. Because most problems cannot now be solved or even addressed by one or two countries alone, states will probably function through alliances.

The next century will not become another German-American century. But the United States and Germany will need to work closely together. As the twentieth century showed, they can do more as friends than as enemies. Yet this will take more effort than during the Cold War.

Berlin will, and even must, henceforth see the world differently from Washington. The Germans and the Americans no longer share a strategic border as they did along the Elbe River. Germany is a European continental state, not a global superpower, and hence Berlin's decisions will be made on a different basis from Washington's.

Washington will also see Berlin differently. During the decade since the breakthrough of the Berlin Wall, American media coverage of Berlin has changed. Whereas American newspaper and television reporters used to speak of West Berlin as "an island of freedom" and of West Berliners as proud U.S. allies, American media now speak mainly of Berlin's Nazi past. By the same token, American coverage of Germany as a whole delves more deeply into the Nazi period than it did during the Cold War.

The new roles of European and American institutions will shift the nature of German-American relations. The growing importance of the European Union, and the important voice that France has in EU policies, can take Germany on different paths from America's. If Germany has to maintain its loyalty to European decisions, it cannot always support the United States. Washington has never fully faced the implications of a united Europe, especially one whose policies might differ from American policies. Neither have most European states—including Germany. Yet a truly united Europe will compel Germany to tilt its loyalties more toward its home continent.

The same applies with respect to NATO. Washington and Berlin will not always see eye to eye on strategic matters. They did not even do so during the final negotiations for German unity.[11] With the implosion of the Soviet Union, they may see even less reason in future.

NATO remains important for Americans and Germans. It helped the United States and Europe address problems in the former Yugoslavia, both in Bosnia or Kosovo, and it will have to continue to do so. But Washington often sees matters more in military and less in political terms than Berlin and other European capitals. Although highly sophisticated U.S. military equipment can work more effectively than European in many conflicts, Europeans will not therefore automatically follow American tactics. And Germany, which has more diplomatic than military assets, will want to use diplomacy more than Washington will. The strategic imperative will not function as it had during the Cold War.

Moscow's Germany expert, Yuli Kvitsinsky, thought that the Germans might welcome U.S. troops less after unification than before. That remains to be tested, but it may turn out to be true. Neither may Washington want so many troops in Europe. Their numbers have already been massively reduced. And Hans-Dietrich Genscher's belief that NATO should be merged into a pan-European structure may yet prove to be correct. Over the long run, Gorbachev's policies and his heritage represent a greater challenge to NATO and the United States than Stalin's, Khrushchev's or Brezhnev's. They cannot help but affect German-American strategic cooperation.

As the new century dawns, Germany will not want to abandon its link with Washington because that link remains essential for German peace, security and prosperity. It is an important part of the Cold War legacy, but it must and will change. Konrad Adenauer, Willy Brandt and Helmut Kohl almost automatically turned to Washington in moments of need. And many American presidents, from Truman to Bush, saw the importance of the German connection. In future no one can take things for granted as in the past. Nor can they expect an automatic turn toward each other.

None of this should evoke any surprise or any alarm, for it marks the normal end of a long process, not only in Germany's relations with America but in its relations with many other states as well. United Germany has more political, strategic and economic alternatives than West Germany had. Its allies do also. All can be grateful for that, but they may have nostalgic moments. De Gaulle once said to the French living in Algeria that *l'Algérie de Papa* had gone forever. So, for Americans, has *l'Allemagne de Papa*. And, for Germans, *l'Amérique de Papa*. For both, NATO is no longer *l'alliance de Papa*.

The true test of the Western alliance in historical terms will not be its victory in the Cold War. That purpose, for which Dean Acheson and Ernest Bevin established the alliance, has been accomplished. The true test will be keeping the peace that follows and making certain that the effort of fifty years of Cold War will not have been in vain.

THE THIRD GERMAN QUESTION

The world has faced two German questions since the dawn of modern European history:

First, how to keep the peace in Germany as others fought over shares of German territory and of the German nation before Bismarck's unification in 1871. The Cold War struggle over Germany became a modern variation of that older German question.

Second, how to keep the peace of Europe and of the world against a united German autocratic state that was not only powerful but often assertive and aggressive. This German problem faced the world during the Wilhelminian Reich and during Hitler's rule.

Now comes the third German question: how to relate to a German state that is united, powerful and at times assertive but that is a fully committed democracy and has no interest in aggression; or, how to relate to a German government that may not have the major elements of national power, such as nuclear weapons, but that still has great influence and will occasionally use it. These questions did not arise during the Cold War when a divided Germany practiced not only a deliberate culture of reticence but also a culture of inaction, leaving major elements of policy to others and only acting within the context of alliances that were mainly guided by others.

Bonn's culture of reticence, its conscious desire to go unnoticed, may pass away with the republic of the same name. Others expect no reticence from France, from Britain, from the United States or from other governments. For decades, though, they have expected it from Germany. But a German democracy also can have national interests and can pursue them as other democracies do.

Thus the third German question can pose problems for Germany and its allies. The Germans will carve out a central place in Europe and a principle role for themselves in the world. They have already begun to do that and will continue to do it, whether under the Schröder government or its successors. Not everyone will like or accept everything the Germans do. But no one has any experience, any prescription or even any historical record for dealing with that kind of Germany. They will have to find their way as Germany, Europe and the world evolve. So will the Germans.

A German chancellor needs to explain matters that other leaders do not need to explain: what is a legitimate German national interest abroad? When should German forces become engaged abroad? To what extent should Germany try to lead? An American or French president or a British prime minister—or even a Japanese premier—does not need to answer that kind of question. Those governments, or others, can and do recognize legitimate national interests. Germany may also have them, but others are still not accustomed to that. Neither are the Germans themselves. A German chancellor must explain more carefully than anyone else what he may perceive as such a national interest. He must explain it abroad as well as at home.

Such questions arise even when Germany acts within international organizations. A German chancellor or foreign minister or even finance minister must serve as a link between many others. Germany is the universal middleman. Increasingly, however, a German chancellor will not want to serve only as a mediator but will want to persuade others to follow German policies and ideas.

The third German question has a less costly answer than the first two, for not so much is at stake. Europe and the world are better off when Germany is neither too weak nor too strong. So, for that matter, are the Germans themselves. But they and their friends need to learn to adjust to new relationships. And the past will get in the way, as people on all sides may fall back into attitudes that may not reflect current reality but may be too deeply rooted to ignore.

Relations will become clearer over time. But they will be difficult at first as the Germans find their new place in Europe and in the world. Each step that Gerhard Schröder, his colleagues and his successors take will set a precedent in shaping Germany's new role. Each will take Germany on a new course. The Germans, and others, need to think about the legacy of the Reich and of the Cold War as well as about the future.

The Germans and their friends can be grateful that they have been able to go beyond the great crises of the Cold War. But the German question remains, as always, a question without an easy answer, for Germans or for others.

The new Berlin Republic will follow certain principles based on Germany's experience during the Cold War:

- Democracy at home. Germans do not want to return to extremism in any form.
- Reliability abroad. Konrad Adenauer established this principle and others have held to it.
- Universal openness in all directions. Willy Brandt established this principle and Schröder wants to maintain it.
- A persistent wish for wider connections, with a determination never to go it alone unless absolutely necessary.

The new Germany has national interests, as did the old, and will pursue them as other states do. It will inevitably come into conflict with the national interests of others. But it will strive to avoid open breaks and outright opposition even if it must differ with another state. Washington may find that Germany shows its disagreement not by taking action against the United States but by taking action without it.

This strategy follows the principles of a shepherd and could legitimately be termed a "shepherd" doctrine. Berlin wants to help guide global and alliance policy. But, like a shepherd, it wants to make sure that all of Germany's friends and partners remain in concert or at least in contact within a circle of diplomacy and, if possible, agreement. The strategy leads to a search for understanding on the widest possible front, toward the East and toward the West. Friends, real and potential, must be brought into the circle. Once they are there, Berlin will try to keep them there. Above all else, it will try to avoid isolation.

Schröder's policy, like that of his successors, must serve this purpose and the reality it reflects. If the Berlin Republic is to be at peace, the Europe of Berlin must be at peace. Schröder must institutionalize stability on all sides, within the European Union, with eastern Europe and Russia, and across the Atlantic.

The new Berlin Republic wants to be what the old Bonn Republic became. It wants to remain a universal link, trying not to direct policy by itself but to keep everybody in step, while keeping its primary allegiance to the democratic West.

Not all of Germany's friends, former occupiers or allies will always approve of German actions. That will be part of the new and third German question. But, whatever problems that third German question may pose, they should prove easier for Europe, America and others than those posed by the two earlier German questions.

NOTES

CHAPTER 1

1. Robert Murphy, *Diplomat among Warriors* (Garden City, NY: Doubleday, 1964), 211.
2. Jochen Laufer, "The Soviet Union and the Zonal Division of Germany," paper presented at a conference entitled "The Soviet Union, Germany, and the Cold War, 1945–1962: New Evidence from Eastern Archives," Essen and Potsdam, June 28-July 3, 1994, 1–3; Wolfgang Pfeiler, "Das Deutschlandbild und die Deutschlandpolitik Josef Stalins," *Deutschland Archiv* (December 1979), 1256–1284.
3. Vladislav Zubok and Constantine Pleshakov, *Inside the Kremlin's Cold War* (Cambridge, MA: Harvard University Press, 1996), 19–21.
4. For contrasting attitudes regarding Germany, see the following sources from which most of this chapter is drawn: John Wheeler-Bennett and Anthony Nicholls, *The Semblance of Peace: The Political Settlement after the Second World War* (New York: Norton, 1974); Winston S. Churchill, *The Second World War* (Boston: Houghton Mifflin, 1953), and especially vol. 5, *Closing the Ring*, and vol. 6, *Triumph and Tragedy*; David S. Painter, *Deciding Germany's Future, 1943–1945*, Case 323, Part A, Pew Case Studies in International Affairs (Washington, D.C.: Institute for the Study of Diplomacy, Georgetown University, n.d.).
5. On the Casablanca Conference: Murphy, *Diplomat among Warriors*, 165–178; Charles E. Bohlen, *Witness to History, 1929–1969* (New York: Norton, 1973), 158; J. K. Snowden, *The German Question* (New York: St. Martin's Press, 1975), 50–56.
6. Wheeler-Bennett and Nicholls, *Semblance of Peace*, 43.
7. Snowden, *German Question*, 58.
8. On the Teheran Conference, see Churchill, *Closing the Ring*, 361–407; U.S. Department of State, *Foreign Relations of the United States: The Conferences at Cairo and Teheran, 1943* (Washington, D.C.: U.S. Government Printing Office, 1961). (Hereafter cited as *FRUS*.)
9. Snowden, *German Question*, 233–236.
10. Wheeler-Bennett and Nicholls, *Semblance of Peace*, 267–271.

11. *FRUS, 1945, Volume 3, The European Advisory Commission; Austria; Germany,* 1–557 and 697–1607.

12. Ibid., 205, 379.

13. Ibid., 175, 208 and 277.

14. U.S. Department of State, *Documents on Germany, 1944–1985* (Washington, D.C.: U.S. Department of State, 1986), 33–40.

15. *FRUS, European Advisory Commission,* 264–265.

16. *Documents on Germany, 1944–1985,* 1–9.

17. Snowden, *German Question,* 67.

18. Ibid., 63–66; Murphy, *Diplomat among Warriors,* 226–227.

19. Bohlen, *Witness to History,* 175–176.

20. Raymond Poidevin, "Die Französische Deutschlandpolitik, 1943–1949," in Claus Scharf and Hans-Jürgen Schröder, eds., *Die Deutschlandpolitik Frankreichs und die Französische Zone, 1945–1949* (Wiesbaden: Franz Steiner, 1983), 15–18.

21. Pierre Maillard, *De Gaulle et l'Allemagne* (Paris: Plon, 1990), 86–93.

22. Churchill, *Triumph and Tragedy,* 227.

23. Ibid.

24. Herbert Tint, *French Foreign Policy since the Second World War* (New York: St. Martin's Press, 1972), 35–39.

25. Snowden, *German Question,* 9; *FRUS, European Advisory Commission,* 318.

26. George C. Herring, *Aid to Russia, 1941–1946* (New York: Columbia University Press, 1973), passim.

27. John H. Backer, *The Decision to Divide Germany* (Durham, N.C.: Duke University Press, 1978), 179.

28. For the Yalta Conference, see: Wheeler-Bennett and Nicholls, *Semblance of Peace,* 174–250; Bohlen, *Witness to History,* 173–201 and 217–239; James MacGregor Burns, *Roosevelt* (New York: Harcourt Brace Jovanovich, 1970), 564–580; James F. Byrnes, *Speaking Frankly* (New York: Harper & Brothers, 1947), 21–45; Churchill, *Triumph and Tragedy,* 327–394; Murphy, *Diplomat among Warriors,* 255–260; Robert E. Sherwood, *Roosevelt and Hopkins* (New York: Harper & Brothers, 1948), 850–869.

29. Alfred M. de Zayas, *Nemesis at Potsdam: The Anglo-Americans and the Expulsion of the Germans* (London: Routledge & Kegan Paul, 1977), 46–52.

30. Ibid., 50.

31. Churchill, *Triumph and Tragedy,* 387.

32. *Documents on Germany, 1944–1985,* 14.

33. Snowden, *German Question,* 75.

34. *Documents on Germany, 1944–1985,* 33–40.

35. For the Potsdam Conference, see: *FRUS, Conference of Berlin (Potsdam), 1945,* vols. 1 and 2, passim; Bohlen, *Witness to History,* 173–201; Backer, *The Decision,* 67–72 and 88–101; Byrnes, *Speaking Frankly,* 65–87; Churchill, *Triumph and Tragedy,* 647–676; David McCullough, *Truman* (New York: Simon & Schuster, 1992), 404–453; Lucius D. Clay, *Decision in Germany* (New York: Doubleday,

1950), 37–49; Murphy, *Diplomat among Warriors*, 245–247; Harry S. Truman, *Memoirs* (Garden City, N.Y.: Doubleday, 1956) 1, 332–412; Wheeler-Bennett and Nicholls, *Semblance of Peace*, 308–343; Zayas, *Nemesis at Potsdam*, 131–141; *Documents on Germany, 1944–1985*, 54–64.

36. *FRUS, Conference of Berlin*, 1.
37. Backer, *The Decision*, 70–71.
38. *Documents on Germany, 1944–1985*, 54–64.
39. Ibid., 55.
40. McCullough, *Truman*, 549.
41. Ibid.; Murphy, *Diplomat among Warriors*, 278–279.
42. Byrnes, *Speaking Frankly*, 54; Wheeler-Bennett and Nicholls, *Semblance of Peace*, 554.
43. McCullough, *Truman*, 452.
44. A. W. DePorte, *De Gaulle's Foreign Policy 1944–1946* (Cambridge, MA: Harvard University Press, 1968), 168–182.
45. Pierre de Senarclens, *From Yalta to the Iron Curtain*, trans. Amanda Pingree, (Oxford: Berg, 1995), 79.

CHAPTER 2

1. The contents of this chapter are based primarily on Allan Bullock, *Ernest Bevin: Foreign Secretary, 1945–1951* (London: Heinemann, 1983), 9–306; James F. Byrnes, *Speaking Frankly* (New York: Harper & Brothers, 1947), 111–149; Anne Deighton, *The Impossible Peace* (Oxford: Clarendon Press, 1993), 54–104; Pierre de Senarclens, *From Yalta to the Iron Curtain*, trans. Amanda Pingree (Oxford: Berg, 1945), 82–120; Wheeler-Bennett and Nicholls, *The Semblance of Peace: The Political Settlement after the Second World War* (New York: Norton, 1974), 419–462.
2. Wheeler-Bennett and Nicholls, *Semblance of Peace*, 429.
3. Byrnes, *Speaking Frankly*, 159–176.
4. Ibid.
5. Deighton, *Impossible Peace*, 81–102; Wilfried Loth, *Stalin's ungeliebtes Kind* (Berlin: Rowohlt, 1994), 85–86.
6. Wolfgang Benz, "Der Strom schien nicht zu versiegen," *Frankfurter Allgemeine Zeitung*, April 6, 1996, 10.
7. John Lewis Gaddis, *We Now Know* (Oxford: Clarendon Press, 1997), 116; Loth, *Stalin's ungeliebtes Kind*, 29.
8. Wladimir S. Semjonov, *Von Stalin bis Gorbatschow: Ein halbes Jahrhundert in diplomatischer Mission, 1939–1991*, trans. Hilde and Helmut Ettinger (Berlin: Nicolai, 1995), 200–201.
9. Material here on the Soviet occupation zone, except where otherwise cited, comes from the following main sources: David Childs, *The GDR: Moscow's German Ally*

(London: George Allen & Unwin, 1983), 1–36; Loth, *Stalin's ungeliebtes Kind*, 13–99; Norman M. Naimark, *The Russians in Germany: A History of the Soviet Zone of Occupation, 1945–1949* (Cambridge, MA: The Belknap Press of Harvard University Press, 1995), 9–204; Semjonov, *Von Stalin bis Gorbatchow*, 206–215; Hermann Weber, *DDR: Grundriss der Geschichte, 1945–1990* (Berlin: Fackelträger, 1991), 18–36; Weber, ed., *DDR: Dokumente zur Geschichte der Deutschen Demokratischen Republik, 1945–1985* (Munich: Deutscher Taschenbuch Verlag, 1986), 17–147.

10. Cited in a report by Wolfgang Leonhard, in Weber, *DDR: Dokumente*, 30.

11. Weber, *DDR: Dokumente*, 51–52.

12. Ruth Fischer, *Stalin und der deutsche Kommunismus* (Berlin: Dietz, 1991), vol. 2, *Die Bolschewisierung des deutschen Kommunismus ab 1925*, 142–143.

13. Loth, *Stalin's ungeliebtes Kind*, 20.

14. Childs, *GDR*, 14–16; "Stalin's reges Interesse an der Bodenreform in der Sowjetzone," *Frankfurter Allgemeine Zeitung*, September 6, 1995, 5.

15. Childs, *GDR*, 15.

16. Naimark, *Russians in Germany*, 168–169.

17. Weber, *DDR: Dokumente*, 43.

18. "Vor- und Frühgeschichte der SED," *Frankfurter Allgemeine Zeitung*, April 29, 1996, 10.

19. Stefan Dietrich, "Die Hand der SPD wurde erst ergriffen, dann abgehackt," *Frankfurter Allgemeine Zeitung*, April 1, 1996, 3; Peter Merseburger, "Es war eine Zwangsvereinigung," *Frankfurter Allgemeine Zeitung*, February 22, 1996, 10; Andreas Malycha, *Auf dem Weg zur SED* (Bonn: Dietz, 1995), passim.

20. Weber, *DDR: Geschichte*, 42; Childs, *GDR*, 22.

21. Fritz Schenk, "Terror gegen ehemalige Sozialdemokraten," in Ilse Spittmann, ed., *Die SED in Geschichte und Gegenwart* (Cologne: Edition Deutschland Archiv, 1987), 177.

22. Wolfgang Leonhard, "Die Abkehr von der Politik des besonderen deutschen Weg zum Sozialismus," in Spittmann, ed., *SED*, 178.

23. Naimark, *Russians in Germany*, 52–60.

24. Ibid., 72; Gaddis, "On Moral Equivalency and Cold War History," *Ethics and International Affairs*, vol. 10, 1996, 141–145.

25. Naimark, *Russians in Germany*, 76.

26. Johann Georg Reissmüller, "Als Ulbricht nirgends mehr eine absolute Mehrheit bekam," *Frankfurter Allgemeine Zeitung*, August 27, 1996, 12.

27. Childs, *GDR*, 17–20.

28. For Ulbricht-Stalin differences, Loth, *Stalin's ungeliebtes Kind*, 58–60; R. C. Raack, "Stalin Plans his Post-War Germany," *Journal of Contemporary History*, vol. 28 (1993), 53–73.

29. John H. Backer, *The Decision to Divide Germany*, (Durham, NC: Duke University Press, 1978), 345.

30. Semjonov, *Von Stalin bis Gorbatschow*, 226–227; Loth, *Stalin's ungeliebtes Kind*, 76–79; and Naimark, *Russians in Germany*, 25–55, cite many Ulbricht-Stalin differences.

31. Naimark, *Russians in Germany*, 49–53.

32. Semjonov, *Von Stalin bis Gorbatschow*, 235–245 and 260–265.

33. Ibid., 261.

34. Backer, *The Decision*, 137.

35. Hannes Adomeit, *Imperial Overstretch* (Baden-Baden: Nomos, 1998), 58.

36. Jacques Attali, *Verbatim III* (Paris: Fayard, 1995), 417.

37. For general Allied policies, see Cyril Black, Jonathan Helmreich, Paul Helmreich, Charles Issawi, and James McAdams, *Rebirth* (Boulder, CO: Westview, 1992), 171–208; Theodor Eschenburg, *Jahre der Besatzung, 1945–1949*, vol. 1 of *Die Geschichte der Bundesrepublik Deutschland* (Stuttgart: Deutsche Verlags-Anstalt, 1985), 77–105.

38. Jean Edward Smith, *Lucius D. Clay* (New York: Henry Holt and Company, 1990), 424–428.

39. Ibid., 396–397.

40. Byrnes, *Speaking Frankly*, 190.

41. Smith, *Clay*, 396–397; John L. Harris, *Remembering and Renewing* (Washington, D.C.: American Institute for Contemporary German Studies, 1998), passim.

42. De Senarclens, *From Yalta*, 147.

43. Smith, *Clay*, 414–415.

44. Deighton, *Impossible Peace*, 62.

45. Ibid., 55–78.

46. Heike Bungert, "A New Perspective on French-American Relations during the Occupation of Germany, 1943–1945: Behind-the-Scenes Diplomatic Bargaining and the Zonal Merger," *Diplomatic History* 18, no. 3 (Summer 1994), 332–352; A. W. DePorte, *De Gaulle's Foreign Policy, 1944–1946* (Cambridge, MA: Harvard University Press, 1968), 250–271; Georges-Henri Soutou, "France and the German Rearmament Problem, 1945–1955," in R. Ahmann, A. M. Birke, and M. Howard, eds., *The Quest for Stability* (Oxford: Oxford University Press, 1993), 487–512; Herbert Tint, *French Foreign Policy since the Second World War* (New York: St. Martin's Press, 1972), 28–43.

47. Lucius D. Clay, *Decision in Germany* (New York: Doubleday, 1950), 263–280; James Bacque, *Verschwiegene Schuld* (Berlin: Ullstein, 1995), passim, suggests that the food shortages may have represented a deliberate policy by Washington and other victorious capitals. Such a policy may well have existed in the minds of some, especially some Americans still committed to carrying out the harsher terms of JCS 1067, but there is no convincing evidence that either Clay or Truman deliberately pursued a starvation policy in the Western occupation zones and there is a lot of evidence that they did not.

CHAPTER 3

1. Eduard Mark, "The War Scare of 1946 and Its Consequences," *Diplomatic History* (Summer 1997), 383–415.

2. Alan Bullock, *Ernest Bevin: Foreign Secretary, 1945–1951* (London: Heinemann, 1983), 288.

3. Wilfried Loth, *Stalin's ungeliebtes Kind* (Berlin: Rowohlt, 1994), 88–93.

4. Ibid.

5. Scott D. Parrish and Mikhail N. Narinsky, *New Evidence on the Soviet Rejection of the Marshall Plan, 1947*, Working Paper no. 9, Cold War International History Project (hereafter cited as CWIHP) (Washington, D.C.: Woodrow Wilson International Center for Scholars, 1994), passim.

6. Charles E. Bohlen, *Witness to History, 1929–1969* (New York: Norton, 1973), 262.

7. Pierre de Senarclens, *From Yalta to the Iron Curtain*, trans. Amanda Pingree (Oxford: Berg, 1995), 217 and 225.

8. Mikhail Narinsky, "Soviet Policy and the Berlin Blockade, 1948," paper presented at a conference entitled "The Soviet Union, Germany, and the Cold War, 1949–1952: New Evidence from Eastern Archives," Essen and Potsdam, June 28–July 3, 1994, 2.

9. Melvyn Leffler, *The Struggle for Germany and the Origins of the Cold War* (Washington, D.C.: German Historical Institute, 1996), 41.

10. Anne Deighton, *The Impossible Peace* (Oxford: Clarendon Press, 1993), 207–222; Bohlen, *Witness to History*, 252; Lucius D. Clay, *Decision in Germany* (New York: Doubleday, 1950), 346–348; Bullock, *Bevin*, 496–497.

11. Loth, *Stalin's ungeliebtes Kind*, 98–99.

12. Ibid.

13. De Senarclens, *From Yalta*, 235.

14. Thomas Paterson, ed., *The Origins of the Cold War* (Lexington, MA: D.C. Heath and Company, 1974), 18.

15. John H. Backer, *The Decision to Divide Germany* (Durham, NC: Duke University Press, 1978), 86–87.

16. Clark Clifford with Richard Holbrooke, *Counsel to the President* (New York: Random House, 1991), 105–110; Spencer Warren, "Churchill's Realism," *The National Interest*, no. 42 (Winter 1995/96), 38–49.

17. Warren, "Churchill's Realism," 47.

18. De Senarclens, *From Yalta*, 135–136.

19. For full texts of cables from various ambassadors, see Kenneth M. Jensen, ed., *Origins of the Cold War*, rev. ed. (Washington, D.C.: U.S. Institute of Peace Press, 1994), 3–67.

20. Ibid., 37.

21. Clifford's memorandum remained secret for twenty years. Arthur Krock learned of it from Truman in 1966 and published it as an appendix to *Memoirs* (New York: Funk & Wagnalls, 1968), 419–482.

22. Viktor Mal'kov, "Commentary," in Jensen, ed., *Origins*, 74–77.

23. Reprinted in *Foreign Affairs* (Spring 1987), 852–868.

24. Walter Isaacson and Evan Thomas, *The Wise Men* (London: Faber and Faber, 1986), 289–290.

25. Andrei Zhdanov, *The International Situation* (Moscow: Foreign Languages Publishing House, 1947).

26. Tony Judt, "Why the Cold War Worked," *New York Review of Books*, October 9, 1997, 39–42.

27. Clay, *Decision in Germany*, 105–164 and 343–353.

28. Wolfgang Pfeiler, "Das Deutschlandbild und die Deutschlandpolitik Josef Stalins," *Deutschland Archiv* (December 1979), 1256–1284.

29. Ibid.

30. Dimitri Simes, "Wir haben es gewusst," *Europäische Rundschau* (Fall 1995), 17.

31. Joseph R. Starobin, "Origins of the Cold War: The Communist Dimension," *Foreign Affairs* (July 1969), 684–685; Vladislav Zubok and Constantine Pleshakov, *Inside the Kremlin's Cold War* (Cambridge, MA.: Harvard University Pres, 1996) 37–75.

CHAPTER 4

1. Anne Deighton, "Cold-War Diplomacy: British Policy towards Germany's Role in Europe, 1945–9," in Ian D. Turner, ed., *Reconstruction in Post-War Germany* (Oxford: Berg, 1989), 32–33.

2. U.S. Department of State, *Documents on Germany, 1944–1985* (Washington, D.C.: Department of State, 1986), 140–141.

3. Herbert Tint, *French Foreign Policy since the Second World War* (New York: St. Martin's Press, 1972), 44–47.

4. Mikhail Narinsky, "Soviet Policy and the Berlin Blockade, 1948," paper presented at a conference entitled "The Soviet Union, Germany, and the Cold War, 1949–1952: New evidence from Eastern Archives," Essen and Potsdam, June 28–July 3, 1994, 6.

5. *Documents on Germany 1944–1985*, 142.

6. Lucius D. Clay, *Decision in Germany* (New York: Doubleday, 1950), 361; author's interview with Clay, Berlin, November 1961.

7. Vladislav Zubok and Constantine Pleshakov, *Inside the Kremlin's Cold War* (Cambridge, MA: Harvard University Press, 1996), 52; Norman M. Naimark, *The Russians in Germany: A History of the Soviet Zone of Occupation, 1945–1949* (Cambridge, MA: The Belknap Press of Harvard University Press, 1995), 6, 306; Narinsky, "Soviet Policy," 5–8.

8. Richard Collier, *Bridge Across the Sky* (London: Macmillan, 1978), 7–8.

9. *Documents on Germany, 1944–1985*, 143–149.

10. Clay, *Decision in Germany*, 361–362; Dean Acheson, *Present at the Creation* (New York: Norton, 1969), 261.

11. Clay interview, November 1961.

12. The record of the early days of the blockade, unless otherwise specified, comes from W. Phillips Davison, *The Berlin Blockade* (Princeton, N.J.: Princeton University

Press, 1958), 91–151; Clay, *Decision in Germany*, 360–362; Alexander George and Richard Smoke, *Deterrence in American Foreign Policy* (New York: Columbia University Press, 1974), 107–137.

13. Davison, *Berlin Blockade*, 22–25.
14. Jean Edward Smith, *Lucius D. Clay* (New York: Henry Holt and Company, 1990), 501.
15. Ibid., 494–497.
16. Davison, *Berlin Blockade*, 110.
17. Ibid., 116.
18. U.S. Department of State, *Foreign Relations of the United States: 1948: Germany and Austria* Washington, D.C.: U.S. Government Printing Office, 1985), 2, 887–921 (Hereafter cites as *FRUS.*).
19. Erich Gniffke, "Beginn der Planwirtschaft," in Ilse Spittmann, ed., *Die SED in Geschichte und Gegenwart* (Cologne: Edition Deutschland Archiv, 1987), 179.
20. Clay interview, October 1961.
21. Smith, *Clay*, 519–523.
22. *FRUS, 1948, Germany and Austria*, 2, 916–917.
23. Narinsky, "Soviet Policy," 2.
24. Wilfried Loth, *Stalin's ungeliebtes Kind* (Berlin: Rowohlt, 1944), 123.
25. Narinsky, "Soviet Policy," 13–14.
26. Richard von Weizsäcker, "Ort der Begegung zweier deutscher Wirklichkeiten," *Frankfurter Allgemeine Zeitung*, June 30, 1990, 10.
27. Collier, *Bridge*, 119.
28. Clay interview, November 1961.
29. Loth, *Stalin's ungeliebtes Kind*, 123–128.
30. The Berlin Air Safety Center (BASC) was established by the four victorious powers after World War II to ensure the safety of Allied and Soviet air traffic in the Berlin area. It had a coordinating function but no control authority over the air corridors and over a wide circular area above and around Berlin itself. Aircraft going in or out of Berlin had to register their flight plans with the BASC and would normally be given a clearance. If they did not receive a clearance, they could still fly but at their own risk. BASC admitted no German aircraft.
31. Collier, *Bridge*, 150.
32. Davison, *Berlin Blockade*, 256.
33. Collier, *Bridge*, 161.
34. Ibid., 162–166.
35. Ibid., 155.

CHAPTER 5

1. For prelude to FRG Basic Law, see Theodor Eschenburg, *Jahre der Besatzung, 1945–1949*, vol. 1 of *Die Geschichte der Bundesrepublik Deutschland* (Stuttgart:

Deutsche Verlags-Anstalt, 1985), 459–513; Lucius D. Clay, *Decision in Germany* (New York: Doubleday, 1950), 392–420.

2. Peter Pulzer, *German Politics 1945–1995* (Oxford: Oxford University Press, 1995), 45–46;

3. Eschenburg, *Jahre der Besatzung*, 469.

4. Hans-Peter Schwarz, *Adenauer—Der Aufstieg: 1876–1952* (Stuttgart: DVA, 1980), passim.

5. Kurt Rabl, Christian Stoll, and Manfred Vasold, *From the U.S. Constitution to the Basic Law of the Federal Republic of Germany* (Gräfelfing: Moos, 1988).

6. Federal Republic of Germany, *Democracy in Germany* (Bonn: Press and Information Office, 1985), 17–24.

7. Alan Bullock, *Ernest Bevin: Foreign Secretary, 1945–1951* (London: Heinemann, 1983), 695.

8. Ibid., 667–670.

9. James Chace, *Acheson* (New York: Simon & Schuster, 1998), 208–209.

10. Wolfgang Leonhard, "Abschied von den Illusionen," in Ilse Spittmann and Gisela Helwig, eds., *DDR Lesebuch* (Cologne: Edition Deutschland Archiv, 1969), 240–243.

11. Ibid.

12. Hermann Weber, *Kleine Geschichte der DDR* (Bonn: Edition Deutschland Archiv, 1980), 45.

13. Ibid.

14. The above account draws on Wilfried Loth, *Stalin's ungeliebtes Kind* (Berlin: Rowohlt, 1994) 31–159, and on Weber, *Kleine Geschichte*, 35–45.

15. Norman M. Naimark, *The Russians in Germany: A History of the Soviet Zone of Occupation, 1945–1949* (Cambridge, MA: The Belknap Press of Harvard University Press, 1995), 56.

16. Loth, *Stalin's ungeliebtes Kind*, 146.

17. David Childs, *The GDR: Moscow's German Ally* (London: George Allen & Unwin, 1983), 23.

18. Naimark, *Russians in Germany*, 57–60.

19. Weber, *Kleine Geschichte*, 42–45.

20. John A. Reed, Jr., *Germany and NATO* (Washington, D.C.: National Defense University Press, 1987), 3–45; Dean Acheson, *Present at the Creation: My Years in the State Department* (New York: W.W. Norton, 1969), 277–284; Chace, *Acheson*, 201; Pierre de Senarclens, *From Yalta to the Iron Curtain*, trans. Amanda Pingree (Oxford: Berg, 1995), 239–260.

21. Bullock, *Bevin*, 700.

22. Thomas H. Etzold and John Lewis Gaddis, *Containment: Documents on American Policy and Strategy, 1945–1950* (New York: Columbia University Press, 1978), 144–152.

23. U.S. Department of State, *Documents on Germany, 1944–1985* (Washington, D.C.: U.S. Department of State, 1986), 209–212.

24. Reed, *Germany and NATO*, 10.
25. W. Taylor Fain III and David S. Painter, "Germany and the Defense of Europe," Pew Case Studies in International Affairs, Case 322, 1989, 1.
26. Ibid.

CHAPTER 6

1. For text of NSC 68, see Ernest R. May, ed., *American Cold War Strategy: Interpreting NSC 68* (Boston: Bedford Books of St. Martin's Press, 1993), 23–82.
2. W. Taylor Fain III and David S. Painter, "Germany and the Defense of Europe," Pew Case Studies in International Affairs, Case 322, 1989, 3–5.
3. Cold War International History Project (hereafter cited as CWIHP), *Bulletin*, Woodrow Wilson International Center for Scholars, Washington, 4 (Fall 1994), 60.
4. Wilfried Loth, "The Korean War and the Reorganization of the European Security System 1948–1955," in R. Ahmann, A.M. Birke, and M. Howard, eds., *The Quest for Stability* (London: Oxford University Press, 1993), 479.
5. U.S. Department of State, *Recent Soviet Pressures on Germany* (Washington: State Department Office of Public Affairs, September, 1951), Department of State Publication 4123, February 1951, 1–2.
6. May, *American Cold War Strategy*, 14.
7. Harry S. Truman, *Memoirs* (New York: Funk & Wagnalls, 1968), 253.
8. James Chace, *Acheson* (New York: Simon & Schuster, 1998), 324–325.
9. Kathryn Weathersby, "Soviet Aims in Korea and the Origins of the Korean War, 1945–1950: New Evidence from Russian Archives," Working Paper #8, CWIHP, Woodrow Wilson International Center for Scholars, Washington, D.C., November, 1993, 30–31; Jian Chen, "The Sino-Soviet Alliance and China's Entry into the Korean War," Working Paper #1, CWIHP, Woodrow Wilson International Center for Scholars, Washington, D.C., June, 1992.
10. Dennis L. Bark and David R. Gress, *From Shadow to Substance, 1945–1963*, vol. 1 of *A History of West Germany* (Oxford: Blackwell, 1989), 275–288; Fain and Painter, "Defense of Europe," 5.
11. Arnulf Baring, *Aussenpolitik in Adenauers Kanzlerdemokratie* (Munich: R. Oldenbourg, 1969), 128–146; Kai Bird, *The Chairman* (New York: Simon & Schuster, 1992), 317–375; Thomas Schwartz, *America's Germany* (Cambridge, MA: Harvard University Press, 1991), 211–278.
12. For citations and summary of Monnet's views, François Duchêne, *Jean Monnet* (New York: Norton, 1994), 181–225.
13. Robert McGeehan, *The German Rearmament Question* (Urbana: University of Illinois Press, 1971), passim.
14. Schwartz, *America's Germany*, 247.
15. Federal Republic of Germany, *Die Sperrmassnahmen der DDR vom Mai 1952* (Bonn: Ministerium für Innerdeutsche Beziehungen, 1953).

16. Ibid., 4; Interview with Stalin's German expert Daniil Melnikov, *Der Spiegel*, no. 49 (1990), 185.

17. Vojtech Mastny, "Stalin's German Illusion," paper presented at a conference entitled "The Soviet Union, Germany, and the Cold War, 1945–1962: New Evidence from Eastern Archives," Essen and Potsdam, June 28-July 3, 1994, 2.

18. *Foreign Relations of the United States, 1952–1954,* (hereafter cited as *FRUS*) vol. 7, 169–172.

19. For Western consultations and texts of East-West notes, see ibid., 172–327.

20. Rolf Steininger, *Eine Chance zur Wiedervereinigung? Die Stalin-Note vom 10. März 1952* (Bonn: Neue Gesellschaft, 1985), 36–37.

21. Ibid., 23–25.

22. Ibid., 85,

23. *FRUS, 1952–1954,* 7, 185.

24. Ibid., 186.

25. Ibid., 250.

26. Ibid., 244.

27. For the strongest single assertion that the West missed a valuable opportunity, see Steininger, *Eine Chance?* published in English as *The German Question: The Stalin-Note of 1952 and the Problem of Reunification* (New York: Columbia University Press, 1990). For opposite case, see Hans-Peter Schwarz, ed., *Die Legende von der verpassten Gelegenheit* (Stuttgart: Belser, 1982). Papers based on recently available documents and supporting Schwarz's view are Ruud van Dijk, "The Stalin-Note: Last Chance for Unification?" paper presented at a conference entitled "The Soviet Union, Germany, and the Cold War, 1945–1962: New Evidence from Eastern Archives," Essen and Potsdam, June 28-July 3, 1994, and Mastny, "Stalin's German Illusion." A former East German official close to the center of power in East Berlin (and also very skeptical) is Fritz Schenk, "Der lange Schatten Josef Stalin's," *Frankfurter Allgemeine Zeitung*, March 10, 1994, 12. For continuing debate, see articles and letters in *Deutschland Archiv* (February and August 1992). For post-unity discussion, see Rolf Steininger, Gerhard Wettig and Hans-Peter Schwarz, *Die Sowjetische Note vom 10. März 1952—Wiedervereinigungsangebot oder Propagandawerkzeug?* (Köln: Bundesinstitut für Ostwissenschaftliche und Internationale Studien, 1981). After unification, Wettig examined pertinent Soviet and East German documents, which, he wrote, reinforced his belief that Stalin had never planned to accept a truly free united Germany.

28. *FRUS, 1952–1954,* 7, 182–183.

29. George Kennan, *Memoirs, 1950–1963* (New York: Boston, Little, 1963), 107.

30. For recent information about the links between Soviet leaders and their policies on Germany, this chapter relies on Vladislav Zubok, "Soviet Foreign Policy in Germany and Austria and the post-Stalin Succession Struggle, 1953–1955," discussion paper presented at a conference entitled "The Soviet Union, Germany, and the Cold War, 1945–1962: New Evidence from Eastern Archives," Essen and Potsdam, June 28-July 3, 1994; and James Richter, "Reexamining Soviet Policy

towards Germany during the Beria Interregnum," Working Paper 3, CWIHP, Woodrow Wilson International Center for Scholars, June, 1992.

31. Dwight D. Eisenhower, *Mandate for Change, 1953–1956* (Garden City, N.Y.: Doubleday, 1963), 143–147; Robert Bowie and Richard Immerman, "Chance for Peace: the Initial U.S. Response to Stalin's Death," discussion paper prepared for a conference entitled "The Year 1953 in the Cold War," Potsdam, November 10–12, 1996.

32. Mastny, "Missed Opportunities after Stalin's Death" and Wettig, "Did Beria Seek Agreement on German Unification? An Old Problem in the Light of New Evidence," discussion papers presented at a conference entitled "The Year 1953 in the Cold War," Potsdam, November 10–12, 1996, 4–5 and 8 respectively.

33. Klaus Larres, *Politik der Illusionen: Churchill, Eisenhower und die deutsche Frage, 1945–1955,* (Göttingen: Vandenhoeck & Ruprecht, 1995); 133–134; Larres, "Great Britain and the East German Uprising of June, 1953," discussion paper prepared for a conference entitled "The Year 1953 in the Cold War," Potsdam, November 10–12, 1996, 3–10.

34. Larres, *Politik der Illusionen,* 135.

35. For Soviet fears about Germany, 1952 and 1953, see Vladislav Zubok, "Soviet Intelligence and the Cold War: The 'Small' Committee of Information, 1952–53," Working Paper 4, CWIHP, Woodrow Wilson International Center for Scholars, December, 1992.

36. Leonid Reshin, "Events of June 17th in GDR seen through the Moscow Archives," discussion paper presented at a conference entitled "The Year 1953 in the Cold War," Potsdam, November 10–12, 1996, translated by Danny Rozas, 3.

37. Peter Przybylski, *Tatort Politburo: Die Akte Honecker* (Berlin: Rowohlt, 1992), 240–249.

38. Christian F. Ostermann, "This Is Not a Politburo, But a Madhouse," CWIHP *Bulletin,* Woodrow Wilson International Center for scholars, 10 (March 1998), 61–110.

39. For details on the debate about Beria's offer and his intent, see following papers presented at a conference entitled "The Year 1953 in the Cold War," Potsdam, November 10–12, 1996: Ruud van Dijk, "The German Question Dropped, Revisited, and Frozen"; Vladislav Zubok, "Unacceptably Rude and Blatant on the German Question: The Succession Struggle after Stalin's Death, Beria and the Significance of the Debate on the GDR in Moscow in April-May, 1953"; Ruud van Dijk, "The Kremlin, the East Germans, and the GDR in 1952–1953." Also see, as basic but perhaps questionable sources: Pavel and Anatoli Sudoplatov, with Jerold and Leona Schecter, *Special Tasks: The Memoirs of an Unwanted Witness, a Soviet Spymaster* (Boston: Back Bay, 1995), 363–364.

40. Malenkov's comments, like other discussion and remarks, are taken from the German translation of the May 27 record. Cited in Mark Kramer, "The Post-Stalin Succession Struggle and the Soviet Bloc: New Courses, Upheavals, and the Beria

Affair," discussion paper prepared for a conference entitled "The Year 1953 in the Cold War," Potsdam, November 10–12, 1996.

41. Hans Wassmund, *Kontinuität im Wandel: Bestimmungsfaktoren sowjetischer Deutschlandpolitik in der Nach-Stalin-Zeit* (Cologne: Bohlau Verlag, 1974), 35–37.

42. Ostermann, "Not a Politburo," 66.

43. Wettig, "Sowjetische Wiedervereinigungsbemühungen im ausgehenden Frühjahr 1953?" *Deutschland Archiv* (September 1992), 947.

44. Ostermann, "Not a Politburo," 66.

45. *Berliner Montags Echo*, July 6, 1953, 1.

46. Much has been written about June 17, 1953. This review draws particularly on two works: Ilse Spittmann and Karl Wilhelm Fricke, eds., *17 Juni 1953* (Cologne: Edition Deutschland Archiv, 1988); and Christian F. Ostermann, "The United States, the East German Uprising of 1953, and the Limits of Rollback," Working Paper 11, CWIHP, Woodrow Wilson International Center for Scholars (December 1994). It also draws on the following recent studies based on Soviet and East German documents and presented at a conference entitled "The Year 1953 in the Cold War," at Potsdam, November 10–12, 1996: Gary Bruce, "The MFS, the West, and the June 17 Uprising"; T. Dietrich, "Militär- und Sicherheitspolitische Aspekte der Stalinistischen Systemkrise 1953 aus DDR-Sicht"; Victor Gobarev, "The German Uprising of 1953 through the Eyes of the Soviet Military"; and Monika Kaiser, "Die SED-Führung und die Krise des Stalinistischen Systems."

47. Radio East Berlin, May 28, 1953; *Neues Deutschland*, June 25, 1953.

48. Christian F. Ostermann, "Die Ostdeutschen an einen langwierigen Kampf gewöhnen," *Deutschland Archiv* (June 1992), 350–368.

49. Larres, *Politik der Illusionen*, 175–212.

50. Wassmund, *Kontinuität im Wandel*, 39.

51. David Childs, *The GDR: Moscow's German Ally* (London: George Allen & Unwin, 1983), 37.

52. Larres, *Politik der Illusionen*, 251–253.

53. Philip Windsor, *Germany and the Management of Detente* (New York: Praeger, 1971), 80.

CHAPTER 7

1. The principal source for this section, unless otherwise indicated, is Anthony Eden, *Full Circle* (Boston: Houghton Mifflin, 1960), 61–174.

2. Michael Guhin, *John Foster Dulles: A Statesman and His Times* (New York: Columbia University Press, 1972), 219.

3. For Eden's talks on European tour, see Eden, *Full Circle*, 174–181.

4. James G. Hershberg, *James B. Conant* (New York: Alfred A. Knopf, 1993), 675.

5. Guhin, *Dulles*, 219.

6. Dwight Eisenhower, *Mandate for Change, 1953–1956* (Garden City, NY: Double-day, 1963), 526; Guhin, *Dulles*, 319.

7. Hermann Weber, ed., *DDR: Dokumente zur Geschichte der Deutschen Demokratischen Republik, 1945–1984* (Munich: Deutscher Taschenbuch Verlag, 1986), 217–218.

8. For Adenauer's attitudes and policies on unification and for record of his initiatives, see Hans-Peter Schwarz, "Adenauers Wiedervereinigungspolitik," *Die Politische Meinung* (November/December 1975), 33–54.

9. Heinrich von Siegler, *The Reunification and Security of Germany* (Munich: Siegler, 1957), 55–120; for GDR views, Gottfried Zieger, *Die Haltung der SED und DDR zur Einheit Deutschlands 1949–1957* (Cologne: Verlag Wissenschaft und Politik, 1988), 7–42.

10. See, for example, the exchanges of January 1958, U.S. Department of State, *Documents on Germany, 1944–1985* (Washington, D.C.: Department of State, 1986), 513–518.

11. For Adenauer visit to Moscow, see Angela Stent, *From Embargo to Ostpolitik* (Cambridge: Cambridge University Press, 1981), 20–47.

12. Rudolf Morsey, "Die Deutschlandpolitik Adenauers," *Vierzig Jahre Deutschlandpolitik im internationalen Kräftefeld* (Bonn: Edition Deutschland Archiv, 1989), 16–32.

CHAPTER 8

1. Howard Trivers, *Three Crises in American Foreign Affairs and a Continuing Revolution* (Carbondale: Southern Illinois University Press, 1970), 3–4.

2. For debates among East European states as well as between Ulbricht and Khrushchev, see Vladislav Zubok, *Khrushchev and the Berlin Crisis (1958–1962)* (Washington, D.C.: Cold War International History Project [hereafter cited as CWIHP], Woodrow Wilson International Center for Scholars, 1993), passim.

3. Honoré M. Catudal, *Kennedy and the Berlin Wall Crisis* (Berlin: Berlin Verlag, 1980), 48.

4. Hope M. Harrison, *Ulbricht and the Concrete "Rose": New Archival Evidence on the Dynamics of Soviet-East German Relations and the Berlin Crisis, 1958–1961* (Washington, D.C.: CWIHP, Woodrow Wilson International Center for Scholars, 1993), 17.

5. Zubok, *Khrushchev and the Berlin Crisis*, 7.

6. Dennis L. Bark and David R. Gress, *From Shadow to Substance, 1945–1963*, vol. 1 of *A History of West Germany* (Oxford: Blackwell, 1989), 435.

7. U.S. Department of State, *Documents on Germany, 1944–1985* (Washington, D.C.: Department of State, 1986), 542–546.

8. Zubok, *Khrushchev and the Berlin Crisis*, 9.

9. For Khrushchev-Ulbricht contrasts, see Wolfgang Heidelmeyer and Günter Hindrichs, *Documents on Berlin, 1943–1963* (Munich: R. Oldenbourg, 1963), 197–204, 233–242; Harrison, *Ulbricht and the Concrete "Rose"*; Zubok, *Khrushchev and the Berlin Crisis,* passim.

10. Hannes Adomeit, *Soviet Risk-Taking and Crisis Behavior,* (Boston: George Allen & Unwin, 1982), 271–272.

11. New sources have added to the literature about the Berlin crisis, on Western as well as on Khrushchev's and Ulbricht's views. See William Burr, "Avoiding the Slippery Slope: The Eisenhower Administration and the Berlin Crisis, November 1958-January 1959," *Diplomatic History,* 18, no. 2 (Spring 1994), 177–205. The U.S. Department of State in 1993 published four volumes in its *Foreign Relations of the United States* series (hereafter cited as *FRUS*), with volumes 8 and 9 of the 1958–1960 series covering the first phase of the crisis (1958–1960) and volumes 14 and 15 covering the second phase (1961–1963); they provide important sources for this and the next three chapters.

12. *FRUS, Berlin Crisis, 1958–1959,* 8, 19.

13. Burr, "Slippery Slope," 195.

14. Ibid., 198.

15. Harold Macmillan, *Pointing the Way, 1959–1961* (London: Macmillan, 1972), 61.

16. *FRUS, Berlin Crisis, 1958–1959,* 8, 568. Foreign Secretary Selwyn Lloyd actually used the "flimsy" phrase but was citing Macmillan's view.

17. Macmillan, *Pointing the Way,* 61–408, gives many examples.

18. Ibid., 78–79.

19. *FRUS, Berlin Crisis, 1958–1959,* 8, 521.

20. Macmillan, *Pointing the Way,* 93–115.

21. *FRUS, Berlin Crisis, 1958–1959,* 8, 426.

22. Ibid., 426, 461, 483, and 651.

23. Ibid., 76–81.

24. Bark and Gress, *Shadow to Substance,* 439.

25. For record of conference, see *FRUS, Berlin Crisis, 1958–1959,* 8, 540–1110.

26. Ibid., 688.

27. Macmillan, *Pointing the Way,* 78.

28. Burr, "Slippery Slope," 189–205.

29. Anatoly Dobrynin, *In Confidence* (New York: Times Books, 1995), 51.

30. Zubok, *Khrushchev and the Berlin Crisis,* 12.

31. Harrison, *Ulbricht and the Concrete "Rose,"* 33–35 and 53.

32. Bark and Gress, *Shadow to Substance,* 454–455.

33. Zubok, *Khrushchev and the Berlin Crisis,* 13–14.

34. Author's interview with John Mapother, American expert on Germany, Washington, August 15, 1998.

35. Zubok, *Khrushchev and the Berlin Crisis,* 13–14; Karl-Heinz Schmidt, *Dialog über Deutschland* (Baden-Baden: Nomos, 1998), 41–44.

36. Zubok, *Khrushchev and the Berlin Crisis,* 14–15.

CHAPTER 9

1. For materials on Kennedy and Berlin and Germany, see Michael R. Beschloss, *The Crisis Years: Kennedy and Khrushchev, 1961–1963* (New York: Edward Burlingam Books, 1991); Frank Mayer, *Kennedy and Adenauer* (New York: St. Martin's Press, 1995); and Richard Reeves, *President Kennedy* (New York: Simon & Schuster, 1992). Author also has recollections from his own service in Berlin during the Kennedy years, as director of several Kennedy visits including the president's and Robert's, and from frequent contacts with White House and State Department officials who knew the views of Kennedy and his advisers.
2. Ole R. Holsti, "The 1914 Case," *American Political Science Review* 54, no. 2 (June 1965) 365–378.
3. Reeves, *Kennedy*, 215.
4. Dean Rusk (as told to Richard Rusk), *As I Saw It* (New York: Norton, 1990), 218.
5. Curtis Cate, *The Ides of August: The Berlin Wall Crisis, 1961* (New York: Evans, 1975), 321–322.
6. Eric Roll, "Harsh Realities of Postwar Britain," *Financial Times*, July 13, 1995, 10.
7. Quoted in Mayer, *Kennedy and Adenauer*, 13–14.
8. *Der Spiegel*, no. 41 (1989), 157.
9. Dennis L. Bark and David R. Gress, *From Shadow to Substance, 1945–1963*, vol. 1 of *A History of West Germany* (Oxford: Blackwell, 1989), 483.
10. Mayer, *Kennedy and Adenauer*, 85.
11. Ibid., 46–48.
12. Vladislav Zubok, *Khrushchev and the Berlin Crisis (1958–1962)* (Washington, D.C.: Cold War International History Project, Woodrow Wilson International Center for Scholars, 1993), (hereafter cited as CWIHP), 246.
13. *Der Spiegel*, no. 40 (1989), 163.
14. Zubok, *Khrushchev and the Berlin Crisis*, 247.
15. Ibid.
16. Beschloss, *Crisis Years*, 211.
17. Rusk, *As I Saw It*, 220–221.
18. Harold Macmillan, *Pointing the Way, 1959–1961* (London: Macmillan, 1972), 356–358.
19. For these quotes, and for an immediately subsequent review of Soviet actions and statements, see Robert M. Slusser, *The Berlin Crisis of 1961* (Baltimore: Johns Hopkins University Press, 1973), 1–20.
20. *Der Spiegel*, no. 41 (1989), 168.
21. Slusser, *Berlin Crisis*, 8. For texts of Khrushchev's speech and of the note he gave to Kennedy in Vienna, see *The Soviet Stand on Germany* (Moscow: Crosscurrents Press, 1961), 17–45.
22. Wjatscheslaw Keworkow, *Der Geheime Kanal* (Berlin: Rowohlt, 1995), 29.
23. Anatoly Dobrynin, *In Confidence* (New York: Times Books, 1995), 43–44.
24. Slusser, *Berlin Crisis*, 10.

25. Rusk, *As I Saw It*, 224.

26. The most detailed account of the pre-Wall consultations among the Soviets, the East Germans and other Warsaw Pact countries is provided by Hope Harrison, *Ulbricht and the Concrete "Rose": New Archival Evidence on the Dynamics of Soviet-East German Relations and the Berlin Crisis, 1958–1961* (Washington, D.C.: Cold War International History Project, Woodrow Wilson International Center for Scholars, 1993, hereafter cited as CWIHP), 30–56. Harrison has consulted many published sources and also has seen East German and Soviet documents as well as interviewed East German and Soviet officials. Her account will be the principal source for this portion of the text; Beschloss, *Crisis Years*, 266–267, contains background on Ulbricht's, Khrushchev's, and Kennedy's attitudes and actions in the period preceding the Wall, but concentrates most on Kennedy whereas Harrison concentrates most on the East.

27. Harrison, *Ulbricht and the Concrete "Rose,"* 36.

28. Alexei Filitov, "Soviet Policy and the Early Years of Two German States, 1949–1961," CWIHP, Woodrow Wilson International Center for Scholars (1994), passim.

29. Reeves, *Kennedy*, 204.

30. For excerpts from and report on Ulbricht speech, see Karl-Heinz Schmidt, *Dialog über Deutschland* (Baden-Baden: Nomos, 1998), 76–86.

31. Filitov, "Soviet Policy," 18.

32. CWIHP, *Bulletin*, Woodrow Wilson International Center for Scholars, 4 (Fall 1994), 28.

33. *Der Spiegel*, no. 41 (1989), 170.

34. Author's interview with John Mapother, former official at the U.S. Mission in Berlin, Washington, November 20, 1998.

35. For most extensive description of Western reaction after August 13, see Cate, *Ides of August*, 205–353.

36. Honoré M. Catudal, *Kennedy and the Berlin Wall Crisis* (Berlin: Berlin Verlag, 1980), 38.

37. Rusk, *As I Saw It*, 225.

38. Jean Edward Smith, *Lucius D. Clay* (New York: Henry Holt and Company, 1990), 637.

39. Reeves, *Kennedy*, 212.

40. Brandt's letter and Kennedy's reply are in U.S. Department of State, *Foreign Relations of the United States: The Berlin Crisis, 1961–1963*, (hereafter cited as *FRUS*), 14, 345–346 and 352–353; Kennedy's reaction to letter is in *Der Spiegel*, no. 48 (1989), 156.

41. Reeves, *Kennedy*, 213; for text of Murrow's letter, see *FRUS, The Berlin Crisis, 1961–1963*, 14, 339–341.

42. Smith, *Clay*, 642.

43. Ibid., 644.

44. Quoted in Cate, *Ides of August*, 448–449.

45. *FRUS, The Berlin Crisis, 1961–1963*, 14, 378–379.

46. Ibid., 375–376.

47. Ibid., 387.

CHAPTER 10

1. Information on General Clay's attitudes and remarks during his Berlin service comes from three principal sources, all of whom spoke to Clay either during his stay in Berlin or afterward: Curtis Cate, *The Ides of August: The Berlin Wall Crisis, 1961* (New York: Evans, 1975), 325–390; Jean Edward Smith, *Lucius D. Clay* (New York: Henry Holt and Company, 1990), 629–665; and the author's own frequent talks with Clay, whom the author served in Berlin as special assistant. Other sources separately cited.

2. For text, U.S. Department of State, *Foreign Relations of the United States, The Berlin Crisis, 1961–1963* (Washington, D.C.: U.S. Government Printing Office, 1994) (hereafter cited as *FRUS*), 14, 387.

3. Karl-Heinz Schmidt, *Dialog über Deutschland* (Baden-Baden: Nomos, 1998), 86–87.

4. Ibid., 87–93.

5. Hope Harrison, *Ulbricht and the Concrete "Rose": New Archival Evidence on the Dynamics of Soviet-East German Relations and the Berlin Crisis, 1958–1961* (Washington, D.C.: Cold War International History Project, Woodrow Wilson International Center for Scholars, 1993) (hereafter cited as CWIHP), 23.

6. Smith, *Clay*, 658–660; author's recollection.

7. Bruce W. Menning, "The Berlin Crisis of 1961 from the Perspective of the Soviet General Staff," paper presented at a conference entitled "The Soviet Union, Germany, and the Cold War, 1945–1962: New Evidence from Eastern Archives," Essen and Potsdam, June 28-July 3, 1994, 13–20.

8. For text of Clay letter, see *FRUS, Berlin Crisis, 1961–1963*, 14, 509–513.

9. Quoted in Cate, *Ides of August*, 476.

10. One of the mysteries of the Berlin crisis was the impact that the Kozlov faction and other opposition groups within the CPSU leadership might have had on Khrushchev's policies. To date, it has not been possible to trace how Soviet domestic politics shaped Khrushchev's tactics on Berlin. Nor has any evidence of links between Ulbricht and Kozlov come to light. But Khrushchev did apparently defeat the Kozlov faction and decide to ease his Berlin deadline by the CPSU congress of October 1961. For background and discussion, see Robert M. Slusser, *The Berlin Crisis of 1961* (Baltimore: Johns Hopkins University Press, 1973), 179–200.

11. The Checkpoint Charlie story has been told many times by different authors. Howard Trivers, *Three Crises in American Foreign Affairs and a Continuing Revolution* (Carbondale: Southern Illinois University Press, 1970), passim, presents the

view of a U.S. official on the scene; Cate, *Ides of August*, 457–495, also has full record.

12. *FRUS, The Berlin Crisis, 1961–1963*, 14, 524.

13. Smith, *Clay*, 661; author's notes and recollections of meeting.

14. In 1964, Robert Kennedy reportedly told an American historian that the president had informed Khrushchev through Robert and a Soviet intelligence official, Georgi Bolshakov, that U.S. tanks would withdraw within half an hour if the Soviets withdrew first. *Der Spiegel*, no. 48 (1989), 159–160, reported the message. So did others, including Peter Wyden, Richard Reeves and Raymond Garthoff. The editors of *Foreign Relations of the United States*, however, wrote that they did not find any evidence of it either in the Kennedy Library or in State Department files (*FRUS, The Berlin Crisis, 1961–1963*, 14, 544). Garthoff has informed the author that a former Soviet ambassador to Germany, Valentin Falin, claimed to have seen the Soviet report, but no one else claims to have seen it. Neither Khrushchev, Robert Kennedy nor any of the early John F. Kennedy biographers reported any such message, although they would have had reason to do so because it showed the president rather than Clay as master of the situation. Many White House officials resented the press attention to Clay and would have been glad to put him down and to play up Kennedy.

Clay told this author and others that he withdrew U.S. tanks because they had served their purpose by bringing the Soviets out of hiding. He had already written Kennedy that he wanted to pull U.S. forces back once he had forced a confrontation. Clay never told the author of any coordinated Soviet-American instruction, although he and the author analyzed the Checkpoint Charlie outcome a number of times and Clay spoke frankly to the author on every other occasion.

The president thus does not appear to have told Clay about any such message to Khrushchev. He appears not to have told any of his closest advisers and early biographers, including Rusk, McNamara, Bundy or the White House officials whom he had instructed to record his presidency. Nor did Khrushchev ever cite such a message, although he would also have had reason to do so (and as he later did with the arrangement under which Kennedy withdrew missiles from Turkey in exchange for Soviet missile withdrawals from Cuba). Therefore, there is reason to question whether any Kennedy-Bolshakov-Khrushchev message on the tanks existed.

Even without a Kennedy message to Khrushchev, all wanted to pull back the tanks: Khrushchev did not like to have Soviet armor in the capital of the nominally independent GDR. Neither did Ulbricht. And Clay had made his point.

15. Kennedy's reaction was reported to the author by Clay himself and by others after Clay returned from Washington. It was also reported by Clay's assistant James P. O'Donnell, who had served in the Kennedy White House and had heard it from his White House friends.

16. Harold Macmillan, *Pointing the Way, 1959–1961* (London: Macmillan, 1972), 405–408. Cate, *Ides of August*, 491.

17. *Der Spiegel*, no. 43 (1989), 160.

18. Schmidt, *Dialog über Deutschland*, 93–96.

19. Ibid.

20. Frank Mayer, *Kennedy and Adenauer* (New York: St. Martin's Press, 1995), 92–93.

21. Macmillan, *Pointing the Way*, 417–425.

22. Mayer, *Kennedy and Adenauer*, 89.

23. Ibid., 77.

24. National Security Archive, *The Berlin Crisis, 1958–1962* (Washington, D.C.: National Security Archive, 1996), 142.

25. Mayer, *Kennedy and Adenauer*, 111–120.

26. Ibid., 86.

27. Ibid., 85.

28. John C. Ausland, *Kennedy, Khrushchev, and Berlin* (Washington: The Foreign Service Institute, n.d.), 17.

29. Ibid., 11–16.

30. Clay interviews by author, Berlin, February-May, 1962.

31. Letter from Clay to Taylor, September 7, 1962, among the Clay papers in the George C. Marshall Research Library, Virginia Military Institute, Lexington, Virginia.

32. For this and subsequent exchanges and statements, see *FRUS, Berlin Crisis, 1961–1963*, 15, 270–348.

33. Anatoly Dobrynin, *In Confidence* (New York: Times Books, 1995), 68.

34. *FRUS, Berlin Crisis, 1961–1963*, 15, 309.

35. Ibid., 370–376, for this part of Kennedy-Gromyko talk.

36. John R. Mapother. "Berlin and the Cuban Crisis," *Foreign Intelligence Literary Scene*, 12, no. 1 (January 1993), 1–3; Ray S. Cline, "Commentary: The Cuban Missile Crisis," *Foreign Affairs* (Fall 1989), 190–196.

37. *FRUS, Berlin Crisis, 1961–1963*, 15, 398–399.

38. Macmillan, *At the End of the Day* (New York: Harper & Row, 1973), 182.

39. Thomas J. Schoenbaum, *Waging Peace and War: Dean Rusk in the Truman, Kennedy, and Johnson Years* (New York: Simon and Schuster, 1988), 354–355.

40. Ernest R. May and Philip D. Zelikow, *The Kennedy Tapes* (Cambridge, MA: Harvard University Press, 1997), 143, 144, 176.

41. Ibid., 148, 172, 177.

42. Ibid., 144.

43. Ibid., 183.

44. Dobrynin, *In Confidence*, 71–73.

45. CWIHP, *Cold War Crises*, The Woodrow Wilson International Center for Scholars (Spring 1995), 59 and 89–92.

46. Arnold L. Horelick, "The Cuban Missile Crisis," *World Politics* 16, no. 3 (April 1964), 369.

47. Mapother, "Berlin and the Cuban Crisis," 3.

48. Cate, *Ides of August*, 493.

49. Horelick, "Cuban Missile Crisis," 388.

50. Dobrynin, *In Confidence*, 81–95.

51. Ibid.

52. Robert Kennedy, *Thirteen Days* (New York: W.W. Norton, 1969), 86–87, although edited by Sorensen, confirms Dobrynin's account that U.S. missiles in Turkey would be withdrawn "shortly after this crisis." The author has not seen what Kennedy might have drafted before Sorensen's editing. Also see CWIHP, *Bulletin*, Woodrow Wilson International Center for Scholars, 5 (Spring 1995), 75–80.

53. *FRUS, Berlin Crisis, 1961–1963*, 15, 469.

54. Memorandum from David Klein, U.S. Mission, Berlin, August 3, 1963, in private files of John Mapother, Washington, D.C.

55. *FRUS, Berlin Crisis, 1961–1963*, 15, 486.

56. For post-Cuba style, see *FRUS, Berlin Crisis, 1961–1963*, 15, 440–452, 465, 469, 496, 500–503, and 506–508.

57. Ibid., 519–520.

CHAPTER 11

1. For Kennedy's concern on Franco-German link, see Frank Mayer, *Kennedy and Adenauer* (New York: St. Martin's Press, 1995), 127–155.

2. Dennis L. Bark and David R. Gress, *From Shadow to Substance, 1945–1963*, vol. 1 of *A History of West Germany* (Oxford: Blackwell, 1989), 493–497.

3. Mayer, *Kennedy and Adenauer*, 144.

4. Full text of Kennedy speech in *Public Papers of the Presidents: John F. Kennedy, 1963* (Washington, D.C.: U.S. Government Printing Office, 1976), 524–525; for summary of Berlin visit and redrafting of speech, see Richard Reeves, *President Kennedy* (New York: Simon & Schuster, 1992), 531–537. Much has been made by old German hands and by some scholars that Kennedy actually said "I am a jelly doughnut," which is what one would get if one asked for "*ein Berliner*" in a German bakery. To be grammatically correct, Kennedy would have had to say "*Ich bin Berliner*" (as a U.S. citizen would say "I am American" or a Frenchman "*je suis français*"). But Kennedy's phrase has been accepted as part of the cult of Berlin despite this modest grammatical misstep.

5. Reeves, *Kennedy*, 535–536.

6. U.S. Department of State, *Foreign Relations of the United States, The Berlin Crisis, 1961–1963* Washington, D.C.: U.S. Government Printing Office, 1994), 15, 525–527; Reeves, *Kennedy*, 533–535.

7. Full speech in *Public Papers of the Presidents, John F. Kennedy, 1963*, 526–528.

8. Reeves, *Kennedy*, 537.

9. Henry Kissinger, *Diplomacy* (New York: Simon & Schuster, 1994), 592.

10. Author's interview with Willy Brandt, Bonn, September 6, 1990.

CHAPTER 12

1. Clay Clemens, *Reluctant Realists: The CDU/CSU and West German Ostpolitik* (Durham, NC: Duke University Press, 1989), 38–39; Werner Link, "Neuanstösse in der Deutschlandpolitik, 1961–1973," in Alexander Fischer, ed., *Vierzig Jahre Deutschlandpolitik im Internationalen Kräftefeld* (Bonn: Edition Deutschland Archiv, 1989), 32–33.

2. *Die Welt*, October 9, 1963, 1.

3. *Frankfurter Allgemeine Zeitung*, April 28, 1964, 1.

4. *Christ und Welt*, July 24, 1964, 1.

5. For German attitudes on MLF and U.S. strategic policy, see Henry A. Kissinger, "The Unsolved Problems of European Defense," *Foreign Affairs* (July 1962), 517–541; John Van Oudenaren, *West German Policymaking and NATO Nuclear Strategy* (Santa Monica, CA: RAND, 1985), 4–8; John A. Reed, Jr., *Germany and NATO* (Washington, D.C.: National Defense University Press, 1987), 118–120.

6. Dennis L. Bark and David R. Gress, *Democracy and its Discontents, 1963–1991*, vol. 2 of *A History of West Germany* (Cambridge, MA: Blackwell, 1993), 24; for German role in NATO nuclear policy, see Dieter Mahnke, *Nukleare Mitwirkung* (Berlin: Walter de Gruyter, 1972), passim.

7. Michael Sodaro, *Moscow, Germany, and the West from Khrushchev to Gorbachev* (Ithaca, NY: Cornell University Press, 1990), 44–71.

8. J. A. Kwizinskij, *Vor dem Sturm* (Cologne: Siedler Verlag, 1992), 221.

9. Willy Brandt, *My Life in Politics* (New York: Viking, 1992), 55–70. This is a translation, by Anthea Bell, of Brandt's sometimes more detailed *Erinnerungen* (Frankfurt: Propyläen, 1989).

10. Text in U.S. Department of State, *Documents on Germany, 1944–1985* (Washington, D.C.: U.S. Department of State, 1986), 860.

11. Jochen Staadt, *Die geheime Westpolitik der SED 1960–1970* (Berlin: Akademie Verlag, 1993), 82–87.

12. Brandt, *My Life*, 83.

13. Author's interview with Willy Brandt, Bonn, September 6, 1990.

14. Egon Bahr, *Zu Meiner Zeit* (Munich: Blessing, 1996), 152–161; Brandt, *Erinnerungen*, 73–77. For texts, see Manfred Uschner, *Die Ostpolitik der SPD* (Berlin: Dietz, 1991), 182–202 and 203–210.

15. Staadt, *Geheime Westpolitik*, 89–96.

16. Horst Osterheld, *Aussenpolitik unter Bundeskanzler Ludwig Erhard, 1963–1966* (Düsseldorf: Droste, 1992), 301–305; Theo Sommer, "Bonn Changes Course," *Foreign Affairs* (April 1967), 480.

17. George C. McGhee, *On the Frontline in the Cold War* (Westport, CT: Praeger, 1997), 176–177.

18. Kurt Georg Kiesinger, *Die Grosse Koalition, 1966–1969* (Stuttgart: Deutsche Verlags-Anstalt, 1979), 6–17; Bark and Gress, *Democracy*, 90–97.

19. Kiesinger, *Grosse Koalition*, 66–67.

20. Ibid., 155–174.
21. Brandt, *Erinnerungen*, 164.
22. Ibid., 167–169.
23. Kiesinger, *Grosse Koalition*, 67; Bark and Gress, *Democracy*, 95.
24. Staadt, *Geheime Westpolitik*, 209.
25. Karl-Heinz Schmidt, *Dialog über Deutschland* (Baden-Baden: Nomos, 1998), 107–111.
26. James McAdams, *East Germany and Détente* (Cambridge: Cambridge University Press, 1984), 74.
27. Gottfried Zieger, *Die Haltung von SED und DDR zur Einheit Deutschlands 1949–1987* (Cologne: Verlag Wissenschaft und Politik, 1988), 110.
28. Philip Windsor, *Germany and the Management of Détente* (New York: Praeger, 1971), 116–119 and 149–153.
29. For summaries and texts, Hermann Weber, ed., *DDR: Dokumente zur Geschichte der Deutschen Demokratischen Republik, 1945–1985* (Munich: Deutscher Taschenbuch Verlag, 1986), 255–308.
30. Staadt, *Geheime Westpolitik*, 242–246.
31. Windsor, *Germany and Détente*, 150–154.
32. McAdams, *East Germany and Détente*, 82–83.
33. Staadt, *Geheime Westpolitik*, 274–276.
34. Windsor, *Germany and Détente*, 184–185.
35. Clemens, *Reluctant Realists*, 47–50.

CHAPTER 13

1. Richard M. Nixon, *The Memoirs of Richard Nixon* (New York: Grosset & Dunlap, 1978), 343–347.
2. Ibid., 143.
3. Henry A. Kissinger, *White House Years* (Boston: Little, Brown, 1979), 147–150.
4. J. A. Kwizinskij, *Vor dem Sturm* (Cologne: Siedler Verlag, 1992), 218–225.
5. Arnulf Baring, *Machtwechsel* (Stuttgart: Deutsche Verlags-Anstalt, 1982), 249–251.
6. Ibid., 247–261.
7. For excerpts, see *Deutsche Aussenpolitik* (Bonn: Bonn Aktuell, 1989), 217–221.
8. Wjatscheslaw Keworkow, *Der Geheime Kanal* (Berlin: Rowohlt, 1995), 50–53.
9. Ibid., 171–173.
10. Quoted in Dennis L. Bark and David R. Gress, *Democracy and its Discontents, 1963–1991*, vol. 2 of *A History of West Germany* (Cambridge, MA: Blackwell, 1993), 177, with a report on the meeting, 172–183.
11. Baring, *Machtwechsel*, 257–283.
12. Egon Bahr, *Zu meiner Zeit* (Munich: Karl Blessing Verlag, 1996), 284–338, for Bahr's Moscow talks.
13. Keworkow, *Der Geheime Kanal*, 76–77.

14. Bahr, *Zu meiner Zeit*, 298–304, 315.

15. Karl-Heinz Schmidt, *Dialog über Deutschland* (Baden-Baden: Nomos, 1998), 228–246.

16. Baring, *Machtwechsel*, 282.

17. Ibid., 314–332.

18. Ibid., 333–349.

19. Michael Sodaro, *Moscow, Germany, and the West from Khrushchev to Gorbachev* (Ithaca, NY: Cornell University Press, 1990), 149–151.

20. Bahr, *Zu meiner Zeit*, 315.

21. Keworkow, *Der Geheime Kanal*, 29 and 47.

22. Author's interview with Günther Van Well, formerly political director in the West German Foreign Office, Bonn, September 8, 1990.

23. Valentin Falin, *Politische Erinnerungen* (Munich: Droemer-Knaur, 1993), 102.

24. Author's interview with Andreas Meyer-Landrut, former West German ambassador in Moscow, Bonn, September 8, 1990.

25. Schmidt, *Dialog über Deutschland*, 246–249.

26. Ibid., 257.

27. For example, see *Europäische Sicherheit und Möglichkeiten der Zusammenarbeit* (Hamburg: Körber Stiftung, 1970).

28. Kwizinskij, *Vor dem Sturm*, 229–231; author's interview with Egon Bahr, Munich, February 6, 1999.

29. Willy Brandt, *Errinerungen* (Frankfurt: Propyläen, 1989), 203–206.

30. For Soviet-German economic relations, see Angela Stent, *From Embargo to Ostpolitik: The Political Economy of West German-Soviet Relations, 1955–1980* (Cambridge: Cambridge University Press, 1981), passim.

31. Ibid., 210.

32. Ibid., 214.

33. For discussion in this chapter of the Warsaw Treaty: Bark and Gress, *Democracy*, 186–189; Brandt's thinking and actions are in Brandt, *Erinnerungen*. 211–224.

34. Brandt, *Erinnerungen*, 216; Brandt interview.

35. Dennis L. Bark, *Agreement on Berlin* (Washington, D.C.: American Enterprise Institute, 1974), 18–19.

36. Bahr, *Zu meiner Zeit*, 310–312.

37. Ibid., 358.

38. This discussion on the Berlin Quadripartite talks between the fall of 1970 and the final agreement is based principally on Honoré M. Catudal, *The Diplomacy of the Quadripartite Agreement on Berlin* (Berlin: Berlin Verlag, 1978), 123–217, and on Bark, *Agreement on Berlin*, passim. Other specific sources cited separately where appropriate.

39. Sodaro, *Moscow, Germany*, 162.

CHAPTER 14

1. Hannes Adomeit, *Imperial Overstretch* (Baden-Baden: Nomos, 1998), 122–123.

2. Jochen Staadt, "Walter Ulbricht's letzter Machtkampf," *Deutschland Archiv*, (September/October 1996), 694.

3. Michael Sodaro, *Moscow, Germany, and the West from Khrushchev to Gorbachev* (Ithaca, NY: Cornell University Press, 1990), 207–210.

4. Author's interview with Hans-Otto Bräutigam, former West German representative to GDR, New York, November 20, 1991.

5. Author's interview with Willy Brandt, Bonn, September 6, 1990.

6. Author's interviews with Karl Kaiser, Professor, Cologne University, Bonn, February 12, 1993, and with Dimitri Simes, expert on Soviet affairs, Washington, August 14, 1995.

7. Author's interview with Egon Bahr, Bonn, September 7, 1990.

8. Adomeit, *Imperial Overstretch*, 123.

9. Markus Wolf, *Spionagechef im Geheimen Krieg* (Düsseldorf: List, 1997), 253–258.

10. Ibid.

11. For Honecker-Brezhnev collaboration to remove Ulbricht, see Heinz Lippmann, *Honecker and the New Politics of Europe*, trans. Helen Sebba (New York: Macmillan, 1972), 190–253; for detailed account from SED documents, see Staadt, "Ulbricht's letzter Machtkampf," 686–700.

12. Staadt, "Ulbricht's letzter Machtkampf," 694.

13. Wolf, *Spionagechef*, 253–258.

14. Adomeit, *Imperial Overstretch*, 121.

15. J. A. Kwizinskij, *Vor dem Sturm* (Cologne: Siedler Verlag, 1992), 255–260.

16. Staadt, "Ulbricht's letzter Machtkampf," 698.

17. Wolf, *Spionagechef*, 253–258; Author's interview with John Mapother, U.S. expert on Germany, Washington, March 31, 1998; Bräutigam interview.

18. Staadt, "Ulbricht's letzter Machtkampf," 698–700.

19. Adomeit, *Imperial Overstretch*, 124.

20. Staadt, "Ulbricht's letzter Machtkampf," 698.

21. Kwizinskij, *Vor dem Sturm*, 260.

22. Ibid., 222–223.

23. Ibid., 246.

24. Mapother interview.

25. William E. Griffith, *The Ostpolitik of the Federal Republic of Germany* (Cambridge, MA: MIT Press, 1973), 206–209.

26. Bahr interview.

27. Ibid.

28. Honoré M. Catudal, *The Diplomacy of the Quadripartite Agreement on Berlin* (Berlin: Berlin Verlag, 1978), 139–140.

29. Ibid., 144.

30. Bahr interview.

31. Willy Brandt, *Erinnerungen* (Frankfurt: Propyläen, 1989), 190.

32. Brandt interview.

33. Brandt, *Erinnerungen*, 191.

34. Brandt interview.

35. Author's interview with Henry Kissinger, former U.S. White House Assistant for National Security Affairs, New York, November 20, 1991.

36. Ibid.

37. Bahr interview.

38. Wjatscheslaw Keworkow, *Der Geheime Kanal* (Berlin: Rowohlt, 1995), 277–278.

39. Dennis L. Bark and David R. Gress, *Democracy and Its Discontents, 1963–1991,* vol. 2 of *A History of West Germany* (Cambridge, MA: Blackwell, 1993), 199–201.

40. For Brandt's account of Oreanda, see Brandt, *Erinnerungen*, 202–210.

41. Ibid.

42. Sodaro, *Moscow, Germany*, 194–200.

43. Brandt, *Erinnerungen*, 202–203.

44. For East-West German negotiations, see Griffith, *Ostpolitik*, 209–229; and Tony Armstrong, *Breaking the Ice* (Washington, D.C.: United States Institute of Peace, 1993), passim.

45. Karl-Heinz Schmidt, *Dialog über Deutschland* (Baden-Baden: Nomos, 1998), 275–278.

46. For German texts, see *Verträge, Abkommen und Vereinbarungen zwischen der Bundesrepublik Deutschland und der Deutschen Demokratischen Republik* (Bonn: Presse- und Informationsamt der Bundesregierung, 1973).

CHAPTER 15

1. Dennis L. Bark and David R. Gress, *Democracy and its Discontents, 1963–1991,* vol. 2 of *A History of West Germany* (Cambridge, MA: Blackwell, 1993), 207–213.

2. Willy Brandt, *My Life in Politics* (New York: Viking, 1992), 267.

3. For Soviet efforts to support Brandt, see Wjatscheslaw Keworkow, *Der geheime Kanal* (Berlin: Rowohlt, 1995), 90–93, 114.

4. Markus Wolf, *Man Without a Face* (New York: Times Books, 1997), 150–170.

5. Author's interview with John Mapother, U.S. expert on Germany, Washington, March 31, 1998.

6. Brandt, *My Life*, 308.

7. Keworkow, *Der Geheime Kanal*, 176–179.

8. Karl-Heinz Schmidt, *Dialog über Deutschland* (Baden-Baden: Nomos, 1998), 288–289.

9. Ibid.

10. Ibid., 289–290.

CHAPTER 16

1. Unless otherwise cited, the information in this section about inner-German relations during the 1970s is drawn from Bundesministerium für innerdeutsche

Beziehungen, *Zehn Jahre Deutschlandpolitik* (Bonn: Bundesministerium für innerdeutsche Beziehungen, 1980), 11–22.

2. Ibid., 11.

3. Dettmar Cramer, "Deutsch-deutsche Bewährungsprobe," *Deutschland Archiv* (May 1980), 449.

4. *Zehn Jahre Deutschlandpolitik*, 41–42; Franz Rösch and Fritz Homann, "Thirty Years of the Berlin Agreement—Thirty Years of Inner-German Trade: Economic and Political Dimensions," *Zeitschrift für die gesamte Staatswissenschaft* 137, (September 1981), 524–556.

5. *New York Times*, October 28, 1979, 1.

6. Gerhard Wettig, *Die Durchführung des Berlin-Transits nach dem Vier-Mächte-Abkommen 1972–1981* (Cologne: Bundesinstitut für ostwissenschaftliche und internationale Studien, 1981), passim.

7. Ibid., 15.

8. Hermann Weber, ed., *DDR: Dokumente zur Geschichte der Deutschen Demokratischen Republik, 1945–1985* (Munich, Deutscher Taschenbuch Verlag, 1986), 355–356.

9. "Wir haben euch Waffen und Brot geschickt," *Der Spiegel*, no. 10 (1980), 42–61.

10. Karl-Heinz Schmidt, *Dialog über Deutschland* (Baden-Baden, Nomos, 1998), 298–299.

11. Ibid., 304–305.

12. Egon Bahr, *Zu meiner Zeit* (Munich: Karl Blessing Verlag, 1996), 332.

13. Wolfgang Jäger and Werner Link, *Republik im Wandel, 1974–1982* (Stuttgart: Deutsche Verlags-Anstalt, 1987), 291. Pages 290–341 serve as a basic source for German-Soviet and German-American policy issues during Schmidt's chancellorship.

14. For German military views on the SS-20 impact on the European balance, see Federal Minister of Defense, *White Paper 1979: The Security of the Federal Republic of Germany and the Development of the Federal Armed Forces* (Bonn: Federal Ministry of Defense, 1979), 107–111.

15. Jonathan Haslam, *The Soviet Union and the Politics of Nuclear Weapons in Europe* (Ithaca, NY: Cornell University Press, 1990), 58–96, gives full background.

16. Harry Gelman. *The Brezhnev Politburo and the Decline of Detente* (Ithaca, NY: Cornell University Press, 1984), 19–104; Michael Sodaro, *Moscow, Germany and the West from Khrushchev to Gorbachev* (Ithaca, NY: Cornell University Press, 1990), 385–409; author's interview with Curt Gasteyger, School of International Studies, Geneva, April 15, 1998.

17. Gelman, *Brezhnev Politburo*, 47.

18. Ibid., 209–212.

19. Wjatscheslaw Keworkow, *Der Geheime Kanal* (Berlin: Rowohlt, 1995), 192–224.

20. Zbigniew Brzezinski, *Power and Principle* (New York: Farrar Strauss Giroux, 1983), 289–315; Helmut Schmidt, *Men and Powers*, trans. Ruth Hein, (New York: Random House, 1959), 181–187; Jimmy Carter, *Keeping Faith* (Toronto: Bantam Books, 1982), 535–537.

21. Cyrus Vance, *Hard Choices* (New York: Simon and Schuster, 1983), 67–68.

22. Helmut Schmidt, *Strategie des Gleichgewichts* (Stuttgart: Seewald, 1969), 21.

23. Marion Dönhoff, "Bonn and Washington: The Strained Relationship," *Foreign Affairs* (Summer 1979), 1064.

24. Helmut Schmidt, *Men and Powers*, 185.

25. Gregor Schöllgen, *Geschichte der Weltpolitik von Hitler bis Gorbatschow, 1941–1991* (Munich: Beck, 1996), 361–363.

26. *Die Zeit*, April 14, 1978, 3.

27. Author's interview with Walther Stützle, former planning chief, West German ministry of defense, Bonn, September, 7, 1990.

28. Carter, *Keeping Faith*, 244–261.

29. Text of Schmidt speech in *Survival* (January/February 1978), 2–10.

30. Julius W. Friend, *The Linchpin: French-German Relations, 1950–1990* (New York: Praeger, 1991), 58–60.

31. Margaret Thatcher, *The Downing Street Years* (New York: Harper Collins, 1993), 240–241.

32. *Is America Becoming Number 2?* (Washington, D.C.: Committee on the Present Danger, 1978); Robert Kilmarx, *Soviet-United States Naval Balance* (Washington, D.C.: Center for Strategic and International Studies, 1975); "Russia's Blue-Water Bid," *Newsweek*, February 21, 1977, 8–13; "Is America Strong Enough?" *Newsweek*, October 27, 1980, 48–54.

33. Karl-Heinz Schmidt, *Dialog über Deutschland*, 313.

34. Alex Alexiev, "U.S. Policy and the War in Afghanistan," *Global Affairs* (Fall 1988), 81–85.

35. Keworkow, *Der geheime Kanal*, 236–249.

36. Karl-Heinz Schmidt, *Dialog über Deutschland*, 307–312.

37. Bahr, *Zu meiner Zeit*, 506–507.

38. Brzezinski, *Power and Principle*, 459–469; Helmut Schmidt, *Men and Powers*, 205–216.

39. Helmut Schmidt, *Men and Powers*, 86–91.

40. Ibid., 92–94.

41. Detlef Nakath and Gerd-Rüdiger Stephan, *Von Hubertusstock nach Bonn* (Berlin: Dietz, 1995), 20–21.

42. For GDR verbatim report of talks and preparation and evaluation, see Nakath and Stephan, *Von Hubertusstock*, 55–75; for West German record, see *Das deutsch-deutsche Treffen am Werbellinsee* (Bonn: Bundesministerium für innerdeutsche Beziehungen, 1982); for background, see Eric Frey, *Division and Détente: The Germanies and their Alliances* (New York: Praeger, 1987), 95–99; and James McAdams, *Germany Divided* (Princeton, NJ: Princeton University Press, 1991), 134–152.

43. Manfred Wilke, Reinhardt Gutsche, and Michael Kubina, "Die SED-Führung und die Unterdrückung der polnischen Oppositionsbewegung 1980/81," *German Studies Review* 17, no. 1 (Spring 1994), 105–152.

44. *New York Times*, May 21, 1981, 21.

CHAPTER 17

1. Charles Krauthammer, "The Reagan Doctrine," *Time*, April 1, 1985, 30–31.
2. Robert McFarlane, *Special Trust* (New York: Cadell & Davies, 1994), 293.
3. Jay Winik, *On the Brink* (New York: Simon and Schuster, 1996), 184; For the "walk in the woods," see ibid., 184–213; also, Strobe Talbott, *The Master of the Game* (New York: Vintage Books, 1988), 174–181.
4. Winik, *On the Brink*, 203; Talbott, *Master of the Game*, 177.
5. J. A. Kwizinskij, *Vor dem Sturm* (Cologne: Siedler Verlag, 1992), 291–357.
6. Ronald Reagan, *An American Life* (New York: Simon and Schuster, 1990), 570.
7. Jonathan Haslam, *The Soviet Union and the Politics of Nuclear Weapons* (Ithaca, NY: Cornell University Press, 1990), 143.
8. McFarlane, *Special Trust*, 295–296.
9. Ibid., 127–131.
10. Wjatscheslaw Keworkow, *Der geheime Kanal* (Berlin: Rowohlt, 1995), 261–262.
11. Roland Smith, *Soviet Policy Towards West Germany* (London: International Institute for Strategic Studies, 1985), Adelphi Paper 203, 24.
12. Ibid.
13. Winik, *On the Brink*, 168.
14. Dennis L. Bark and David R. Gress, *Democracy and Its Discontents*, vol. 2 of *A History of West Germany* (Cambridge, MA: Blackwell, 1993), 406–7.
15. Haslam, *Soviet Union and Nuclear Weapons*, 131–138. The following quotes are taken from this source.
16. Ibid.; Theo Sommer, "The Germanies Must Cooperate," *Newsweek*, January 7, 1985, 44.
17. *Frankfurter Allgemeine Zeitung*, August 4, 1984, 1.
18. For strategic analysis of INF deployment, see Cristoph Bertram, "The Implications of Theater Nuclear Weapons in Europe," *Foreign Affairs* (Winter 1981–82), 305–326.
19. Federal Republic of Germany, *Bulletin*, December 14, 1982, 9–15.
20. For Bitburg visit, see George P. Shultz, *Turmoil and Triumph* (New York: Scribner's, 1993), 539–560.
21. For Soviet quotes, see *Europa-Archiv*, October 25, 1985, 566–571.
22. Ibid.
23. Bundesminister der Verteidigung, *SDI: Fakten und Bewertungen; Fragen und Antworten; Dokumentation* (Bonn: FRG Ministry of Defense, June, 1986), 54–55.
24. For texts and summaries of Kohl and other German statements, see ibid., 53, 56–58.
25. *International Herald Tribune*, March 5, 1985. Cited in Louis Deschamps, *The SDI and European Security Interests* (Paris: The Atlantic Institute for International Affairs, 1987), 26.
26. *Die Welt*, July 2, 1986, 1.

27. McFarlane, *Special Trust*, 295–296; Don Oberdorfer, *The Turn* (New York: Poseidon Press, 1991), 38 and 74.

28. Oberdorfer, *Turn*, 62.

29. *Newsweek*, November 2, 1992, 58.

30. Mikhail Gorbachev, *Memoirs*, trans. Georges Peronansky and Tatjana Varsavsky (New York: Doubleday, 1995), 18–170.

31. William Griffith, "Brezhnev's Foreign Policy," *Problems of Communism* (March-April 1985), 106–109.

32. Hubert Védrine, *Les Mondes de François Mitterrand* (Paris: Fayard, 1996), 371–375.

33. Principal sources for Reagan-Gorbachev negotiations from 1985 through 1988 are Oberdorfer, *Turn*, 109–386; Gorbachev, *Memoirs*, 401–463; McFarlane, *Special Trust*, 298–322; Reagan, *American Life*, 545–723; and Shultz, *Turmoil and Triumph*, 340–380, 463–607, 751–782, 863–900, 993–1015, and 1080–1108. For INF treaty text, see *Treaty between the United States and the Union of Soviet Socialist Republics on the Elimination of their Intermediate-range and Shorter-range Missiles* (Washington, D.C.: U.S. Department of State, 1987).

34. Richard Perle, "Reykjavik as a Watershed in U.S.-Soviet Arms Control," *International Security*, no. 11 (Summer 1987), 175–179.

35. *The Washington Post*, November 2, 1986, 1.

36. Oberdorfer, *Turn*, 321.

37. Reagan, *American Life*, 706; for text of speech, see *New York Times*, June 13, 1987, 3.

38. For Gorbachev's initial attitude toward Kohl, see David Shumaker, *Gorbachev and the German Question* (Boulder, CO: Westview, 1996), 9–28.

39. Egon Bahr, *Zu meiner Zeit* (Munich: Karl Blessing Verlag, 1996), 525–546.

40. Karl-Rudolf Korte, *Deutschlandpolitik in Helmut Kohls Kanzlerschaft* (Stuttgart: DVA, 1998), 206.

41. *Frankfurter Rundschau*, February 13, 1987, 1–2.

42. Shumaker, *Gorbachev and the German Question*, 42–45.

43. Federal Republic of Germany, *Statements and Speeches*, vol. 10, no. 3, February 6, 1987, 1–5.

44. Kohl *ARD* interview, April 3, 1987.

45. Teltschik *Deutschlandfunk* interview, March 16, 1987.

46. Richard von Weizsäcker, *Remembrance, Sorrow and Reconciliation* (Bonn: Press and Information Office of the Federal Republic of Germany, 1985), 57–73.

47. For reports on visit, see Richard von Weizsäcker, *Vier Zeiten* (Berlin: Siedler Verlag, 1997), 339–347; Shumaker, *Gorbachev and the German Question*, 47–49.

48. Shumaker, *Gorbachev and the German Question*, 62.

49. Vyacheslav Dashichev, untitled paper presented at the American Institute for Contemporary German Studies, Washington, D.C., July 17, 1991, 4.

50. Shumaker, *Gorbachev and the German Question*, 68–69.

51. Eugene B. Rumer, *A German Question in Moscow's "Common European Home"* (Santa Monica, CA: RAND, 1991), Rand Note N-3220-USDP, 6–12; and Dimitri

Simes, "Gorbachev: A New Foreign Policy?" *Foreign Affairs, America and the World, 1986*, 477–500.

52. *Kölnische Rundschau*, August 8, 1986, 3.

53. Nineteenth All-Union Conference of the CPSU, *Documents and Materials* (Washington, D.C.: Soviet Embassy, 1988), 129.

54. Shumaker, *Gorbachev and the German Question*, 74–79.

55. Jeffrey Gedmin, *The Hidden Hand: Gorbachev and the Collapse of East Germany* (Washington, D.C.: AEI Press, 1992), 52.

56. *The Economist*, June 17, 1989, 37.

57. Moscow Television Service, June 15, 1989.

58. Vienna Television Service, June 15, 1989.

59. For list of agreements, see *Frankfurter Allgemeine Zeitung*, June 13, 1989, 2; for description of visit, see *Die Begegnungen von Moskau und Bonn* (Bonn: Presse- und Informationsamt der Bundesregierung).

60. Gorbachev, *Memoirs*, 503.

61. Bergedorfer Gesprächskreis zu Fragen der freien industriellen Gesellschaft, *Systemöffnende Kooperation?* Protokoll no. 84 (March 1988).

62. Bergedorfer Gesprächskreis zu Fragen der freien industriellen Gesellschaft, *Das gemeinsame Europäische Haus—aus der Sicht der Sowjetunion und der Bundesrepublik Deutschland*, Protokoll no. 86 (December 1988).

63. Unless otherwise cited, information for this section comes from *Innerdeutsche Beziehungen: Die Entwicklung der Beziehungen zwischen der Bundesrepublik Deutschland und der Deutschen Demokratischen Republik, 1980–1986* (Bonn: Bundesministerium für innerdeutsche Beziehungen, 1986); also see Heinrich Potthoff, *Die "Koalition der Vernunft"* (Munich: Deutscher Taschenbuch Verlag, 1995); Detlef Nakath and Gerd-Rüdiger Stephan, *Von Hubertusstock nach Bonn* (Berlin: Dietz Verlag, 1995), passim; less comprehensive and more analytical: Ernst Martin, *Deutschlandpolitik der 80er Jahre* (Stuttgart: Bonn Aktuell, 1986).

64. Korte, *Deutschlandpolitik*, 196–198 and 211–214.

65. Smith, *Soviet Policy toward Germany*, 25–26.

66. Hannes Adomeit, *Imperial Overstretch* (Baden-Baden: Nomos, 1998), 171.

67. Korte, *Deutschlandpolitik*, 164.

68. Michael Sodaro, *Moscow, Germany, and the West from Khrushchev to Gorbachev* (Ithaca, NY: Cornell University Press, 1990), 298.

69. Smith, *Soviet Policy toward Germany*, 26.

70. Ernest D. Plock, *West German - East German Relations and the Fall of the GDR* (Boulder, CO: Westview, 1993), 47.

71. Sodaro, *Moscow, Germany*, 307.

72. Adomeit, *Imperial Overstretch*, 169–170.

73. For Chernenko-Gromyko-Honecker talk, see ibid., 175–185.

74. *International Herald Tribune*, September 5, 1984, 1.

75. *Frankfurter Allgemeine Zeitung*, December 1, 1984, 1.

76. *Frankfurter Allgemeine Zeitung*, April 4, 1986, 2.

77. Bundesminister für innerdeutsche Beziehungen, *Informationen*, February 12, 1988, 9–10.

78. *Frankfurter Rundschau*, January 6, 1987, 1.

79. *Frankfurter Allgemeine Zeitung*, April 14, 1987, 1.

80. *Tagesspiegel*, September 11, 1986.

81. For the West German official record of Honecker's visit, see *Der Besuch von Generalsekretär Honecker in der Bundesrepublik Deutschland* (Bonn: Bundesministerium für innerdeutsche Beziehungen, 1987). Honecker's own records of his talks with West German officials are in Erich Honecker, *Moabiter Notizen* (Berlin: edition ost, 1994), 105–235.

82. *U.S. News & World Report*, September 14, 1987, 40.

83. "The Balance of Payments of the Federal Republic of Germany with the German Democratic Republic," *Monthly Report of the Deutsche Bundesbank* (January 1990), 15.

84. Hanns-D. Jacobsen and Heinrich Machowski, "Die wirtschaftsbeziehungen zwischen beiden deutschen Staaten," in Jacobsen, Machowski, and Dirk Sager, eds., *Perspektiven für Sicherheit und Zusammenarbeit in Europa* (Bonn: Bildungszentrale für politische Bildung, 1988), 374–5.

85. Plock, *West German - East German Relations*, 41–66.

86. Deutsche Bank, *Special: East Germany* (Frankfurt: Deutsche Bank, 1990), 7–11.

87. For a summary of the 5,000-page West German report on KoKo, see *Frankfurter Allgemeine Zeitung*, June 22, 1994, pp. 1–2.

88. Peter Przybylski, *Tatort Politbüro: Die Akte Honecker* (Berlin: Rowohlt, 1991), 367–375.

89. Ibid., 294–295.

90. Armin Volze, "Geld und Politik in den innerdeutschen Beziehungen 1970–1989," *Deutschland Archiv* (March 1990), 386–7.

91. Elizabeth Pond, *Beyond the Wall* (Washington, D.C.: Brookings, 1991), 80.

92. *Washington Post*, August 12, 1993, A22.

93. For new *Ostpolitik*, see Timothy Garten Ash, *We, the People* (Cambridge: Granta Books, 1990), 313–342.

94. Ibid., 342.

CHAPTER 18

1. Timothy Garten Ash, *We, the People* (Cambridge: Granta Books, 1990), 133.

2. Elizabeth Pond, *Beyond the Wall* (Washington, D.C.: Brookings, 1991), 88.

3. Ash, *We, the People*, 47–52.

4. Charles S. Maier, *Dissolution: The Crisis of Communism and the End of East Germany* (Princeton, NJ: Princeton University Press, 1997), 131.

5. Karl-Rudolf Korte, *Deutschlandpolitik in Helmut Kohls Kanzlerschaft* (Stuttgart: DVA, 1998), 452.

6. Günter Schabowski, *Der Absturz* (Berlin: Rowohlt, 1992), 228–232.

7. Ilse Spittmann, "Der 17. Januar und die Folgen," *Deutschland Archiv* (March 1988), 227–232.

8. *Financial Times*, December 31, 1987, 5; *Der Spiegel*, no. 21 (1987), 78–92.

9. Hans Kleinschmid, "Symptome eines Syndroms," *Deutschland Archiv* (March 1988), 232–236.

10. Material for the remainder of this chapter comes mainly from the following sources: Hannes Bahrmann and Christoph Links, *Chronik der Wende* (Berlin: Links Verlag, 1994); Robert Darnton, *Berlin Journal* (New York: Norton, 1991); Volker Gransow and Konrad H. Jarausch, eds., *Die Deutsche Vereinigung: Dokumente* (Cologne: Verlag Wissenschaft und Politik, 1991), 52–110; Cornelia Heins, *The Wall Falls* (London: Grey Seal, 1994), 181–249; Ekkehard Kuhn, *Gorbatschow und die deutsche Einheit* (Bonn: Bouvier, 1993); Christoph Links and Hannes Bahrmann, *Wir sind das Volk* (Wuppertal: Peter Hammer Verlag, 1990); Maier, *Dissolution*, 108–215; Elizabeth Pond, *After the Wall* (New York: Priority Press, 1990), 1–153; Ralf Georg Reuth and Andreas Bönte, *Das Komplott* (Munich: Piper, 1993); and from the author's observations during visits to Berlin at the time.

11. Reuth and Bönte, *Komplott*, 27.

12. Spittmann, "Der 17. Januar," 227.

13. Reuth and Bönte, *Komplott*, 46.

14. Author's interview with J. D. Bindenagel, former minister at U.S. Embassy in East Berlin, Washington, August 20, 1998.

15. Reuth and Bönte, *Komplott*, 91–92.

16. Text of appeal in Gransow and Jarausch, eds., *Deutsche Vereinigung*, 60–61.

17. Vyacheslav Dashichev, untitled paper presented at the American Institute for Contemporary German Studies, Washington, D.C., July 17, 1991, 8.

18. Reuth and Bönte, *Komplott*, 108–109.

19. Kuhn, *Gorbatschow*, 44.

20. Schabowski, *Absturz*, 249–252,

21. Text in Gransow and Jarausch, eds., *Deutsche Vereinigung*, 76–77.

22. Schabowski, *Absturz*, 262–271.

23. Ibid., 121–122.

24. Kuhn, *Gorbatschow*, 55–56.

25. Reuth and Bönte, *Komplott*, 137–139.

26. Dashichev, untitled paper, 6.

27. Material for this section comes from the author's own travels to Berlin and East Germany during the fall of 1989 and from: Hannes Bahrmann and Christoph Links, *Chronik der Wende*; Darnton, *Berlin Journal*; Gransow and Jarausch, eds., *Deutsche Vereinigung*, 52–110; Heins, *The Wall Falls*, 181–249; Links and Bahrmann, *Wir sind das Volk*; Maier, *Dissolution*, 108–215; Pond, *After the Wall* 1–153; Reuth and Bönte, *Das Komplott*, passim.

28. Bahrmann and Links, *Chronik der Wende*, 89–91.

29. The most detailed review of events in East Berlin and along the Wall on November 9, 1989, is in Hans-Hermann Hertle, *Chronik des Mauerfalls* (Berlin: Ch. Links, 1997), 118–212. For text of regulation, see Gransow and Jarausch, eds., *Deutsche Vereinigung*, 93–94.

30. Maier, *Dissolution*, 160.

31. Schabowski, *Absturz*, 305–309.

32. Bindenagel interview.

33. George Kennan, *The German Problem: A Personal View* (Washington, D.C.: American Institute for Contemporary German Studies, 1989), 6.

34. Egon Bahr, *Zu meiner Zeit* (Munich: Karl Blessing Verlag, 1996), 570–574.

35. James McAdams, "The GDR at Forty: the Perils of Success," *German Politics and Society* (Summer 1989), 14–26.

36. Theo Sommer, ed., *Reise ins andere Deutschland* (Reinbek: Rowohlt, 1986).

37. Vernon A. Walters, *Die Vereinigung war voraussehbar* (Berlin: Siedler Verlag, 1994), passim.

38. Schabowski, *Absturz*, 311.

CHAPTER 19

1. J. A. Kwizinskij, *Vor dem Sturm* (Berlin: Siedler Verlag, 1993), 15; Ekkehard Kuhn, *Gorbatschow und die deutsche Einheit* (Bonn: Bouvier Verlag, 1993), 69; Egon Bahr, *Zu meiner Zeit* (Munich: Karl Blessing Verlag, 1996), 573; Hannes Adomeit, *Imperial Overstretch* (Baden-Baden: Nomos, 1998), 437.

2. Willy Brandt, ". . . *was zusammengehört*" (Bonn: Dietz, 1993), 33–39.

3. Kuhn, *Gorbatschow*, 77–78.

4. Ibid., 96–97.

5. Author's interview with Horst Teltschik, Munich, April 20, 1998.

6. Kwizinskij, *Vor dem Sturm*, 16–17; Helmut Kohl, *Ich wollte Deutschlands Einheit* (Berlin: Propyläen, 1996), 141.

7. Teltschik interview.

8. Horst Teltschik, *329 Tage* (Berlin: Siedler Verlag, 1992), 109; as general sources of information for this chapter, see *ibid.*, 42–147, and Kohl, *Deutschlands Einheit*, 125–283; for comprehensive later review, see Werner Weidenfeld, with Peter M. Wagner and Elke Bruck, *Aussenpolitik für die deutsche Einheit: Die Entscheidungsjahre, 1989/90* (Stuttgart: Deutsche Verlags-Anstalt, 1999), passim.

9. Philip Zelikow and Condoleezza Rice, *Germany Unified and Europe Transformed* (Cambridge, MA: Harvard University Press, 1995), 139–141.

10. Ibid.; George Bush and Brent Scowcroft, *A World Transformed* (New York: Knopf, 1998), 201–202; Robert L. Hutchings, *American Diplomacy and the End of the Cold War* (Washington, D.C.: Wilson Center Press, 1997), 107–108.

11. Hutchings, *American Diplomacy*, 112.

12. Teltschik, *329 Tage*, 105.

13. Author's interview with Robert Zoellick, former counselor of the U.S. State Department, Washington, September 15, 1998; Hutchings, *American Diplomacy*, 97.

14. Michael R. Beschloss and Strobe Talbott, *At the Highest Levels* (Boston: Little, Brown, 1991), 137.

15. Kuhn, *Gorbatschow*, 125.

16. Teltschik, *329 Tage*, 81–84.

17. Hans-Dietrich Genscher, *Erinnerungen* (Berlin: Siedler Verlag, 1995), 686–688.

18. Kohl, *Deutschlands Einheit*, 215, 301; Teltschik, *329 Tage*, 87–91. For details on the Dresden events and discussions, see Weidenfeld, *Aussenpolitik für die deutsche Einheit*, 201–204.

19. Zelikow and Rice, *Germany Unified*, 151–153.

20. Ibid., *Germany Unified*, 117.

21. Teltschik, *329 Tage*, 106–108.

22. German Information Service, *Statements and Speeches*, vol. 12, no. 25, December 19, 1989, contains the full official translation of the ten points. The summary version cited here is drawn from Zelikow and Rice, *Germany Unified*, 119–120.

23. G. Jonathan Greenwald, *Berlin Witness* (University Park: Pennsylvania State University Press, 1993), 288.

24. Bush and Scowcroft, *A World Transformed*, 244.

25. Teltschik, *329 Tage*, 112–113.

26. Ibid., 141–144.

27. Ibid., 145.

28. *The Economist*, May 26, 1990, 56.

29. Greenwald, *Berlin Witness*, 292.

30. Kuhn, *Gorbatschow*, 85.

31. James A. Baker III with Thomas M. DeFrank, *The Politics of Diplomacy* (New York: Putnam's, 1995), 234.

32. Zelikow and Rice, *Germany Unified*, 81 and 117.

33. Ibid., 131–132.

34. Ibid., 133.

35. Ibid., 142–143; Zoellick interview.

36. Beschloss and Talbott, *At Highest Levels*, 186–187.

37. Zoellick interview; Hutchings, *American Diplomacy*, 100, 115.

38. Hutchings, *American Diplomacy*, 167.

39. Adomeit, *Imperial Overstretch*, 218.

40. Ibid., 216–217.

41. Mikhail Gorbatschow, *Erinnerungen*, trans. Igor Petrowitsch Gorodetzkij (Berlin: Siedler Verlag, 1993), 709; the English version is Mikhail Gorbachev, *Memoirs*, trans. Georges Peronansky and Tatjana Varsavsky (New York: Doubleday, 1995).

42. Eduard Shevardnadze, *Die Zukunft gehört der Freiheit*, trans. Novosti Information Agency (Hamburg: Rowohlt, 1991), 233

43. Zelikow and Rice, *Germany Unified*, 266.

44. Ibid., 161–163.

45. For a detailed analysis of the Soviet debate, see Rafael Biermann, "Machtgefüge im Umbruch," in Elke Bruck, Peter M. Wagner, eds., *Wege zum "2+4"-Vertrag* (Munich: Forschungsgruppe Deutschland, 1996), 92–105.

46. Hubert Védrine, *Les Mondes de François Mitterrand* (Paris: Fayard, 1996), 428; Julius W. Friend, *The Linchpin* (New York: Praeger, 1991), 81–84.

47. Jaques Attali, *Verbatim III* (Paris: Fayard, 1995), 390. For a detailed report on Mitterrand's efforts in Kiev to persuade Germany to veto German unification, see Weidenfeld, *Aussenpolitik für die deutsche Einheit,* 153–159.

48. Védrine, *Mitterrand,* 430; Hutchings, *American Diplomacy,* 105.

49. Védrine, *Mitterrand,* 431–433.

50. Dominique Moisi, "The French Answer to the German Question," *Foreign Affairs* (Spring 1990), 30–35.

51. Teltschik, *329 Tage,* 86.

52. *La Politique Étrangère de la France: Textes et Documents* (January-February 1990), 86.

53. Thatcher's actions regarding Germany and her relations with Kohl are summarized in Margaret Thatcher, *The Downing Street Years* (New York: Harper Collins, 1993), 263, 548–549, 747–748 and 784–789; see also Weidenfeld, *Aussenpolitik für die deutsche Einheit,* 69–74.

54. Hutchings, *American Diplomacy,* 68–69, 108.

55. Thatcher, *Downing Street Years,* 792–793.

56. Ibid., 748.

57. Paul Sharp, *Thatcher's Diplomacy* (London: Macmillan, 1997), 218–219.

58. Attali, *Verbatim III,* 369, 400.

59. Védrine, *Mitterrand,* 440–441.

60. Teltschik, *329 Tage,* 153.

61. Ibid., 159.

62. Zoellick interview.

63. Beschloss and Talbott, *At Highest Levels,* 185.

64. Zelikow and Rice, *Germany Unified,* 176–177.

65. Ibid., 180–184.

66. Ibid., 226–229; The most complete collection of public documents and press reports on the talks is the multivolume series by Stiftung Wissenschaft und Politik, *"Zwei + Vier": Die Frage der äusseren Aspekte der deutschen Einheit* (Ebenhausen: Stiftung Wissenschaft und Politik, 1990); for a personal Two-plus-Four German memoir, see Hans-Dietrich Genscher, *Erinnerungen* (Berlin: Siedler Verlag, 1995), 709–895.

67. Zoellick interview.

68. Zelikow and Rice, *Germany Unified,* 243–248.

69. Author's interview with Igor Maximychev, Deputy Chief of Mission at Soviet Embassy in East Berlin, Potsdam, June 2, 1990.

70. Bush and Scowcroft, *A World Transformed,* 269.

71. Zelikow and Rice, *Germany Unified,* 275–285. The following quotes are taken from this text.

72. Ibid., 278.

73. Gorbatschow, *Erinnerungen*, 722–723.

74. Bush and Scowcroft, *A World Transformed*, 281–283.

75. Attali, *Verbatim III*, 497.

76. Beschloss and Talbott, *At Highest Levels*, 221.

77. Ibid., 289.

78. Ibid., 295–303.

79. Ibid., 296.

80. Ibid., 303.

81. Hutchings, *American Diplomacy*, 45, 120.

82. Zelikow and Rice, *Germany Unified*, 174–175.

83. Teltschik interview.

84. Bush and Scowcroft, *A World Transformed*, 243, 246; Hutchings, *American Diplomacy*, 387, n.75; Zoellick and Bindenagel interviews.

85. Attali, *Verbatim III*, 432, 435, 439 and 520.

86. Genscher, *Erinnerungen*, 773–782.

87. Hans Tietmeyer, "Errinerungen an die Vertragsverhandlungen," in Theo Waigel and Manfred Schell, eds., *Tage, die Deutschland und die Welt veränderten* (Munich: Bruckmann, 1994), 57–117.

88. David Schoenbaum and Elizabeth Pond, *The German Question* (New York: St. Martin's Press, 1996), 157.

89. Harry Maier, "Gefährliche Schlagseite," *Die Zeit*, May 20, 1998, 35.

90. W. R. Smyser, *The German Economy* (New York: St. Martin's Press, 1993), 149–174.

91. Wolfgang Schäuble, *Der Vertrag* (Stuttgart: Deutsche Verlags- Anstalt, 1991), passim; treaty text in *Frankfurter Allgemeine Zeitung*, September 5, 1990, B1-B6.

92. For full record of inner-German negotiations, see Schäuble, *Der Vertrag*, passim.

93. Teltschik, *329 Tage*, 192.

94. Kohl, *Deutschlands Einheit*, 556–557; Kwizinskij, *Vor Dem Sturm*, 19.

95. Teltschik, *329 Tage*, 248.

96. Teltschik interview.

97. Teltschik, *329 Tage*, 231–232.

98. Zelikow and Rice, *Germany Unified*, 325–327.

99. For the path to the new NATO, Zelikow and Rice, *Germany Unified*, 303–324.

100. Bush and Scowcroft, *A World Transformed*, 244.

101. Zoellick interview; Zelikow and Rice, *Germany Unified*, 316.

102. Ibid., 324–325.

103. Giulietto Chiesa, "The 28th Congress of the CPSU," *Problems of Communism* (July-August 1990), 24–38.

104. David H. Shumaker, *Gorbachev and the German Question* (Westport, CT: Praeger, 1995), 135–137.

105. Jack F. Matlock, Jr., *Autopsy of an Empire* (New York: Random House, 1995), 386–388.

106. Adomeit, *Imperial Overstretch*, 511–516.

107. Matlock, *Autopsy*, 389; Moscow television, July 7, 1990.

108. Kuhn, *Gorbatschow*, 127–128.

109. Mikhail Gorbatschow, *Gipfel-Gespräche* (Berlin: Rowohlt, 1993), 161–180.

110. Teltschik, *329 Tage*, 313–342.

111. Gorbatschow, *Erinnerungen*, 726.

112. Zelikow and Rice, *Germany Unified*, 329.

113. Ibid., 344.

114. Ibid.; *Deutsche Aussenpolitik, 1990/91* (Bonn: Foreign Office, 1991), 244–246.

115. Kwizinskij, *Vor dem Sturm*, 59.

116. Full text of treaty is in *Deutsche Aussenpolitik, 1990/91*, 237–243.

117. Friend, *Linchpin*, 87.

118. Beschloss and Talbott, *At Highest Levels*, 240.

119. Zelikow and Rice, *Germany Unified*, 346–352; Teltschik, *329 Tage*, 352–362.

120. Adomeit, *Imperial Overstretch*, 541–554.

121. Text in Curt Gasteyger, ed., *Europa von der Spaltung zur Einigung* (Bonn: Bundeszentrale für politische Bildung, 1997), 452–456.

122. Ibid., 413–419.

123. Ibid., 456–459.

124. Ibid., 469–499.

CHAPTER 20

1. For example, Peter Schweizer, *Victory* (New York: Atlantic Monthly Press, 1994).

2. Stephen Rosenfeld, "Star Wars: Scandal and Coup?" *Washington Post*, August 20, 1993, A17; Robert McFarlane, "Consider What Star Wars Accomplished," *New York Times*, August 23, 1993, 21; Jacques Attali, *Verbatim III* (Paris: Fayard, 1995), 305.

3. Author's interview with Ambassador Vernon Walters, Washington, November 4, 1994; Anatoly Dobrynin, *In Confidence* (New York: Times Books, 1995), 527, 609.

4. Carl Bernstein and Marco Politi, *His Holiness* (New York: Doubleday, 1996), 269–275; Adrian Karatnycky, "How We Helped Solidarity Win," *Washington Post*, August 27, 1989, C1.

5. Paul Sharp, *Thatcher's Diplomacy* (New York: St. Martin's Press, 1997), 202–225.

6. *Deutschland Archiv* (December 1990), 1935.

7. Eduard Shevardnadze, *Die Zukunft gehört der Freiheit*, trans. Novosti Press Agency (Hamburg: Rowohlt, 1991), 238.

8. Ekkehard Kuhn, *Gorbatschow und die deutsche Einheit* (Bonn: Bouvier Verlag, 1993), 167.

9. Author's interview with Willy Brandt, Bonn, September 6, 1990.

10. Wolfgang Bergsdorf, "Deutschland 1871 und 1991," *Geschichte*, No. 4 (1991): 4–7; "The Week in Germany," German Information Service, New York, April 16, 1999, 1–3; *Focus*, No. 16, 1999, 20–42; for the German role in peace-keeping operations, see Auswärtiges Amt, *25 Jahre deutsche Beteiligung an Friedenserhaltenden Massnahmen der Vereinten Nationen* (Bonn: Foreign Office, 1998).

11. Robert L. Hutchings, *American Diplomacy and the End of the Cold War* (Washington, D.C.: Woodrow Wilson Center Press, 1997), 278–279.

INDEX